Absolute Proof
That the Book of Mormon is a Fake

by
Timothy W. Henline

For ordering information or to contact the author:
E-mail: timothyhenline@absoluteproofthebook.com
Web site: www.absoluteproofthebook.com

Unless otherwise noted all Scripture quotations are from the King James English Version (KJV)

Published by
Fern Mountain Publishing
P.O. Box 104
Rock Cave, WV 26234

International Standard Book Number: 0-9787914-0-1
ISBN 13: 978-0-9787914-0-7

Printed in the United States of America

First Edition 2006

Dedication

I dedicate this book to all those who seek the truth, no matter how difficult the process of finding that truth or how hard that truth may be to accept.

Table of Contents

INTRODUCTION

For over 175 years now millions upon millions of people have read the Book of Mormon. Scanning its pages many millions have come to believe that it is the inspired word of God and in general a history of the early forbears of the Native Americans, North, South and Central Americans to be precise. As of this writing there are approximately 12.2 million members, world wide of The Church of Jesus Christ of Latter-Day Saints or the Mormons, as they are more commonly known. This statistic comes from the church's official website. Needless to say the overall reach and extent of involvement the church has in the lives of humans all over the world is immeasurable.

Since its inception as an organization in 1830 the church has continued to grow and can now be found in most countries of the world. This impact, without doubt, can trace its beginnings to two things; first Joseph Smith, the founder of Mormonism, and second and more directly, the book I will prove that he himself wrote, the Book of Mormon. Even though Mr. Smith claims he received the book from an angel named Moroni and that God himself instructed him to translate the plates of gold, purportedly written and buried by the ancestors of the American Indians, I will prove not only that he wrote the Book of Mormon himself, but I will also prove how he did it.

So, for the first time in approximately 175 years someone has proven, without doubt, that the Book of Mormon is a work of fiction and that it was indeed written at the hands of Joseph Smith. I know that this will appear as an astonishing claim to many but as I have state numerous times in the writing of this book, "If you read my book all the way through and if then you still believe that the Book of Mormon isn't a fake and that Joseph Smith didn't write it, then I believe you need serious, and I do mean serious, psychological help." This is how sure I am that what you have here in your hands is the evidence to prove my claims.

It has taken me many years and countless thousands of hours to complete this work, of which this book is only a small part. In fact my original work is so large that it is well over 2200 pages. As you can imagine this would not make for an easily readable nor practical book for the masses that I hoped it would reach. So what you have here in your hand is a condensed and explanatory version of that massive work which required me to sacrifice much of my life to complete. I spent almost every single day for many years working on this project. My thinking as I was spending most of my available time on this book was that I might possibly save tens of thousands and yes even millions of people time over the years with their mostly inevitable attempt to try to "find the truth". You see one of the most intriguing parts of what Mormons talk to potential members about is "truth" and the seeking of it, this appeals to many who are in that "mode" of truth finding. I was one of those people. Therefore I felt this book and my sacrifice of time would save countless millions from seeking the truth but only ending up finding falsehood.

You might ask how and why I was able to come up with this "absolute proof" and for over 175 years no one else has. Well I will chalk it up to a series of events that only I have experienced. That is not to say that somewhere twenty, thirty or even 130 years from now someone else might not have been able to find the same thing. I found it at this moment in time precisely because of those series of events that transpired in my life to make it occur. Just as many of the discoveries of our planet took a unique set of circumstances for those discoveries to come about, I had just such a unique set of circumstances. I had studied religion all my life from the time I was only 13 years old. I studied the Bible inside and out. And among the many religions I became a part of in the process of my own search for truth, I became a Mormon and was even a Mormon missionary for a year when, while on my mission, I started to have doubts as to the validity of what the Book of Mormon claimed. The second aspect of my life that was an ingredient of those "unique set of circumstances" was, perhaps most importantly, that I am a computer expert. These circumstances more particularly and others including my love of Sherlock Holmes and deductive reasoning, led me to this "absolute truth" and thus this book which you now hold.

Now I want to make it clear from the start that if you are Mormon you may not want to read this book if you want to continue to be Mormon. That is how sure I am that this book will affect your beliefs. After all I titled it "Absolute Proof". But if regardless of the fact that you are a Mormon you truly seek truth, as I have and do, then you have nothing to fear from reading this book.

I also want to make it clear before you begin that this book is in no way intended to be a medium to persecute anyone, particularly Mormons. Some of the best people I have ever met in my life were and are Mormons. They, as was I, are only on the path of trying to find the truth. To hurt them in any way for trying to do that, I believe, only hurts you. They are not "evil" people, they are not a part of some secret "satanic" society, and for the most part they are a very caring and loving people and want only the best for you and our society. So please, I beg you, do not use this book as a means to vent your own angers, inadequacies and doubts of your own faith.

So whether you are Mormon or of some other religion I hope you will read this book based on a premise I came up with for myself many years ago, "truth is truth and it will always be truth and you can't change it just because you don't like it".

Chapter One

In the Beginning

Rather than go into protracted detail on the history of the Book of Mormon and how it came to be, I have always hated reading books where I had to sift through a significant amount of background before getting to the "meat" of the book, I will briefly touch on the beginnings of the Book of Mormon how I know now it came to be and what led Joseph Smith to write it. In other words I will focus on that which accounts for this book you are reading. For any additional history I would direct you to reputable websites and books on the subject. I might note here that the reason I use the word "reputable" is that I know from experience that there are many misleading and in some cases completely fabricated works on the Mormon Church.

It might also be worth noting here that some of what you read in the next few chapters will not be entirely clear to you until you finish reading this book. It might therefore be appropriate to finish the book and return to the first few chapters for some, "Now I know what he means".

Also before we begin let me state some obvious facts as they relate to this book you are now reading and give you that brief understanding of the background. First I would like to state emphatically that Joseph Smith wrote the Book of Mormon. And second I will show you how he did it.

Joseph Smith states that in the spring of 1820 when he was 14 years old he went to the woods to pray near his home in the town of Palmyra in the State of New York. While there he claims that "God the Father" and his "Son Jesus Christ" appeared to him. The official church website describes what happened to him while there;

> "Wondering which of the many churches to join, Joseph had followed the counsel in the Bible's book of James: "If any of you lack wisdom, let him ask of God." The Lord told Joseph "that all the religious denominations were believing in incorrect doctrines" and that he was to await further instructions from on high. "In a state of calmness and peace indescribable," Joseph left that sacred grove knowing the reality of our Father in Heaven and His resurrected Son, Jesus Christ."

Again, this is not the full account to learn more please visit the churches website or other accurate histories regarding the presumed event.

It wasn't until approximately three more years had passed that Joseph's next event would occur. On the night of September 21, 1823 while praying Joseph states that the angel Moroni appeared to him. The church website fills us in on what happened next:

"Moroni, a messenger sent from God, stood before him. In mortal life Moroni had been the last of ancient American prophets having authority from God and whose teachings were recorded for our time. Moroni declared "that the time was at hand for the Gospel in all its fullness to be preached in power, unto all nations" and that Joseph was "to be an instrument in the hands of God" in that work. He quoted ancient prophets who had foreseen that this time would come. As Moroni stood before him Joseph was shown in vision "the place where the plates were deposited.""

The website continues:

"Every September for four years, Joseph went to the Hill Cumorah and was taught by Moroni. In September 1827 Joseph met Moroni at the hill and received the gold plates. Twenty-one months later, having completed the translation, Joseph returned the plates to Moroni."

Now this is the story as the church relates it to us and also, we believe, by Joseph Smith himself. Now when you finish reading this book you will understand more clearly what I am about to say here. Joseph Smith actually gives us hints as to the time frame of his coming up with the idea for the Book of Mormon and its actual writing. I have learned over the years when investigating truth from people, especially when I interrogated people as part of police work I had done, that most people, when they are lying, use part of the truth to tell their story. In Joseph Smith's case this is no different. He tells us that at 14 years old he wanted to know the truth of religion from God. This is perfectly plausible as I myself at 13 did the very same thing. I used to go to the hill behind my parent's house, 2000 feet up, and pray to God to know the same thing. That part of Joseph Smith's story I believe to be true, the part where God and Jesus visit him I believe to be a fabrication.

Next we are told that when he was around 17 years of age he was visited by the Angel Moroni and then visited by this angel every September for an additional four years this would make him approximately 21 years of age. I believe during this time Joseph Smith was still seeking to understand religion and what was going on in his life, this is the period that he would have started the writing of the Book of Mormon. Not necessarily at 17 but the ideas were brewing during this time. Mr. Smith states that he was visited every September by the angel Moroni to receive instruction or to be taught by the angel. This of course in truth was not when he was receiving instruction from the angel but when he himself began to write the Book of Mormon and compile it himself. This is the partial truth I was talking about earlier the "instruction" by the angel was in fact his own instruction as he compiled the Book of Mormon.

Now one argument I have heard countless times is that it would be impossible for one person to write the Book of Mormon let alone someone as young as Joseph Smith. In fact this could not be farther from the truth. While researching this book I understood how easy it would have been and indeed by looking at every single word I came to the conclusion that it would have been relatively simple, indeed it could have been done by just about anyone with the ability to read and write. Someone with limited education and a good imagination and actually as you will see someone would only need a relatively simple imagination as most of the Book of Mormon and its ideas are from other sources. I am confident when you finish this book you will agree.

Now another 21 months later and the book was published. It is important to note that it only took him three months to "translate" it. During this additional 21 months time he also wrote the Book of Mormon and made additions and modifications to his work. So Joseph Smith had approximately five and a half years to write the Book of Mormon. And when you finish reading this book you will see how this is more than enough time to accomplish such a work. One thing you need to keep in mind is that there were no televisions, no radios, movies, games, etc…Joseph Smith had plenty of time to come up with and write this book. And as you will see he had a lot of help in writing it. Five and a half years is a long time when it comes to writing any book as I am aware of as a writer.

To get back to the "three months" to translate, it is interesting to note how he translated it. This also gives us indications that he himself wrote it but I will not give you those details until the 12th chapter as it will then be clearer to you after you read how Joseph Smith came up with and compiled the Book of Mormon.

Now that you have a basic understanding of the early history of the Book of Mormon let's move on to the beginning of the ideas for the Book of Mormon.

Chapter Two

The Idea Takes Hold

Joseph Smith's idea for the Book of Mormon came from a combination of events that were transpiring at his time in history. During the early 1830's there was an almost obsessive struggle under way to try to figure out where the American Indians came from. Many ideas were put forth in an attempt to come up with an answer but the most popular idea by far was that they were a part of the lost ten tribes of Israel. Joseph Smith would have been well aware of this debate as it was even in the newspapers of the time. Several years ago while in New York state I did some research of the newspapers of Joseph's Smith's day and encountered articles on just such a debate; including one in New York making the argument that the American Indians were indeed of the lost tribes of Israel. In addition to newspapers, many books were written on the subject including one known as *The View of the Hebrews*, written by a pastor in 1823 by the name of Ethan Smith. Many groups believe Joseph Smith used this book to write the Book of Mormon, but as you will see, I believe this is not the case. I have read the claims related to the connection but they are particularly flimsy and do not hold up to scrutiny. Again, as you will soon see you will be shown what he did use. Now we can not of course say that Joseph Smith did not read this book and possibly utilize it in some fashion in his quest to write the Book of Mormon, but we cannot also say that he did not use many of the countless newspaper articles, journals, and books also circulating at the time which all fostered the idea that Indians were from the lost ten tribes of Israel. Please note that you will be made aware of several of these throughout this book.

Now Joseph Smith would have been caught up, at least in his own mind, with the debate over where the Indians came from. During the same time and under his own admission, Joseph Smith was debating the "many religions" and trying to find out for himself what the "truth" was. During his studies he would have done what we ourselves do in modern times, consult other books. He of course was studying the Bible and naturally would have used books on the Bible including commentaries. There were a few that were extremely common at the time. *Matthew Henry's Commentary on the Whole Bible* originally written in 1706, *John Wesley's Explanatory Notes on the Whole*

Bible produced between 1754 and 1765, John Gill's *Exposition of the Entire Bible* (1690-1771), and Adam Clarke's *Commentary on the Bible* 1826. I think it is important to note here that I looked at literally hundreds of book, commentaries, sermons, and other possible sources. And as you will see the evidence here alone eliminates the others.

So Joseph Smith was of the right age and alive at the exact same time that America was debating the lineage of the American Indians. And the most accepted belief was that those American Indians were of the lost tribes of Israel. Joseph Smith then would have studied these commentaries and found ideas in them that would have supported that idea and the book he intended to right. As you will see he also utilized these books as the framework for the Book of Mormon itself.

I think it is important to note here that the evidence I will present that shows that Joseph Smith used these commentaries is substantial and overwhelming. It is therefore important that you restrain yourself from complete judgment until you finish this entire book. Snap judgments either for or against will only lead you, in either case, to a whimsical understanding of just what it is I present here. What you will read has far reaching effects on our world not only as it has played out in our history for millions of people but also as it will play out for millions more. Please take the time to develop an opinion based on a complete reading of this book and if necessary additional study.

It is my belief that while reading one of the commentaries mentioned above Joseph Smith came up with the idea for the Book of Mormon. Adam Clarke's commentaries were published at the exact time Joseph Smith would have begun the writing of the Book of Mormon. So it isn't surprising that we come across Clarke's commentary on the Indians. In Clarke's commentary on Hosea chapter nine verse 17 Clarke states the following:

> "And where they have wandered to, who can tell? and in what nations to be found, no man knows. **Wanderers** they are; and perhaps even now unknown to themselves. Some have thought they have found them in one country; some, in another; and a very pious writer, in a book entitled, The Star in the West, (*by Boudinot*) thinks he has found their descendants in the American Indians; among whom he has discovered many customs, apparently the same with those of the ancient Jews, and commanded in the Law."

As you can see Clarke clearly outlines the entire idea behind the Book of Mormon at the exact same time that Joseph Smith would have begun its writing. In addition Mr. Smith uses some of the same ideas related to this commentary in the Book of Mormon itself. Notice in Alma chapter 26 verse 36 the same idea.

"Now if this is boasting, even so will I boast; for this is my life and my light, my joy and my salvation, and my redemption from everlasting wo. Yea, blessed is the name of my God, who has been mindful of this people, who are a branch of the tree of Israel, and has been lost from its body in a strange land; yea, I say, blessed be the name of my God, who has been mindful of us, **wanderers** in a strange land."

In fact he uses the word "wanderers" three times in the Book of Mormon to describe the characters of the Book of Mormon, which we have seen is what Clarke calls them.

Also during the time of Joseph's coming up with and writing the Book of Mormon a poem was published entitled *Traits of the Aborigines of America. A Poem* Cambridge: From the University Press, Hillard and Metcalf Printers, Sold by Cummings & Hillard, No. 1 Cornhill, Boston. 1822. In this poem many of the thoughts and ideas of the Book of Mormon can be found. Here are some highlights of this rather lengthy poem. The first quote even mentions Judge Boudinot and his belief as mentioned in the quote above from Clarke's commentary.

"Scatter'd from Jewish altars.

Let the heart, That deems such semblance but the baseless dream Of blind
credulity, survey the trace
Of similarity, bid Truth's clear light
Beam o'er the misty annal, note the facts,
Compare the language, weigh the evidence,
And answer for itself.

The chrystal tube
Of calm inquiry, to thy patient eye,
Meek Boudinot! reveal'd an unknown star
Upon this western cloud. Its trembling beam
Guided thy soul to Zion's sacred hill"

Another quote:

"That God would gather from the utmost bound,
The children of his Friend, of the cold North
And glowing South, his fugitives require;
From Gush and Elam, from the sea-green isles,
And from the western regions, bring again

His banish'd; bid the fearful desert bloom
And sing before them, while their blinded hearts
Illumin'd, catch the knowledge and the love
Of Jesus Christ."

Another quote:

"—To them replied
The elder Chief:
"We bear upon our minds
Past times, and other days. This beauteous land
Was once our fathers'. Here, in peace they dwelt;
For the Great Spirit gave it as a gift
To them, and to their sons. But to this shore
Once came a vast canoe, which white men steer'd
Feebly, against the blast."

As you can see the idea of the Indians being part of the lost tribes of Israel was widespread. Especially at the time Joseph Smith came up with and wrote the Book of Mormon. In fact Judge Boudinot believed that evidence for his belief that the Indians came from the lost tribes could be found in the Apocrypha which would have been also available to Joseph Smith. In it Esdras has a vision of the ten tribes,

"in his vision beheld the ten tribes who were carried captive by ShAlmanezer, in the time of Hosea their king, taking counsel to leave the multitude, and go into a country where mankind never dwelt, that they might keep the statues which they never kept **in their own land**, and remain there until the latter times."— 2 Esdras, xiii, 40.

This is again the main idea behind the Book of Mormon. The idea that parts of the lost ten tribes were scattered and "kept in their own land" "until the latter times".

From the Book of Mormon, 2 Nephi 24:1;

"For the Lord will have mercy on Jacob, and will yet choose Israel, and set them **in their own land**; and the strangers shall be joined with them, and they shall cleave to the house of Jacob."

Also from the Book of Mormon, Alma 15:12;

"Yea, I say unto you, that in the **latter times** the promises of the Lord have been extended to our brethren, the Lamanites; and notwithstanding the many afflictions which they shall have, and notwithstanding they shall be driven to and fro upon the face of the earth, and be hunted, and shall be smitten and scattered abroad, having no place for refuge, the Lord shall be merciful unto them."

Now the Poem mentioned previously, states that Judge Boudinot and others during the time of Joseph's compiling and writing the Book of Mormon believed in one of the premises of the Book of Mormon that the Indians were indeed from the lost ten tribes of Israel. It is also clear that those beliefs made their way into the commentaries of the time including Clarke's commentary.

Since Joseph Smith utilized the commentaries to write the Book of Mormon we will now see how he utilized another commentary popular at the time to add to his *Book of* Mormon structure and ideas. In John Gill's Commentary we are made aware of the phrase "isles of the sea" which Joseph Smith utilized in order to claim that the "isles of the sea" included the Americas and thus the natives found there are from the lost tribes of Israel. In addition the commentaries made use of the term Gentiles which Joseph Smith turned into those who became what is now America.

For example here is a quote from Gill's commentary which outlines a belief that the particular verse in Isaiah, which Joseph Smith extensively copied from to write the Book of Mormon, is a prophecy of a future event and that the Gentiles are in the "isles of the sea", the bold here is from the KJV of the Bible: To make it easier to keep track of what comes from where, before each item I will use three letters to signify where each comes from. **COM** for the commentaries, **KJV** for the King James Version of the Bible and **BOM** for the Book of Mormon. I will add italics for emphasis on those thoughts.

> **COM** Gill: Isa 51:5 "**the isles shall wait upon me**; upon Christ, for his coming; for his salvation and righteousness; for his Gospel, the truths, promises, and blessings of it; and in his house and ordinances, for his presence. *This is a prophecy of the conversion of the Gentiles, even in the isles of the sea, those afar off, as ours of Great Britain and Ireland, in which there have been and are many waiting upon him:*"

And…

> **COM** Gill: <u>Isa 41:1</u> "**Keep silence before me, O islands**,.... The great controversy in the world after the coming of Christ, which is expressly spoken of in the preceding chapter, was, as Cocceius observes, whether he was a divine Person; this was first objected to by the Jews, and afterwards by many that bore the Christian name; some, in the times of the apostles, especially the Apostle John; and others in later ages; some affirmed that he was a mere man, as Ebion and Cerinthus; others that he was a created God, as Arius; and others a God by office, as Socinus and his followers; now these are called upon, *wherever they were, whether on the*

continent, or in the isles of the sea; and especially all such places which were separated from Judea by the sea, or which they went to by sea, were called islands, perhaps the European nations and isles are more particularly intended; and now, as when the judge is on the bench, and the court is set, and a cause just going to be tried, silence is proclaimed; so here, Jehovah himself being on the throne, and a cause depending between him and men being about to be tried, they are commanded silence;"

And…

COM Gill: Isa 24:15 "**the name of the Lord God of Israel, in the isles of the sea**; *whose name will now be known, not in Israel, or among the Jews only, but in all distant and foreign countries, which are sometimes meant by the isles of the sea;* and in all islands, even the most remote, who will have reason to join with them on the continent to glorify God, whose name will now be great in all the earth."

And…

COM Gill: Isa 24:14 "**for the majesty of the Lord, they shall cry aloud from the sea**: so the Hebrew accents distinguish these clauses; and the sense is, *that from the west,* as Kimchi and Ben Melech interpret it, *from the western nations, where Protestantism chiefly prevails;* or from the Mediterranean Sea, which lay west of Judea; from the maritime countries, the countries bordering upon it, *where at this time will appear many that will embrace the Gospel of Christ; or from the isles of the sea,* as the phrase is explained in the next verse Isa 24:15, such as our isles of Great Britain and Ireland;"

And…

COM Gill: Psa 97:1 "**let the multitude of isles be glad thereof**; *the isles of the sea are many, even many thousands: Columbus, when he first discovered America,* sailing by Cuba westward, gave names, as he passed along, to seven hundred islands, leaving three thousand more without names (r): Gejerus reports, from some writers, that an Indian king, in 1553, was converted to the Christian faith, that ruled over eleven thousand islands; and that in Maldivar there are reckoned to be sixteen thousand: well may the text speak of a multitude of them: or, "let the great islands", &c. such as ours of Great Britain and Ireland; *these isles are said to wait for Christ and his doctrine,* Isa 42:4 and therefore must be glad to hear of his coming and kingdom: the Gospel was very early sent to the isles, as to Cyprus, Crete, &c. see Act 13:4 and to our northern isles likewise, who have great reason to be glad at its coming among us, continuance with us, and the success it has had; and that it is yet in the midst of us for further usefulness; and that Christ reigns, and will reign evermore."

Note here; as I stated previously, how Joseph Smith utilized Gill's use of "isles of the sea" in order to make the claim in the Book of Mormon that the new continent of America was an "isle of the sea". In addition Joseph Smith utilized the term Gentiles, as it is found in Gill, as pointing not just to Europe but to the America's. So let us look now at how Joseph Smith used these ideas as found in Gill's commentary in the Book of Mormon itself.

He utilizes these ideas in the Book of Mormon in *The Second Book of Nephi* chapter 10 verse 20. What is accounted here is the time when the Jewish group of the Book of Mormon leaves Jerusalem and lands in the Americas which Joseph Smith calls an "isle of the sea".

> "And now, my beloved brethren, seeing that our merciful God has given us so great knowledge concerning these things, let us remember him, and lay aside our sins, and not hang down our heads, for we are not cast off; nevertheless, we have been driven out of the land of our inheritance; but we have been led to a better land, for the Lord has made the sea our path, and we are upon an **isle of the sea**."

Here they have landed in the America's and Joseph Smith makes sure we know it is an "isle of the sea" What is interesting is that if they had indeed landed anywhere in the Americas how could they call it an "isle of the sea" when they would have not know whether or not it was indeed and island which of course it was and is not. Remember what we just read from some of Gill's commentary, *"wherever they were, whether on the continent, or in the isles of the sea; and especially all such places which were separated from Judea by the sea, or which they went to by sea, were called islands,"*. Can you see how this is exactly what Joseph Smith is saying here in 2 Nephi quoted above. He even clarifies for us that it is America earlier in 2 Nephi chapter 10 verse 11 by using a common phrase of the time that signified America,

> "And this land shall be **a land of liberty** unto the Gentiles, and there shall be no kings upon the land, who shall raise up unto the Gentiles."

In fact in 2 Nephi chapter 10 in verse 8 Smith uses the same phrase as does Henry in his commentary on the Gentiles and Henry's commentary even spells out what Smith claims.

> "And it shall come to pass that they shall be gathered in from their long **dispersion**, from **the isles of the sea**, and from the four parts of the earth; and **the nations of the Gentiles** shall be great in the eyes of me, saith God, in carrying them forth to the lands of their inheritance."

Now note the same idea and phrases in Matthew Henry's commentary.
COM Henry: Eze 39:1-7 "in **the isles**, that is, **the nations of the Gentiles**."

This verse is even linked to a commentary by Henry that even seems to point out the entire premise of the Book of Mormon but also uses the same words as this verse in Nephi above.

> **COM** Henry: Isa 24:13-15 "Those who have made, or are making, their escape from the land (that being emptied and made desolate) to the sea and **the isles of the sea**, shall thence cry aloud; their **dispersion** shall help to spread the knowledge of God, and they shall make even remote shores to ring with his praises."

Also note as you will learn in a later chapter that the word "dispersion" does not appear in the King James Bible and is used here in the Book of Mormon verse as above and also used in Henry's commentary. Note here that the entire premise of the Book of Mormon is found; escaping from "the land", going to "the isles of the sea" or America by "dispersion" and "the knowledge of God" being "spread" to them."

Now in 1 Nephi Joseph Smith makes up a prophet so that he can utilize the phrase "isles of the sea", 1 Nephi 19: 10, 12, 16

> [**10**] And the God of our fathers, who were led out of Egypt, out of bondage, and also were preserved in the wilderness by him, yea, the God of Abraham, and of Isaac, and the God of Jacob, yieldeth himself, according to the words of the angel, as a man, into the hands of wicked men, to be lifted up, according to the words of Zenock, and to be crucified, according to the words of Neum, and to be buried in a sepulchre, according to the words of Zenos, which he spake concerning the three days of darkness, which should be a sign given of his death unto those who should inhabit **the isles of the sea**, more especially given unto those who are of the house of Israel.
>
> [**12**] And all these things must surely come, saith the prophet Zenos. And the rocks of the earth must rend; and because of the groanings of the earth, many of the kings of **the isles of the sea** shall be wrought upon by the Spirit of God, to exclaim: The God of nature suffers.
>
> [**16**] Yea, then will he remember **the isles of the sea**; yea, and all the people who are of the house of Israel, will I gather in, saith the Lord, according to the words of the prophet Zenos, from the four quarters of the earth.

Here Smith starts out the Book of Mormon with a made up prophet, the prophet Zenos, which by the way he took from either or all of the commentaries; Henry, Gill, Wesley or Clarke, all use the word Zeno. Of course all Joseph Smith needed to do was add the "s" to Zeno to create the prophet Zenos. As you will see in a latter chapter Joseph Smith utilized the commentaries to come up with some of the names he employs in the Book of Mormon. Below is a quote from Henry's commentary showing this name.

> **COM** Henry: Rom 1:19-32 "for which many of the heathen, even of those among them who passed for wise men, as Solon and **Zeno**, were infamous, against the plainest and most obvious dictates of natural light."

In verse 10 of 1 Nephi, as we outlined above, Joseph Smith wrote that the prophet Zenos said that the sign will be "given of his (Jesus) death unto those who should inhabit **the isles of the sea**, more especially given unto those who are of the house of Israel." This of course he knew was to be written into the Book of Mormon when Jesus appears to the forerunners of the Native Americans. Here is more confirmation that he is saying they are "of the house of Israel" which again is the premise of the Book of Mormon that he again verifies in verse 16.

Again in 1 Nephi 22 verse 4 he gives more confirmation of his reading of the commentaries.

> "And behold, there are many who are already lost from the knowledge of those who are at Jerusalem. Yea, the more part of all the tribes have been led away; and they are scattered to and fro upon **the isles of the sea**; and whither they are none of us knoweth, save that we know that they have been led away."

It is interesting how similar this verse in 1 Nephi 22 is to Clarke's commentary that we outlined in the beginning of this chapter.

> **COM** Clarke: Hosea 9:17 "And where they have wandered to, who can tell? and in what nations to be found, no man knows. **Wanderers** they are; and perhaps even now unknown to themselves. Some have thought they have found them in one country; some, in another; and a very pious writer, in a book entitled, The Star in the West, (*by Boudinot)* thinks he has found their descendants in the American Indians; among whom he has discovered many customs, apparently the same with those of the ancient Jews, and commanded in the Law."

Here we see that Smith believed that all the lost tribes were led away to the "isles of the sea" not just those who ended up in the Americas. As noted above the commentaries stated that many lands where the "isles of the sea". Smith clarifies this idea in 2 Nephi 10 verse 21;

> "But great are the promises of the Lord unto them who are upon **the isles of the sea**; wherefore as it says isles, there must needs be more than this, and they are inhabited also by our brethren.

And again he shows the premise of the Book of Mormon in 2 Nephi 29:7. Here he is saying there are not just those in Jerusalem who will see or be taken care of by Jesus but those in the "isles of the sea" in other words the "other sheep I have" idea found elsewhere in the Book of Mormon.

> "Know ye not that there are more nations than one? Know ye not that I, the Lord your God, have created all men, and that I remember those who are upon **the isles of the sea**; and that I rule in the heavens above and in the earth beneath; and I bring forth my word unto the children of men, yea, even upon all the nations of the earth?"

At one time Joseph Smith, making up an entire paragraph as he occasionally did, made the mistake of using the more modern form of the words "isles of the sea" by using "islands of the sea". As you will note in a future chapter Joseph Smith made this mistake of utilizing modern phrases by error when most of the time he was trying to use King James style English to make his work sound "more religious". It is important to note here that both the King James Version of the Bible and the commentaries use the phrase "isles of the sea" and not "islands of the sea". Hence he made this mistake in a hasty attempt to add this to the Book of Mormon as a defense for the Book of Mormon as these words are supposed to be direct quotes from God. The mistake we are now talking about appears in 2 Nephi 29:11.

> "For I command all men, both in the east and in the west, and in the north, and in the south, and in **the islands of the sea**, that they shall write the words which I speak unto them; for out of the books which shall be written I will judge the world, every man according to their works, according to that which is written."

What is particularly interesting is that Joseph Smith wanted his premise of the "isles of the sea" to fit so much that he changed Isaiah, which he quotes, in order to make it fit this idea. Let us look at Isaiah 49:8. In order to make it easier to see the differences between the verses as they appear in the Bible and the Book of Mormon I will bold the differences in each. In the Isaiah verse I will bold what is the same and not bold what has changed and in the Book of Mormon verse I will do the opposite.

> **KJV** Isaiah 49:8 **"Thus saith the LORD, In an acceptable time have I heard thee, and in a day of salvation have I helped thee: and I will preserve thee, and give thee for a covenant of the people, to establish the earth, to cause to inherit the desolate heritages;"**

Now let us look at the Book of Mormon*'s* version of this verse found in **BOM** 1 Nephi 21:8.

> "Thus saith the Lord: In an acceptable time have I heard thee, **O isles of the sea**, and in a day of salvation have I helped thee; and I will preserve thee, and give thee **my servant** for a covenant of the people, to establish the earth, to cause to inherit the desolate

heritages;"

Note the additions which I have bolded. Joseph Smith wanted to change this verse in Isaiah to meet his story premise. So he added "O isles of the sea" and as we will discuss later "my servant" signifying himself. "In an acceptable time" meaning to Joseph Smith his day and the Book of Mormon. In other words a person supposedly living around 600 BC is quoting Isaiah, which the Book of Mormon claims they have copies of, but somehow adds the words "O isles of the sea" and "my servant". Something a Jew would not have done. But of course we know that this is nothing more than evidence that Joseph Smith wrote the Book of Mormon to fit his premise which he came up with through studying the aforementioned commentaries.

Joseph Smith changed much of Isaiah to fit this premise and remember many of the ideas we outlined above and will outline come from these commentaries comments on Isaiah. Let us take a look at some of those changes. First let us look at another verse this time in

> **KJV** Isaiah 48:3. "**I have declared the former things from the beginning; and they went forth out of my mouth, and I shewed them; I did them suddenly,** and they came to pass."

And now **BOM** 1 Nephi 20:3

> "**Behold**, I have declared the former things from the beginning; and they went forth out of my mouth, and I showed them. I did **show** them suddenly.

Note here that Joseph Smith leaves off "and they came to pass". He does this throughout his quotations of Isaiah to change the tense. He cannot have it ending with a comment that would indicate it had already been fulfilled because it needs to be in the future or in 1800's America to be precise.

I would like to stress a point before I continue here. This type of change alone is considerable evidence the Book of Mormon is a fake and points to the fact that Joseph Smith wrote it, especially with phrases like the addition of "my servant" above and as we will see later, but the evidence you will see next and the evidence compiled throughout this and my much lager work is evidence beyond doubt in other words it is "Absolute Proof" that Joseph Smith wrote the Book of Mormon and that it is a fake. But of course due to space constraints I will not go into every detail.

And now another significant addition: **KJV** Isaiah 49:13

> "**Sing, O heavens; and be joyful, O earth; and break forth into singing, O mountains: for the LORD hath comforted his people, and will have mercy upon his afflicted.**"

BOM 1 Nephi 21:13

> "Sing, O heavens; and be joyful, O earth; **for the feet of those who are in the east shall be established**; and break forth into singing, O mountains; **for they shall be smitten no more;** for the

Lord hath comforted his people, and will have mercy upon his afflicted."

Note the changes in tense here, both additions need to signify a future event. For Joseph Smith it needs to be changed so it can fit with the premise of the Book of Mormon so he added; "shall be established", "shall be smitten no more" and "the feet of those are in the east shall be established" Those in the east are those who left Israel the ten lost tribes. The implication that they are of the east implies that they shall at least be established in the west and thus America and elsewhere or as Joseph Smith wants us to believe "the isles of the sea". How can we know that it is America? Well he clarifies that it is a future event and that "they shall be smitten no more" in Joseph Smith's time America was developing tremendously and had not seen any major wars from rival nations.

And another: **KJV** Isaiah 48:14:

> "**All ye, assemble yourselves, and hear**; which **among them hath declared these things? The LORD hath loved him: he will do his pleasure on Babylon, and his arm shall be on the Chaldeans.**"

And now **BOM** 1 Nephi 21:14

> "All ye, assemble yourselves, and hear; **who** among them hath declared these things **unto them**? The Lord hath loved him; **yea, and he will fulfill his word which he hath declared by them; and** he will do his pleasure on Babylon, and his arm shall come upon the Chaldeans."

Again if we look at the additions in bold in the Nephi quote we can see that he changed "which" to "who" thus signifying himself. For this same reason he added "unto them" meaning us who receive Joseph Smith's words and the Book of Mormon which explains the next addition, "**yea, and he will fulfill his word which he hath declared by them; and**" which again is signifying the Book of Mormon. Note also here that he is manipulating the tense; it says "will fulfill". Joseph Smith does this in order to tell us that it will be a future event. After all this is supposed to be 600BC and the Book of Mormon does not come into existence until 1830 AD. Now Joseph Smith changed the tense in several of his quotes from Isaiah and he did so in order not just to change the meaning but to make it fit his premise.

Let us look at: **KJV** Isaiah 48:16

> "**Come ye near unto me**, hear ye this; **I have not spoken in secret from the beginning; from the time that it was**, there am I: **and** now **the Lord GOD, and his Spirit, hath sent me.**"

Now **BOM** 1 Nephi 21:16

> "Come ye near unto me; I have not spoken in secret; from the beginning, from the time that it was **declared have I spoken**; and

the Lord God, and his Spirit, hath sent me."

Notice he eliminates the tense word in Isaiah that would indicate the present tense. Again he needs it to be a future event and thus eliminates "now". In addition he eliminates the present tense phrase "there am I".

Let us look at more: **KJV** Isaiah 48:17

> **"Thus saith the LORD, thy Redeemer, the Holy One of Israel; I** am **the LORD thy God which teacheth thee to profit, which leadeth thee by the way that thou shouldest go."**

Now **BOM** 1 Nephi 21:17

> **"And** thus saith the Lord, thy Redeemer, the Holy One of Israel; I **have sent him**, the Lord thy God who teacheth thee to profit, who leadeth thee by the way thou shouldst go, **hath done it."**

Note that the elimination of "am" and the addition of "have sent him" completely changes the meaning of the verse. The "have sent him" is a reference to Joseph Smith himself as well as the "hath done it". Joseph Smith wants us to believe the "who leadeth thee" is indeed himself. In reality it is "the Lord" that this verse refers to. Joseph Smith is saying here that God is saying this to the future people who read it. When in fact it was directed to those of the days of Isaiah.

Now let us look at another: **KJV** Isaiah 48:14

> **"All ye, assemble yourselves, and hear;** which **among them hath declared these things? The LORD hath loved him: he will do his pleasure on Babylon, and his arm shall be on the Chaldeans."**

BOM 1 Nephi 20:14

> "All ye, assemble yourselves, and hear; **who** among them hath declared these things **unto them**? The Lord hath loved him; **yea, and he will fulfill his word which he hath declared by them; and** he will do his pleasure on Babylon, and his arm shall come upon the Chaldeans."

Note here the change from "which" to "who" signifying Joseph Smith who is saying "declared these things unto them? The addition "unto them" signifies us in "the latter-day" and he adds **"yea, and he will fulfill his word which he hath declared by them;"** The word of the Book of Mormon that he declared by those of the Book of Mormon.

And the very next verse: **KJV** Isaiah 48:15

> **"I, even I, have spoken; yea, I have called him: I have brought him, and he shall make his way prosperous."**

BOM 1 Nephi 20:15

> **Also, saith the Lord; I the Lord, yea**, I have spoken; yea, I have called him **to declare**, I have brought him, and he shall make his way prosperous.

Again note the change in tense with the use of "to declare" in other words he is saying Joseph Smith will declare.

And another: **KJV** Isaiah 48:17

> **"Thus saith the LORD, thy Redeemer, the Holy One of Israel; I** am **the LORD thy God which teacheth thee to profit, which leadeth thee by the way that thou shouldest go."**

BOM 1 Nephi 20:17

> **And** thus saith the Lord, thy Redeemer, the Holy One of Israel; I **have sent him,** the Lord thy God who teacheth thee to profit, who leadeth thee by the way thou shouldst go, **hath done it.**

Adding again the idea that the Lord is saying to those in the future "I have sent him" meaning Joseph Smith and that he has lead us and that Joseph Smith "hath done it".

And another: **KJV** Isaiah 48:22

> **"There is no peace, saith the LORD, unto the wicked."**

BOM 1 Nephi 20:22

> **"And notwithstanding he hath done all this, and greater also, there** is no peace, saith the Lord, unto the wicked."

Joseph Smith continues with the additions which reference him, "he hath done all this".

And another more significant addition: **KJV** Isaiah 49:1

> **"Listen, O isles, unto me; and hearken, ye people, from far; The LORD hath called me from the womb; from the bowels of my mother hath he made mention of my name."**

BOM 1 Nephi 21:1

> **"And again: Hearken, O ye house of Israel, all ye that are broken off and are driven out because of the wickedness of the pastors of my people; yea, all ye that are broken off, that are scattered abroad, who are of my people, O house of Israel.** Listen, O isles, unto me, and hearken ye people from far; the Lord hath called me from the womb; from the bowels of my mother hath he made mention of my name."

Again God talking to us in the future or the "latter days" we "are broken off" and "are scattered abroad" and again clarifying that we in the "isles" are of the "house of Israel".

And another: **KJV** Isaiah 49:5

> **"And now, saith the LORD that formed me from the womb to be his servant, to bring Jacob again to him, Though Israel be not gathered, yet shall I be glorious in the eyes of the LORD, and my God shall be my strength."**

BOM 1 Nephi 21:5

> "And now, saith the Lord -- that formed me from the womb **that I**

should be his servant, to bring Jacob again to him -- though Israel be not gathered, yet shall I be glorious in the eyes of the Lord, and my God shall be my strength."

Joseph Smith's importance again emphasized in this addition to Isaiah "that I should".

And another: **KJV** Isaiah 49:9

"That thou mayest say to the prisoners, Go forth; to them that are in darkness, Shew yourselves. They shall feed in the ways, and their pastures shall be in all high places."

BOM 1 Nephi 21:9

"That thou mayest say to the prisoners: Go forth; to them that **sit** in darkness: Show yourselves. They shall feed in the ways, and their pastures shall be in all high places."

A simple change but an important one Joseph Smith had to change the tense "are" to "sit". It is also a change that shows how desperate Joseph Smith was to make Isaiah fit the idea that he was a bringer of knowledge and the Book of Mormon.

Another simple addition to say that it is a future event:

KJV Isaiah 49:12

"Behold, these shall come from far: and, lo, these from the north and from the west; and these from the land of Sinim."

BOM 1 Nephi 21:12

"And then, O house of Israel, behold, these shall come from far; and lo, these from the north and from the west; and these from the land of Sinim."

Let us look at another: Incidentally he quotes continuously from Isaiah from Isaiah 48:1 through Isaiah 49:26 with his additions and subtractions from those verses.

KJV Isaiah 49:18

"Lift up thine eyes round about, and behold: all these gather themselves together, and come to thee. As I live, saith the LORD, thou shalt surely clothe thee with them all, as with an ornament, and bind them on thee, **as a bride** doeth."

BOM 1 Nephi 21:18

"Lift up thine eyes round about and behold; all these gather themselves together, and **they shall** come to thee. And as I live, saith the Lord, thou shalt surely clothe thee with them all, as with an ornament, and bind them on **even** as a bride."

Note again the tense addition "they shall".

Now let us look at an additional section of the Book of Mormon in 2 Nephi chapter 7 were Joseph Smith quotes from Isaiah 49:23 through 50:1-7 skips verse 8 and 9 and picks back up with Isaiah 50:10 through 52:2

Isn't it interesting that with the two verses of 2 Nephi chapter 6 verses 6 and 7 and then again in 2 Nephi chapter 6 starting with verse 6 Joseph Smith picks up essentially where he left off in 1 Nephi many many chapters earlier. The last verse he quotes of Isaiah in 1 Nephi chapter 21 is Isaiah 49:25 and when he picks back up in 2 Nephi chapter 6 quoting directly Isaiah verse after verse, he starts with Isaiah 49:22. Now in-between these two sections from 1 Nephi to 2 Nephi he utilizes phrases and direct quotes from Isaiah many times.

Now the first time he quotes Isaiah 49:25 in 1 Nephi 21:25 he quotes it exactly as it appears in Isaiah 49:25 but the second time Joseph Smith quotes Isaiah 49:25 in 2 Nephi 6:17 he makes additions:

KJV Isaiah 49:25

> **"But thus saith the LORD, Even the captives of the mighty shall be taken away, and the prey of the terrible shall be delivered: for I will contend with him that contendeth with thee, and I will save thy children."**

BOM 1 Nephi 21:25

> "But thus saith the Lord, even the captives of the mighty shall be taken away, and the prey of the terrible shall be delivered; for I will contend with him that contendeth with thee, and I will save thy children."

"Now the second time he quotes Isaiah 49:25 in 2 Nephi 6:17 he makes additions:" Of course if the first one was a quote from *The Book of* Isaiah which Joseph Smith claims is from a copy of Isaiah the Nephites had, then why would the second have an addition and subtraction, which of course it does not in reality. Notice those changes:

KJV Isaiah 49:25

> **"But thus saith the LORD, Even the captives of the mighty shall be taken away, and the prey of the terrible shall be delivered: for I will contend with him that contendeth with thee**, and I will save thy children."

BOM 1 Nephi 6:17

> "But thus saith the Lord: Even the captives of the mighty shall be taken away, and the prey of the terrible shall be delivered; **for the Mighty God shall deliver his covenant people. For thus saith the Lord:** I will contend with them that contendeth with thee"

This is a significant error and again shows us that the Book of Mormon is a fake and that Joseph Smith wrote it. Now back to the variations in 2 Nephi:

KJV Isaiah 50:4

> **"The Lord GOD hath given me the tongue of the learned, that I should know how to speak a word in season to** him that is **weary: he wakeneth morning by morning, he wakeneth mine ear to hear as the learned."**

BOM 1 Nephi 7:4

"The Lord God hath given me the tongue of the learned, that I should know how to speak a word in season unto **thee, O house of Israel. When ye are** weary he waketh morning by morning. He waketh mine ear to hear as the learned."

Here he changes the singular "him" to the plural by adding "O house of Israel. When ye are" again he did this to fit the premise of the Book of Mormon. This person is Joseph Smith himself so he needed it to be to all the house of Israel.

And another:

KJV Isaiah 50:9

"**Behold, the Lord GOD will help me; who** is he that **shall condemn me?** lo, **they all shall wax old as a garment;** the **moth shall eat them up.**"

BOM 1 Nephi 7:9

"**For** the Lord God will help me. **And all they** who shall condemn me, behold, all they shall wax old as a garment, **and** the moth shall eat them up."

He makes a significant change in meaning here. In the original the question is "who is he" Joseph Smith makes it "all they" singular to plural.

And another:

KJV Isaiah 51:18

"There is **none to guide her among all the sons** whom **she hath brought forth; neither** is there any **that taketh her by the hand of all the sons that she hath brought up.**"

BOM 1 Nephi 7:18

"**And** none to guide her among all the sons she hath brought forth; neither that taketh her by the hand, of all the sons she hath brought up."

Another attempt here to change the meaning from present tense by removing "there is" and "is there any".

And now another set of verses with significant changes in meaning to fit the Book of Mormon premise.

KJV Isaiah 51:19

"**These two** things **are come unto thee; who shall be sorry for thee? desolation, and destruction, and the famine, and the sword: by whom shall I comfort thee?**"

BOM 1 Nephi 7:19

"These two **sons** are come unto thee, who shall be sorry for thee -- **thy** desolation and destruction, and the famine and the sword -- **and** by whom shall I comfort thee?"

Note here that Joseph Smith is choosing the word "sons" to imply the sons of Nephi instead of "things". This makes this verse make little sense for as we are told the "two things" are; "desolation and destruction," and "famine and the sword". Now he continues this onto the next verse:

KJV Isaiah 51:20

> **"Thy sons have fainted, they lie at the head of all the streets, as a wild bull in a net: they are full of the fury of the LORD, the rebuke of thy God."**

BOM 1 Nephi 7:20

> "Thy sons have fainted, **save these two**; they lie at the head of all the streets; as a wild bull in a net, they are full of the fury of the Lord, the rebuke of thy God."

Now again Joseph Smith wants to say that there are two sons, the two sons of Nephi of the Book of Mormon, so he can't say that they have fainted because they are supposed to be faithful so he adds the clarifier "save these two".

We now again skip many many chapters where again Joseph Smith starts quoting Isaiah. He begins this in 2 Nephi 12:2 by quoting Isaiah 2:1 all the way through, believe it or not, Isaiah 14:32. Here again we will look at the changes made and we will see that he made these changes to fit his addition of himself and the Book of Mormon and its premise into Isaiah.

KJV Isaiah 2:5

> **"O house of Jacob, come ye, and let us walk in the light of the LORD."**

BOM 1 Nephi 12:5

> "O house of Jacob, come ye and let us walk in the light of the Lord; **yea, come, for ye have** all gone astray, every one to his **wicked** ways."

KJV Isaiah 53:6

> **"All** we like sheep **have gone astray**; we **have** turned **every one to his own way**; and the LORD hath laid on him the iniquity of us all."

Note that Joseph Smith had to add this sentence to the end of this verse, which he modified from Isaiah 53:6. He did so in order to make his premise work, in other words everyone was bad in Jerusalem and Israel and so Lehi had no choice but to leave. Also note: he is stating that he is reading from Isaiah which would not have had these modifications let alone an addition of a verse written toward the end of Isaiah in reality written many years later. In the very next verse he makes more modifications along this line.

KJV Isaiah 2:6

> **"Therefore thou hast forsaken thy people the house of Jacob, because they be replenished from the east, and are soothsayers like the Philistines, and they please themselves in the children**

of strangers."
BOM 1 Nephi 12:6

"Therefore, **O Lord**, thou hast forsaken thy people, the house of Jacob, because they be replenished from the east, **and hearken unto** soothsayers like the Philistines, and they please themselves in the children of strangers."

Joseph Smith changed this verse from "and are" to "and hearken unto" again he can not make them utterly bad or else Lehi leaving Jerusalem would be counted among them and thus the descendents and those coming to America thus destroying his premise.

And yet another:
KJV Isaiah 2:9

"**And the mean man boweth down, and the great man humbleth himself: therefore forgive them not**."

BOM 1 Nephi 12:9

"And the mean man boweth **not** down, and the great man humbleth himself **not**, therefore, forgive him not."

Joseph Smith did not understand the meaning behind this verse and therefore changed the meaning by adding "not", The meaning was supposed to be that now, after the Lord is in his mountain, the mean man bows down and the great man humbles himself so, don't forgive them now just because they do it because the Lord is in his mountain. Again he had to change this in order to keep with his premise it didn't make much sense to him if the "mean man" did not bow down and the "great man" would not humble himself nor would it make sense to the premise of the Book of Mormon.

More evidence that he had to change the verse to meet his premise:
KJV Isaiah 2:10

"**Enter into the rock, and hide thee in the dust, for fear of the LORD**, and **for the glory of his majesty**."

BOM 1 Nephi 12:10

"**O ye wicked ones**, enter into the rock, and hide thee in the dust, for **the** fear of the Lord and the glory of his majesty **shall smite thee**."

Again Joseph Smith had to change this verse to match his premise, not Lehi's people and descendents just the "wicked ones". It would not fit the Book of Mormon story if they were all wicked.

And in the very next verse he adds to the beginning of the verse to make it a future event.
KJV Isaiah 2:11

"**The lofty looks of man shall be humbled, and the haughtiness of men shall be bowed down, and the LORD alone shall be exalted in that day.**"

BOM 1 Nephi 12:11

"**And it shall come to pass that** the lofty looks of man shall be humbled, and the haughtiness of men shall be bowed down, and the Lord alone shall be exalted in that day."

And he continues the addition of future tense words and phrases in the next two verses:

KJV Isaiah 2:12

"**For the day of the LORD of hosts** shall be **upon every one** that is **proud and lofty, and upon every one that is lifted up; and he shall be brought low:**"

BOM 1 Nephi 12:12

"For the day of the Lord of Hosts **soon cometh** upon **all nations, yea**, upon every one; **yea, upon the** proud and lofty, and upon every one who is lifted up, and he shall be brought low."

Again he had to change this so it did not mean Lehi and his descendents but "all nations" and in addition it had to be a future event and not a present one.

KJV Isaiah 2:13

"And **upon all the cedars of Lebanon,** that **are high and lifted up, and upon all the oaks of Bashan,**"

BOM 1 Nephi 12:13

"**Yea, and the day of the Lord shall come** upon all the cedars of Lebanon, **for they** are high and lifted up; and upon all the oaks of Bashan;"

Joseph Smith is using terms like "shall come" and "soon cometh" and "the day of the Lord" above because he is trying to say it hasn't happened yet, from his day 1820's AD.

And another:

KJV Isaiah 2:14

"**And upon all the high mountains, and upon all the hills** that **are lifted up,**"

BOM 1 Nephi 12:14

"And upon all the high mountains, and upon all the hills, **and upon all the nations which** are lifted up, **and upon every people;**"

Again, he had to add the above statements to keep within his premise, please see the above explanation.

More tense changes to signify a future event. Note that he also adds the exact same phrases to 2 Nephi 12:21;

KJV Isaiah 2:19

"**And they shall go into the holes of the rocks, and into the caves of the earth, for fear of the LORD, and** for **the glory of**

his majesty, when he ariseth to shake terribly the earth."
BOM 1 Nephi 12:19

"And they shall go into the holes of the rocks, and into the caves
of the earth, for the fear of the Lord **shall come upon them** and
the glory of his majesty **shall smite them**, when he ariseth to
shake terribly the earth."

More changes in tense:

KJV Isaiah 3:8

"**For Jerusalem is ruined, and Judah is fallen: because their
tongue and their doings** are **against the LORD, to provoke the
eyes of his glory.**"

BOM 1 Nephi 13:8

"For Jerusalem is ruined, and Judah is fallen, because their
tongue**s** and their doings **have been** against the Lord, to provoke
the eyes of his glory."

Notice the change in tense. Joseph Smith needed for Jerusalem to already
be in ruin and Judah to already have fallen so there doings can't be in present
tense.

And more:

KJV Isaiah 3:11

"**Woe unto the wicked!** it **shall** be ill with him: **for the reward of**
his hands **shall be** given him."

BOM 1 Nephi 13:11

"Wo unto the wicked, **for they shall perish;** for the reward of
their hands shall be **upon** them!"

Again changing tense and singular to plural also note instead of "ill" he
changes it to "perish" again to maintain his premise.

And more:

KJV Isaiah 3:18

"**In that day the Lord will take away the bravery of their
tinkling ornaments** about their feet, **and** their **cauls, and** their
round tires like the moon,"

BOM 1 Nephi 13:18

"In that day the Lord will take away the bravery of their tinkling
ornaments, and cauls, and round tires like the moon;"

Here Joseph Smith left off "about their feet" because he knew that in his
time the 1830's people did not wear "tinkling ornaments about there feet".

Now another interesting change:

KJV Isaiah 5:9

"**In mine ears said the LORD of hosts, Of a truth many houses
shall be desolate,** even **great and fair, without inhabitant.**"

BOM 1 Nephi 15:9

"In mine ears, said the Lord of Hosts, of a truth many houses shall be desolate, and great and fair **cities** without inhabitant."

Joseph Smith added the word "cities" to make it more people.

Next a simple change but an important one:

KJV Isaiah 6:9

"And he said, Go, and tell this people, Hear ye indeed, but understand not; and see ye indeed, but perceive not."

BOM 1 Nephi 16:9

"And he said: Go and tell this people -- Hear ye indeed, but they understood not; and see ye indeed, but they perceive**d** not."

Again he had to change the tense so that their inability was in the past not in the present, hence the addition of a single "d" to the end of the word "perceive".

And now another change:

KJV Isaiah 6:13

"But yet in it **shall be a tenth, and** it **shall return, and shall be eaten: as a teil tree, and as an oak, whose substance is in them, when they cast their leaves: so the holy seed shall be the substance thereof."**

BOM 1 Nephi 16:13

"But yet **there** shall be a tenth, and **they** shall return, and shall be eaten, as a teil-tree, and as an oak whose substance is in them when they cast their leaves; so the holy seed shall be the substance thereof."

Again changing the tense and singular state, it is interesting that in this one he changed a singular "in it" to a tense "there" to make the verse about a future event instead of a thing. If you read the previous verse in Isaiah the "it" is "the land" thus changing the entire meaning of the verse and in reality making it not make much sense. For example let's look at what it is really, "But yet in the land shall be a tenth, and the land shall return" instead of "in the future there shall be a tenth" and "in the future they shall return."

And now a small but significant change:

KJV Isaiah 9:3

"Thou hast multiplied the nation, and not **increased the joy: they joy before thee according to the joy in harvest, and as men rejoice when they divide the spoil."**

BOM 1 Nephi 19:3

"Thou hast multiplied the nation, and increased the joy -- they joy before thee according to the joy in harvest, and as men rejoice when they divide the spoil."

Joseph Smith left out "not" here and in the process completely changes the meaning of the verse and also negates the whole meaning of the very next verse:

KJV Isaiah 9:4

"For thou hast broken the yoke of his burden, and the staff of his shoulder, the rod of his oppressor, as in the day of Midian."

BOM 1 Nephi 19:4

"For thou hast broken the yoke of his burden, and the staff of his shoulder, the rod of his oppressor."

Joseph Smith left off "as in the day of Midian" because in the day of Midian the Jews defeated Midian and there was peace for forty years. This story isn't even close to what Joseph Smith is trying to portray for "America" and the coming forth of the restored church, which he knew from the commentaries but chose to ignore.

And another change:

KJV Isaiah 9:17

"Therefore the LORD shall have no joy in their young men, neither shall have mercy on their fatherless and widows: for every one is an hypocrite and an evildoer, and every mouth speaketh folly. For all this his anger is not turned away, but his hand is stretched out still."

BOM 1 Nephi 19:17

"Therefore the Lord shall have no joy in their young men, neither shall have mercy on their fatherless and widows; for every one **of them** is **a** hypocrite and an evildoer, and every mouth speaketh folly. For all this his anger is not turned away, but his hand is stretched out still."

Here Joseph Smith changes this verse in Isaiah from everyone meaning all people to only "them", this he does again to not signify him or his people or the people of Nephi since they cannot be hypocrites.

And again he wants the plural in the next verse:

KJV Isaiah 9:18

"For wickedness burneth as the fire: it shall devour the briers and thorns, and shall kindle in the thickets of the forest, and they shall mount up like the lifting up of smoke."

BOM 1 Nephi 19:18

"For wickedness burneth as the fire; it shall devour the briers and thorns, and shall kindle in the thickets of the forests, and they shall mount up like the lifting up of smoke."

Again he needs to make it everywhere and not just one place hence the plural "forests".

Another interesting change:

KJV Isaiah 10:5

"O Assyrian, the rod of mine anger, and the staff in their hand

is mine **indignation.**"
BOM 1 Nephi 20:15
"O Assyrian, the rod of mine anger, and the staff in their hand is **their** indignation."
This change takes the indignation out of the hand of God and places it in the hand of the enemy with "their" instead of "mine" something that would never be the case to Isaiah.
Here is another significant change:
KJV Isaiah 10:13
"**For he saith, By the strength of my hand I have done** it, **and by my wisdom**; for I am prudent: and I have removed the bounds **of the people, and have robbed their treasures, and I have put down the inhabitants like a valiant man:**"
BOM 1 Nephi 20:13
"For he saith: By the strength of my hand and by my wisdom I have done **these things;** for I am prudent; and I have **moved the borders** of the people, and have robbed their treasures, and I have put down the inhabitants like a valiant man;"
Many changes here; changing "it" the singular to the plural "these things" and Joseph Smith changed "removed the bounds" which actually means remove the chains that hold them to "moved the borders of the people" so that he could say that the borders of the people were moved to the America's but changed the entire meaning of the verse to make it have this meaning and to again fit his premise.
Another change in which Joseph Smith did not understand the original meaning, after all, the original writer knew what he was trying to say.
KJV Isaiah 13:3
"**I have commanded my sanctified ones, I have also called my mighty ones for mine anger**, even **them that rejoice in my highness.**"
BOM 1 Nephi 23:3
"I have commanded my sanctified ones, I have also called my mighty ones, for mine anger **is not upon** them that rejoice in my highness."
This verse apparently did not make sense to Joseph Smith so he changed it, he must have not been able to reconcile the fact that it stated that God would be angry with his "mighty ones" of course Joseph Smith did not understand the thought behind the verse. His "mighty ones" were to destroy enemies in fulfillment of his anger.
A rather long addition to a verse in Isaiah:
KJV Isaiah 13:22
"**And the wild beasts of the islands shall cry in their desolate**

houses, and dragons in their pleasant palaces: and her time is near to come, and her days shall not be prolonged."

BOM 1 Nephi 23:22

"And the wild beasts of the islands shall cry in their desolate houses, and dragons in their pleasant palaces; and her time is near to come, and her day shall not be prolonged. **For I will destroy her speedily; yea, for I will be merciful unto my people, but the wicked shall perish.**"

Joseph Smith added the last sentence to fit his premise. The verse sounded as though it would be all over so he added the clarification that the merciful would be spared but the wicked would parish.

And another significant change:

KJV Isaiah 14:2

"**And the people shall take them, and bring them to their place: and the house of Israel shall possess them** in the **land of the LORD for servants and handmaids: and they shall take them captives,** whose **captives they were; and they shall rule over their oppressors.**"

BOM 1 Nephi 24:2

"And the people shall take them and bring them to their place; **yea, from far unto the ends of the earth; and they shall return to their lands of promise.** And the house of Israel shall possess them, **and** the land of the Lord shall be for servants and handmaids; and they shall take them captives unto **whom** they were captives; and they shall rule over their oppressors."

Joseph Smith added to the first sentence to fit his premise, "from far unto the ends of the earth and they shall return to their lands of promise" this is all those who immigrated to the US. And instead of "in the land of the Lord" he changed it to "the land of the Lord" as he had intimated earlier that "the land of the Lord" was America.

Time change again in the next two verses:

KJV Isaiah 14:3

"**And it shall come to pass in** the **day that the LORD shall give thee rest from thy sorrow, and from thy fear, and from the hard bondage wherein thou wast made to serve,**"

BOM 1 Nephi 24:3

"And it shall come to pass in **that** day that the Lord shall give thee rest, from thy sorrow, and from thy fear, and from the hard bondage wherein thou wast made to serve."

Joseph Smith changed "the" to "that" to show a specific time and to fit his premise.

KJV Isaiah 14:4

"**That thou shalt take up this proverb against the king of Babylon, and say, How hath the oppressor ceased! the golden city ceased!**"

BOM 1 Nephi 24:4

"**And it shall come to pass in that day**, that thou shalt take up this proverb against the king of Babylon, and say: How hath the oppressor ceased, the golden city ceased!"

As in the previous verse Joseph Smith added the beginning line to denote a time and to fit his premise.

Now another change in tense:

KJV Isaiah 14:16

"**They that see thee shall narrowly look upon thee, and consider thee,** saying, **Is this the man that made the earth to tremble, that did shake kingdoms;**"

BOM 1 Nephi 24:16

"They that see thee shall narrowly look upon thee, and **shall** consider thee, **and shall** say: Is this the man that made the earth to tremble, that did shake kingdoms?"

Here Joseph Smith takes the present tense word "saying" and changes that present tense meaning by adding "shall" and "shall say".

Another significant change:

KJV Isaiah 14:19

"**But thou art cast out of thy grave like an abominable branch, and as the** raiment **of those that are slain, thrust through with a sword, that go down to the stones of the pit; as a carcase trodden under feet.**"

BOM 1 Nephi 24:19

"But thou art cast out of thy grave like an abominable branch, and the **remnant** of those that are slain, thrust through with a sword, that go down to the stones of the pit; as a carcass trodden under feet."

This is an immense change here to fit his premise: Joseph Smith changed the word "raiment" which is obviously clothing to "remnant".

Another significant change:

KJV Isaiah 14:25

"**That I will** break **the Assyrian in my land, and upon my mountains tread him under foot: then shall his yoke depart from off them, and his burden depart from off their shoulders.**"

BOM 1 Nephi 24:25

"That I will **bring** the Assyrian in my land, and upon my mountains tread him under foot; then shall his yoke depart from off them, and his burden depart from off their shoulders."

Joseph Smith changed "break" to "bring" so that it would sound as though God were brining the Assyrians to America as many people from many nations came to America, this changes the entire meaning of the verse.

Another small but significant change:

KJV Isaiah 14:32

"What shall one then answer the messengers of the nation? That the LORD hath founded Zion, and the poor of his people shall trust in it."

BOM 1 Nephi 24:32

"What shall then answer the messengers of the nations? That the Lord hath founded Zion, and the poor of his people shall trust in it."

Again, an attempt to change the singular into the plural but this little change completely changes the meaning. Instead of just one nation the change makes it many nations. America is made up of many nations. Joseph Smith knew this hence the change.

And now to end this section let's look at a verse from 2 Nephi:

BOM 2 Nephi 25:1

"Now I, Nephi, do speak somewhat concerning the words which I have written, which have been spoken by the mouth of Isaiah. For behold, Isaiah spake many things which were hard for many of my people to understand; for they know not concerning the manner of prophesying among the Jews."

Now in this verse it clearly states that Nephi had written down what Isaiah had spoken, he couldn't possibly have remembered which means he could only have gotten it from a written source, which source is what we have from the Bible today, hence there should not be any of the changes outlined above. The last sentence is there to tell us that Joseph Smith actually knows what it prophesies about, in other words his premise about America is true. This shows that Joseph Smith actually is the one that made the changes and not a character from a book who lived hundreds of years before.

Now to continue our look at Isaiah Joseph Smith starting with 2 Nephi 26 verse 15 starts quoting from Isaiah chapter 29. What is interesting is that as before he does not quote exactly but utilizes Isaiah chapter 29 to fill in the story he is making up. In order to more easily clarify the distinctions between Isaiah and Nephi I will bold words that match. Note in these quotes how Joseph Smith only uses part of the verses of Isaiah to make up his story. Note that he creates these stories to fit the premise of the Book of Mormon and its coming forth in the "latter days". Again this is more proof that Joseph Smith made up the Book of Mormon.

KJV Isaiah 29:3

And I will **camp against thee round about**, and will **lay siege against thee with a mount, and** I will **raise forts against thee.**
KJV Isaiah 29:4
And thou shalt **be brought down**, and shalt speak out of the ground, and thy speech shall be low out of **the dust**, and thy voice shall be, as of one that hath a familiar spirit, out of the ground, and thy speech shall whisper out of the dust."
BOM 2 Nephi 26:15
"After my seed and the seed of my brethren shall have dwindled in unbelief, and shall have been smitten by the Gentiles; yea, after the Lord God shall have **camp**ed **against** them **round about**, and shall have laid **siege against** them **with a mount, and raised forts against them**; and after they shall have been **brought down** low in **the dust**, even that they are not, yet the words of the righteous shall be written, and the prayers of the faithful shall be heard, and all those who have dwindled in unbelief shall not be forgotten."
And...
KJV Isaiah 29:4
"And thou shalt be brought down, and **shalt speak out of the ground**, and thy **speech shall be low out of the dust, and** thy **voice shall be, as** of **one that hath a familiar spirit**, out **of the ground, and** thy **speech shall whisper out of the dust.**"
BOM 2 Nephi 26:16
"For those who shall be destroyed **shall speak** unto them **out of the ground**, and their **speech shall be low out of the dust, and** their **voice shall be as one that hath a familiar spirit**; for the Lord God will give unto him power, that he may whisper concerning them, even as it were **out of the ground; and** their **speech shall whisper out of the dust.**"
Notice Joseph Smith is changing the singular "thy" to the plural "them" this is an obvious reference to the Book of Mormon, hence the change from "thy" to "they" so it could mean those of the Book of Mormon.
KJV Isaiah 29:5
"Moreover the multitude of thy strangers shall be like small dust, **and the multitude of the terrible ones shall be as chaff that passeth away: yea, it shall be at an instant suddenly.**"
KJV Isaiah 29:20
"For the **terrible one** is brought to nought, and the scorner is consumed, and all that watch for iniquity are cut off:"
BOM 2 Nephi 26:18
"Wherefore, as those who have been destroyed have been destroyed speedily; **and the multitude of their terrible ones shall**

be as chaff that passeth away -- yea, thus saith the Lord God: **It shall be at an instant, suddenly**"

Now in-between this verse and the next verse where he picks up again with Isaiah 29:6 he uses significant phrases from other parts of Isaiah, including : Isaiah 57:14, Isaiah 10:13, Isaiah 3:15, Isaiah 45:22, and Isaiah 55:1.

KJV Isaiah 29:6

"Thou shalt **be visited of the LORD of hosts with thunder, and with earthquake, and great noise, with storm and tempest, and the flame of devouring fire.**"

BOM 1 Nephi 27:2

"And when that day shall come, they shall be visited of the Lord of Hosts, with thunder and with earthquake, and with a great noise, and with storm, and with tempest, and with the flame of devouring fire."

Joseph Smith also used the idea that his book the Book of Mormon was a "marvelous work" spoken of in Isaiah.

KJV Isaiah 29:14

"Therefore, behold, I **will proceed to do a marvellous work among** this people, even a **marvellous work and a wonder**: for the wisdom of their wise men shall perish, and the understanding of their prudent men shall be hid."

BOM 1 Nephi 22:8

"And after our seed is scattered the Lord God **will proceed to do a marvelous work among the** Gentiles, which shall be of great worth unto our seed; wherefore, it is likened unto their being nourished by the Gentiles and being carried in their arms and upon their shoulders."

As you can see he changed "this people" to "the Gentiles" in order of course to say that this would be the Book of Mormon that would come to the "isle of the sea" or as we have already noted "the Gentiles".

BOM 1 Nephi 14:7

"For the time cometh, saith the Lamb of God, that I will work a great and a **marvelous work** among the children of men; a work which shall be everlasting, either on the one hand or on the other -- either to the convincing of them unto peace and life eternal, or unto the deliverance of them to the hardness of their hearts and the blindness of their minds unto their being brought down into captivity, and also into destruction, both temporally and spiritually, according to the captivity of the devil, of which I have spoken."

This "marvelous work" is according to Joseph Smith the Book of Mormon.

Now if you look at the commentaries they talk about the "marvelous work". I won't go into great detail here on the use of the phrase "marvelous work" as it is used in both commentaries and the Book of Mormon. We are limited on space and we need to move onto the next chapter. I would refer you to the commentaries for more research. I will leave you with one quote here from the commentary of Gill.

> **COM** Gill: Isaiah 4:5 "and this will be all the Lord's doing, a work of his almighty power, and therefore signified by a "creation"; it will be a new, strange, and **marvellous work**; wonderful in the eyes of the saints, and in the eyes of the world, that those who have been forsaken and hated should be made an eternal excellency, and the joy of many generations,"

Chapter Three

The Sources of the Book of Mormon: A Detailed Look

As you are already aware Joseph Smith used the commentaries I outlined to create the Book of Mormon. We saw how the commentaries contained the idea of the Indians being descendents of the lost tribes of Israel and thus of "the House of Judah". And we also saw how Joseph Smith utilized the commentaries ideas of "the isles of the sea" and other ideas as fodder for the main ideas behind the Book of Mormon itself and its overall structure, in other words the framework of the Book of Mormon. We also looked at how he modified Isaiah to fit those premises. Now we will look at some of the more blatant uses of the commentaries found in the Book of Mormon.

Before we continue I would like to bring some statistics to your attention. Joseph Smith copied extensively from the King James Version of the Bible. In fact when I do a computer analysis of five word phrases used both in the Book of Mormon and the King James Version of the Bible, the results equal 37,291 matches. This means that there were 37,291 five word phrases that were found in both the King James Version of the Bible and the Book of Mormon. What is interesting is that when we compare the commentaries in the same fashion. We make an interesting discovery. I believe after completing my study, Joseph Smith used the commentary of Gill more than any of the other commentaries and the statistics bear this fact out. Using the same five word phrase comparison the Book of Mormon matches 58,995 found in Gill. This is significantly more than the results of those comparisons to the Bible. This comes out to 20% of the Book of Mormon, compared to the King James matching only 14% of the Book of Mormon. Obviously, statistically the King James Version of the Bible should be the higher percentage. Now when we compare Henry, Clarke and Wesley under the same criteria we have the following statistics; Henry 9572 or 3% of the Book of Mormon, Clarke, 29,768 or 10% of the Book of Mormon, and Wesley

Joseph Smith was smart enough not to copy entire paragraphs word for word from the commentaries in fact he knew that he needed to use as little as possible from the commentaries so it would be, at the least, very difficult to find out where he did indeed get the ideas for the Book of Mormon from. In fact it would have been of paramount importance that he not copy word for word too much from any source as to not be found out. For this reason it has been difficult for anyone to find the sources of the Book of Mormon. This is in fact the reason that it has been over 175 years since anyone has figured out what sources Joseph Smith used to come up with the Book of Mormon. As I stated in the beginning of this book, it wasn't until the advent of computers and that someone came along with certain computer skills, and was someone also learned in theology, that it could more readily be discerned which sources Joseph Smith used to create his work. But he actually did, having such a large work to undertake, make the mistake of copying some phrases and parts of entire paragraphs and even utilizing whole ideas from the commentaries to produce the Book of Mormon. Again, as with other chapters in this book, outlining all such instances would require a book many times bigger than the Book of Mormon itself and thus would be impractical to say the least. I will therefore only outline a few instances here and suggest that if you require further detail please see my companion CD I hope to create or the alternate website to see more of these details. So just to make it clear, what I will present here is a minute fraction of the evidence for my claims.

Now the first use of the commentaries I will outline is somewhat complex but can be followed with a little skill. It centers on an oft-quoted part of the Book of Mormon in Mormon circles. It is a story of a vision by Lehi in 1 Nephi chapter 8 known as "The Vision of The Tree of Life" or by some "The Vision of The Rod of Iron".

Before we begin I want to explain how I set this up. I will bold the words in the Book of Mormon that match words in *The King James Version* of the Bible. In addition I use the following to explain the number of times each is used, first in the KJV and second in the Book of Mormon. So it will look like this (1/1) the first number is how many times the word or phrase appears in the King James Version of the Bible the second is how many times the word or phrase appears in the Book of Mormon. Now if it looks like this (1NT/1) it means that the used quote only appears in the New Testament and does not appear in the Old Testament. Now I follow the structure of the Book of Mormon but if you would like to skip to the instances of Joseph Smith's use of the commentaries that I find to be the most intriguing please look for the following *** in front of those sections. Even though they are all proof of his use of the commentaries. I will start these *** after the first section which ends on page 56.

We will start with 1 Nephi 11 verses 22-28 to read the entire story I refer you to the entire chapter:

> **BOM** 1 Nephi 11:22 "And I answered him, saying: Yea, it is **the love of God**, which **shed**deth itself **abroad in** the **hearts** of the

children of men; wherefore, it is the most desirable above all things."

Now the first thing you must know about this verse is that it is based on Romans 5:5 of the New Testament, which means that this verse in 1 Nephi which is based on Romans 5:5 was written over 600 to 700 years before *The Book of Romans* was even compiled, a highly unlikely proposition. In fact the statistical probability that the words created in 600 to 700 BC on another continent would somehow match those written 600 to 700 years later in another part of the word would be too high to even contemplate. You will see more of this in the chapter on the use of the New Testament. Here is that Romans verse in King James English:

> **KJV (1NT/1)** Romans 5:5 And hope maketh not ashamed; because **the love of God** is **shed abroad in** our **hearts** by the Holy Ghost which is given unto us.

And now here is Gill's commentary for Revelations 1:14. You will see later why the commentary is a part of *The Book of Revelations*:

> **COM** Gill: Rev 1:14 "and also Christ's eyes of love upon his own people, which have both heat and light; Christ's **love** never waxes cold, and, being **shed abroad in the hearts of** his people, warms theirs; and in the light of his gracious countenance do they see light; and his **love**, like flames of fire, melts their souls into a true and genuine repentance for sin:"

Notice how this commentary actually says the same thing without the King James English, "love" and the phrase "shed abroad in the hearts of" matches what Joseph Smith wrote. Again you will see a little later why it comes from a commentary on Revelations. Let me remind you of the key, so-to-speak, of what I have done here. BOM stands for the Book of Mormon and KJV stands for the King James Version of the Bible. So I will give you the Book of Mormon verse and following that verse I will give you the matching words and phrases Joseph Smith used from the King James Version of the Bible. Remember the (1/9) for example, means that the phase appears once in the King James Version of the Bible and 9 times in the Book of Mormon. Also remember that for example (2NT/7) means that the word or phrase only appears 2 times and only in the New Testament. The bold is where words or phrases match those of the King James Version of the Bible. To clarify what this means the (1/9) means that Joseph Smith used the bolded KJV words or phrases in the BOM 9 times even though it only appears in the KJV once.

BOM 1 Nephi 11:23 And he **spake unto me**, saying: Yea, and the most joyous to the soul.

> **KJV** (1/9) Ezekiel 2:2 And the spirit entered into me when **he spake unto me**, and set me upon my feet, that I heard him that spake unto me.)

BOM 1 Nephi 11:24 And after **he had said these words,** he said unto me: Look! **And I looked, and I beheld the Son of God (43NT/49)** going forth **among the children of men**; **and I** saw many fall down **at his feet and worship him**.

> **KJV (2NT/7)** John 7:9 When **he had said these words** unto them, he abode still in Galilee.)
>
> **KJV** (Revelation 14:14 **And I looked, and** behold a white cloud, and upon the cloud one sat like unto the Son of man, having on his head a golden crown, and in his hand a sharp sickle.)
>
> **KJV** (2/30) Psalm 21:10 Their fruit shalt thou destroy from the earth, and their seed from **among the children of men**.)
>
> **KJV (1NT/2)** Revelation 19:10 **And I fell at his feet** to **worship him**. And he said unto me, See thou do it not: I am thy fellowservant, and of thy brethren that have the testimony of Jesus: worship God: for the testimony of Jesus is the spirit of prophecy.)

As you can see he utilizes parts of the KJV of the Bible and in addition he uses a significant amount of phrases from Revelations and as we have already stated the (1NT/2) means it only appears once in the New Testament, in this case only in Revelations.

Now in the next example we will keep the same uses as noted above but in this example, and from then on, the words in italics are those that also match the commentaries. The (3) as an example, in front of the phase is how many times Joseph Smith uses this phrase in the Book of Mormon. The (15th Century) and the word directly preceding it, as an example, is the date the word is first used in our in history. In this example that means that the word "representation" first came about in the 15th century. It also means that the word does not appear anywhere in the KJV of the Bible. The KJV was published in 1611. The COM denotes that what follows comes from one of the commentaries. The (Henry, Clarke) at the end of a verse denotes that the same word or phrase is also found in those commentaries.

BOM 1 Nephi 11:25 And **it came to pass** (452/1353) that I beheld that the **rod of iron,** which my father had seen, was **the word of God,** (45/89) which led to **the fountain of living waters,** or to **the tree of life**; which waters are *(3) a representation* (15th Century) *of the* **love of God**; and I also beheld that the tree of life was *(3) a representation* (15th Century) *of the* love of God.

> **KJV** (4/8) Revelation 19:15 And out of his mouth goeth a sharp sword, that with it he should smite the nations: and he shall rule them with a **rod of iron**: and he treadeth the winepress of the fierceness and wrath of Almighty God.)
>
> **KJV** (2/1) Jeremiah 2:13 For my people have committed two evils; they have forsaken me **the fountain of living waters**, and hewed them out cisterns, broken cisterns, that can hold no water.)

KJV (6/15) Revelation 22:2 In the midst of the street of it, and on either side of the river, was there **the tree of life**, which bare twelve manner of fruits, and yielded her fruit every month: and the leaves of the tree were for the healing of the nations.)

KJV (13NT/9) Luke 11:42 But woe unto you, Pharisees! for ye tithe mint and rue and all manner of herbs, and pass over judgment and the **love of God**: these ought ye to have done, and not to leave the other undone.)

KJV (6/15) Revelation 22:2 In the midst of the street of it, and on either side of the river, was there **the tree of life**, which bare twelve manner of fruits, and yielded her fruit every month: and the leaves of the tree were for the healing of the nations)

COM Gill: Rev 22:2 "By **the tree of life** is meant not the Gospel, nor godliness, nor eternal life, nor any other of the divine Persons, but Christ, who is the author of life, natural, spiritual, and eternal; See Gill on Rev 2:7 and its situation between the street of the city, where the saints commune and converse together, and the **river of God**'s everlasting **love**, which in this state will appear in its fulness and glory, shows that Christ will be seen and enjoyed by all in the most delightful and comfortable manner that can be wished for:" **COM** Gill: Rev 22:1 "rather, therefore, by this **river** is meant the everlasting **love of God**")

Now I hope you have understood that Joseph Smith made up this story by using the Book of Revelations in the King James Bible and the commentaries. You will note that he utilized the "rod of iron" and the "tree of life". The "tree of life" can be found in Revelations 22:2 and the commentary of Gill on Revelations 22:2 not only tells us what the tree of life is but it also tells us, including the commentary on Revelations 22:1, that the river is the "love of God", the very same thing Joseph Smith states that the waters are. "Which waters are a representation of the love of God." Now again I hope it is obvious to you that Joseph Smith created this story by using Revelations and the commentary of Gill of this very same verse. This is beyond coincidence as Joseph Smith uses the same phrases from Revelations and the meanings exactly from Gill.

Now let us look at the next verse of Nephi.

BOM 1 Nephi 11:26 And the angel said unto me again: Look and behold the *(2) (5) condescension (1647 AD) of God!*

COM Clarke: Eph 3:8 "and the amazing ***condescension of God,***" (Wesley, Henry, Gill)

This verse adds a phrase with a word that was created 36 years after the King James Version of the Bible was published. This phrase "the condescension of God" is also found in the commentaries. The word "condescension" is found in Gill in his commentary on Revelations 22:9 "and shows the great **condescension of** the angel to put himself," now it doesn't specifically state "condescension of God" but this served as a reminder to him to utilize this oft quoted phrase of not only Joseph Smith's time but also of the commentaries themselves, which he had no doubt come across many times. By the way the (2) in front of the phrase "condescension of God" means that phrase was used in the Book of Mormon two times. The (5) in front of the word "condescension" means Joseph Smith used the word "condescension" five times in the Book of Mormon. Again this is beyond coincidence and there is no way a word from 1647 AD and the corresponding phrase could be quoted in a book from approximately 600 BC.

Now that you have an understanding of where and how Joseph Smith came up with this vision for Lehi let us go back a little to 1 Nephi chapter 8 where the vision is first told. The chapter we just looked at 1 Nephi chapter 11 was an explanation of that vision. Again I cannot possibly go into each detail but will outline a few for you here. First let us look at 1 Nephi 8:10-11. Note again the use of the Book of Revelations.

BOM 1 Nephi 8:10 And **it came to pass** (452/1353) that I beheld a tree, whose **fruit** was desirable to make one **happy**.

> **COM** Same idea here: Gill: Rev 22:2 "which is expressive of the **fruit**s and spiritual blessings of grace from Christ, enjoyed by saints in the present state, and of that variety of **happiness** and pleasures to be had in this glorious state,"

As you can see we are using Gill's commentary again and the same commentary of Revelations 22:2. Notice how similar the idea between the commentary and the verse in 1 Nephi 8:10. Remember the commentary of Revelations 22:2 was also used to create the explanation for the vision in 1 Nephi.

BOM 1 Nephi 8:11 And **it came to pass** (452/1353) that I did go forth and (17) partake of the fruit thereof; **and I beheld** that it was most sweet, above all that I ever before tasted. Yea, and I beheld that *the fruit thereof* was white, to exceed all the (6) whiteness (before 12th Century) that I had ever seen.

> **KJV** (**Note**: Only in Rev.) (**6NT/22**) Revelation 13:11 **And I beheld** another beast coming up out of the earth; and he had two horns like a lamb, and he spake as a dragon.)
>
> **KJV** (Genesis 3:6 And when the woman saw that the tree was good for food, and that it was pleasant to the eyes, and a tree to be desired to make one wise, she took of **the fruit thereof**, and did eat, and gave also unto her husband with her; and he did eat.)

Again notice the use of Revelations phrases only found in Revelations.

Now we will skip down to verse 31. In between these there are other uses of Revelations phrases and commentary uses but space can not allow us to go into all of them here.

BOM 1 Nephi 8:31 And he also saw other multitudes **feeling** their way towards that *(3) great and spacious (14ᵗʰ Century)* building.

> **COM** Clarke: Rev 22:2 "As this was a **great and spacious** city")

Notice that the phrase "great and spacious" comes from the same Revelations verse chapter 22:2 but this time from Clarke's commentary. Also note that the word "spacious" is not found in the King James Version of the Bible.

And now verse 37 where we have another oft quoted phrase in the Mormon Church.

BOM 1 Nephi 8:37 And he did **exhort** them then *with all the* **feeling** *of a (1) tender parent*, that they would hearken to his words, that **perhaps** the Lord would be merciful to them, and not cast them off; yea, my father did **preach unto them**.

> **KJV (1NT/13)** Revelation 14:6 And I saw another angel fly in the midst of heaven, having the everlasting gospel to **preach unto them** that dwell on the earth, and to every nation, and kindred, and tongue, and people,)
>
> **COM** Henry: Prov 23:19-28 "**with all the** affection **of a tender parent**")
>
> **COM** This is cross referenced in Gill from Rev 7:17: Gill: Isa 25:8 Rev 7:17, Rev 21:4 the allusion is to **a tender parent**, that takes a handkerchief, and wipes the face of its child, when it has been crying, and quiets and comforts it:" (Henry)

Although the phrase "a tender parent" is to many Mormon's a wonderful phrase unique to the Book of Mormon and one quoted many times by Mormon writers, leaders and general members themselves, as you can see, it actually comes from the commentaries. What is interesting here is that even though it is part of the vision of Lehi of the "tree of life" and "rod of iron" and found in Gill's commentary in Isaiah 25:8, it is cross-referenced from Revelations chapter 7:17. Even notice that this cross-referenced idea is the same as what is found in the "tender parent" verse of 1 Nephi. Notice the Isaiah 25:8 cross reference below.

> **COM** Rev 7:17 "**And God shall wipe away all tear, from their eyes**; or "out of their eyes", as the Alexandrian copy reads; see Isa 25:8. The sense is, that that which is now the occasion of tears will cease, as the sin and corruptions of God's people, which now are the cause of many tears; as also Satan's temptations, the hidings of God's face, and the various afflictions of this life, and the persecutions of the men of the world; there will be no more of either of these;")

And now we will look at verses 34-36:

BOM 1 Nephi 8:34 And after he was slain I saw the multitudes of the earth, that they were **gathered together to fight** against **the apostles of the Lamb**; for thus were **the twelve** called by the angel of the Lord.

> **KJV** (1/2) 1 Samuel 13:5 And the Philistines **gathered** themselves **together to fight** with Israel, thirty thousand chariots, and six thousand horsemen, and people as the sand which is on the sea shore in multitude: and they came up, and pitched in Michmash, eastward from Bethaven.)

> **KJV (1NT/9)** Revelation 21:14 And the wall of the city had twelve foundations, and in them the names of **the twelve apostles of the Lamb**.)

Again Joseph Smith tries to explain how someone more than 600 years before the event happened could possibly know about the event by using the phrase, "called by the angel of the Lord". He used phrases like this as he often did, to explain how he could possibly know that there would be twelve apostles hundreds of years before they existed. It is interesting that the only part of the Bible that calls them "apostles of the Lamb" is found in Revelations which Joseph has been using all along to create this section of 1 Nephi.

BOM 1 Nephi 8:35 And the multitude of the earth was gathered together; **and I beheld** that they were in a large and (*10*) *spacious* (*14th Century*) building, like unto the building which my father saw. And the angel of the (124/11) Lord spake unto me again, saying: Behold the world and the wisdom thereof; yea, behold the house of Israel hath **gathered together to fight** against **the twelve apostles of the Lamb**.

> **KJV (6NT/22)** Revelation 13:11 **And I beheld** another beast coming up out of the earth; and he had two horns like a lamb, and he spake as a dragon.)

It is interesting that the phrase "And I beheld" is only found in the Book of Revelations in the Bible and that Joseph Smith utilizes it here when he has been using Revelations all along. It is also interesting that this time Joseph Smith actually utilizes the entire phrase from Revelations "the twelve apostles of the Lamb".

> **KJV (1NT/9)** Revelation 21:14 And the wall of the city had twelve foundations, and in them the names of **the twelve apostles of the Lamb**.)

Again the use of the "spacious building", remember that the word "spacious" is not found in the King James Version of the Bible. Here again is the use in one of the commentaries again in Revelations 22:2

> **COM** Clarke: Rev 22:2 "As this was a great **and spacious** city" (Henry, Wesley)

BOM 1 Nephi 8:36 And it came to pass (452/1353) that I saw and **bear record**, that the (*3*) *great and spacious* (*14th Century*) building was the pride of the world; and it fell, and the fall thereof was exceedingly great And the angel of the (124/11) Lord spake unto me again, saying: Thus shall be the destruction of **all nations, kindreds, tongues, and people** that shall fight against **the twelve apostles of the Lamb**.

> KJV **(4NT/30)** John 8:14 Jesus answered and said unto them, Though I **bear record** of myself, yet my record is true: for I know whence I came, and whither I go; but ye cannot tell whence I come, and whither I go.)

Notice this time that Joseph Smith actually uses the same phrase "great and spacious"

> COM Clarke: Rev 22:2 "As this was a **great and spacious** city")
> Note again the obvious use of Revelations.
> KJV **(1NT/8)** Revelation 7:9 After this I beheld, and, lo, a great multitude, which no man could number, of **all nations, and kindreds, and people, and tongues**, stood before the throne, and before the Lamb, clothed with white robes, and palms in their hands;)
> KJV **(1NT/9)** Revelation 21:14 And the wall of the city had twelve foundations, and in them the names of **the twelve apostles of the Lamb**.)

This verse tells us that the building represents "the pride of the world" and that it "fell" just as the explanation in Gill's commentary in Revelations concerning the "proud".

> COM Gill: Rev 18:7 "And acted the proud and haughty part in exalting herself above all emperors, kings, and princes, above all kingdoms and states, and also above all churches, assuming arrogant titles, and even blasphemous names; see Rev 13:1 and lived deliciously: in a very luxuriant manner, as the popes, cardinals, archbishops, bishops, priests, monks, and friars have done; some being clothed in purple and scarlet, and in gold and silver, and all living upon the fat of the land, and in rioting and drunkenness, in chambering and wantonness: so much torment and sorrow give her: by pulling down her **pride**, which goes before a **fall**, than which nothing could more torment and afflict her; by stripping her of her fine clothes and rich apparel; and by taking away her fat benefices from her, which will cut her to the heart; and by burning her with fire, which will be very excruciating:")

Now to end this section on the vision of Nephi and its interpretation given in chapter 8 and 10 and 11 of 1 Nephi let us look at the commentary of Clarke on Revelations 22:2 in a little more detail. Here you will note, which I have bolded, many of the same phrases and the basic ideas behind the entire vision and its interpretation. I recommend reading this chapter of Nephi to grasp the entire understanding of the vision of Nephi. The use of the commentaries on

Revelations and the use of key phrases from the Book of Revelations clearly points to their use by Joseph Smith to create this "vision" story.

> **COM** Clarke: <u>Rev 22:2</u> "In the midst of the street of it - That is, of the city which was described in the preceding chapter.
>
> **The tree of life** - An allusion to <u>Gen 2:9</u>. As this **tree of life** is stated to be in the streets of the **city**, and on each **side of the river**, **tree** must here be an enallage of the singular for the plural number, **tree**s **of life**, or **tree**s which yielded **fruit** by which **life** was preserved. The account in Ezekiel is this: "And **by the river**, upon the bank thereof, on this side and on that side, shall grow all trees for meat, whose leaf shall not fade - it shall bring forth new **fruit**, according to his months - and the **fruit** thereof shall be for meat, and the leaf thereof for medicine;" <u>Eze 47:12</u>.**Twelve** manner of **fruit**s - Καρπους δωδεκα· **Twelve fruit**s; that is, **fruit twelve** times in the year, as is immediately explained, yielded her **fruit** every month. As this was a **great and spacious city**, one **fountain** was not sufficient to provide **water** for it, therefore a **river** is mentioned; a great river, by which it was sufficiently watered. Some think that by this **tree of life** the Gospel is indicated; the **twelve fruit**s are **the twelve apostles**; and the leaves are **Gospel** doctrines by which the **nations** - the **Gentiles**, are healed of the disease of sin. But this seems to be a fanciful interpretation.")

Now it is also very interesting that Joseph Smith in his story of "the rod of iron" which is found in Psalms and Revelations, calls the "rod of iron" the "word of God" when that is what Gill and Henry in their commentary call it.

BOM 1 Nephi 11:25 And it came to pass that I beheld that **the rod of iron**, which my father had seen, was **the word of God**, which led to *the fountain of living waters*, or to **the tree of life**; which waters are a representation of the love of God; and I also beheld that the tree of life was a representation of the love of God.

> **COM** Henry: <u>Psa 23:1-6</u> "streams which flow from **the fountain of living waters** and make glad the city of our God.")
>
> **KJV** (2/1) <u>Jeremiah 2:13</u> For my people have committed two evils; they have forsaken me **the fountain of living waters**, and hewed them out cisterns, broken cisterns, that can hold no water.)

BOM 1 Nephi 15:23-24 And they said unto me: What meaneth the *rod of iron* which our father saw, that led to the tree? And I said unto them that it was *the word of God*, and whose would hearken unto *the word of God*, and would hold fast unto it, they would **never perish**; neither could the temptations and **the fiery darts of the** adversary overpower them unto blindness, to lead them away to destruction.

> **COM** Gill: <u>Rev 2:27</u> - And he shall rule them with a **rod of iron**,....

Either with **the Gospel**, which is the rod of Christ's strength, and is the power of God unto salvation,)

COM Henry: <u>Isa 44:9-20</u> "As the **rod of** God is of use to enforce the word, so **the word of God** is of use to explain the rod,"

KJV (1NT/3) <u>John 10:28</u> And I give unto them eternal life; and they shall **never perish**, neither shall any man pluck them out of my hand.)

KJV (1NT/1) <u>Ephesians 6:16</u> Above all, taking the shield of faith, wherewith ye shall be able to quench all **the fiery darts of the** wicked.)

Now the brothers also asked their brother to explain what the water was. I won't list here all of the uses from the Bible and commentaries so that you can read without interruption these verses of 1 Nephi.

BOM 1 Nephi 15:26-36

[26] And they said unto me: What meaneth the river of water which our father saw?

[27] And I said unto them that the water which my father saw was filthiness; and so much was his mind swallowed up in other things that he beheld not the filthiness of the water.

[28] And I said unto them that it was an awful gulf, which separated the wicked from the tree of life, and also from the saints of God.

[29] And I said unto them that it was a representation of that awful hell, which the angel said unto me was prepared for the wicked.

[30] And I said unto them that our father also saw that the justice of God did also divide the wicked from the righteous; and the brightness thereof was like unto the brightness of a flaming fire, which ascendeth up unto God forever and ever, and hath no end.

[31] And they said unto me: Doth this thing mean the torment of the body in the days of probation, or doth it mean the final state of the soul after the death of the temporal body, or doth it speak of the things which are temporal?

[32] And it came to pass that I said unto them that it was a representation of things both temporal and spiritual; for the day should come that they must be judged of their works, yea, even the works which were done by the temporal body in their days of probation.

[33] Wherefore, if they should die in their wickedness they must be cast off also, as to the things which are spiritual, which are pertaining to righteousness; wherefore, they must be brought to stand before God, to be judged of their works; and if their works have been filthiness they must needs be filthy; and if they be filthy it must needs be that they cannot dwell in the kingdom of God; if so, the kingdom of God must be filthy also.

[34] But behold, I say unto you, the kingdom of God is not filthy, and there cannot any unclean thing enter into the kingdom of God; wherefore there

must needs be a place of filthiness prepared for that which is filthy.

[**35**] And there is a place prepared, yea, even that awful hell of which I have spoken, and the devil is the preparator of it; wherefore the final state of the souls of men is to dwell in the kingdom of God, or to be cast out because of that justice of which I have spoken.

[**36**] Wherefore, the wicked are rejected from the righteous, and also from that tree of life, whose fruit is most precious and most desirable above all other fruits; yea, and it is the greatest of all the gifts of God. And thus I spake unto my brethren. Amen.

You will note that here in Nephi the water was called "filthiness" and that it was a "representation of that awful hell" and later that the "filthiness" is the bad "works" of the wicked. Now Gill in his commentary uses the same idea. Notice that Gill says that this water lies "in the way to the heavenly paradise" and Joseph Smith tells us that the water is "an awful gulf, which separated the wicked from the tree of life, and also from the saints of God". In addition Gill says that it may be "a representation of the pollutions and defilements of sin" which is the same idea that Joseph Smith puts forth in his explanation to the brothers.

> **COM** Gill: Joh 18:1 The blood, the **filth** and soil of it, which so discoloured the **water**, as to give it the name of the Black Brook, used to be sold to the gardeners to dung their gardens with (s). It was an emblem of this world, and the darkness and **filthiness** of it, and of the exercises and troubles of the people of God in it, which *lie in the way to the heavenly paradise* and Mount of Zion, through which Christ himself went, drinking "of the brook in the way", Psa_110:7; and through which also all his disciples and followers enter into the kingdom of heaven: it may also be a figure of the dark valley of the shadow of death, through which Christ and all his members pass to the heavenly glory. And I see not why this black and unclean brook may not be a representation of the pollutions and defilements of sin; which being laid on Christ when he passed over it, made him so heavy and sore amazed in the human nature, as to desire the cup might pass from him.)

And now so you can see that Joseph Smith continues his use of the Book of Revelations I will give a brief section of the next chapter of 1 Nephi that of 1 Nephi chapter 12:1-11.

BOM 1 Nephi 12

BOM 1 Nephi 12:1 And it came to pass (452/1353) that the angel said unto me: Look, and behold thy seed, and also the seed of thy brethren. **And I** looked and **beheld the land of promise; and I beheld multitudes of people**, yea, even as it were **in number** as many **as the sand of the sea.**

KJV (*Note: Only in Rev.*) (**6NT/22**) Revelation 13:11 **And I beheld**

another beast coming up out of the earth; and he had two horns like a lamb, and he spake as a dragon.)

KJV (1NT/2) Revelation 20:8 And shall go out to deceive the nations which are in the four quarters of the earth, Gog, and Magog, to **gather** them **together to battle**: the **number** of whom is **as the sand of the sea.**)

KJV (1NT/22) Hebrews 11:9 By faith he sojourned in **the land of promise**, as in a strange country, dwelling in tabernacles with Isaac and Jacob, the heirs with him of the same **promise**:)

KJV (1NT/3) Matthew 4:25 And there followed him great **multitudes of people** from Galilee, and from Decapolis, and from Jerusalem, and from Judaea, and from beyond Jordan.)

Notice that he continues to use Revelations. I might point out again that this was over 600 years before Revelations was even created.

BOM 1 Nephi 12:2 And it came to pass (452/1353) that I beheld multitudes **gathered together to battle,** (*Note: See Rev 20:8 verse above)* **one against the other**; (*Note: The KJV always puts it "one against another" which Joseph Smith utilizes four times*) **and I beheld wars, and rumors of wars,** (*Note: How can you behold "rumors of war"*) and (*1) great slaughters* (Note: plural form not used in the Bible) with the sword among my people.

KJV (6NT/22) Revelation 13:11 **And I beheld** another beast coming up out of the earth; and he had two horns like a lamb, and he spake as a dragon.)

KJV (2NT/6) Matthew 24:6 And ye shall hear of **wars and rumours of wars**: see that ye be not troubled: for all these things must come to pass, but the end is not yet.)

COM Clarke: Rev 16:16 "the valley of which was remarkable for two **great slaughters**:" (Henry)

BOM 1 Nephi 12:3 And it came to pass (452/1353) that I beheld many generations pass away, **after the manner of** (*23) wars and contentions* in the land; **and I beheld** many cities, yea, even that I did not number them.

KJV (18/33) Genesis 18:11 Now Abraham and Sarah were old and well stricken in age; and it ceased to be with Sarah **after the manner of** women.)

COM Clarke: Dan 2:45 "producing, not **wars and contentions**, but glory to God in the highest,")

KJV (*Note: Only in Rev.)* **(6NT/22)** Revelation 13:11 **And I beheld** another beast coming up out of the earth; and he had two horns like a lamb, and he spake as a dragon.)

Please note that this part of the Book of Daniel according to the commentaries is also about the "end times" as is Revelations.

BOM 1 Nephi 12:4 And it came to pass (452/1353) that I saw a **mist of**

darkness on the face of the land of promise; and I saw **lightnings**, and I heard **thunderings, and earthquakes**, and all manner of tumultuous noises; and I saw the **earth and the rocks**, that they **rent**; and I saw mountains (1) tumbling (14ᵗʰ Century) into pieces; and I saw the plains of earth, that they were broken up; and I saw many cities that they were sunk; and I saw many that they were burned with fire; and I saw many that did (7) tumble (1300AD) to the earth, because of the quaking thereof.

> **KJV (3NT/5)** Revelation 8:5 And the angel took the censer, and filled it with fire of the altar, and cast it into the earth: and there were voices, and **thunderings, and lightnings, and** an **earthquake**.)
>
> **KJV (1NT/4)** 2 Peter 2:17 These are wells without water, clouds that are carried with a tempest; to whom the **mist of darkness** is reserved for ever)
>
> **KJV (4/1)** Genesis 6:1 And it came to pass, when men began to multiply **on the face of the** earth, and daughters were born unto them,)
>
> **KJV (1NT/22)** Hebrews 11:9 By faith he sojourned in the **land of promise**, as in a strange country, dwelling in tabernacles with Isaac and Jacob, the heirs with him of the same **promise**:)
>
> **KJV** (1/4) Isaiah 13:4 The noise of a multitude in the mountains, like as of a great people; a **tumultuous noise** of the kingdoms of nations **gathered together**: the LORD of hosts mustereth the host of the battle.)
>
> **KJV (1NT/4)** Matthew 27:51 And, behold, the veil of the temple was rent in twain from the top to the bottom; and the **earth did quake, and the rocks rent**;) 1 Kings 19:11 And he said, Go forth, and stand upon the mount before the LORD. And, behold, the LORD passed by, and a great and strong wind **rent** the mountains, and brake in pieces the **rocks** before the LORD; but the LORD was not in the wind: and after the wind an earthquake; but the LORD was not in the earthquake:)

BOM 1 Nephi 12:5 And it came to pass (452/1353) after I saw these things, I saw the **vapor of** darkness, that it passed from off the face of the earth; and behold, I saw multitudes who had not fallen *because of **the great and terrible** judgments of the Lord.

> **KJV (1NT/5)** Acts 2:19 And I will shew wonders in heaven above, and signs in the earth beneath; blood, and fire, and **vapour of** smoke:)
>
> **COM** Henry: Joe 1:1-7 "**because of the great and terrible** execution they do.")
>
> **KJV** (Joel 2:31 The sun shall be turned into darkness, and the moon into blood, before **the great and terrible** day of the LORD come.)

Please also note that the book of Joel is also considered to be about the "end times" and that Joseph Smith quotes from it and uses a phrase from the commentary of Henry from the same book.

BOM 1 Nephi 12:6 And I **saw the heavens open, and the Lamb of God descending out of heaven**; and he came down and showed himself unto them.

>   **KJV (1NT/4)** Revelation 21:10 And he carried me away in the spirit to a great and high mountain, and shewed me that great city, the holy Jerusalem, **descending out of heaven** from God,)

>   **KJV (1NT/5)** Mark 1:10 And straightway coming up out of the water, **he saw the heavens open**ed, **and the** Spirit like a dove **descending** upon him:)

>   **KJV (2NT/35)** John 1:29 The next day John seeth Jesus coming unto him, and saith, Behold **the Lamb of God**, which taketh away the sin of the world.)

BOM 1 Nephi 12:7 And I also saw and **bear record** that the **Holy Ghost (89NT/95)** fell upon twelve others; and they were **ordained of God**, and chosen.

>   **KJV (4NT/30)** John 8:14 Jesus answered and said unto them, Though I **bear record** of myself, yet my record is true: for I know whence I came, and whither I go; but ye cannot tell whence I come, and whither I go.)

>   **KJV (2NT/1)** Acts 10:42 And he commanded us to preach unto the people, and to testify that it is he which was **ordained of God** to be the Judge of quick and dead.)

BOM 1 Nephi 12:8 And the **angel spake unto me**, saying: Behold the **twelve** disciples **of the Lamb**, who are chosen to minister unto thy seed.

>   **KJV** (1/12) 1 Kings 13:18 He said unto him, I am a prophet also as thou art; and an **angel spake unto me** by the word of the LORD, saying, Bring him back with thee into thine house, that he may eat bread and drink water. But he lied unto him.)

BOM 1 Nephi 12:9 And he said unto me: **Thou rememberest the twelve apostles of the Lamb**? Behold they are they who shall **judge the twelve tribes of Israel**; wherefore, the twelve ministers of thy seed shall be judged of them; for ye are of the house of Israel.

>   **KJV (1NT/9)** Revelation 21:14 And the wall of the city had twelve foundations, and in them the names of **the twelve apostles of the Lamb**.)

>   **KJV** (1/1) Psalm 88:5 Free among the dead, like the slain that lie in the grave, whom **thou rememberest** no more: and they are cut off from thy hand.)

>   **KJV (2NT/1)** Matthew 19:28 And Jesus said unto them, Verily I say unto you, That ye which have followed me, in the regeneration when the Son of man shall sit in the throne of his glory, ye also shall sit upon twelve thrones, **judging the twelve tribes of Israel**.)

Please note that this account in Matthew and in Revelations is also about the end times and both cross reference each other in Clarke and Gill. And Henry cross-references the Matthew verse from the commentary on the Book of Daniel.

BOM 1 Nephi 12:10 And these twelve ministers whom thou beholdest shall judge thy seed. And, behold, they are righteous forever; for *(10) because of their faith* in **the Lamb of God** their garments are made **white in** his **blood**.

> **KJV (1NT/2)** Revelation 7:14 And I said unto him, Sir, thou knowest. And he said to me, These are they which came out of great tribulation, and have washed their robes, and made them **white in** the **blood** of the Lamb.)
>
> **KJV (2NT/35)** John 1:29 The next day John seeth Jesus coming unto him, and saith, Behold **the Lamb of God**, which taketh away the sin of the world.)
>
> **COM** Clarke: Gal 3:16 "those who were like himself **because of their faith**.")

BOM 1 Nephi 12:11 And the angel said unto me: Look! And I looked, and beheld three generations pass away in righteousness; and their *garments* were *white* even like unto **the Lamb of God**. And the angel said unto me: These are *made white in the blood of the Lamb*, *(10) because of their faith* in him.

> **KJV (1NT/2)** Revelation 7:14 And I said unto him, Sir, thou knowest. And he said to me, These are they which came out of great tribulation, and have washed their robes, and **made** them **white in the blood of the Lamb**.)
>
> **KJV (2NT/35)** John 1:29 The next day John seeth Jesus coming unto him, and saith, Behold **the Lamb of God**, which taketh away the sin of the world.)
>
> **COM** Gill: Rev 19:14 "not the horses, but the armies on them; which designs not their inward purity, which was very glorious; nor their outward conversation **garments**, washed and **made white in the blood of the Lamb**;")

Notice that this verse in Gill matches what Joseph Smith wrote including the word "garments".

BOM 1 Nephi 14:9 And it came to pass (452/1353) that he said unto me: Look, and behold that great and abominable church (76/259), which is **the mother of abominations**, whose founder is **the devil**.

> **KJV (1NT/4)** Revelation 17:5 And upon her forehead was a name written, MYSTERY, BABYLON THE GREAT, THE **MOTHER OF** HARLOTS AND **ABOMINATIONS** OF THE EARTH.)
>
> **KJV (44NT/94)** Matthew 4:1 Then was Jesus led up of the Spirit into the wilderness to be tempted of **the devil**.)

BOM 1 Nephi 14:10 And he said unto me: Behold there are save two churches only; the one is the church (76/259) of **the Lamb of God**, and the other is the church (76/259) of **the devil**; wherefore, whoso belongeth not to the church (76/259) of **the Lamb of God** belongeth to that great church (76/259), which is **the mother of abominations**; and she is **the whore of** all **the earth**.

> **KJV (1NT/4)** Revelation 17:5 And upon her forehead was a name written, MYSTERY, BABYLON THE GREAT, **THE MOTHER OF** HARLOTS AND **ABOMINATIONS OF THE EARTH**.)
>
> **KJV** (Revelation 17:15 And he saith unto me, The waters which thou sawest, where **the whore** sitteth, are peoples, and multitudes, and nations, and tongues.)
>
> **KJV (2NT/35)** John 1:29 The next day John seeth Jesus coming unto him, and saith, Behold **the Lamb of God**, which taketh away the sin of the world.)

BOM 1 Nephi 14:11 And it came to pass (452/1353) that I looked and beheld **the whore** of all **the earth**, and **she sat upon many waters**; and she had *dominion over* all the earth, among **all nations, kindreds, tongues, and people**.

> **COM** Gill: Rev 17:1 "her **sitting** here may be in allusion to the posture of harlots plying of men; or may denote her ease, rest, and grandeur, sitting as a queen; and is chiefly expressive of her power and **dominion over** the kings and **nations of the earth**,")
>
> **KJV (1NT/2)** Revelation 17:1 And there came one of the seven angels which had the seven vials, and talked with me, saying unto me, Come hither; I will shew unto thee the judgment of the great **whore that sitteth upon many waters**:)
>
> **KJV (1NT/8)** Revelation 7:9 After this I beheld, and, lo, a great multitude, which no man could number, of **all nations, and kindreds, and people, and tongues**, stood before the throne, and before the Lamb, clothed with white robes, and palms in their hands;)

BOM 1 Nephi 14:12 And it came to pass (452/1353) that I beheld the church (76/259) of **the Lamb of God**, and its numbers were few, because of the wickedness and **abominations** of **the whore** who **sat upon many waters**; nevertheless, I beheld that the church (76/259) of **the Lamb,** who were *(4) the saints of God,* were also upon all the face of the earth; and their dominions upon the face of the earth were small, because of the wickedness **of the great whore** whom I saw.

> **KJV (1NT/2)** Revelation 17:1 And there came one of the seven angels which had the seven vials, and talked with me, saying unto me, Come hither; I will shew unto thee the judgment of the great **whore that sitteth upon many waters**:)
>
> **COM** Wesley: Rev 18:6 "Others; in particular, **the saints of God**." (Henry, Clarke)

KJV (2NT/1) <u>Revelation 17:1</u> And there came one of the seven angels which had the seven vials, and talked with me, saying unto me, Come hither; I will shew unto thee the judgment **of the great whore** that sitteth **upon many waters**:)

BOM <u>1 Nephi 14:13</u> And it came to pass (452/1353) that I beheld that the great **mother of abominations** did *gather together* multitudes upon the face of all the earth, among all *(7) the nations of the Gentiles, to fight against the* Lamb of God.

> **COM** Also notice how this fits with the next few verses. Gill: <u>Rev 16:14</u> "that is, they will persuade them to **gather together, to fight against the saints**, the **Gentile** Christians in the several parts of the world, and the Jewish Christians, now settled in their own land; and this will be the battle of the Lord, who is God Almighty, and it will be fighting against him; and therefore the attempt must be vain and fruitless, and issue in the ruin of those who are gathered to it, who will be deceived and drawn into it by these diabolical spirits: and this is called "the battle of that great day of God"; not of the day of judgment, for it will be before that time; but of **that day** of vengeance upon all the remains of his and his church's enemies, both Pagan, Papal, and Mahometan, who will for this purpose be gathered together; "which", as the Ethiopic version renders it, "God has appointed".)
>
> **KJV (1NT/4)** <u>Revelation 17:5</u> And upon her forehead was a name written, MYSTERY, BABYLON THE GREAT, THE **MOTHER OF** HARLOTS AND **ABOMINATIONS** OF THE EARTH.)
>
> **COM** Henry: Eze 39:1-7 "in the isles, that is, **the nations of the Gentiles**." (Clarke)

BOM <u>1 Nephi 14:14</u> And **it came to pass** (452/1353) that I, Nephi, beheld the power of **the Lamb of God**, that it descended upon the saints of the **church** (76/259) of the Lamb, and upon the covenant people of the Lord, who were **scattered upon all the face of the earth**; and they were armed with righteousness and with **the power of God** in **great glory.**

Notice that the commentary outlined above of Gill has the same ideas as in this verse in Nephi.

> **COM** Gill states: <u>Rev. 16:14</u> "the Gentile Christians in the several parts of the world, and the Jewish Christians, now settled in their own land;" and Joseph Smith says "it descended upon the saints of the church of the Lamb, and upon the covenant people of the Lord, who were scattered upon all the face of the earth;" This is the exact same thing just said in a different way. "The Gentile Christians" are the "the saints of the church of the Lamb" and the "Jewish Christians" are the "the covenant people of the Lord". In addition both are in

different places of the world. Gill says they are "the several parts of the world" and Joseph Smith says they are, "scattered upon all the face of the earth".

KJV (1/6) <u>Genesis 11:8</u> So the LORD **scattered** them abroad from thence **upon the face of all the earth**: and they left off to build the city.)

KJV (11NT/48) <u>Matthew 22:29</u> Jesus answered and said unto them, Ye do err, not knowing the scriptures, nor **the power of God**.)

KJV (2NT/6) <u>Matthew 24:30</u> And then shall appear the sign of the Son of man in heaven: and then shall all the tribes of the earth mourn, and they shall see the Son of man coming in the clouds of heaven with **power and great glory**.)

BOM <u>1 Nephi 14:15</u> And **it came to pass** (452/1353) that I beheld that **the wrath of God** was **poured out** upon that great and abominable **church** (76/259), **insomuch** (20/181) that there were **wars and rumors of wars** among all the **nations and kindreds of the earth**.

> **KJV (1NT/1)** <u>Revelation 14:10</u> The same shall drink of the wine of **the wrath of God**, which is **poured out** without mixture into the cup of his indignation; and he shall be tormented with fire and brimstone in the presence of the holy angels, and in the presence of the Lamb:)

> **KJV (2NT/6)** <u>Matthew 24:6</u> And ye shall hear of **wars and rumours of wars**: see that ye be not troubled: for all these things must come to pass, but the end is not yet.)

BOM <u>1 Nephi 14:16</u> And as there began to be **wars and rumors of wars** among all the nations which belonged to the **mother of abominations**, the angel spake unto me, saying: Behold, **the wrath of God** is upon the **mother of harlots**; and behold, thou seest all these things –

> **KJV (1NT/4)** <u>Revelation 17:5</u> And upon her forehead was a name written, MYSTERY, BABYLON THE GREAT, THE **MOTHER OF** HARLOTS AND **ABOMINATIONS** OF THE EARTH.)

> **KJV (1NT/3)** <u>Revelation 17:5</u> And upon her forehead was a name written, MYSTERY, BABYLON THE GREAT, THE **MOTHER OF HARLOTS** AND ABOMINATIONS OF THE EARTH.)

BOM <u>1 Nephi 14:17</u> And when **the day cometh that the wrath of God is poured out** upon the **mother of harlots**, which is the great and abominable church (76/259) **of all the earth**, whose founder is **the devil**, then, at that day, *(5) the work of the Father* shall (17) commence (1340 AD) (***Note: Henry, Wesley, Clarke**, Gill*), in preparing the way for the fulfilling of his covenants, which he hath made to his people who are of the house of Israel.

> **KJV (1NT/1)** <u>Revelation 14:10</u> The same shall drink of the wine of **the wrath of God, which is poured out** without mixture into the cup of his indignation; and he shall be tormented with fire and brimstone

in the **presence** of the holy angels, and in the **presence** of the Lamb:)

KJV (1NT/3) <u>Revelation 17:5</u> And upon her forehead was a name written, MYSTERY, BABYLON THE GREAT, THE **MOTHER OF HARLOTS** AND ABOMINATIONS **OF THE EARTH**.)

KJV (1/9) <u>Malachi 4:1</u> For, behold, **the day cometh, that** shall burn as an oven; and all the proud, yea, and all that do wickedly, shall be stubble: and **the day that cometh** shall burn them up, saith the LORD of hosts, that it shall leave them neither root nor branch.)

COM Henry: <u>Col 1:12-29</u> "It is spoken of as **the work of the Father**,")

BOM <u>1 Nephi 14:18</u> And it came to pass (452/1353) that the angel spake unto me, saying: Look!

BOM <u>1 Nephi 14:19</u> And I looked and beheld a man, and he was dressed in a **white robe**.

KJV (3NT/3) <u>Revelation 7:9</u> After this I beheld, and, lo, a great multitude, which no man could number, of all nations, and kindreds, and people, and tongues, stood before the throne, and before the Lamb, clothed with **white robe**s, and palms in their hands;)

BOM <u>1 Nephi 14:20</u> And the angel said unto me: Behold one **of the twelve apostles of the Lamb**.

KJV (1NT/9) <u>Revelation 21:14</u> And the wall of the city had twelve foundations, and in them the names **of the twelve apostles of the Lamb**.)

BOM <u>1 Nephi 14:21</u> Behold, he shall see and write the remainder of these things; yea, and also many things which have been.

BOM <u>1 Nephi 14:22</u> And he shall also write concerning **the end of the world**.

KJV (Note even though this phrase exists twice in the Old Testament it does not have the same meaning as it has in the New Testament verses: **(5NT/2)** <u>Matthew 13:49</u> So shall it be at **the end of the world**: the angels shall come forth, and sever the wicked from among the just,)

Note: This is obviously a reference to John and *the* Book of Revelations, which of course Joseph Smith has been quoting from.

BOM <u>1 Nephi 14:23</u> Wherefore, the things which he shall write are **just and true**; and behold they are written in the book which thou beheld proceeding out of the mouth of the Jew; and at the time they proceeded out of the mouth of the Jew, or, at the time the book proceeded out of the mouth of the Jew, the things which were written were *(1) plain and pure,* and **most precious** and easy to the understanding of all men.

KJV (1NT/6) <u>Revelation 15:3</u> And they sing the song of Moses the servant of God, and the song of the Lamb, saying, Great and marvellous are thy works, Lord God Almighty; **just and true** are thy ways, thou King of saints.)

COM Henry: <u>1Co 3:18-20</u> "**plain and pure** Christianity will be likely to be despised by those who can suit their doctrines to the corrupt taste of their hearers,")

KJV (2NT/10) <u>Revelation 18:12</u> The merchandise of gold, and silver, and precious stones, and of pearls, and fine linen, and purple, and silk, and scarlet, and all thyine wood, and all manner vessels of ivory, and all manner vessels of **most precious** wood, and of brass, and iron, and marble,)

BOM <u>1 Nephi 15:3</u> For he truly spake many great **things** unto them, **which** were **hard to be understood**, save a man should inquire of the Lord; and they being hard in their hearts, therefore they did not look unto the Lord as they ought.

KJV (1NT/1) <u>2 Peter 3:16</u> As also in all his epistles, speaking in them of these **things**; in **which** are some things **hard to be understood**, which they that are unlearned and unstable wrest, as they do also the other scriptures, unto their own destruction.)

Note: It is interesting that this part of 2 Peter is speaking of the end times and Joseph Smith quotes from it as he has been talking about the "end times" all along. The writer of 2 Peter describes the "end times" and the "heresies" that would arise. It is also interesting that Gill cross references this section of 2 Peter many times in his commentary on Revelations which Joseph Smith quotes above: Gill: Rev 20:4 "the present earth will be burnt up, and a new one formed, in which these righteous persons will dwell, <u>2Pe 3:13</u>")

BOM <u>1 Nephi 15:12</u> Behold, I say unto you, that the house of Israel was compared unto an **olive-tree**, by the Spirit of the Lord which was in our father; and behold are we not broken off from the house of Israel, and are we not a branch of the house of Israel?

BOM <u>1 Nephi 15:13</u> And now, the thing which our father meaneth concerning the **grafting** in of **the natural branches** through **the fulness of the Gentiles**, is, that **in the latter days**, when our seed shall have (26) dwindled (1596 AD) in unbelief, yea, **for the space of** many years, and many generations after the Messiah shall be *manifested in body* unto the *children of men (23/131)*, then shall the *(3) fulness of the Gospel, (**Note: The BOM?**)* of the Messiah come unto the Gentiles, and from the Gentiles unto the remnant of our seed –

As you may remember the reference to the "olive-tree" and "the natural branches" and "grafting" will later be completely more detailed in the Book of Mormon in Jacob and is talked about in Romans. Here we are told that they know about this "olive-tree" by "the Spirit of the Lord". As I have mentioned and as you will continue to see when Joseph Smith knew that what he was saying stretched credulity and came from the New Testament, such as Jesus name and that he would be baptized by John and his mother would be Mary, that we would have a hard time believing it, he would offer up "the Spirit of the Lord" or an "Angel of the Lord" told or said.

KJV (1NT/1) Romans 11:24 For if thou wert cut out of the olive tree which is wild by nature, and wert **grafted** contrary to nature into a good **olive tree**: how much more shall these, which be **the natural branches**, be grafted into their own **olive tree**?)

KJV (1NT/2) Romans 11:25 For I would not, brethren, that ye should be ignorant of this mystery, lest ye should be wise in your own conceits; that blindness in part is happened to Israel, until **the fulness of the Gentiles** be come in.)

KJV (11/5) Numbers 24:14 And now, behold, I go unto my people: come therefore, and I will advertise thee what this people shall do to thy people **in the latter days**.)

COM Note: Joseph Smith uses dwindle and dwindled interchangeable, and both are in Henry, while dwindle is in all (Henry: Mar 14:53-65: "Peter followed at a distance, such a degree of cowardice was his late courage **dwindled** into,"

COM Clarke: Rom 11:23 "Fallen as they are and degraded, God can, in the course of his providence and mercy, restore them to all their forfeited privileges; and this will take place if they abide not **in unbelief**: which intimates that God has furnished them with all the power and means necessary for faith, and that they may believe on the Lord Jesus whenever they will."

KJV (3NT/26) Romans 11:23 And they also, if they abide not still **in unbelief,** shall be grafted in: for God is able to graft them in again.)

KJV (1NT/69) Acts 19:8 And he went into the synagogue, and spake boldly **for the space of** three months, disputing and persuading the things concerning the kingdom of God.)

KJV (9NT/9) 1 John 1:2 (For the life was **manifested**, and we have seen it, and bear witness, and shew unto you that eternal life, which was with the Father, and was **manifested** unto us;)

COM Wesley: 2Co 4:10 "That the life also of Jesus might be **manifested in** our **body**")

BOM 1 Nephi 15:14 And at that day shall the remnant of our seed know that they are of the house of Israel, and that they are the covenant people of the Lord; and then shall they know and **come to the knowledge of** their forefathers, and also to the knowledge of the gospel of their Redeemer, which was ministered unto their fathers by him; wherefore, they shall **come to the knowledge of** their Redeemer and the very (5) *points of his doctrine,* that they may know how to come unto him **and be saved**.

KJV (1NT/10) 2 Timothy 3:7 Ever learning, and never able to **come**

to the knowledge of the truth.)
COM Clarke: <u>Rom 14:1</u> "than with curious disquisitions on speculative **points of doctrine**." (Gill)
KJV (1NT/7) <u>Luke 8:12</u> Those by the way side are they that hear; then cometh the devil, and taketh away the word out of their hearts, lest they should believe **and be saved**.)

Doesn't the phrase "points of doctrine" even sound modern? It most definitely is and Joseph Smith got it from the commentaries.
BOM <u>1 Nephi 15:15</u> And then at that day will they not rejoice and give praise unto their **everlasting God**, their **rock and** their **salvation**? Yea, at that day, will they not receive the strength and **nourishment** from **the true vine**? Yea, will they not come unto the true *(4) fold of God?*
> **KJV** (3/5) <u>Genesis 21:33</u> And Abraham planted a grove in Beersheba, and called there on the name of the LORD, the **everlasting God**.)
> **KJV** (1/1) **Psa 62:2** - He only *is* **my Rock and my salvation…**)
> **KJV (1NT/3)** <u>Colossians 2:19</u> And not holding the Head, from which all the body by joints and bands having **nourishment** ministered, and knit together, increased with the increase of God.)
> **KJV (1NT/2)** <u>John 15:1</u> I am **the true vine**, and my Father is the husbandman.)
> **COM** Clarke: <u>Mat 10:6</u> "The Jewish Church was the ancient **fold of God**;")

BOM <u>1 Nephi 15:16</u> Behold, I say unto you, Yea; they shall be remembered again among the house of Israel; they shall **be grafted in**, being a **natural branch** of the **olive-tree**, into the true **olive-tree**.
> **KJV (2NT/3)** <u>Romans 11:19</u> Thou wilt say then, The branches were broken off, that I might **be grafted in**.)
> **KJV (1NT/1)** <u>Romans 11:24</u> For if thou wert cut out of the olive tree which is wild by nature, and wert grafted contrary to nature into a **good olive tree**: how much more shall these, which be the **natural branches**, be **grafted** into their own **olive tree**?)
> **COM** Here in Gill is the entire meaning behind the verses of the "natural branch" above in which Joseph Smith also quotes exact phrases from Romans 11 in which the "natural branch" story appears. Gill: <u>Rom 11:24</u> - For if thou wert cut out of **the olive tree**,.... As the apostle argues the possibility of bringing the Jews into a Gospel church state, from the power of God; so here the probability of it, or the easiness and likelihood of its being performed, from the in**grafting of the Gentiles**; who were originally like an **olive tree**, which is wild by nature, grows in the field, bears no fruit, and is useless and unprofitable; so they by nature were sinners of **the**

Gentiles, children of wrath, full of unrighteousness, without any fruit of holiness; being not within the pale of the Jewish church and commonwealth; but in the wide field of the world, worthless, and of no account; and yet many were "cut out of" this wild olive tree; were, through the ministration of the Gospel, by the power of divine grace separated from the rest of the world; were effectually called and brought into a Gospel church state; God took out from among them a people for his name. This their being cut out of the wild olive, as it expresses the power and grace of God towards them, it might teach them humility, as it led them to observe their original state and condition: and wert **grafted**, contrary to nature, into a good olive tree: for an **olive tree** being full of fatness, will not admit of in**grafting**; nor was it ever usual to ingraft upon olive; hence the Jews say (y) זתים אין בהן הרכבה, "there is no ingrafting on olives": besides, it is contrary to nature, use, and custom, to ingraft wild scions, or grafts of any sort into a good stock; but always good scions or grafts into a wild stock, for in wild hungry stocks, grafts grow best: but in the in**grafting of the Gentiles** into a Gospel church state, just such a method was taken, as if a wild graft were let into a good stock; so that this ingrafting was not of nature, it was contrary to it; but of pure grace, and, sovereign good will and pleasure; and the apostle's argument is this, that if **the Gentiles**, who were originally as a **wild olive tree**; if some as grafts were taken out from among them, and, quite contrary to their own nature, and the nature of things, were, by the goodness and grace of God, **grafted into** a good **olive**, the Gospel church state; how much more shall these which be **the natural branches**, be **grafted into their own olive tree**? that there is a greater likelihood, and more easily may it be, according to all appearance of things, that the Jews, **the natural branches** or descendants of Abraham, should be brought into a Gospel church state, which first began among them, and which at first only consisted of some of their nation. The Gospel church is called "their own **olive tree**", in allusion to Israel, or the Jewish church, which is often so called in their writings."

BOM 1 Nephi 15:17 And this is what our father meaneth; and he meaneth that it will not come to pass until after they are scattered by the Gentiles; (***Note: Again the Europeans almost destroying the American Indians.)*** and he meaneth that it shall come by way of the Gentiles, that the Lord may show his power unto the Gentiles, for the very cause that he shall be rejected of the Jews, or of the house of Israel.

BOM 1 Nephi 15:18 Wherefore, our father hath not spoken of our seed alone, but also of **all** the house of **Israel**, (4) pointing (14th Century) to *the covenant* which should be fulfilled **in the latter days; which covenant the Lord made to our father Abraham, saying: In thy seed shall all the kindreds of the earth be blessed**.

> **KJV (1NT/1)** Romans 11:26 And so **all Israel** shall be saved: as it is written, There shall come out of Sion the Deliverer, and shall turn away ungodliness from Jacob:)
>
> **KJV (11/5)** Numbers 24:14 And now, behold, I go unto my people: come therefore, and I will advertise thee what this people shall do to thy people **in the latter days**.)
>
> **KJV (1NT/1)** Acts 3:25 Ye are the children of the prophets, and **of the covenant which God made with our fathers, saying unto Abraham**, And **in thy seed shall all the kindreds of the earth be blessed**.)
>
> **COM** Henry's commentary cross references this verse in his commentary on Romans 11 and also Isaiah (see the next verse) Henry: Rom 11:1-32 "For this is my covenant with them - this, that the deliverer shall come to them - this, that my Spirit shall not depart from them, as it follows, Isa 59:21. God's gracious intentions concerning Israel were made the matter of a **covenant**, which the God that cannot lie could not but be true and faithful to. They were the children of **the covenant**, Act 3:25.")
>
> **Note:** Joseph Smith makes a big mistake here by using the quote in Acts 3:25 about Abraham instead of the one he should have known in Genesis 22:18 – "And in thy seed shall all nations of the earth be blessed ..." Although he gets this part correct he mistakenly uses what Acts 3:25 says **"of the covenant which God made with our fathers, saying unto Abraham"**

BOM 1 Nephi 15:18 version **"which covenant the Lord made to our father Abraham, saying"**.

> **Note:** Notice how this is the same as Acts 3:25 when if it was written around 600BC it should have come from Genesis. This shows that Joseph Smith created the Book of Mormon and wrote this from Acts of the New Testament.

BOM 1 Nephi 15:19 And **it came to pass** (452/1353) that I, Nephi, spake much unto them concerning these things; yea, I spake unto them concerning *(2) the restoration (19) of the Jews **in the latter days.

> **COM** Gill: Jer 23:7 "nor with **the restoration of the Jews in the latter day**, which will be a most wonderful and amazing event, Rom 11:15. (Henry, Clarke)
>
> **KJV (11/5)** Numbers 24:14 And now, behold, I go unto my people: come therefore, and I will advertise thee what this people shall do to thy people **in the latter days**.)

Note: Notice the phrase "restoration of the Jews" which is a modern phrase and should not be found in a 600BC document. The phrase is found in Gill's commentary on Romans which Joseph Smith has been using to point out his "olive-tree" hypothesis. In addition why would Nephi a Jew use the phrase "restoration of the Jews in the latter days" when he would, as a Jew, have said something like "the restoration of our people the latter days". Also note that this phrase in Gill cross-references Romans 11 which Joseph Smith has been using throughout this section.

BOM 1 Nephi 15:20 And I did rehearse unto them the words of Isaiah, who spake concerning (2) *the restoration* (19) *of the Jews*, or of the house of Israel; and after they were restored they should no more be confounded, neither should they be (1) *scattered again.* And **it came to pass** (452/1353) that I did speak many words unto my brethren, that they were **pacified** and did humble themselves before the Lord.

 COM Note that Romans continues by quoting Isaiah which is clarified here in this quote from Gill in bold text which is the quote from Romans. Gill: Rom 11:26 **"as it is written, Isa_59:20, there shall come out of Zion the Deliverer: the words of the prophet are, "and the Redeemer shall come to Zion":"**

 COM Henry: Jer 31:10-17 "from being **scattered again**")

 KJV (2/6) Esther 7:10 So they hanged Haman on the gallows that he had prepared for Mordecai. Then was the king's wrath **pacified**.)

***BOM 1 Nephi 17:41 And he did **straiten them** in the wilderness **with his rod**; for they hardened their hearts, even as ye have; and the Lord straitened them because of their iniquity. He sent *fiery flying serpents* **among** them; and after they *were bitten* he prepared a way that they might be healed; and the labor which they had to perform was to look; and because of the (2) simpleness (13th Century) of the way, or the (3) easiness (13th Century) of it, there were many who perished.

 KJV (1/1) Jeremiah 19:9 And I will cause them to eat the flesh of their sons and the flesh of their daughters, and they shall eat every one the flesh of his friend in the siege and straitness, wherewith their enemies, and they that seek their lives, shall **straiten them**.)

 KJV (2/1) Exodus 8:17 And they did so; for Aaron stretched out his hand **with his rod**, and smote the dust of the earth, and it became lice in man, and in beast; all the dust of the land became lice throughout all the land of Egypt.)

 KJV (2/1) Numbers 21:6 And the LORD sent **fiery serpents among** the people, and they bit the people; and much people of Israel died.)

 COM It is interesting that the Bible does not call them "flying serpents" but Henry and Gill both do. Henry: Num 21:4-9 "They had impudently flown in the face of God himself, and the poison of asps was under their lips, and now these **fiery serpents** (which, it should seem, were **flying serpents**," Gill: <u>Num 21:6</u> "as before related from Diodorus Siculus, their bites were altogether incurable; and Solinus (y) says, of the same Arabian **flying serpents**, that their poison is so quick, that death follows before the pain can be felt;

COM Henry: <u>Joh 3:1-21</u> "Being thus lifted up, it was appointed for the cure of those that **were bitten** by **fiery serpents**. He that sent the plague provided the remedy.")

COM Henry: <u>2Ki 5:15-19</u> "He valued the cure, not by the **easiness of it** to the prophet,")

Note: As you can see the KJV does not call them "flying serpents" but the commentaries do.

***BOM** <u>1 Nephi 19:12</u> And all these things must surely come, **saith the prophet** Zenos. And **the rocks** of the earth must **rend**; and because of the groanings of the earth, many of the kings of **the isles of the sea** shall be **wrought upon** by the Spirit of God, to (6) exclaim (1570 AD) *(1) The God of nature suffers*.

KJV (1NT/7) <u>Acts 7:48</u> Howbeit the most High dwelleth not in temples made with hands; as **saith the prophet,**)

KJV (1NT/4) <u>Matthew 27:51</u> And, behold, the veil of the temple was rent in twain from the top to the bottom; and the **earth** did quake, and **the rocks rent**;)

KJV (2/8) <u>Isaiah 24:15</u> Wherefore glorify ye the LORD in the fires, even the name of the LORD God of Israel in **the isles of the sea**.)

KJV (1/12) <u>2 Kings 12:11</u> And they gave the money, being told, into the hands of them that did the work, that had the oversight of the house of the LORD: and they laid it out to the carpenters and builders, that **wrought upon** the house of the LORD,)

COM Gill: <u>Act 17:34</u> ""It is reported of him, that being at Heliopolis in Egypt, along with Apollophanes, a philosopher, at the time of Christ's sufferings, he should say concerning the unusual eclipse that then was, that "a God unknown, and clothed with flesh, suffered", on whose account the whole world was darkened; or, as, others affirm, he said, "either **the God of nature suffers**, or the frame of the world will be dissolved":")

COM Wesley: <u>Mat 27:45</u> ""Either **the God of nature suffers**, or the frame of the world is dissolved." Also note: "The God of nature" is also found in Clarke and Henry.)

COM Note how verses 10-12 above fit the entire comments of Wesley here: <u>Mat 27:45</u> "From the sixth hour, there was darkness over all the earth unto the ninth hour - Insomuch, that even a heathen philosopher seeing it, and knowing it could not be a natural eclipse, because it was at the time of the full moon, and continued **three hours** together, cried out, "Either **the God of nature suffers**, or the frame of the world is dissolved." By this darkness God testified his abhorrence of the wickedness which was then committing. It likewise intimated Christ's sore conflicts with the Divine justice, and with all the powers of darkness.)

Note: Obviously this phrase "the God of nature suffers" is very unique and has its own history as you will note here in the commentaries. As a result of this history it is quite improbable that someone in 600 BC would use this phrase. Joseph Smith knowing that he got it from the commentaries did what he always had done when he utilized the improbable and so applies this knowledge to the kings of the earth being "**wrought upon** by the Spirit of God".

BOM 1 Nephi 22:5 And since they have been led away, these things have been prophesied concerning them, and also concerning all those who shall hereafter be scattered and be confounded, because of the Holy One of Israel; for against him will they harden their hearts; wherefore, they shall be (*3*) *scattered among all nations* and **shall be hated of all men**.

COM Clarke: Deu 30:5 "As this promise refers to a return from a captivity in which they had been **scattered among all nations**,")

KJV Zechariah 7:14 But I **scattered** them with a whirlwind **among all** the **nations** whom they knew not. Thus the land was desolate after them, that no man passed through nor returned: for they laid the pleasant land desolate.)

KJV (3NT/1) Matthew 10:22 And ye **shall be hated of all men** for my name's sake: but he that endureth to the end shall be saved.)

BOM 1 Nephi 22:13 And the blood of that great and abominable church (76/259), which is *the whore* of all **the earth**, shall turn **upon their own heads**; for they shall war among themselves, and the sword of their own hands shall fall **upon their own heads, and they shall be drunken with their own blood**.

KJV (1/6) Ezekiel 11:21 But as for them whose heart walketh after the heart of their detestable things and their abominations, I will recompense their way **upon their own heads**, saith the Lord GOD.)

KJV (1/1) Isaiah 49:26 And I will feed them that oppress thee with their own flesh; **and they shall be drunken with their own blood**, as with sweet wine: and all flesh shall know that I the LORD am thy Saviour and thy Redeemer, the mighty One of Jacob.)

COM Gill: Note the same ideas here: Isa 49:26 "It will be a righteous thing with God to give **the whore** of Rome her **own blood** to drink, even so as to be made drunk with it as it is with wine, who has been drunk already with the blood of the saints, Rev 16:6.")

COM Henry: Isa 49:24-26 ""I will feed those that oppress thee with their own flesh, and they shall be drunken with their own blood. The proud Babylonians shall become not only an easy, but an acceptable, prey to one another. God will send a dividing spirit among them, and their ruin, which was begun by a foreign invasion, shall be completed by their intestine divisions. They shall bite and devour one another, till they are consumed one of another. They shall greedily and with delight prey upon those that are their own flesh and blood." God can make the oppressors of his church to be their own tormentors and their own destroyers."

BOM 1 Nephi 22:14 And every nation which shall **war against thee**, O house of Israel, shall be turned **one against another**, and they **shall fall into the pit** which they digged to (2) ensnare (1576) the people of the Lord.

And **all that fight against** Zion shall be destroyed, and that great whore, who hath **pervert**ed **the right ways of the Lord**, yea, that great and abominable church (76/259), shall (7) tumble (1300AD) **to the dust and great shall be the fall of it.**

COM Gill: Isa 24:18 - **And it shall come to pass,** *that* **he who fleeth from the noise of the fear,**.... From the fearful noise that will be made, the voices and thunderings heard in the heavens above, the sea and waves roaring below; or from wars, and rumours of wars, and terrible armies approaching and pursuing, Luk 21:25 or rather at the report of an object to be feared and dreaded by wicked men, even the Son of Man coming in the clouds of heaven, Rev 1:7, **shall fall into the pit**; of ruin and destruction, dug for the wicked, Psa 94:13 just as the kings of Sodom and Gomorrah fell into the slime pits, when they fled from their conquerors, Gen 14:10,

KJV (1/1) Isaiah 41:12 Thou shalt seek them, and shalt not find them, even them that contended with thee: they that **war against thee** shall be as nothing, and as a thing of nought.)

KJV (8/4) Genesis 15:10 And he took unto him all these, and divided them in the midst, and laid each piece **one against another**: but the birds divided he not.)

COM Henry: Jer 18:18-23 "Those that think to **ensnare** others will justly be themselves ensnared in an evil time." (Clarke, Gill, Wesley)

KJV (1/1) Isaiah 29:7 And the multitude of all the nations that fight against Ariel, even **all that fight against** her and her munition, and that distress her, shall be as a dream of a night vision.)

COM It is interesting here that Joseph Smith changes Ariel to Zion as we are told in Henry: Isa 29:1-8 That it is Jerusalem which is here called Ariel is agreed, for that was the city where David dwelt; that part of it which was called Zion was in a particular manner the city of David,")

KJV (**1NT/2**) <u>Acts 13:10</u> And said, O full of all subtilty and all mischief, thou child of the devil, thou enemy of all righteousness, wilt thou not cease to **pervert the right ways of the Lord**?)

KJV (4/5) <u>Isaiah 25:12</u> And the fortress of the high fort of thy walls shall he bring down, lay low, and bring to the ground, even **to the dust**.)

KJV (**1NT/1**) <u>Matthew 7:27</u> And the rain descended, and the floods came, and the winds blew, and beat upon that house; and it fell: and **great** was **the fall of it**.)

COM Gill: <u>Pro 14:11</u> "though they lean upon it and would hold it fast, but it shall fall, **and great shall be the fall of it;** and particularly the apostate church of Rome, that synagogue of Satan,")

Note: Notice that this explanation in Gill of Isaiah 24:18 is about the end time and is cross-referenced with Revelations, again this is what he has been using all along.

BOM <u>2 Nephi 1:14</u> **Awake!** and **arise from the dust**, and hear the words of a trembling parent, whose (5) limbs (12th Century) ye must soon lay down (*1*) *in the cold and silent grave,* from whence (*1*) *no traveler* can *return*; a few more days and **I go the way of all the earth.**

> **Note:** And now something very important we must look into. Many critics of Joseph Smith and the Book of Mormon think that Joseph Smith was quoting Shakespeare in the pages of the Book of Mormon and they use as an example the verse above but in actuality I doubt very much that he would have made such a colossal mistake as to knowingly quote Shakespeare. As you will see, by using the commentary of Clarke, he did not realize that it was Shakespeare he was using for this verse in 2 Nephi. Clarke, instead of stating that this quote came from Shakespeare, said it came from "a poet" and never clarified the name of the poet. Clarke says the following in his commentary, *"I give this long quotation from a poet who was well acquainted with all the workings of the human heart; and one who could not have described scenes of distress and anguish of mind so well, had he not passed through them."* As you can see he did not state that the poem came from Shakespeare just "a poet". Below is the exact quote of the Shakespeare "poet" that Joseph Smith copied from by using Clarke.
>
> **COM** Clarke: <u>Heb 2:15</u> "The undiscovered country from whose bourn **No traveler return**s, - puzzles the will; And makes us rather bear those ills we have,")
>
> **COM** Henry: <u>Joh 19:38-42</u> "Thus without pomp or solemnity is the

body of Jesus laid **in the cold and silent grave.**")

KJV (1NT/1) Ephesians 5:14 Wherefore he saith, **Awake** thou that sleepest, and **arise from the** dead, and Christ shall give thee light.)

KJV (1/1) 1 Kings 2:2 **I go the way of all the earth**: be thou strong therefore, and shew thyself a man;)

BOM 2 Nephi 1:15 But behold, the Lord **hath redeemed my soul** from hell; I have **beheld his glory**, and I am (20) encircled (15ᵗʰ Century) about *eternally in the arms of his love.*

> **KJV** (2/2) 1 Kings 1:29 And the king sware, and said, As the LORD liveth, that **hath redeemed my soul** out of all distress,)
>
> **KJV (1NT/1)** John 1:14 And the Word was made flesh, and dwelt among us, (and we **beheld his glory,** the glory as of the only begotten of the Father,) full of grace and truth.)
>
> **COM** Gill: Mat 28:6 "Christ, as the Son of God, lay in the bosom of his Father, and **in the arms of his love,** from all **eternity**")

BOM 2 Nephi 1:21 And now that my soul might have joy in you, and that my heart might (*1) leave this world with* gladness because of you, that I might not be brought down with (*1) grief and sorrow* to the grave, arise from the dust, my sons, and be men, and be determined in one mind and (*1) in one heart, (1) united in all things,* that ye may not come down into captivity;

> **COM** Henry: Deu 34:1-4 "Those may **leave this world with** a great deal of cheerfulness that die in the faith of Christ," (Wesley)
>
> **COM** Henry: Rev 5:1-5 "Such desires, not presently answered, turn to **grief and sorrow.**")
>
> **COM** Henry: Eph 4:2-16 "but **in one heart** and one soul.")
>
> **COM** Clarke: Gen 11:4 "Being therefore strictly **united in all things,**")

***BOM** 2 Nephi 1:22 That ye may not be cursed with a (*5) sore cursing;* and also, that ye may not (*1) incur (15ᵗʰ Century) the displeasure of* a just *God* upon you, unto the destruction, yea, the (*1) eternal destruction of* **both soul and body**.

> **COM** Clarke: Jer 33:9 "and tremble lest they should **incur the displeasure of** your **God** by doing you any kind of evil." (Henry, Gill)
>
> **COM** Clarke: Joh 5:30 "He who has no better reason to give for his conduct than his own will shall in the end have the same reason to give for his **eternal destruction.**" (Henry, Wesley)
>
> **KJV (1NT/4)** (Note: Same context: Matthew 10:28 And fear not them which kill the body, but are not able to kill the soul: but rather fear him which is able to destroy **both soul and body** in hell.)

BOM 1 Nephi 1:23 Awake, my sons; put on the **armor of righteousness.** (*2) Shake off the chains* of with which ye are bound, and come forth **out of**

obscurity, and arise from the dust.

> **KJV (1NT/1)** <u>2 Corinthians 6:7</u> By the word of truth, by the power of God, by the **armour of righteousness** on the right hand and on the left,)
>
> **COM** Henry: <u>Pro 23:29-35</u> "Much ado he has to **shake off the chains** of his drunken sleep")
>
> **KJV** (1/3) <u>Isaiah 29:18</u> And in that day shall the deaf hear the words of the book, and the eyes of the blind shall see **out of obscurity**, and out of darkness.)

***BOM** <u>1 Nephi 1:24</u> Rebel no more against your brother, whose (*3*) *views* (*1523 AD*) have been glorious, and who hath kept the commandments from the time that we left Jerusalem; and who hath been (*5*) *an instrument in the hands of God,* in bringing us forth into the **land of promise**; for were it not for him, we must have (*1*) *perished with hunger in the wilderness;* nevertheless, ye (*11*) *sought to take away his life;* yea, and he hath suffered **much sorrow** because of you.

> **COM** Clarke: <u>Gen 12:1</u> "The apostle assures us that in all this Abram had spiritual **views**;" (Henry, Wesley)
>
> **COM** Clarke: <u>Jdg 8:22</u> "and now, dazzled with the success of a man who was only **an instrument in the hands of God** to deliver them from their enemies,")
>
> **KJV (1NT/22)** <u>Hebrews 11:9</u> By faith he sojourned in the **land of promise**, as in a strange country, dwelling in tabernacles with Isaac and Jacob, the heirs with him of the same **promise**:)
>
> **COM** Henry: <u>Amo 2:9-16</u> "That he led thee forty years through a desert land, and fed thee in a **wilderness**, where thou wouldst otherwise **have perished with hunger**.")
>
> **COM** Clarke: <u>Gen 20:7</u> "his townsmen **sought to take away his life**:")
>
> **KJV** (1/6) <u>Ecclesiastes 5:17</u> All his days also he eateth in darkness, and he hath **much sorrow** and wrath with his sickness.

BOM <u>1 Nephi 1:25</u> And I *exceedingly fear and tremble* because of you, lest he shall suffer again; for behold, ye have accused him that he sought **power and authority over** you; but I know that he hath not sought for power nor authority over you, but he hath sought the glory of God, and your own (*1*) *eternal welfare.*

> **KJV (1NT/1)** <u>Hebrews 12:21</u> And so terrible was the sight, that Moses said, **I exceedingly fear and** quake:)
>
> **COM** Clarke: <u>Heb 12:18-21</u> "and even to Moses, who held the highest intimacy with Jehovah, the revealed glories, the burning fire, the blackness, the darkness, the tempest, the loud-sounding trumpet, and the voice of words, were so terrible that he said, **I exceedingly**

fear and tremble.")

KJV (2NT/5) Luke 9:1 Then he called his twelve disciples together, and gave them **power and authority over** all devils, and to cure diseases.)

COM Henry: Luk 16:1-18 "in order to promote our future and **eternal welfare**," (Clarke)

*****BOM** 2 Nephi 2:7 Behold, he (*1) offereth himself a sacrifice for sin,* to (*5) answer the ends of the law,* unto all those who have **a broken heart and a contrite spirit**; and unto none else can (*5) the ends of the law be answered.*

> **Note:** I hope I don't need to state how improbable it would be for the modern phrases "offering himself a sacrifice for sin" and the phrase where it clarifies that Jesus answers the "ends of the law" to appear in a book written between approximately 600 BC to 400 AD. Especially when these are phrases used by those who delve deeply into the intricacies of Christianity such as those who write commentaries, hence the reason these phrases are found in the commentaries Joseph Smith used.
>
> **COM** Gill: 1Ti 1:15 "by his obedience, sufferings, and death, by fulfilling the law, bearing its penalty, **offering himself a sacrifice for sin**, thereby finishing it, making reconciliation for it, and bringing in an everlasting righteousness:" (Clarke)
>
> **COM** Henry: Joh 13:31-35 "**The ends of the law** were abundantly **answer**ed, and the glory of his government effectually asserted and maintained.")
>
> **KJV** (1/6) Psalm 34:18 The LORD is nigh unto them that are of **a broken heart**; **and** saveth such as be of **a contrite spirit**.)
>
> **COM** Henry: Psa 34:11-22 "It is the character of the righteous, whose prayers God will hear, that they are of **a broken heart and a contrite spirit**")

*****BOM** 2 Nephi 2:18 And because he had **fallen from heaven**, and had become miserable forever, he sought also the misery of all mankind. Wherefore, he said unto Eve, yea, even **that** *old serpent,* who is *the devil,* who is the *father of all lies*, wherefore he said: (*17) partake of the (6) forbidden fruit, and* **ye shall not die**, but **ye shall be as God, knowing good and evil.**

> **KJV** (1/3) Isaiah 14:12 How art thou **fallen from heaven**, O Lucifer, son of the morning! how art thou cut down to the ground, which didst weaken the nations!)
>
> **KJV (2NT/2)** Revelation 12:9 And the great dragon was cast out, **that old serpent**, called **the Devil**, and Satan, which deceiveth the whole world: he was cast out into the earth, and his angels were cast out with him.)
>
> **KJV (1NT/2)** John 8 44 Ye are of your father the devil, and the lusts

of your father ye will do. He was a murderer from the beginning, and abode not in the truth, because there is no truth in him. When he speaketh a lie, he speaketh of his own: **for he is a liar, and the father of it.**)

COM Gill: Rev 12:15 "since the old serpent, the devil, **is the father of all lies**, and errors:")

COM Phrase not found in the OT but is a phrase started in 1662 AD, hence it is as many phrases Joseph Smith has used a modern phrase. Henry: Joe 1:1-7 "and when they are going to **partake of the forbidden fruit** a prohibition of another nature shall come between the cup and the lip, and cut off the wine from their mouth." (Clarke, Gill, Wesley)

KJV (1/1) Genesis 3:3-4 And the **serpent** said unto the woman, **Ye shall not** surely **die**: For God doth know that in the day ye eat thereof, then your eyes shall be opened, and **ye shall be as god**s, **knowing good and evil**.)

Note: The phase "father of all lies" is a modern one and one taken from the commentaries.

BOM 2 Nephi 2:19 And after Adam and Eve had (*5*) *partaken* (*16ᵗʰ Century*) *of the* (*6*) *forbidden fruit,* they were *driven out of the garden of Eden*, to till the earth.

COM Henry: Hos 9:1-6 "it was like **driving** our first parents **out of the garden of Eden**,)

***BOM 2 Nephi 25:20 **And now**, my **brethren**, I have spoken plainly that ye (*3*) *cannot err*. And as the Lord God liveth that brought Israel up out of the land of Egypt, and gave unto Moses power that he should heal the nations after they had been *bitten by* the (6) *poisonous* (*1580*) *serpents* if they would (*14*) *cast their eyes* unto the serpent which he did raise up before them, and also gave him power that he should **smite the rock and** the **water** should come forth; yea, behold I say unto you, that as these things are true, and as the Lord God liveth, **there is none other name given under heaven** save it be this Jesus Christ, **of which I have spoken**, **whereby** man can **be saved**.

KJV (**3NT/19**) Acts 3:17 **And now**, **brethren**, I wot that through ignorance ye did it, as did also your)

COM Gill: Rev 13:6 "giving out that he **cannot err**" (Clarke, Henry)

COM Gill: Deu 32:24 "could not escape falling into the hands of wild beasts, and of meeting with **poisonous serpents** that go upon their bellies," (Clarke)

COM Henry: Joh 3:1-21 "Being thus lifted up, it was appointed for the cure of those that were **bitten by** fiery **serpents**.")

COM Clarke: Isa 8:21 "And he shall **cast his eyes** upward" (Henry)

KJV (1/1) Exodus 17:6 Behold, I will stand before thee there upon the rock in Horeb; and thou shalt **smite the rock, and** there shall come **water** out of it, that the people may drink. And Moses did so in the sight of the elders of Israel.)

KJV (1/13) Exodus 32:34 Therefore now go, lead the people unto the place **of which I have spoken** unto thee: behold, mine Angel shall go before thee: nevertheless in the day when I visit I will visit their sin upon them.)

KJV (1NT/1) Acts 4:12 Neither is there salvation in any other: for **there is none other name under heaven given** among men, **whereby** we must **be saved**.)

Note: Notice again the use of the serpents in the Moses story. Notice also again that the KJV does not call them "poisonous" but the commentaries do.

BOM 2 Nephi 26:4 Wherefore, **all** those who are **proud, and that do wickedly, the day that cometh shall burn them up, saith the Lord of Hosts**, for they **shall be** as **stubble**.

KJV This verse in Malachi was written 150 years after Lehi left Jerusalem for the Americas: Malachi 4:1 For, **behold**, the day cometh, that **shall** burn **as** an oven; and **all** the **proud**, yea, **and all that do wickedly, shall be stubble**: and **the day that cometh shall burn them up, saith the LORD of hosts**, that it shall leave them neither root nor branch.)

***BOM 2 Nephi 26:5 And they that kill the prophets, and the saints, **the depths of the earth shall swallow them up**, saith the Lord of Hosts; and mountains shall cover them, and **whirlwinds** shall carry them away, and **buildings shall** (*1*) *fall upon them and crush them to pieces and* **grind** *them* **to** *powder*.

KJV (1/4) Psalm 71:20 Thou, which hast shewed me great and sore troubles, shalt quicken me again, and shalt bring me up again from **the depths of the earth**.)

KJV (2/1) Psalm 21:9 Thou shalt make them as a fiery oven in the time of thine anger: the LORD **shall swallow them up** in his wrath, and the fire shall devour them.)

COM Cross referenced in Henry from Malachi 4:1: Mal 4:1-3 "In both Christ is a consuming fire to those that rebel against him. The day of his coming shall burn as an oven; it shall be a day of wrath, of fiery indignation. This was foretold concerning the Messiah, Psa_21:9,")

KJV (2/4) Zechariah 9:14 And the LORD shall be seen over them, and his arrow shall go forth as the lightning: and the LORD God shall blow the trumpet, and shall go with **whirlwinds** of the south.)

KJV (3NT/13) Mark 13:2 And Jesus answering said unto him, Seest thou these great **buildings**? there shall not be left one stone upon another, that shall not be thrown down.)

COM Henry: Luk 20:9-19 "he will **fall upon them and crush them to pieces** - will **grind them to powder.**")

KJV (1NT/1) Matthew 21:44 And whosoever shall fall on this stone shall be broken: but on whomsoever it shall **fall**, it will **grind** him **to powder.**)

Note: Now I hope you can see that this, as many of the others we have looked at and will look at, is beyond coincidence. First the phrase related to "grinding to powder" comes from the New Testament written half a decade later but secondly Joseph Smith almost uses word for word what Henry uses in his commentary. This again is beyond coincidence. Notice that the New Testament phrase says "it shall fall, it will grind him to powder" yet Joseph Smith uses almost exactly what Henry states in his commentary. This is beyond coincidence why would he use other New Testament verses word for word and then all of a sudden not. Because he copied it from Henry instead.

BOM 2 Nephi 26:10 And when these things have passed away a (*3) speedy destruction,* cometh unto my people; for, notwithstanding the pains of my soul, I have seen it; wherefore, I know that it shall come to pass; and they sell themselves for naught; for, for the reward of their pride and their foolishness they shall *reap destruction*; **for because** they **yield unto the devil (44NT/94)** and choose **works of darkness rather than light**, therefore they must go **down to hell**.

COM Clarke: Phi 4:23 "fighting under the Captain of our salvation, expect the **speedy destruction** of every inward foe;")

COM Clarke: Pro 22:8 "If he sow to the flesh, shall he not of the flesh **reap destruction**?")

KJV (Ephesians 5:6 Let no man deceive you with vain words: **for because** of these things cometh the wrath of God upon the children of disobedience.)

KJV (Acts 23:21 But do not thou **yield unto** them: for there lie in wait for him of them more than forty men, which have bound themselves with an oath, that they will neither eat nor drink till they have killed him: and now are they ready, looking for a promise from thee.)

KJV (2NT/13) Romans 13:12 The night is far spent, the day is at hand: let us therefore cast off the **works of darkness**, and let us put on the armour of light.)

KJV (John 3:19 And this is the condemnation, that **light** is come into the world, and men loved **darkness rather than light**, because their deeds were evil.)

KJV (Ephesians 5:8 For ye were sometimes **darkness**, but now are ye **light** in the Lord: walk as children of light:)

KJV (6/11) Isaiah 14:15 Yet thou shalt be brought **down to hell**, to the sides of the pit.)

BOM 2 Nephi 26:11 For the **Spirit** of the **Lord** will **not always strive with man**. And when the Spirit ceaseth to strive with man then cometh (*3) speedy destruction,* and this grieveth my soul.

> **KJV** Genesis 6:3 And the LORD said, My **spirit** shall **not always strive with man**, for that he also is flesh: yet his days shall be an hundred and twenty years.
>
> **COM** This verse Genesis 6:3 is cross-referenced in John 3:19 above: Joh 3:1-21 "We are here told what we are: We are flesh, not only corporeal but corrupt, **Gen_6:3.** The soul is still a spiritual substance, but so wedded to the flesh, so captivated by the will of the flesh, so in love with the delights of the flesh, so employed in making provision for the flesh, that it is mostly called flesh;")
>
> **COM** Clarke: Phi 4:23 "fighting under the Captain of our salvation, expect the **speedy destruction** of every inward foe;")

BOM 2 Nephi 26:20 And the Gentiles are *lifted up in the pride of their* eyes, and have stumbled, because of the greatness of their **stumbling block**, that they have built up many **churches**; nevertheless, they **put down the** power and miracles of God, and *preach up* unto themselves their own wisdom and their own learning, that they may **get gain** and **grind** upon **the face of the poor**.

> **COM** Henry: Job 24:18-25 "and **lifted up in the pride of their** own spirits.")
>
> **KJV** Isaiah 57:14 And shall say, Cast ye up, cast ye up, prepare the way, take up the **stumblingblock** out of the way of my people.)
>
> **KJV** (3/2) Isaiah 10:13 For he saith, By the strength of my hand I have done it, and by my wisdom; for I am prudent: and I have removed the bounds of the people, and have robbed their treasures, and I have **put down the** inhabitants like a valiant man:)
>
> **KJV** (1NT/18) James 4:13 Go to now, ye that say, To day or to morrow we will go into such a city, and continue there a year, and buy and sell, and **get gain**:)
>
> **KJV** Isaiah 3:15 What mean ye that ye beat my people to pieces, and **grind the face**s **of the poor**? saith the Lord GOD of hosts.
>
> **COM** This is the same meaning and also uses some of the same phrases: Clarke: Act 20:30 "The superintendents lose the life of God, neglect the souls of the people, become greedy of gain, and, by secular extortions, oppress the people. The members of the **Church**,

thus neglected, oppressed, and irritated, get their minds alienated from their rapacious pastors. Men of sinister views take advantage of this state of distraction, foment discord, **preach up** the necessity of division, and thus the people become separated from the great body, and associate with those who profess to care for their souls, and who disclaim all secular views.")

***BOM 2 Nephi 26:21 And there are many **churches** *built up* which cause **envyings**, and **strifes**, and **malice**.

> **KJV (2NT/8)** 2 Corinthians 12:20 For I fear, lest, when I come, I shall not find you such as I would, and that I shall be found unto you such as ye would not: lest there be debates, **envyings**, wraths, **strifes**, backbitings, whisperings, swellings, tumults:)
>
> **KJV** (Colossians 3:8 But now ye also put off all these; anger, wrath, **malice**, blasphemy, filthy communication out of your mouth.)
>
> **KJV** (Colossians 2:7 - Rooted and **built up** in him…)
>
> **COM** Henry: **Rom 2:17-29** "but pulled down with their lives what they **built up** with their preaching;"

***BOM 2 Nephi 26:22 And there are also *(18)* secret *(21)* combinations *(14ᵗʰ Century)*, even as in **times of old**, according to the (21) combinations (14ᵗʰ Century) of **the devil (44NT/94)**, for he is the founder of all these things; yea, the founder of murder, and **works of darkness**; yea, and he **leadeth them** by the neck with a (1) flaxen (15ᵗʰ Century) cord, until he bindeth them with his strong cords forever.

> **COM** Gill: Job 12:22 "likewise the **secret** plots, counsels, and **combinations** of wicked men,")
>
> **KJV** (1/5) Psalm 44:1 We have heard with our ears, O God, our fathers have told us, what work thou didst in their days, in the **times of old**.)
>
> **KJV (2NT/13)** Romans 13:12 The night is far spent, the day is at hand: let us therefore cast off the **works of darkness**, and let us put on the armour of light.)
>
> **KJV (2NT/4)** Mark 9:2 And after six days Jesus taketh with him Peter, and James, and John, and **leadeth them** up into an high mountain apart by themselves: and he was transfigured before them.)
>
> **COM** Gill: Exo 35:25 "that is, yarn of these several colours, and **flaxen** thread,")
>
> **Note:** From verse 20-22 Joseph Smith uses the present tense showing us that it was written in his day and directed toward the items described in his day. Further proof of this is that he uses such phrases as "they have built up many churches", "preach up unto themselves", "many churches built up", "and there are also secret combinations", "that they may get gain" all of these are modern concepts of Joseph

Smith's day. In addition many critics of Joseph Smith believe that his use of "secret combinations" and other "combinations" found in the Book of Mormon came from groups in Joseph Smith's day such as the Masons. In fact as you can see and will see it came from the commentaries.

BOM 2 Nephi 27:6 And it shall come to pass that the Lord God shall bring forth **unto you the words of a book**, and they shall be the words of them which have *slumber*ed.

> **Note:** Joseph Smith really changed this verse to fit his premise: the book of course is the Book of Mormon hence the quantity of changes. Please note that this verse in Isaiah clearly states "<u>as</u> the words of a book" not actually as a book as Joseph Smith is implying with his changes, he also changes the idea of the fictional book from a "book that is sealed" to words from people who have slept, in other words the Book of Mormon coming out of the ground containing the words of Nephi and his descendents, again this changes the meaning of Isaiah from fictional to real, not the intent at all.

> **KJV** Isaiah 29:11 And the vision of all is become **unto you** as **the words of a book** that is sealed, which men deliver to one that is learned, saying, Read this, I pray thee: and he saith, I cannot; for it is sealed:)

> **COM** Henry: This section of commentary in Henry on the section of Isaiah 29:10 has the idea of rejecting, as in "rejecting the prophets" above (See 2 Nephi 27:5) and also the idea of slumbering. Isa 29:9-16 "(Isa 29:10), that he who bids them awake and open their eyes should yet lay them to sleep and shut their eyes; but it is in a way of righteous judgment, to punish them for their loving darkness rather than light, their loving sleep. When God by his **prophets** called them they said, Yet a little sleep, a little **slumber**; and therefore he gave them up to strong delusions, and said, Sleep on now. This is applied to the unbelieving Jews, who **rejected** the gospel of Christ, and were justly hardened in their infidelity, till wrath came upon them to the uttermost. Rom 11:8, God has given them the **spirit of slumber**.")

BOM 2 Nephi 28:11 Yea, **they** have **all gone out of the way; they** have **become** corrupted.

> **COM** Clarke tells us that in this verse "unprofitable" is "what is termed the corruption of human nature;" hence what Joseph Smith has above.)

> **KJV (1NT/1)** Romans 3:12 **They** are **all gone out of the way, they** are together **become** unprofitable; there is none that doeth good, no, not one.)

***BOM** 2 Nephi 29:6 And then **shall they rejoice**; for they shall know that it is a blessing unto them **from the hand of God**; and their *scales of darkness* shall begin *to fall from their eyes*; and many generations shall not pass away among them, **save they** shall be a pure and **delightsome** people.

> KJV (1/1) Psalm 89:16 In thy name **shall they rejoice** all the day: and in thy righteousness shall they be exalted.)
>
> KJV (1/1) Ecclesiastes 2:24 There is nothing better for a man, than that he should eat and drink, and that he should make his soul enjoy good in his labour. This also I saw, that it was **from the hand of God.)**
>
> NOTE: Again I hope I don't have to point out how improbable it is that this modern phrase should appear in a supposed ancient book.
>
> COM Gill: Col 1:13 "This deliverance is wrought out for them in the effectual calling, when they are internally called, and powerfully brought out of this darkness, by introducing light into them, revealing Christ in them, causing the prince of darkness to flee from them, and the **scales of darkness** and blindness to **fall from their eyes**;")
>
> KJV (1NT/14) Matthew 19:11 But he said unto them, All men cannot receive this saying, **save they** to whom it is given.)
>
> KJV (1/8) Malachi 3:12 And all nations shall call you blessed: for ye shall be a **delightsome** land, saith the LORD of hosts.)
>
> Note: Another phrase that would be impossible to be just coincidence. "The scales of darkness fall from their eyes" this phrase is very unique and Joseph Smith used it from the commentary of Gill.

BOM 2 Nephi 30:8 And it shall come to pass that the Lord God shall (17) commence (1340 AD) his work among **all nations, kindreds, tongues, and people** to bring about the *(1) (19) restoration (14ᵗʰ Century) of his people* upon the earth.

> KJV (1NT/8) Revelation 7:9 After this I beheld, and, lo, a great multitude, which no man could number, of **all nations, and kindreds, and people, and tongues**, stood before the throne, and before the Lamb, clothed with white robes, and palms in their hands;)
>
> COM Note how well this commentary by Gill fits with what is being said: Gill: Jer 16:19 "calling upon God, and exercising faith in him; having received the promise of the **restoration of his people** to their land, and a view of the future conversion of the Gentiles;." (Clarke, Henry)

***BOM** 2 Nephi 31:5 And now, if **the Lamb of God**, *he being holy*, should have need to be baptized by water, **to fulfil all righteousness**, O then, how much more need have we, being unholy, to be baptized, yea, even by water!

> KJV (2NT/35) John 1:29 The next day John seeth Jesus coming unto him, and saith, Behold **the Lamb of God**, which taketh away the sin of the world.)

KJV (1NT/2) <u>Matthew 3:15</u> And Jesus answering said unto him, Suffer it to be so now: for thus it becometh us **to fulfil all righteousness**. Then he suffered him.)

COM Note the same idea here: Gill: <u>Jam 1:17</u> "wherefore **he being holy**, cannot turn to that which is evil; nor can he, who is the fountain of light, be the cause of darkness, or admit of any in him; and since every good and perfect gift comes from him, evil cannot proceed from him, nor can he tempt any to it. ")

COM Clarke: <u>Heb 7:26</u> "**He was holy**; We, **unholy**. He was harmless; We, harmful, injuring both ourselves and others." (Henry)

Note: As you will see again later. He uses a present tense phrase as a description of Jesus "he being holy" yet they are writing this hundreds of years before he was baptized by John.

BOM <u>2 Nephi 31:6</u> And now, *(6) I would ask* of you, **my beloved brethren**, wherein **the Lamb of God** did **fulfil all righteousness** in being baptized by water?

COM Clarke: <u>Joh 12:24</u> "But, **I would ask**, has ever a more correct philosophy on this point appeared?")

KJV (4NT/60) <u>James 1:19</u> Wherefore, **my beloved brethren**, let every man be swift to hear, slow to speak, slow to wrath:)

KJV (2NT/35) <u>John 1:29</u> The next day John seeth Jesus coming unto him, and saith, Behold **the Lamb of God**, which taketh away the sin of the world.)

KJV (1NT/2) <u>Matthew 3:15</u> And Jesus answering said unto him, Suffer it to be so now: for thus it becometh us to **fulfil all righteousness**. Then he suffered him.)

Note: Joseph Smith made a tense mistake: "did fulfill" see note below.

***BOM** <u>2 Nephi 31:7</u> **Know ye not that** *he was holy?* But notwithstanding *he being holy*, he showeth unto **the children of men** (22/131) that, **according to the flesh** he humbleth himself before the Father, and **witnesseth** unto the Father that he would be obedient unto him in keeping his commandments.

KJV (10/11) <u>2 Samuel 3:38</u> And the king said unto his servants, **Know ye not that** there is a prince and a great man fallen this day in Israel?)

Note: Joseph Smith made a big mistake here as he has many times by using the wrong tense, indicating that it was written after the event in this case after Jesus lived on earth, "he was holy". He made this mistake, as other times because he was copying the idea from the commentaries.

COM Clarke: <u>Heb 7:26</u> "**He was holy**; We, unholy. He was harmless; We, harmful, injuring both ourselves and others." (Gill,

Henry)

COM Gill: <u>Jam 1:17</u> "wherefore **he being holy**, cannot turn to that which is evil;")

KJV (*Note: KJV uses "sheweth"* <u>Psalm 19:1</u> The heavens declare the glory of God; and the firmament sheweth his handywork.)

KJV (7NT/12) <u>Acts 2:30</u> Therefore being a prophet, and knowing that God had sworn with an oath to him, that of the fruit of his loins, **according to the flesh**, he would raise up Christ to sit on his throne;)

KJV (2NT/1) <u>John 5:32</u> There is another that beareth witness of me; and I know that the witness which he **witnesseth** of me is true.)

Note: We in our modern society are used to saying "in the form of a dove" but this is a modern interpretation of what appears in the New Testament.

BOM <u>2 Nephi 31:8</u> Wherefore, after he was baptized with water the **Holy Ghost (89NT/95) descended** upon him in the *(2) form of a dove.*

KJV (1NT/1) <u>Luke 3:22</u> And **the Holy Ghost descended** in a bodily shape like **a dove** upon him, and a voice came from heaven, which said, Thou art my beloved Son; in thee I am well pleased.

COM Gill: <u>Luke 3:22</u>: like a **dove upon him**; either **in the form of a dove**, or this corporeal form, whatever it was, descended and hovered on him as a dove does:)

Note: The KJV states that it was like a dove the more modern way of saying this is "form of a dove" just as Gill and the Book of Mormon.

BOM <u>2 Nephi 31:9</u> And again, it showeth unto **the children of men** (22/131) the *straightness* of the path, and the *narrowness* of **the gate**, by which they should enter, he having set the **example** before them.

COM Gill: <u>Mat 7:28</u> the **straitness** and **narrowness** of the way to eternal life, and the largeness and breadth of the way to destruction; concerning false prophets, and the right hearing of the word.)

KJV (1NT/1) <u>Matthew 7:14</u> Because **strait** is the gate, **and narrow** is the way, which leadeth unto life, and few there be that find it.)

KJV (4NT/8) <u>John 13:15</u> For I have given you an **example**, that ye should do as I have done to you.)

Note: The KJV uses the words "strait" and "narrow" but the commentary of Gill states "straitness" and "narrowness" just as the BOM.

BOM <u>2 Nephi 31:10</u> And he said unto **the children of men** (22/131): **Follow thou me.** Wherefore, **my beloved brethren**, can we follow Jesus save we shall be willing to keep *the (2) commandments of the Father*?

KJV (1NT/1) <u>John 21:22</u> Jesus saith unto him, If I will that he tarry till I come, what is that to thee? **follow thou me.**)

KJV (4NT/60) <u>James 1:19</u> Wherefore, **my beloved brethren**, let

every man be swift to hear, slow to speak, slow to wrath:)
COM Gill: <u>Joh 15:10</u> **The commandments of the Father** kept by Christ were not only the precepts of the moral law.)
BOM <u>Jacob 1:7</u> Wherefore we labored diligently among our people, that we might *(2) persuade them to* come unto Christ, and *(17) partake of **the goodness of God**,* that they might **enter into his rest, lest by any means** he should *(1) swear in his wrath* they should not enter in, **as in the provocation in the days of temptation** while the children of Israel were **in the wilderness**.

> **COM** Henry: <u>Gal 5:1-12</u> "To **persuade them to** stedfastness in the doctrine and liberty of the gospel" (Wesley)
>
> **COM** Clarke: <u>1Co 13:13</u> "Without faith it is impossible to please God; and without it, we can not **partake of the** grace of our Lord Jesus:" (Henry, Gill, Wesley)
>
> **KJV** (2/5) <u>Psalm 52:1</u> Why boastest thou thyself in mischief, O mighty man? **the goodness of God** endureth continually.)
>
> **KJV (1NT/3)** <u>Hebrews 3:18</u> And to whom sware he that they should not **enter into his rest**, but to them that believed not?)
>
> **KJV (3NT/7)** <u>1 Corinthians 8:9</u> But take heed **lest by any means** this liberty of yours become a stumblingblock to them that are weak.)
>
> **COM** Note how this fits with the verse and the use of Hebrew phrases, phrases found only found in Hebrews: Henry: <u>Heb 3:7-19</u> "God's wrath will discover itself in its righteous resolution to destroy the impenitent; he will **swear in his wrath**, not rashly, but righteously, and his wrath will make their condition a restless condition; there is no resting under the wrath of God.")
>
> **Note** Notice how unique the phrase "as in the provocation" is. Obviously he has been utilizing the New Testament throughout the Book of Mormon but this use, because of this phrase, is as they say "above and beyond".
>
> **KJV (1NT/1)** <u>Hebrews 3:8</u> Harden not your hearts, **as in the provocation, in the day of temptation in the wilderness:**)

BOM <u>Jacob 2:19</u> And after ye have obtained a **hope in Christ** ye shall obtain riches, if ye seek them; and ye will seek them for the intent to do good -- *to clothe the naked,* and *to feed the hungry,* and to liberate the captive, and administer relief to the sick and the afflicted.

> **COM** Henry: <u>Mat 25:31-46</u> "Now the good works here mentioned are such as we commonly call works of charity to the poor: not but that many will be found on the right hand who never were in a capacity **to feed the hungry,** or **clothe the naked,** but were themselves fed and clothed by the charity of others;" (Gill)

BOM <u>Jacob 4:11</u> Wherefore, beloved brethren, *be reconciled unto him* through the *(4) atonement of Christ,* **his Only Begotten Son,** and ye may obtain a resurrection, according to the power of the resurrection **which is in Christ**, and be presented as the *first-fruits of Christ* unto God, having faith, and obtained *a good hope of glory* in him before he (2) manifesteth (***Note: Not found in Henry, Clarke, Wesley,*** Gill, ***KJV, or Dictionary)*** himself in the flesh.

> **COM** Henry: <u>2Co 13:11-14</u> "He hath loved us, and is willing to be at peace with us; he commands us to love him, and to **be reconciled to him**,")
>
> **COM** Clarke: <u>Joh 14:16</u> "As the death and **atonement of Christ** will be necessary to man till the conclusion of the world" (Gill)
>
> **KJV (5NT/5)** <u>John 3:16</u> For God so loved the world, that he gave **his only begotten Son**, that whosoever believeth in him should not perish, but have everlasting life.)
>
> **KJV (7NT/8)** <u>Romans 8:39</u> Nor height, nor depth, nor any other creature, shall be able to separate us from the love of God, **which is in Christ** Jesus our Lord.)
>
> **COM** Henry: <u>Joh 1:37-42</u> "and these are the **first-fruits of Christ**'s disciples;")
>
> **COM** Gill: <u>1Co 15:10</u> "being a believer in Christ through faith, as a gift of God's grace, and having **a good hope of** eternal **glory** the same way;")
>
> **Note:** Notice how unique the phase "a good hope of" is. In addition it should be obvious that the phrase "first-fruits of Christ" is a modern concept. You should also note that it does not appear in the KJV. In addition the phrase "be reconciled to him" is also modern, hence the reason all these phrases are found in the commentaries. More evidence that the BOM is a modern creation. In fact as he copied these from the commentaries the BOM is a modern fabrication.

***BOM <u>Jacob 7:27</u> And I, Jacob, saw that I must soon **go down to** my **grave**; wherefore, I said unto my son Enos: Take these plates. And I told him the things which my brother Nephi had commanded me, and he *promised obedience* unto the commands. And I **make an end of** my writing upon these plates, which writing has been small; and *to the (1) reader (12th Century)* I **bid farewell**, hoping that many of my brethren may read my words. Brethren, (1) adieu. (14th Century)

> **KJV** (<u>Job 21:13</u> - They spend their days in wealth, and in a moment **go down to the grave**;)
>
> **COM** Gill: <u>Rom 2:13</u> "when he read it to them, and they hearkened to it, and **promised obedience**;" (Clarke)
>
> **KJV** (8/16) <u>Job 18:2</u> How long will it be ere ye **make an end of** words? mark, and afterwards we will speak.)
>
> **COM** Clarke: <u>Mat 20:15</u> "may render it as useful **to the reader** as

any thing else that has been written on it." (Henry, Gill)

KJV (1NT/4) Luke 9:61 And another also said, Lord, I will follow thee; but let me first go **bid** them **farewell**, which are at home at my house.)

COM Henry: Act 15:29 "God be with you! corrupted now into good by to ye! And of the same meaning with **adieu**! a Dieu, to God; that is, I commend you to God. All these terms savour not only of good will, or benevolence, but also of piety." Gill: Job 2:9 "take thy farewell of him (l); bid **adieu** to him and all religion, and so die;"

Note: It is highly unlikely that a Jewish man living around 500 BC would know such a word. It cannot be just an interpretation of a word that a Jewish man would have used as there are many other words utilized in the King James Version of the Bible that mean "farewell" including "farewell" even though it is only found in the New Testament, but why break with precedent here. It is also interesting to note that Henry, Clarke, and Gill all use the word. Why would Joseph Smith make the mistake of using this word? As with many of the mistakes that should have been obvious, he was used to seeing this word in the commentaries, especially in conjunction with "I bid".

BOM Mosiah 3:15 And many *signs, and wonders, and (2) types (15th Century), and shadows* showed he unto them, concerning his coming; and also **holy prophets spake** unto them concerning his coming; and yet they hardened their hearts, and understood not that the law of Moses **availeth nothing** except it were through the atonement of his blood.

COM Gill: Luk 2:31 "and in the promises and prophecies of the Old Testament, and in all the **types**, **shadows**, **and** sacrifices, of that dispensation;… by the miracles, wonders, **and signs**, which God did by Christ," (Clarke, Henry)

Note: "Types and Shadows" is a modern concept found in the commentaries.

KJV (1NT/1) Luke 1:70 As he **spake** by the mouth of his **holy prophets**, which have been since the world began:)

KJV (1/3) Esther 5:13 Yet all this **availeth** me **nothing**, so long as I see Mordecai the Jew sitting at the king's gate.)

Note: Again the concepts of "types and shadows" is a modern concept hence its source is Gill.

BOM Mosiah 4:5 For behold, if the knowledge of **the goodness of God** at this time has (8) awakened (12th Century) you *to a sense of* your (3) *nothingness (1631)*, and your worthless and (7) *fallen state* --

KJV (2/8) Psalm 52:1 Why boastest thou thyself in mischief, O mighty man? **the goodness of God** endureth continually.)

COM Gill: 1Sa 7:3 "they began to be **awakened to a sense of** their sins," (Henry, Clarke)

Note: Obviously the phrase "sense of nothingness" is quite unique and just as obvious copied form the commentaries.

COM Gill: 2Sa 7:20 "to express his **sense of** his own **nothingness and un**worth**iness**," (Clarke)

COM Clarke: Gen 3:1 "That man is **in a fallen state**")

BOM Mosiah 4:13 And ye will not *have a mind to* injure one another, but to **live peaceably**, and to **render to every man according to** that which is **his** due.

COM Henry: Rom 15:22-29 "God's dearest servants are not always gratified in every thing that they **have a mind to**." (Gill)

KJV (1NT/1) Romans 12:18 If it be possible, as much as lieth in you, **live peaceably** with all men.)

KJV (1NT/1) Romans 2:6 Who will **render to every man according to his** deed.)

COM Clarke: Rom 5:7 "These may be considered the just, who **render to every man his due**;")

Note: It is interesting that Romans, something that should not be quoted from hundreds of years before it was written, states "render to every man according to his *deed*" while the BOM says it exactly as Clarke does "render to every man his *due*" (emphasis added to "deed" and "due").

***BOM Mosiah 9:9 And we began to till the ground, yea, even with all manner of seeds, with seeds of **corn**, and of **wheat**, and of **barley**, and with neas, and with sheum, and with seeds of all manner of fruits; and we did begin to multiply and prosper in the land.

COM Notice that this part of Gill uses the same vegetables in the same order: and if you just take away the b in beans and move the "n" you get neas. In addition Joseph Smith ends with "all manner of fruits" and this ends with a similar idea "and various fruits" you could also take the word "pease" which Gill uses and remove the "p" in the beginning the "e" on the end and add the "n" you have "neas" in any case it didn't use "pease" because he didn't know what it was so he changed it around to make his own word. Gill: Gen 1:29 "and both these take in all kind of vegetables, all herbs, plants, roots, even **corn**, **wheat**, **barley**, pease, beans, &c. and the various **fruits** of all sorts of trees,")

BOM Mosiah 3:17 And moreover, I say unto you, that there shall be **no other name given** nor any *other way* nor *means* **whereby salvation** can come unto **the children of men** (22/131), only in and through **the name of Christ, the Lord Omnipotent**.

COM Gill: Act 4:12 "and determined he would save them by him, and by no other, and in **no other way**")

COM Clarke: Act 4:12 "Not only no other person, but no name except that divinely appointed one, Mat_1:21, by which salvation from sin can be expected - none given under heaven - **no other means** ever devised by God himself for the salvation of a lost world.")

KJV (1NT/1) Acts 4:12 Neither is there **salvation** in any **other**: for there is **none other name** under heaven **given** among men, **whereby** we must be saved.)

KJV (2NT/23) 1 Peter 4:14 If ye be reproached for **the name of Christ**, happy are ye; for the spirit of glory and of God resteth upon you: on their part he is evil spoken of, but on your part he is glorified.)

KJV (1NT/4) Revelation 19:6 And I heard as it were the voice of a great multitude, and as the voice of many waters, and as the voice of mighty thunderings, saying, Alleluia: for **the Lord** God **omnipotent** reigneth.)

Note: Notice that Joseph Smith uses the modern way of saying what Acts does. Again something that shouldn't happen as this BOM verse was written on a different continent at a different time.

BOM Introduction to Alma: The account of Alma, who was the son of Alma the first, and chief judge over the people of Nephi, and also the high priest *over the Church* (76/259). **An account** of the reign of the judges, and the *(23) wars and contentions* among the people. And also **an account** of a war between the Nephites and the Lamanites, according to the record of Alma, *(2) the first and chief* judge.

COM Clarke: 1Ti 3:2 "A bishop has to watch **over the Church**,")

KJV (2NT/29) Luke 16:2 And he called him, and said unto him, How is it that I hear this of thee? give **an account** of thy stewardship; for thou mayest be no longer steward.)

COM Clarke: Dan 2:45 "producing, not **wars and contentions**, but glory to God in the highest,")

COM Gill: Col 1:18 "or might be **the first and chief** over all persons, angels, and men;" (Henry)

Note: The phrase "the first and chief" is unique and it is interesting that a phrase from the commentaries are found in the introductions to each book of the BOM.

BOM Mormon 5:2 But behold, I was without hope, for I knew the judgments of the Lord which should come upon them; for they repented not of their iniquities, but did struggle for their lives without calling upon *that Being* who created them.

COM Col 1:16-17 "it would have been for **that Being who** gave him that office,")

BOM 1 Nephi 17:26 Now ye know that **Moses** was commanded of the **Lord** to do **that great work**; and ye know that by his word **the waters** of **the Red Sea were divided hither and thither**, and they **passed through on dry ground**.

> **KJV** (1/1) Exodus 14:31 And Israel saw **that great work** which the **LORD** did upon the Egyptians: and the people feared the **LORD**, and believed the **LORD**, and his servant **Moses**.)
>
> **KJV** (*Note: Verse of note: An apparent mix of these two verses:* Hebrews 11:29 By faith they **passed through the Red sea** as by **dry** land: which the Egyptians assaying to do were drowned.)
>
> **KJV** (2/5) 2 Kings 2:8 And Elijah took his mantle, and wrapped it together, and smote the waters, and they **were divided hither and thither**, so that they two went over **on dry ground**.)
>
> **COM** Henry: Heb 11:4-31 "By faith they **passed through the Red Sea** as **on dry** land;" It is also interesting to note that this section of Henry cross references Exodus 14 "The story we have in Exodus, ch. 14. Observe,")

BOM 1 Nephi 17:27 But ye know that the (*1) Egyptians were drowned* in *the Red Sea*, who were the armies of Pharaoh.

> **COM** Clarke: 1Co 10:1-5 "They were miraculously conducted through **the Red Sea**, where the pursuing **Egyptians were drowned**:")

BOM 1 Nephi 17:28 And ye also know that they were *fed with **manna in the wilderness***.

> **KJV** (1NT/1) John 6:49 Your fathers did eat **manna in the wilderness**, and are dead.)
>
> **COM** Gill: Psa 103:7 "his works, his wonderful works; his plagues on their enemies **the Egyptians**; his redemption of them out of the house of bondage; his leading them through **the Red sea** as on dry land; his feeding **them with manna in the wilderness**,")

BOM Mosiah 10:18 For this very cause has king Laman, by his *cunning, and lying craftiness*, and his (*2) fair promises,* deceived me, that I have brought this my people up into this land, that they may destroy them; yea, and we have suffered these many years in the land.

> **COM** Henry: Eze 13:10-16 "What has become of all the fine soft words and **fair promises** wherewith you flattered your wicked neighbours, and all the assurances you gave them that the troubles of the nation should soon be at an end?"" (Gill, Wesley)
>
> **COM** Gill: Eze 13:4 "and such are comparable to foxes, for their **craftiness** and **cunning**, and **lying** in wait to deceive, as these seduced the Lord's people,")

BOM <u>Mosiah 12:12</u> And again, he saith thou shalt be as *the* blossoms *of* a thistle, *which, when* it is fully ripe, if the wind *bloweth*, it is driven forth upon the face of the land. And he pretendeth (***Note: Not found)*** the Lord hath spoken it. And he saith all this shall come upon thee except thou repent, (*30*) *and this because* of thine iniquities.

    KJV (3/2) <u>2 Kings 14:9</u> And Jehoash the king of Israel sent to Amaziah king of Judah, saying, The **thistle** that was in Lebanon sent to the cedar that was in Lebanon, saying, Give thy daughter to my son to wife: and there passed by a wild beast that was in Lebanon, and trode down the **thistle**.)

    KJV (1/8) <u>Job 30:5</u> They were **driven forth** from among men, (they cried after them as after a thief;)

    COM Note the same idea here in Gill: <u>Isa 17:13</u> "Jarchi interprets it of the flower of thorns; that is, **the** down **of** the **thistle, which, when blown** off, rolls up, and, being exceeding light, is carried away at once;")

    COM Clarke: <u>2Ki 13:23</u> "**and this because of** his covenant with their fathers:" (Henry)

*****BOM** <u>Mosiah 13:10</u> But this much I tell you, what you do with me, after this, shall be as *a type and a shadow of* things which are to come.

    COM Gill: <u>Num 19:2</u> "who intended it as **a type and shadow of** the blood and sacrifice of Christ," (Henry, Clarke)

    Note: Again "a type and a shadow of" is a modern concept.

BOM <u>Mosiah 15:8</u> And thus God breaketh (*12*) *the bands of death, having gained the victory* over death; giving the Son power to **make intercession for the children of men** (22/131) –

    COM Henry: <u>Act 2:14-36</u> "Christ was imprisoned for our debt, was thrown into **the bands of death**; but, divine justice being satisfied, it was not possible he should be detained there," (Wesley, Gill)

    COM Clarke: <u>Lev 16:10</u> "and **having gained the victory** upon a battle,)

    KJV (1NT/2) <u>Hebrews 7:25</u> Wherefore he is able also to save them to the uttermost that come unto God by him, seeing he ever liveth to **make intercession for** them.)

    Note: Here we have two phrases, as with many of the others, that is extremely unlikely to have been made up by Joseph Smith and just as unlikely or really impossible, to have been written by someone so long ago.

*****BOM** <u>Mosiah 15:9</u> Having *ascended into heaven,* having the (*3*) *bowels of mercy; being filled with compassion* towards the children of men (22/131); *standing betwixt them* and justice; having broken (*12*) *the bands of death,* taken upon himself their iniquity and their transgressions, *having redeemed* *them*, and *satisfied the demands of justice.*

> **COM** Gill: Mat 19:28 "as he did when he **ascended into heaven**," (Henry, Clarke, Wesley)
>
> **COM** Gill: Mat 15:32 "and accustom them to show **bowels of mercy and compassion**" (Henry, Clarke)
>
> **COM** Gill: Act 7:21 "and **being filled with compassion** to it,")
>
> **COM** Henry: Act 2:14-36 "Christ was imprisoned for our debt, was thrown into **the bands of death**; but, divine justice being satisfied, it was not possible he should be detained there," (Wesley, Gill)
>
> **COM** Henry: Deu 27:11-26 "so near as that the priests **standing betwixt them** might be heard by those that were next them on both sides;")
>
> **COM** Gill: Mat 18:14 "and **having redeemed them** by Christ" (Henry)
>
> **COM** Henry: Heb 10:1-6 "Could they have **satisfied the demands of justice**,")
>
> **Note:** Again unlikely phrases especially "satisfied the demands of justice.

BOM Mosiah 15:10 **And now I say unto you, who shall declare his generation**? Behold, I say unto you, that when *his soul* has been *made an offering for sin* **he shall see his seed**. And now **what say ye**? And who shall be his seed?

> **KJV (1NT/18)** Acts 5:38 **And now I say unto you**, Refrain from these men, and let them alone: for if this counsel or this work be of men, it will come to nought:)
>
> **KJV** (2/1) Isaiah 53:8 He was taken from prison and from judgment: and **who shall declare his generation?** for he was cut off out of the land of the living: for the transgression of my people was he stricken.)
>
> **COM** Gill: Heb 10:10 "that **his soul** should be **made an offering for sin**;")
>
> **KJV** (Isaiah 53:10 Yet it pleased the LORD to bruise him; he hath put him to grief: when thou shalt make his soul an offering for sin, **he shall see his seed**, he shall prolong his days, and the pleasure of the LORD shall prosper in his hand.)
>
> **KJV** (Judges 18:8 - And they came unto their brethren to Zorah and Eshtaol, and their brethren said unto them, **what say ye?**)
>
> **Note:** Here we have a statistical improbability that the BOM would have the same modern phrase and this much of one from the commentary of Gill, "his soul...made an offering for sin."

BOM Mosiah 16:13 And now, **ought ye not to** tremble and repent of your sins, and remember that only *in and through Christ* ye can be saved?

> **KJV** (Neh 5:9 - Also I said, it is not good that ye do, **ought ye not to**

walk in the fear of our God;)
COM Gill: <u>Joh 17:26</u> "nor is anything of God to be known savingly, but **in and through Christ;**" (Henry, Clarke)
BOM <u>Mosiah 17:20</u> And now, when Abinadi had said these words, he fell, having suffered death by fire; yea, having been put to death because he would not deny the commandments of God, having *sealed the truth* of his words by his death.

> **COM** Clarke: <u>Rev 12:11</u> "and thus **sealed the truth** of what they spake with their blood.")
> **Note:** Notice that this idea from Clarke is exactly the same. "sealed the truth"..."of his words"..."of what they spake"..."with his death"... "with their blood". Clarke clarifies that "with their blood" was also their death.

BOM <u>Mosiah 21:16</u> And it came to pass (452/1353) that they began to prosper *(2) by degrees* in the land, and began to raise grain more abundantly, and flocks, and herds, that they did not suffer with hunger.

> **COM** Gill: <u>Rev 9:14</u> "and from hence, **by degrees**, as before observed, a large empire was raised." (Henry, Wesley, Clarke)
> **Note:** Again a very unique saying "by degrees".

BOM <u>Mosiah 22:11</u> And it came to pass (452/1353) that the people of king Limhi did depart by night into the wilderness with their flocks and their herds, and they went round about the land of Shilom in the wilderness, and *bent their course* towards the land of Zarahemla, being led by Ammon and his brethren.

> **KJV** (1/11) <u>Amos 3:11</u> Therefore thus saith the Lord GOD; An adversary there shall be even **round about the land**; and he shall bring down thy strength from thee, and thy palaces shall be spoiled.)
> **COM** Gill: <u>Gen 31:21</u> "he travelled and **bent his course** that way: this, was a mountain on the border of the land of Canaan,")
> **Note:** "bent their course" what a unique phrase but it is found in Gill.

***BOM <u>Mosiah 23:14</u> And also trust no one to be your teacher nor your minister, except he be a man of God, *walking in his ways and keeping his commandments.*

> **COM** Gill: <u>Rom 8:8</u> "There are many things which are pleasing to him, such as prayer, praise, giving of alms, **keeping his commandments, and walking in his ways**; but these unregenerate men cannot do in any acceptable manner to God; for they are without the Spirit, without Christ, without faith; and in all they do have no view to the glory of God: they have neither grace, nor strength, nor right principles, nor right ends.")
> **Note:** Again a long phrase not likely to have been thought up by Joseph Smith or the speaker in Mosiah.

BOM <u>Mosiah 23:15</u> Thus did Alma teach his people, that every man *should* *love his neighbor as himself,* that there should be no contention among them.

> **COM** Even though the phase "love thy neighbour as thy self" appears many times in the KJV it is interesting that Joseph Smith uses the exact phrasing as Clarke: Pro 12:26 "One would hope these translators meant not exclusively; he **should love his neighbor as himself.**")

***BOM** Mosiah 25:11 And again, when they thought upon the Lamanites, who were their brethren, of *their sinful and polluted state,* they were filled with pain and anguish *for the welfare of their souls.*

> **COM** Gill: Ecc 3:18 "He thought of the condition of the children of men, **their sinful and polluted state;**")
>
> **COM** Gill: Zec 11:5 "those who should have been concerned **for the welfare of their souls** had no compassion on them." (Clarke, Henry)
>
> **Note:** Again another unique and modern phrase "their sinful and polluted state."

BOM Mosiah 27:1 And now it came to pass (452/1353) that the persecutions which were inflicted on the church (76/259) by the unbelievers became so great that the church (76/259) began to murmur, and complain to their leaders concerning the matter; and they did complain to Alma. And Alma *laid the case before* their *king,* Mosiah. And Mosiah consulted with his priests.

> **COM** Gill: Jer 38:4 "**laid the case before** the **king,** and addressed him upon it in the following manner:" (Henry)

BOM Mosiah 27:22 And he caused that the priests should assemble themselves together; and they began to fast, and to pray to the Lord their God that he would open the mouth of Alma, that he might speak, and also that his (5) limbs (12th Century) might receive their strength -- that the eyes of the people might be opened to see and know of *the goodness and glory of God.*

> **COM** Gill: Exo 33:19 "the more clearly and fully does **the goodness and glory of God** pass before them.")

BOM Mosiah 27:31 Yea, **every knee shall bow, and every tongue confess** before him. Yea, even **at the last day,** when all men shall stand to be judged of him, then shall they *confess that he is* God; then shall they confess, *who live without God in the world,* that the judgment of an **everlasting punishment** is just upon them; and they shall quake, and tremble, and (6) shrink (13th Century) (***Note: Henry, Clarke, Wesley***) beneath the (3) *glance (15th Century) of* his (2) *all-searching eye.*

> **COM** (Gill: Mat 26:64 "will see him also, and *confess that he is* Lord and Christ, and the Son of God." (Henry)
>
> **KJV** (**1NT/1**) Romans 14:11 For it is written, As I live, saith the Lord, **every knee shall bow** to me, **and every tongue shall confess** to God.)
>
> **KJV** (**5NT/49**) John 6:44 No man can come to me, except the Father

which hath sent me draw him: and I will raise him up **at the last day**.)
COM Gill: Mat 15:1-9 "he does not stand at that distance which those are at, **who live without God in the world**," (Henry, Clarke)
KJV (1NT/1) Ephesians 2:12 That at that time ye were without Christ, being aliens from the commonwealth of Israel, and strangers from the covenants of promise, having no hope, **and without God in the world**:)
KJV (1NT/2) Matthew 25:46 And these shall go away into **everlasting punishment**: but the righteous into life eternal.)
 Note: (Isaac Watts (1674-1748) Pastor who wrote many hymns and poems: "But his **all-searching eye** reveals The secrets of the night." John Wesley also in his sermons used the same phrase: *Sermons on Several Occasions* "Where are they, whom his **all-searching eye** discerns to be truly humble; to abhor themselves in dust and ashes, in the presence of God their Saviour;"). **COM** Clarke: Son 4:9 ""Even one of thine eyes, or one **glance of** thine **eye**s, has been sufficient to deprive me of all power; it has completely overcome me;" for glance may be understood, and such forms of speech are common in all languages, when speaking on such subjects.")
Note: The phrase "and without God in the world" is a modern phrase. In fact Wesley in created an entire sermon on this "On Living Without God" sermon number 125 in which he starts out with the phrase "without God in the world". In this sermon he states that this phrase could better be translated "atheists in the world" which is exactly how Joseph Smith uses this phrase in Mosiah.
BOM Mosiah 28:4 And thus did the Spirit of the Lord work upon them, for they were the very *vilest of sinners*. And the Lord saw fit *in his infinite mercy* to spare them; nevertheless they suffered much *(3) anguish of soul* because of their iniquities, suffering much and fearing that they should be **cast off forever**.

> **COM** Gill: Heb 12:3 "some of them the **vilest of sinners**," (Henry, Clarke)
> **COM** Clarke: Jam 5:20 "him back to God, who, **in his infinite mercy**" (Henry)
> **COM** Gill: Job 7:11 "but great **anguish of soul**;" (Henry, Clarke)
> **KJV (2/4)** Lamentations 3:31 For the LORD will not **cast off for ever**:)
> **Note:** Several modern terms.

BOM Mosiah 29:35 And he also unfolded unto them all the *(1) disadvantages (14th Century) they labored under*, by having an unrighteous king to rule over them;

COM Henry: <u>Luk 2:25-40</u> "hat now the mystery of that should be **unfolded**, when in Christ we should as it were see God face to face" (Clarke, Wesley)

COM Henry: <u>Act 11:19-26</u> "considering the outward **disadvantages they laboured under:**")

Note: Again a long unique phrase.

BOM <u>Alma 1:30</u> And thus, in their *(2) prosperous circumstances,* they did not send away any who were **naked**, or that were **hungry**, or that were **athirst**, or that were **sick**, or that had not been nourished; and they did not *set their hearts upon riches*; therefore they were *liberal to all*, both old and young, both bond and free, both male and female, whether out of the **church** (76/259) or in the **church** (76/259), having **no respect** to **persons** as to those who *stood in need.*

COM Gill: <u>Jam 5:13</u> "as well as in **prosperous circumstances**" (Henry)

KJV (1NT/1) <u>Matthew 25:44</u> Then shall they also answer him, saying, Lord, when saw we thee an **hungred**, or **athirst**, or a stranger, or **naked**, or **sick**, or in prison, and did not minister unto thee?)

COM Gill: <u>Mar 10:24</u> "as that he was to be understood of such that trusted in their **riches**, **set their hearts upon** them,")

COM Note how these comments in Gill fit these two paragraphs: Gill: <u>Rom 16:23</u> "of the church at Corinth, to whom he was kind and hospitable, even to as many as **stood in need** of his assistance; or of the church of Christ in general, being beneficent and **liberal to all** Christian strangers that came that way, lodged them at his house, and provided every thing proper and convenient for them.")

KJV (**3NT/1**) <u>Romans 2:11</u> For there is **no respect** of **persons** with God.)

BOM <u>Alma 5:10</u> And now I ask of you on what **conditions** are they saved? Yea, *what grounds* had they to *hope for salvation*? What is the cause of their *being loosed* from (*12) the bands of death,* yea, and also the chains of hell?

KJV (**1NT/1**) <u>Luke 14:32</u> Or else, while the other is yet a great way off, he sendeth an ambassage, and desireth **conditions** of peace.)

COM Henry: <u>1Th 5:6-10</u> "Having mentioned salvation and the hope of it, the apostle shows **what grounds** and reasons Christians have to **hope for** this **salvation**,")

COM Gill: <u>Act 16:28</u> "that they took no notice of their **bands being loosed**," (Clarke, Henry)

COM Henry: <u>Act 2:14-36</u> "Christ was imprisoned for our debt, was thrown into **the bands of death**; but, divine justice being satisfied, it was not possible he should be detained there," (Wesley, Gill)

Note: Again the phrase "what grounds...hope for salvation" is quite unique and found in Henry.

***BOM Alma 5:15 Do ye *(4) exercise faith* in the redemption of him who created you? Do you *look forward with an eye of faith,* and view this mortal body raised in immortality, and this **corruption raised in incorruption**, to **stand before God**, to be judged **according to** the **deeds** which have been done in the mortal body?

> **COM** Henry: Gen 22:15-19 "Note, If we **exercise faith**, God will encourage it." (Wesley
>
> **COM**: Henry: Psa 37:1-6 "When we **look forward with an eye of faith** we shall see no reason to envy wicked people their prosperity,")
>
> **KJV (1NT/1)** 1 Corinthians 15:42 So also is the resurrection of the dead. It is sown in **corruption**; it is **raised in incorruption**:)
>
> **KJV (1NT/8)** Revelation 20:12 And I saw the dead, small and great, **stand before God**; and the books were opened: and another book was opened, which is the book of life: and the dead were judged out of those things which were written in the books, according to their works.)
>
> **KJV (1NT/1)** Romans 2:6 Who will render to every man **according to his deeds**:)
>
> **Note:** The phrase "look forward with an eye of faith" is quite unique and as with many phrases I searched countless books that existed at the time and before, and the only place this phrase appeared was in the commentary of Henry and I want to emphasize written before Joseph Smith wrote the BOM.

BOM Alma 5:18 Or otherwise, can ye imagine yourselves brought *before the (1) tribunal (1526) of God* with your souls *filled with guilt and (3) remorse (14th Century)*, having a remembrance of all your guilt, yea, a perfect remembrance of all your wickedness, yea, a remembrance that ye have *(3) set at (3) defiance (15th Century)* the commandments of God?

> **COM** Clarke: Mat 26:39 "The whole world are here represented as standing guilty and condemned **before the tribunal of God**;" (Gill, Henry)
>
> **COM** Gill: Joh 4:29 "and her conscience was **filled with guilt and remorse**, and her soul with shame and confusion;")
>
> **COM** Henry: Jer 48:14-47 "The Moabites preferred Chemosh before Jehovah, and thought themselves a match for the God of Israel, whom they **set at defiance**.")
>
> **Note:** Again the phrase "before the tribunal of God", is another rare phrase and modern especially since the word tribunal did not come into existence until 1526 AD.

***BOM Alma 5:26 And now behold, I say unto you, my brethren, if ye have experienced a change of heart, and if ye have felt to *sing the song of redeeming love, (6) I would ask* , can ye feel so now?

COM Gill: <u>Psa 68:4</u> "and therefore should **sing the song of redeeming love**, with grace and melody in their hearts, unto him;")

COM Clarke: <u>Joh 12:24</u> "But, **I would ask**, has ever a more correct philosophy on this point appeared?")

Note: The song of redeeming love is just that a song, it is a modern song, and was song during the time of Joseph Smith but Joseph Smith unaware of this used the phrase from Gill.

***BOM** <u>Alma 7:23</u> And now **I would that ye** should be humble, and be submissive and *gentle*; *easy to be entreated*; full of *patience* and *long-suffering*; being **temperate in all things**; being diligent in keeping the commandments of God at all times; asking for whatsoever things ye stand in need, (*1*) *both spiritual and temporal*; always *returning thanks unto God* for whatsoever things ye do receive.

KJV (2NT/56) <u>Colossians 2:1</u> For **I would that ye** knew what great conflict I have for you, and for them at Laodicea, and for as many as have not seen my face in the flesh;)

KJV (1NT/2) <u>1 Corinthians 9:25</u> And every man that striveth for the mastery is **temperate in all things**. Now they do it to obtain a corruptible crown; but we an incorruptible.)

COM Clarke: <u>1Jo 4:7</u> "And ever be ready to promote each other's welfare, **both spiritual and temporal**." (Henry)

KJV (1NT/27) <u>2 Corinthians 4:18</u> While we look not at the things which are seen, but at the things which are not seen: for the things which are seen are **temporal**; but the things which are not seen are eternal.)

COM Gill: <u>Luk 12:17</u> "and was still further off of thinking of **returning thanks to God for** it:" (Henry, Clarke)

COM <u>Gal 5:13-26</u> "He particularly recommends to us, love, to God especially, and to one another for his sake, - joy, by which may be understood cheerfulness in conversation with our friends, or rather a constant delight in God, - peace, with God and conscience, or a peaceableness of temper and behaviour towards others, - **long-suffering**, **patience** to defer anger, and a contentedness to bear injuries, - **gentle**ness, such a sweetness of temper, and especially towards our inferiors, as disposes us to be affable and courteous, and **easy to be entreated** when any have wronged us, - goodness (kindness, beneficence), which shows itself in a readiness to do good to all as we have opportunity, - faith, fidelity, justice, and honesty, in what we profess and promise to others, - meekness, wherewith to govern our passions and resentments, so as not to be easily provoked, and, when we are so, to be soon pacified, - and temperance, in meat and drink, and other enjoyments of life, so as not to be excessive and immoderate in the use of them. Concerning these things, or those in whom these fruits of the Spirit are found, the apostle says, There is no law against them, to condemn and punish them.")

Note: Notice how the above quote from Gill fits with what Joseph Smith wrote in Alma.

BOM <u>Alma 10:17</u> Now they knew not that Amulek could know of their designs. But **it came to pass** (452/1353) as they **began to question him**, he **perceived their thoughts**, and he said unto them: (*4*) *O ye wicked and perverse generation*, ye **lawyers** and **hypocrites**, for ye are laying the foundation of the devil; for ye are laying *traps and snares* to catch the holy ones of God.

> **KJV (1NT/1)** <u>Luke 5:22</u> But when Jesus **perceived their thoughts**, he answering said unto them, What reason ye in your hearts?)
>
> **COM Note:** The King James Version of the Bible tells us that Jesus said "faithless and perverse" but the Book of Mormon gives us this exact phrase match for Gill: <u>Mat 27:40</u> "and no other but that sign was to be given to that **wicked and perverse generation**,")
>
> **KJV (2NT/1)** <u>Matthew 17:17</u> Then Jesus answered and said, **O** faithless and **perverse generation**, how long shall I be with you? how long shall I suffer you? bring him hither to me.)
>
> **KJV (5NT/17)** <u>Luke 7:30</u> But the Pharisees and **lawyers** rejected the counsel of God against themselves, being not baptized of him.)
>
> **KJV (1NT/1)** <u>Matthew 16:3</u> And in the morning, It will be foul weather to day: for the sky is red and lowering. **O ye hypocrites**, ye can discern the face of the sky; but can ye not discern the signs of the times?)
>
> **COM** Gill: <u>Son 3:6</u> "and because of the **traps and snares** that are in it, through evil men,")

BOM <u>Alma 10:25</u> But Amulek **stretched forth his hand**, and cried the mightier unto them, saying: (*4*) *O ye wicked and perverse generation*, why hath Satan got such great hold upon your hearts? Why will ye yield yourselves unto him that he may have power over you, to blind your eyes, that ye will not understand the words which are spoken, according to their truth?

> **KJV** (7/12) <u>Exodus 10:22</u> And Moses **stretched forth his hand** toward heaven; and there was a thick darkness in all the land of Egypt three days:)
>
> **COM** The KJV tells us that Jesus said "faithless and perverse" but Gill gives us this exact phrase: <u>Mat 27:40</u> "and no other but that sign was to be given to that **wicked and perverse generation**,")
>
> **KJV (2NT/1)** <u>Matthew 17:17</u> Then Jesus answered and said, **O** faithless and **perverse generation**, how long shall I be with you? how long shall I suffer you? bring him hither to me.)

BOM Alma 12:22 Now Alma said unto him: **This is the thing which** I **was about to** explain, now we see that Adam did fall by the (5) partaking of the (*6*) *forbidden fruit, according* to **the word of God** (45/89); and thus we see, that by his fall, **all mankind** became a lost and fallen people.

> **KJV** (Exo 16:16 - **This is the thing which** the Lord hath commanded...)
>
> **KJV (3/21)** Acts 20:3 And there abode three months. And when the Jews laid wait for him, as he **was about to** sail into Syria, he purposed to return through Macedonia.)
>
> **COM** Phrase not found in the Old Testament but is a phrase started in 1662 AD. Henry: Joe 1:1-7 "and when they are going to **partake of the forbidden fruit** a prohibition of another nature shall come between the cup and the lip, and cut off the wine from their mouth." (Clarke, Wesley)
>
> **KJV** (1/20) Job 12:10 In whose hand is the soul of every living thing, and the breath of **all mankind**.)

BOM Alma 12:27 But behold, it was not so; but it was *appointed* **unto men** that they must **die**; and *after death, they* must *come to judgment*, even that same judgment of which we have spoken, which is the end.

> **KJV (1NT/1)** Hebrews 9:27 And as it is **appointed unto men** once to **die**, but **after** this the **judgment**;)
>
> **COM** Henry: Heb 9:23-28 "It is **appointed to men that after death they** shall **come to judgment**,")
>
> **Note:** Even though this idea is found in Hebrews which means it should not be in the BOM, Joseph Smith actually matches more what Henry says in his commentary.

BOM Alma 13:15 And it was this same Melchizedek to whom *Abraham paid tithes*; yea, even our father *Abraham paid tithes* of one-**tenth part of all** he possessed.

> **COM** Gill: Heb 7:4 "how great then must **Melchizedek** be, to whom he **paid tithes**?")
>
> **KJV** (Genesis 14:20 And blessed be the most high God, which hath delivered thine enemies into thy hand. And he gave him tithes of all.)
>
> **KJV (1NT/1)** Hebrews 7:2 To whom also Abraham gave a **tenth part of all**; first being by interpretation King of righteousness, and after that also King of Salem, which is, King of peace;)
>
> **Note:** It is interesting that the King James Version of the Bible's account in Genesis says "gave him tithes of all" while here, supposedly having a copy of Genesis Joseph Smith says what Gill says instead of the Bible's version, "paid tithes". In addition it is also interesting that he uses the words out of the book of Hebrews from the New Testament "a tenth part of all".

BOM Alma 13:16 Now these ordinances were given **after this manner did**, that thereby the people might look forward on **the Son of God, (43NT/49)** it being a *type of his order*, or it being *his order*, and this that they might look forward to him for a remission of their sins, that they might enter into the rest of the Lord.

> **KJV** (16/34) Genesis 39:19 And it came to pass, when his master heard the words of his wife, which she spake unto him, saying, **After this manner did** thy servant to me; that his wrath was kindled.)

Notice that Joseph Smith continues to use Gill's commentary on Hebrew chapter seven which talks about Abraham and Melchizedek, by using the idea that the order of Melchizedek is a "type" of Jesus' order. This as you can see is exactly what Gill tells us in his commentary, and Joseph Smith even uses the phrase "type of" again a modern concept.

COM Gill: Heb 7:13 "and in the **type of** him **Melchizedek**, in the preceding verses; for not **Melchizedek** is here meant, but the Lord Jesus Christ,")

COM Gill: Heb 7:1 "but he is expressly said to be like unto him, and Christ is said to be of **his order**;")

KJV (1NT/8) Luke 1:77 To give knowledge of salvation unto his people by the **remission of their sins**,)

COM Gill: Heb 7:28 "which declared Christ an high priest after the **order** of **Melchizedek**")

Note: If you will notice we are maintaining the Melchizedek comparison in the BOM. In addition Joseph Smith continues to use Hebrews both from the KJV and the commentaries to create this section on Melchizedek. Notice that Joseph Smith calls Melchizedek "a type of his order" when Gill says the same thing. You will see this continuance of the use of the commentaries to create this section of the BOM on Melchizedek below.

BOM Alma13:18 But **Melchizedek** having exercised mighty faith, and *received the office of* the *high priesthood* according to the holy order of *God*, did preach repentance unto his people. And behold, they did repent; and **Melchizedek** did (*6) establish peace* in the land in his days; therefore he was **called the prince of peace,** for he was the **king of Salem**; and he did reign under his father.

> Notice that Joseph Smith continues to use the commentaries on chapter seven of Hebrews. He even uses the same idea and words.
>
> **COM** Henry: Heb 7:1-10 "and it is well observed that Levi **paid tithes** to Melchisedec in Abraham, Heb 7:9. Now Levi **received the office of** the **priesthood** from **God**, as to a greater and **high**er **priest** than himself; therefore that **high priest** who should afterwards

appear, of whom **Melchisedec** was **a type**, must be much superior to any of the Levitical priests, who **paid tithes**, in **Abraham**, to **Melchisedec**.")

COM Gill: <u>1Ki 5:12</u> "in order to continue and **establish peace** and friendship between them," (Henry)

KJV (1/1) <u>Isaiah 9:6</u> For unto us a child is born, unto us a son is given: and the government shall be upon his shoulder: and his name shall be **called** Wonderful, Counsellor, The mighty God, The everlasting Father, **The Prince of Peace**.)

KJV (**1NT/1**) <u>Hebrews 7:1</u> For this Melchisedec, **king of Salem**, priest of the most high God, who met Abraham returning from the slaughter of the kings, and blessed him;)

KJV (**1NT/1**) <u>Hebrews 7:2</u> To whom also Abraham gave a tenth part of all; first being by interpretation King of righteousness, and after that also **King of Salem**, which is, King of peace;) **KJV** (1/1) <u>Genesis 14:18</u> And **Melchizedek king of Salem** brought forth bread and wine: and he was the priest of the most high God.)

COM Gill: <u>Heb 7:13</u> "but the Lord Jesus Christ, as appears by what follows; the antitype of **Melchizedek**, the Lord our righteousness, **the Prince of peace**, the priest of God, that lives for ever, without father, without mother, &c.")

BOM <u>Alma 13:19</u> Now, there were many before him, and also there were many afterwards, but none were greater; therefore, of him they have (*2*) *more particularly made mention.*

KJV (**2NT/4**) <u>Acts 21:19</u> And when he had saluted them, he declared **particularly** what things God had wrought among the Gentiles by his ministry.)

Notice below the same idea in the commentaries as is said here of Melchizedek. Basically that he was the greatest.

COM Henry: <u>Heb 7:1-10</u> "Melchisedec's greater honour - in that it was his place and privilege to bless Abraham; and it is an uncontested maxim *that the less is blessed of the greater,* <u>Heb 7:7</u>. He who gives the blessing is greater than he who receives it;")

COM Gill: <u>Heb 7:9</u> "that is, to Melchizedek; and therefore Melchizedek must be greater than they, and his priesthood a more excellent one than theirs; since they who receive tithes from others gave tithes to him.")

COM Gill: <u>Heb 7:3</u> "and this (Peleg) was the father of Heraclim, the father of Melchizedek;" and in a preceding chapter, his pedigree is **more particularly** set forth: (Clarke, Henry)

COM Gill: <u>Heb 7:3</u> "afterwards he begat Melchizedek, the priest whom we have now **made mention** of.")

Note: Obviously he continues the use of the commentaries on Hebrews chapter 7 to create this verse also.

BOM <u>Alma 22:14</u> And since man had fallen he could not *(2) merit (14th Century) anything* of himself; but the sufferings and death of Christ atone for their sins, through faith and repentance, and so forth; and that he breaketh *(12) the bands of death*, that the grave shall have no **victory**, and that the **sting** of **death** should be **swallowed up** in the *hopes of glory*; and Aaron did expound all these things unto the king.

> **COM** Gill: <u>Rom 11:35</u> "hence no man can **merit anything** at the hands of God,")
>
> **COM** Henry: <u>Act 2:14-36</u> "Christ was imprisoned for our debt, was thrown into **the bands of death**; but, divine justice being satisfied, it was not possible he should be detained there," (Wesley, Gill)
>
> **KJV (1NT/1)** <u>1 Corinthians 15:55</u> "Where, O **death**, is your **victory**? Where, O **death**, is your **sting**?")
>
> **KJV (1NT/1)** <u>1 Corinthians 15:54</u> When the perishable has been clothed with the imperishable, and the mortal with immortality, then the saying that is written will come true: "**Death** has been **swallowed up** in **victory**.")
>
> **COM** Gill: <u>Col 1:27</u> "he is the ground and foundation of their **hopes of glory**." (Henry, Clarke)

***BOM <u>Alma 23:7</u> For they became *(10) a righteous people;* they did *lay down* the *weapons of* their *rebellion*, that they did not fight *against God* any more, neither against any of their brethren.

***BOM <u>Alma 23:13</u> And these are the names of the cities of the Lamanites which were converted unto the Lord; and these are they that *laid down the weapons of their rebellion*, yea, all their weapons of war; and they were all Lamanites.

> **COM** Henry: <u>Zec 8:1-8</u> "they shall be **a righteous people** and shall abound in the fruits of righteousness," (Wesley)
>
> **COM** Gill: <u>Job 13:24</u> "but he was now reconciled unto God, the enmity of his heart was slain, and he had **laid down** his **weapons of rebellion**, and ceased committing hostilities **against God**, and was become subject to him and to his law, through the power of efficacious grace;")
>
> **Note:** "laid down...weapons of rebellion" again a unique phrase taken from the commentaries. Notice that in Alma 23:7 it is the same idea of laying down the weapons of rebellion against God, but in Alma 23:13 he varies its use.

BOM <u>Alma 30:16</u> Ye look forward and say that ye see a remission of your sins.

But behold, it is the effect of a (1) frenzied (1796) mind; and this *(1)* *derangement (1776) of your mind*s comes because of the **traditions of** your **fathers**, which lead you away into a belief of things which are not so.

> **COM** Clarke: <u>Act 12:25</u> "This argues such blindness of understanding, hardness of heart, and **derangement of mind**,")
>
> **KJV (1NT/20)** <u>Galatians 1:14</u> And profited in the Jews' religion above many my equals in mine own nation, being more exceedingly zealous of the **traditions of** my **fathers**.)
>
> **Note:** "derangement of mind" is very unique and all the more so because the word "derangement" did not come into our history until almost 60 years before the BOM was even written. You will see an explanation of the types of words in a later chapter.

BOM** <u>Alma 30:42</u> Behold, I know that thou believest, but *thou art possessed with **a lying spirit, and ye have put off the Spirit of God that it may have **no place in you**; but **the devil** has power over you, and he doth *carry you about*, working devices that he may destroy the children of God.

> **KJV (4/1)** <u>1 Kings 22:23</u> Now therefore, behold, the LORD hath put **a lying spirit** in the mouth of all these thy prophets, and the LORD hath spoken evil concerning thee.)
>
> **COM** Henry: <u>Joh 7:14-36</u> ""Thou hast a devil, **thou art possessed with a lying spirit**,")
>
> **KJV (1NT/7)** <u>John 8:37</u> I know that ye are Abraham's seed; but ye seek to kill me, because my word hath **no place in you**.)
>
> **COM** Henry: <u>Mat 21:1-11</u> "he might have had an ass of his own, to **carry him about**;")
>
> **Note:** "thou are possessed with a lying spirit" a very long phrase taken from Henry.

BOM <u>Alma 30:44</u> But Alma said unto him: Thou hast had signs enough; will ye tempt your God? Will ye say, Show unto me a sign, when ye have the testimony of all these thy brethren, and also all the holy prophets? The **scriptures** are laid before thee, yea, and all things (1) denote (1592) (***Note: Henry, Clarke,** Gill, **Wesley)** there is a God; yea, even the earth, and *all things* that are upon the face of it, yea, and *its motion*, yea, and also all the planets which move in their regular form do witness that there is a *Supreme Creator*.

> **KJV (21NT/41)** <u>Matthew 21:42</u> Jesus saith unto them, Did ye never read in the **scriptures**, The stone which the builders rejected, the same is become the head of the corner: this is the Lord's doing, and it is marvellous in our eyes?)
>
> **COM** Gill: <u>Isa 40:22</u> "Or, "the globe (z)" of it; for the earth is spherical or globular: not a flat plain, but round, hung as a ball in the air; here Jehovah sits as the Lord and Sovereign; being the Maker of it, he is above it, orders and directs **its motion**, and governs **all things** in it:")

COM Henry: <u>Dan 5:10-29</u> "and it is more his honour to be a subject to the **supreme Creator** than to be lord of the inferior creatures.")

Note: Please note before these verses and into the next chapter Joseph Smith quotes from Matthew often.

Note: Joseph Smith uses the title from Henry "surpreme Creator" you will see Joseph Smith's use of titles in a future chapter.

BOM <u>Alma 32:38</u> But if ye **neglect** the tree, and **take no thought** for its **nourishment**, behold it will not get any root; and when *the heat of the sun* cometh and (1) *scorcheth* it, **because** it hath **no root** it *withers* **away**, and ye pluck it up and cast it out.

KJV (3NT/7) <u>Matthew 18:17</u> And if he shall **neglect** to hear them, tell it unto the church: but if he **neglect** to hear the church, let him be unto thee as an heathen man and a publican.)

KJV (5NT/1) <u>Matthew 6:25</u> Therefore I say unto you, **Take no thought** for your life, what ye shall eat, or what ye shall drink; nor yet for your body, what ye shall put on. Is not the life more than meat, and the body than raiment?)

KJV (1NT/3) <u>Colossians 2:19</u> And not holding the Head, from which all the body by joints and bands having **nourishment** ministered, and knit together, increaseth with the increase of God.)

Note: Notice the exact same meaning here including the use of the some of the same words as the verse above; "having no depth of earth" and "will not get any root" along with "because it hath no root" and then of course the copying of the same words.

COM Henry: <u>Mat 13:1-23</u> "How they fell away, so that no fruit was brought to perfection; no more than the corn, that having no depth of earth from which to draw moisture, is **scorched** and **withered** by **the heat of the sun**.")

COM Note: And note later in the same commentary of Matthew by Henry <u>Mat 13:1-23</u> ...the same sun which warms and cherishes that which was well rooted, withers and burns up that which wanted root.")

KJV (1NT/1) <u>Matthew 13:6</u> And when the sun was up, they were **scorched**; and **because** they had **no root**, they **withered away**.)

BOM <u>Alma 32:39</u> Now, this is not because the seed was not good, neither is it because the fruit thereof would not be desirable; but it is because your ground is barren, and ye will not nourish the tree, therefore ye cannot have the fruit thereof.

COM Henry: <u>Mat 13:1-23</u> "[2.] The *stony ground. Some fell upon stony places...")*

Note: We are even told in Henry in this part of the commentary what part of ground the seeds are in;

***BOM Alma 32:40 And thus, if ye will not nourish the word, *(2) looking forward with an eye of faith* to the *fruit* thereof, ye can never pluck of the *fruit* of **the tree of life**;

> **COM** This phrase does not make sense to use here, looking forward with an eye of faith to fruit? Henry: Psa 37:1-6 When we **look forward with an eye of faith** we shall see no reason to envy wicked people their prosperity,")
>
> **KJV** (6/15) Genesis 2:9 And out of the ground made the LORD God to grow every tree that is pleasant to the sight, and good for food; **the tree of life** also in the midst of the garden, and the tree of knowledge of good and evil.)

BOM Alma 32:41 But if ye will nourish the word, yea, nourish the tree as it (11) beginneth (***Note: Not found in Wesley, Clarke,*** Gill***, Henry, KJV)*** to grow, by your faith with great diligence, and with patience, looking forward to the *fruit* thereof, it shall take *root*; and behold it shall be a tree *springing up unto everlasting life.*

> **Note:** Notice the same meaning here in Gill for the verses above and note that Joseph Smith has been using Matthew phrases also. In addition space constraints make it impossible to do here but if you read the commentary of Henry in its entirety, as outlined above, you will grasp more fully the same meaning behind what Joseph Smith has made up her. Also notice he uses the same unique phrase "springing up unto everlasting life". Joseph Smith used this entire section of Gill to make up this section of the BOM.
>
> **COM** Gill: Mat 13:6 "they were offended with what they met with, for the sake of Christ, and the profession of his word; and therefore, not being rooted in him, nor in the love of God, nor having the root of the matter, true grace, in themselves, or, as Luke says, "lacked moisture", of divine grace, of the dews and waterings of it, fell away finally and totally. This is no instance of the apostasy of real saints, or any proof of true believers falling away finally and totally; since these were not **rooted**, and grounded in the everlasting and unchangeable love of God, were not interested in it, or were partakers of the effects of it; had they been so, they could never have been separated from it; tribulation, distress, and persecution could never have done it; none of these would ever have moved them; had they had the love of God shed abroad in their hearts, they would have gloried in tribulation: nor were they united to Christ, rooted and built up in him; had they, they would have continued to have derived life and **nourishment** from him; in him the life of believers is hid, and because he lives they live also; as long as there is life in the **root**, the branches will not die; he is the **root** that bears the branches, the **root** of the righteous that yields

fruit, and is never moved: nor had these the truth of grace, which is an incorruptible seed, a well of living water **springing up to everlasting life**; had they, they could never have withered away; to such God gives more grace, he himself is as the dew unto them, and he waters them every moment.")

BOM Alma 32:42 And because of your diligence and your faith and your patience with the word in nourishing it, that it may take *root* in you, behold, *by and by* ye shall pluck the fruit thereof, which is *most precious*, which is sweet above all that is sweet, and which is white above all that is white, yea, and pure above all that is pure; and ye shall feast upon this fruit even until ye are filled, that ye **hunger** not, **neither shall** ye **thirst**.

> **KJV (1NT/5)** Matthew 13:21 Yet hath he not root in himself, but dureth for a while: for when tribulation or persecution ariseth because of the word, **by and by** he is offended.)
>
> **COM Henry:** Mat 13:1-23 "Observe how soon they fall away, **by and by**; as soon rotten as they were ripe;")
>
> **KJV (2NT/10)** Revelation 18:12 The merchandise of gold, and silver, and precious stones, and of pearls, and fine linen, and purple, and silk, and scarlet, and all thyine wood, and all manner vessels of ivory, and all manner vessels of **most precious** wood, and of brass, and iron, and marble,)
>
> **COM** Henry: Mat 13:24-43 "In the field of this world good people are the wheat, the **most precious** grain, and the valuable part of the field.")
>
> **KJV (1NT/1)** Revelation 7:16 They shall hunger no more, neither thirst any more; neither shall the sun light on them, nor any heat.)

***BOM Alma 34:16 And thus mercy can *satisfy the demands of justice*, and *encircles them in the arms of safety*, while he that exercises no faith unto repentance is exposed to the whole law of *the demands of justice*; therefore only unto him that has faith unto repentance is brought about the great and eternal *(17) plan of redemption.*

> **COM** Henry: Heb 10:7-18 "but as a priest to **satisfy the demands of justice**, and to fulfil all righteousness.")
>
> **COM** Gill: Psa 125:2 "he encompasses them with his favour and lovingkindness as a shield; he **encircles them in the arms of** everlasting love; he guards them by his providence all around, and keeps a wakeful and watchful eye over them, that nothing hurts them: he keeps them,")
>
> **COM** Clarke: Rom 7:25 "the Divine **plan of redemption** by Jesus Christ." (Gill)
>
> **Note:** "satisfy the demands of justice" and "plan of redemption" are modern concepts.

BOM <u>Alma 34:33</u> And now, as I said unto you before, as ye have had so many witnesses, therefore, I beseech of you that ye do not *(4) procrastinate (1588)* the day of your repentance until the end; for after this *day of life*, which is given us *to prepare for eternity*, behold, if we do not *improve our time* while in this life, then cometh the *(2) night of darkness* wherein there can be no labor performed.

> **COM** Gill: <u>Eze 13:22</u> "and that it is in their power to **repent** when they please, and therefore **procrastinate** it to the last." (Henry)
>
> **COM** Gill: <u>Joh 9:4</u> "while the **day of life** lasts, for in the grave there is no work nor device:" (Henry, Wesley)
>
> **COM** Henry: <u>2Pe 3:11-18</u> "but that men may have time **to prepare for eternity.**")
>
> **COM** Gill: <u>Rom 13:12</u> "a little while, and the **night of darkness**, affliction, and disconsolation will be over, and the day of glory will succeed,")
>
> **COM** Henry: <u>Psa 115:9-18</u> "We ourselves must shortly go to the land of silence; but, while we do live, we will bless the Lord, will **improve our time** and work that work of him that sent us into the world to praise him before the **night comes**, and because the night comes, wherein **no** man can work.")
>
> **Note:** Many modern phrases here.

BOM <u>Alma 37:34</u> Teach them to *never be weary of* **good works**, but to be **meek and lowly in heart**; for such **shall find rest to their souls**.

> **KJV (16NT/11)** <u>Matthew 5:16</u> Let your light so shine before men, that they may see your **good works**, and glorify your Father which is in heaven.)
>
> **COM** Gill: <u>Psa 106:3</u> "we should **never be weary of** well doing, but be always abounding in **good works;**")
>
> **KJV (1NT/1)** <u>Matthew 11:29</u> Take my yoke upon you, and learn of me; for I am **meek and lowly in heart**: and ye **shall find rest** unto **your souls.**)
>
> **Note:** "never be weary of good works" is the same meaning as "never be weary of well doing". Joseph Smith repeatedly changes phrases from the commentaries to have the same meaning but different wording.

***BOM <u>Alma 40:26</u> But behold, an (47) awful (13th Century) (*Henry, Clarke, Wesley)* death cometh upon the wicked; for they die as to **things pertaining to** things of righteousness; for they are unclean, and *no unclean thing* can **inherit the kingdom of God**; but they are cast out, and (9) consigned (1528) to *(17) partake of the fruits of their labors* or their works, which have been evil; and they *drink the dregs* of a *bitter cup.*

> **KJV (4NT/9)** <u>Acts 1:3</u> To whom also he shewed himself alive after

his passion by many infallible proofs, being seen of them forty days, and speaking of the **things pertaining to** the kingdom of God)

KJV (4NT/13) <u>1 Corinthians 6:9</u> Know ye not that the unrighteous shall not **inherit the kingdom of God**? Be not deceived: neither fornicators, nor idolaters, nor adulterers, nor effeminate, nor abusers of themselves with mankind,)

COM Clarke: <u>Mat 4:1-11</u> "but, blessed be God, into the Jerusalem above, that holy city, **no unclean thing shall** enter;")

COM Gill: <u>2Th 2:3</u> "but because they are by the righteous judgment of God appointed and **consigned to** everlasting destruction;" (Clarke, Wesley, Henry)

COM Clarke: <u>1Co 13:13</u> "Without faith it is impossible to please God; and without it, we can not **partake of the** grace of our Lord Jesus:"(Henry, Gill, Wesley)

COM Clarke: <u>Joh 4:37</u> "Others have labored - the patriarchs and prophets, and ye are entered into the **fruits of their labors**.")

COM Henry: <u>2Sa 24:10-17</u> "The country had drunk of the **bitter cup**, but Jerusalem must **drink the dregs**.")

Note: I hope I don't need to clarify how rare drinking the dregs of a bitter cup is.

*****BOM** <u>Alma 41:1</u> And now, my son, **I have somewhat to say** concerning the (19) restoration (14th Century) of which has been spoken; for behold, some have *(1) wrested (12th Century) the scriptures*, and have gone far astray because of this thing. And **I perceive that** thy mind has been (3) worried (13th Century) (*Note: Clarke, Henry, Gill)* also **concerning this thing**. But behold, I will explain it unto thee.

KJV (2/4) <u>1 Kings 2:14</u> He said moreover, **I have somewhat to say** unto thee. And she said, Say on.)

COM Clarke: <u>Isa 45:1</u> "in his decree for the **restoration** of the Jews, to have been given to him by Jehovah, the God of heaven" (Henry, Wesley)

COM Gill: <u>1Ti 1:7</u> "**wrested the Scriptures** to their own destruction, and that of others; they were ignorant of the things they talked of,")

KJV (21NT/41) <u>Matthew 21:42</u> Jesus saith unto them, Did ye never read in the **scriptures**, The stone which the builders rejected, the same is become the head of the corner: this is the Lord's doing, and it is marvellous in our eyes?)

KJV (11/17) <u>2 Kings 4:9</u> And she said unto her husband, Behold now, **I perceive** that this is an holy man of God, which passeth by us continually.)

KJV (3/6) <u>Genesis 19:21</u> And he said unto him, See, I have accepted thee **concerning this thing** also, that I will not overthrow this city, for the which thou hast spoken.)

Note: "wrested the Scriptures" is a modern thought.

BOM Alma 41:11 And now, my son, all men that are *in a state of nature*, or I would say, in a *(3) carnal state*, are **in the gall of bitterness and in the bonds of iniquity**; *they are without God in the world*, and *they* have *gone contrary to the nature of God*; therefore, they are in a state *(2) contrary to the nature of* (30) happiness (15th Century) (Note: Henry, Clarke, Wesley***).

> **COM** Gill: Act 8:23 "and signifying, that he was **in a state of nature** and unregeneracy;" (Henry, Clarke, Wesley)
>
> **Note:** What a unique phrase "a state of nature" notice that it comes from the same commentary in Gill for Acts 8:23 as does the phrase he quotes from the New Testament, Acts 8:23.
>
> **KJV (1NT/3)** Acts 8:23 For I perceive that thou art **in the gall of bitterness, and in the bond of iniquity**.)
>
> **COM** Henry: Rom 7:1-6 "When we were in the flesh, that is, in a **carnal state**, under the reigning power of sin and corruption" (Gill, Clarke)
>
> **COM** Clarke: Dan 2:45 "He that giveth to those poor (emphatically poor, for **they are without God in the world**, and consequently without the true riches) lendeth unto the Lord;")
>
> **KJV (1NT/1)** Ephesians 2:12 That at that time ye were **without Christ**, being aliens from the commonwealth of Israel, and strangers from the covenants of promise, having no hope, **and without God in the world**:)
>
> **COM** Henry: Jer 24:1-10 "and boasted that though therein **they** had **gone contrary to the** command **of God** yet they had acted prudently for themselves.")
>
> **COM** Gill: Rom 3:7 "nothing is more **contrary to the nature of** God," (Henry, Wesley, Clarke)

BOM Alma 42:10 Therefore, as they had become *carnal,* ***sensual,*** *and* ***devilish***, by nature, this *(3) (4) probationary* (*15th Century) state* became a state for them to prepare; it became a (4) preparatory (15th Century) (***Note:*** Gill, ***Henry, Clarke, Wesley)*** state.

> **COM** Gill: Jam 3:17 "it is pure in itself, it is free from everything that is earthly, **carnal**, or **sensual**, or **devilish**;")
>
> **KJV (1NT/6)** James 3:15 This wisdom descendeth not from above, but is earthly, **sensual, devilish**.)
>
> **COM** Clarke: "Gen 2:17 - Of the tree of the knowledge - thou shalt not eat - This is the first positive precept God gave to man; and it was given as a test of obedience, and a proof of his being in a dependent, **probationary state**.")
>
> **Note:** "probationary state" is a modern phrase and concept.

***BOM <u>Alma 43:6</u> And now, as the Amalekites were of a more wicked and (3) *murderous (1535)* **disposition** than the Lamanites were, *in and of themselves*, therefore, Zerahemnah appointed **chief captains** over the Lamanites, and they were all Amalekites and Zoramites.

> **COM** Clarke: <u>Eze 19:14</u> "A vindictive and **murderous disposition** has taken hold:")
>
> **Note:** Notice that the word "murderous" is not in the KJV. Hence the entire phrase "murderous disposition" from Clarke.
>
> **KJV (1NT/3)** <u>Acts 7:53</u> Who have received the law by the **disposition** of angels, and have not kept it.)
>
> **COM** Gill: <u>Gal 2:16</u> "and such works are designed, as are performed by sinful men **in and of themselves**," (Henry)
>
> **KJV (2NT/22)** <u>Acts 25:23</u> And on the morrow, when Agrippa was come, and Bernice, with great pomp, and was entered into the place of hearing, with the **chief captains**, and principal men of the city, at Festus' commandment Paul was brought forth.)

BOM <u>Alma 43:7</u> Now this he did **that he might preserve** their hatred towards the Nephites, that he might bring them into subjection to *the accomplishment of his designs*.

> **KJV (1/3)** <u>Deuteronomy 6:24</u> And the LORD commanded us to do all these statutes, to fear the LORD our God, for our good always, **that he might preserve** us alive, as it is at this day.)
>
> **COM** Clarke: <u>Est 4:11</u> "might stand much in the way of **the accomplishment of his designs**")

BOM <u>Alma 45:18</u> And when Alma had done this he departed out of the land of Zarahemla, as if to go into the land of Melek. And it came to pass (452/1353) that he was (3) *never heard of more*; as to his death or burial we know not of.

> **COM** Henry: <u>Gen 37:23-30</u> "he would be lost, and **never heard of more**.")
>
> **Note:** This is obviously a reference from that of Moses and the belief by some that he did not die but was taken into heaven and his death and burial was not known of, see below.

BOM <u>Alma 45:19</u> Behold, this we know, that he was a righteous man; and the saying **went abroad in** the church (76/259) that he was taken up by the Spirit, or *buried by the* hand of the *Lord,* even as Moses. But behold, the **scriptures** saith the Lord took Moses unto himself; and we suppose that he has also received Alma in the spirit, unto himself; therefore, **for this cause** we know nothing concerning his death and burial.

> **KJV (1NT/1)** <u>Matthew 9:26</u> And the fame hereof **went abroad in**to all that land.)
>
> **COM** Gill: <u>Mat 17:3</u> "and why this should not be the case of Moses,

or why he should appear in another body, and not his own, I see not; for though he died, yet he was **buried by the Lord**, and no man ever knew the place of his sepulchre; and there was a dispute about his body, between Michael and the devil, all which are uncommon circumstances: so that it might be, that his body was, quickly after his death, raised and restored to him; or at this time, as a pledge of the resurrection of the dead, as Christ's transfiguration was of his glory. The Jews have a notion that Moses is not dead, but is ascended, and stands and ministers to God, in the highest heavens (e):")

COM Gill: "Deu 34:6 - And he buried him,.... Aben Ezra says he buried himself, going into a cave on the top of the mount, where he expired, and so where he died his grave was; but though he died on the mount, he was buried in a valley: Jarchi and so other Jewish writers (d) say, **the Lord buried him**; it may be by the ministry of angels: an Arabic writer says (e), he was buried by angels: it is very probable he was buried by Michael, and who is no other than the archangel or head of principalities and powers, our Lord Jesus Christ, for a reason that will be hereafter suggested, see Jud_1:9, in a valley in the land of Moab, over against Bethpeor; where stood a temple dedicated to the idol Peor, see Deu_3:29, but *no man knoweth of his sepulchre unto this day*; to the time when Joshua wrote this, or, as others think, Samuel: if Moses is the same with the Osiris of the Egyptians, as some think (f), it may be observed, that his grave is said to be **unknown** to the Egyptians, as Diodorus Siculus (g) and Strabo (h) both affirm; and the grave of Moses is **unknown**, even unto this our day: for though no longer ago than in the year 1655, in the month of October, it was pretended to be found by some Maronite shepherds on Mount Nebo, with this inscription on it in Hebrew letters, "**Moses** the servant of the Lord"; but this story was confuted by Jecomas, a learned Jew, who proved it to be the grave of another Moses (i), whom Wagenseil conjectures was Moses Maimonides (k); but some think the whole story is an imposition: the reason why the grave of Moses was kept a secret was, as Ben Gersom suggests, lest, because of his miracles, succeeding generations should make a god of him and worship him, as it seems a sort of heretics called Melchisedecians.")

KJV (21NT/41) Matthew 21:42 Jesus saith unto them, Did ye never read in the scriptures, The stone which the builders rejected, the same is become the head of the corner: this is the Lord's doing, and it is marvellous in our eyes?)

***BOM** Alma 51:21 And thus Moroni put an end to those king-men, that there were not any *known by the (1) appellation (15th Century)* of king-men; and thus he put an end to the stubbornness and the pride of those people who professed the blood of nobility; but they were brought down to humble themselves like unto their brethren, and to *fight valiantly* for their freedom from bondage.

> **COM** Clarke: <u>Act 8:3</u> "and are **known** in ecclesiastical history **by the appellation of** Zealots or Sicarii.")
>
> **COM** Clarke: <u>2Ch 26:13</u> "they were ready to fight, and **fight valiantly**, whenever the king had any occasion for them, or the land was invaded.")

BOM <u>Alma 52:21</u> And **it came to pass** (452/1353) that Moroni, having no hopes of meeting them upon fair grounds, therefore, he resolved upon a plan that he might *(2) decoy (1641)* the Lamanites out of their strongholds.

> **Note:** These next few verses of the BOM match perfectly this story including using the word "decoy":
>
> **COM** Clarke: <u>Jos 8:10</u> "There is no doubt that Joshua had left the rest of the army so disposed and ready, part of it having probably advanced towards Ai, that he might easily receive reinforcements in case of any disaster to the thirty thousand which had advanced against the city; and this consideration will serve to remove a part of the difficulty which arises from <u>Jos 8:1</u>, <u>Jos 8:3</u>, <u>Jos 8:10</u>, collated with other parts of this chapter. Had he brought all his troops in sight, the people of Ai would not have attempted to risk a battle, and would consequently have kept within their walls, from which it was the object of Joshua to **decoy** them. See the preceding observations, particularly <u>Jos 8:10-12</u> (note).")

BOM <u>Alma 52:22</u> Therefore he caused that Teancum should take *(7) a small number of men* and march down near the seashore; and Moroni and his army, by night, marched in the wilderness, on the west of the city Mulek; and thus, **on the morrow**, when the (30) guards (15th Century) of the Lamanites had discovered Teancum, they ran and told it unto Jacob, their leader.

> **COM** Gill: <u>Dan 11:23</u> "either he went into the heart of Syria with **a small number of men** at first,")
>
> **KJV** (39/38) <u>Genesis 19:34</u> And it came to pass **on the morrow**, that the firstborn said unto the younger, Behold, I lay yesternight with my father: let us make him drink wine this night also; and go thou in, and lie with him, that we may preserve seed of our father.)
>
> Alma 52:23 And it came to pass (452/1353) that the armies of the Lamanites did march forth against Teancum, **supposing** by their numbers to (22) overpower (1593 AD) Teancum because of the smallness of his numbers. And as Teancum saw the armies of the Lamanites coming out against him he began to retreat down by the seashore, northward.
>
> **KJV** (7NT/14) <u>1 Timothy 6:5</u> Perverse disputings of men of corrupt

minds, and destitute of the truth, **supposing** that gain is godliness: from such withdraw thyself.)

> **COM** Henry: Jer 50:33-46 "he can **overpower** all the force that is against them," (Clarke, Wesley)

BOM Alma 52:24 And it came to pass (452/1353) that when the Lamanites saw that he began to flee, they took courage and pursued them with (3) vigor, (14th Century) (*Note: Clarke, Wesley*). And while Teancum was thus leading away the Lamanites who were pursuing them in vain, behold, Moroni commanded that a part of his army who were with him should march forth into the city, and take possession of it.

BOM Alma 52:25 And thus they did, and slew all those who had been left to protect the city, yea, all those who would not yield up their weapons of war.

BOM Alma 52:26 And thus Moroni had obtained possession of the city Mulek with a part of his army, while he marched with the remainder to meet the Lamanites when they should return from the pursuit of Teancum.

> (**Note:** This is the exact same story found in Joshua chapter 8)

BOM Alma 54:12 And behold, if you do not this, I will come against you with my armies; yea, even I will arm my women and my children, and I will come against you, and I will follow you even into your own land, which is the land of our first inheritance; yea, and it shall be *blood for blood*, yea, *life for life*; and I will give you battle even until you are (3) *destroyed from off the face of the earth*.

> **COM** Gill: Gen 9:6 "for this is but the law of retaliation, a just and equitable one, **blood for blood**, or **life for life**;)
>
> **Note:** Both phrases together and in Gill, unlikely to be coincidence.
>
> **COM** Gill: Mar 13:20 "that nation and race of men must have been utterly **destroyed from off the face of the earth**:" (Clarke)

BOM Alma 16:17 For behold, the Lord had blessed them so long with **the riches of the world** that they had not been stirred up to anger, to wars, nor to bloodshed; therefore they began to set their hearts upon their riches; yea, they began to seek to **get gain** that they might be lifted *up one above another*; therefore they began to commit (5) *secret murders*, and to *rob and* to (12) *plunder* (*1632*), that they might get gain.

> **KJV** (**1NT/1**) Romans 11:12 Now if the fall of them be **the riches of the world**, and the diminishing of them the riches of the Gentiles; how much more their fulness?")
>
> **KJV** (**1NT/18**) James 4:13 Go to now, ye that say, To day or to morrow we will go into such a city, and continue there a year, and buy and sell, and **get gain**:)
>
> **COM** Gill: Mat 18:4 "it being common to children to behave towards one another, as on a level; not to envy one another, or to set **up one above another**, or be vainly elated with the distinctions of birth and

fortune.")
COM Clarke: <u>Isa 26:20-21</u> "**Secret murders**, and other secret wickednesses, shall be discovered, sooner or later.")
COM Gill: <u>2Ki 13:21</u> "one of the bands of the Moabites, which came to **rob and plunder**, and which was about the place where they intended to bury the man;" (Clarke)
BOM <u>Alma 16:18</u> And now behold, those murderers and plunderers were a band who had been formed by Kishkumen and Gadianton. And now it had come to pass that there were many, even among the Nephites, of Gadianton's band. But behold, they were more numerous among the more wicked part of the Lamanites. And they were called Gadianton's *robbers and murderers.*
COM Clarke: <u>Mat 27:35</u> "It was the punishment of **robbers and murderers**" (Gill, Wesley)
BOM <u>Alma 16:19</u> And it was they who did murder the chief judge Cezoram, and his son, while in **the judgment-seat**; and behold, they were not found.
KJV **(10NT/56)** <u>Romans 14:10</u> But why dost thou judge thy brother? or why dost thou set at nought thy brother? for we shall all stand before **the judgment seat** of Christ.)
BOM <u>Alma 16:20</u> And now **it came to pass** (452/1353) that when the Lamanites found that there were robbers among them they were *(14) exceedingly sorrowful* ; and they did *use every means in their power to destroy* them off the face of the earth.
BOM <u>Alma 16:20</u> But behold, Satan did stir up the hearts of **the more part** of the Nephites, insomuch (20/181) that they did unite with those *bands of robbers,* and did enter into their covenants and their oaths, that they would protect and preserve one another in whatsoever *(2) difficult circumstances* they should be placed, that they should not suffer for their murders, and their plunderings, and their stealings.
COM Henry: <u>Gen 3:17-19</u> "Did sorrow come in with sin? He was a man of sorrows, his soul was, in his agony, **exceedingly sorrowful**.")
COM Clarke: <u>Rom 3:15</u> "They make **use** of **every means in their power to destroy** the reputation and lives of the innocent.")
KJV **(2NT/26)** <u>Acts 19:32</u> Some therefore cried one thing, and some another: for the assembly was confused: and **the more part** knew not wherefore they were come together. Words in OT but not exact phrase)
COM Henry: <u>Jdg 6:1-6</u> "quarter themselves upon it, and enrich themselves with its spoils - **bands of robbers**, and no better." (Clarke, Gill)
COM Gill: <u>2Th 1:11</u> "and in encouraging, supporting, and maintaining it under the most **difficult circumstances**," (Clarke)
BOM <u>Alma 16:22</u> And **it came to pass** (452/1353) that they did have their

signs, yea, their secret signs, and their secret words; and this that they might (2) distinguish (1561) (*Note; Henry, Clarke, Wesley,* Gill*)* a brother who had entered into the covenant, that whatsoever wickedness his brother should do he should not be injured by his brother, nor by those who did belong to his band, who had taken this covenant.

BOM <u>Alma 16:23</u> And thus they might murder, and (12) plunder (1632), and steal, and **commit wholesome** and (*9) all manner of wickedness,* contrary to the laws of their country and also the laws of their God.

> **COM** Gill: <u>2Ki 13:21</u> "one of the bands of the Moabites, which came to rob and **plunder**, and which was about the place where they intended to bury the man;" (Clarke)
>
> **KJV** (2/8) <u>Ezekiel 23:43</u> Then said I unto her that was old in adulteries, Will they now **commit whoredoms** with her, and she with them?)
>
> **COM** Gill: <u>Rev 17:5</u> "of abominable doctrines and practices; **all manner of wickedness** that is to be found in the earth," (Henry)

BOM <u>Alma 16:24</u> And whosoever of those who belonged to their band should reveal **unto the world** of their wickedness and their abominations, should be tried, not according to the laws of their country, but according to the laws of their wickedness, which had been given by Gadianton and Kishkumen.

BOM <u>Alma 16:25</u> Now behold, it is these secret oaths and covenants which Alma commanded his son should not go forth **unto the world, lest they should** *be a means of bringing down* the people unto destruction.

> **KJV** (**5NT/17**) <u>Matthew 18:7</u> Woe **unto the world** because of offences! for it must needs be that offences come; but woe to that man by whom the offence cometh!)
>
> **KJV** (11/17) <u>Deuteronomy 32:27</u> Were it not that I feared the wrath of the enemy, lest their adversaries should behave themselves strangely, and **lest they should** say, Our hand is high, and the LORD hath not done all this.)
>
> **COM** Gill: <u>Rom 12:20</u> "not to aggravate his condemnation, as if this would **be a means of bringing down** the wrath of God the more fiercely on him," (Wesley)

BOM <u>Alma 16:26</u> Now behold, those secret oaths and covenants did not come forth unto Gadianton from the records which were delivered unto Alma; but behold, they were put into the heart of Gadianton by that same being who did entice our (*13) first parents* (20NT/22) to (*17) partake of the* (*6) forbidden fruit, –*

> **COM** Henry: <u>Gen 2:25</u> "of which the condition of **our first parents** in the garden of paradise is justly supposed to have been an expressive emblem.")
>
> **COM** (Note: Phrase not found in the OT but is a phrase started in

1662 AD. Henry: <u>Joe 1:1-7</u> "and when they are going to **partake of the forbidden fruit** a prohibition of another nature shall come between the cup and the lip, and cut off the wine from their mouth." (Clarke, Gill, Wesley)

Note: We, in modern times, call it "forbidden fruit" and therefore next to impossible to be to be written hundreds of years ago. In addition "our first parents" is also a modern phrase.

BOM <u>Alma 16:27</u> Yea, that same being who did plot with Cain, that if he would murder his brother Abel it should not be known **unto the world**. And he did plot with Cain and his followers **from that time forth**.

> **KJV (5NT/17)** <u>Matthew 18:7</u> Woe **unto the world** because of offences! for it must needs be that offences come; but woe to that man by whom the offence cometh!)

> **KJV (3/10)** <u>Nehemiah 4:16</u> And it came to pass **from that time forth**, that the half of my servants wrought in the work, and the other half of them held both the spears, the shields, and the bows, and the habergeons; and the rulers were behind all the house of Judah.)

BOM <u>Alma 16:28</u> And also it is that same being who put it into the hearts of the people to build a tower sufficiently high that they might get to heaven. And it was that same being who led on the people who came from that tower into this land; who spread the **works of darkness** and abominations over all the face of the land, until he dragged the people down to *an entire destruction*, and to an everlasting hell.

> **KJV (2NT/13)** <u>Romans 13:12</u> The night is far spent, the day is at hand: let us therefore cast off the **works of darkness**, and let us put on the armour of light.)

> **COM** Gill: <u>2Ki 11:18</u> "made **an entire destruction** of them all,")

BOM <u>Alma 16:29</u> Yea, it is that same being who put it into the heart of Gadianton to still carry on the work of darkness, and of secret murder; and he has brought it forth from the beginning of man even down to this time.

BOM <u>Alma 16:30</u> And behold, it is he who is the *author of* all *sin*. And behold, he doth carry on his **works of darkness** and secret murder, and doth hand down *(2) their plots* , and their oaths, and their covenants, and their plans of (47) awful (13th Century) (*Henry, Clarke, Wesley)* wickedness, **from generation to generation** according as he can get hold upon **the hearts of the children of men**.

> **COM** Henry: <u>Rom 13:1-6</u> "The usurpation of power and the abuse of power are not of God, for he is not **the author of sin**; but the power itself is." (Clarke, Gill)

> **KJV (2NT/13)** <u>Romans 13:12</u> The night is far spent, the day is at hand: let us therefore cast off the **works of darkness**, and let us put on the armour of light.)

COM Clarke: Act 6:15 "yet counterworks all **their plots** and designs," (Gill, Henry, Wesley)

KJV (2/14) Isaiah 13:20 It shall never be inhabited, neither shall it be dwelt in **from generation to generation**: neither shall the Arabian pitch tent there; neither shall the shepherds make their fold there.)

KJV (2/14) Proverbs 15:11 Hell and destruction are before the LORD: how much more then **the hearts of the children of men**?)

***BOM** Alma 16:31 And now behold, he had got great hold upon the hearts of the Nephites; yea, insomuch (20/181) that they had become (*3) exceedingly wicked* ; yea, **the more part** of them *had **turned out of the way** of righteousness*, and did **trample under their feet** the commandments of God, and did turn unto their own ways, and did build up unto themselves idols of their gold and their silver.

COM Clark: Jer 51:35 "yet in return they, being themselves **exceedingly wicked**, shall suffer for all the carnage they have made, and for all the blood they have shed." (Henry)

KJV (**2NT/26**) Acts 19:32 Some therefore cried one thing, and some another: for the assembly was confused: and **the more part** knew not wherefore they were come together. Words in OT but not exact phrase)

KJV (2/1) Job 31:7 If my step hath **turned out of the way**, and mine heart walked after mine eyes, and if any blot hath cleaved to mine hands;)

COM Gill: Job 31:8 "If what he had before said was not true; but he **had turned out of the way of righteousness**,")

Note: A unique phrase to Gill.

KJV (**1NT/6**) Matthew 7:6 Give not that which is holy unto the dogs, neither cast ye your pearls before swine, lest they **trample them under their feet**, and turn again and rend you.)

BOM Alma 16:32 And **it came to pass** (452/1353) that all these iniquities did come unto them in the space of not many years, insomuch that a more part of it had come unto them in the sixty and seventh year of the reign of the judges over the people of Nephi.

BOM Alma 16:33 And they did grow in their iniquities in the sixty and eighth year also

BOM Alma 16:34 And (*17) thus we see that* the Nephites did begin to (26) dwindle (1596 AD) **in unbelief**, and grow in wickedness and abominations, while the Lamanites began to (*4) grow exceedingly* in the knowledge of their God; yea, they did begin to keep his statutes and commandments, and to **walk in truth** and uprightness before him.

COM Clarke: Act 26:18 "**Thus we see that** not only this salvation comes through Christ," (Henry)

KJV (3NT/26) <u>Romans 11:23</u> And they also, if they abide not still **in unbelief**, shall be grafted in: for God is able to graft them in again.)

KJV (1NT/1) <u>3 John 1:4</u> I have no greater joy than to hear that my children **walk in truth**.)

***BOM** <u>Alma 8:14</u> Yea, did he not **bear record** that **the Son of God (43NT/49)** should come? And as he *lifted up the brazen serpent in the wilderness*, even so shall he be lifted up who should come.

KJV (4NT/30) <u>John 8:14</u> Jesus answered and said unto them, Though I **bear record** of myself, yet my record is true: for I know whence I came, and whither I go; but ye cannot tell whence I come, and whither I go.)

KJV (1/1) <u>2 Kings 18:4</u> He removed the high places, and brake the images, and cut down the groves, and brake in pieces the **brasen serpent** that Moses had made: for unto those days the children of Israel did burn incense to it: and he called it Nehushtan.)

Note: Notice that Henry here says it exactly like Joseph Smith.

COM Henry: <u>Joh 12:27-36</u> "or to the setting up of a standard, which draws soldiers together; or, rather, it refers to the **lifting up** of **the brazen serpent in the wilderness**," ("brazen serpent" Clarke, Wesley, Henry)

***BOM** <u>Alma 8:15</u> And as many as should **look upon** that **serpent** should **live**, even so as many as should look upon **the Son of God (43NT/49)** with faith, having a contrite spirit, might live, even unto that life which is eternal.

KJV (1/1) <u>Numbers 21:8</u> And the LORD said unto Moses, Make thee a fiery **serpent**, and set it upon a pole: and it shall come to pass, that every one that is bitten, when he **look**eth **upon** it, shall **live**.)

COM Obviously this is a common interpretation of our modern times and is in each of the commentaries. As an example Henry: <u>Joh 8:21-30</u> "*When you have lifted up the Son of man,* lifted him up upon the cross, as the **brazen serpent** upon the pole (<u>Joh 3:14</u>), as the sacrifices under the law (for Christ is the great sacrifice),"

BOM <u>Alma 13:29</u> *(4) O ye wicked and perverse generation*; ye hardened and ye stiffnecked people, **how long** will ye suppose that the Lord will **suffer you**? Yea, **how long** will ye **suffer** yourselves to be led by foolish and **blind guides**? Yea, how long will ye choose **darkness rather than light**?

Note: The King James Version of the Bible tells us that Jesus said "faithless and perverse" but Gill, in his commentary, gives us this exact phrase that Joseph Smith uses: Mat 27:40 "and no other but that sign was to be given to that **wicked and perverse generation**,")

KJV (2NT/1) <u>Matthew 23:16</u> Woe unto you, ye **blind guides**, which say, Whosoever shall swear by the temple, it is nothing; but whosoever shall swear by the gold of the temple, he is a debtor!)

KJV (1NT/1) <u>John 3:19</u> And this is the condemnation, that light is come into the world, and men loved **darkness rather than light**, because their deeds were evil.)

KJV (2NT/1) <u>Matthew 17:17</u> Then Jesus answered and said, **O** faithless and **perverse generation, how long** shall I be with you? **how long** shall I **suffer you**? bring him hither to me.)

BOM <u>Alma 14:5</u> And behold, there shall *a new star* arise, **such an one as** ye never have beheld; **and this** also **shall be a sign unto you**.

COM Gill: <u>Hag 2:6</u> "at his birth **a new star** appeared in the heavens,")

KJV (3/10) <u>Psalm 50:21</u> These things hast thou done, and I kept silence; thou thoughtest that I was altogether **such an one as** thyself: but I will reprove thee, and set them in order before thine eyes.)

KJV (<u>Luke 2:12</u> **And this shall be a sign unto you**; Ye shall find the babe wrapped in swaddling clothes, lying in a manger.)

BOM <u>3 Nephi 5:6</u> And thus they did *put an end to all* (***Note: Clarke,*** Gill, ***Henry)*** those *wicked,* and *secret,* and abominable (21) *combinations* (14th Century), in the which there was so much wickedness, and so many murders committed.

COM Gill: <u>Job 12:22</u> "also the depths of Satan, his deep laid schemes, his wiles and stratagems, to draw into sin, and so to ruin; these are unknown to natural men, but saints are made acquainted with them, so that they are not altogether ignorant of his devices, <u>Rev 2:24</u>; likewise the **secret** plots, counsels, and **combinations** of **wicked** men,") (Henry, Clarke)

BOM <u>3 Nephi 6:7</u> And it came to pass (452/1353) that there were many *cities built anew*, and there were many old cities *repaired*.

COM Gill: <u>Num 32:37</u> "this shows that those **cities** were not **built anew** properly, only **repaired**,")

Note: Uniquely the same.

BOM <u>3 Nephi 6:8</u> And there were many *highways cast up*, and many roads made, which led from city to city, and from land to land, and from place to place.

COM Gill: <u>Isa 49:11</u> "being conspicuous and visible; and, like causeways, or, **highways cast up**,")

BOM** <u>3 Nephi 6:13</u> Some were **lifted up** in **pride**, and others were (*1*) *exceedingly humble;* some did *return **railing for railing, while others would receive railing and persecution and all manner of afflictions, and would **not** turn and **revile again**, but were humble and penitent before God.

KJV (1NT/4) <u>1 Timothy 3:6</u> Not a novice, lest being **lifted up** with **pride** he fall into the condemnation of the devil.)

KJV (1NT/1) <u>1 Peter 3:9</u> Not rendering evil for evil, or **railing for**

railing: but contrariwise blessing; knowing that ye are thereunto called, that ye should inherit a blessing.)

KJV (1NT/1) 1 Peter 2:23 Who, when he was **reviled, reviled not again**; when he suffered, he threatened not; but committed himself to him that judgeth righteously:)

COM Gill: Isa 37:15 "He did not **return railing for railing**, but committed himself and his cause to him that judgeth righteously")

Note: It is interesting that the KJV says "rendering...railing for railing" will Gill says exactly what Joseph Smith says "return railing for railing".

BOM 3 Nephi 11:40 And whoso shall declare **more** or less **than** this, and establish it for my doctrine, the same **cometh of evil**, and is not built upon my rock; but he buildeth upon a *sandy foundation*, and **the gates of hell** *stand open to receive* such when the *floods come and the winds beat upon* them.

KJV (1NT/1) Matthew 5:37 But let your communication be, Yea, yea; Nay, nay: for whatsoever is **more than** these **cometh of evil**.)

COM It is interesting that the phrase "sandy foundation" is found in the commentaries. Gill: 1Pe 2:4 "refused him as a foundation stone, and left him out of the building; and laid another foundation, even their own works of righteousness, on which **sandy foundation** they built themselves,")

KJV (1NT/4) Matthew 16:18 And I say also unto thee, That thou art Peter, and upon this rock I will build my church; and **the gates of hell** shall not prevail against it.)

KJV (2NT/1) Matthew 7:25 And the rain descended, and **the floods came, and the winds** blew, and **beat upon** that house; and it fell not: for it was founded **upon** a rock.)

COM Gill: Isa 60:11 "and **the gates** of the church will **stand open** always **to receive** them;")

COM Gill: Job 8:15 "or the hope and confidence laid upon it is like a house built on the sand, and, when rain falls, **floods come, and winds beat upon** it, it falls; and great is the fall of it")

BOM 3 Nephi 26:18 And many of them saw *and heard (3) unspeakable (14th Century) things*, which are *not lawful to be* written.

COM Notice how similar this verse is to Gill's commentary below. Also note that the word "unspeakable" is not found in the King James Bible. Gill: Phi 3:13 "and even though he had been caught up into the third heaven, and had **heard unspeakable** words, **not lawful to be** uttered" (See 2 Cor 12:4)

BOM 3 Nephi 27:11 But if it be not built upon **my gospel**, and is *built upon the works of men*, or upon *the works of the devil*, **verily I say unto you** (48NT/46) they have joy in their works for a season, *(3) and by and by* the end cometh, and they are **hewn down and cast into the fire**, *from whence there is no return.*

> KJV (**3NT/17**) <u>Romans 2:16</u> In the day when God shall judge the secrets of men by Jesus Christ according to **my gospel.**)
>
> COM Gill: <u>Rom 9:28</u> "not **upon the works of men**, but upon the absolute, sovereign, and efficacious will of God;")
>
> COM Gill: <u>Rom 16:20</u> "who has not only destroyed **the works of the devil**,")
>
> COM Clarke: <u>Jam 5:7</u> "The seed of your deliverance is already sown, **and by and by** the harvest of your salvation will take place." (Henry, Wesley, Gill)
>
> KJV (**2NT/13**) <u>Matthew 7:19</u> Every tree that bringeth not forth good fruit is **hewn down, and cast into the fire.**)
>
> COM Gill: <u>Job 10:21</u> "to the grave, his long home, **from whence there is no return** to this world")

BOM <u>3 Nephi 28:13</u> And behold, **the heavens were opened**, and they were *caught up into heaven*, and saw *and heard (3) unspeakable (14th Century) things.*

> KJV (2/1) <u>Ezekiel 1:1</u> Now it came to pass in the thirtieth year, in the fourth month, in the fifth day of the month, as I was among the captives by the river of Chebar, that **the heavens were opened**, and I saw visions of God.)
>
> COM Gill: <u>Phi 3:13</u> "and even though he had been **caught up into** the third **heaven, and** had **heard unspeakable** words, **not lawful to be** uttered")
>
> Note: This commentary in Gill is very much the same as this BOM verse.

BOM <u>3 Nephi 29:2</u> And ye may know that **the words** of the Lord, which have been **spoken by the holy prophets**, shall all be fulfilled; and **ye need not** say that the *Lord delays his coming* unto the children of Israel.

> KJV (**1NT/2**) <u>2 Peter 3:2</u> That ye may be mindful of **the words** which were **spoken** before **by the holy prophets**, and of the commandment of us the apostles of the Lord and Saviour:)
>
> KJV (**2NT/10**) <u>1 Thessalonians 4:9</u> But as touching brotherly love **ye need not** that I write unto you: for ye yourselves are taught of God to love one another.)
>
> KJV (**2NT/1**) <u>Matthew 24:48</u> But and if that evil servant shall say in his heart, My lord **delay**eth **his coming**;)
>
> COM Henry: <u>Mat 24:32-51</u> "The cause of his wickedness; and that is, a practical disbelief of Christ's second coming; He hath said in his heart, My **Lord delays his coming**;")

***BOM <u>Mormon 2:10</u> And **it came to pass** (452/1353) that the Nephites began to repent of their iniquity, and began to cry even as had been prophesied by Samuel the prophet; for behold no man could keep that which was his own, for the thieves, and the robbers, and the murderers, and *the magic art*, and the witchcraft which was in the land.

> **COM** Gill: 2Ti 3:8 "and famous for their skill in **the magic art;**" (Henry, Wesley)
>
> **Note:** Many critics of the Book of Mormon believe that phrases like this one "the magic art" came from Joseph Smith's area in his state of New York, when in fact they as every other unique phrases came from the commentaries.

BOM Mormon 7:5 Know ye that ye must **come to the knowledge of** your fathers, and repent of all your **sins and iniquities**, and believe in *Jesus Christ*, that he is **the Son of God**, (43NT/49) and that he *was slain by the Jews*, and *by the power of the Father* he hath risen *again*, whereby he hath *gained the victory over* the **grave**; and also in him is **the sting of death swallowed up**.

> **KJV (1NT/10)** 2 Timothy 3:7 Ever learning, and never able to **come to the knowledge of** the truth.)
>
> **KJV (1NT/9)** Hebrews 10:17 And their **sins and iniquities** will I remember no more.)
>
> **COM** Clarke: 2Ti 2:8 "let us remember that **Jesus Christ**, who **was slain by the Jews**, rose **again** from the dead, and his resurrection is the proof and pledge of ours")
>
> **Note:** This is the exact same idea as what Joseph Smith wrote.
>
> **COM** Henry: Rom 6:1-23 "Christ was raised up from the dead by the glory of the Father, that is, **by the power of the Father.**")
>
> **COM** Clarke: Luk 9:31 "The death of Jesus was his glory, because, by it, he **gained the victory over** sin, death, and hell,")
>
> **KJV (1NT/2)** 1 Corinthians 15:54 So when this corruptible shall have put on incorruption, and this mortal shall have put on immortality, then shall be brought to pass the saying that is written, **Death** is **swallowed up** in **victory**.)
>
> **KJV (1NT/1)** 1 Corinthians 15:55 O **death**, where is thy **sting**? O **grave**, where is thy victory?
>
> **KJV (1NT/1)** 1 Corinthians 15:56 **The sting of death** is sin; and the strength of sin is the law.)

BOM Ether 8:14 And **it came to pass** (452/1353) that they all sware unto him, **by the God of heaven**, and also *by the heavens*, and also *by* the *earth*, and *by their heads*, that whoso should vary from the assistance which Akish desired should lose his head; and whoso should (1) divulge (15th Century) whatsoever thing Akish made known unto them, the same should lose his life.

> (1/1) Ezra 7:23 Whatsoever is commanded **by the God of heaven**, let it be diligently done for the house of the God of heaven: for why

should there be wrath against the realm of the king and his sons?)

COM Clarke: <u>Mat 5:37</u> "'If any **swear by heaven, by earth**, by the sun, etc.,… "They swore **by their** own **Heads**.")

Note: Swearing by all three the same.

COM Henry: <u>Eph 5:3-20</u> "and which none were permitted to **divulge** upon pain of death.")

BOM <u>Ether 8:25</u> For it cometh to pass that whoso buildeth it up seeketh to overthrow the freedom of all lands, nations, and countries; and it bringeth to pass the destruction of all people, for it is built up by **the devil**, who is the **father of all lies**; even that same liar who *(2) beguiled our (13) first parents,* (20NT/22) yea, even that same liar who hath caused man to commit **murder from the beginning**; who hath hardened the hearts of men that they have murdered the prophets, and stoned them, and cast them out from the beginning.

KJV (1NT/1) <u>John 8 44</u> Ye are of your father **the devil**, and the lusts of your father ye will do. He was a **murderer from the beginning**, and abode not in the truth, because there is no truth in him. When he speaketh a lie, he speaketh of his own: **for he is a liar, and the father of it**.)

COM Gill: <u>Rev 20:2</u> That old serpent; so called with respect to his cunning and subtlety, as well as his antiquity, being from the beginning of the creation, and having as early **beguiled our first parents**;")

Note: Again a modern idea, including the phrase "bequiled our first parents".

BOM <u>Ether 8:26</u> Wherefore, I, Moroni, am commanded to write these things that evil may **be done away**, and that the time may come that Satan may have no power upon **the hearts of the children of men**, but that they may be persuaded to do good continually, that they may come unto *(3) the fountain of all righteousness!* **and be saved**.

KJV (2NT/7) <u>1 Corinthians 13:10</u> But when that which is perfect is come, then that which is in part shall **be done away**.)

KJV (2/14) <u>Proverbs 15:11</u> Hell and destruction are before the LORD: how much more then **the hearts of the children of men**?)

COM A very unique phrase in Clarke: Mat 23:23 "And faith in God as **the fountain of all righteousness**, mercy, and truth."(Gill)

KJV (1NT/7) <u>Luke 8:12</u> Those by the way side are they that hear; then cometh the devil, and taketh away the word out of their hearts, lest they should believe **and be saved**.)

BOM <u>Moroni 7:11</u> For behold, *a bitter fountain* cannot bring forth good *water*; neither can a good fountain bring forth bitter water; wherefore, a man being a servant of the devil cannot follow Christ; and if he follow Christ he cannot be a servant of the devil.

> **COM** Clarke: <u>Gen 5:3</u> "unless we could suppose it possible that **a bitter fountain** could send forth sweet **waters**,")
>
> **Note:** The same idea

BOM <u>Moroni 7:28</u> For he hath *(5) answered the ends of the law,* and he (5) claimeth (Note: Not found) all those who have faith in him; and they who have faith in him will cleave unto every good thing; wherefore he (1) advocateth (***Note: Not in KJV, commentaries or dictionary)*** the cause of the children of men (22/131); and he dwelleth **eternally in the heavens.**

> **COM** Henry: <u>Joh 13:31-35</u> "**The ends of the law** were abundantly **answered**, and the glory of his government effectually asserted and maintained.")
>
> **Note:** Again we have the answering of the law.
>
> **KJV (1NT/2)** <u>2 Corinthians 5:1</u> For we know that if our earthly house of this tabernacle were dissolved, we have a building of God, an house not made with hands, **eternal in the heavens.**)

BOM <u>Moroni 7:46</u> Wherefore, **my beloved brethren**, if ye **have not charity**, ye are **nothing**, for **charity never faileth**. Wherefore, cleave unto charity, which is *the greatest of all*, for *all* things must *fail* --

> **KJV (4NT/60)** <u>James 1:19</u> Wherefore, **my beloved brethren**, let every man be swift to hear, slow to speak, slow to wrath:)
>
> **KJV (1NT/2)** <u>1 Corinthians 13:2</u> And though I have the gift of prophecy, and understand all mysteries, and all knowledge; and though I have all faith, so that I could remove mountains, and **have not charity**, I am **nothing**.)
>
> **KJV (1NT/1)** <u>1 Corinthians 13:8</u> **Charity never faileth**: but whether there be prophecies, they shall fail; whether there be tongues, they shall cease; whether there be knowledge, it shall vanish away.)
>
> **COM** Gill: <u>1Co 12:31</u> "or particularly the grace of **charity**, or love to the saints, may be intended by the more excellent way; which is the evidence of a man's passing from death and life; the new commandment of Christ, and the fulfilling of the law; without which, a man, though he has never such great gifts, he is nothing as a Christian, nor in the business of salvation; and is **the greatest of all** the graces of the Spirit; and is of such a nature, that when prophecies, tongues, knowledge, and **all** external gifts shall **fail**,")
>
> **Note:** Both Gill and Joseph Smith here state that charity is "the greates of all".

BOM <u>Moroni 7:47</u> But charity is the *pure love* of Christ, and it endureth forever; and whoso is found *possessed of it* **at the last day, it shall be well with him.**

> **COM** Gill: <u>1Co 9:17</u> "nor in **pure love** to Christ, and the good of

souls," Clarke, Henry)

COM Gill: <u>1Co 13:4</u> "Charity suffereth long,.... The apostle, in this and some following verses, enumerates the several properties and characters of the grace of love; and all along represents it as if it was a person, and no doubt designs one who is **possessed of it**,")

KJV (5NT/49) <u>John 6:44</u> No man can come to me, except the Father which hath sent me draw him: and I will raise him up **at the last day**.)

KJV (7/4) <u>Isaiah 3:10</u> Say ye to the righteous, that **it shall be well with him**: for they shall eat the fruit of their doings.)

***BOM** <u>Moroni 8:3</u> *I am mindful of you always in my prayers*, continually praying unto God the Father in the name of his **Holy Child, Jesus**, that he, through his (*4*) *infinite goodness and grace*, will keep you through the endurance of faith on his name to the end.

> **COM** Gill: <u>1Th 1:2</u> "The Ethiopic version renders this clause in the singular number, "and **I am mindful of you always in my prayer**";")
>
> **Note:** It is interesting that Joseph Smith uses the exact phrase of an Ethiopic version of 1 Thessalonians 1:2 that is found in Gill.
>
> **KJV (1NT/1)** <u>Acts 4:27</u> For of a truth against thy **holy child Jesus**, whom thou hast anointed, both Herod, and Pontius Pilate, with the Gentiles, and the people of Israel, were gathered together,)
>
> **COM** Clarke: <u>Gen 1:1</u> "from his **infinite goodness**, can do nothing but what is eternally just, right, and kind."(Henry, Gill, Wesley)
>
> **COM** Gill: <u>1Th 2:13</u> "were owing to the **goodness and grace** of God,")

BOM <u>Moroni 8:8</u> Listen to the words of Christ, your Redeemer, your Lord and your God. Behold, I **came** into **the world not to call the righteous but sinners to repentance; the whole need no physician, but they that are sick**; wherefore, *little* children **are whole**, for they *are not capable of* committing sin; wherefore *the curse of Adam* is taken from them in me, that it **hath no power** over them; and *the law of circumcision* is done away in me.

> **KJV (1NT/1)** <u>Mark 2:17</u> When Jesus heard it, he saith unto them, They that **are whole** have **no need of** the **physician, but they that are sick**: I **came not to call the righteous, but sinners to repentance**.)
>
> **COM** Gill: <u>Mat 18:6</u> "which cannot be said of infants, or **little** ones in age, and who also **are not capable of** offence;")
>
> **KJV (1NT/2)** <u>Revelation 20:6</u> Blessed and holy is he that hath part in the first resurrection: on such the second death **hath no power**, but they shall be priests of God and of Christ, and shall reign with him a thousand years.)
>
> **COM** Gill: <u>1Co 7:19</u> "to him that hath not **the law of circumcision**;"

(Henry, Clarke)

Note: The argument regarding baptism and children has been around a long time notice how John Calvin (1509-1564) in his Institutes of the Christian Religion talks about this argument. Book 4, chapter 16, Part B: "Every one whom Christ blesses is exempted from **the curse of Adam**, and the wrath of God. Therefore, seeing it is certain that infants are blessed by him, it follows that they are freed from death."

***BOM** <u>Moroni 8:24</u> Behold, my son, this thing ought not to be; for repentance is unto them that are *(5) under condemnation*, and *under the curse of a broken law*.

COM Clarke: <u>Joh 20:23</u> "They who believed on the Son of God, in consequence of their preaching, had their sins remitted; and they who would not believe were declared to lie **under condemnation**." (Henry)

COM Again note how unique the phrase "under the curse of a broken law". Clarke: <u>Psa 13:2</u> "Satan appears to triumph while the soul lies **under the curse of a broken law**")

Note: A fitting one to end in this chapter with as it is next to impossible that the modern phrase "under the curse of a broken law" should appear in the BOM.

Chapter Four

The Use of the Commentaries in Short

As I have explained, it would be quite impossible to detail all of the instances in which Joseph Smith used the commentaries to create the Book of Mormon. As I also explained if I were to do this the book you now hold in your hands would be bigger than the Bible and impossible to get published. Therefore in this chapter I will give, and definitely not all, short uses of the commentaries by Joseph Smith so you will be able to clearly see their use in the completion of the Book of Mormon by Joseph Smith. Again if you want to skip to the most intriguing items now I have added *** in front of them.

***BOM 1 Nephi 1:4 For **it came to pass** (452/1353) in (*32*) *the commencement* (*1314AD*) *of* the (*2*) *first year of the* **reign of Zedekiah, king of Judah**, my father, Lehi, having **dwelt** at **Jerusalem** in **all his days**; and in **that same year** there came **many prophets**, prophesying unto the people that they must repent, or **the great city Jerusalem** (*3*) *must be destroyed.*

> **Note**: The King James Version of the Bible uses this phrase "it came to pass" 452 times while the BOM utilizes it 1353 times. A scripture reference will not be shown for this but the numbers will. You will see more about this use of the phrase "it came to pass" and other phrases in a future chapter.
> **COM** Clarke: Jer 50:4 "In the times in which Babylon shall be opposed by the Medes and Persians, both Israel and Judah, seeing **the commencement of the** fulfilling of the prophecies," (Clarke, Henry)
> **COM** Clarke: Jer 24:1 "This prophecy was undoubtedly delivered in **the first year of the reign of Zedekiah.**")
> **Note:** Note here that instead of using the words of the OT "in the beginning" Joseph Smith uses the exact words of Clarke: "the first year of".
> **KJV** (Jeremiah 28:1 And it came to pass the same year, in the beginning **of the reign of Zedekiah king of Judah,**)
> **KJV** (1 Kings 2:38 And Shimei said unto the king, The saying is

good: as my lord the king hath said, so will thy servant do. And Shimei **dwelt** in **Jerusalem** many days.)

KJV (10/18) <u>1 Kings 15:14</u> But the high places were not removed: nevertheless Asa's heart was perfect with the LORD **all his days.**)

KJV (2NT/7) <u>John 11:49</u> And one of them, named Caiaphas, being the high priest **that same year**, said unto them, Ye know nothing at all,)

KJV (2NT/6) <u>Matthew 13:17</u> For verily I say unto you, That **many prophets** and righteous men have desired to see those things which ye see, and have not seen them; and to hear those things which ye hear, and have not heard them.)

KJV (<u>Revelation 21:10</u> And he carried me away in the spirit to a great and high mountain, and shewed me that **great city**, the holy **Jerusalem**, descending out of heaven from God,)

COM Henry: <u>Isa 17:1-5</u> "Damascus itself, the head city of Syria, **must be destroyed**;" (Clarke, Wesley)

BOM <u>1 Nephi 1:18</u> Therefore, **I would that ye** should know, that after the Lord had (*29*) *shown* (12th Century) so many marvelous things unto my father, Lehi, yea, (*3*) *concerning the destruction of Jerusalem,* behold he **went forth among the** people, and (*5*) *began to prophesy* and to **declare unto them** *concerning the things* **which he had** both **seen and heard**.

KJV (2NT/56) <u>Colossians 2:1</u> For **I would that ye** knew what great conflict I have for you, and for them at Laodicea, and for as many as have not seen my face in the flesh;)

COM Gill: <u>Jer 1:12</u> "in like manner the Lord says he would hasten to perform what he had said or should say by him **concerning the destruction of Jerusalem**," (Clarke, Henry, Wesley)

Note: Notice that the above is from the commentary of Gill Jeremiah chapter 1 as well as the "began to prophesy" phrase below. It is interesting that in this chapter of Nephi Lehi is doing this at the same time Joseph Smith claims they left Jerusalem. It is also interesting that he uses these key phrases from the commentaries from the same book at the same time Joseph Smith claims these events are happening.

KJV (1/5) <u>Ezekiel 16:14</u> And thy renown **went forth among the** heathen for thy beauty: for it was perfect through my comeliness, which I had put upon thee, saith the Lord GOD.)

COM Gill: <u>Jer 1:1-2</u> "and Jeremiah **began to prophesy**," (Henry)

COM Henry: <u>Eze 24:15-27</u> "When we are enquiring **concerning the things** of God our enquiry must be, "What are those thing to us?"(Clarke, Gill)

KJV (1NT/1) <u>1 John 1:3</u> That **which** we have **seen and heard**

declare we **unto** you, that ye also may have fellowship with us: and truly our fellowship is with the Father, and with his Son Jesus Christ.) **KJV** (Jeremiah 36:13 Then Michaiah **declared unto them** all the words that **he had heard**, when Baruch read the book in the ears of the people.)

*****BOM** 1 Nephi 1:20 And **when the Jews** heard these things they were angry with him; yea, even as with (*4) the prophets of old,* whom they had cast out, and stoned, and slain; and they also sought his life, that they might take it away. But behold, I, Nephi, will show unto you that *the tender mercies of the Lord* are over all those whom he hath chosen, (*10) because of their faith*, to make them mighty even unto the power of deliverance.

> **KJV** (7/1) Nehemiah 4:12 And it came to pass, that **when the Jews** which dwelt by **them** came, **they** said unto us ten times, From all places **whence** ye shall return unto us **they** will be upon you.)
>
> **COM** Henry: Mat 18:1-6 "Christ often taught by signs or sensible representations (comparisons to the eye), as **the prophets of old**.")
>
> **Note:** This is an interesting phrase to use in 600BC as they were alive during "the prophets of old" hence the reason Henry and Gill in their work use the phrase only in their commentary of the NT.
>
> **KJV** (1/1) Jeremiah 44:30 Thus saith the LORD; Behold, I will give Pharaohhophra king of Egypt into the hand of his enemies, and into the hand of them that seek his life; as I gave Zedekiah king of Judah into the hand of Nebuchadrezzar king of Babylon, his enemy, and that **sought his life**.)
>
> **KJV** (4/1) 1 Kings 19:10 And he said, I have been very jealous for the LORD God of hosts: for the children of Israel have forsaken thy covenant, thrown down thine altars, and slain thy prophets **with** the sword; and I, even I only, am left; and **they** seek my **life**, to **take it away**.)
>
> **COM** Henry 1Ki 19:9-18 "Gracious souls are more affected by **the tender mercies of the Lord** than by his terrors.")
>
> **KJV** (1/3) Psalm 145:9 The LORD is good to all: and his **tender mercies are over all** his works.)
>
> **KJV** (3/2) Psalm 33:12 Blessed is the nation whose God is the LORD; and the people **whom he hath chosen** for his own inheritance.)
>
> **COM** Clarke: Gal 3:16 "those who were like himself **because of their faith**.")

*****BOM** 1 Nephi 2:9 And when my father saw that **the waters of the river** emptied into **the fountain of the** Red Sea, he spake unto Laman, **saying: O that thou mightest be like unto** this river, (*1) continually running* into (*3) the fountain of all righteousness*!

KJV (4/2) <u>Jeremiah 2:18</u> And now what hast thou to do in **the** way of Egypt, to drink the waters of Sihor? or what hast thou to do in the way of Assyria, to drink **the waters of the river**?)

KJV (2/1) <u>Joshua 15:9</u> And the border was drawn from the top of the hill unto **the fountain of the** water of Nephtoah,)

KJV (5/15) <u>Daniel 4:31</u> While the word was in the king's mouth, there fell a voice from heaven, **saying, O** king Nebuchadnezzar, to thee it is spoken; The kingdom is departed from thee.)

KJV (12/6) <u>Psalm 51:4</u> Against thee, thee only, have I sinned, and done this evil in thy sight: **that thou mightest** be justified when **thou** speakest, and be clear when **thou** judgest.)

KJV (4/8) <u>Isaiah 19:16</u> In that day shall Egypt **be like unto** women: and it shall be afraid and fear because of the shaking of the hand of the LORD of hosts, which he shaketh over it.)

COM Clarke: <u>Mat 23:23</u> "And faith in God as **the fountain of all righteousness**, mercy, and truth." (Gill)

BOM <u>1 Nephi 4:13</u> Behold the Lord slayeth the wicked to bring forth *(1) his righteous purposes.* It is better **that one man should perish** than that a **nation** should (26) dwindle (1596 AD) and *(1)* **perish in unbelief.**

COM Henry: <u>Eze 14:1-11</u> "When God has served **his** own **righteous purposes** by him he shall be reckoned with for his unrighteous purposes.")

COM Joseph Smith uses dwindle and dwindled interchangeable, and both are in Henry, while dwindle is in all (Henry: <u>Mar 14:53-65</u>: "Peter followed at a distance, such a degree of cowardice was his late courage **dwindled** into,")

COM Henry: <u>Rom 9:14-24</u> "while the greatest part of the Jews are left to **perish in unbelief**,")

KJV How similar these verses: <u>John 11:50</u> Nor consider that it is expedient for us, **that one man should die** for the people, and that the whole **nation perish** not.")

BOM <u>1 Nephi 4:18</u> Therefore I did obey *(2) the voice of the Spirit,* and took Laban *(1) by the hair of the head,* and I **smote off his head** *(4) with his own sword.*

COM Clarke: <u>Act 2:5-13</u> "when they resolved not to believe **the voice of the Spirit** in the apostles' preaching,")

COM Clarke: <u>Act 8:39</u> "who was taken up **by the hair of the head**, and carried from Judea to Babylon!")

KJV (1/1) <u>Judges 5:26</u> She put her hand to the nail, and her right hand to the workmen's hammer; and with the hammer she **smote** Sisera, she **smote off his head**,)

COM Henry: <u>Jdg 5:24-31</u> "We read it she smote off his head, probably **with his own sword,**" (Clarke)

BOM 1 Nephi 4:34 And I also spake unto him, saying: **Surely the Lord hath** commanded us to do this thing; and shall we not be diligent in keeping the commandments of the Lord? Therefore, if thou wilt go down into the wilderness to my father thou shalt (*5*) *have place* with us.

> **KJV** (1/1) Genesis 29:32 And Leah conceived, and bare a son, and she called his name Reuben: for she said, **Surely the LORD hath** looked upon my affliction; now therefore my husband will love me.)
>
> **COM** Clarke: 1Ki 13:31 "and he is willing to **have place with** him in the general resurrection." (Henry, Wesley)

***BOM 1 Nephi 5:11 And he beheld that they did contain *the five books of Moses,* which **gave an account of the creation of the world**, and also of Adam and Eve, who were our (*13*) *first parents;* (20NT/22)

> **COM** Exo 12:40 Clarke: "The Samaritan Pentateuch is allowed by many learned men to exhibit the most correct copy of **the five books of Moses**;" (Henry, Wesley) See also 1 Nephi 19:23
>
> **Note:** There are many problems with using the phrase "the five books of Moses" but the main one is that the phrase would not have been used in the time this was supposed to have been written as the Jews would not have called it that. Known to Jews today as the Torah.
>
> **COM** Henry: Jos 22:21-29 "They **gave an account of** the fears they had lest,")
>
> **KJV** (1NT/5) Romans 1:20 For the invisible things of him from **the creation of the world** are clearly seen, being understood by the things that are made, even his eternal power and Godhead; so that they are without excuse:)
>
> **COM** Henry: Gen 2:25 "of which the condition of **our first parents** in the garden of paradise is justly supposed to have been an expressive emblem.")
>
> **Note:** Henry, Clarke and Wesley all use the phrase "first parents" many times although the phrase is not found in the King James Version of the Bible and used in the Book of Mormon 13 times. The singular and plural form of the word parent is only found in the NT but found in the BOM 22 times.

BOM 1 Nephi 7:13 And (*37*) *if it so be* that (*1*) *we are faithful to him,* we shall obtain the **land of promise**; and ye shall know at some (*1*) *future* (*14th Century*) *period* (*1530 AD*) that **the word of** the Lord **shall be fulfilled** (*3*) *concerning the destruction of Jerusalem,* for **all things** which the Lord hath spoken (*3*) *concerning the destruction of Jerusalem,* **must be fulfilled.**

> **COM** Wesley: 1Ch 28:20 "in like manner, if **we are faithful to him,** go along with us in our day, and will never fail us.")
>
> **KJV** (1NT/22) Hebrews 11:9 By faith he sojourned in the **land of**

promise, as in a strange country, dwelling in tabernacles with Isaac and Jacob, the heirs with him of the same **promise**:)
COM Clarke: <u>Rom 9:33</u> "to which, at a certain **future period**, they shall again be restored.")
KJV (1NT/1) <u>Revelation 17:17</u> For God hath put in their hearts to fulfil his will, and to agree, and give their kingdom unto the beast, until **the word**s of God **shall be fulfilled**.)
COM Gill: <u>Jer 1:12</u> "in like manner the Lord says he would hasten to perform what he had said or should say by him **concerning the destruction of Jerusalem**," (Clarke, Henry, Wesley)
KJV (1NT/2) <u>Luke 24:44</u> And he said unto them, These are the words which I spake unto you, while I was yet with you, that **all things must be fulfilled**, which were written in the law of Moses, and in the prophets, and in the psalms, concerning me.)
BOM <u>1 Nephi 7:16</u> And **it came to pass** (452/1353) that when I, Nephi, **had spoken these words** unto my brethren, they were angry with me. And **it came to pass** (452/1353) that they did lay their hands upon me, for behold, they were (*7*) *exceedingly wroth*, and they did **bind me with cords**, for they (*11*) *sought to take away* **my** *life*, that they might leave me in the wilderness *to be devoured by wild beasts.*

    KJV (2/19) <u>Job 42:7</u> And it was so, that after the LORD **had spoken these words** unto Job, the LORD said to Eliphaz the Temanite, My wrath is kindled against thee, and against thy two friends: for ye have not spoken of me the thing that is right, as my servant Job hath.)
    KJV (1/2) <u>Psalm 118:27</u> God is the LORD, which hath shewed us light: **bind** the sacrifice **with cords**, even unto the horns of the altar.)
    COM Clarke: <u>Gen 20:7</u> "his townsmen **sought to take away** his **life:**")
    KJV (1/5) <u>Psalm 31:13</u> For I have heard the slander of many: fear was on every side: while they took counsel together against me, they devised **to take away my life**.)
    COM Clarke: <u>Eze 16:5</u> "who exposed those children in the open fields **to be devoured by wild beasts** who had any kind of deformity, or whom they could not support.")
BOM <u>1 Nephi 8:21</u> And I saw (4) numberless (13th century) (3) concourses (14th Century) of people, many of whom were (*3*) (*3*) *pressing* (*14th Century*) *forward,* that they **might obtain** the path which led unto the tree by which I stood.

    COM Clarke: <u>Gen 24:12</u> "but there are **numberless** cases," (Henry, Gill, Wesley)
    COM Similar: Clarke: <u>Jer 46:7</u> "The vast **concourse of people** is here represented as a river:" (Henry, Wesley)

COM Henry: <u>Num 9:15-23</u> "though no doubt they were very desirous to be **pressing forward** in their journey towards Canaan")

KJV (1NT/9) <u>Hebrews 11:35</u> Women received their dead raised to life again: and others were tortured, not accepting deliverance; that they **might obtain** a better resurrection:)

BOM <u>1 Nephi 10:3</u> That after they should be destroyed, even **that great city** Jerusalem, and many be **carried away captive into Babylon,** according to the *(10) own due time* of the Lord, they should return again, yea, even be brought back out of captivity; and after they should be brought back out of captivity they should possess again *(12) the land of their inheritance.*

KJV (10/10) <u>Jonah 1:2</u> Arise, go to Nineveh, **that great city**, and cry against it; for their wickedness is come up before me.)

KJV (1/4) <u>Jeremiah 39:9</u> Then Nebuzaradan the captain of the guard **carried away captive into Babylon** the remnant of the people that remained in the city, and those that fell away, that fell to him, with the rest of the people that remained.)

COM Henry: <u>Psa 44:17-26</u> "that God would, in his **own due time**, work deliverance for them.")

COM Note how similar this last part of this verse and this use in Henry: <u>Jer 4:1-2</u> "If thou wilt return to me, then thou shalt **return**, that is, thou shalt be **brought back out of** thy **captivity** into thy own land again, as was of old promised,")

COM Henry: <u>1Pe 1:3-5</u> "Besides, they were most of them Jews, and so had a great affection to the land of Canaan, as **the land of their inheritance,**")

***BOM <u>1 Nephi 10:14</u> And after the house of Israel should be *scattered* they should be *gathered together again;* or, *(19) in fine,* after the Gentiles had received the *(3) fulness of the Gospel, (**Note: The BOM?**)* **the natural branches of the olive-tree**, or the remnants of the house of Israel, should be **grafted in**, or **come to the knowledge of the** *(3) true Messiah,* their Lord and their Redeemer.

COM Henry: <u>Psa 147:1-11</u> "He opens a door for their return; many that were missing, and thought to be lost, are brought back, and those that were **scattered** in the cloudy and dark day are **gathered together again.**")

COM Clarke: <u>Heb 7:26</u> "most under-foot and down-trodden vassals of perdition." Milton on Reformation, **in fine.**" (Henry, Wesley)

Note: This is very interesting as no OT or NT personage would have used this phrase "in-fine" as it is a modern invention, meaning "in short".

KJV (1NT/1) <u>Romans 11:24</u> For if thou wert cut out **of the olive tree** which is wild by nature, and wert grafted contrary to nature into a good **olive tree**: how much more shall these, which be **the natural branches**, be **grafted in**to their own **olive tree?**)

KJV (1NT/10) 2 Timothy 3:7 Ever learning, and never able to **come to the knowledge of the** truth.)

COM Henry: Act 2:14-36 "that Christ Jesus is **the true Messiah** and Saviour of the world;" (Clarke, Wesley)

Note: The idea of a "true Messiah" comes in history after there were many claiming they were the Messiah, in other words much later in time than when this was supposedly written.

BOM 1 Nephi 10:19 For **he that diligently seeketh**) **shall find**; and the **mysteries of God** shall be unfolded (4) unto them, by **the power of the Holy Ghost (89NT/95)**, as well in these times as in **times of old**, and as well in **times of old** as *(1) in times to come;* wherefore, *(3) the course of the* Lord is one *(3) eternal round.*

KJV (1/1) Proverbs 11:27 **He that diligently seeketh** good procureth favour: but he that seeketh mischief, it shall come unto him.

KJV (Verse of note: Luke 11:10 For every one that asketh receiveth; and he that seeketh **findeth**; and to him that knocketh it **shall** be opened.)

KJV (1NT/8) 1 Corinthians 4:1 Let a man so account of us, as of the ministers of Christ, and stewards of **the mysteries of God**.)

COM Henry: Luk 2:25-40 "hat now the **mystery** of that should **be unfolded**, when in Christ we should as it were see God face to face" (Clarke, Wesley)

KJV (1NT/24) Romans 15:13 Now the God of hope fill you with all joy and peace in believing, that ye may abound in hope, through **the power of the Holy Ghost**.)

KJV (1/5) Psalm 44:1 We have heard with our ears, O God, our fathers have told us, what work thou didst in their days, in the **times of old**.)

COM Henry: Exo 12:43-51 "as it should be observed **in times to come**." (Wesley)

COM Henry: Pro 19:16 "that will walk in the way of their hearts and after **the course of the** world" (Wesley, Clarke)

COM Clarke: Psa 102:27 "but God's **eternal round** has no completion.")

Note: The phrase "one eternal round" as with several items Joseph Smith used for the BOM comes from a hymn.

***BOM** 1 Nephi 10:21 Wherefore, if ye have *(1) sought to do* wickedly in the days of your (9) probation, (15ᵗʰ Century) then ye are found unclean *(1) before the judgment-seat of God;* and no unclean thing can *(4) dwell with God;* wherefore, ye must be cast off forever.

COM Henry: <u>Amo 5:4-15</u> "and **sought to do** them mischief.")

COM Clarke: <u>Mat 8:12</u> "and now the **day of probation** is ended,)

COM Clarke: 1Sa 25:44 "or in going to appear **before the judgment-seat of God**,")

Note: It is interesting here that judgment seat is only found in the NT 10 times but Joseph Smith uses it in the BOM 56 times.

COM Henry: <u>Heb 10:19-39</u> "but fallen man cannot **dwell with God** without a high priest," (Gill, Clarke)

***BOM** 1 Nephi 11:16 And he said unto me: Knowest thou the *(2) (5) condescension (1647 AD) of God?*

COM Clarke: <u>Eph 3:8</u> "and the amazing **condescension of God**," (Wesley, Henry)

***BOM** 1 Nephi 11:18 And he said unto me: Behold, the virgin whom **thou seest** is the mother of **the Son of God, (43NT/49)** after *(1) the manner of the flesh.*

KJV (15/10) <u>Genesis 13:15</u> For all the land which **thou seest**, to thee will I give it, and to thy seed for ever.)

COM Clarke: <u>Gal 4:23</u> "Hebrew phrase, על דרך בשר al derec basar, according to **the manner of the flesh**, i.e. naturally, according to the common process of nature.")

Note: This entire section of Clarke is about Jesus being born "after the flesh" and Joseph Smith uses an exact quote from that section.

BOM 1 Nephi 11:33 And I, Nephi, saw that *(1) he was lifted up upon the cross* and slain *(10) for the sins of the world.*

COM Henry: <u>Num 21:4-9</u> "**He was lifted up upon the cross**")

COM <u>Clarke: 1Jo 5:6</u> "He shed his blood **for the sins of the world**;" (Henry)

***BOM** 1 Nephi 13:26 And after they go forth by the hand of **the twelve apostles of the Lamb,** from the Jews unto the Gentiles, **thou seest** *(3) the (4) formation* (15th Century) *of a* great and abominable **church (76/259),** (Constantine, Catholic Church?) which is *(4) most abominable (2) above all other churches;* for behold, they have taken away from the gospel of the Lamb many parts which are plain and **most precious;** and also many covenants of the Lord have they taken away.

KJV (**1NT/9**) <u>Revelation 21:14</u> And the wall of the city had twelve foundations, and in them the names of **the twelve apostles of the Lamb.**)

KJV (15/10) <u>Genesis 13:15</u> For all the land which **thou seest**, to thee will I give it, and to thy seed for ever.)

COM Clarke: <u>Psa 119:176</u> "as the different alphabetical letters under which it is arranged are to **the formation of a** complete alphabet.")

COM <u>Rev 17:4</u> Clarke: "to diffuse their **most abominable** system of idolatry over the whole earth, and to extend the sphere of their domination. Here we have also an illustration of that remarkable passage in Rev 16:10, the kingdom of the beasts, i.e., the kingdom of the Latin kingdom;" (Henry, Wesley)

Note: Clarke says exactly the same thing about the Catholic church, which of course is what Joseph Smith is saying here in 1 Nephi 13.

KJV (5NT/4) Matthew 15:9 But in vain they do worship me, teaching for **doctrines** the commandments of men.)

COM Wesley: Isa 2:2 "being advanced **above all other churches and kingdoms**.")

KJV (2NT/10) Revelation 18:12 The merchandise of gold, and silver, and precious stones, and of pearls, and fine linen, and purple, and silk, and scarlet, and all thyine wood, and all manner vessels of ivory, and all manner vessels of **most precious** wood, and of brass, and iron, and marble,)

COM Many in Joseph Smith day believed this of the Catholic Church. Hence Clarke's commentary. Rev 17:5 "as the **church** of Rome has been; of corporeal fornication, by commanding celibacy, and forbidding marriage to priests, and setting up of brothel houses; and of spiritual fornication or idolatry, everywhere required and encouraged by it: and of "the abominations of the earth"; of **abominable** doctrines and practices; all manner of wickedness that is to be found in the earth, as murder, adultery, sodomy, perjury, &c. these, with everything that is vile and wicked, are practised and connived at by her.")

BOM 1 Nephi 14:11 And **it came to pass (452/1353)** that I looked and beheld **the whore** of all the earth, and **she sat upon many waters**; and she had **dominion over all the earth**, among **all nations, kindreds, tongues, and people.**

KJV (1NT/2) Revelation 17:1 And there came one of the seven angels which had the seven vials, and talked with me, saying unto me, Come hither; I will shew unto thee the judgment of the great **whore that sitteth upon many waters**:)

KJV (1/1) Genesis 1:26 And God said, Let us make man in our image, after our likeness: and let them have **dominion** over the fish of the sea, and over the fowl of the air, and over the cattle, and **over all the earth**, and over every creeping thing that creepeth upon the earth.)

KJV (1NT/8) Revelation 7:9 After this I beheld, and, lo, a great multitude, which no man could number, of **all nations, and kindreds, and people, and tongues**, stood before the throne, and before the Lamb, clothed with white robes, and palms in their hands;)

COM Gill: <u>Rev 17:1</u> "her sitting here may be in allusion to the posture of harlots plying of men; or may denote her ease, rest, and grandeur, sitting as a queen; and is chiefly expressive of her power and **dominion over** the kings and **nations of the earth**,")

BOM <u>1 Nephi 15:29</u> And I said unto them that it was a *(1) (5) representation (15th Century) of that* (47) awful (13th Century) (***Henry, Clarke, Wesley***) hell, which the angel said unto me was ***prepared for the*** *wicked*.

    COM Clarke: <u>Mat 8:3</u> "This action of Christ is a **representation of that** invisible hand which makes itself felt by the most insensible heart;" (Henry)

    KJV (***Verse of note:*** <u>Matthew 25:41</u> Then shall he say also unto them on the left hand, Depart from me, ye cursed, into everlasting fire, **prepared for the** devil and his angels:)

    COM Gill: <u>Gen 15:17</u> "the Jewish paraphrases make this to be a **representation of hell**, which is **prepared for the wicked** in the world to come,")

BOM <u>1 Nephi 16:10</u> And **it came to pass (452/1353)** that as my father arose in the morning, and went forth to the tent door, to his **great astonishment** he beheld upon the ground a round ball of *(3) curious workmanship;* and it was of **fine brass**. And within the ball were two (2) spindles; (1570) and the one pointed the way whither we should go into the wilderness. (Compass?)

    KJV (1NT/5) <u>Mark 5:42</u> And straightway the damsel arose, and walked; for she was of the age of twelve years. And they were astonished with a **great astonishment**.)

    COM Clarke: <u>Gen 35:2</u> "But it is more natural to suppose that these gods found now in Jacob's family were images of silver, gold, or **curious workmanship**," (Wesley)

    KJV (2NT/1) <u>Revelation 1:15</u> And his feet like unto **fine brass**, as if they burned in a furnace; and his voice as the sound of many waters.)

    COM Clarke: <u>Jer 18:3</u> "the **spindle** of the moving stone being placed on a stone below, on which it turned, and supported the stone above, on which the vessel was manufactured, and which alone had a rotatory motion." (Henry)

BOM <u>1 Nephi 16:18</u> And **it came to pass (452/1353)** that as I, Nephi, went forth to slay food, behold, I did *break* my **bow**, which was made *of* fine ***steel***; and after I did break my bow, behold, my brethren were angry with me because of the loss of my bow, for we did obtain no food.

    KJV (<u>2 Samuel 22:35</u> He teacheth my hands to war; so that a **bow of steel** is broken by mine arms. <u>Psalm 18:34</u> He teacheth my hands to war, so that a **bow of steel** is broken by mine arms.)

    COM Henry: <u>Psa 18:29-50</u> "God girded him with strength (<u>Psa 18:32</u>, <u>Psa 18:39</u>), to such a degree that he could **break** even a

bow of steel, <u>Psa 18:34</u>.")
***BOM 1 Nephi 16:29 And (*17*) *thus we see that* by (*4*) *small means* the Lord can (*1*) *bring about great things.*

> **COM** Clarke: <u>Act 26:18</u> "**Thus we see that** not only this salvation comes through Christ," (Henry)
> **COM** Clarke: <u>Psa 59:16</u> "When I came with **small means** and feeble help,")
> **COM** Clarke: <u>Zec 4:1-10</u> "Note, In God's work the day of **small** things is not to be despised. Though the instruments be weak and unlikely, God often chooses such, by them to **bring about great things**.")
> **Note:** Notice the same concept here and even the same ending "bring about great things".

***BOM <u>1 Nephi 17:20</u> And thou art like unto our father, led away by the **foolish** (*2*) *imaginations of his heart;* yea, he hath led us out of the land of Jerusalem, and we have wandered in the wilderness for these many years; and our women **have toiled**, being (*1*) *big* (*14th Century) with child;* and they have borne children in the wilderness and suffered all things, (*76*) *save it were* death; and (*2*) *it would have been better* that they had died before they came out of Jerusalem than to have suffered these afflictions.

> **KJV** (<u>Romans 1:21</u> Because that, when they knew God, they glorified him not as God, neither were thankful; but became vain in their **imaginations**, and their **foolish heart** was darkened.)
> **COM** Clarke: <u>Job 21:19</u> "It is, however, very natural to suppose that children brought up without the fear of God will walk in the sight of their own eyes, and according to the **imaginations** of their own **hearts**.")
> **KJV** (**1NT/2**) <u>Luke 5:5</u> And Simon answering said unto him, Master, we **have toiled** all the night, and have taken nothing: nevertheless at thy word I will let down the net.)
> **COM** Gill: <u>Rom 8:22</u> "it was like a woman **big with child**, ready to bring forth many sons to God;," (Henry, Clarke)
> **Note:** Please notice that the word "big" is not found in the KJV of the Bible. Which means the phrase "big with child" should not be a part of the BOM except for the fact that it comes from the commentaries.
> **COM** Gill: <u>Isa 30:7</u> "that **it would have been better** for the ambassadors to have spared all their toil, and labour, and strength, in going down to Egypt, and have remained quiet and easy in their own country:")

BOM <u>1 Nephi 18:17</u> Now my father, Lehi, had said many things unto them, and also unto the sons of Ishmael; but, behold, they did **breathe out** much **threatenings against** anyone that should speak for me; and my parents being

stricken in years, and having suffered **much grief** because of their children, they were brought down, yea, even *(1) upon their (1) sick-beds. (14th Century)*

> **KJV** (1/3) <u>Psalm 27:12</u> Deliver me not over unto the will of mine enemies: for false witnesses are risen up against me, and such as **breathe out** cruelty.)

> **KJV (1NT/5)** <u>Acts 9:1</u> And Saul, yet **breathing out threatenings** and slaughter **against** the disciples of the Lord, went unto the high priest,)

> **KJV** (4/1) <u>Joshua 13:1</u> Now Joshua was old and **stricken in years**; and the LORD said unto him, Thou art old and **stricken in years**, and there remaineth yet very much land to be)

> **KJV** (1/1) <u>Ecclesiastes 1:18</u> For in much wisdom is **much grief**: and he that increaseth knowledge increaseth sorrow.)

> **COM** Henry: <u>Psa 149:1-5</u> "**Upon their sick-beds**, their death-beds, let them sing the praises of their God.")

> **Note:** Notice again that the word "sick-beds" is not in the KJV of the Bible.

***BOM** <u>1 Nephi 18:18</u> Because of their grief and **much sorrow**, and the iniquity of my brethren, they were brought near even to be carried out of this time *(2) to meet their God;* yea, their **grey hairs** were about to be brought down *(1) to lie low* in the dust; yea, even they were near to be cast with sorrow into *(1) a watery grave. (12th Century)*

> **KJV** (1/6) <u>Ecclesiastes 5:17</u> All his days also he eateth in darkness, and he hath **much sorrow** and wrath with his sickness.)

> **COM** Wesley: <u>Mat 25:7</u> "They trimmed their lamps - They examined themselves and prepared **to meet their God**." (Henry, Clarke)

> **KJV** (5/1) <u>Genesis 44:29</u> And if ye take this also from me, and mischief befall him, ye shall bring down my **gray hairs** with sorrow to the)

> **COM** Henry: <u>Eze 2:1-5</u> "It therefore became him, and all of his order, to humble themselves, and **to lie low**, as sons of men, common men.")

> **COM** Clarke: <u>Act 27:42</u> "Though, through the providence of God, those poor men had escaped **a watery grave**,")

> **Note:** The phrase "a watery grave" is a modern creation.

BOM 1 Nephi 18:22 And **it came to pass (452/1353)** that I, Nephi, did guide the ship, that we **sailed** again towards *(13) the promised land.*

> **KJV (14NT/2)** <u>Luke 8:23</u> But as they sailed he fell asleep: and there came down a storm of wind on the lake; and they were filled with water, and were in jeopardy.)

> **COM** The phrase "the promised land" is not in the King James Version of the Bible it is a modern concept. Wesley: <u>Heb 3:10</u> "Into

my rest - **In the promised land.**" (Henry, Clarke)

BOM 2 Nephi 1:28 And now my son, Laman, and also Lemuel and Sam, and also my sons who are the sons of Ishmael, behold, if ye will hearken unto the voice of Nephi ye shall not perish. And if ye will hearken unto him I leave unto you a blessing, yea, even my *(2) first blessing.*

> **COM** Henry: Gen 4:1-2 "he preserved to them the benefit of that **first blessing** of increase.")

BOM 2 Nephi 1:29 But if ye will not hearken unto him I take away my *(2) first blessing*, yea, even my blessing, and it shall rest upon him.

> **COM** Henry: Gen 4:1-2 "he preserved to them the benefit of that **first blessing** of increase.")

BOM 2 Nephi 1:30 And now Zoram, I speak unto you: Behold, thou art the servant of Laban; nevertheless, thou hast been brought out of the land of Jerusalem, and I know that thou art *(2) a true friend* unto my son, Nephi, forever.

> **COM** Henry: Mat 11:1-6 "for he was **a true friend** of the Bridegroom," (Clarke, Wesley)

***BOM 2 Nephi 2:4 And thou hast beheld **in thy youth** his glory; wherefore, thou art blessed even as they unto whom he shall minister in the flesh; for the Spirit is **the same, yesterday, today, and forever.**

And the way is prepared from the fall of man, and *(1) salvation is free.*

> **KJV** (1/5) Ecclesiastes 11:9 Rejoice, O young man, **in thy youth**; and let thy heart cheer thee in the days of thy youth, and walk in the ways of thine heart, and in the sight of thine eyes: but know thou, that for all these things God will bring thee into judgment.)
>
> **KJV** (1NT/6) Hebrews 13:8 Jesus Christ **the same yesterday**, and **to day, and for ever**.)
>
> **COM** Clarke: Rom 5:15 "That is, Christ Jesus died for every man; **salvation is free** for all;")
>
> **Note:** The phrase "salvation is free" is very unique.

***BOM 2 Nephi 2:12 Wherefore, it **must needs have** been created for **a thing of naught**; wherefore there would have been no purpose in *(1) the end of its creation.* Wherefore, this thing must needs destroy the wisdom of God and *(2) his eternal purposes,* and also the power, and the mercy, and the *(12) justice of God.*

> **KJV** (2NT/5) Acts 17:3 Opening and alleging, that Christ **must needs have** suffered, and risen again from the dead; and that this Jesus, whom I preach unto you, is Christ.)
>
> **KJV** (4/4) Isaiah 29:21 That make a man an offender for a word, and lay a snare for him that reproveth in the gate, and turn aside the just for **a thing of nought**.)
>
> **COM** Henry: Gen 1:31 "Good, for it answers **the end of its creation,**

and is fit for the purpose for which it was designed." (Clarke, Wesley)

Note: What a unique phrase "the end of its creation". Hence it comes from the commentaries.

KJV (6NT/14) Mark 10:6 But from the beginning of the **creation** God made them male and female.)

COM Clarke: Eph 1:5 "**his eternal purposes** could not be fulfilled;")

COM Henry: Rev 18:9-24 "yet they had reason to rejoice in the discoveries of the glorious **justice of God**." (Clarke, Wesley)

***BOM 2 Nephi 2:15 And to bring about *(2) his eternal purposes,* in the *(2) end of man,* after he had *created our (13) first* **parents,** **(20NT/22)** and the *beasts of the field and the fowls of the air,* **and** *(19)* **in fine,** all things which are created, **it must needs be that** there was an opposition; even *the (6) forbidden fruit* in opposition to **the tree of life**; the one being sweet and the other bitter.

COM Clarke: Eph 1:5 "**his eternal purposes** could not be fulfilled;")

COM Clarke: 1Co 1:19 "and whose highest discoveries amount to nothing in comparison of the grand truths relative to God, the invisible world, and the true **end of man**" (Henry, Wesley)

COM Clarke: Gen 3:6 "God had undoubtedly **created our first parents** not only very wise and intelligent, but also with a great capacity and suitable propensity to increase in knowledge.")

COM Clarke: Jer 7:32 "or becoming food for the **beasts of the field and the fowls of the air,**")

Note: It is interesting that the OT uses the phrase beasts of the field and fowls of the heavens" but Clarke uses the same as Joseph Smith:

COM Clarke: Heb 7:26 "most under-foot and down-trodden vassals of perdition." Milton on Reformation, **in fine.**" (Henry, Wesley)

Note: This is very interesting as no OT or NT personage would have used this phrase as it is a modern invention, meaning "in short".

COM "forbidden fruit" is a modern phrase. Clarke: Gen 2:23 "God had said that in the day they ate of **the forbidden fruit**, dying they should die," (Henry, Gill, Wesley)

KJV (1NT/14) Matthew 18:7 Woe unto the world because of offences! for **it must needs be that** offences come; but woe to that man by whom the offence cometh!)

KJV (6/15) Genesis 2:9 And out of the ground made the LORD God to grow every tree that is pleasant to the sight, and good for food; **the tree of life** also in the midst of the garden, and the tree of knowledge of good and evil.)

***BOM 2 Nephi 2:23 And they would have had no children; wherefore they would have remained *(1) in a state of (1) innocence, (14th Century)* having no joy, for they knew no misery; doing no good, for they knew no sin.

> **COM** Gill: <u>Gen 2:17</u> "and may have regard to more deaths than one; not only a corporeal one, which in some sense immediately took place, man became at once a mortal creature, who otherwise continuing **in a state of innocence**, and by eating of the tree of life, he was allowed to do, would have lived an immortal life;" (Henry, Wesley, Clarke)
>
> **Note:** Another highly unique phrase and modern concept "in a state of innocence".

*****BOM** <u>2 Nephi 2:27</u> Wherefore, men are free **according to the flesh**; and **all things are** given them which are **expedient** unto man. And they are free to choose liberty and **eternal life**, through *(2) the great Mediator* of all **men**, or to choose captivity and death, according to the captivity and power of **the devil**; for he seeketh that all men might be *(1) miserable like unto himself.*

> **KJV (1NT/1)** <u>1 Corinthians 10:23</u> **All things are** lawful for me, but **all things** are not **expedient**: all things are lawful for me, but all things edify not.)
>
> **KJV (26NT/25)** <u>Matthew 19:16</u> And, behold, one came and said unto him, Good Master, what good thing shall I do, that I may have **eternal life?**)
>
> **COM** Clarke: <u>Joh 16:24</u> "Ye have not as yet considered me **the great Mediator** between God and man;" (Henry, Wesley)
>
> **KJV** (<u>1 Timothy 2:5</u> For there is one God, and one **mediator** between God and **men**, the man Christ Jesus;)
>
> **KJV (44NT/94)** <u>Matthew 4:1</u> Then was Jesus led up of the Spirit into the wilderness to be tempted of **the devil**.)
>
> **COM** Henry: <u>Job 18:5-10</u> "He, as the tempter, lays snares for sinners in the way, wherever they go, and he shall prevail. If he make them sinful like himself, he will make them **miserable like himself**.")
>
> **KJV (7NT/12)** <u>Acts 2:30</u> Therefore being a prophet, and knowing that God had sworn with an oath to him, that of the fruit of his loins, **according to the flesh**, he would raise up Christ to sit on his throne;)

BOM <u>2 Nephi 2:28</u> And now, my sons, **I would that ye** should look to *(2) the great Mediator* of all **men**, and hearken unto his great commandments; and be faithful unto his words, and choose **eternal life**, according to the will of his Holy Spirit;

> **KJV (2NT/56)** <u>Colossians 2:1</u> For **I would that ye** knew what great conflict I have for you, and for them at Laodicea, and for as many as have not seen my face in the flesh;)
>
> **COM** Clarke: <u>Joh 16:24</u> "Ye have not as yet considered me **the great Mediator** between God and man;" (Henry, Wesley)
>
> **Note**: Hearken to what great commandments and words? They

haven't been spoken yet nor have the sons heard them in a "vision". He even talks about it as a future event.

KJV (26NT/25) Matthew 19:16 And, behold, one came and said unto him, Good Master, what good thing shall I do, that I may have **eternal life**?)

BOM 2 Nephi 2:29 And not choose *(1) eternal death,* according to **the will of the flesh** and the evil which is therein, which giveth *(4) the spirit of* ***the devil*** power to (1) captivate, (1555 AD) **(*Note: Henry, Clarke, Wesley*)** to bring you **down to hell**, that he may reign over you in his own kingdom.

> **COM** Clarke: 2Ti 2:17 "it terminates in the bitter pains of an **eternal death**" (Henry, Wesley)
>
> **KJV (1NT/1)** John 1:13 Which were born, not of blood, nor of **the will of the flesh**, nor of the will of man, but of God.)
>
> **COM** Clarke: Mat 12:31 "by the power of God, to **the spirit of the devil**.")
>
> **Note:** Another very unique phrase "the spirit of the devil".
>
> **KJV (44NT/94)** Matthew 4:1 Then was Jesus led up of the Spirit into the wilderness to be tempted of **the devil**.)
>
> **KJV** (6/11) Isaiah 14:15 Yet thou shalt be brought **down to hell**, to the sides of the pit.)

***BOM** 2 Nephi 9:2 That he has **spoken** unto the Jews, **by the mouth of his holy prophets, even from the beginning** own, **from generation to generation**, *until the time comes* that they shall be restored *(1) to the true* **church (76/259)** and *(4) fold of God*; when they shall be *(3) gathered home* to *(19) the lands of their inheritance,* and **shall be established** in all their lands of promise.

> **KJV (1NT/1)** Luke 1:70 As he spake **by the mouth of his holy prophets**, which have been since the world began:)
>
> **KJV** (1/5) Isaiah 48:5 I have **even from the beginning** declared it to thee; before it came to pass I shewed it thee: lest thou shouldest say, Mine idol hath done them, and my graven image, and my molten image, hath commanded them.)
>
> **KJV** (2/14) Isaiah 13:20 It shall never be inhabited, neither shall it be dwelt in **from generation to generation**: neither shall the Arabian pitch tent there; neither shall the shepherds make their fold there.)
>
> **COM** Gill: Mat 23:39 "till ye shall say, blessed is he that cometh in the name of the Lord; that is, **until the time comes**, that the fulness of the Gentiles shall be brought in, and all Israel shall be saved, the Jews shall be converted, and seek the Lord their God,")
>
> **COM** Clarke: Col 4:5 "belong **to the true Church** of Christ.
>
> **Note:** Henry, Clarke and Wesley all use the phrase "true church" a concept that obviously did not occur until the break offs of the

Catholic Church in our modern times. The phrase "true church" is used three times in the BOM and because of the history of the Christian Church, which didn't begin until hundreds of years after this verse in the BOM was written and even over a thousand years since the church began to break up and thus the phrase "true church" then had meaning.

COM Clarke: Mat 10:6 "The Jewish Church was the ancient **fold of God**;")

COM Henry: Ecc 1:1-3 "**gathered home** to his duty, and come at length to himself.")

COM Henry: 1Pe 1:3-5 "Besides, they were most of them Jews, and so had a great affection to the land of Canaan, as **the land of their inheritance**, settled upon them by God himself;")

KJV Verse of note: Note how similar these verses are, also note that Joseph Smith would have used the verse in Acts as it would relate in his mind to our day and the coming of the BOM and the "true church (76/259)" The Mormon Church (76/259). Incidentally the concept of a "true church (76/259)" is a modern concept that came about after the Protestant Reformation. Luke 1:70 As he spake **by the mouth of his holy prophets, which have been since the world began**: Acts 3:21 Whom the heaven must receive until the times of restitution of all things, which God hath **spoken by the mouth of all** his **holy prophets since the world began**.

KJV (18/6) Leviticus 25:30 And if it be not redeemed within the space of a full year, then the house that is in the walled city **shall be established** for ever to him that bought it throughout his generations: it shall not go out in the jubile.)

BOM 2 Nephi 9:3 Behold, **my beloved brethren**, I speak unto you these things that **ye may rejoice**, and **lift up your heads** forever, because of the blessings which the Lord God shall bestow upon your children.

KJV (**4NT/60**) James 1:19 Wherefore, **my beloved brethren**, let every man be swift to hear, slow to speak, slow to wrath:)

KJV (**1NT/1**) Philippians 2:28 I sent him therefore the more carefully, that, when ye see him again, **ye may rejoice**, and that I may be the less sorrowful.)

KJV (3/5) Psalm 24:7 **Lift up your heads**, O ye gates; and be ye lift up, ye everlasting doors; and the King of glory shall come in.)

BOM 2 Nephi 9:4 For I know that ye have searched much, many of you, to know **of things to come**; wherefore I know that ye know that our flesh must **waste away and die**; nevertheless, *(1) in our bodies* we shall see God.

KJV (2/8) Isaiah 45:11 Thus saith the LORD, the Holy One of Israel, and his Maker, Ask me **of things to come** concerning my sons, and concerning the work of my hands command ye me.)

KJV (Job 14:10 But man **dieth, and waste**th **away**: yea, man giveth up the ghost, and where is he?)

COM Henry: Mat 6:9-15 "wrongs done to us **in our bodies,**"(Gill)

***BOM** 2 Nephi 9:7 Wherefore, **it must needs be** an infinite atonement -- save it should be an infinite atonement **this corruption** could not **put on incorruption**. Wherefore, the first judgment which came upon man **must needs have** remained to an *(1) endless (2) duration.* *(14th Century)* And if so, this flesh must have laid down to rot and to (2) crumble (1570AD) to its *(3) mother earth,* to **rise no more**.

KJV (**1NT/7**) Matthew 18:7 Woe unto the world because of offences! for **it must needs** be that offences come; but woe to that man by whom the offence cometh!)

KJV (**1NT/1**) 1 Corinthians 15:53 For this corruptible must **put on incorruption**, and this mortal must put on immortality.)

COM Gill: 1Pe 1:4 "in order to inherit it, **corruption** must **put on incorruption**, in every sense;")

Note: Notice that the NT verse, which should not be quoted from anyway, states "corruptible must put on incorruption" but Joseph Smith uses exactly what Gill says "corruption ...put on incorruption".

KJV (**2NT/5**) Acts 17:3 Opening and alleging, that Christ **must needs have** suffered, and risen again from the dead; and that this Jesus, whom I preach unto you, is Christ.)

COM Clarke: Rev 1:4 "the **endless duration** that shall be when time is no more." (Henry)

COM Gill: Jer 8:2 "that is, they should **lie** and **rot** upon the face of the earth, and **crumble** into dust, and become dung for it;" (Henry)

COM Clarke: Job 1:21 "That **mother earth** was a common expression in different nations, I allow; but I believe no such metaphor was now in the mind of Job." (Gill)

Note: What a unique phrase "mother earth".

KJV (1/3) Jeremiah 25:27 Therefore thou shalt say unto them, Thus saith the LORD of hosts, the God of Israel; Drink ye, and be drunken, and spue, and fall, and **rise no more**, because of the sword which I will send among you.)

BOM 2 Nephi 9:8 O the wisdom of God, his mercy and grace! For behold, if the flesh should **rise no more** our spirits must become subject to that angel who fell from before the presence of the *Eternal God*, and became **the devil**, to **rise no more**.

KJV (1/3) Jeremiah 25:27 Therefore thou shalt say unto them, Thus saith the LORD of hosts, the God of Israel; Drink ye, and be drunken, and spue, and fall, and **rise no more**, because of the sword which I will send among you.)

COM Henry: <u>Gen 11:5-9</u> "The counsels and resolves of the **Eternal God** concerning this matter")

KJV (44NT/94) <u>Matthew 4:1</u> Then was Jesus led up of the Spirit into the wilderness to be tempted of **the devil**.)

KJV (1/3) <u>Jeremiah 25:27</u> Therefore thou shalt say unto them, Thus saith the LORD of hosts, the God of Israel; Drink ye, and be drunken, and spue, and fall, and **rise no more**, because of the sword which I will send among you.)

***BOM** <u>2 Nephi 9:9</u> And our spirits must have **become like unto** him, and we become devils, angels to a devil, to be shut out from the (*1*) *presence of our God,* and to remain with *the father of lies*, in misery, like unto himself; yea, to that being who **beguiled** our (*13*) *first parents,* (**20NT/22**) who transformeth (*Note: Not found)* himself nigh unto **an angel of light**, and stirreth up the children of men unto (*18*) *secret* (*21*) *combinations* (*14th Century)* of murder and all manner of secret **works of darkness**.

COM Henry: <u>Gen 39:1-6</u> "yet cannot deprive us of the gracious **presence of our God**." (Wesley)

COM Gill: Psa 69:4 "for Satan is the **father of lies** and falsehood;" (Clarke, Gill, Henry)

Note: Although we think this phrase, "father of lies", is in the KJV, it is actually a modern invention, father of lies can be found in the more modern translations.

KJV (<u>John 8:44</u> Ye are of your **father** the **devil**, and the lusts of your **father** ye will do. He was a murderer from the beginning, and abode not in the truth, because there is no truth in him. When he speaketh a lie, he speaketh of his own: *for he is a liar, and the **father** of it.*)

KJV (1NT/1) <u>2 Corinthians 11:14</u> And no marvel; for Satan himself is **transformed into an angel of light**.)

KJV (<u>Genesis 3:13</u> And the LORD God said unto the woman, What is this that thou hast done? And the woman said, The serpent **beguiled** me, and I did eat. <u>2 Corinthians 11:3</u> But I fear, lest by any means, as the serpent **beguiled** Eve through his subtilty, so your minds should be corrupted from the simplicity that is in Christ.)

COM Gill: <u>Psa 72:4</u> "who **beguiled our first parents**, and deceives mankind.")

COM Gill: <u>Job 12:22</u> "likewise the **secret** plots, counsels, and **combinations** of wicked men,")

KJV (2NT/13) <u>Romans 13:12</u> The night is far spent, the day is at hand: let us therefore cast off the **works of darkness**, and let us put on the armour of light.)

COM Note how well this sentence from Henry fits the previous verse: Henry: <u>Gen 1:3-5</u> "The works of Satan and his servants are **works of darkness**;")

***BOM** <u>2 Nephi 9:26</u> For the atonement satisfieth *(1) the demands of his justice* upon all those who have not the law given to them, that they are delivered from that (47) awful (13th Century) (**Henry, Clarke, Wesley**) monster, **death and hell**, **and the devil**, and **the lake of fire and brimstone**, which is endless **torment**; and they are restored to that God who gave them breath, which is the Holy One of Israel.

> **COM** Clarke: <u>Joh 19:30</u> "As if he had said: "I have executed the great designs of the Almighty - I have **satisfied the demands of his justice** - I have accomplished all that was written in the prophets, and suffered the utmost malice of my enemies; and now the way to the holy of holies is made manifest through my blood." (Gill, Henry)
> **Note:** Interestingly the word "justice" is not used in the NT. And satisfying the demands of justice is a modern concept.
> **KJV (44NT/94)** <u>Matthew 4:1</u> Then was Jesus led up of the Spirit into the wilderness to be tempted of **the devil**.)
> **COM** Clarke: <u>Psa 115:18</u> "The word hell among our ancestors meant originally the covered, or hidden obscure place, from helan, to cover or conceal: it now expresses only the place of **endless torment**." (Henry)
> **KJV (1NT/1)** <u>Revelation 20:10</u> **And the devil** that deceived them was cast into **the lake of fire and brimstone**, where the beast and the false prophet are, and shall be **torment**ed day and night for ever and ever.
> **KJV (1NT/1)** <u>Revelation 20:14</u> And **death and hell** were cast into **the lake of fire**. This is the second **death**.)

***BOM** <u>2 Nephi 9:35</u> Wo unto the murderer who deliberately (15th Century:) **killeth**, for he shall die.

> **Note**: "Deliberately" is a modern word, Joseph Smith obviously wanted to make a distinction here that you can kill accidentally; the problem is that murder is never an accident.
> **KJV** (*Note: Verse of note:* <u>Numbers 35:30</u> Whoso **killeth** any person, the **murderer** shall be put to death by the mouth of witnesses: but one witness shall not testify against any person to cause him to die.)

BOM <u>2 Nephi 9:39</u> O, **my beloved brethren**, remember the (2) awfulness (13th Century) in transgressing against that Holy God, and also the (2) awfulness (13th Century) of yielding to the **enticings** of that *cunning one*. Remember, **to be carnally-minded is death**, and **to be spiritually-minded is life** eternal.

> **KJV (4NT/60)** <u>James 1:19</u> Wherefore, **my beloved brethren**, let

every man be swift to hear, slow to speak, slow to wrath:)

COM Henry: <u>Rev 13:9</u> "These words are evidently introduced to impress the reader with the **awfulness** of what has just been spoken" (Clarke)

KJV (2NT/4) <u>1 Corinthians 2:4</u> And my speech and my preaching was not with **enticing** words of man's wisdom, but in demonstration of the Spirit and of power:)

COM Gill: <u>Eph 6:11</u> "that ye may be able to stand against the wiles of the devil; who is the grand enemy of Christ and his people, and a very powerful and **cunning one** he is;")

Note: Again we will get into the use of titles in a future chapter.

KJV (1NT/1) <u>Romans 8:6</u> For **to be carnally minded is death; but to be spiritually minded is life and peace**.)

BOM <u>2 Nephi 25:16</u> And after they have been scattered, and the Lord God hath scourged them by other nations **for the space of** many generations, yea, even down **from generation to generation** until they shall be (*1*) *persuaded to believe in Christ,* **the Son of God**, **(43NT/49)** and the atonement, which is infinite for **all mankind** -- and (*3*) *when that day shall come* that they shall believe in Christ, and **worship the Father** in his name, with **pure hearts and clean hands**, and look not forward any more for another Messiah, then, at that time, the day will come that **it must needs be expedient** that they should believe these things.

KJV (1NT/69) <u>Acts 19:8</u> And he went into the synagogue, and spake boldly **for the space of** three months, disputing and persuading the things concerning the kingdom of God.)

KJV (2/14) <u>Isaiah 13:20</u> It shall never be inhabited, neither shall it be dwelt in **from generation to generation**: neither shall the Arabian pitch tent there; neither shall the shepherds make their fold there.)

COM Henry: <u>Act 19:8-12</u> "There were some that were **persuaded to believe in Christ**;")

KJV (1/20) <u>Job 12:10</u> In whose hand is the soul of every living thing, and the breath of **all mankind**.)

COM Henry: <u>Rev 6:9-17</u> "so God has his day of righteous wrath; and, **when that day shall come**, the most stout-hearted sinners will not be able to stand before him:")

KJV (1NT/2) <u>John 4:21</u> Jesus saith unto her, Woman, believe me, the hour cometh, when ye shall neither in this mountain, nor yet at Jerusalem, **worship the Father**.)

KJV (1/2) <u>Psalm 24:4</u> He that hath **clean hands**, **and** a **pure heart**; who hath not lifted up his soul unto vanity, nor sworn deceitfully.)

COM Henry: <u>Act 2:14-36</u> "This is that effusion of the Spirit upon all flesh which should come, and we are to look for no other, **no more**

than we are to look **for another Messiah**;)

KJV (1NT/7) Matthew 18:7 Woe unto the world because of offences! for **it must needs be** that offences come; but woe to that man by whom the offence cometh!)

KJV (7NT/62) John 11:50 Nor consider that it is **expedient** for us, that one man should die for the people, and that the whole nation perish not.)

*****BOM** 2 Nephi 25:21 Wherefore, **for this cause** hath the Lord God promised unto me that these things which I write shall be *(10) kept and preserved,* and *(18) handed down* unto my seed, **from generation to generation**, that the promise may be fulfilled unto Joseph, that his seed should **never perish** *as long as the earth* should stand.

> **KJV (26/27)** Exodus 9:16 And in very deed **for this cause** have I raised thee up, for to shew in thee my power; and that my name may be declared throughout all the earth.)
>
> **COM** Henry: 1Pe 1:3-5 "It is certain, a reversion in another world, safely **kept and preserved** till we come to the possession of it." (Clarke)
>
> **COM** Clarke: Mat 15:2 "that had been successively **handed down from** Moses through every **generation**, but not committed to writing.")
>
> **KJV (1NT/3)** John 10:28 And I give unto them eternal life; and they shall **never perish**, neither shall any man pluck them out of my hand.)
>
> **COM** Henry: Mat 28:20 "**The promise** takes in not only the primitive apostles, but also all their successors in the Christian ministry, **as long as the earth** shall endure." (Gill)

*****BOM** 2 Nephi 25:29 And now behold, I say unto you that the right way is to believe in Christ, and deny him not; and *(1) Christ is the Holy One of Israel;* wherefore ye must bow down before him, and worship him **with all** your might, **mind**, and **strength**, and your whole **soul**; and if ye do this ye shall **in nowise** be **cast out**.

> **COM** Henry: Psa 89:15-18 "**Christ is the Holy One of Israel**, that holy thing;")
>
> **Note:** A highly unique and long title, hence its origin is the commentary of Henry.
>
> **KJV (1NT/1)** Mark 12:30 And thou shalt love the Lord thy God with all thy heart, and with all thy **soul**, and with all thy **mind**, and with all thy **strength**: this is the first commandment.)
>
> **KJV (1NT/1)** John 6:37 All that the Father giveth me shall come to me; and him that cometh to me I will **in no wise cast out**.)

BOM 2 Nephi 25:30 And, inasmuch as it shall be **expedient**, ye must keep the

*(6) performances (15ᵗʰ Century) (**Note: Henry, Clarke, Wesley**) and **ordinances of** of* God until the law shall be fulfilled which was given unto Moses.

> **KJV (7NT/62)** <u>John 11:50</u> Nor consider that it is **expedient** for us, that one man should die for the people, and that the whole nation perish not.)
>
> **KJV (1NT/2)** <u>Luke 1:6</u> And they were both righteous before God, walking in all the commandments **and ordinances of** the Lord blameless.)
>
> **COM** Clarke: <u>Act 17:34</u> "and Paul grants that they were much addicted to religious **performances**:" Rom 2:29 "taught every considerate man among them that God could be pleased with their rites and external **performances**")
>
> **Note:** Where did Joseph Smith get the idea for "performances" and their relation to "ordinances" as the word "performances" is not found in the King James Version of the Bible, we can see in Henry, Clarke and Wesley that correlation.

***BOM** <u>2 Nephi 28:11</u> Yea, **they** have **all gone out of the way; they** have **become** corrupted.

> **Note:** Clarke tells us that in this verse "unprofitable" is "what is termed the corruption of human nature;" hence what Joseph Smith has above.
>
> **KJV (1NT/1)** <u>Romans 3:12</u> **They** are **all gone out of the way, they** are together **become** unprofitable; there is none that doeth good, no, not one.)

***BOM** <u>2 Nephi 28:21</u> And others will he **pacify**, and *(1) lull (1650 AD)* them away into *(1) carnal security*, that they will say: **All is well** in Zion; yea, Zion prospereth, **all is well** -- and thus **the devil** (1) cheateth (Cheat 1590 AD) *(**Note: Not found**)* their souls, and **leadeth them** away carefully **down to hell**.

> **KJV (1/3)** <u>Proverbs 16:14</u> The wrath of a king is as messengers of death: but a wise man will **pacify** it.)
>
> **COM** Clarke: <u>Zep 3:4</u> "and **lull** the people into spiritual slumber." (Henry)
>
> **COM** Gill: <u>Rev 14:13</u> "when coldness, lukewarmness, and **carnal security** will seize upon men, and Christ will come upon them at an unawares;"(Clarke, Henry)
>
> **Note:** Another very unique phrase, "carnal security".
>
> **KJV (1NT/11)** <u>Acts 17:9</u> And when they had taken **security** of Jason, and of the other, they let them go.)
>
> **KJV (2/4)** <u>2 Kings 5:22</u> And he said, **All is well**. My master hath sent me, saying, Behold, even now there be come to me from mount Ephraim two young men of the sons of the prophets: give them, I

pray thee, a talent of silver, and two changes of garments.)

KJV (2/4) 2 Kings 5:22 And he said, **All is well**. My master hath sent me, saying, Behold, even now there be come to me from mount Ephraim two young men of the sons of the prophets: give them, I pray thee, a talent of silver, and two changes of garments.)

KJV (**44NT/94**) Matthew 4:1 Then was Jesus led up of the Spirit into the wilderness to be tempted of **the devil**.)

KJV (**2NT/4**) Mark 9:2 And after six days Jesus taketh with him Peter, and James, and John, and **leadeth them** up into an high mountain apart by themselves: and he was transfigured before them.)

KJV (6/11) Isaiah 14:15 Yet thou shalt be brought **down to hell**, to the sides of the pit.)

BOM 2 Nephi 28:22 And behold, others he **flattereth** away, and **telleth** them there is no hell; and he saith unto them: I am no devil, for there is none -- and thus he (2) whispereth (***Note: Not found***) in their ears, until he (*4*) *grasps* (*16ᵗʰ Century*) them *with his* (*47*) *awful* (*13ᵗʰ Century*) chains, from whence there is no deliverance.

KJV (6/1) Psalm 36:2 For he **flattereth** himself in his own eyes, until his iniquity be found to be hateful.)

KJV (7/2) Psalm 101:7 He that worketh deceit shall not dwell within my house: he that **telleth** lies shall not tarry in my sight.)

COM Clarke: Exo 4:17 "But first he **grasps with**in his **awful hand**") (Note: see above for the previous)

***BOM 2 Nephi 31:21 And now, behold, **my beloved brethren**, this is the way; and **there is none other** way nor **name given under heaven whereby** man can **be saved** in the kingdom of God. And now, behold, this is **the doctrine of Christ**, and the only and (*1*) *true doctrine of the Father*, **and of the Son, and of the Holy Ghost** (**89NT/95**), which is one God, **without end. Amen**.

KJV (**4NT/60**) James 1:19 Wherefore, **my beloved brethren**, let every man be swift to hear, slow to speak, slow to wrath:)

KJV (**1NT/1**) Acts 4:12 Neither is there salvation in any other: for **there is none other name under heaven given** among men, **whereby** we must **be saved**.)

KJV (**2NT/7**) 2 John 1:9 Whosoever transgresseth, and abideth not in **the doctrine of Christ**, hath not God. He that abideth in **the doctrine of Christ**, he hath both the Father and the Son.)

COM (Gill: 1Jo 2:23 "Such an one does not hold the **true doctrine of the Father**, and does not appear to have true faith in him, true love unto him, or real interest in him, only by profession:")

KJV (**1NT/2**) Matthew 28:19 Go ye therefore, and teach all nations, baptizing them in the name of the Father, **and of the Son, and of the**

Holy Ghost:)
KJV (**1NT/1**) <u>Ephesians 3:21</u> Unto him be glory in the church by Christ Jesus throughout all ages, world **without end. Amen**.)
BOM <u>2 Nephi 32:9</u> But behold, I say unto you that ye must **pray always**, and **not faint**; that ye must not perform any thing unto the Lord save **in the first place** ye shall pray unto the Father (*7) in the name of Christ* that he will consecrate thy **performance** unto thee, that thy **performance** may be for the *welfare of thy soul.*

KJV (**2NT/3**) <u>Luke 21:36</u> Watch ye therefore, and **pray always**, that ye may be accounted worthy to escape all these things that shall come to pass, and to stand before the Son of man.)

COM Gill: <u>2Ti 1:3</u> "it becomes us to pray without ceasing: to **pray always, and not faint** and give out")

KJV (1/5) <u>Numbers 10:14</u> **In the first place** went the standard of the camp of the children of Judah according to their armies: and over his host was Nahshon the son of Amminadab.)

COM Clarke: <u>Joh 16:23</u> "in the name of Jesus the Savior, because I have died to redeem you - **in the name of Christ** the Anointer, because I have ascended to send down the gift of the Holy Ghost."(Henry, Wesley, Gill)

KJV (**2NT/2**) <u>2 Corinthians 8:11</u> Now therefore perform the doing of it; that as there was a readiness to will, so there may be a **performance** also out of that which ye have.)

COM Gill uses the phrase "welfare of the soul" many times: <u>1Ti 4:8</u> "to the health of the body, and the **welfare** of the **soul**;")

***BOM <u>2 Nephi 33:9</u> I also have charity for the Gentiles. But behold, for none of these can I hope except they shall be **reconciled** unto Christ, and enter into the **narrow gate**, and walk in the **strait** path **which leads to life**, and *continue in the path* until *the end* of *the day of (9) probation.* (15th Century)

KJV (**1NT/1**) <u>Romans 5:10</u> For if, when we were enemies, we were **reconciled** to God by the death of his Son, much more, being **reconciled**, we shall be saved by his life.)

KJV (**1NT/1**) <u>Matthew 7:14</u> Because **strait** is **the gate, and narrow** is the way, which **leadeth** unto **life**, and few there be that find it.)

COM Clarke: <u>Mat 8:12</u> "and now the **day of probation** is ended,)

COM Clark: <u>Gen 19:38</u> "To begin in the good way is well; to **continue in the path** is better; and to persevere **unto the end**, best of all.")

BOM <u>2 Nephi 33:11</u> And if they are not the words of Christ, **judge ye** -- for Christ will show unto you, **with power and great glory**, that they are his words, **at the last day**; and you and I shall stand face to face before *his bar*; and ye shall know that I have been commanded of him to write these things, notwithstanding my **weakness.**

> **KJV (3NT/5)** <u>Acts 4:19</u> But Peter and John answered and said unto them, Whether it be right in the sight of God to hearken unto you more than unto God, **judge ye.**)
>
> **KJV (2NT/5)** <u>Matthew 24:30</u> And then shall appear the sign of the Son of man in heaven: and then shall all the tribes of the earth mourn, and they shall see the Son of man coming in the clouds of heaven **with power and great glory.**)
>
> **KJV (5NT/49)** <u>John 6:44</u> No man can come to me, except the Father which hath sent me draw him: and I will raise him up **at the last day.**)
>
> **COM** Gill: <u>Mat 24:48</u> "or by death, to summon him to **his bar**; or at judgment, to give in his account of his stewardship." (Clarke)
>
> **Note:** As we have seen preveiosuly the concept of being before "his bar" is a modern concept.
>
> **KJV (7NT/19)** <u>1 Corinthians 1:25</u> Because the foolishness of God is wiser than men; and the **weakness** of God is stronger than men.)

***BOM <u>2 Nephi 33:14</u> And you that will not (*17) partake of the* **goodness of God**, and respect the *words of the Jews*, and also my words, and the words which shall **proceed forth out of the mouth** of **the Lamb of God,** behold, **I bid you** an *everlasting farewell*, for these words shall condemn you **at the last day**.

> **COM** Clarke: <u>1Co 13:13</u> "Without faith it is impossible to please God; and without it, we can not **partake of the** grace of our Lord Jesus:"(Henry, Gill, Wesley)
>
> **KJV (2/8)** <u>Psalm 52:1</u> Why boastest thou thyself in mischief, O mighty man? **the goodness of God** endureth continually.)
>
> **COM** Clarke: <u>Joh 8:57</u> "but their foundation, which is no other than these **words of the Jews**, is but a very uncertain one.")
>
> **KJV (**<u>Matthew 15:18</u> But those things which **proceed out of the mouth** come **forth** from the heart; and they defile the man.)
>
> **KJV (2NT/35)** <u>John 1:29</u> The next day John seeth Jesus coming unto him, and saith, Behold **the Lamb of God**, which taketh away the sin of the world.)
>
> **KJV (1/2)** <u>Joshua 6:10</u> And Joshua had commanded the people, saying, Ye shall not shout, nor make any noise with your voice, neither shall any word **proceed out of** your **mouth**, until the day **I bid you** shout; then shall ye shout.)
>
> **COM** Henry: <u>Gen 48:8-22</u> "and **bid**ding **an everlasting farewell** to sin and sorrow.")
>
> **Note:** To bid and everlasting farewell is very unique and obviously from Henry.

KJV (5NT/49) <u>John 6:44</u> No man can come to me, except the Father which hath sent me draw him: and I will raise him up **at the last day**.)

***BOM <u>Intro to the Book of Jacob</u> The words of his preaching unto his brethren. He (2) confoundeth (*Note: Not in Commentaries or KJV*) a man who seeketh to (*2*) *overthrow the doctrine of* Christ. A few words concerning the (6) history (1485 AD) (*Note: Clarke, Henry, Wesley*) of the people of Nephi.

> **COM** Gill: <u>Mat 23:37</u> "In order to set aside, and **overthrow the doctrine of** grace,)
>
> **Note:** How very unique this phrase is, "overthrow the doctrine of".
>
> **KJV (2NT/7)** <u>Hebrews 6:1</u> Therefore leaving the principles of **the doctrine of Christ**, let us go on unto perfection; not laying again the foundation of repentance from dead works, and of faith toward God,)

***BOM <u>Jacob 1:15</u> And now **it came to pass (452/1353)** that the people of Nephi, under the reign of the second king, began to grow hard in their hearts, and (*2*) *indulge (1623) themselves* somewhat in (*1*) *wicked practices,* such as like unto David of old desiring many wives and concubines, and also Solomon, his son.

> **COM** Gill: <u>Job 21:7</u> "and **indulge themselves in** all the gratifications of sensual pleasures and delights;" (Clarke, Henry)
>
> **COM** Henry: <u>Amo 8:4-10</u> "By such **wicked practices** as these men show such a greediness of the world, such a love of themselves, such a contempt of mankind in general," (Clarke, Gill)
>
> **Note**: It is interesting that here the taking of many wives is called "wicked practices".

***BOM <u>Jacob 2:10</u> But, notwithstanding the greatness of the task, I must do according to the (13) strict (15th Century) (*Note: Henry, Clarke, Wesley*) commands of God, and tell you concerning your wickedness and abominations, in the presence of **the pure in heart**, and the broken heart, and under the (*3*) *glance (15th Century) of the piercing eye of the* Almighty God

> **KJV (1NT/5)** <u>Matthew 5:8</u> Blessed are **the pure in heart**: for they shall see God.)
>
> **COM**: Isaac Watts (1674-1748) Pastor who wrote many hymns and poems: "But his **all-searching eye** reveals The secrets of the night.").
>
> **COM** Clarke: <u>Son 4:9</u> ""Even one of thine eyes, or one **glance of thine eyes**, has been sufficient to deprive me of all power; it has completely overcome me;" for glance may be understood, and such forms of speech are common in all languages, when speaking on such subjects.")
>
> **COM** Henry: <u>Rom 2:17-29</u> "A form of knowledge may deceive men, but cannot impose upon **the piercing eye of the** heart-searching

God.")

Note: You can tell the sections were Joseph Smith completely makes up his own thoughts, because there are very few phrases from the King James Version of the Bible or the commentaries.

***BOM Jacob 2:13 And (*1*) *the hand of providence* hath smiled upon you most pleasingly, that you have obtained many riches; and because some of you have obtained more abundantly than that of your brethren ye are lifted up in the pride of your hearts, and wear **stiff neck**s and high heads because of the **costliness** of your apparel, and persecute your brethren because ye suppose that ye are better than they.

> **COM** Henry: Jer 17:5-11 "whereas they are but instruments in **the hand of Providence**." (Clarke, Gill)
>
> **Note:** Again "the hand of providence" is a modern phrase.
>
> **KJV** (2/2) Psalm 75:5 Lift not up your horn on high: speak not with a **stiff neck**.)
>
> **KJV** (**1NT/1**) Revelation 18:19 And they cast dust on their heads, and cried, weeping and wailing, saying, Alas, alas that great city, wherein were made rich all that had ships in the sea by reason of her **costliness**! for in one hour is she made desolate.)

BOM Jacob 2:15 O that he would show you that he can pierce you, and with one (3) glance (15th Century) of his eye he can smite you **to the dust**!

> **KJV** (4/5) Isaiah 25:12 And the fortress of the high fort of thy walls shall he bring down, lay low, and bring to the ground, even **to the dust**.)

***BOM Jacob 3:11 O my brethren, **hearken unto my words**; (*3*) *arouse* (*1593*) *the* (*3*) *faculties* (*14th Century*) *of* your *souls*; shake yourselves that ye may awake from the slumber of death; and loose yourselves from **the pains of hell** that ye may not become angels to **the devil**, to be **cast into** that **lake of fire and brimstone** which **is the second death**.

> **KJV** (1/14) Deuteronomy 18:19 And it shall come to pass, that whosoever will not **hearken unto my words** which he shall speak in my name, I will require it of him.)
>
> **COM** Gill: Luk 18:13 "and he did this to **arouse** and stir up all **the** powers and **faculties of** his **soul**, to call upon God.")
>
> **Note:** How very unique.
>
> **KJV** (1/4) Psalm 116:3 The sorrows of death compassed me, and **the pains of hell** gat hold upon me: I found trouble and sorrow.)
>
> **KJV** (**44NT/94**) Matthew 4:1 Then was Jesus led up of the Spirit into the wilderness to be tempted of **the devil**.)
>
> **KJV** (**1NT/1**) Revelation 20:14 And death and hell were cast into the **lake of fire**. This **is the second death**.) (**2NT/1**) Revelation 20:10 And the devil that deceived them was **cast into the lake of fire and**

brimstone, where the beast and the false prophet are, and shall be tormented day and night for ever and ever.)

***BOM <u>Jacob 4:2</u> But whatsoever things we write upon anything save it be upon plates must perish and vanish away; but we can write a few words upon plates, which will give our children, and also our beloved brethren, *(1) a small degree of knowledge* concerning us, or concerning their fathers –

> **COM** Gill: <u>Son 2:15</u> "and these, having but **a small degree of knowledge**, are more easily imposed upon and seduced by false teachers;")

***BOM <u>Jacob 4:8</u> Behold, **great and marvelous** are the works of the Lord. **How unsearchable are the depth**s of the mysteries of him; and *(1) it is impossible that man should* **find out** all **his ways**. And **no man knoweth** of his ways save it be revealed unto him; wherefore, brethren, despise not the **revelations of** God.

> **KJV (1NT/25)** <u>Revelation 15:3</u> And they sing the song of Moses the servant of God, and the song of the Lamb, saying, **Great and marvellous** are thy works, Lord God Almighty; just and true are thy ways, thou King of saints.)
>
> **COM** Gill: <u>Jer 31:37</u> "as **it is impossible that man should** know the measure of the heavens above;")
>
> **Note:** Notice that these are exactly the same concept using the same phrase, "it is impossible that man should…".
>
> **KJV** (*Note: Note how similar these verses are:* **(1NT/1)** <u>Romans 11:33</u> O the depth of the riches both of the wisdom and knowledge of God! **how unsearchable are** his judgments, and **his ways** past **finding out!**)
>
> **KJV (6/5)** <u>Deuteronomy 34:6</u> And he buried him in a valley in the land of Moab, over against Bethpeor: but **no man knoweth** of his sepulchre unto this day.)
>
> **KJV (1NT/5)** <u>2 Corinthians 12:1</u> It is not expedient for me doubtless to glory. I will come to visions and **revelations of** the Lord.)

***BOM <u>Jacob 4:17</u> And now, my beloved, *(3) How is it possible* that these, after having rejected the **sure foundation**, can ever build upon it, that it may become *the head of their corner*?

> **COM** Henry: <u>Isa 23:1-14</u> "And **how is it possible** that its ruin should be effected?""(Clarke, Gill)
>
> **Note**: Note here that in the commentary in Henry, he cross references 1 Peter 2:7 which Joseph Smith uses at the end of this verse: <u>Isa 28:14-22</u> "The promise of Christ in particular; for to him this is expressly applied in the New Testament, <u>1Pe 2:6-8</u>. He is that stone which has become **the head of the corner**.")
>
> **KJV** (<u>1 Peter 2:7</u> Unto you therefore which believe he is precious:

but unto them which be disobedient, the stone which the builders disallowed, the same is made **the head of the corner**,)

***BOM** Jacob 5:3 For behold, thus saith the Lord, I will liken thee, O house of Israel, like unto a **tame** olive-tree, which a man took and nourished in his vineyard; and it grew, and *waxed old, and began to decay.*

> **KJV (2NT/5)** James 3:8 But the tongue can no man **tame**; it is an unruly evil, full of deadly poison.)
>
> **KJV (4/3)** Genesis 18:12 Therefore Sarah laughed within herself, saying, After I am **waxed old** shall I have pleasure, my lord being old also?)
>
> **COM** Henry: Psa 89:38-52 "and yet **waxed old and began to decay** already.")

***BOM** Jacob 6:8 Behold, will ye reject these words? Will ye reject **the words of the prophets**; and will ye reject all the words which have been spoken concerning Christ, after so many have spoken concerning him; and deny *the good word of Christ*, and **the power of God**, and **the gift of the Holy Ghost (89NT/95)**, and quench **the Holy Spirit**, and **make a mock** of (*17) the great plan of redemption,* which hath been laid for you?

> **KJV (5/14)** 2 Chronicles 18:12 And the messenger that went to call Micaiah spake to him, saying, Behold, **the words of the prophets** declare good to the king with one assent; let thy word therefore, I pray thee, be like one of their's, and speak thou good.)
>
> **COM** Gill: Ecc 2:26 "and who have **the good word of Christ** dwelling in them," (Clarke)
>
> **Note:** The phrase "the good word of Christ" is very unique.
>
> **KJV (11NT/48)** Matthew 22:29 Jesus answered and said unto them, Ye do err, not knowing the scriptures, nor **the power of God**.)
>
> **KJV (2NT/3)** Acts 2:38 Then Peter said unto them, Repent, and be baptized every one of you in the name of Jesus Christ for the remission of sins, and ye shall receive **the gift of the Holy Ghost**.)
>
> **KJV (2NT/11)** Ephesians 4:30 And grieve not **the holy Spirit** of God, whereby ye are sealed unto the day of redemption.)
>
> **COM** Henry: 1Th 5:16-22 "so we must be careful not to **quench the Holy Spirit** by indulging carnal lusts and affections, or minding only earthly things.")
>
> **KJV (1/2)** Proverbs 14:9 Fools **make a mock** at sin: but among the righteous there is favour.)
>
> **COM** Gill: Tit 2:14 "and **the plan of redemption** being drawn in the everlasting council, and the whole adjusted and fixed in the covenant of peace;" (Clarke)

BOM Jacob 6:12 O be wise; *what can I say more?*

> **COM** Gill: Joh 21:16 "expressing himself in the same language as

before; and it is, as if he should say, Lord, **what can I say more?** I can say no more than I have done, and by that I abide:")

***BOM** Jacob 6:13 Finally, I **bid** you **farewell**, until I shall *meet* you before the pleasing *bar of God*, which bar **striketh** the **wicked** with (47) awful (13th Century) dread and fear. Amen.

> **KJV (1NT/4)** Luke 9:61 And another also said, Lord, I will follow thee; but let me first go **bid** them **farewell**, which are at home at my house.)
>
> **COM** Gill: Pro 22:2 "and the wicked rich and poor meet together to commit sin; and they meet together in the grave (q), where there is no difference; and they will **meet** at the **bar of God** at the last day, and in hell, where they will be together for evermore;")
>
> **KJV (1/1)** Job 34:26 He **striketh** them as **wicked** men in the open sight of others;)
>
> **COM** Henry: 2Ch 7:1-11 "They bowed their faces to the ground and worshipped, thus expressing their **awful dread** of the divine majesty, their cheerful submission to the divine authority," (Wesley)

BOM Jacob 7:2 And **it came to pass (452/1353)** that he began to preach among the people, and to declare unto them that there should be no Christ. And he preached many things which were flattering unto the people; and this he did that he might (2) *overthrow* **the doctrine of Christ**.

> **COM** Gill: Mat 23:37 "In order to set aside, and **overthrow the doctrine of** grace,)
>
> **KJV (2NT/7)** Hebrews 6:1 Therefore leaving the principles of **the doctrine of Christ**, let us go on unto perfection; not laying again the foundation of repentance from dead works, and of faith toward God,)

BOM Jacob 7:19 And he said: **I fear lest** I have committed *the (2) unpardonable (15th Century) sin*, for I have lied unto God; for I denied the Christ, and said that I believed the **scriptures**; and they truly testify of him. And because I have thus lied unto God *I greatly fear* lest my case shall be (47) awful (13th Century) (***Henry, Clarke, Wesley)***; but I confess unto God.

> **KJV (2NT/6)** 2 Corinthians 11:3 But **I fear, lest** by any means, as the serpent beguiled Eve through his subtilty, so your minds should be corrupted from the simplicity that is in Christ.)
>
> **COM** Gill: Mar 3:30 "they knew in their own consciences they were works which were wrought by the finger and Spirit of God, and so were guilty of the sin against the Holy Ghost; **the unpardonable sin**, for which there is no remission:" (Henry, Clarke)
>
> **KJV (21NT/41)** Matthew 21:42 Jesus saith unto them, Did ye never read in the **scriptures**, The stone which the builders rejected, the same is become the head of the corner: this is the Lord's doing, and it is marvellous in our eyes?)

COM Gill: <u>1Sa 20:10</u> "**I greatly fear** he will chide thee for my sake;")

BOM <u>Words of Mormon 1:11</u> And they were (*18*) *handed down* from king Benjamin, from generation to generation until they have fallen into my hands. And I, Mormon, pray to God that they may be preserved from this time henceforth. And I know that they will be preserved; for there are great things written upon them, out of which my people and their brethren shall be judged at the (*6*) *great and last day*, according to **the word of God (45/89)** which is written.

COM Clarke: <u>Mat 15:2</u> "that had been successively **handed down from** Moses through every **generation**, but not committed to writing.")

COM Gill: <u>Mat 13:39</u> "or else the day of judgment, **the great and last day**, when the heavens and the earth,")

*****BOM** <u>Mosiah 2:39</u> **And now I say unto you**, that mercy hath no (*15*) claim (14th Century) on that man; therefore his *final* (*2*) *doom* (*12th Century*) (*Note: Clarke, Henry, Wesley,* Gill*) is to endure a never-ending torment.

KJV (**1NT/18**) <u>Acts 5:38</u> **And now I say unto you**, Refrain from these men, and let them alone: for if this counsel or this work be of men, it will come to nought:)

COM Henry: <u>Rom 14:1-23</u> "expecting our **final doom** from him, which will be eternally conclusive.")

Note: "Final doom" is a modern phrase.

BOM <u>Mosiah 3:5</u> For behold, **the time cometh**, and (*3*) *is not far distant*, that **with power, the Lord Omnipotent** who **reigneth**, who **was, and is** from all eternity to all eternity, shall come down from heaven **among the children of men**, and shall dwell in a tabernacle of clay, and shall go forth amongst men, working (*11*) *mighty miracles*, such as **heal**ing **the sick, rais**ing **the dead,** causing **the lame to walk, the blind to** receive their sight, and **the deaf to hear** and curing **all manner of disease**s.

KJV (**2NT/15**) <u>John 16:2</u> They shall put you out of the synagogues: yea, **the time cometh**, that whosoever killeth you will think that he doeth God service.)

COM Clarke: <u>Hab 2:3</u> "it will not tarry longer than the prescribed time, and this time **is not far distant**. Wait for it.")

KJV (9/10) <u>Psalm 65:6</u> Which by his strength setteth fast the mountains; being girded **with power**:)

KJV (**1NT/4**) <u>Revelation 19:6</u> And I heard as it were the voice of a great multitude, and as the voice of many waters, and as the voice of mighty thunderings, saying, Alleluia: for **the Lord** God **omnipotent reigneth**.)

KJV (**1NT/1**) <u>Revelation 4:8</u> And the four beasts had each of them six wings about him; and they were full of eyes within: and they rest not day and night, saying, Holy, holy, holy, LORD God Almighty, which **was, and is**, and is to come.)

KJV (2/30) Psalm 21:10 Their fruit shalt thou destroy from the earth, and their seed from **among the children of men**.)

COM Clarke: Deu 33:23 "through Christ's constant residence, and the **mighty miracles** he wrought in it,")

KJV (1NT/2) Matthew 10:8 **Heal the sick**, cleanse the lepers, **raise the dead**, cast out devils: freely ye have received, freely give.)

KJV (1NT/2) Matthew 15:31 Insomuch that the multitude wondered, when they saw the dumb to speak, the maimed to be whole, **the lame to walk, and the blind to** see: and they glorified the God of Israel.)

KJV (1NT/2) Mark 7:37 And were beyond measure astonished, saying, He hath done all things well: he maketh both **the deaf to hear**, and the dumb to speak.)

KJV (2NT/4) Matthew 10:1 And when he had called unto him his twelve disciples, he gave them power against unclean spirits, to cast them out, and to heal all manner of sickness and **all manner of** disease.)

*****BOM** Mosiah 3:8 And he shall be called **Jesus Christ, the Son of God** the Father of heaven and earth, *(2) the Creator of all things* from the beginning; and his mother shall be called Mary.

KJV (1NT/11) Mark 1:1 The beginning of the gospel of **Jesus Christ, the Son of God**;)

COM Clarke: Rev 22:16 "for he is **the Creator of all things**," (Gill, Henry, Wesley)

BOM Mosiah 3:9 And lo, he cometh unto his own, that salvation might come unto **the children of men (22/131)** even through faith on his name; and even **after all this** they shall consider him a man, **and say** that **he hath a devil**, and shall **scourge him**, and shall **crucify him**.

KJV (2/4) 2 Chronicles 21:18 And **after all this** the LORD smote him in his bowels with an incurable disease.)

KJV (3NT/2) Luke 7:33 For John the Baptist came neither eating bread nor drinking wine; **and ye say, He hath a devil**.)

KJV (2NT/3) Luke 18:33 And they shall **scourge him**, and put him to death: and the third day he shall rise again.)

COM Note here that Joseph Smith uses a paraphrase of Henry's compilation of what Matthew says: Henry: Mat 20:17-19 "and delivered to the Gentiles, that they shall mock him, and **scourge him, and crucify him**."

KJV (Matthew 20:19 And shall deliver him to the Gentiles to mock, and to **scourge**, and to **crucify him**: and the third day he shall rise again.*)*

***BOM Mosiah 4:3 And **it came to pass (452/1353)** that after they **had spoken these words**, the Spirit of the Lord came upon them, and they **were filled with joy**, having received a **remission of their sins**, and having *peace of (5) conscience (13th Century)*, because of the **exceeding faith** which they had in Jesus Christ who should come, *(40) according to the words* which king Benjamin had spoken unto them.

> KJV (2/19) Job 42:7 And it was so, that after the LORD **had spoken these words** unto Job, the LORD said to Eliphaz the Temanite, My wrath is kindled against thee, and against thy two friends: for ye have not spoken of me the thing that is right, as my servant Job hath.)

> KJV (**2NT/9**) Acts 13:52 And the disciples **were filled with joy**, and with the **Holy Ghost**.)

> KJV (**1NT/8**) Luke 1:77 To give knowledge of salvation unto his people by the **remission of their sins**,)

> COM Gill: 1Ti 1:2 "and by "peace" he may design **peace of conscience** through the blood of Christ," (Clarke, Henry, Wesley)

> Note: How unique is the phrase "peace of conscience". Notice that the word "conscience" is not in the KJV.

> KJV (**1NT/11**) 1 Timothy 1:14 And the grace of our Lord was **exceeding** abundant with **faith** and love which is in Christ Jesus.)

> COM Henry: Hos 6:4-11 "I have slain them by my judgments, **according to the words** of my mouth." (Clarke, Gill)

BOM Mosiah 4:9 Believe in God; **believe that he is, and that he** created all things, both in heaven and in earth; believe that he has all wisdom, and *all power, both in heaven and in earth;* believe that man doth not comprehend all the things which the Lord can comprehend.

> KJV (**1NT/1**) Hebrews 11:6 But without faith it is impossible to please him: for he that cometh to God must **believe that he is, and that he** is a rewarder of them that diligently seek him.)

> COM Gill: Rev 10:8 "Jesus Christ, who has **all power both in heaven and in earth**;" (Clarke, Henry)

***BOM Mosiah 4:18 But I say unto you, **O man**, whosoever doeth this the same hath great cause to repent; and except he repenteth of that which **he hath done** he perisheth forever, and hath no *interest in the kingdom of God*.

> KJV (**1NT/1**) Romans 9:20 Nay **but, O man**, who art thou that repliest against God? Shall the thing formed say to him that formed it, Why hast thou made me thus?)

> KJV (38/6) Isaiah 12:5 Sing unto the LORD; for **he hath done** excellent things: this is known in all the earth.)

> COM Henry: Luk 12:54-59 "of securing to yourselves an **interest in the kingdom of God** and the privileges of that kingdom?")

BOM Mosiah 4:26 And now, for the sake of these things which I have spoken unto you -- that is, for the sake of retaining a remission of your sins **from day to day**, that ye may walk **guiltless** before God -- **I would that ye** should impart of your substance to the poor, every man according to that which he hath, such as *feeding the hungry, clothing the naked, visiting the* sick and administering to their relief, both spiritually and (5) temporally (14th Century), according to their wants.

> **KJV** (6/10) 1 Chronicles 16:23 Sing unto the LORD, all the earth; shew forth **from day to day** his salvation.)
>
> **KJV** (10/8) Exodus 20:7 Thou shalt not take the name of the LORD thy God in vain; for the LORD will not hold him **guiltless** that taketh his name in vain.)
>
> **KJV** (**2NT/56**) Colossians 2:1 For **I would that ye** knew what great conflict I have for you, and for them at Laodicea, and for as many as have not seen my face in the flesh;)
>
> **COM** Gill: Jam 3:17 "of compassion and beneficence to the poor; **feeding the hungry, clothing the naked, visiting the** widows and fatherless in their affliction; and doing all other good works and duties, both with respect to God and man, as fruits of grace, and of the Spirit:")

***BOM Mosiah 4:27 And see that **all** these **things** are **done in wisdom** and order; for it is not requisite that a man should run faster than he has strength. And again, it is **expedient** that he should be diligent, that thereby he might *win the prize*; therefore, **all things** must **be done in order**.

> **KJV** (**7NT/62**) John 11:50 Nor consider that it is **expedient** for us, that one man should die for the people, and that the whole nation perish not.)
>
> **COM** Gill: Ecc 9:11-12 "One would think that the lightest of foot should, in running, **win the prize**; and yet the race is not always to the swift;")
>
> **Note:** Wining a prize is again a modern concept.
>
> **KJV** (**1NT/1**) 1 Corinthians 14:40 Let **all things be done** decently and **in order**.)

***BOM Mosiah 5:7 And now, because of the covenant which ye have made ye shall be called (3) *the children of Christ*, his sons, and his daughters; for behold, this day he hath *spiritually begotten* you; for ye say that your hearts are changed through faith on his name; therefore, ye are born of him and have become his sons and his daughters.

> **COM** Gill: Psa 127:5 "**the children of Christ** and of the church;")
>
> **Note:** Obviously the phrase "the children of Christ" is modern because the idea did not take place until after Christ, especially since this phrase in Mosiah was supposed to have been written in

approximately 127 BC.

    COM Clarke: <u>1Pe 1:3</u> "and none are children of God till they are **spiritually begotten** and born again.")

BOM <u>Mosiah 6:27</u> And because he said unto them that Christ was the God, *the Father of all things,* and said that he should **take upon** him the image of man, and it should be the image after which man was created in the beginning; or *(13) in other words,* he said that man was created after the image of God, and that God should come down **among the children of men**, and **take upon** him **flesh and blood**, and go forth **upon the face of the earth-**

    COM Clarke: <u>1Co 1:23</u> ""They count us mad, that after the eternal God, **the Father of all things**,")

    KJV (**1NT/26**) <u>2 Corinthians 8:4</u> Praying us with much intreaty that we would receive the gift, and **take upon** us the fellowship of the ministering to the saints.)

    COM Clarke: <u>Gen 25:34</u> "**in other words**, let us now believe-love-obey."(Henry, Wesley)

    KJV (2/30) <u>Psalm 21:10</u> Their fruit shalt thou destroy from the earth, and their seed from among the **children of men**.)

    KJV (**5NT/9**) <u>Matthew 16:17</u> And Jesus answered and said unto him, Blessed art thou, Simon Barjona: for **flesh and blood** hath not revealed it unto thee, but my Father which is in heaven.)

    KJV (12/26) <u>Numbers 12:3</u> Now the man Moses was very meek, above all the men which were **upon the face of the earth**.)

***BOM <u>Mosiah 8:17</u> But **A seer** can know of things which are past, and also of things which are to come, and by them shall all things be revealed, or, rather, shall **secret things** be made manifest, and **hidden things** shall come **to light**, and things which are not known *(10) shall be made known* by them, and also things *(10) shall be made known* by them *which otherwise could not be known.*

    KJV (2/5)<u>1 Samuel 9:9</u> (Beforetime in Israel, when a man went to enquire of God, thus he spake, Come, and let us go to the seer: for he that is now called a Prophet was beforetime called **a Seer**.)

    KJV (2/1) <u>Daniel 2:22</u> He revealeth the deep and **secret things**: he knoweth what is in the darkness, and the light dwelleth with him.)

    KJV (1NT/1) <u>1 Corinthians 4:5</u> Therefore judge nothing before the time, until the Lord come, who both will bring **to light** the **hidden things** of darkness, and will make manifest the counsels of the hearts: and then shall every man have praise of God.)

    COM Henry: <u>Act 4:5-14</u> "and it **shall be made known** to all the people of Israel," (Clarke)

    COM Gill: <u>Dan 9:22</u> "to teach thee the knowledge and give thee the understanding of **secret things, which otherwise could not be**

known;"
Note: Notice that this quote from Gill above matches the same concepts in this verse of Mosiah and as with many of Joseph Smith's duplications from the commentaries ends the same "which otherwise could not be know".

BOM Mosiah 12:2 Yea, wo be unto this generation! And the Lord said unto me: **Stretch forth thy hand** and prophesy saying: Thus saith the Lord, it shall come to pass that this generation, because of their iniquities, shall be brought into bondage, and shall *be smitten on the cheek*; yea, and shall be driven by men, and shall be slain; and **the vultures** of the air, and the dogs, yea, and the wild beasts, shall devour their flesh.

> **KJV (1NT/1)** Luke 6:10 And looking round about upon them all, he said unto the man, **Stretch forth thy hand**. And he did so: and his hand was restored whole as the other.)
> **COM** Gill: Job 16:10 "to be **smitten on the cheek** is a reproach itself," (Henry)
> **KJV** (2/1) Psalm 3:7 Arise, O LORD; save me, O my God: for thou hast **smitten** all mine enemies upon the **cheek** bone; thou hast broken the teeth of the ungodly.)
> **KJV** (1/2) Isaiah 34:15 There shall the great owl make her nest, and lay, and hatch, and gather under her shadow: there shall **the vultures** also be gathered, every one with her mate.)

BOM Mosiah 16:3 For they are *carnal and devilish*, and **the devil** has power over them; yea, even **that old serpent** that did **beguile** our *(13) first parents,* **(20NT/22)** which was the cause of their fall; which was the cause of **all mankind** becoming carnal, **sensual, devilish, knowing evil** from **good,** *(4) subjecting* (*14th Century) themselves to* **the devil**

> **KJV (1NT/6)** James 3:15 This wisdom descendeth not from above, but is earthly, **sensual, devilish**.)
> **COM** Clarke: Exo 1:22 "through which he becomes **carnal and devilish**.")
> **KJV (2NT/2)** Revelation 12:9 And the great dragon was cast out, **that old serpent**, called the Devil, and Satan, which deceiveth the whole world: he was cast out into the earth, and his angels were cast out with him.)
> **KJV (2NT/1)** Colossians 2:4 And this I say, lest any man should **beguile** you with enticing words.)
> **COM** Henry: Gen 2:25 "of which the condition of **our first parents** in the garden of paradise is justly supposed to have been an expressive emblem.")
> **KJV** (1/20) Job 12:10 In whose hand is the soul of every living thing, and the breath of **all mankind**.)

KJV (1/1) <u>Genesis 3:5</u> For God doth know that in the day ye eat thereof, then your eyes shall be opened, and ye shall be as gods, **knowing good** and **evil**.)

COM Gill: <u>Mat 10:32</u> "and **subjecting themselves to** his ordinances," (Henry)

BOM <u>Mosiah 16:4</u> Thus **all mankind** were lost; and behold, they would have been *(1) endlessly (12th century) lost* were it not that God redeemed his people from their lost and *(7) fallen state.*

KJV (1/20) <u>Job 12:10</u> In whose hand is the soul of every living thing, and the breath of **all mankind**.)

COM Clarke: <u>1Co 15:54</u> "God is represented as swallowing him up; or that eternity gulps him down; so that he is **endlessly lost** and absorbed in its illimitable waste.")

COM Clarke: <u>Gen 3:1</u> "That man is in a **fallen state**")

BOM <u>Mosiah 17:13</u> And **it came to pass (452/1353)** that they **took** him **and bound him, and scourged** his skin with *(1) faggots (14th Century),* yea, **even unto death**.

KJV (*Note: Continuing the same use of John as above:* **(1NT/1)** <u>John 18:12</u> Then the band and the captain and officers of the Jews **took** Jesus, **and bound him**,)

KJV (*Note: Again continuing the same:* <u>John 19:1</u> Then Pilate therefore took Jesus, **and scourged** him)

COM Gill: <u>Pro 12:10</u> "as they call them, are dark dungeons and stinking prisons, racks and tortures, fire and **faggots**;" (Clarke)

KJV (3/5) <u>Psalm 48:14</u> For this God is our God for ever and ever: he will be our guide **even unto death**.)

BOM <u>Mosiah 21:13</u> And they did **humble themselves even to the dust,** *(4) subjecting themselves to the yoke of* bondage, **submitting** themselves to be smitten, and to be driven **to and fro**, and burdened, according to the desires of their enemies.

KJV (1/25) <u>2 Chronicles 7:14</u> If my people, which are called by my name, shall **humble themselves**, and pray, and seek my face, and turn from their wicked ways; then will I hear from heaven, and will forgive their sin, and will heal their land.)

KJV (4/5) <u>Isaiah 25:12</u> And the fortress of the high fort of thy walls shall he bring down, lay low, and bring to the ground, **even to the dust**.)

COM Gill: <u>Col 2:23</u> "or rather in **subjecting themselves to the yoke of** the law,)

KJV **(1NT/1)** <u>Ephesians 5:21</u> **Submitting** yourselves one to another in the fear of God.)

KJV (23/6) <u>Genesis 8:7</u> And he sent forth a raven, which went forth

to and fro, until the waters were dried up from off the earth.)

BOM <u>Mosiah 22:12</u> And they had taken all their gold, and silver, and their precious things, which they could carry, and also their (37) provisions with them, into the wilderness; and they *pursued their journey.*

> **KJV** (***The words gold, silver and precious things are used in the BOM 22 times.*** (8/22) <u>2 Chronicles 21:3</u> And their father gave them great gifts of **silver**, and of **gold, and** of **precious things**, with fenced cities in Judah:)
>
> **COM** Gill: <u>Mat 2:10</u> "and they **pursued their journey** with inexpressible delight, till they came to the place where the illustrious person was they were seeking after.")

BOM <u>Mosiah 24:5</u> And they were a people (*1) friendly one with another;* nevertheless they knew not God; neither did the brethren of Amulon teach them anything concerning the Lord their God, neither the law of Moses; nor did they teach them the words of Abinadi;

> **COM** Henry: <u>Eph 4:2-16</u> "and makes them live **friendly one with another**.")

BOM <u>Mosiah 24:15</u> And now **it came to pass (452/1353)** that the burdens which were laid upon Alma and his brethren were made light; yea, the Lord did strengthen them that they could bear up their burdens with ease, and they did submit *cheerfully and with patience* to all the will of the Lord.

> **COM** Gill: <u>1Pe 5:9</u> "and therefore should not be surprised and staggered by them, nor think them strange, but endure them without murmuring, **and with patience** and **cheerfulness**; since they are the "same afflictions" and trials which others have been exercised with in all ages:")

BOM <u>Mosiah 24:19</u> **And** in the morning **the Lord caused a deep sleep to** come upon the Lamanites, yea, and all their task-masters were *in a profound sleep.*

> **KJV** (1/1) <u>Genesis 2:21</u> **And the LORD** God **caused a deep sleep to** fall upon Adam, and he slept: and he took one of his ribs, and closed up the flesh instead thereof;)
>
> **COM** Henry: <u>Jdg 5:26</u> "Observing him to be **in a profound sleep**")

BOM <u>Mosiah 25:8</u> For they *knew not what to think*; for when they beheld those that had been delivered (*26) out of bondage* they were filled with (*11) exceedingly great joy* .

> **COM** Gill: <u>Gen 45:26</u> "it amazed him, he **knew not what to think**, or say or believe about it;")
>
> **COM** Henry: <u>Isa 49:7-12</u> "but they are applicable to that guidance of divine grace which all God's spiritual Israel are under, from their release **out of bondage** to their settlement in the heavenly Canaan." (Clarke, Wesley)

BOM Mosiah 26:31 And ye shall also *forgive one another* your *trespasses*; for **verily I say unto you (48NT/46)**, he that forgiveth not his neighbor's trespasses when he says that he repents, the same hath brought himself *(5) under condemnation.*

> **COM** Gill: Mat 18:35 "and should also pray to God that he would forgive also. It is certainly the will of God, that we should **forgive one another** all **trespasses** and offences.")
>
> **COM** Clarke: Joh 20:23 "They who believed on the Son of God, in consequence of their preaching, had their sins remitted; and they who would not believe were declared to lie **under condemnation.**" (Henry)

BOM Mosiah 26:37 And **it came to pass (452/1353)** that Alma did *(1) regulate (15th Century) all the affairs of the church* **(76/259)**; and they began again to have peace and to *(8) prosper exceedingly* in *(3) the affairs of the church (76/259),* **walk**ing **circumspectly** before God, receiving many, and baptizing many.

> **COM** Clarke: 1Co 4:17 "This person will also inform you of the manner in which I **regulate all the Church**es;")
>
> **COM** Gill: 2Co 2:12 "who was to give him an account of **the affairs of the church** at Corinth," (Henry, Wesley, Clarke)
>
> **KJV (1NT/1)** Ephesians 5:15 See then that ye **walk circumspectly**, not as fools, but as wise,)

BOM Mosiah 27:9 And he became a great hinderment (*Note: Not in KJV or Dictionary or Commentaries)* to *the prosperity* of **the church (76/259) of God**; *stealing away the hearts* of the people; causing much **dissension** among the people; giving a chance for the enemy of God to exercise his power over them.

> **COM** Similar: Gill: Pro 26:1 "and **hinder the prosperity** of the commonwealth;")
>
> **KJV (8NT/31)** Acts 20:28 Take heed therefore unto yourselves, and to all the flock, over the which the Holy Ghost hath made you overseers, to feed **the church of God**, which he hath purchased with his own blood.)
>
> **COM** Gill: Joh 10:24 "or **stealing away** their **heart**,")
>
> **KJV** (*Note: Only in Acts:* **(3NT/23)** Acts 15:2 When therefore Paul and Barnabas had no small **dissension** and disputation with them, they determined that Paul and Barnabas, and certain other of them, should go up to Jerusalem unto the apostles and elders about this question.)

BOM Mosiah 27:18 And now Alma and those that were with him fell again **to the earth**, for great was their astonishment; for with their own eyes they had beheld an angel of the Lord; and his **voice** was as thunder, which shook the earth; and they knew that there was nothing save **the power of God** that could shake the earth and cause it to tremble as though it would *part asunder.*

> **KJV (*Note: Again the same story of Paul:* (1NT/1)** <u>Acts 26:14</u> And when we were all fallen **to the earth**, I heard a **voice** speaking unto me, and saying in the Hebrew tongue, Saul, Saul, why persecutest thou me? it is hard for thee to kick against the pricks.)
>
> **KJV (11NT/48)** <u>Matthew 22:29</u> Jesus answered and said unto them, Ye do err, not knowing the scriptures, nor **the power of God**.)
>
> **COM** Gill: Amo 6:11 "either with an earthquake, so that they shall **part asunder** and fall;")

***BOM <u>Mosiah 27:28</u> Nevertheless, after wading through **much tribulation**s, repenting **nigh unto death**, the Lord in mercy hath seen fit to snatch me out of *an everlasting burning*, and I am **born of God**.

> **KJV (1NT/4)** <u>Acts 14:22</u> Confirming the souls of the disciples, and exhorting them to continue in the faith, and that we must through **much tribulation** enter into the kingdom of God.)
>
> **KJV (2NT/1)** <u>Philippians 2:27</u> For indeed he was sick **nigh unto death**: but God had mercy on him; and not on him only, but on me also, lest I should have sorrow upon sorrow.)
>
> **COM** Gill: <u>Isa 33:14</u> "So the Targum interprets it of the place where the ungodly are to be judged and delivered into hell, **an everlasting burning**.")
>
> **KJV (5NT/9)** <u>1 John 3:9</u> Whosoever is **born of God** doth not commit sin; for his seed remaineth in him: and he cannot sin, because he is **born of God**.)

***BOM <u>Mosiah 29:10</u> And now let us be wise and look forward to these things, and do that which will *make for the peace of* this people.

> **COM** Gill: <u>Act 15:29</u> "it will be doing a good thing, and **make for the peace of** the churches;")

BOM <u>Mosiah 29:19</u> And were it not for the (1) interposition (14th Century) (*Note:* Gill**, Clarke, Henry, Wesley)** of their all-wise Creator, (*30) and this because* of their sincere repentance, they (*5) must (6) unavoidably (1577)* remain in bondage until now.

> **COM** <u>2Ki 13:23</u> Clarke: "**and this because of** his covenant with their fathers:" (Henry)
>
> **COM** Henry: <u>Jer 50:21-32</u> "Babylon's pride **must unavoidably** be her ruin;" (Clarke, Wesley)

BOM <u>Alma 1:1</u> Now **it came to pass (452/1353)** that in the first year of the reign of the judges over the people of Nephi, (*3) from this time forward*, king *****BOM Mosiah** having gone **the way of all the earth**, having warred **a good warfare**, *walking uprightly before* God, leaving none to **reign in his stead**; nevertheless he had established laws, and they were acknowledged by the people; *therefore they were (7) obliged (14th Century) to abide by the laws* which he had made.

> **COM** Gill: <u>Mat 22:46</u> "captious, and troublesome generation of men, **from this time forward**, to the time of his sufferings," (Henry, Clarke)
> **KJV** (2/5) <u>1 Kings 2:2</u> I go **the way of all the earth**: be thou strong therefore, and shew thyself a man;)
> **KJV** (**1NT/1**) <u>1 Timothy 1:18</u> This charge I commit unto thee, son Timothy, according to the prophecies which went before on thee, that thou by them mightest war **a good warfare**;)
> **COM** Clarke: <u>1Pe 5:9</u> "and **walking uprightly before** him.")
> **KJV** (1/12) <u>2 Chronicles 1:8</u> And Solomon said unto God, Thou hast shewed great mercy unto David my father, and hast made me to **reign in his stead**.)
> **COM** Clarke: <u>Mat 19:9</u> "and as the question was not settled by the schools of Shammai and Hillel, so as to ground national practice on it **therefore they were obliged to abide by** the positive declaration of the law,")

BOM <u>Alma 1:3</u> And he had gone about among the people, preaching to them that which he termed to be **the word of God (45/89)**, *(2) bearing down (**Note: Henry, Clarke, Wesley,** Gill)* against the **church (76/259)**; declaring unto the people that every priest and teacher ought *to become (3) popular (1548);* and they ought not to labor with their hands, but that they ought to be *(7) supported (14th Century)* by the people.

> **COM** Clarke: <u>1Co 2:4</u> "I used none of the means of which great orators avail themselves in order **to become popular**, and thereby to gain fame." (Henry, Wesley)

***BOM <u>Alma 1:15</u> And **it came to pass (452/1353)** that they took him; and his name was Nehor; and they carried him upon the top of the hill Manti, and there *he was caused*, or rather did acknowledge, *between the heavens and the earth*, that what he had taught to the people was *(1) contrary to **the word of God (45/89)**; and there he suffered *an (1) ignominious (15th Century) death*.

> **COM** Gill: <u>Psa 119:74</u> "on which **he was caused** to hope;" (Henry)
> **COM** Gill: <u>Joh 12:32</u> "and men, being lifted up **between the heavens and the earth**;")
> **COM** Henry: <u>Gen 3:1-5</u> "It was **contrary to the word of God**,")
> **COM** Henry: <u>Luk 24:36-49</u> "Redeemer that it dares face those daring enemies of his that had put him to **an ignominious death**," (Henry, Clarke)
> **Note:** How unique and modern the phrase "an ingnominious death".

***BOM <u>Alma 1:22</u> Nevertheless, there were many among them who began to be proud, and began to contend warmly with their adversaries, even unto blows; yea, they would smite one another *with their fists.*

COM Gill: Jer 37:15 "and **smote** him; either **with their fists,**")

******BOM** Alma 1:27 And they did impart of their substance, every man according to that which he had, to the poor, and the needy, and the sick, and the afflicted; and they did not wear *(8) costly apparel,* yet they were *neat and comely.*

COM Gill: 1Pe 3:4 "wearing of gold, or any **costly apparel,** can give to the body:" (Clarke, Wesley)

COM Gill: Lam 4:7 "appeared very **neat and comely,**")

BOM Alma 3:26 And in one year were *thousands and tens of thousands* of souls sent to *the eternal world,* that they might reap their rewards **according to their works,** whether they were good or whether they were bad, to reap *eternal (30) happiness (15th Century) or eternal misery,* according to the spirit which they **listed KJV (2NT/1)** Matthew 17:12 But I say unto you, That Elias is come already, and they knew him not, but have done unto him whatsoever they **listed.** Likewise shall also the Son of man suffer of them.) to obey, whether it be a good spirit or a bad one.

COM Gill: Psa 148:2 "And great numbers there are of them, **thousands and tens of thousands,**")

COM Clarke: Num 9:23 "he may call thee to march into **the eternal world**" (Henry)

KJV (3NT/13) Revelation 20:13 And the sea gave up the dead which were in it; and death and hell delivered up the dead which were in them: and they were judged every man **according to their works.**)

COM Clarke: Gen 25:23 "where the words are quoted; for it proves to a demonstration that this cannot be meant of God's arbitrary predestination of particular persons to **eternal happiness or misery,**")

BOM Alma 4:6 And **it came to pass (452/1353)** in the eighth year of the reign of the judges, that the people of the **church (76/259)** began to wax proud, because of their **exceeding riches,** and their fine silks, and their fine-twined linen, and because of their many flocks and herds, and their *gold* and their *silver,* and all manner of *precious things,* which **they had obtained** *by their industry*; and in all these things were they lifted up in the pride of their eyes, for they began to wear very *(8) costly apparel.*

KJV (1NT/4) Ephesians 2:7 That in the ages to come he might shew the **exceeding riches** of his grace in his kindness toward us through Christ Jesus.)

KJV (*Note: The words gold, silver and precious things are used in the BOM 22 times.* (8/22) 2 Chronicles 21:3 And their father gave them great gifts of **silver,** and of **gold, and** of **precious things,** with fenced cities in Judah:)

KJV (**1NT/4**) <u>Acts 27:13</u> And when the south wind blew softly, supposing that **they had obtained** their purpose, loosing thence, they sailed close by Crete.)

COM Henry: <u>1Ch 4:11-23</u> "got a good livelihood **by their industry**,")

COM Gill: <u>1Pe 3:4</u> "wearing of gold, or any **costly apparel**, can give to the body:" (Clarke, Wesley)

*****BOM** <u>Alma 4:8</u> For they saw and beheld with great sorrow that the people of the **church (76/259)** began to be lifted up in the pride of their eyes, and to *set their hearts* upon *riches* and upon (*9*) *the vain things of the world*, that they began to be **scornful**, one towards another, and they began to persecute those that did not believe *according to their own will and pleasure*.

COM Clarke: <u>Job 1:22</u> "He saw many who, when **riches** increased, **set their hearts** on them, and forgot God.")

COM Gill: <u>Pro 30:8</u> "and his affections taken off from **the vain things of the world**,")

KJV (**3/1**) <u>Psalm 1:1</u> Blessed is the man that walketh not in the counsel of the ungodly, nor standeth in the way of sinners, nor sitteth in the seat of the **scornful**.)

COM Gill: <u>Deu 20:10</u> "or were provoked to by their enemies; which was their own choice, and **according to their own will and pleasure**;")

*****BOM** <u>Alma 5:14</u> And now behold, I ask of you, my brethren of the **church (76/259)**, have ye spiritually been **born of God**? Have ye received his image in your countenances? Have ye experienced this *mighty change in* your *hearts*?

KJV (**5NT/9**) <u>1 John 3:9</u> Whosoever is **born of God** doth not commit sin; for his seed remaineth in him: and he cannot sin, because he is **born of God**.)

COM Henry: <u>Eph 1:15-23</u> ""We have heard him ourselves, we have felt a **mighty change in** our **hearts**,"")

*****BOM** <u>Alma 5:21</u> I say unto you, ye will know at that day that **ye cannot be saved**; for there can no man be saved except his *garments are washed white*; yea, his garments must be purified until they are cleansed from all stain, through the blood of him of whom it has been spoken by our fathers, who should come *to redeem his people from* their *sins*.

KJV (**2NT/9**) <u>Acts 15:1</u> And certain men which came down from Judaea taught the brethren, and said, Except ye be circumcised after the manner of Moses, **ye cannot be saved**.)

COM Gill: <u>Eph 2:13</u> "and their **garments are washed**, and made **white**;")

COM Gill: <u>Psa 111:9</u> "and Christ **to redeem his people from sin**,")

BOM <u>Alma 5:27</u> Have ye **walk**ed, keeping yourselves **blameless before God**? Could ye say, if ye were *called to die* at this time, within yourselves, that ye have been sufficiently humble? That your *garments* have been cleansed and *made white through the blood of Christ,* who will come to redeem his people from their sins?

> **KJV (1NT/1)** <u>Luke 1:6</u> And they were both righteous **before God**, **walk**ing in all the commandments and ordinances of the Lord **blameless.**)

> **COM** Gill: <u>Zec 1:8</u> "who, though not **called to die** for Christ, yet suffer persecution in various ways,")

> **COM** Gill: <u>Ecc 9:8</u> "the conversation **garments** of the saints are **made white in the blood of** Christ,")

BOM <u>Alma 6:5</u> Now **I would that ye** should understand that **the word of God (45/89)** was liberal unto all, that none were *deprived of the privilege of* assembling themselves together **to hear the word of God (45/89).**

> **KJV (2NT/56)** <u>Colossians 2:1</u> For **I would that ye** knew what great conflict I have for you, and for them at Laodicea, and for as many as have not seen my face in the flesh;)

> **COM** Henry: <u>Num 9:1-14</u> "Israelites that were thus **deprived of the privilege of** the passover,")

> **KJV (5NT/3)** <u>Luke 5:1</u> And it came to pass, that, as the people pressed upon him **to hear the word of God**, he stood by the lake of Gennesaret,)

BOM <u>Alma 7:7</u> For behold, I say unto you there be many things to come; and behold, there is one thing which is of more importance than they all -- for behold, the *time is not far distant,* that the Redeemer liveth and cometh among his people.

> **COM** Clarke: <u>Hab 2:3</u> "it will not tarry longer than the prescribed time, and this **time is not far distant**. Wait for it.")

BOM <u>Alma 7:20</u> **I perceive that** it has been made known unto you, by the testimony of his word, that he cannot walk in **crooked paths**; neither doth he vary from that which he hath said; neither hath he a **shadow of turning** from *the right* to the *left,* or from that which is right to that which is wrong; therefore, his course is one (*3) eternal round.*

> **KJV (1/1)** <u>Isaiah 59:8</u> The way of peace they know not; and there is no judgment in their goings: they have made them **crooked paths**: whosoever goeth therein shall not know peace.)

> **COM** Note the same meaning in "doth not vary" and this verse in James "with whom is no variableness")

> **KJV (1NT/1)** <u>James 1:17</u> Every good gift and every perfect gift is from above, and cometh down from the Father of lights, with whom is no variableness, neither **shadow of turning**.)

COM Gill: <u>Job 23:11</u> "from the way of God, did not turn aside from it to **the right** or **left**, or go into **crooked paths** with wicked men, or wickedly depart from his God, his ways and worship,")

COM Clarke: <u>Psa 102:27</u> "but God's **eternal round** has no completion.")

***BOM <u>Alma 8:10</u> Nevertheless Alma labored much in the spirit, *wrestling with God in* mighty *prayer*, that he would pour out his Spirit upon the people who were in the city; that he would also grant that he might baptize them unto repentance.

COM Henry: <u>Mat 20:29-34</u> "This **wrestling with God in prayer**, and makes us the fitter to receive mercy;" (Gill, Wesley)

BOM <u>Alma 8:14</u> And **it came to pass (452/1353)** that while he was journeying thither, being *(3) weighed down with sorrow*, wading through **much tribulation** and *(3) anguish of soul*, because of *(9) the wickedness of the people* who were in the city of Ammonihah, **it came to pass (452/1353)** while Alma was thus *(3) weighed down with sorrow*, behold an angel of the Lord appeared unto him, saying:

COM Wesley: <u>Mat 26:41</u> "How gentle a rebuke was this, and how kind an apology! especially at a time when our Lord's own mind was so **weighed down with sorrow**.")

KJV (1NT/4) <u>Acts 14:22</u> Confirming the souls of the disciples, and exhorting them to continue in the faith, and that we must through **much tribulation** enter into the kingdom of God.)

COM Gill: <u>Job 7:11</u> "but great **anguish of soul**;" (Henry, Clarke)

COM Wesley: <u>Num 25:6</u> "Bewailing the **wickedness of the people**, and the dreadful judgments of God," (Clarke, Henry)

COM Wesley: <u>Mat 26:41</u> "How gentle a rebuke was this, and how kind an apology! especially at a time when our Lord's own mind was so **weighed down with sorrow**.")

***BOM <u>Alma 9:8</u> Behold, *(4) O ye wicked and **perverse generation**, how have ye forgotten the tradition of your fathers; yea, how soon ye have forgotten the commandments of God.

COM The King James Version of the Bible tells us that Jesus said "faithless and perverse" but Gill gives us this exact phrase: <u>Mat 27:40</u> "and no other but that sign was to be given to that **wicked and perverse generation**,")

KJV *(2NT/1)* <u>Matthew 17:17</u> Then Jesus answered and said, **O** faithless and **perverse generation**, how long shall I be with you? how long shall I suffer you? bring him hither to me.)

BOM <u>Alma 9:24</u> For behold, the promises of the Lord are extended to the Lamanites, but they are not unto you if ye transgress; for has not the Lord expressly promised and firmly decreed, that if ye will *(6) rebel against him* that ye shall *utterly* be *destroyed from off the face of the earth*?

    COM <u>Exo 8:17</u> Henry: "God can fetch a scourge, with which to correct those that **rebel against him**."(Clarke, Wesley)

    KJV (8/16) <u>Joshua 1:18</u> Whosoever he be that doth **rebel against** thy commandment, and will not hearken unto thy words in all that thou commandest him, he shall be put to death: only be strong and of a good courage.)

    COM Gill: <u>Mar 13:20</u> "that nation and race of men must have been **utterly destroyed from off the face of the earth**:" (Clarke)

BOM <u>Alma 10:13</u> Nevertheless, there were some among them who thought to **question** them, that by their *cunning devices* they might catch them in their words, that they might find witness against them, that they might deliver them to their judges that they might be judged according to the law, and that they might be slain or **cast into prison**, according to the crime which they could make appear or witness against them.

    KJV (**14NT/14**) <u>Matthew 22:35</u> Then one of them, which was a lawyer, asked him a **question**, tempting him, and saying,)

    COM Gill: <u>2Co 11:14</u> "it is in this way he has succeeded in his enterprises and temptations; these are his wiles, stratagems, and **cunning devices**."

    KJV (**5NT/23**) <u>Matthew 4:12</u> Now when Jesus had heard that John was **cast into prison**, he departed into Galilee;)

BOM <u>Alma 10:14</u> Now it was those men who sought to destroy them, who were **lawyers,** who were hired or appointed by the people to administer the law at their times of trials, or at the trials of the crimes of the people before the judges.

    KJV (**5NT/17**) <u>Luke 7:30</u> But the Pharisees and **lawyers** rejected the counsel of God against themselves, being not baptized of him.)

    Note: This form of judicial process did not exist until modern times. But of course Joseph Smith new it existed.

***BOM <u>Alma 10:15</u> Now these **lawyers** were learned in all the *arts and cunning* of the people; and this was to enable them that they might be skilful in their profession.

    COM Clarke: <u>Ecc 7:27</u> "his powers of reason with her **arts and cunning**;")

BOM <u>Alma 10:19</u> Yea, well did Mosiah say, who was our last king, when he **was about to** deliver up the kingdom, having no one to (*17) confer (1570)* it upon, causing that this people should be governed by their own voices -- yea, well did he say that if the time should come that the voice of this people should choose iniquity, that is, if the time should come that this people should fall into transgression, they would be (*2) ripe for destruction.*

    KJV (**3/21**) <u>Acts 20:3</u> And there abode three months. And when the

Jews laid wait for him, as he **was about to** sail into Syria, he purposed to return through Macedonia.)

COM Gill: <u>Gen 27:25</u> "and in a good temper and disposition of mind to **confer** the blessing." (Henry, Clarke, Wesley)

COM Gill: <u>Rev 19:15</u> "who being **ripe for destruction**, are cast into it, and pressed, squeezed, and trodden down by the mighty power of Christ," (Henry, Clarke, Wesley)

***BOM <u>Alma 10:27</u> And now behold, I say unto you, that *the foundation of the destruction of* this people is beginning to be laid by the unrighteousness of your **lawyers** and your judges.

COM Gill: <u>Dan 11:2</u> "who laid **the foundation of the destruction of** the Persian monarchy by the Grecians.")

KJV (5NT/17) <u>Luke 7:30</u> But the Pharisees and **lawyers** rejected the counsel of God against themselves, being not baptized of him.)

BOM <u>Alma 11:45</u> Now, behold, I have spoken unto you concerning the death of the mortal body, and also concerning the resurrection of the mortal body. I say unto you that this mortal body is raised to an **immortal** body, that is from death, even from *(3)* the *first death* unto life, that they can die no more; their spirits (4) uniting (15th Century) (*Note: Clarke, Henry,* Gill*, Wesley)* with their bodies, never to be divided; thus the whole becoming spiritual and **immortal**, that they can no more see corruption.

KJV (1NT/19) <u>1 Timothy 1:17</u> Now unto the King eternal, **immortal**, invisible, the only wise God, be honour and glory for ever and ever. Amen.)

COM Gill: <u>Rev 2:11</u> "The phrase is Jewish, and is opposed to **the first death**, or the death of the body; which is the effect of sin, and is appointed of God, and which the people of God die as well as others; but the second death is peculiar to wicked men." (Henry, Clarke, Wesley)

BOM <u>Alma 12:3</u> Now Zeezrom, seeing that thou hast been taken in thy lying and craftiness, for **thou hast not lied unto men** only but thou hast lied **unto God**; for behold, he *knows all* thy *thoughts,* and **thou seest** that thy thoughts are made known unto us by his Spirit;

KJV (1NT/1) <u>Acts 5:4</u> Whiles it remained, was it not thine own? and after it was sold, was it not in thine own power? why hast thou conceived this thing in thine heart? **thou hast not lied unto men, but unto God**.)

COM Clarke: <u>Amo 4:13</u> "He formed the earth; he created the wind; **he knows** the inmost **thoughts** of the heart;") **COM** Gill: <u>Act 1:24</u> "for none **knows** the hearts of men, but God, who is the Maker of them; and he **knows all** the **thoughts**, counsels, and purposes of them, and the good or bad that is in them:")

KJV (15/10) <u>Genesis 13:15</u> For all the land which **thou seest**, to thee will I give it, and to thy seed for ever.)

*****BOM** <u>Alma 12:4</u> And **thou seest** that we know that thy plan was a very subtle plan, as to (*1) the (2) subtlety, (14th Century) of the devil, for to lie* and to deceive this people **that thou mightest** set them against us, to **revile** us and to cast us out –

KJV (15/10) <u>Genesis 13:15</u> For all the land which **thou seest**, to thee will I give it, and to thy seed for ever.)

COM Clarke: <u>Eph 5:33</u> "**the subtlety of the devil** in deceiving Eve." (word subtlety Henry, Wesley)

KJV (**44NT/94**) <u>Matthew 4:1</u> Then was Jesus led up of the Spirit into the wilderness to be tempted of **the devil**.)

COM Gill: <u>Tit 1:12</u> "Hence, with the Grecians, to "cretize", is proverbially used **for to lie**; this is a sin, than which nothing makes a man more like the devil, or more infamous among men, or more abominable to God.")

KJV (12/6) <u>Psalm 51:4</u> Against thee, thee only, have I sinned, and done this evil in thy sight: **that thou mightest** be justified when **thou** speakest, and be clear when **thou** judgest.)

KJV (2/25) <u>Exodus 22:28</u> Thou shalt not **revile** the gods, nor curse the ruler of thy people.)

*****BOM** <u>Alma 12:6</u> And behold I say unto you all that this was a snare of the adversary, which he has laid to catch this people, that he might *bring you into subjection* unto him, that he might encircle you about with his chains, that he might chain you down to **everlasting destruction**, according to the power of his captivity.

COM Clarke: <u>Rom 6:13</u> "Satan himself cannot force you to sin: till he wins over your will, he cannot **bring you into subjection**.")

KJV (**1NT/9**) <u>2 Thessalonians 1:9</u> Who shall be punished with **everlasting destruction** from the presence of the Lord, and from the glory of his power;)

BOM <u>Alma 12:10</u> And therefore, he that will harden his heart, the same receiveth the lesser portion of the word; and he that will not harden his heart, to him is given *the greater portion* of the word, until it is given unto him to know **the mysteries of God** until he know them in full.

COM Clarke: <u>Rom 8:39</u> "and consequently they have been deprived of **the greater portion** of the happiness designed for them by their bountiful Creator." (Gill)

KJV (**1NT/8**) <u>1 Corinthians 4:1</u> Let a man so account of us, as of the ministers of Christ, and stewards of **the mysteries of God**.)

*****BOM** <u>Alma 12:12</u> And Amulek hath spoken plainly concerning death, and being raised from this mortality to *a state of immortality*, and being brought before *(5) the bar of God*, to be judged according to our works.

> COM Gill: <u>Mat 22:30</u> "This was an usual way of speaking with them, to compare saints in **a state of immortality**,")
>
> **Note:** How very unique the phrase "a state of immortality".
>
> COM Gill: <u>Heb 10:31</u> "and signifies to be arrested by justice as a criminal, and be brought to **the bar of God**, and receive the sentence of condemnation;" (Clarke, Henry)

BOM <u>Alma 12:13</u> Then if our hearts have been hardened, yea, if we have *hardened* our *hearts against the word*, **insomuch (20/181)** that it has not been found in us, then will our state be (47) awful (13th Century) (Henry, Clarke, Wesley***), for then we shall be condemned.

> COM Henry: <u>Jer 6:9-17</u> "Nay, and this **hardened** their **hearts against the word** of God and his prophets.")

BOM <u>Alma 12:15</u> But this cannot be; we must come forth and stand before him in his glory, and in his power, and in his might, majesty, and dominion, and acknowledge to our *everlasting shame* that all *(2) his judgments are just*; that he is just in all his works, and that he is merciful unto **the children of men (22/131)**, and that he has all power to save every man that believeth on his name and **bring**eth **forth fruit meet for repentance**.

> COM Gill: <u>Rom 6:21</u> "shall be brought to **everlasting shame** and confusion hereafter." (Henry)
>
> COM Henry: <u>Joh 12:37-41</u> "Justa sunt judicia ejus, sed occulta - **His judgments are just**, but hidden.")
>
> KJV (**1NT/1**) <u>Matthew 3:8</u> **Bring forth** therefore **fruit**s **meet for repentance**:)

BOM <u>Alma 13:23</u> And they are made known unto us *in plain terms*, that we may understand, that we *(3) cannot err*; *(30) and this because* of our being wanderers in a strange land; therefore, we are thus **highly favored**, for we have these glad tidings declared unto us in all parts of our vineyard.

> COM Gill: <u>2Pe 3:10</u> "speak of it **in plain terms**." (Henry)
>
> COM Gill: <u>Rev 13:6</u> "giving out that he **cannot err**" (Clarke, Henry)
>
> COM <u>2Ki 13:23</u> Clarke: "**and this because** of his covenant with their fathers:" (Henry)
>
> KJV (**1NT/7**) <u>Luke 1:28</u> And the angel came in unto her, and said, Hail, thou that art **highly favoured**, the Lord is with thee: blessed art thou among women.)

***BOM <u>Alma 13:25</u> And now we only wait to hear *the joyful news* declared unto us **by the mouth of** angels, of his coming; for **the time cometh**, *we know not how soon*. Would to God that it might be in my day; but let it be *(2) sooner or later,* in it I will rejoice.

> COM Gill: <u>Mar 16:10</u> "when Mary brought them **the joyful news** of Christ's resurrection from the dead." (Clarke)

COM Clarke: <u>Rth 1:6</u> "**by the mouth** of an **angel**, says the Targum.")

KJV (**2NT/15**) <u>John 16:2</u> They shall put you out of the synagogues: yea, **the time cometh**, that whosoever killeth you will think that he doeth God service.)

COM Henry: <u>Joh 14:28-31</u> "**We know not how soon** our breath may be stopped," (Gill)

COM Henry: <u>Isa 45:20-25</u> "One way or other, **sooner or later**," (Clarke, Wesley),

*****BOM** <u>Alma 14:17</u> Therefore, after Alma having established the **church (76/259)** at Sidom, seeing *a great check*, yea, seeing that the people were (1) checked (14th Century) as to (*10*) *the pride of their hearts*, and began to **humble themselves** before God, and began to assemble themselves together at their sanctuaries to worship God before the altar, watching and praying continually, that they might be delivered from Satan, and from death, and from destruction –

COM Henry: <u>Jdg 16:22-31</u> "This would give **a great check** to the insolence of the survivors,")

"**Note:** "a great check" is very unique.

COM Gill: <u>Joh 8:44</u> "this he and his associates, in the **pride of their hearts**," (Henry)

KJV (**1/25**) <u>2 Chronicles 7:14</u> If my people, which are called by my name, shall **humble themselves**, and pray, and seek my face, and turn from their wicked ways; then will I hear from heaven, and will forgive their sin, and will heal their land.)

BOM <u>Alma 15:10</u> But behold, in one day *it was left desolate*; and the carcasses were mangled by dogs and wild beasts of the wilderness.

COM Gill: <u>Mal 1:3</u> "though this was the case of Judea, that **it was left desolate**," (Henry)

BOM <u>Alma 17:2</u> Now these sons of Mosiah were with Alma at the time the angel first appeared unto him; therefore Alma did **rejoice exceedingly** to see his brethren; and what added more to his joy, they were still his brethren in the Lord; yea, and they had **waxed strong** in **the knowledge of the truth**; for they were men *of a sound understanding* and they had searched the **scriptures** diligently, **that they might know the word of God (45/89)**.

KJV (**1/9**) <u>Job 3:22</u> Which **rejoice exceedingly**, and are glad, when they can find the grave?)

KJV (**2NT/5**) <u>Luke 1:80</u> And the child grew, and **waxed strong** in spirit, and was in the deserts till the day of his shewing unto Israel.)

KJV (**3NT/15**) <u>1 Timothy 2:4</u> Who will have all men to be saved, and to come unto the **knowledge of the truth**.)

COM Clarke: <u>Act 13:7</u> "A man of good sense, **of a sound**

understanding, and therefore wished to hear the doctrine taught by these apostles; he did not persecute the men for their preaching, but sent for them that he might hear for himself.")

KJV (21NT/41) Matthew 21:42 Jesus saith unto them, Did ye never read in the **scriptures**, The stone which the builders rejected, the same is become the head of the corner: this is the Lord's doing, and it is marvellous in our eyes?)

KJV (3/8) Ezekiel 20:12 Moreover also I gave them my sabbaths, to be a sign between me and them, **that they might know** that I am the LORD that sanctify them.)

***BOM** Alma 17:5 Now these are *the circumstances which attended* them in their journeyings, for they had **many afflictions (0/8)**; they did suffer much, both in body and in mind, such as hunger, thirst and (7) fatigue (1669), and also much labor in the spirit.

COM Clarke: Act 27:14 "from N.E. round by the E. to S.E. The euroclydon, from **the circumstances which attended** it," (Gill)

***BOM** Alma 17:18 Now Ammon being the chief among them, or rather he did administer unto them, and he departed from them, after having blessed them according *to their several stations*, having imparted **the word of God (45/89)** unto them, or administered unto them before his departure; and thus they took their several journeys throughout the land.

COM Gill: Eph 4:10 "and all with gifts and graces suitable **to their several stations** and work.")

***BOM** Alma 18:30 And Ammon said unto him: The *heavens* is a place *where God dwells* and all his holy angels.

COM Gill: Heb 11:10 "or else the ultimate glory of the saints in **heaven, where God dwells**, and keeps his palace; and which will be the dwelling place of the saints" (Henry)

BOM Alma 19:6 Now, this was what Ammon desired, for he knew that king Lamoni was under **the power of God**; he knew that the *dark veil of* unbelief was being cast away from his mind, and the light which did light up his mind, which was *the light of the glory of God*, which was a *(4) marvelous light* of his goodness -- yea, this light had (1) infused (1526) such joy into his soul, the cloud of darkness having been (1) dispelled (15th Century) , and that the light of everlasting life was lit up in his soul, yea, he knew that this had overcome his natural frame, and he was carried away in God –

KJV (11NT/48) Matthew 22:29 Jesus answered and said unto them, Ye do err, not knowing the scriptures, nor **the power of God**.)

COM Gill: Psa 78:49 "they were scattered under a **dark veil of** forgetfulness," (Clarke)

COM Clarke: 1Jo 2:27 "the same Spirit from whom they had already received **the light of the glory of God**," (Gill, Henry)

COM Gill: <u>Eph 2:10</u> "He has saved us that we may show forth the virtues of Him who called us from darkness into his **marvelous light**." (Henry)
COM Gill: <u>1Co 6:11</u> "which lies in a principle of spiritual life **infused into** the **soul**, in a spiritual light in the understanding,")
COM Gill: <u>Rom 13:11</u> "and that the dawn of grace, and day of spiritual light had broke in upon their souls, and **dispelled the darkness** of sin, ignorance and unbelief; that the darkness was past, and the true light shined, and the sun of righteousness was risen on them:")

*****BOM** <u>Alma 21:9</u> Now Aaron began to open the **scriptures** unto them concerning the coming of Christ, and also concerning **the resurrection of the dead**, and that there could be no redemption for mankind (*76*) *save it were* through *the death and sufferings of Christ*, and the atonement of his blood.

KJV (21NT/41) <u>Matthew 21:42</u> Jesus saith unto them, Did ye never read in the **scriptures**, The stone which the builders rejected, the same is become the head of the corner: this is the Lord's doing, and it is marvellous in our eyes?)
KJV (6NT/17) <u>Matthew 22:31</u> But as touching **the resurrection of the dead**, have ye not read that which was spoken unto you by God, saying,)
COM Henry: <u>Act 3:12-26</u> "but because in particular **the death and sufferings of Christ** were for the remission of sins,")

BOM <u>Alma 21:21</u> And he did rejoice over them, and he did teach them many things. And he did also declare unto them that they were a people who were under him, and that they were (*4*) *a free people*, that they were free from the oppressions of the king, his father; for that his father had granted unto him that he might reign over the people who were in the land of Ishmael, and in all the land round about.

COM Henry: <u>Exo 5:10-14</u> "and what reason we have to be thankful to God that we are **a free people**, and not oppressed." (Clarke, Gill)

BOM <u>Alma 22:32</u> And now, it was only the distance of *a day and a half's journey* for a Nephite, on the line Bountiful and the land Desolation, from the east to the west sea; and thus the land of Nephi and the land of Zarahemla were (*2*) (*13*) nearly (*1561*) (*18*) *surrounded* (circa 1616*) by water*, there being a small (*2*) *neck of land* between the land northward and the land southward. (*Note: Obviously a description of North and South America.*)

COM Gill: <u>Exo 2:15</u> "which is about **a day and a half's journey** southeast from Mount Sinai, is the place where Jethro lived.")
COM Clarke: <u>Job 28:28</u> "Though this has been already explained, let the reader farther consider that, as fishes are **surrounded by water**, and live and move in it, which is a much denser medium than our

atmosphere;)

> **COM** Clarke: 1Co 9:24 "were celebrated every fifth year on the isthmus, or narrow **neck of land**, which joins the Peloponnesus, or Morea, to the main land; and were thence termed the Isthmian games." (Henry, Gill)

BOM Alma 23:5 *And thousands were* brought to the knowledge of the Lord, yea, thousands were brought to believe in the traditions of the Nephites; and they were taught the records and prophecies which were (*18) handed down* even to the **present time.**

> **COM** Henry: Num 28:16-31 "**and thousands were** converted by the preaching of the apostles,")
>
> **KJV** (**3NT/7**) Luke 18:30 Who shall not receive manifold more in **this present time**, and in the world to come life everlasting.)
>
> **COM** Clarke: Rev 2:17 "This was carefully preserved, and **handed down even to** posterity in the same family;)

***BOM** Alma 23:18 And they began to be a very **industrious** people; yea, and they were friendly with the Nephites; therefore, they *did open a* (*4) correspondence (15th Century) with* them, and the curse of God did no more follow them.

> **KJV** (1/4) 1 Kings 11:28 And the man Jeroboam was a mighty man of valour: and Solomon seeing the young man that he was **industrious**, he made him ruler over all the charge of the house of Joseph.)
>
> **COM** Henry: Luk 3:21-38 "to **open a correspondence with** the heavenly Canaan.")

***BOM** Alma 24:4 And the king *died in that selfsame year that* the Lamanites began to make (*9) preparations for war* against the people of God.

> **COM** Gill: 2Ki 13:20 "**in that selfsame year that** Elisha **died;**")
>
> **Note:** As with much of what you have read this is beyond coincidence, "in that selfsame year that…died".
>
> **COM** Henry: Jer 12:7-13 "ashamed that they have depended so much upon their **preparations for war** and particularly upon their ability to bear the charges of it" (Clarke)

BOM Alma 24:10 And **I** also **thank my God**, yea, my great God, that he hath granted unto us that we might repent of these things, and also that he hath forgiven us of those our many sins and murders which we have committed, and taken away the guilt from our hearts, (*3) through the* (*5) merits, (14th Century)* of his Son.

> **KJV** (**5NT/3**) Romans 1:8 First, **I thank my God** through Jesus Christ for you all, that your faith is spoken of throughout the whole world.)
>
> **COM** Clarke: Mar 10:50 "to be saved only **through the merits** of

Christ." (Henry)

BOM <u>Alma 24:13</u> Behold, I say unto you, Nay, let us retain our swords that they be not *stained with the blood of* our brethren; for **perhaps**, if we should stain our swords again they can no more be washed bright through the blood of the Son of **our great God**, which shall be shed for the atonement of our sins.

> **COM** Gill: <u>Isa 64:1</u> "as a triumphant conqueror, **stained with the blood of** his enemies;" (Henry, Clarke)
>
> **KJV (3NT/43)** <u>Acts 8:22</u> Repent therefore of this thy wickedness, and pray God, if **perhaps** the thought of thine heart may be forgiven thee.)
>
> **KJV (1NT/2)** <u>Titus 2:13</u> while we wait for the blessed hope—the glorious appearing of **our great God** and Savior, Jesus Christ,)

***BOM <u>Alma 24:30</u> And thus we can plainly discern, that after a people have been *once enlightened by the Spirit of God*, and have had *(6) great knowledge*, of **things pertaining to** righteousness, and then have *(2) fallen away* into sin and transgression, they become more hardened, and thus their state becomes worse than though they had never known these things.

> **KJV (1NT/2)** <u>Hebrews 6:4</u> For it is impossible for those who were **once enlightened**, and have tasted of the heavenly gift, and were made partakers of the Holy Ghost,)
>
> **COM** Gill: <u>Joh 4:25</u> "and from a common prevailing notion among the Jews, that the times of the Messiah would be times of **great knowledge**, founded on several prophecies,")
>
> **KJV (4NT/9)** <u>Acts 1:3</u> To whom also he shewed himself alive after his passion by many infallible proofs, being seen of them forty days, and speaking of the **things pertaining to** the kingdom of God)
>
> **COM** Clarke: <u>Joh 10:28</u> "And having **fallen away**." (Henry, Wesley)
>
> **COM** Gill: <u>Heb 6:4</u> "there are some who are savingly **enlightened by the Spirit of God**, to see the impurity of their hearts and actions, and their impotency to perform that which is good, the imperfection of their own righteousness to justify them, their lost state and condition by nature, and to see Christ and salvation by him, and their interest in it; and these being "once" enlightened, never become darkness, or ever so fall as to perish;")
>
> **COM** Henry: <u>Joh 6:60-71</u> "They walked no more with him, returned no more to him and attended no more upon his ministry. It is hard for those who have been **once enlightened**, and have tasted the good word of God, if they fall away, to renew them again to repentance")

***BOM <u>Alma 25:5</u> And the remainder, having fled into the east wilderness, and having *(2) usurped (14th Century) the* **power and authority** over the Lamanites, caused that many of the Lamanites should perish by fire because of their belief –

COM Gill: 2Th 2:4 "and over which he **usurped power and authority**;")
KJV (**2NT/5**) Luke 9:1 Then he called his twelve disciples together, and gave them **power and authority** over all devils, and to cure diseases.)

***BOM Alma 25:15 Yea, and they did keep the law of Moses; for it was **expedient** that they should keep the law of Moses as yet, for it was not all fulfilled. But (2) *notwithstanding the law of Moses,* they did look forward to the coming of Christ, considering that the law of Moses was *a type of his* coming, and **believing** that they must keep those *outward* (6) *performances* (*15th Century*) **until the time** that he should be revealed unto them.

KJV (**7NT/62**) John 11:50 Nor consider that it is **expedient** for us, that one man should die for the people, and that the whole nation perish not.)
COM Clarke: Rth 2:2 "The words seem to intimate that, **notwithstanding the law of Moses,**")
COM Gill: Dan 9:19 "Jerusalem, the city of the great King, Christ, and a **type of his** church and people, who are also called by his name, and call upon him")
KJV (**8NT/13**) Matthew 21:22 And all things, whatsoever ye shall ask in prayer, **believing,** ye shall receive.)
COM Henry: Phi 3:1-3 "They have no confidence in the flesh, in those carnal ordinances and **outward performances**." (Clarke, Gill, Wesley)
KJV (6/12) Psalm 105:19 **Until the time** that his word came: the word of the LORD tried him.)

***BOM Alma 25:17 And now behold, Ammon, and Aaron, and Omner, and Himni, and their brethren did **rejoice exceedingly**, for the success which they had had among the Lamanites, seeing that the Lord had granted unto them according to their prayers, and that he had also verified his word unto them (1) *in every particular.*

KJV (1/9) Job 3:22 Which **rejoice exceedingly**, and are glad, when they can find the grave?)
KJV (**2NT/10**) 1 Corinthians 12:27 Now ye are the body of Christ, and members in **particular**.)
COM Henry: Exo 25:31-40 "but the will of God must be religiously observed **in every particular**." Clarke, Gill, Wesley)

***BOM Alma 26:3 Behold, I answer for you; for our brethren, the Lamanites, were in darkness, yea, even in the darkest abyss, but behold, how many of them are brought to behold the (4) *marvelous light* of God! And this is the blessing which hath been **bestowed upon us**, that we have been made (3) *instruments in the hands of God* to *bring about this great work.*

COM Gill: Eph 2:10 "He has saved us that we may show forth the virtues of Him who called us from darkness into his **marvelous light**." (Henry)

COM Clarke: Luk 2:20 "preaching these mysteries with the fullest conviction of their truth, they become **instruments in the hands of God** of begetting the same faith in their hearers;" (Gill)

COM Henry: Hos 3:1-5 "He that has here promised that they shall do it will enable them to do it, and **bring about this great work** in his own way and time, in the latter days of the last times,")

***BOM** Alma 26:17 Who could have *supposed* that our God would have been so merciful as to have snatched us from our (47) awful (13th Century) (*Henry, Clarke, Wesley), sinful, and polluted state*?

> **KJV (8NT/33)** Matthew 20:10 But when the first came, they **supposed** that they should have received more; and they likewise received every man a penny.)

> **COM** Gill: Ecc 3:18 "He thought of the condition of the children of men, their **sinful and polluted state**")

***BOM** Alma 26:19 Oh then, why did he not (1) *consign* (1528) us *to* an (47) awful (13th Century) (*Henry, Clarke, Wesley) destruction*, yea, why did he not let (*2) the sword of his justice* fall upon us, and (2) doom (12th Century) (*Note: Clarke, Henry, Wesley,* Gill) us to eternal despair?

> **COM** Clarke: Rev 17:16 "and in the end **consign** her **to** utter **destruction**.")

> **COM** Henry: Isa 34:1-8 "When the day of God's abused mercy and patience is over **the sword of his justice** gives no quarter, spares none." (Gill)

***BOM** Alma 26:24 For **they said unto us**: Do ye suppose that ye can bring the Lamanites to **the knowledge of the truth**? Do ye suppose that ye can convince the Lamanites of the incorrectness of the **traditions of** their **fathers**, as stiffnecked a people as they are; whose hearts delight in the shedding of blood; whose days have been spent in *the (1) grossest (14th Century) iniquity*; whose ways have been the ways of a **transgressor from the** beginning? Now my brethren, ye remember that this was their language.

> **KJV** (1/1) Nehemiah 4:12 And it came to pass, that when the Jews which dwelt by them came, **they said unto us** ten times, From all places whence ye shall return unto us they will be upon you.)

> **KJV (3NT/15)** 1 Timothy 2:4 Who will have all men to be saved, and to come unto the **knowledge of the truth**.)

> **KJV (1NT/20)** Galatians 1:14 And profited in the Jews' religion above many my equals in mine own nation, being more exceedingly zealous of the **traditions of** my **fathers**.)

> **COM** Gill: Mic 2:1 "they do not pray to him, and therefore are bold

and daring to perpetrate **the grossest iniquity**,")

KJV (1/1) <u>Isaiah 48:8</u> Yea, thou heardest not; yea, thou knewest not; yea, from that time that thine ear was not opened: for I knew that thou wouldest deal very treacherously, and wast called a **transgressor from the** womb.)

*****BOM** <u>Alma 26:28</u> And now behold, we have come, and been forth amongst them; and we have been patient in our sufferings, and we have suffered *every (1) privation (14th Century)*; yea, we have traveled from house to house, (5) relying (1574) (*Note: Clarke, Wesley, Henry,* Gill*)* upon the mercies of the world -- not upon the mercies of the world alone but upon the mercies of God.

> **COM** Clarke: <u>1Ki 21:4</u> "**Every privation** and cross makes an unholy soul unhappy;"
>
> **Note:** Remember that the date with this word means that it is not found in the KJV.

*****BOM** <u>Alma 26:30</u> And we have suffered all manner of afflictions, and all this, that **perhaps** we might *be the means of saving* some *soul*; and we **supposed** that our joy would be full if **perhaps** we could *be the means of saving* some.

> **KJV** (**3NT/43**) <u>Acts 8:22</u> Repent therefore of this thy wickedness, and pray God, if **perhaps** the thought of thine heart may be forgiven thee.)
>
> **COM** Gill: <u>Jam 5:20</u> "and he will **be the means of saving** "a soul",")
>
> **KJV** (**8NT/33**) <u>Matthew 20:10</u> But when the first came, they **supposed** that they should have received more; and they likewise received every man a penny.)
>
> **KJV** (**3NT/43**) <u>Acts 8:22</u> Repent therefore of this thy wickedness, and pray God, if **perhaps** the thought of thine heart may be forgiven thee.)

BOM <u>Alma 26:35</u> Now have we not reason to rejoice? Yea, I say unto you, there never were men that had so *(5) great reason* to rejoice as we, **since the world began**; yea, and my joy is carried away, even unto boasting in my God; for he has all power, all wisdom, and all understanding; he *comprehendeth* all things, and he is a *merciful Being*, even unto salvation, to those who will repent and **believe on his name**.

> **COM** Gill: <u>Gen 1:18</u> "and therefore have **great reason** to be thankful," (Clarke, Wesley, Henry)
>
> **KJV** (**4NT/1**) <u>Romans 16:25</u> Now to him that is of power to stablish you according to my gospel, and the preaching of Jesus Christ, according to the revelation of the mystery, which was kept secret **since the world began**,)
>
> **COM** Henry: <u>1Co 2:6-16</u> "The light shineth in darkness, and the

darkness **comprehendeth** it not," (Clarke)

COM Clarke: <u>Exo 34:6</u> "Rachum, the **merciful Being**, who is full of tenderness and compassion.")

KJV (1NT/12) <u>John 1:12</u> But as many as received him, to them gave he power to become the sons of God, even to them that **believe on his name**:)

*****BOM** <u>Alma 27:18</u> Now was not this exceeding joy? Behold, this is joy which none receiveth save it be the *truly penitent and humble* seeker of (30) happiness (15th Century) (*Note: Henry, Clarke, Wesley*).

    COM Henry: <u>Jam 4:1-10</u> "If we be **truly penitent and humble** under the marks of God's displeasure, we shall in a little time know the advantages of his favour;")

*****BOM** <u>Alma 27:27</u> And they were among the people of Nephi, and also **numbered among** the people who were of **the church (76/259) of God**. And they were also (9) distinguished (1561) for their zeal towards God, and also towards men; for they were perfectly *honest and upright in all* things; and they were *firm in the faith* of Christ, even unto the end.

    KJV (3/30) <u>Numbers 1:47</u> But the Levites after the tribe of their fathers were not **numbered among** them.)

    KJV (8NT/31) <u>Acts 20:28</u> Take heed therefore unto yourselves, and to all the flock, over the which the Holy Ghost hath made you overseers, to feed **the church of God**, which he hath purchased with his own blood.)

    COM Gill: <u>Psa 15:4</u> "he that is **honest and upright in all** his dealings.")

    COM Clarke: <u>Deu 31:6</u> "Stand **firm in the faith**;")

*****BOM** <u>Alma 27:28</u> And they did look upon shedding the blood of their brethren with the *greatest* (2) *abhorrence* (1660); and they never could be prevailed upon to (9) *take up arms against* their brethren; and they never did look upon death with any *degree of terror*, for their hope and (3) *views* (1523 AD) of Christ and the resurrection; therefore, **death** was **swallowed up** to them by the **victory** of Christ over it.

    COM Henry: <u>Rom 6:1-23</u> "are to be rejected with the **greatest abhorrence**;)

    COM Henry: <u>Jer 20:7-13</u> "God's being a mighty God bespeaks him a terrible God to all those that **take up arms against** him or any one that,")

    COM Henry: <u>Luk 1:5-25</u> "even to a **degree of terror**,")

    COM Gill: <u>Isa 56:7</u> "by giving them **views of Christ**, his love and loveliness, fulness, grace, and righteousness: by favouring them with the consolations of his Spirit, and his gracious influences; and by showing them their interest in the blessings of grace and glory:")

KJV (1NT/2) <u>1 Corinthians 15:54</u> So when this corruptible shall have put on incorruption, and this mortal shall have put on immortality, then shall be brought to pass the saying that is written, **Death** is **swallowed up** in **victory**.)

BOM <u>Alma 27:29</u> Therefore, they would suffer death in the most (*1*) *aggravating* (*1530*) and (*1*) *distressing* (*14ᵗʰ Century*) manner which could be inflicted by their brethren, before they would take the sword or (*11*) cimeter (*1548*) to smite them.

> **COM** Gill: <u>Mar 9:44</u> "**aggravating** them, tormenting them for them, filling them with dreadful anguish **and** misery, with twinging remorses, and severe reflections, and which will never have an end. This will be always the case; conscience will be ever **distressing**, racking, and torturing them;")

***BOM <u>Alma 28:11</u> And the bodies of many thousands are *laid low in the* earth, while the bodies of many thousands are (*2*) moldering (*1531*) *in heaps* **upon the face of the earth**; yea, and many thousands are mourning for the loss of their kindred, because they have reason to fear, according to the promises of the Lord, that they are (*9*) (*9*) *consigned* (*1528*) *to* a *state of endless* wo.

> **COM** Gill: <u>Isa 5:15</u> "**laid low in the** dust,")
>
> **Note:** Again here we have the typical Joseph Smith slight variation in wording but the same meaning, "laid low in the earth" vs. "laid low in the dust" of course the same meaning. He did this often and I have not pointed out every instance.
>
> **COM** Clarke: <u>Job 3:14</u> "but the monuments which they have raised to contain their corrupting flesh, **moldering** bones, and dust.")
>
> **COM** Gill: <u>Jdg 15:16</u> "that is, with such an instrument he had slain heaps of men, who lay dead **in heaps upon** one another;")
>
> **KJV** (12/26) <u>Numbers 12:3</u> Now the man Moses was very meek, above all the men which were **upon the face of the earth**.)
>
> **COM** Gill: <u>2Th 2:3</u> "but because they are by the righteous judgment of God appointed and **consigned to** everlasting destruction;" (Clarke, Wesley, Henry)
>
> **COM** Henry: <u>Mat 25:31-46</u> "If they must be doomed to such a **state of endless** misery, yet may they not have some good company there?")
>
> **COM** <u>Clarke: Eze 3:18</u> "How many loads of **endless wo** must such have to bear!")

BOM <u>Alma 28:12</u> While many thousands of others *truly mourn* for the loss of their kindred, yet they rejoice and (*1*) *exult* (*1570*) *in the hope*, and even know, according to the promises of the Lord, that they are raised to dwell **at the right hand of God,** in a state of never-ending (30) happiness (15ᵗʰ Century) (***Note:***

Henry, Clarke, Wesley).

    COM Gill: <u>Job 42:6</u> "and never do any more **truly mourn** for sin and repent of it,")

    COM Clarke: <u>Heb 3:6</u> "and **exult in the** enjoyment of that **hope**.)

    KJV (1NT/4) <u>Romans 8:34</u> Who is he that condemneth? It is Christ that died, yea rather, that is risen again, who is even **at the right hand of God**, who also maketh intercession for us.)

BOM <u>Alma 29:3</u> But behold, I am a man, and do sin in my wish; for I *ought to be content with* the things which the Lord hath allotted unto me.

    COM Note the same idea here. Note: Gill: <u>1Co 12:18</u> "and therefore each member **ought to be content with** his place, gift, and usefulness, be they what they will;" (Henry)

***BOM <u>Alma 29:4</u> I ought not to *harrow up* (5) in my desires, the **firm decree** of a just God, for I know that he (2) granteth (*Not in KJV, or works)* unto men *according to their desire*, whether it be unto death or unto life; yea, I know that he allotteth (*Note: Not found in KJV or works)* unto men, yea, decreeth (*Note: Not found in KJV or works)* unto them *decrees* which *are* (2) *unalterable* (*1611*), according to their wills, whether they be unto salvation or unto destruction.

    COM Clarke: <u>Gen 37:32</u> "What deliberate cruelty to torture the feelings of their aged father, and thus **harrow up** his soul!")

    KJV (1/1) <u>Daniel 6:7</u> All the presidents of the kingdom, the governors, and the princes, the counsellors, and the captains, have consulted together to establish a royal statute, and to make a **firm decree**, that whosoever shall ask a petition of any God or man for thirty days, save of thee, O king, he shall be cast into the den of lions.)

    COM Gill: <u>1Co 10:6</u> "for though the Lord gave them flesh **according to their desire**,")

    COM Henry: Num 23:13-30 "All his **decrees are unalterable**, and all his promises inviolable.")

***BOM <u>Alma 29:5</u> Yea, and I know that good and evil have come before all men; he that knoweth not good from evil is blameless; but he that knoweth good and evil, to him it is given according to his desires, whether he desireth good or evil, life or death, joy or (3) *remorse* (*14ᵗʰ Century) of conscience*.

    COM Note the similarity of meaning here: Gill: <u>1Jo 3:21</u> "Which must be understood, not of a stupidity of mind, as is in unregenerate men, who have no sense of sin, no sorrow for it, or **remorse of conscience** on account of it; or as is in them who are past feeling; having their consciences seared as with a red hot iron; such cannot be entitled to the advantages that follow; nor is it of persons the apostle speaks, but of himself, and Christians, the beloved of the Lord, and one another, who had an experience of the grace of God upon their souls, and made a profession of religion: nor does it design such a purity of heart and life in believers, as that their hearts do not smite, reproach, and condemn them for sin at any time, for such a state of perfection is not to be attained to and expected in this life; but rather a conscience purged by the blood of Christ, or an heart sprinkled from an evil conscience by that blood, which speaks peace and pardon, so that there is no more conscience of sin,")

BOM Alma 29:13 Yea, and *that same God* did establish his **church (76/259)** among them; yea, and *that same God* hath **called** me by a **holy calling**, to **preach the word unto this people**, and hath given me *(4) much success, in the which* my joy is full.

> **KJV (1NT/6)** 2 Timothy 1:9 Who hath saved us, and **called** us with an **holy calling**, not according to our works, but according to his own purpose and grace, which was given us in Christ Jesus before the world began,)
>
> **KJV (2NT/20)** 2 Timothy 4:2 **Preach the word**; be instant in season, out of season; reprove, rebuke, exhort with all long suffering and doctrine.)
>
> **KJV (9/43)** Jeremiah 21:8 And **unto this people** thou shalt say, Thus saith the LORD; Behold, I set before you the way of life, and the way of death.)
>
> **COM** Gill: Act 15:3 "and in the latter Philip the evangelist had **preached** with much success")
>
> **KJV (14/28)** Genesis 1:29 And God said, Behold, I have given you every herb bearing seed, which is upon the face of all the earth, and every tree, **in the which** is the fruit of a tree yielding seed; to you it shall be for meat.)

BOM Alma 29:16 Now, when I think of the success of these my brethren my soul is carried away, even to the *separation* of it *from the body*, as it were, so great is my joy.

> **COM** Henry: Mat 16:24-28 "The soul is the spiritual and immortal part of man, which thinks and reasons, has a power of reflection and prospect, which actuates the body now, and will shortly act in a **separation from the body**.")

BOM Alma 30:2 Now their dead were not numbered because of *(7) the greatness of their numbers*; neither were the dead of the Nephites numbered -- but **it came to pass (452/1353)** after they had buried their dead, and also after the days of *fasting, and mourning, and prayer*, (and it was in the sixteenth year of the reign of the judges over the people of Nephi) there began to be continual peace throughout all the land.

> **COM** Gill: Isa 29:5 "is not used to express the weakness of them, but

the greatness of their number,")
COM Gill: <u>Joe 2:16</u> "and betake themselves to **fasting mourning, and prayer;**")
BOM <u>Alma 30:23</u> Now the high priest's name was Giddonah. And Korihor said unto him: Because I do not teach the foolish **traditions of** your **fathers**, and because I do not teach this people to bind themselves down under the foolish *ordinances and (6) performances* (15th Century) which are laid down by *ancient priests*, **to usurp power and authority over** them, *to keep them in ignorance*, that they may not lift up their heads, but be brought down according to thy words.

> **KJV (1NT/20)** <u>Galatians 1:14</u> And profited in the Jews' religion above many my equals in mine own nation, being more exceedingly zealous of the **traditions of** my **fathers**.)
> **COM** Henry: Phi 3:1-3 "They have no confidence in the flesh, in those carnal **ordinances and** outward **performances**." (Clarke, Wesley)
> **COM** Gill: <u>Dan 9:26</u> "in whom the succession of the **ancient priests** terminated")
> **KJV (1NT/5)** <u>1 Timothy 2:12</u> But I suffer not a woman to teach, nor **to usurp authority** over the man, but to be in silence.)
> **KJV (2NT/5)** <u>Luke 9:1</u> Then he called his twelve disciples together, and gave them **power and authority over** all devils, and to cure diseases.)
> **COM** Gill: <u>Gen 3:1</u> "and therefore God had forbid it, **to keep them in ignorance:**" (Henry)

BOM <u>Alma 30:31</u> And he did rise up in **great swelling words** before Alma, and did **revile** against the priests and teachers, accusing them of leading away the people after the silly **traditions of** their **fathers**, for the sake of (1) glutting (14th Century) on the labors of the people.

> **KJV (2NT/1)** <u>2 Peter 2:18</u> For when they speak **great swelling words** of vanity, they allure through the lusts of the flesh, through much wantonness, those that were clean escaped from them who live in error.)
> **KJV (2/25)** <u>Exodus 22:28</u> Thou shalt not **revile** the gods, nor curse the ruler of thy people.)
> **KJV (1NT/20)** <u>Galatians 1:14</u> And profited in the Jews' religion above many my equals in mine own nation, being more exceedingly zealous of the **traditions of** my **fathers**.)
> **COM** Gill: <u>Rev 9:3</u> "**glutting** themselves with the spoils of others,")

BOM <u>Alma 30:57</u> Now the knowledge of what had happened unto Korihor was **immediately published throughout all the** land; yea, the proclamation was sent forth by the chief judge to all the people in the land, declaring unto those who had believed in the words of Korihor that they must *(2) speedily repent, lest the same* judgments would *come* unto *them.*

> **KJV (55NT/18)** <u>Matthew 24:29</u> **Immediately** after the tribulation of those days shall the sun be darkened, and the moon shall not give her light, and the stars shall fall from heaven, and the powers of the heavens shall be shaken:)
>
> **KJV (1NT/1)** <u>Acts 13:49</u> And the word of the Lord was **published throughout all the** region.)
>
> **COM** Clarke: <u>Luk 13:4</u> "if ye do not **speedily repent**, and turn to God." (Henry)
>
> **COM** Gill: <u>Zep 3:7</u> "and fear to offend me, **lest the same** calamities should **come** upon **them**;" (Henry)

BOM <u>Alma 31:5</u> And now, as the preaching of the word had a *great (1) tendency (1628)* to lead the people to do that which was just -- yea, *it had had* more powerful effect upon the minds of the people than the sword, or anything else, which had happened unto them -- therefore Alma thought it was **expedient** that they should try the *(1) virtue of **the word of God** (45/89)*.

> **COM** Henry: <u>Mar 6:7-13</u> "The great design of the gospel preachers, and the **great tendency** of gospel preaching, should be, to bring people to repentance," (Clarke)
>
> **COM** Henry: <u>Mar 11:12-26</u> "so that it could not be pretended that **it had had** fruit,")
>
> **KJV (7NT/62)** <u>John 11:50</u> Nor consider that it is **expedient** for us, that one man should die for the people, and that the whole nation perish not.)
>
> **COM** Clarke: <u>Heb 4:12</u> "he sets before them the efficacy and **virtue of the word of God**,")

BOM <u>Alma 31:28</u> Behold, O my God, their *(8) costly apparel*, and their (1) ringlets (1555), and their bracelets, and their **ornaments of gold**, and all their precious things which they are (3) ornamented (1720) with; and behold, their hearts are set upon them, and yet they cry unto thee and say -- **We thank thee**, O God, for we are a chosen people unto thee, while others shall perish.

> **COM** Gill: <u>1Pe 3:4</u> "wearing of gold, or any **costly apparel**, can give to the body:" (Clarke, Wesley)
>
> **COM** Gill: <u>Exo 28:22</u> "not of circles and **ringlets** of gold coupled together, but of golden wires twisted together, as ropes are." (Clarke)
>
> **KJV (2/1)** <u>Jeremiah 4:30</u> And when thou art spoiled, what wilt thou do? Though thou clothest thyself with crimson, though thou deckest thee with **ornaments** of **gold**, though thou rentest thy face with painting, in vain shalt thou make thyself fair; thy lovers will despise thee, they will seek thy life.)
>
> **COM** Gill: <u>Exo 15:22</u> "**ornamented with** gold and silver, and

precious stones; or as others," (Clarke)

KJV (1/3) <u>1 Chronicles 29:13</u> Now therefore, our God, **we thank thee**, and praise thy glorious name.)

***BOM** <u>Alma 32:3</u> Therefore they were not **permitted** to enter into their synagogues to worship God, being esteemed as filthiness; therefore they were poor; yea, they were esteemed by their brethren as **dross**; therefore they were *poor as to things of the world*; and also they were *(3) poor in heart.*

KJV (**2NT/8**) <u>Acts 26:1</u> Then Agrippa said unto Paul, Thou art **permitted** to speak for thyself. Then Paul stretched forth the hand, and answered for himself:)

COM Note same idea here: Henry: <u>1Co 4:7-13</u> "They suffered in their persons and characters as the very worst and vilest men, as the most proper to make such a sacrifice: or else as the very dirt of the world, that was to be swept away: nay, as the off-scouring of all things, the **dross**, the filings of all things.")

KJV (7/2) <u>Psalm 119:119</u> Thou puttest away all the wicked of the earth like **dross**: therefore I love thy testimonies.)

COM Gill: <u>Gal 2:10</u> "but properly and literally the **poor as to the things of** this **world**;")

COM Henry: <u>Mat 5:3-12</u> "The pure in heart are happy (<u>Mat 5:8</u>); Blessed are the **poor in heart**, for they shall see God.")

BOM <u>Alma 32:7</u> Therefore he did say no more to the other multitude; but he **stretched forth his hand**, and cried unto those whom he beheld, who were *truly penitent and humble*, and said unto them:

KJV (7/12) <u>Exodus 10:22</u> And Moses **stretched forth his hand** toward heaven; and there was a thick darkness in all the land of Egypt three days:)

COM Henry: <u>Jam 4:1-10</u> "If we be **truly penitent and humble** under the marks of God's displeasure, we shall in a little time know the advantages of his favour;" (Clarke, Henry, Wesley)

BOM <u>Alma 32:28</u> Now, we will compare the word unto a seed. Now, if ye **give place**, that a seed may be planted in your heart, behold, if it be a true seed, or a **good seed**, if ye do not cast it out by your unbelief, that ye will resist the Spirit of the Lord, behold, it will begin to swell within your breasts; and when you feel these swelling motions, ye will begin to say within yourselves -- **it must needs be that** this is a **good seed**, or that the word is good, for it (11) beginneth (*Note: Not found in Wesley, Clarke,* Gill, *Henry, KJV*) to enlarge my soul; yea, it (11) beginneth (*Note: Not found in Wesley, Clarke,* Gill, *Henry, KJV*) to *enlighten my understanding*, yea, it (11) beginneth (*Note: Not found in Wesley, Clarke,* Gill, *Henry, KJV*) to be delicious to me.

KJV (4/4) <u>Isaiah 49:20</u> The children which thou shalt have, after thou hast lost the other, shall say again in thine ears, The place is too strait for me: **give place** to me that I may dwell.)

KJV (**4NT/4**) <u>Matthew 13:24</u> Another parable put he forth unto them, saying, The kingdom of heaven is likened unto a man which sowed **good seed** in his field:)

KJV (**1NT/14**) <u>Matthew 18:7</u> Woe unto the world because of offences! for **it must needs be that** offences come; but woe to that man by whom the offence cometh!)

KJV (**4NT/4**) <u>Matthew 13:24</u> Another parable put he forth unto them, saying, The kingdom of heaven is likened unto a man which sowed **good seed** in his field:)

COM Henry: <u>Psa 119:35-36</u> "He had before prayed to God to **enlighten his understanding**, that he might know his duty, and not mistake concerning it;")

*****BOM** <u>Alma 33:1</u> Now after Alma **had spoken these words**, they sent forth unto him **desiring to** know whether they should believe in one God, that they **might obtain** this fruit of which he had spoken, or how they should plant *the seed*, or *the word* of which he had spoken, which he said must be *planted in their hearts*; or in what manner they should begin to exercise their faith.

KJV (**2/19**) <u>Job 42:7</u> And it was so, that after the LORD **had spoken these words** unto Job, the LORD said to Eliphaz the Temanite, My wrath is kindled against thee, and against thy two friends: for ye have not spoken of me the thing that is right, as my servant Job hath.)

KJV (**8NT/4**) <u>Matthew 12:46</u> While he yet talked to the people, behold, his mother and his brethren stood without, **desiring to** speak with him.)

KJV (**1NT/9**) <u>Hebrews 11:35</u> Women received their dead raised to life again: and others were tortured, not accepting deliverance; that they **might obtain** a better resurrection:)

COM Clarke: <u>Luk 8:18</u> "The word of God, the Divine **seed**, was **planted in their hearts**.")

BOM <u>Alma 34:28</u> And now behold, **my beloved brethren**, I say unto you, do not suppose that this is all; for after ye have done all these things, if ye turn away the needy, and the naked, and visit not the sick and afflicted, and *impart of* your *substance*, if ye have, *to those who stand in need* -- I say unto you, if ye do not any of these things, behold, your prayer is vain, and **availeth** you **nothing**, and ye are as hypocrites who do deny the faith.

KJV (**4NT/60**) <u>James 1:19</u> Wherefore, **my beloved brethren**, let every man be swift to hear, slow to speak, slow to wrath:)

COM Gill: <u>Gal 6:6</u> "such as are under their instructions ought to **impart of** their worldly **substance** to them,")

COM Henry: <u>Luk 16:1-18</u> "to the duty of beneficence and doing good **to those who stand in need** of any thing that either we have or can do for them.")

KJV (1/3) <u>Esther 5:13</u> Yet all this **availeth** me **nothing**, so long as I see Mordecai the Jew sitting at the king's gate.)

*****BOM** <u>Alma 36:28</u> And I know that he **will raise** me **up at the last day**, to *dwell with him in glory*; yea, and I will praise him forever, for he has brought our fathers out of Egypt, and he has **swallowed up** *the Egyptians in the Red Sea*; and he led them by his power into *(13) the promised land*; yea, and he has delivered them *(26) out of bondage* and captivity **from time to time**.

KJV (5NT/49) <u>John 6:44</u> No man can come to me, except the Father which hath sent me draw him: and I **will raise** him **up at the last day**.)

COM Clarke: <u>1Co 6:14</u> "that we may **dwell with him in glory** for ever.")

KJV (14/15) <u>Exodus 7:12</u> For they cast down every man his rod, and they became serpents: but Aaron's rod **swallowed up** their rods.)

COM Gill: <u>Isa 43:3</u> "he drowned **the Egyptians in the Red sea**," (Henry)

COM The phrase "the promised land" is not in the King James Version of the Bible it is a modern concept. Wesley: <u>Heb 3:10</u> "Into my rest - **In the promised land**." (Henry, Clarke)

COM Henry: <u>Isa 49:7-12</u> "but they are applicable to that guidance of divine grace which all God's spiritual Israel are under, from their release **out of bondage** to their settlement in the heavenly Canaan." (Clarke, Wesley)

KJV (3/12) <u>1 Chronicles 9:25</u> And their brethren, which were in their villages, were to come after seven days **from time to time** with them.)

*****BOM** <u>Alma 37:18</u> For he promised unto them that he would preserve these things for a *(7) wise purpose* in him, that he might *(7) show forth his power* unto *(7) (10) future (14th Century) generations*.

COM Henry: <u>Luk 17:1-10</u> "and the **wise purpose** and counsel of God," (Clarke)

COM Clarke: <u>Joh 11:3</u> "to induce our Lord to **show forth his power** and goodness:")

COM Clarke: <u>Jer 36:2</u> "that they may serve for a testimony to **future generations**." (Henry, Gill, Wesley)

BOM <u>Alma 38:9</u> And now, my son, I have told you this that ye may learn wisdom, that ye may **learn of me** that *there is no other way or means whereby man can be saved, only in and through Christ*. Behold, *he is the life* and **the light of the world**. Behold, he is the word of truth and righteousness.

KJV (1NT/2) <u>Matthew 11:29</u> Take my yoke upon you, and **learn of me**; for I am meek and lowly in heart: and ye shall find rest unto your souls.)

COM Henry: <u>Act 4:12</u> "by which salvation from sin can be expected - none given under heaven - **no other means** ever devised by God himself for the salvation of a lost world.")

COM Gill: <u>Act 13:40</u> "no other way, but **in and through Christ**;")

COM Gill: <u>Eph 3:14</u> "and **there is no other way** of coming to him but by Christ;")

COM Gill: <u>Deu 32:3</u> "and his name only; for there is no other under heaven **whereby man can be saved**:")

COM Henry: <u>1Ti 2:1-8</u> "Christ is the way and the truth, and so **he is the life**." (Clarke, Gill)

KJV (**2NT/1**) <u>John 8:12</u> Then spake Jesus again unto them, saying, I am **the light of the world**: he that followeth me shall not walk in darkness, but shall have the light of life.)

***BOM <u>Alma 39:15</u> And now, my son, I would say **somewhat** unto you concerning the coming of Christ. Behold, I say unto you, that it is he that surely shall come to **take away the sins of the world**; yea, he cometh to declare *glad tidings of salvation* unto his people.

KJV (**1NT/7**) <u>John 1:29</u> The next day John seeth Jesus coming unto him, and saith, Behold the Lamb of God, which **taketh away the sin of the world**.)

COM Gill: <u>2Co 10:14</u> "they came with the good news and **glad tidings of salvation** by Christ;" (Henry, Wesley, Clarke)

BOM <u>Alma 39:13</u> And then shall it come to pass, that *the spirits of the wicked*, yea, who are evil -- for behold, they *have no part nor portion* of the Spirit of the Lord; for behold, they chose **evil** works **rather than good**; therefore (*4*) *the spirit of **the devil did enter into them, and take possession of their house -- and these **shall be cast out into outer darkness**; there shall be **weeping, and wailing**, and **gnashing of teeth**, (*30*) *and this because* of their own iniquity, being *led captive by the will of **the devil***.

COM Gill: <u>Ecc 9:6</u> "and the **spirits of the wicked** dead will still continue to love sin,")

COM Gill: <u>Jer 4:14</u> "without the washing of regeneration, there is no seeing nor entering into the kingdom of God; and unless we are washed by Christ, and in his blood, we can have **no part nor portion** with him in the heavenly glory; none shall ascend the holy hill, or dwell in the holy place, but such who have clean hands, and a pure heart;")

KJV (**1/1**) <u>Psalm 52:3</u> Thou lovest **evil** more **than good**; and lying **rather than** to speak righteousness. Selah.)

COM Clarke: <u>Mat 12:31</u> "by the power of God, to **the spirit of the devil**.")

KJV (44NT/94) <u>Matthew 4:1</u> Then was Jesus led up of the Spirit into the wilderness to be tempted of **the devil.**)

KJV (1NT/1) <u>Matthew 8:12</u> But the children of the kingdom **shall be cast out into outer darkness**: there shall be weeping and gnashing of teeth.)

KJV (7NT/2) <u>Matthew 8:12</u> But the children of the kingdom shall be cast out into outer darkness: there shall be **weeping** and **gnashing** of **teeth.**)

KJV (<u>Matthew 13:42</u> And shall cast them into a furnace of fire: there shall be **wailing** and gnashing of teeth.)

COM <u>2Ki 13:23</u> Clarke: "**and this because of** his covenant with their fathers:" (Henry)

COM Henry: <u>2Ti 2:22-26</u> "those who before were **led captive by the devil** at his **will** come to be led into the glorious liberty of the children of God," (Clarke)

BOM <u>Alma 39:14</u> Now this is the state of the souls of the wicked, yea, in darkness, and a state of (47) awful (13th Century) (***Henry, Clarke, Wesley***), **fearful looking for** the **fiery indignation** of **the wrath of God** upon them; thus they *remain in this state*, as well as *the righteous in* **paradise**, **until the time** of their resurrection.

KJV (1NT/1) <u>Hebrews 10:27</u> But a certain **fearful looking for** of judgment and **fiery indignation**, which shall devour the adversaries.)

KJV (10/14) <u>Psalm 78:31</u> **The wrath of God** came upon them, and slew the fattest of them, and smote down the chosen men of Israel.)

COM Gill: <u>Psa 148:2</u> "and happy in the enjoyment of God, in whose presence they always are, and whose face they continually behold; and will ever **remain in this state**,")

COM Gill: <u>Mat 22:12</u> ""Esau the wicked, will veil himself with his garment, and sit among **the righteous in paradise**, in the world to come;")

KJV (3NT/5) <u>Luke 23:43</u> And Jesus said unto him, Verily I say unto thee, Today shalt thou be with me in **paradise.**)

KJV (6/12) <u>Psalm 105:19</u> **Until the time** that his word came: the word of the LORD tried him.)

BOM <u>Alma 40:18</u> Behold, I say unto you, Nay; but it meaneth *the (1) reuniting (15th Century) of the soul* with the *body*, of those from the days of Adam down to **the resurrection of Christ**.

COM Henry: <u>Psa 49:15-20</u> "**The reuniting of the soul and body** at the resurrection.")

KJV (1NT/8) <u>Acts 2:31</u> He seeing this before spake of **the resurrection of Christ**, that his soul was not left in hell, neither his flesh did see corruption.)

BOM <u>Alma 40:19</u> Now, whether *the souls and the bodies* of those of whom has been spoken *shall* all *be (4) reunited (15ᵗʰ Century)* at once, the wicked as well as the righteous, I do not say; let it suffice; that I say that they all come forth; or *(13) in other words,* their resurrection cometh to pass before the resurrection of those who die after **the resurrection of Christ**.

> **COM** Gill: <u>Mat 22:30</u> "At the time of the resurrection, and in that state; when **the bodies and souls** of men **shall be reunited**," (Clarke, Henry)
>
> **COM** Clarke: <u>Gen 25:34</u> "**in other words**, let us now believe-love-obey."(Henry, Wesley)
>
> **KJV (1NT/8)** <u>Acts 2:31</u> He seeing this before spake of **the resurrection of Christ**, that his soul was not left in hell, neither his flesh did see corruption.)

***BOM** <u>Alma 41:5</u> The one raised to (30) happiness (15ᵗʰ Century) (*Note: Henry, Clarke, Wesley*) according to his desires of (30) happiness (15ᵗʰ Century) (*Note: Henry, Clarke, Wesley*), or good according to his desires of good; and the other to evil according to his desires of evil; for as he has desired to do evil **all the day long** even so *shall* he *have* his *reward of evil* when **the night cometh**.

> **KJV** (13/12) <u>Psalm 35:28</u> And my tongue shall speak of thy righteousness and of thy praise **all the day long**.)
>
> **COM** Gill: <u>Pro 24:20</u> "No reward of good things, such as is for the righteous in a way of grace; but he **shall have** a **reward of evil** things, a just recompence of reward for his sins:")
>
> **KJV (1NT/1)** <u>John 9:4</u> I must work the works of him that sent me, while it is day: **the night cometh**, when no man can work.)

BOM <u>Alma 41:13</u> O, my son, this is not the case; but *(2) the **meaning of** the word (19) restoration (14ᵗʰ Century)* is to bring back again *evil for evil*, or carnal for carnal, or **devilish** for **devilish** -- *good for* that which is *good*; righteous for that which is righteous; just for that which is just; merciful for that which is merciful.

> **KJV (1NT/7)** <u>1 Corinthians 14:11</u> Therefore if I know not the **meaning of** the voice, I shall be unto him that speaketh a barbarian, and he that speaketh shall be a barbarian unto me.)
>
> **COM** Wesley: <u>Isa 59:15</u> "The translators reach **the meaning of the word** by prey" (Henry, Clarke)
>
> **COM** Clarke: <u>Isa 45:1</u> "in his decree for the **restoration** of the Jews, to have been given to him by Jehovah, the God of heaven" (Henry, Wesley)
>
> **KJV (1NT/6)** <u>James 3:15</u> This wisdom descendeth not from above, but is earthly, sensual, **devilish**.)
>
> **COM** Henry: <u>Jer 18:18-23</u> ""Shall evil be recompensed for good, and

shall it go unpunished? Wilt not thou recompense me good for that evil?" 2Sa 16:12. To render **good for good** is human, **evil for evil** is brutish, good for evil is Christian, but evil for good is **devilish**; it is so very absurd and wicked a thing that we cannot think but God will avenge it")

***BOM** Alma 42:18 Now, there was a punishment *(6) affixed, (1533 AD)*, and a *just law* given, which brought *(3) remorse (14ᵗʰ Century) of conscience* unto man.

> **COM** Clarke: Joh 3:33 "and such instrument is considered as fully confirmed by having the testator's seal **affixed** to it," (Henry, Gill, Wesley)
>
> **COM** Clarke: 1Pe 3:19 "The inhabitants of the antediluvian world, who, having been disobedient, and convicted of the most flagrant transgressions against God, were sentenced by his **just law** to destruction." (Henry)
>
> **COM** Clarke: Luk 16:23 "and find themselves in torments, under dreadful gnawings, and **remorse of conscience**; and having a terrible sensation of divine wrath" (Gill, Henry, Wesley)

BOM Alma 42:24 For behold, justice exerciseth all his demands, and also mercy (5) claimeth (***Note: Not found)*** all which is her own; and thus, none but the *truly penitent and humble* are saved.

> **COM** Henry: Jam 4:1-10 "If we be **truly penitent and humble** under the marks of God's displeasure, we shall in a little time know the advantages of his favour;" (Clarke, Wesley)

***BOM** Alma 42:30 O my son, **I desire that ye** should deny the *(12) justice of God* no more. Do not *(1) endeavor to **excuse** yourself in the least point because of your sins, by denying the *(12) justice of God*; but do you let the *(12) justice of God*, and his mercy, and his long-suffering have *full sway in* your *heart*; and let it bring you down **to the dust** in humility.

> **KJV (1NT/10)** Ephesians 3:13 Wherefore **I desire that ye** faint not at my tribulations for you, which is your glory.)
>
> **COM** Henry: Rev 18:9-24 "yet they had reason to rejoice in the discoveries of the glorious **justice of God**." (Clarke, Wesley)
>
> **COM** Clarke: 1Ki 11:3 "We may **endeavor to excuse** all this by saying,")
>
> **KJV (3NT/5)** Luke 14:18 And they all with one consent began to make **excuse**. The first said unto him, I have bought a piece of ground, and I must needs go and see it: I pray thee have me **excused**.)
>
> **COM** Clarke: Exo 4:21 "and God chose to permit these dispositions to have their **full sway in** his **heart** without check or restraint from Divine influence:")
>
> **KJV (4/5)** Isaiah 25:12 And the fortress of the high fort of thy walls

shall he bring down, lay low, and bring to the ground, even **to the dust**.)

***BOM** Alma 43:14 Now those descendants were as numerous, (13) nearly (1561), as were the Nephites; and thus the Nephites were *(7) obliged (14th Century) to contend* with their brethren, even unto bloodshed.

> **COM** Clarke: 2Ti 1:18 "triumphing over sufferings and death; perfectly unshaken, unstumbled, with the evils with which he is **obliged to contend**,")

***BOM** Alma 43:30 And he also knowing that it was the only desire of the Nephites to preserve their lands, and their liberty, and their **church (76/259)**, therefore he *thought it no sin* that he should defend them *by (7) stratagem (15th Century)*; therefore, he found by his spies which course the Lamanites were to take.

> **COM** Henry: Psa 31:9-18 "One would think they **thought it no sin** to tell a deliberate lie if it might but serve to expose a good man either to hatred or contempt.")
>
> **COM** Gill: Jer 51:41 "for it was taken **by stratagem** and surprise," (Clarke, Henry, Wesley)

BOM Alma 43:51 Now, the Lamanites were more *numerous*, yea, by *more than double* the number of the Nephites; nevertheless, they were driven **insomuch (20/181)** that they were gathered together in one body in the valley, upon the bank by the river Sidon.

> **COM** Henry: Num 1:17-43 "That Judah is the most **numerous** of them all, **more than double** to Benjamin and Manasseh,")

***BOM** Alma 46:21 And **it came to pass (452/1353)** that when Moroni had proclaimed these words, behold, the people came running together with their armor **girded about** their **loins**, *rend*ing *their garments in token*, or as a covenant, that they would not forsake the Lord their God; or, *(13) in other words,* if they should transgress the commandments of God, or fall into transgression, and be ashamed to **take upon** them **the name of Christ**, the Lord should rend them even as they had rent their garments.

> **KJV (1NT/5)** Luke 12:35 Let your **loins** be **girded about**, and your lights burning;)
>
> **COM** Gill: Jer 36:24 "nor did they **rend their garments in token** of sorrow and mourning on account of either, as used to be when anything blasphemous was said or done, or any bad news were brought.")
>
> **Note:** Notice how extremely unique this phrase is, "rend their garments in token".
>
> **COM** Clarke: Gen 25:34 "**in other words**, let us now believe-love-obey."(Henry, Wesley)
>
> **KJV (1NT/26)** 2 Corinthians 8:4 Praying us with much intreaty that

we would receive the gift, and **take upon** us the fellowship of the ministering to the saints.)

KJV (2NT/23) 1 Peter 4:14 If ye be reproached for **the name of Christ**, happy are ye; for the spirit of glory and of God resteth upon you: on their part he is evil spoken of, but on your part he is glorified.)

***BOM Alma 46:29 And **it came to pass (452/1353)** that when Amalickiah saw that the people of Moroni were more numerous than the Amalickiahites -- and he also saw that his people were doubtful concerning the justice of the cause in which they had undertaken -- therefore, fearing that he should not *gain the point*, he took those of his people who would and departed into the land of Nephi.

COM Henry: Deu 30:15-20 "so prudent, so affectionate, and every way so apt to **gain the point**," (Gill)

***BOM Alma 46:36 And **it came to pass (452/1353)** also, that he caused the title of liberty to be (1) hoisted (15th Century) (*Note: Clarke, Gill, Henry)* upon every tower which was in all the land, which was possessed by the Nephites; and thus Moroni *planted the* standard of liberty among the Nephites.

COM Clarke: Rom 16:18 "who have neither grace nor gifts to **plant the standard of** the cross on the devil's territories,")

BOM Alma 46:39 And **it came to pass (452/1353)** that there were many who died, *firmly believing* that their souls were redeemed by the Lord Jesus Christ; thus they *went out of the world* rejoicing.

COM Gill: Mat 20:30 "being eagerly desirous of having their sight, and **firmly believing** that he was able to restore it to them." (Henry, Clarke)

KJV (8NT/13) Matthew 21:22 And all things, whatsoever ye shall ask in prayer, **believing**, ye shall receive.)

COM Gill: Job 10:21 "Before he **went out of the world**, the way of all flesh, to the grave, his long home, from whence there is no return to this world," (Henry, Wesley)

***BOM Alma 47:23 And **it came to pass (452/1353)** that the king put forth his hand to raise them, as was the custom with the Lamanites, as *a token of peace*, which custom they had taken from the Nephites.

COM Gill: Psa 46:9 "the Targum renders it "round shields" (z): and the destroying of all these military weapons and carriages is **a token of peace**, and of war's being caused to cease, there being no more use for them;")

BOM Alma 48:13 Yea, and he was a man who was *firm in the faith* of Christ, and he **had sworn with an oath** to defend his people, his rights, and his country, and his religion, even to the loss of his blood.

COM Clarke: Deu 31:6 "Stand **firm in the faith**;")

KJV (1NT/2) <u>Acts 2:30</u> Therefore being a prophet, and knowing that God **had sworn with an oath** to him, that of the fruit of his loins, according to the flesh, he would raise up Christ to sit on his throne;)

***BOM** <u>Alma 48:24</u> Nevertheless, they could not suffer to lay down their lives, that their wives and their children should be (1) massacred (1581) by the **barbarous** cruelty of those who were once their brethren, yea, and had dissented from their **church (76/259)**, and had left them and had gone to destroy them by joining the Lamanites.

KJV (1NT/1) <u>Acts 28:2</u> And the **barbarous** people shewed us no little kindness: for they kindled a fire, and received us every one, because of the present rain, and because of the cold.)

COM Henry: <u>1Sa 22:6-19</u> "**Barbarous cruelty**, and such as one cannot think of without horror!" (Clarke, Wesley)

***BOM** <u>Alma 49:11</u> But behold, Amalickiah did not come down himself to battle. And behold, his **chief captains** *durst not attack* the Nephites at the city of Ammonihah, for Moroni had altered *the management of affairs* among the Nephites, **insomuch (20/181)** that the Lamanites were disappointed in their *(2) places of retreat* and they could not come upon them.

KJV (2NT/22) <u>Acts 25:23</u> And on the morrow, when Agrippa was come, and Bernice, with great pomp, and was entered into the place of hearing, with the **chief captains**, and principal men of the city, at Festus' commandment Paul was brought forth.)

COM Henry: <u>Jdg 15:1-8</u> "Samson himself they **durst not attack**, and therefore,")

COM Gill: <u>Act 23:5</u> "though he had got **the management of affairs** in his hands," (Clarke, Wesley)

COM Henry: <u>Mat 10:16-42</u> "in providing **places of retreat** and shelter for them;" (Clarke)

BOM <u>Alma 49:21</u> And **it came to pass (452/1353)** that the captains of the Lamanites brought up their armies before the place of entrance, and began to contend with the Nephites, to get into their *place of **security*** but behold, they were **driven back from time to time, insomuch (20/181)** that they were slain *with an immense slaughter*.

KJV (1NT/11) <u>Acts 17:9</u> And when they had taken **security** of Jason, and of the other, they let them go.)

COM Clarke: <u>Mat 24:20</u> "they could not expect admission into any **place of security** in the land." (Henry)

KJV (2/13) <u>Psalm 114:3</u> The sea saw it, and fled: Jordan was **driven back**.)

KJV (3/12) <u>1 Chronicles 9:25</u> And their brethren, which were in their villages, were to come after seven days **from time to time** with them.)

COM Clarke: <u>Jer 46:2</u> "Nabopolassar sent his son Nebuchadnezzar with an army against him, defeated him **with immense slaughter** near the river Euphrate")

BOM <u>Alma 50:19</u> And *(3) thus we see how merciful* and just are all the *dealings of the Lord*, to the fulfilling of all his words unto **the children of men (22/131)**; yea, we can behold that his **words are verified**, even at this time, which he spake unto Lehi, saying:

> **COM** Gill: <u>Mat 26:47</u> "**Thus we see how** diligent wicked men are in the accomplishment of their evil designs," (Henry)
>
> **COM** Clarke: <u>Exo 13:22</u> "that the **merciful dealings of the Lord** may never be forgotten." (Gill)
>
> **KJV** (1/1) <u>2 Chronicles 6:17</u> Now then, O LORD God of Israel, let thy **word be verified**, which thou hast spoken unto thy servant David.)

*****BOM** <u>Alma 51:2</u> Nevertheless, they did not long maintain an *entire peace* in the land, for there began to be a contention among the people concerning the chief judge Pahoran; for behold, there were a part of the people who desired that a few **particular** *points of the law* should be altered.

> **COM** Gill: <u>Isa 11:13</u> "shall cease among the people of God, and there shall be **entire peace** and harmony among them.")
>
> **KJV** (**2NT/10**) <u>1 Corinthians 12:27</u> Now ye are the body of Christ, and members in **particular**.)
>
> **COM** Clarke: <u>Jam 3:16</u> "altercations about the different **points of the law**,")

*****BOM** <u>Alma 51:16</u> For it was *his first care* to put an end to such contentions and **dissensions** among the people; for behold, this had been hitherto a cause of all their destruction. And **it came to pass (452/1353)** that it was granted according to **the voice of the people**.

> **COM** Henry: <u>Gen 8:20-22</u> "one would have thought, **his first care** would have been to build a house for himself;" Gill, Wesley)
>
> **KJV** (*Note: Only in Acts:* (**3NT/23**) <u>Acts 15:2</u> When therefore Paul and Barnabas had no small **dissension** and disputation with them, they determined that Paul and Barnabas, and certain other of them, should go up to Jerusalem unto the apostles and elders about this question.)
>
> **KJV** (1/24) <u>1 Samuel 8:7</u> And the LORD said unto Samuel, Hearken unto **the voice of the people** in all that they say unto thee: for they have not rejected thee, but they have rejected me, that I should not reign over them.)

*****BOM** <u>Alma 51:17</u> And **it came to pass (452/1353)** that Moroni commanded that his army should go against those king-men, to pull down their pride and their nobility and *level them with the earth*, or they should take up arms and **support** the cause of liberty.

>COM Henry: Amo 9:1-10 "if professors liken themselves to the world, God will **level them with the** world.")
>
>**Note:** Again we have another phrase match where Joseph Smith just varies the ending but maintains the same meaning, "level them with the world" vs. "level them with the earth".
>
>**KJV (2NT/35)** 1 Thessalonians 5:14 Now we exhort you, brethren, warn them that are unruly, comfort the feebleminded, **support** the weak, be patient toward all men.)

BOM Alma 52:1 And now, **it came to pass (452/1353)** in the twenty and sixth year of the reign of the judges over the people of Nephi, behold, when the Lamanites awoke on the first morning of the first month, behold, they found Amalickiah was dead in his own tent; and they also saw that Teancum was ready to *(3) give them battle* on that day.

>COM Gill: Gen 14:8 "With his armed men to meet the four kings, and **give them battle**" (Clarke)

BOM Alma 52:20 And **it came to pass (452/1353)** they sent *(1) embassies (1534)* to the army of the Lamanites, which protected the city of Mulek, to their leader, whose name was Jacob, desiring him that he would come out with his armies to meet them upon the plains between the two cities. But behold, Jacob, who was a Zoramite, would not come out with his army to meet them upon the plains.

>COM Gill: Isa 39:1 "he sent letters and a present to Hezekiah; by his ambassadors, which was always usual in **embassies** and visits" (Henry)

BOM Alma 53:6 And **it came to pass (452/1353)** that Moroni had thus gained a victory over one of the greatest of the armies of the Lamanites, and had obtained possession of the city of Mulek, which was one of *the strongest holds of* the Lamanites in the land of Nephi; and thus he had also built a stronghold to retain his prisoners.

>COM Henry: Act 21:15-26 "for the grace of God can break down **the strongest holds of** Satan.")

BOM Alma 54:7 Yea, I would tell you these things if ye were capable of hearkening unto them; yea, I would tell you concerning that (47) awful (13th Century) (*Henry, Clarke, Wesley*) hell that awaits to receive such murderers as thou and thy brother have been, **except ye repent** and withdraw your *(3) murderous (1535) purposes*, and return with your armies to your own lands.

>**KJV (2NT/19)** Luke 13:3 I tell you, Nay: but, **except ye repent**, ye shall all likewise perish.)
>
>COM Clarke: Gen 34:14 "Thus far they were perfectly right; but to make this holy principle a cloak for their deceitful and **murderous purposes**, was the full sum of all wickedness")

***BOM Alma 55:3 Behold, I know the place where the Lamanites do guard my people whom they have taken prisoners; and as Ammoron would not grant unto me mine **epistle**, behold, I will give unto him according to my words; yea, I will seek death among them until they shall *sue for peace*.

> KJV (**15NT/41**) Romans 16:22 I Tertius, who wrote this **epistle**, salute you in the Lord.)
>
> COM Henry: Gen 32:3-8 "and to **sue for peace** as well as right." (Clarke, Gill, Wesley)

BOM Alma 55:11 For, said they: We are weary, therefore let us take of the wine, (*3*) *and by and by* we shall receive wine for our rations, which will strengthen us to go against the Nephites.

> COM Clarke: Jam 5:7 "The seed of your deliverance is already sown, **and by and by** the harvest of your salvation will take place." (Henry, Wesley, Gill)

BOM Alma 55:17 Yea, even to their women, and all those of their children, as many as were able to use a weapon of war, when Moroni had armed all those prisoners; and all those things were done in *a profound silence*.

> COM Gill: Act 15:12 "there was **a profound silence** in the whole assembly" (Henry, Clarke)

BOM Alma 55:31 But behold, the Nephites were not slow to remember the Lord their God in this their time of affliction. They could not *be taken in their snares*; yea, they would not partake of their wine, **save they** had first given to some of the Lamanite prisoners.

> COM Henry: Eze 23:36-49 "lest they **be taken in their snares**;")
>
> KJV (**1NT/14**) Matthew 19:11 But he said unto them, All men cannot receive this saying, **save they** to whom it is given.)

BOM Alma 56:12 And the Lamanites had also retained many prisoners, all of whom are **chief captains**, for none other have they (*2*) *spared alive*. And we suppose that they are now at this time in the land of Nephi; it is so if they are not slain.

> KJV (**2NT/22**) Acts 25:23 And on the morrow, when Agrippa was come, and Bernice, with great pomp, and was entered into the place of hearing, with the **chief captains**, and principal men of the city, at Festus' commandment Paul was brought forth.)
>
> COM Gill: Lev 16:10 "though **spared alive** for a while,")

BOM Alma 56:17 And now they were determined to *conquer* in this place *or die*; therefore you may well suppose that this *little force* which I brought with me, yea, those sons of mine, gave them (*2*) *great hopes* and much joy.

> COM Gill: Jer 6:23 "to engage in battle, and **conquer or die**;" (Henry, Clarke)
>
> COM Henry: 1Sa 14:16-23 "He, and all the **little force** he had, made a vigorous attack upon the enemy;")

COM Gill: <u>1Sa 23:7</u> "he had no **great hopes** of finding him out," (Henry, Wesley)

***BOM <u>Alma 56:39</u> And **it came to pass (452/1353)** that before *the dawn of the morning*, behold, the Lamanites were pursuing us. Now we were not sufficiently strong to contend with them; yea, I **would not suffer** that my little sons should fall into their hands; therefore we did continue our march, and we took our march into the wilderness.

> **COM** Gill: <u>2Sa 23:4</u> "was as **the dawn of the morning;**")
>
> **KJV** (4/15) <u>Judges 1:34</u> And the Amorites forced the children of Dan into the mountain: for they **would not suffer** them to come down to the valley:)

***BOM <u>Alma 56:50</u> The army of Antipus being weary, because of their long march *in so short a space of time*, were about to fall into the hands of the Lamanites; and had I not returned with my two thousand they would have **obtained their purpose**.

> **COM** Gill: <u>Mat 26:40</u> "was there an occasion for it; and yet, **in so short a space of time**," (Clarke)
>
> **KJV** (**1NT/1**) <u>Acts 27:13</u> And when the south wind blew softly, supposing that they had **obtained their purpose**, loosing thence, they sailed close by Crete.)

BOM <u>Alma 57:12</u> And **it came to pass (452/1353)** that not many days had passed away before the Lamanites began to lose *all hopes of (7) succor (13th Century)*; therefore they **yielded up** the city unto our hands; and thus we had accomplished our designs in obtaining the city Cumeni.

> **COM** Clarke: <u>1Ki 20:43</u> "the Calesians saw clearly that **all hopes of succor** were at an end; which occasioned them so much sorrow and distress that the hardiest could scarcely support it.")
>
> **KJV** (3/5) <u>Genesis 49:33</u> And when Jacob had made an end of commanding his sons, he gathered up his feet into the bed, and **yielded up** the ghost, and was gathered unto his people.)

***BOM <u>Alma 57:20</u> And as the remainder of our army were about to give way before the Lamanites, behold, those two thousand and sixty were *firm and (1) undaunted (1587)*.

> **COM** Gill: <u>Gen 49:24</u> "and so his posterity were unmoved and unshaken, and stood **firm and undaunted**, notwithstanding the powerful enemies they had to deal with, until they were wholly subdued")

***BOM <u>Alma 57:26</u> And now, their *(3) preservation (14th Century)* was astonishing to our whole army, yea, that they should be spared while there was a thousand of our brethren who were slain. And we do justly *ascribe it to the miraculous power of God*, because of their **exceeding faith** in that which they had been taught to believe -- that there was a just God, and whosoever did not doubt, that they should be preserved by his marvelous power.

> **COM** Gill: <u>Dan 6:24</u> "would not **ascribe it to the** providence **of God,**")
>
> **KJV (1NT/11)** <u>1 Timothy 1:14</u> And the grace of our Lord was **exceeding** abundant with **faith** and love which is in Christ Jesus.)

***BOM <u>Alma 58:4</u> And **it came to pass (452/1353)** that I thus did send *an (3) embassy (1534)* to the governor of our land, to acquaint him concerning the affairs of our people. And **it came to pass (452/1353)** that we did wait to receive provisions and strength from the land of Zarahemla.

> **COM** Gill: <u>2Sa 10:1</u> "David sent **an embassy** to their king," Henry, Clarke, Wesley)

BOM <u>Alma 58:6</u> And the Lamanites were *(1) sallying (1560)* forth against us **from time to time,** resolving *by (7) stratagem (15ᵗʰ Century)* to destroy us; nevertheless we could not come to battle with them, because of their (1) retreats (14ᵗʰ Century) and their strongholds.

> **COM** Gill: <u>Jer 14:18</u> "who by **sallying** out of the city upon them," (Henry, Wesley, Clarke)
>
> **KJV** (3/12) <u>1 Chronicles 9:25</u> And their brethren, which were in their villages, were to come after seven days **from time to time** with them.)
>
> **COM** Gill: <u>Jer 51:41</u> "for it was taken **by stratagem** and surprise," (Clarke, Henry, Wesley)
>
> **COM** Clarke: <u>1Sa 4:2</u> "There is no doubt that both the Philistines and Israelites had what might be called the art of war, according to which they marshalled their troops in the field, constructed their camps, and conducted **their retreats**, sieges, etc.; but we know not the principles on which they acted." (Henry)

BOM <u>Alma 59:7</u> And thus being *(4) exceedingly numerous*, yea, and receiving strength **from day to day**, by the command of Ammoron they came forth against the people of Nephihah, and they did begin to slay them with an *(2) exceedingly great slaughter* .

> **COM** Clarke: <u>Isa 3:7</u> "The daily provision for Solomon's household, whose attendants were **exceedingly numerous**, was proportionately great," (Henry)
>
> **KJV** (6/10) <u>1 Chronicles 16:23</u> Sing unto the LORD, all the earth; shew forth **from day to day** his salvation.)

***BOM <u>Alma 59:8</u> And their armies were so numerous that the remainder of the people of Nephihah were *(7) obliged (14ᵗʰ Century) to flee* before them; and they came even and joined the army of Moroni.

> **COM** Gill: <u>2Sa 23:12</u> "made a **great slaughter** among them, entirely routed them, so that they that escaped his sword were **obliged to flee**:"(Henry)

BOM Alma 60:21 Or do ye suppose that the Lord will still deliver us, while we sit upon our thrones and do not *make use of the means which* the Lord has provided for us?

> **COM** Gill: Act 23:17 "yet he thought it his duty to **make use of the means, which** providence had put in his way, for his preservation and safety")
>
> **Note:** Again a variation with the same meaning.

BOM Alma 60:24 And now, except ye do repent of that which ye have done, and begin to be *up and doing*, and send forth food and men unto us, and also unto Alma, that he may **support** those parts of our country which he has regained, and that we may also recover the remainder of our possessions in these parts, behold it will be **expedient** that we contend no more with the Lamanites until we have first cleansed our inward vessel, yea, even the great head of our government.

> **COM** Henry: Pro 27:23-27 "We must be diligent and take pains; not only sit down and contrive, but be **up and doing:**" (Gill)
>
> **KJV** (**2NT/35**) 1 Thessalonians 5:14 Now we exhort you, brethren, warn them that are unruly, comfort the feebleminded, **support** the weak, be patient toward all men.)
>
> **KJV** (**7NT/62**) John 11:50 Nor consider that it is **expedient** for us, that one man should die for the people, and that the whole nation perish not.)

BOM Alma 60:27 And I will come unto you, and if there be any among you that has a desire for freedom, yea, if there be even a spark of freedom remaining, behold I will *stir up insurrections among* you, even until those who have desires **to usurp** power and **authority** shall become extinct.

> **COM** Clarke: 1Ki 1:52 "**stir up insurrections among** the people,")
>
> **KJV** (**1NT/5**) 1 Timothy 2:12 But I suffer not a woman to teach, nor **to usurp authority** over the man, but to be in silence.)

BOM Alma 60:32 Behold, can you suppose that the Lord will spare you and come out in judgment against the Lamanites, when it is the tradition of their fathers that has caused their hatred, yea, and it has been (1) redoubled (15th Century) by those who have dissented from us, while your iniquity is for the cause of your love of glory and (9) *the vain things of the world*?

> **COM** Gill: Jer 34:22 "that it should return to Jerusalem again, and carry on the siege with **redoubled** rigour:" (Henry, Clarke, Wesley)
>
> **COM** Gill: Pro 30:8 "and his affections taken off from **the vain things of the world**,")

BOM Alma 62:20 And when the night came, Moroni went forth in *the darkness of the night*, and came upon the top of the wall to **spy out** in what part of the city the Lamanites did camp with their army.

> **COM** Gill: Jer 39:4 "and they took the advantage of the **darkness of**

the night to make their escape:" (Henry, Clarke, Wesley)

KJV (9/2) Numbers 13:17 And Moses sent them to **spy out** the land of Canaan, and said unto them, Get you up this way southward, and go up into the mountain:)

***BOM Alma 62:43 And Moroni **yielded up** the command of his armies into the hands of his son, whose name was Moronihah; and he retired to his own house that he might spend *the remainder of his days in peace.*

> **KJV** (3/5) Genesis 49:33 And when Jacob had made an end of commanding his sons, he gathered up his feet into the bed, and **yielded up** the ghost, and was gathered unto his people.)
>
> **COM** Gill: Jer 15:11 "that it should be well with him in his latter end; **the remainder of his days** should be comfortable or be spent **in peace** and prosperity")

BOM Alma 2:7 And **it came to pass (452/1353)** that he met Kishkumen, and he gave unto him a sign; therefore Kishkumen (*1*) *made known unto him the* (*6*) *object* (*14ᵗʰ Century*) (***Note: As a thing: Clarke, Henry, Wesley)*** *of his desire,* (desiring that he would conduct him to the **judgment-seat** that he might murder Alma.

> **COM** Clarke: Gen 4:26 "which was **made known unto him** by prophecy"(Henry, Wesley)
>
> **COM** Clarke: Pro 18:1 ""He who is separated shall seek the desired thing, (i.e., **the object of his desire**)," (Henry)
>
> **KJV** (**10NT/56**) Romans 14:10 But why dost thou judge thy brother? or why dost thou set at nought thy brother? for we shall all stand before the **judgment seat** of Christ.)

BOM Alma 3:35 Nevertheless they did fast and pray oft, and did wax stronger and stronger in their humility, and firmer and firmer in the faith of Christ, unto the filling their souls with **joy and consolation**, yea, even to the purifying and the *sanctification of their hearts,* which sanctification cometh because of their yielding their hearts unto God.

> **KJV** (**1NT/1**) Philemon 1:7 For we have great **joy and consolation** in thy love, because the bowels of the saints are refreshed by thee, brother.)
>
> **COM** Gill: Rom 9:23 "and in putting his grace in them; or in other words, in justifying them by the imputation and application of the righteousness of his Son unto them, and by the regeneration, renovation, and **sanctification of their hearts,** by his Spirit.")

BOM Alma 4:12 And it was **because of the pride of** their hearts, because of their **exceeding riches**, yea, it was because of their oppression to the poor, withholding their food from the hungry, withholding their clothing from the naked, and *smiting* their humble brethren *upon the cheek, making a mock* of that which was sacred, denying **the spirit of prophecy** and of revelation, murdering, (11) plundering (1632) (*Note: **Henry, Clarke, Wesley,** Gill*), lying, stealing, committing adultery, rising up in (*4*) *great contentions* , and deserting away into the land of Nephi, among the Lamanites –

> **KJV** (1/3) Job 35:12 There they cry, but none giveth answer, **because of the pride of** evil men.)
>
> **KJV** (**1NT/4**) Ephesians 2:7 That in the ages to come he might shew the **exceeding riches** of his grace in his kindness toward us through Christ Jesus.)
>
> **COM** Gill: Psa 3:7 "to **smite** anyone **upon the cheek** is reckoned reproachful, and is casting contempt upon them;")
>
> **COM** Gill: Pro 14:9 "they are so far from **making a mock** at sin,")
>
> **KJV** (1/18) Revelation 19:10 And I fell at his feet to worship him. And he said unto me, See thou do it not: I am thy fellowservant, and of thy brethren that have the testimony of Jesus: worship God: for the testimony of Jesus is **the spirit of prophecy**.
>
> **COM** Henry: 2Ch 24:15-27 "probably on occasion of some solemn feast, when this Zechariah, being filled with **the spirit of prophecy**, and known (it is likely) to be a prophet,")
>
> **COM** Gill: Luk 12:51 "through the sin of man, the occasion of **great contention**, discord, and division." (Henry)

BOM Alma 4:23 And because of their iniquity the **church (76/259)** had begun to (26) dwindle; (1596 AD) and they began to (5) disbelieve (1644) (*Note:* Gill*, Clarke, Henry, Wesley)* in **the spirit of prophecy** and in **the spirit of revelation**; and the judgments of God did *stare them in the face*.

> **COM** Joseph Smith uses dwindle and dwindled interchangeable, and both are in Henry, while dwindle is in all (Henry: Mar 14:53-65: "Peter followed at a distance, such a degree of cowardice was his late courage **dwindled** into,")
>
> **KJV** (1/18) Revelation 19:10 And I fell at his feet to worship him. And he said unto me, See thou do it not: I am thy fellowservant, and of thy brethren that have the testimony of Jesus: worship God: for the testimony of Jesus is **the spirit of prophecy**.
>
> **COM** Henry: 2Ch 24:15-27 "probably on occasion of some solemn feast, when this Zechariah, being filled with **the spirit of prophecy**, and known (it is likely) to be a prophet,")
>
> **KJV** (**1NT/9**) Ephesians 1:17 That the God of our Lord Jesus Christ, the Father of glory, may give unto you **the spirit of** wisdom and **revelation** in the knowledge of him:)
>
> **COM** Gill: Act 9:6 "so persons under first convictions "tremble" at the sight of their sins, which rise up like so many ghosts, and **stare them in the face**, and load their consciences with guilt")

***BOM** Alma 5:8 And now my sons, behold I have **somewhat** more to desire of you, which desire is, that ye may not do these things that ye may boast, but that ye may do these things to **lay up for yourselves** a **treasure in heaven**, yea, which is eternal, and which **fadeth not away**; yea, that ye may have that *precious (1) gift of eternal life*, which *we (2) have reason to suppose* hath been given to our fathers.

> **KJV (1NT/1)** <u>Matthew 6:20</u> But **lay up for yourselves treasure**s in **heaven**, where neither moth nor rust doth corrupt, and where thieves do not break through nor steal;)
>
> **KJV (2NT/1)** <u>1 Peter 1:4</u> To an inheritance incorruptible, and undefiled, and that **fadeth not away**, reserved in heaven for you,)
>
> **COM** Clarke: <u>Joh 6:68</u> "and none can confer the **gift of eternal life** but thou alone.") (Clarke: <u>1Pe 1:2</u> "They who receive the **precious gift of** faith thereby become the sons of God; and, being sons, they shall receive the Spirit of holiness, to walk as Christ also walked.")
>
> **KJV (26NT/25)** <u>Matthew 19:16</u> And, behold, one came and said unto him, Good Master, what good thing shall I do, that I may have **eternal life**?)
>
> **COM** Henry: <u>Luk 2:41-52</u> "**We have reason to suppose** that Joseph went up likewise at the feasts of pentecost and tabernacles;" (Clarke)

***BOM <u>Alma 5:9</u> O remember, remember, my sons, the words which king Benjamin spake unto his people; yea, remember that there is no other way nor means whereby man can be saved, only through *the atoning blood of Jesus Christ*, who shall come, yea, remember that he cometh to redeem the world.

> **COM** Clarke: <u>1Pe 1:2</u> "**the atoning blood of Jesus Christ** which was typified by the sprinkling of the blood of sacrifices under the law,")

BOM <u>Alma 5:12</u> And now, my sons, remember, remember that it is upon the rock of our Redeemer, who is Christ, **the Son of God**, **(43NT/49)** that ye must build your foundation; that when **the devil** shall send forth his mighty winds, yea, his shafts in the whirlwind, yea, when all his hail and his mighty storm shall beat upon you, it shall have no power over you to drag you down to the **gulf** of misery and *endless wo, (3)* because of the rock upon which ye are built, which is *a sure foundation*, a *foundation* whereon if men build they cannot fall.

> **KJV (1NT/6)** <u>Luke 16:26</u> And beside all this, between us and you there is a great **gulf** fixed: so that they which would pass from hence to you cannot; neither can they pass to us, that would come from thence.)
>
> **COM** Clarke: <u>Eze 3:18</u> "How many loads of **endless wo** must such have to bear!")
>
> **COM** Clarke: <u>1Pe 2:4</u> "I lay in Zion for a foundation a stone, a tried stone, a precious corner stone, **a sure foundation**. Jesus Christ is, in

both the prophet and apostle, represented as the foundation on which the Christian Church is built")

BOM Alma 6:2 For behold, there were many of the Nephites who had become **hardened and impenitent** and (*2*) *grossly* (*14th Century*) *wicked*, **insomuch (20/181)** that they did (*1*) *reject the word of God* and all the preaching and prophesying which did come among them.

> **KJV (1NT/1)** Romans 2:5 But after thy **hard**ness **and impenitent** heart treasurest up unto thyself wrath against the day of wrath and revelation of the righteous judgment of God;)
>
> **COM** Henry: 1Pe 4:1-3 "It is a Christian's duty not only to abstain from what is **grossly wicked**,")
>
> **COM** Clarke: Gen 40:23 "and lead them to **reject the word of God** entirely,")

***BOM** Alma 6:20 And now **it came to pass (452/1353)** that when the Lamanites found that there were robbers among them they were (*14*) *exceedingly sorrowful*; and they did *use every means in their power to destroy* them off the face of the earth.

But behold, Satan did stir up the hearts of **the more part** of the Nephites, **insomuch (20/181)** that they did unite with those *bands of robbers*, and did enter into their covenants and their oaths, that they would protect and preserve one another in whatsoever (*2*) *difficult circumstances* they should be placed, that they should not suffer for their murders, and their plunderings, and their stealings.

> **COM** Henry: Gen 3:17-19 "Did sorrow come in with sin? He was a man of sorrows, his soul was, in his agony, **exceedingly sorrowful**.")
>
> **COM** Clarke: Rom 3:15 "They make **use** of **every means in their power to destroy** the reputation and lives of the innocent.")
>
> **KJV (2NT/26)** Acts 19:32 Some therefore cried one thing, and some another: for the assembly was confused: and **the more part** knew not wherefore they were come together. Words in OT but not exact phrase)
>
> **COM** Henry: Jdg 6:1-6 "quarter themselves upon it, and enrich themselves with its spoils - **bands of robbers**, and no better." (Clarke, Gill)
>
> **COM** Gill: 2Th 1:11 "and in encouraging, supporting, and maintaining it under the most **difficult circumstances**," (Clarke)

***BOM** Alma 6:31 And now behold, he had got great hold upon the hearts of the Nephites; yea, **insomuch (20/181)** that they had become (*3*) *exceedingly wicked*; yea, **the more part** of them *had turned out of the way of righteousness*, and did **trample under their feet** the commandments of God, and did turn unto their own ways, and did build up unto themselves idols of their gold and their silver.

> **COM** Clark: <u>Jer 51:35</u> "yet in return they, being themselves **exceedingly wicked**, shall suffer for all the carnage they have made, and for all the blood they have shed." (Henry)
>
> **KJV (2NT/26)** <u>Acts 19:32</u> Some therefore cried one thing, and some another: for the assembly was confused: and **the more part** knew not wherefore they were come together. Words in OT but not exact phrase)
>
> **KJV (2/1)** <u>Job 31:7</u> If my step hath **turned out of the way**, and mine heart walked after mine eyes, and if any blot hath cleaved to mine hands;)
>
> **KJV (1NT/6)** <u>Matthew 7:6</u> Give not that which is holy unto the dogs, neither cast ye your pearls before swine, lest they **trample them under their feet**, and turn again and rend you.)
>
> **COM** Gill: <u>Job 31:8</u> "If what he had before said was not true; but he **had turned out of the way of righteousness**,")

BOM <u>Alma 7:19</u> And behold, instead of gathering you, except ye will repent, behold, he shall scatter you forth that ye shall become *meat for dogs* and wild beasts.

> **COM** Henry: <u>1Ki 21:17-29</u> "particularly that those who died in the city should be **meat for dogs** and those who died in the field meat for birds")

BOM <u>Alma 7:24</u> For behold, they are more righteous than you, for they have not sinned against that *(6) great knowledge*, which ye have received; therefore the Lord will be merciful unto them; yea, he will *lengthen out their days* and increase their seed, even when thou shalt be **utterly destroyed** except thou shalt repent.

> **COM** Gill: uses this phrase many times: <u>Joh 4:25</u> "and from a common prevailing notion among the Jews, that the times of the Messiah would be times of **great knowledge**, founded on several prophecies,")
>
> **COM** Henry: <u>Jer 15:15-21</u> "Take me not away by a sudden stroke, but in thy long-suffering **lengthen out** my days." (Wesley, Clarke)
>
> **KJV (21/3)** <u>Exodus 22:20</u> He that sacrificeth unto any god, save unto the LORD only, he shall be **utterly destroyed**.)

BOM <u>Alma 8:24</u> And now, seeing ye know these things and cannot deny them except ye shall lie, therefore in this **ye have sinned**, for ye have rejected all these things, notwithstanding *so many evidences* which ye have received; yea, even ye have received all things, both **things in heaven, and** all **things** which are **in the earth**, as a witness that they are true.

> **KJV (4/1)** <u>Exodus 32:30</u> And it came to pass on the morrow, that Moses said unto the people, **Ye have sinned** a great sin: and now I will go up unto the LORD; peradventure I shall make an atonement

for your sin.)

COM Clarke: <u>Gen 42:38</u> "How strange is it that our faith, after so **many evidences** of his goodness, should still be so weak;" Henry, Gill)

KJV (**2NT/1**) <u>Philippians 2:10</u> That at the name of Jesus every knee should bow, of **things in heaven, and things in earth**, and things under the earth;)

BOM <u>Alma 12:5</u> Yea, how quick to be **lifted up** in **pride**; yea, how quick to boast, and do all manner of that which is iniquity; and how slow are they to remember the Lord their God, and to give ear unto his counsels, yea, how slow to walk *in wisdom's paths*!

KJV (**1NT/4**) <u>1 Timothy 3:6</u> Not a novice, lest being **lifted up** with **pride** he fall into the condemnation of the devil.)

COM Gill: <u>Psa 119:35</u> "in the law of God, after the inward man; in the commandments of Christ, which are not grievous; **in wisdom's** ways and **paths**, which are pleasantness and peace")

BOM <u>Alma 12:14</u> Yea, if he say unto the earth -- Thou shalt go back, that it *lengthen out the day* for many hours -- it is done;

COM Henry: <u>Jer 15:15-21</u> "Take me not away by a sudden stroke, but in thy long-suffering **lengthen out** my **days**." (Wesley, Clarke)

COM Henry: <u>Jos 10:7-14</u> "He bids the **sun stand still** (See next verse) upon Gibeon, the place of action and the seat of war, intimating that what he designed in this request was the advantage of Israel against their enemies; it is probable that the sun was now declining, and that he did not call for the **lengthen**ing **out** of **the day** until he observed it hastening towards it period.")

BOM <u>Alma 12:15</u> And thus, (*16*) *according to his word* the earth goeth back, and it appeareth unto man that the sun **standeth still**; yea, and behold, this is so; for surely it is the earth that moveth and not the sun.

COM Clarke: <u>Luk 1:38</u> "Done unto her **according to his word**." (Henry)

KJV (1/1) <u>Zechariah 11:16</u> For, lo, I will raise up a shepherd in the land, which shall not visit those that be cut off, neither shall seek the young one, nor heal that that is broken, nor feed that that **standeth still**: but he shall eat the flesh of the fat, and tear their claws in pieces.)

BOM <u>Alma 12:24</u> And (*7) may God grant*, in his great fulness, that men might be brought unto repentance and **good works**, that they might be restored unto *grace for grace*, **according to their works**.

COM Clarke: <u>2Th 3:16</u> "**May God grant** you prosperity always, and everywhere.")

KJV (**16NT/11**) <u>Matthew 5:16</u> Let your light so shine before men, that they may see your **good works**, and glorify your Father which is in heaven.)

COM Gill: Mat 12:35 "and who has the grace of God implanted in him: for "the good treasure the heart", is not what he is naturally possessed of, but what is put into him: and is no other than the superabundant grace of God, or that **grace for grace**, which he has received out of Christ's **fulness**, and the rich experience of it he is blessed with" (Clarke, Henry, Wesley)

KJV (3NT/13) Revelation 20:13 And the sea gave up the dead which were in it; and death and hell delivered up the dead which were in them: and they were judged every man **according to their works**.)

***BOM Alma 12:26 Yea, who shall be *(9)* (9) consigned (1528) *to a state of endless misery*, fulfilling the words which say: **They that have done good** shall have everlasting **life; and they that have done evil** shall have everlasting **damnation**. And **thus it is**. Amen.

COM Gill: 2Th 2:3 "but because they are by the righteous judgment of God appointed and **consigned to** everlasting destruction;" (Clarke, Wesley, Henry)

COM Henry: Mat 25:31-46 "If they must be doomed to such **a state of endless misery**, yet may they not have some good company there?")

KJV (1NT/1) John 5:29 And shall come forth; **they that have done good**, unto the resurrection of **life**; and **they that have done evil**, unto the resurrection of **damnation**.)

KJV (2NT/6) Luke 24:46 And said unto them, **Thus it is** written, and thus it behooved Christ to suffer, and to rise from the dead the third day:)

BOM Alma 13:25 And now when ye talk, ye say: If our days had been *in the days of* our *fathers of old*, we would not have slain the prophets; we would not have stoned them, and cast them out.

COM Henry: Mal 3:7-12 "either as **in the days of** their **fathers of old**, who were sent into captivity for their disobedience," (Gill, Clarke)

BOM Alma 13:38 But behold, your *days of probation (15th Century)* are past; ye have *(4) procrastinated (1588)* the day of your salvation until it is (1) everlastingly (13th Century) (*Note: Clarke*, Gill, *Henry, Wesley)* too late, and your destruction is made sure; yea, for ye have sought all the days of your lives for that which ye could not obtain; and ye have sought for (30) happiness (15th Century) (*Note: Henry, Clarke, Wesley)* in doing iniquity, which thing is *(2) contrary to the nature of* that righteousness which is in our great and *Eternal Head*.

COM Clarke: Mat 8:12 "and now the **day of probation** is ended,)

COM Gill: Eze 13:22 "and that it is in their power to **repent** when they please, and therefore **procrastinate** it to the last." (Henry)

COM Gill: Rom 3:7 "nothing is more **contrary to the nature of God**," (Henry, Wesley, Clarke)

COM Clarke: Luk 9:62 "So that the appointment of any 'vicar on earth,' to represent that rock or **eternal head** of the Church whose continual presence")

BOM Alma 14:13 And if ye **believe on his name** ye will repent of all your sins, that thereby ye may have a remission of them *through his (5) merits, (14ᵗʰ Century)*

KJV (1NT/12) John 1:12 But as many as received him, to them gave he power to become the sons of God, even to them that **believe on his name**:)

COM Clarke: Mar 10:50 "to be saved only **through** the **merits** of Christ." (Clarke: Phi 3:8 "That superior light, information, and blessedness which come through the Gospel of Jesus Christ; justification through his blood, sanctification by his Spirit, and eternal glory **through his merits** and intercession.") (Henry)

BOM Alma 14:18 Yea, and it bringeth to pass the *condition of repentance,* that whosoever repenteth the same is not **hewn down and cast into the fire**; but whosoever repenteth not is **hewn down and cast into the fire**; and there cometh upon them again a *(8) spiritual death,* yea, a **second death**, for they are cut off again as to **things pertaining to** righteousness.

COM Gill: Jer 39:16 "not what promised good, on **condition of repentance** and amendment;")

KJV (2NT/13) Matthew 7:19 Every tree that bringeth not forth good fruit is **hewn down, and cast into the fire**.)

COM Clarke: Mat 8:22 "Natural death is the separation of the body and soul; **spiritual death**, the separation of God and the soul:" (Henry, Gill, Wesley)

KJV (4NT/6) Revelation 20:14 And death and hell were cast into the lake of fire. This is the **second death**.)

KJV (4NT/9) Acts 1:3 To whom also he shewed himself alive after his passion by many infallible proofs, being seen of them forty days, and speaking of the **things pertaining to** the kingdom of God)

***BOM Alma 15:6 Yea, I say unto you, that **the more part** of them are doing this, and they are **striving** with *(1) unwearied (13ᵗʰ Century) diligence* that they may bring the remainder of their brethren to **the knowledge of the truth**; therefore there are many who do add to their numbers daily.

KJV (2NT/26) Acts 19:32 Some therefore cried one thing, and some another: for the assembly was confused: and **the more part** knew not wherefore they were come together.)

KJV (3NT/6) <u>Hebrews 12:4</u> Ye have not yet resisted unto blood, **striving** against sin.)

COM (Henry: <u>Rom 15:17-21</u> "His **unwearied diligence** and industry in his work. He was one that laboured more abundantly than they all.")

KJV (3NT/15) <u>1 Timothy 2:4</u> Who will have all men to be saved, and to come unto the **knowledge of the truth**.)

BOM <u>Alma 16:12</u> And there was **but *little (1)* alteration (*14th Century*)** in the affairs of the people, *(76) save it were* the people began to be more hardened in iniquity, and do more and more of that which was contrary to the commandments of God, in the eighty and ninth year of the reign of the judges.

KJV (1/7) <u>Deuteronomy 28:38</u> Thou shalt carry much seed out into the field, and shalt gather **but little** in; for the locust shall consume it.)

COM Clarke: <u>Joh 17:12</u> "with very **little alteration**:" (Henry, Gill)

Note: "save it were" This phrase is quite unique and found in works such as The Scarlet Letter, and Geofffrey Chaucer, The Canterbury Tales, The Reeves Prologue noted here: "**Save it were** only old Oswald the reeve, Because he was a carpenter by craft." It appears in the BOM 76 times.)

BOM <u>Alma 16:18</u> That *it is not reasonable that such a being as* a Christ shall come; if so, and he be **the Son of God, (43NT/49)** the **Father of heaven and of earth,** as it has been spoken, why will he not show himself unto us as well as unto them who shall be at Jerusalem?

COM Gill: <u>Num 32:6</u> "**it is not reasonable that** your brethren should be left by you and engage in a war with your common enemies,")

COM Henry: <u>1Co 15:35-50</u> "The first Adam was made a living soul, **such a being as** ourselves,")

KJV (2NT/5) <u>Matthew 11:25</u> At that time Jesus answered and said, I thank thee, O **Father**, Lord **of heaven and earth**, because thou hast hid these things from the wise and prudent, and hast revealed them unto babes.)

BOM <u>3 Nephi 1:24</u> And there were no contentions, *(76) save it were* a few that began to preach, *(2) endeavoring (15th Century) to prove* by the **scriptures** that it was no more **expedient** to observe the law of Moses. Now in this thing they did **err**, having **not** understood **the scriptures**.

COM Clarke: <u>2Co 2:16</u> "and **endeavoring to prove** that he has excluded the major part even of their own world")

KJV (21NT/41) <u>Matthew 21:42</u> Jesus saith unto them, Did ye never read in the **scriptures**, The stone which the builders rejected, the same is become the head of the corner: this is the Lord's doing, and it is marvellous in our eyes?)

KJV (7NT/62) John 11:50 Nor consider that it is **expedient** for us, that one man should die for the people, and that the whole nation perish not.)

KJV (1NT/1) Matthew 22:29 Jesus answered and said unto them, Ye do **err, not** knowing **the scriptures**, nor the power of God.)

***BOM** 3 Nephi 1:27 And **it came to pass (452/1353)** that the ninety and third year did also pass away in peace, (76) save it were for the Gadianton robbers, who dwelt upon the mountains, who did (2) (2) infest (1602) the land; for so strong were their holds and their secret places that the people could not (22) overpower (1593 AD) them; therefore they did commit many murders, and did do much slaughter among the people.

> **COM** Clarke: Exo 8:3 "The expression, bring forth abundantly, not only shows the vast numbers of those animals, which should now **infest the land**,")

> **COM** Henry: Jer 50:33-46 "he can **overpower** all the force that is against them," (Clarke, Wesley)

***BOM** 3 Nephi 2:12 Therefore, all the Lamanites who had become converted unto the Lord did unite with their brethren, the Nephites, and were compelled, *for the safety of their lives* and their women and their children, to (9) *take up arms against* those Gadianton robbers, yea, and also to maintain their rights, and the (10) privileges (12th Century) of their **church (76/259)** and of their worship, and their freedom and their liberty.

> **COM** Gill: Jer 48:6 "giving counsel to the Moabites to betake themselves to flight **for the safety of their lives**, these being in great danger;")

> **COM** Henry: Jer 20:7-13 "God's being a mighty God bespeaks him a terrible God to all those that **take up arms against** him or any one that,")

> **COM** Henry: 1Co 9:19-23 "will not plead and insist upon **rights and privileges** in bar to this design." (Clarke, Gill)

BOM 3 Nephi 2:13 And **it came to pass (452/1353)** that before this thirteenth year had passed away the Nephites were *threatened with* **utter destruction** because of this war, which had become (15) *exceedingly sore.*

> **KJV (2/12)** 1 Kings 20:42 And he said unto him, Thus saith the LORD, Because thou hast let go out of thy hand a man whom I appointed to **utter destruction**, therefore thy life shall go for his life, and thy people for his people)

> **COM** Henry: Hos 10:9-15 "They are **threatened with utter destruction**,")

BOM 3 Nephi 3:5 Therefore I have written this **epistle**, sealing it **with mine own hand**, **feeling** for your welfare, because of your (9) firmness (14th

Century) in that which ye believe to be right, and your *noble spirit in the field of battle.*

> **KJV (15NT/41)** <u>Romans 16:22</u> I Tertius, who wrote this **epistle**, salute you in the Lord.)
>
> **KJV (8/9)** <u>1 Samuel 25:33</u> And blessed be thy advice, and blessed be thou, which hast kept me this day from coming to shed blood, and from avenging myself **with mine own hand.**)
>
> **KJV (2NT/7)** <u>Ephesians 4:19</u> Who being past **feeling** have given themselves over unto lasciviousness, to work all uncleanness with greediness.)
>
> **COM** Clarke: <u>Heb 10:33</u> "This was a **noble spirit;**" (Henry)

BOM 3 Nephi 3:9 And behold, I am Giddianhi; and I am the governor of this the secret society of Gadianton; which society and the works thereof I know to be good; and they are *(2) of ancient date;* and they have been *(18) handed down* unto us.

> **COM** Gill: <u>Phi 4:22</u> "are spurious, though **of ancient date**, being made mention of by Austin and Jerom" (Henry, Clarke)
>
> **COM** Clarke: <u>Mat 15:2</u> "that had been successively **handed down from** Moses through every **generation**, but not committed to writing.")

BOM <u>3 Nephi 4:7</u> And **it came to pass (452/1353)** that they did come up to battle; and it was in the sixth month; and behold, **great and terrible** was the day that they did come up to battle; and they were **girded about after the manner of** robbers; and they had a lamb-skin about their **loins**, and they were *dyed in blood*, and their **heads** were **shorn**, and they had head-plates upon them; and **great and terrible** was the appearance of the armies of Giddianhi, because of their armor, and because of their being *dyed in blood.*

> **KJV (7/16)** <u>Deuteronomy 1:19</u> And when we departed from Horeb, we went through all that **great and terrible** wilderness, which ye saw by the way of the mountain of the Amorites, as the LORD our God commanded us; and we came to Kadeshbarnea.)
>
> **KJV (18/33)** <u>Genesis 18:11</u> Now Abraham and Sarah were old and well stricken in age; and it ceased to be with Sarah after the manner of women.)
>
> **KJV (1NT/5)** <u>Luke 12:35</u> Let your **loins** be **girded about**, and your lights burning;)
>
> **COM** Gill: <u>Isa 63:1</u> ""with dyed garments", or "stained" (q); that is, with the blood of his enemies; so Jarchi interprets it **dyed in blood**, or dipped in it;")
>
> **KJV (1NT/3)** <u>Acts 18:18</u> And Paul after this tarried there yet a good while, and then took his leave of the brethren, and sailed thence into Syria, and with him Priscilla and Aquila; having **shorn** his **head** in

Cenchrea: for he had a vow.)

BOM 3 Nephi 4:23 And **it came to pass (452/1353)** that Zemnarihah did give command unto his people that they should withdraw themselves from the siege, and march into the (1) *furthermost (15ᵗʰ Century) parts of* the land northward.

> **COM** Gill: Isa 13:5 "from the ends of the earth; the **furthermost parts of** it,")

***BOM 3 Nephi 4:29 May the Lord preserve his people in *righteousness* and in *holiness of heart,* that they may cause to be *felled to the earth* all who shall seek to slay them because of power and *(18) secret (21) combinations (14ᵗʰ Century),* even as this man hath been *felled to the earth.*

> **COM** Clarke: Rom 2:29 "with their rites and external performances no farther than they led to **holiness of heart and righteousness** of life.")
>
> **COM** Clarke: Jer 22:7 "there being no resistance, every tree is soon **felled to the earth**.")
>
> **COM** Gill: Job 12:22 "likewise the **secret** plots, counsels, and **combinations** of wicked men,")

BOM 3 Nephi 4:33 And their hearts were **swollen** with joy, unto the *(1) gushing (15ᵗʰ Century) out* of many *tears,* because of the **great goodness** of God in delivering them out of the hands of their enemies; and they knew it was because of their repentance and their humility that they had been delivered from an **everlasting destruction**.

> **KJV (1NT/7)** Acts 28:6 Howbeit they looked when he should have **swollen**, or fallen down dead suddenly: but after they had looked a great while, and saw no harm come to him, they changed their minds, and said that he was a god.)
>
> **COM** Gill: Eze 24:16 "neither shall thy **tears** run down; his cheeks, by which vent would be given to his grief, and his mind somewhat eased; but all care was to be taken to prevent any **gushing** of them out of his eyes," (Gill: Isa 48:21 "their **gushing out** denotes the abundance of it")
>
> **KJV** (4/3) Nehemiah 9:25 And they took strong cities, and a fat land, and possessed houses full of all goods, wells digged, vineyards, and oliveyards, and fruit trees in abundance: so they did eat, and were filled, and became fat, and delighted themselves in thy **great goodness**.)
>
> **KJV (1NT/9)** 2 Thessalonians 1:9 Who shall be punished with **everlasting destruction** from the presence of the Lord, and from the glory of his power;)

***BOM 3 Nephi 5:20 I am Mormon, and a pure *(25) descendant (1600 AD) of* Lehi. I have *reason to bless* my *God* and my Savior Jesus Christ, that he brought our fathers out of the land of Jerusalem, (and no one knew it *(76) save it were* himself and those whom he brought out of that land) and that he hath given me and my people so much knowledge unto *(3) the salvation of our souls.*

> **COM** Clarke: <u>Heb 4:14</u> "That this high priest is Jesus, the Son of God; not a son or **descendant of** Aaron, nor coming in that way, but in a more transcendent line.")
>
> **COM** Henry: <u>Mat 15:29-39</u> "we have as much **reason to bless God** as if we had been cured of them;" (Gill)
>
> **COM** Henry: <u>1Co 15:20-34</u> "This is the very end of our faith, even the **salvation of our souls** (<u>1Pe 1:9</u>), not only what it will issue in, but what we should aim at." (Clarke, Gill)

*****BOM** <u>3 Nephi 6:15</u> Now the cause of this iniquity of the people was this -- Satan had great power, unto the stirring up of the people to do *(9) all manner of iniquity,* and to the *puffing* them *up with pride*, tempting them to seek for power, and authority, and riches, and *(9) the vain things of the world*.

> **COM** Henry: <u>Eze 5:5-17</u> "A contempt of the word and law of God opens a door to **all manner of iniquity**.")
>
> **COM** Henry: <u>Joh 13:1-17</u> "instead of **puffing** a man **up with pride**,")
>
> **COM** Gill: <u>Pro 30:8</u> "and his affections taken off from **the vain things of the world**,")

*****BOM** <u>3 Nephi 6:18</u> Now they did not *sin ignorantly*, for they knew the will of God **concerning them**, for it had been taught unto them; therefore they did **wilfully** *(2) rebel against* God.

> **COM** Gill: <u>Num 15:31</u> "paying no regard to it as a law of his; otherwise such who **sin ignorantly** break the commandment of God:")
>
> **KJV** (5/16) <u>Numbers 32:28</u> So **concerning them** Moses commanded Eleazar the priest, and Joshua the son of Nun, and the chief fathers of the tribes of the children of Israel:)
>
> **KJV** (1NT/1) <u>Hebrews 10:26</u> For if we sin **wilfully** after that we have received the knowledge of the truth, there remaineth no more sacrifice for sins,)
>
> **COM** Clarke: <u>Jer 4:14</u> "Whilst thou continuest a **rebel against God**" (Henry, Wesley)

BOM <u>3 Nephi 7:9</u> Now this *(18) secret combination*, which had brought so great iniquity upon the people, did gather themselves together, and did place at their head a man whom they did call Jacob;

> **COM** Gill: <u>Job 12:22</u> "likewise the **secret** plots, counsels, and **combinations** of wicked men,")

*****BOM** <u>3 Nephi 7:17</u> And **he** did **minister many things unto** them; and all of them cannot be written, and a part of them *would not suffice*, therefore they are not written in this book. And Nephi did minister **with power and with** great **authority**.

> **KJV (1NT/1)** 2 Timothy 1:18The Lord grant unto him that he may find mercy of the Lord in that day: and in how **many things he minister**ed **unto** me at Ephesus, thou knowest very well.)
>
> **COM** Clarke: Joh 21:25 "He composed such a great number of precepts and lessons, that if the heavens were paper, and all the trees of the forest so many pens, and all the children of men so many scribes, they **would not suffice** to write all his lessons!"
>
> **Note:** You will notice that this has exactly the same meaning as the verse outlined above in 3 Nephi 7:17.
>
> **KJV (1NT/4)** Luke 4:36 And they were all amazed, and spake among themselves, saying, What a word is this! for **with authority and power** he commandeth the unclean spirits, and they come out.)

BOM 3 Nephi 8:2 And now **it came to pass (452/1353)**, if there was no mistake made by this man in the *reckoning of* our *time*, the thirty and third year had passed away;

> **COM** Gill: Psa 90:12 "nor is this to be understood of calculating or re**ckoning of time** to come;")

BOM 3 Nephi 8:3 And the people began to look *with great (1) earnestness (12th Century)* for the sign which had been given by the prophet Samuel, the Lamanite, yea, for the time that there should be darkness **for the space of** three days over the face of the land.

> **COM** Luk 11:27 "in the hearing of all the people, and **with great earnestness** and fervour:")
>
> **KJV (1NT/69)** Acts 19:8 And he went into the synagogue, and spake boldly **for the space of** three months, disputing and persuading the things concerning the kingdom of God.)

BOM 3 Nephi 10:13 And they were spared and were not sunk and buried up in the earth; and they **were** not **drowned in the depths of the sea**; and they were not burned by fire, neither were they fallen upon and *crushed to death*; and they were not carried away in the whirlwind; neither were they (6) overpowered (1593) (*Note: Clarke, Henry, Gill, Wesley*) by the **vapor of smoke** and of darkness.

> **KJV (1NT/3)** Matthew 18:6 But whoso shall offend one of these little ones which believe in me, it were better for him that a millstone were hanged about his neck, and that he **were drowned in the depth of the sea.**)
>
> **COM** Henry: Jdg 16:22-31 "and indeed few of either could escape being either stifled or **crushed to death.**" (Gill)
>
> **KJV (1NT/5)** Acts 2:19 And I will shew wonders in heaven above,

and signs in the earth beneath; blood, and fire, and **vapour of smoke:**)

***BOM 3 Nephi 10:18 And **it came to pass (452/1353)** that in the ending of the thirty and fourth year, behold, I will show unto you that the people of Nephi who were spared, and also those who had been called Lamanites, who had been spared, did have great favors (*29) shown* (12th Century) unto them, and great blessings poured out upon their heads, **insomuch (20/181)** that soon after *the (4) ascension (14th Century) of Christ into heaven* he did truly manifest himself unto them –

> **COM** Gill: Joh 3:14 "and may point out **the ascension of Christ into heaven**," (Henry)

BOM 3 Nephi 11:29 For **verily, verily I say unto you,** he that hath the *spirit of contention* is not of me, but is of the devil, who is the father of contention, and he stirreth up the hearts of men to contend with (*3) anger, **one with another**.*

> **Note**: It is interesting that the use of two verilys is only found in John which book Joseph Smith has been using all along for this section it is also interesting that Joseph Smith uses it 23 times and with only one exception in Alma, this is the first time he uses this phrase from John:
>
> **KJV (1NT/23)** John 5:24 **Verily, verily, I say unto you, He that** heareth my word, and believeth on him that sent me, hath everlasting life, and shall not come into condemnation; but is passed from death unto life.)
>
> **COM** Clarke: Mat 12:19 "The spirit of Christ is not a **spirit of contention**, murmuring, clamor, or litigiousness. He who loves these does not belong to him." (Henry)

BOM 3 Nephi 12:1 And **it came to pass (452/1353)** that **when Jesus had spoken these words** unto Nephi, and to those who had been called, (*now the number of* them who had been called, and received power and authority to baptize, *was* twelve) and behold, he **stretched forth his hand** unto the multitude, and cried unto them, saying: Blessed are ye if ye shall **give heed** unto the words of these twelve whom I have chosen from among you to minister unto you, and to be your servants; and unto them I have given power that they may **baptize you with water**; and after that ye are **baptized with water**, behold, I will **baptize you with fire and with the Holy Ghost (89NT/95)**; therefore blessed are ye if ye shall **believe in me** and be baptized, after that ye have seen me and know that I am.

> **KJV (1NT/10)** John 18:1 **When Jesus had spoken these words**, he went forth with his disciples over the brook Cedron, where was a garden, into the which he entered, and his disciples.)
>
> **COM** Gill: 1Jo 5:7 "**Now the number of** these witnesses **was** three,

there being so many persons in the Godhead;" (Henry)

KJV (7/12) Exodus 10:22 And Moses **stretched forth his hand** toward heaven; and there was a thick darkness in all the land of Egypt three days:)

KJV (3/12) Jeremiah 18:19 **Give heed** to me, O LORD, and hearken to the voice of them that contend with me.)

KJV (1NT/1) Acts 11:16 Then remembered I the word of the Lord, how that he said, John indeed **baptized with water**; but ye shall be **baptized with the Holy Ghost**.)

KJV (1NT/1) Matthew 3:11 I indeed **baptize** you **with** water unto repentance. but he that cometh after me is mightier than I, whose shoes I am not worthy to bear: he shall **baptize you with the Holy Ghost, and with fire**:)

KJV (2NT/8) Matthew 18:6 But whoso shall offend one of these little ones which **believe in me**, it were better for him that a millstone were hanged about his neck, and that he were drowned in the depth of the sea.)

BOM 3 Nephi 16:10 And thus commandeth the Father that I should say unto you: At that day when the Gentiles shall sin against **my gospel**, and shall reject the fulness of **my gospel**, and shall be lifted up in (*10*) *the pride of their hearts* above all nations, and above all the people of the whole earth, and shall be filled with all manner of (9) lyings (***Note: Note in KJV, commentaries or dictionary***), and of deceits, and **of mischief**s, and all manner of hypocrisy, and murders, and *priestcrafts*, and whoredoms, and of secret abominations; and if they shall do all those things, and shall reject the fulness of **my gospel**, behold, saith the Father, I will bring the fulness of **my gospel** from among them.

KJV (3NT/17) Romans 2:16 In the day when God shall judge the secrets of men by Jesus Christ according to **my gospel**.)

COM Gill: Joh 8:44 "this he and his associates, in the **pride of their hearts**," (Henry)

KJV (1/2) Proverbs 24:2 For their heart studieth destruction, and their lips talk **of mischief**.)

COM Gill: Psa 123:3 "reckon an engine of state, to keep people in awe of the civil magistrate; or a piece of **priestcraft**, to serve the lucrative views of a set of men;")

***BOM 3 Nephi 17:6 And he said unto them: Behold, my *bowels* are filled with *compassion* towards you.

COM Henry: Mat 23:13-33 "and at the same time to shut up the **bowels of compassion**" (Clarke, Gill, Wesley)

BOM 3 Nephi 18:8 And **it came to pass (452/1353)** that when he said these words, he commanded his disciples that they should take of the wine of the cup and *drink of it*, and that they should also give unto the multitude that they might *drink of it.*

    COM Gill: <u>Luk 22:17</u> "and said, take this and divide it among yourselves; that is, every one **drink of it**." (Henry, Wesley, Clarke)

BOM <u>3 Nephi 18:9</u> And **it came to pass (452/1353)** that they did so, and did *drink of it* and were filled; and they gave unto the multitude, and they did drink, and they were filled.

    COM Gill: <u>Luk 22:17</u> "and said, take this and divide it among yourselves; that is, every one **drink of it**." (Henry, Wesley, Clarke)

BOM <u>3 Nephi 18:13</u> But whoso among you shall do more or less than these are not **built upon** my **rock**, but are **built upon** a **sandy** foundation; and when the **rain descends, and the floods** come, **and the winds** blow, **and beat upon** them, they shall **fall**, and **the gates of hell** are *ready open to receive them.*

    KJV (1NT/1) <u>Matthew 7:27</u> And the **rain descend**ed, **and the floods** came, **and the winds** blew, **and beat upon** that house; and it fell: and great was the **fall** of it.)

    KJV (1NT/4) <u>Matthew 16:18</u> And I say also unto thee, That thou art Peter, and upon this rock I will build my church; and **the gates of hell** shall not prevail against it.)

    COM Gill: <u>Pro 30:16</u> "the grave is the house appointed for all living; it stands **ready** for them, it is **open to receive them** when dead;")

    KJV (1NT/1) <u>Matthew 7:24</u> Therefore whosoever heareth these sayings of mine, and doeth them, I will liken him unto a wise man, which **built** his house **upon** a **rock**:)

BOM <u>3 Nephi 19:25</u> And **it came to pass (452/1353)** that Jesus blessed them as they did pray unto him; and his countenance did *smile upon them,* and *the light of his countenance* did shine upon them, and behold they were as **white** as the countenance and also the garments of Jesus; and behold the (6) whiteness (before 12th Century) thereof did **exceed** all the (6) whiteness (before 12th Century), yea, even there could be nothing upon **earth** so **white** as the (6) whiteness (before 12th Century) thereof.

    COM Henry: <u>Pro 23:17-18</u> "at the providence of God, though it seem to **smile upon them**," (Clarke, Gill, Wesley)

    COM Clarke: <u>Luk 15:8</u> "till he restore to him **the light of his countenance**." (Henry, Gill, Wesley)

    COM Clarke: <u>Rev 1:14</u> "for the **whiteness** or splendor of his head and hair doubtless proceeded from the rays of light and glory which encircled his head, and darted from it in all directions." (Henry, Wesley)

    KJV (1NT/1) <u>Mark 9:3</u> And his raiment became shining, **exceeding white** as snow; so as no fuller on **earth** can **white** them.)

BOM <u>3 Nephi 20:26</u> The Father having raised me up unto you first, and sent me to bless you in turning away every one of you from his iniquities; (*30) and* *this because* ye are the *children of the covenant* –

> COM 2Ki 13:23 Clarke: "**and this because of** his covenant with their fathers:" (Henry)
>
> COM Gill: Act 3:25 "so the phrase בני ברית, "**children of the covenant**", is used by the Jews, as peculiar to themselves;" (Henry)

BOM 3 Nephi 21:26 And then shall (*5) the work of the Father* (17) commence (1340 AD) (*Note: Henry, Wesley, Clarke, Gill*) at that day, even when **this gospel shall be preached** among the remnant of this people. **verily I say unto you (48NT/46)**, at that day shall (*5) the work of the Father* (17) commence (1340 AD) (*Note: Henry, Wesley, Clarke, Gill*) among all the dispersed of my people, yea, even the tribes which have been lost, which the Father hath led away out of Jerusalem.

> COM Henry: Col 1:12-29 "It is spoken of as **the work of the Father**,")
>
> KJV (**2NT/1**) Matthew 26:13 Verily I say unto you, Wheresoever **this gospel shall be preached** in the whole world, there **shall** also this, that this woman hath done, be told for a memorial of her.)

BOM 3 Nephi 21:28 Yea, and then shall the work (17) commence (1340 AD) (*Note: Henry, Wesley, Clarke, Gill*), with the Father among all nations in preparing the way whereby his people may be (*3) gathered home* to (*12) the land of their inheritance.*

> COM Gill: Isa 57:1 "that there are evil times coming, great calamities, and sore judgments upon men; and therefore these righteous ones are gathered out of the world, and are **gathered home**, and safely housed in heaven, that they may escape the evil coming upon a wicked generation;")
>
> COM Henry: 1Pe 1:3-5 "Besides, they were most of them Jews, and so had a great affection to the land of Canaan, as **the land of their inheritance**,")

BOM 3 Nephi 26:9 And when they shall have received this, which is **expedient** that they should have first, *to try their faith*, and if it shall so be that they shall believe these things then shall the greater things be made manifest unto them.

> KJV (**7NT/62**) John 11:50 Nor consider that it is **expedient** for us, that one man should die for the people, and that the whole nation perish not.)
>
> COM Gill: Mat 14:16 "however, to **try their faith**, and make way for the working of the following miracle," (Henry, Wesley)

BOM 3 Nephi 27:14 And my Father sent me that I might (*2) be **lifted up** upon the cross*; and after that I had been ***lifted up** upon the cross*, that I might **draw all men unto** me, that as I have been lifted up by men even so should men be lifted up by the Father, to stand before me, to be judged of their works,

whether they **be good or whether** they **be evil–**

> **COM** Gill: <u>Joh 8:28</u> "meaning himself, who was to **be lifted up upon the cross**," (Henry)
>
> **KJV (1NT/1)** <u>John 12:32</u> And I, if I **be lifted up** from the earth, will **draw all men unto me**.)
>
> **KJV** (2/5) <u>Ecclesiastes 12:14</u> For God shall bring every work into judgment, with every secret thing, **whether** it **be good, or whether** it **be evil**.)

BOM <u>3 Nephi 27:33</u> And **it came to pass (452/1353)** that **when Jesus had ended these sayings** he said unto his disciples: **Enter ye in at the strait gate**; for **strait is the gate, and narrow is the way** that leads **to life, and few there be that find it**; but **wide is the gate, and broad the way** *which leads to death*, **and many there be** that **travel** therein, until **the night cometh**, wherein **no man can work**.

> **KJV (1NT/1)** <u>Matthew 7:28</u> And it came to pass, **when Jesus had ended these sayings**, the people were astonished at his doctrine:)
>
> **KJV (1NT/1)** <u>Matthew 7:13</u> **Enter ye in at the strait gate**: for **wide is the gate, and broad** is **the way**, that **lead**eth to destruction, **and many there be** which go in thereat:)
>
> **KJV (1NT/1)** <u>Matthew 7:14</u> Because **strait is the gate, and narrow is the way**, which **lead**eth un**to life, and few there be that find it**.)
>
> **COM** Henry: <u>2Pe 2:10-22</u> "They have gone into a wrong way: they have erred and strayed from the way of life, and gone over into the path **which leads to death**, and takes hold of hell;" (Clarke, Gill)
>
> **KJV (1NT:13)** <u>Acts 19:29</u> And the whole city was filled with confusion: and having caught Gaius and Aristarchus, men of Macedonia, Paul's companions in **travel**, they rushed with one accord into the theatre.)
>
> **KJV (1NT/1)** <u>John 9:4</u> I must work the works of him that sent me, while it is day: **the night cometh**, when **no man can work**.)

BOM <u>3 Nephi 28:15</u> And **whether** they were **in the body or out of the body**, they could not **tell**; for it did seem unto them like a (2) transfiguration (*Note: Clarke, Gill, Henry, Wesley)* of them, that they were changed from this *body of flesh* into an **immortal** state, that they could behold **the things of God**.

> **KJV (2NT/1)** <u>2 Corinthians 12:2</u> I knew a man in Christ above fourteen years ago, (**whether in the body**, I cannot tell; **or** whether **out of the body**, I cannot **tell**: God knoweth;) such an one caught up to the third heaven.)
>
> **COM** Henry: <u>2Co 5:1-11</u> "The **body of flesh** is a heavy burden, the calamities of life are a heavy load." (Clarke, Gill)
>
> **KJV (1NT/19)** <u>1 Timothy 1:17</u> Now unto the King eternal, **immortal**, invisible, the only wise God, be honour and glory for ever

and ever. Amen.)

KJV (1NT/7) <u>1 Corinthians 2:11</u> For what man knoweth the things of a man, save the spirit of man which is in him? even so **the things of God** knoweth no man, but the Spirit of God.)

***BOM** <u>3 Nephi 28:35</u> And **it** would be **better for** them if they **had not been born**. For do ye suppose that ye can get rid of the justice *of an offended God*, who hath been trampled under feet of men, that thereby salvation might come?

KJV (1NT/1) <u>Matthew 26:24</u> The Son of man goeth as it is written of him: but woe unto that man by whom the Son of man is betrayed! **it** had **been** good **for** that man **if** he **had not been born**.)

COM Clarke: <u>Pro 9:12</u> "But if thou scorn - refuse to receive - the doctrines of wisdom, and die in thy sins, thou alone shalt suffer the vengeance **of an offended God**." (Henry)

***BOM** <u>3 Nephi 29:4</u> And when ye shall see these sayings coming forth among you, then **ye need not** any longer (3) spurn (12th Century) at the doings of the Lord, for *(2) the sword of his justice* is in his right hand; and behold, at that day, if ye shall (3) spurn (12th Century) at his doings he will cause that it *shall soon overtake* you.

KJV (2NT/10) <u>1 Thessalonians 4:9</u> But as touching brotherly love **ye need not** that I write unto you: for ye yourselves are taught of God to love one another.)

COM Henry: <u>Rom 13:1-6</u> "And those who **spurn at** their power reflect upon God himself." (Clarke, Gill)

COM Henry: <u>Isa 34:1-8</u> "When the day of God's abused mercy and patience is over **the sword of his justice** gives no quarter, spares none." (Gill)

COM Henry: <u>Jer 24:1-10</u> "shall be sent after them, **shall soon overtake** them,")

BOM <u>4 Nephi 1:17</u> There were no robbers, nor murderers, neither were there Lamanites, nor any manner of -ites; but they were in one, *(3) the children of Christ*, and **heirs** to **the kingdom** of God.

COM Gill: <u>Psa 127:5</u> "**the children of Christ** and of the church;")

KJV (1NT/1) <u>James 2:5</u> Hearken, my beloved brethren, Hath not God chosen the poor of this world rich in faith, and **heirs** of **the kingdom** which he hath promised to them that love him?)

BOM <u>4 Nephi 1:20</u> And he kept it eighty and four years, and there was still peace in the land, *(76) save it were a small part of the people who* had revolted from the **church (76/259)** and taken upon them the name of Lamanites; therefore there began to be Lamanites again in the land.

COM Clarke: <u>Act 11:30</u> "in any sense of the word, for it contains but **a small part of the people who** profess Christianity." (Henry,

Wesley)

BOM <u>4 Nephi 1:27</u> And **it came to pass (452/1353)** that when two hundred and ten years had passed away there were many **churches** in the land; yea, there were many **churches** which *professed to know* the Christ, and yet they did deny **the more parts** of his gospel, **insomuch (20/181)** that they did receive *(9) all manner of wickedness*, and did administer that which was sacred unto him to whom it had been forbidden because of unworthiness.

> **COM** Henry: <u>Heb 10:19-39</u> "Here he refers to their own consciences, to judge how much sorer punishment the despisers of Christ (after they have **professed to know** him) are likely to undergo;" (Gill)
>
> **KJV (2NT/26)** <u>Acts 19:32</u> Some therefore cried one thing, and some another: for the assembly was confused: and **the more part** knew not wherefore they were come together. Words in OT but not exact phrase)
>
> **COM** Gill: <u>Rev 17:5</u> "of abominable doctrines and practices; **all manner of wickedness** that is to be found in the earth," (Henry)

BOM <u>Mormon 1:18</u> And these Gadianton robbers, who were among the Lamanites, did *(2) (2) infest (1602) the land*; **insomuch (20/181)** that **the inhabitants thereof** began to hide up their treasures in the earth; and they became **slippery**, because the Lord had cursed the land, that they could not hold them, nor retain them again.

> **COM** Clarke: <u>Exo 8:3</u> "The expression, bring forth abundantly, not only shows the vast numbers of those animals, which should now **infest the land**,")
>
> **KJV (20/17)** <u>Job 26:5</u> Dead things are formed from under **the** waters, and **the inhabitants thereof**.)
>
> **KJV (3/4)** <u>Jeremiah 23:12</u> Wherefore their way shall be unto them as **slippery** ways in the darkness: they shall be driven on, and fall therein: for I will bring evil upon them, even he year of their visitation, saith the LORD.)

***BOM <u>Mormon 2:15</u> And **it came to pass (452/1353)** that my sorrow did return unto me again, and I saw that *the day of grace* was *passed* with them, both *(5)* temporally (14th Century) and spiritually; for I saw thousands of them hewn down in *open rebellion against their God*, and heaped up as dung upon the face of the land. And thus three hundred and **forty and four** years had passed away.

> **COM** Gill: <u>1Th 5:8</u> "since **the day of grace** has **passed** upon us,)
>
> **COM** Henry: <u>Psa 1:1-3</u> "they break out into **open rebellion against God** and engage in the service of sin and Satan.")
>
> **KJV (4NT/4)** <u>Revelation 7:4</u> And I heard the number of them which were sealed: and there were sealed an hundred and **forty and four** thousand of all the tribes of the children of Israel.)

BOM <u>Mormon 3:10</u> And they did *swear by the heavens*, and also by the throne of God, that they would go up to battle against their enemies, and would cut them off from the face of the land.

>**COM** Henry: <u>Jam 5:12-20</u> "Hence it was that **swearing by the heavens**, and by the earth, and by the other oaths the apostle refers to, came to be in use." (Clarke, Gill)

BOM <u>Mormon 3:20</u> And these things doth the Spirit manifest unto me; therefore **I write unto you** all. And **for this cause I write unto you**, that ye may know that ye must all **stand before the judgment-seat of Christ**, yea, every soul who *belongs to the whole human* family of Adam; and ye must stand to be **judg**ed of your **work**s, **whether** they **be good or evil**;

>**KJV (7NT/5)** <u>1 John 2:13</u> **I write unto you**, fathers, because ye have known him that is from the beginning. **I write unto you**, young men, because ye have overcome the wicked one. **I write unto you**, little children, because ye have known the Father.)

>**KJV** (26/27) <u>Exodus 9:16</u> And in very deed **for this cause** have I raised thee up, for to shew in thee my power; and that my name may be declared throughout all the earth.)

>**KJV (1NT/4)** <u>Romans 14:10</u> But why dost thou judge thy brother? or why dost thou set at nought thy brother? for we shall all **stand before the judgment seat of Christ**.)

>**COM** Clarke: <u>Exo 38:8</u> "(though this **belongs to the whole human** race, and not exclusively to woman)")

>**KJV** (1/1) <u>Ecclesiastes 12:14</u> For God shall bring every **work** into judgment, with every secret thing, **whether** it **be good, or whether** it **be evil**.)

BOM <u>Mormon 4:10</u> And **it came to pass (452/1353)** that the three hundred and sixty and sixth year had passed away, and the Lamanites came again upon the Nephites to battle; and yet the Nephites **repented not of the** evil they had done, but *persisted in their wickedness* continually.

>**KJV (1NT/1)** <u>Revelation 9:20</u> And the rest of the men which were not killed by these plagues yet **repented not of the** works of their hands, that they should not worship devils, and idols of gold, and silver, and brass, and stone, and of wood: which neither can see, nor hear, nor walk:)

>**COM** Henry: <u>Mat 21:33-46</u> "How they **persisted in their wickedness**.")

BOM <u>Mormon 4:18</u> And from this time forth did the Nephites gain no power over the Lamanites, but began to be swept off by them even as a dew before the sun.

>**COM** Clarke: <u>Gen 27:28</u> "And Hushal compares an army ready to fall upon its enemies to a **dew** falling on the ground, <u>2Sa 17:12</u>,

which gives us the idea that this fluid fell in great profusion, so as to saturate every thing.")

COM Henry: "<u>1Sa 14:16-23</u> The Philistines were, by the power of God, set against one another. They melted away like snow **before the sun**")

BOM <u>Mormon 5:18</u> But now, behold, they are led about by Satan, even **as chaff is driven** before **the wind**, or as a vessel is *tossed about* upon *the waves*, without sail or anchor, or without anything wherewith to (3) steer (12th Century) her; and even as she is, so are they.

> **KJV** (1/1) <u>Hosea 13:3</u> Therefore they shall be as the morning cloud and as the early dew that passeth away, **as** the **chaff** that **is driven** with **the** whirl**wind** out of the floor, and as the smoke out of the chimney.)
>
> **COM** Gill: <u>Mar 6:48</u> "being **tossed about** with **the waves** of the sea,")
>
> **COM** Henry: <u>Mar 4:35-41</u> He doth preserve it, he doth **steer**, Ev'n when the boat seems most to reel." (Clarke, Wesley)

BOM <u>Mormon 6:6</u> And **it came to pass (452/1353)** that when we had gathered in all our people in one to the land of Cumorah, behold I, Mormon, began to be old; and knowing it to be the *last struggle* of my people, and having been commanded of the Lord that I should not suffer the records which had been (*18) handed down* by our fathers, which were sacred, to fall into the hands of the Lamanites, (for the Lamanites would destroy them) therefore I made this record out of the plates of Nephi, and (*10) hid up* in the hill Cumorah all the records which had been (5) entrusted (1602) (***Note: Clarke,*** Gill*, **Henry)** to me by the hand of the Lord, (*76) save it were* these few plates which I gave unto my son Moroni.

> **COM** Clarke: <u>2Co 13:4</u> "he gave up his life, none could take it away from him; and in his **last struggle**," (Gill)
>
> **COM** Clarke: <u>Mat 15:2</u> "that had been successively **handed down** from Moses through every generation, but not committed to writing.")
>
> **COM** Gill: <u>Amo 5:15</u> "in the stores of grace he has **hid up** for them;")

BOM <u>Mormon 7:7</u> And he hath **brought to pass** (*2) the redemption of the world*, whereby he that is found **guiltless** before him at the judgment day hath it given unto him to dwell **in the presence of God** in his kingdom, to sing (*1) ceaseless (1586) praises with the choirs above,* (***Note: This is from a hymn.*** *"ceaseless praises" and "with the choirs above")* unto *the Father*, and unto *the Son*, and unto *the **Holy** Ghost* (**89NT/95**), which *are one God*, in a (*3) state of* (*30) happiness* (15th Century) which hath no end.

> **KJV** (<u>1 Corinthians 15:54</u> So when this corruptible shall have put on

incorruption, and this mortal shall have put on immortality, then shall be **brought to pass** the saying that is written, Death is swallowed up in victory.)

COM Henry: Luk 2:8-20 "but the **redemption of the world** is for his glory in the highest." (Clarke, Wesley)

KJV (10/8) Exodus 20:7 Thou shalt not take the name of the LORD thy God in vain; for the LORD will not hold him **guiltless** that taketh his name in vain.)

KJV (**2NT/2**) Luke 1:19 And the angel answering said unto him, I am Gabriel, that stand **in the presence of God**; and am sent to speak unto thee, and to shew thee these glad tidings.)

COM Clarke: Mat 6:32 "his soul is never satisfied - give! give! is the **ceaseless** language of his earth-born heart.")

COM "Gill: Exo 20:3 "since though **the Father** is God, **the Son** is God, **and the Holy** Spirit is God, there are not three Gods, but three Persons, and these three **are one God**,")

COM Clarke: Luk 20:38 "which proves that the best informed Jews believed that the souls of righteous men were in the presence of God in **a state of happiness**." (Henry, Wesley)

BOM Mormon 8:15 For none can have power to bring it to light save it be given him of God; for God wills that it shall be done with an *eye single* to his glory, or the welfare of the ancient and long dispersed covenant people of the Lord.

COM Henry: Psa 5:1-6 "That he will have his **eye single** and his heart intent in the duty:")

Note: The phrase "with an eye single to his glory" was a common phrase in Joseph Smith's day.

BOM Mormon 8:19 For behold, the same that judgeth **rashly** shall be judged **rashly** again; for according to his works shall his *wages be*; therefore, **he that smiteth** shall be smitten again, of the Lord.

KJV (**1NT/2**) Acts 19:36 Seeing then that these things cannot be spoken against, ye ought to be quiet, and to do nothing **rashly**.)

COM Henry: Pro 16:27-28 "Those are bad men, and bad women too, that do such ill offices; they are doing the devil's **work**, and his will their **wages be**.")

Note: Notice again this has the same meaning including "wages be".

KJV (5/1) Exodus 21:12 **He that smiteth** a man, so that he die, shall be surely put to death.)

BOM Mormon 8:22 For the (*5*) *eternal purposes*; of the Lord shall roll on, until all his promises shall be fulfilled.

COM Gill: Rev 7:10 "resolved upon it in his **eternal purposes** and decrees," (Clarke)

BOM Mormon 8:24 And he knoweth their prayers, that they were in behalf of their brethren. And he knoweth their faith, for in his name could they **remove mountains**; and in his name could they cause the earth to shake; and *(6) by the power of his word* did they cause prisons to (7) tumble (1300AD) to the earth; yea, even the **fiery furnace** could not harm them, neither *wild beasts* nor *(6) poisonous (1580) serpents,* because of *(2) the power of his word.*

> **KJV** (1NT/1) 1 Corinthians 13:2 And though I have the gift of prophecy, and understand all mysteries, and all knowledge; and though I have all faith, so that I could **remove mountains**, and have not charity, I am nothing.)
>
> **COM** Gill: Heb 1:3 "the Syriac version renders it, **"by the power of his word"** (Henry)
>
> **COM** Clarke: Jer 51:25 "I will **tumble** thee from the rocky base on which thou restest." (Henry)
>
> **KJV** (8/1) Daniel 3:17 If it be so, our God whom we serve is able to deliver us from the burning **fiery furnace**, and he will deliver us out of thine hand, O king.)
>
> **COM** Gill: Deu 32:24 "could not escape falling into the hands of **wild beasts**, and of meeting with **poisonous serpents** that go upon their bellies," (Clarke)

BOM Mormon 8:26 And no one need say they shall not come, for they surely shall, for the Lord hath spoken it; for out of the earth shall they come, by the hand of the Lord, *and none can stay it*; and it shall come in a day when it shall be said that miracles are done away; and it shall come even as if one should speak from the dead.

> **COM** Gill: Deu 30:4 "whose eye is omniscient, and reaches every part of the world; and whose arm is omnipotent, **and none can stay it**,")

BOM Mormon 8:33 O ye wicked **and perverse** and stiffnecked people, why have ye built up **churches** unto yourselves to **get gain**? Why have ye **transfigured** *the holy word of God,* that ye might *bring **damnation** upon* your souls? Behold, look ye unto the **revelations of** God; for behold, **the time cometh** at that day when **all these things must be fulfilled**.

> **KJV** (2NT/1) Matthew 17:17 Then Jesus answered and said, **O** faithless **and perverse** generation, how long shall I be with you? how long shall I suffer you? bring him hither to me.)
>
> **KJV** (1NT/18) James 4:13 Go to now, ye that say, To day or to morrow we will go into such a city, and continue there a year, and buy and sell, and **get gain**:)
>
> **KJV** (2NT/1) Matthew 17:2 And was **transfigured** before them: and his face did shine as the sun, and his raiment was white as the light.)
>
> **COM** Gill: Mat 7:6 "and is generally understood of not delivering or

communicating **the holy word of God**," (Clarke, Henry, Wesley)
KJV (**11NT/10**) Matthew 23:14 Woe unto you, scribes and Pharisees, hypocrites! for ye devour widows' houses, and for a pretence make long prayer: therefore ye shall receive the greater **damnation**.)
COM Clarke: 1Co 11:27 "can neither **bring damnation upon** themselves by so doing,")
KJV (**1NT/5**) 2 Corinthians 12:1 It is not expedient for me doubtless to glory. I will come to visions and **revelations of** the Lord.)
KJV (**2NT/15**) John 16:2 They shall put you out of the synagogues: yea, **the time cometh**, that whosoever killeth you will think that he doeth God service.)
KJV (**1NT/2**) Luke 24:44 And he said unto them, These are the words which I spake unto you, while I was yet with you, that **all things must be fulfilled**, which were written in the law of Moses, and in the prophets, and in the psalms, concerning me.)

BOM Mormon 9:6 O then ye **unbelieving**, turn ye unto the Lord; **cry mightily** unto the Father **in the name of Jesus**, that **perhaps** ye may be found (*13*) *spotless* (*14th* Century), *pure*, fair, *and white*, having been cleansed by **the blood of the Lamb**, at that (*6*) *great and last day.*

KJV (**5NT/4**) Acts 14:2 But the **unbelieving** Jews stirred up the Gentiles, and made their minds evil affected against the brethren.)
KJV (1/8) Jonah 3:8 But let man and beast be covered with sackcloth, and **cry mightily** unto God: yea, let them turn every one from his evil way, and from the violence that is in their hands.)
KJV (**3NT/43**) Acts 8:22 Repent therefore of this thy wickedness, and pray God, if **perhaps** the thought of thine heart may be forgiven thee.)
KJV (**1NT/1**) Revelation 7:14 And I said unto him, Sir, thou knowest. And he said to me, These are they which came out of great tribulation, and have washed their robes, and made them **white** in **the blood of the Lamb**.)
COM Gill: Rev 15:6 "and denotes their being clothed with the **pure and spotless** robe of Christ's righteousness, which is fine linen, clean **and white**, and the righteousness of the saints,")
COM Gill: Mat 13:39 "or else the day of judgment, the **great and last day**, when the heavens and the earth,")

BOM Mormon 9:13 And because of *the redemption of man*, which came by Jesus Christ, they are brought back into **the presence of the Lord**; yea, this is wherein all men are redeemed, because the death of Christ bringeth to pass the resurrection, which bringeth to pass a redemption from an *endless sleep*, from which sleep all men shall be (8) awakened (12th Century) by **the power of God** when **the trump shall sound**; and they shall come forth, **both small and**

great, and all shall stand *before his bar*, being redeemed and *loosed* from this eternal *band of death*, which death is a *(7) **temporal** death.*

> **COM** Clarke: Job 14:12 "When once we die, unknown in earth's dark womb Sleep long and drear, the **endless sleep** of death. J. B. B. C.")

> **COM** Gill: 1Sa 7:3 "they began to be **awakened** to a sense of their sins," (Henry, Clarke)

> **KJV (11NT/48)** Matthew 22:29 Jesus answered and said unto them, Ye do err, not knowing the scriptures, nor **the power of God**.)

> **KJV (1NT/1)** 1 Corinthians 15:52 In a moment, in the twinkling of an eye, at the last **trump**: for the trumpet **shall sound**, and the dead shall be raised incorruptible, and we shall be changed.)

> **KJV** (*Note: Same idea:* **(2NT/1)** Revelation 13:16 And he causeth all, **both small and great**, rich and poor, free and bond, to receive a mark in their right hand, or in their foreheads:)

> **COM** Henry: Joh 18:28-40 "We by sin were become liable to the judgment of God, and were to be brought **before his bar**;")

> **COM** Henry: 1Co 15:51-57 "There is a day coming when the grave shall open, the **bands of death** be **loosed**, the dead saints revive, and become incorruptible and immortal, and put out of the reach of death for ever.")

> **KJV (1NT/27)** 2 Corinthians 4:18 While we look not at the things which are seen, but at the things which are not seen: for the things which are seen are **temporal**; but the things which are not seen are eternal.)

> **COM** Clarke: Act 5:10 "calls a sin unto death; a sin which must be punished with **temporal death**, or the death of the body," (Henry, Wesley)

****BOM** Mormon 9:19 And if there were miracles **wrought** then, why has God ceased to be a God of miracles and yet be an *unchangeable Being*? And behold, I say unto you he changeth not; if so he would *(4) cease to be God*; and he ceaseth not to be God, and is a God of miracles.

> **COM** Gill: Isa 48:12 "phrases expressive of the self-existence, supremacy, eternity, and immutability of Christ, Rev 1:8, and what is it that such a sovereign, eternal and **unchangeable Being** cannot do?")

> **COM** Gill: 1Co 15:28 "my meaning is not that he will **cease to be God**")

****BOM** Ether 1:33 Which Jared came forth with his brother and their families, with some others and their families, from the great tower, at the time the Lord confounded the language of the people, and *(3) swore in his wrath that* they should be **scattered upon all the face of the earth**; and according to the word of the Lord the people were scattered.

> **COM** Gill: Heb 3:18 "for which reason God **swore in his wrath that** they should not enter into the good land." (Henry)
>
> **KJV** (1/6) Genesis 11:8 So the LORD **scattered** them abroad from thence **upon the face of all the earth**: and they left off to build the city.)

BOM Ether 2:7 And the Lord **would not suffer** that they should stop beyond the sea in the wilderness, but he would that they should come forth even unto **the land of promise**, which was choice (*9) above all other lands,* which the Lord God had preserved for (*10) a righteous people.*

> **KJV** (4/15) Judges 1:34 And the Amorites forced the children of Dan into the mountain: for they **would not suffer** them to come down to the valley:)
>
> **KJV** (**1NT/22**) Hebrews 11:9 By faith he sojourned in **the land of promise**, as in a strange country, dwelling in tabernacles with Isaac and Jacob, the heirs with him of the same **promise**:)
>
> **COM** Henry: Deu 11:8-17 "See how Moses here magnifies the land of Canaan **above all other lands**,")
>
> **COM** Henry: Zec 8:1-8 "they shall be **a righteous people** and shall abound in the fruits of righteousness," (Wesley)

BOM Ether 3:1 And **it came to pass (452/1353)** that the brother of Jared, (now the number of the vessels which had been prepared was eight) went forth unto the mount, which they called the mount Shelem, because of its exceeding height, and did **molten** out of a rock sixteen small *stones*; and they were *white and clear*, even **as transparent glass**; and he did carry them in his hands upon the top of the mount, and cried again unto the Lord, saying:

> **KJV** (39/6) Exodus 34:17 Thou shalt make thee no **molten** gods.)
>
> **COM** Gill: Lam 4:7 "or rather "than precious **stones**"; and particularly "than pearls", which Bochart (q) proves at large are designed by the word used, which are white, and not red; and the word should be rendered, "clearer" or "whiter than pearls", as it is by Lyra and others (r); and the word in the Arabic language signifies **white and clear** (s), as pearls are;")
>
> **KJV** (**1NT/1**) Revelation 21:21 And the twelve gates were twelve pearls: every several gate was of one pearl: and the street of the city was pure gold, **as** it were **transparent glass**.)

BOM Ether 3:2 O Lord, thou hast said that we must be (*3) encompassed (14th Century) about by* the floods. Now behold, O Lord, and do not be angry with thy servant because of his **weakness** before thee; for **we know that thou art holy** and **dwellest in the heavens**, and that we are unworthy before thee; because of the fall our natures have become **evil continually**; nevertheless, O Lord, thou hast given us a commandment that we must call upon thee, that from thee we may receive according to our desires.

    COM Gill: <u>Psa 31:8</u> "and **encompassed about by** Saul and his army,")

    KJV (7NT/19) <u>1 Corinthians 1:25</u> Because the foolishness of God is wiser than men; and the **weakness** of God is stronger than men.)

    KJV (3NT/6) <u>Matthew 22:16</u> And they sent out unto him their disciples with the Herodians, saying, Master, **we know that thou art** true, and teachest the way of God in truth, neither carest thou for any man: for thou regardest not the person of men.)

    KJV (1/1) <u>Psalm 22:3</u> But **thou art holy**, O thou that inhabitest the praises of Israel.)

    KJV (1/1) <u>Psalm 123:1</u> Unto thee lift I up mine eyes, O thou that **dwellest in the heavens**.)

    KJV (1/3) <u>Genesis 6:5</u> And God saw that the wickedness of man was great in the earth, and that every imagination of the thoughts of his heart was only **evil continually**.)

*****BOM** <u>Ether 4:3</u> And now, after that, they have all (26) dwindled (1596 AD) **in unbelief;** and there is none save it be the Lamanites, and they have *rejected the gospel of Christ*; therefore I am commanded that I should hide them up again in the earth.

    COM Joseph Smith uses dwindle and dwindled interchangeable, and both are in Henry, while dwindle is in all (Henry: Mar <u>14:53-65</u>: "Peter followed at a distance, such a degree of cowardice was his late courage **dwindled** into,")

    KJV (3NT/26) <u>Romans 11:23</u> And they also, if they abide not still **in unbelief**, shall be grafted in: for God is able to graff them in again.)

    COM Henry: <u>Isa 29:9-16</u> "This is applied to the unbelieving Jews, who **rejected the gospel of Christ**,")

    KJV (11NT/5) <u>Romans 1:16</u> For I am not ashamed of **the gospel of Christ**: for it is the power of God unto salvation to every one that believeth; to the Jew first, and also to the Greek.)

*****BOM** <u>Ether 4:15</u> Behold, when ye shall rend that *(2) veil of unbelief* which doth cause you to remain in your *(2) (47) awful (13th Century) state of* wickedness, and **hardness of heart**, and blindness of mind, then shall the **great and marvelous** things which have been *(10) hid up* **from the foundation of the world** from you -- yea, when ye shall call upon the Father in my name, with **a broken heart and a contrite spirit**, then shall ye know that the Father hath remembered the covenant which he made unto your fathers, O house of Israel.

    COM Gill: <u>2Co 3:16</u> "the veil of blindness and ignorance, respecting themselves, case, state, and condition, and the way of salvation by Christ; the **veil of unbelief**,")

COM Clarke: <u>Heb 6:4</u> "to warn them against such an **awful state of** perdition,")

KJV (1NT/1) <u>Mark 16:14</u> Afterward he appeared unto the eleven as they sat at meat, and upbraided them with their unbelief and **hardness** of **heart**, because they believed not them which had seen him after he was risen.)

KJV (1NT/25) <u>Revelation 15:3</u> And they sing the song of Moses the servant of **God**, and the song of the Lamb, saying, **Great and marvellous** are thy works, Lord God Almighty; just and true are thy ways, thou King of saints.)

COM Gill: <u>Amo 5:15</u> "in the stores of grace he has **hid up** for them;")

KJV (6NT/22) <u>Matthew 13:35</u> That it might be fulfilled which was spoken by the prophet, saying, I will open my mouth in parables; I will utter things which have been kept secret **from the foundation of the world.**)

KJV (1/6) <u>Psalm 34:18</u> The LORD is nigh unto them that are of **a broken heart; and** saveth such as be of **a contrite spirit.**)

*****BOM** <u>Ether 5:5</u> And (*37)* if it so be* that they repent and come unto the Father in the name of Jesus, they *shall be received into the kingdom of God.*

COM Clarke: <u>Rom 11:31</u> "**shall be received into the kingdom of God** again.")

*****BOM** <u>Ether 6:7</u> And **it came to pass (452/1353)** that when they were buried in the deep there was no water that could hurt them, their vessels being tight like unto a dish, and also they were tight like unto *the ark of Noah*; therefore when they were (*3) encompassed (14th Century) about by* **many waters** they did **cry unto the Lord**, and he did **bring them forth** again upon the top of the waters.

COM Gill: <u>Gen 8:4</u> "Now this mountain seems plainly to have its name from **the ark of Noah**,")

COM Gill: <u>Psa 31:8</u> "and **encompassed about by** Saul and his army,")

KJV (14/12) <u>2 Samuel 22:17</u> He sent from above, he took me; he drew me out of **many waters**;)

KJV (7/20) <u>Psalm 107:19</u> Then they **cry unto the LORD** in their trouble, and he saveth them out of their distresses.)

KJV (3/5) <u>Isaiah 41:22</u> Let them **bring them forth**, and shew us what shall happen: let them shew the former things, what they be, that we may consider them, and know the latter end of them; or declare us things for to come.)

BOM <u>Ether 6:12</u> And they did land upon the shore of (*13) the promised land.* And when they had set their feet upon the shores of (*13) the promised land* they bowed themselves down upon the face of the land, and did **humble themselves** before the Lord, and did shed *tears of joy* before the Lord, because of **the multitude of** his **tender mercies** over them.

> **COM** The phrase "the promised land" is not in the King James Version of the Bible it is a modern concept. Wesley: <u>Heb 3:10</u> "Into my rest - **In the promised land.**" (Henry, Clarke)
>
> **KJV** (1/25) <u>2 Chronicles 7:14</u> If my people, which are called by my name, shall **humble themselves**, and pray, and seek my face, and turn from their wicked ways; then will I hear from heaven, and will forgive their sin, and will heal their land.)
>
> **COM** Henry: <u>Luk 7:36-50</u> "Nay, she washed them with her tears, **tears of joy**;" (Gill, Wesley)
>
> **KJV** (2/1) <u>Psalm 51:1</u> Have mercy upon me, O God, according to thy lovingkindness: according unto **the multitude of** thy **tender mercies** blot out my transgressions.)

***BOM <u>Ether 9:15</u> And after that he had anointed Emer to be king he saw peace in the land **for the space of** two years, and he died, having seen *(4) exceedingly many* days, which were full of sorrow. And **it came to pass (452/1353)** that Emer did **reign in his stead**, and did fill *(2) the steps of his father*.

> **KJV (1NT/69)** <u>Acts 19:8</u> And he went into the synagogue, and spake boldly **for the space of** three months, disputing and persuading the things concerning the kingdom of God.)
>
> **COM** Clarke: <u>Eze 47:1-12</u> "so that there shall be a very great multitude of fish, according to their kinds, as the fish of the great sea, **exceedingly many**.")
>
> **KJV** (1/12) <u>2 Chronicles 1:8</u> And Solomon said unto God, Thou hast shewed great mercy unto David my father, and hast made me to **reign in his stead**.)
>
> **COM** Gill: <u>1Ki 16:13</u> "By which it appears that the son trod in **the steps of his father**" (Henry)

BOM <u>Ether 9:23</u> And **it came to pass (452/1353)** that Coriantum did walk *in (2) the steps of his father*, and did build many mighty cities, and did administer that which was good unto his people in **all his days**. And **it came to pass (452/1353)** that he had no children even until he was *(3) exceedingly old*.

> **COM** Gill: <u>1Ki 16:13</u> "By which it appears that the son trod **in the steps of his father**" (Henry)
>
> **KJV** (10/18) <u>1 Kings 15:14</u> But the high places were not removed: nevertheless Asa's heart was perfect with the LORD **all his days**.)

BOM <u>Ether 10:5</u> And **it came to pass (452/1353)** that Riplakish did not do that which was right in the sight of the Lord, for he did have many wives and concubines, and did lay that upon men's shoulders which was **grievous to be**

borne; yea, he did tax *them with heavy taxes*; and with the taxes he did build many *(2) (10) spacious (14th Century* **buildings**.

> **KJV (2NT/5)** <u>Matthew 23:4</u> For they bind heavy burdens and **grievous to be borne**, and lay them on men's shoulders; but they themselves will not move them with one of their fingers.)
>
> **COM** Gill: <u>Eze 34:3</u> "oppressed **them with heavy taxes**, and got their substance into their own hands." (Henry, Clarke, Wesley)
>
> **COM** Gill: <u>Eze 28:7</u> "their beautiful city and **spacious buildings**, the palaces of their king and nobles,")
>
> **KJV (3NT/13)** <u>Mark 13:2</u> And Jesus answering said unto him, Seest thou these great **buildings**? there shall not be left one stone upon another, that shall not be thrown down.)

BOM <u>Ether 10:20</u> And they built a great city by the *narrow neck of land*, by the place where the sea divides the land.

> **COM** Clarke: <u>1Co 9:24</u> "were celebrated every fifth year on the isthmus, or **narrow neck of land**, which joins the Peloponnesus, or Morea, to the main land; and were thence termed the Isthmian games." (Henry, Gill)

*****BOM** <u>Ether 12:4</u> Wherefore, whoso believeth in God might with surety hope for *a better world*, yea, even a place **at the right hand of God, which hope** cometh of faith, maketh **an anchor** to **the soul**s of men, which would make them *sure and steadfast,* **always abounding in good works**, being led to glorify God.

> **COM** Henry: <u>Act 20:36-38</u> "we hope to see them again in **a better world**," (Clarke, Wesley)
>
> **KJV (1NT/4)** <u>Romans 8:34</u> Who is he that condemneth? It is Christ that died, yea rather, that is risen again, who is even **at the right hand of God**, who also maketh intercession for us.)
>
> **KJV (1NT/1)** <u>Hebrews 6:19</u> **Which hope** we have as **an anchor** of **the soul**, both sure and stedfast, and which entereth into that within the veil;)
>
> **KJV (1NT/1)** <u>1 Corinthians 15:58</u> Therefore, my beloved brethren, be ye stedfast, unmoveable, **always abounding in** the work of the Lord, forasmuch as ye know that your labour is not in vain in the Lord.)
>
> **COM** Henry: <u>Mat 7:21-29</u> "His profession will not wither; his comforts will not fail; they will be his strength and song, as an anchor of the soul, **sure and steadfast**.")
>
> **KJV (16NT/11)** <u>Matthew 5:16</u> Let your light so shine before men, that they may see your **good works**, and glorify your Father which is in heaven.)

*****BOM** <u>Ether 12:19</u> And there were many whose faith was so *(6)* *exceedingly strong,* even before Christ came, who could not be kept from *(3) within the veil;,* but truly saw with their eyes the things which they had beheld *with an eye of faith,* and they were glad.

> COM Clarke: <u>Rev 18:19</u> "The lamentation over this great ruined city, <u>Rev 18:9-19</u>, is **exceedingly strong** and well drawn.")
>
> COM Henry: <u>Exo 40:34-38</u> "and the glory of the Lord retired **within the veil**," (Gill, Clarke, Wesley)
>
> COM Another example of an exact duplication of a phrase of Henry beyond coincidence: Henry: <u>Psa 37:1-6</u> "When we look forward **with an eye of faith** we shall see no reason to envy wicked people their prosperity,")

BOM <u>Ether 13:16</u> And now Coriantumr, having (2) studied (15th Century) (Note: Clarke,*** Gill, ***Henry, Wesley),*** himself, in all *the arts of war* and all the cunning of the world, wherefore he gave battle unto them who sought to destroy him.

> COM Henry: <u>2Sa 17:1-14</u> "men of celebrated bravery and versed in all **the arts of war**." (Gill)

BOM <u>Ether 15:2</u> He saw that there had been slain by the sword already (13) nearly (1561) *two millions of* his people, and he began to sorrow in his heart; yea, there had been slain *two millions of* mighty men, and also their wives and their children.

> COM Clarke: <u>Nah 1:12</u> "Sennacherib invaded Judea with an army of **nearly two** hundred thousand men.")
>
> COM Clarke: <u>Exo 12:37</u> "Such a company moving at once, and emigrating from their own country, the world never before nor since witnessed; no doubt upwards of **two millions of** souls,")

BOM <u>Ether 15:16</u> And **it came to pass (452/1353)** that when it was night they were weary, and retired to their camps; and after they had retired to their camps they took up a howling and a lamentation for the loss of the slain of their people; and so great were their cries, their *howlings and lamentations,* that they did *(1) rend the air exceedingly.*

> COM Gill: <u>Deu 28:32</u> "what **howlings and lamentations** were made by the women;")

BOM <u>Moroni 6:4</u> And after they had been received unto baptism, and were **wrought upon** and cleansed by **the power of the Holy Ghost (89NT/95),** they were **numbered among** the people of **the church (76/259) of** Christ; and their names were taken, that they might be remembered and nourished by **the good word of God,** *to keep them in the right way,* to keep them continually watchful unto prayer, (5) relying (1574) (***Note: Clarke, Wesley, Henry,*** Gill*)* alone *(2) upon the (5) merits (15th Century)* of Christ, who was **the author and the finisher of** their **faith.**

> **KJV** (1/12) <u>2 Kings 12:11</u> And they gave the money, being told, into

the hands of them that did the work, that had the oversight of the house of the LORD: and they laid it out to the carpenters and builders, that **wrought upon** the house of the LORD,)

KJV (1NT/24) <u>Romans 15:13</u> Now the God of hope fill you with all joy and peace in believing, that ye may abound in hope, through **the power of the Holy Ghost** .)

KJV (3/30) <u>Numbers 1:47</u> But the Levites after the tribe of their fathers were not **numbered among** them.)

KJV (1NT/4) <u>Romans 16:16</u> Salute one another with an holy kiss. **The churches of Christ** salute you.)

KJV (1NT/2) <u>Hebrews 6:5</u> And have tasted **the good word of God**, and the powers of the world to come,)

COM Hos 7:8-16 "He had given them his laws, which were all holy, just, and good, by which he designed **to keep them in the right way;**"

COM Henry: <u>Heb 9:1-7</u> "grounded **upon the merits** and satisfaction of his sacrifice,")

COM Gill: <u>Rom 14:19</u> "on the free grace of God and **merits of Christ:**" (Clarke, Wesley, Henry)

KJV (1NT/1) <u>Hebrews 12:2</u> Looking unto Jesus **the author and finisher of** our **faith**; who for the joy that was set before him endured the cross, despising the shame, and is set down at the right hand of the throne of God.)

***BOM** <u>Moroni 7:3</u> Wherefore, I would speak unto you that are of the **church (76/259),** that are the peaceable **followers of Christ**, and that have obtained a sufficient hope by which ye can enter into the rest of the Lord, from this time henceforth un*til* ye shall *rest with him in heaven.*

> **COM** Henry: <u>Act 7:54-60</u> "When the **followers of Christ** are for his sake" (Clarke, Wesley)
>
> **KJV (1NT/2)** <u>1 Corinthians 11:1</u> Be ye followers of me, even as I also am of Christ.)
>
> **COM** Henry: <u>Heb 4:1-10</u> "resting from the servitude of sin, and reposing ourselves in God **till** we are prepared to **rest with him in heaven.**")

BOM <u>Moroni 7:31</u> And *the office of their ministry* is to call men unto repentance, and to fulfill and to do the work of the covenants of the Father, which he hath made unto **the children of men (22/131),** to prepare the way **among the children of men**, by declaring **the word of Christ** unto *the chosen vessels of* the Lord, that they may *(3) bear testimony* of him.

> **COM** Gill: <u>Act 13:25</u> "John entered on **the office of his ministry** before him,")
>
> **KJV** (2/30) <u>Psalm 21:10</u> Their fruit shalt thou destroy from the earth,

and their seed from **among the children of men**.)

KJV (1NT/5) Colossians 3:16 Let **the word of Christ** dwell in you richly in all wisdom; teaching and admonishing one another in psalms and hymns and spiritual songs, singing with grace in your hearts to the Lord.)

COM Gill: Act 17:1 "there being none of **the chosen vessels of** salvation to be called there,")

COM Henry: Joh 1:29-36 "John had continued to **bear testimony** to him")

BOM Moroni 7:32 *(2) And by so doing*, the Lord God prepareth the way **that the residue of men** may have **faith in Christ**, that the **Holy Ghost (89NT/95)** may *(5) have place* in their hearts, according to the power thereof; and **after this manner did** bringeth to pass the Father, the covenants which he hath made unto **the children of men (22/131)**.

COM Gill: Col 4:5 "**and by so doing**, they will heap up coals of fire on their heads.")

KJV (1NT/1) Acts 15:17 **That the residue of men** might seek after the Lord, and all the Gentiles, upon whom my name is called, saith the Lord, who doeth all these things.)

KJV (4NT/11) Galatians 3:26 For ye are all the children of God by **faith in Christ** Jesus.)

COM Clarke: 1Ki 13:31 "and he is willing to **have place** with him in the general resurrection." (Henry, Wesley)

KJV (16/34) Genesis 39:19 And it came to pass, when his master heard the words of his wife, which she spake unto him, saying, **After this manner did** thy servant to me; that his wrath was kindled.)

BOM Moroni 7:36 Or have angels ceased to appear unto **the children of men (22/131)**? Or has he withheld **the power of the Holy Ghost (89NT/95)** from them? Or will he, so *long as time shall last*, or the earth shall stand, or there shall be one man upon the face thereof to be saved?

KJV (1NT/24) Romans 15:13 Now the God of hope fill you with all joy and peace in believing, that ye may abound in hope, through **the power of the Holy Ghost**.)

COM Henry: Jud 1:3-7 "wholly free from such men and such practices as **long as time shall last**." (Clarke)

COM Clarke: Heb 7:21 "as **long as time shall** run, and the generations of men be continued on **earth**.")

BOM Moroni 7:39 But behold, **my beloved brethren**, I judge better things of you, for I judge that ye have **faith in Christ** because of your meekness; for if ye have not faith in him then ye are *not fit to be* **numbered among** the people of his **church (76/259)**.

KJV (4NT/60) James 1:19 Wherefore, **my beloved brethren**, let

every man be swift to hear, slow to speak, slow to wrath:)

KJV (4NT/11) <u>Galatians 3:26</u> For ye are all the children of God by **faith in Christ** Jesus.)

KJV (3/30) <u>Numbers 1:47</u> But the Levites after the tribe of their fathers were not **numbered among** them.)

COM Gill: <u>1Co 11:16</u> "is **not fit to be** a **church** member; nor ought he to be suffered to continue in the communion of the church," (Clarke, Henry, Wesley)

***BOM** <u>Moroni 8:6</u> And now, my son, **I desire that ye** should labor diligently, that this *gross error* should be removed from among you; for, *(6) for this intent* I have written this **epistle.**

KJV (1NT/10) <u>Ephesians 3:13</u> Wherefore **I desire that ye** faint not at my tribulations for you, which is your glory.)

COM Gill: <u>Joh 8:35</u> "sometimes suffered to fall into some foul sin, or into some **gross error** and heresy," (Clarke)

COM Gill: <u>Rom 3:25</u> **"for this intent,** in his eternal purposes and decrees;")

KJV (15NT/41) <u>Romans 16:22</u> I Tertius, who wrote this **epistle,** salute you in the Lord.)

BOM <u>Moroni 8:12</u> But little children are *alive in Christ,* even **from the foundation of the world**; if not so, God is a partial God, and also a changeable God, and a **respecter to persons**; for how many little children have died without baptism!

COM Henry: <u>1Co 15:20-34</u> "but the meaning is not that, as all men died in Adam, so all men, without exception, shall be made **alive in Christ**;")

KJV (6NT/22) <u>Matthew 13:35</u> That it might be fulfilled which was spoken by the prophet, saying, I will open my mouth in parables; I will utter things which have been kept secret **from the foundation of the world.**)

KJV (1NT/1) <u>Acts 10:34</u> Then Peter opened his mouth, and said, Of a truth I perceive that God is no **respecter of persons**:)

BOM <u>Moroni 8:26</u> And the **remission of sins** bringeth *(2) meekness, and (4) lowliness of heart;* and because of *(2) meekness, and (4) lowliness of heart;* cometh the visitation of the **Holy Ghost (89NT/95)**, which **Comforter** filleth with hope and **perfect love**, which love endureth by diligence unto prayer, until the end shall come, when all the saints shall *(4) dwell with God.*

COM Henry: <u>Eph 4:2-16</u> "was eminent for **meekness and lowliness of heart**,")

KJV (1NT/4) <u>Philippians 2:3</u> Let nothing be done through strife or vain glory; but in **lowliness of** mind let each esteem other better than themselves.)

KJV (4NT/1) <u>John 14:16</u> And I will pray the Father, and he shall give you another **Comforter**, that he may abide with you for ever;)

KJV (1NT/1) <u>1 John 4:18</u> There is no fear in love; but **perfect love** casteth out fear: because fear hath torment. He that feareth is not made perfect in love.)

COM Henry: <u>Heb 10:19-39</u> "but fallen man cannot **dwell with God** without a high priest," (Gill, Clarke)

BOM <u>Moroni 9:4</u> Behold, I am laboring with them continually; and when I *(2) speak **the word of God** (45/89) with* **sharpness** they tremble and anger against me; and when I use no **sharpness** they **harden their hearts** against it; wherefore, **I fear lest** the Spirit of the Lord hath ceased **striving** with them.

COM Henry: <u>Act 4:23-31</u> "but enabled to **speak the word of God with** boldness," (Clarke)

KJV (1NT/6) <u>2 Corinthians 13:10</u> Therefore I write these things being absent, lest being present I should use **sharpness**, according to the power which the Lord hath given me to edification, and not to destruction.)

KJV (1/24) <u>Joshua 11:20</u> For it was of the LORD to **harden their hearts**, that they should come against Israel in battle, that he might destroy them utterly, and that they might have no favour, but that he might destroy them, as the LORD commanded Moses.)

KJV (2NT/6) <u>2 Corinthians 11:3</u> But **I fear, lest** by any means, as the serpent beguiled Eve through his subtilty, so your minds should be corrupted from the simplicity that is in Christ.)

KJV (3NT/6) <u>Hebrews 12:4</u> Ye have not yet resisted unto blood, **striving** against sin.)

***BOM** <u>Moroni 9:10</u> And after they had done this thing, they did murder them in a *most cruel manner, torturing* their bodies **even unto death**; and after they have done this, they devour their flesh like unto wild beasts, **because of the hardness of** their **hearts**; and they do it for a token of bravery.

COM Henry: <u>Act 10:9-18</u> "choose rather to be **tortured** to death in the **most cruel manner** that ever was than to eat swine's flesh,")

KJV (3/5) <u>Psalm 48:14</u> For this God is our God for ever and ever: he will be our guide **even unto death**.)

KJV (1NT/13) <u>Matthew 19:8</u> He saith unto them, Moses **because of the hardness of** your **hearts** suffered you to put away your wives: but from the beginning it was not so.)

BOM <u>Moroni 10:27</u> And I **exhort** you to remember these things; for the time speedily cometh that ye shall know that **I lie not**, for ye shall see me at *(5) the bar of God*; and the Lord God will say unto you: Did I not declare my words unto you, which were written by this man, like as one crying from the dead, yea, even as one speaking out of the dust?

KJV (16NT/29) <u>Acts 2:40</u> And with many other words did he testify and **exhort**, saying, Save yourselves from this untoward generation.)

COM Clarke: <u>Rom 14:12</u> "We shall not, at **the bar of God**, be obliged to account for the conduct of each other" (Gill, Henry)

BOM <u>Moroni 10:33</u> And again, if ye **by the grace of God** are **perfect in Christ**, and deny not his power, then **are** ye **sanctified in Christ by the grace of God**, through *the shedding of* **the blood of Christ**, which is in the *covenant* of the Father unto the remission of your sins, that ye become holy, **without spot**.

KJV (3NT/5) <u>1 Corinthians 15:10</u> But **by the grace of God** I am what I am: and his grace which was bestowed upon me was not in vain; but I laboured more abundantly than they all: yet not I, but the grace of God which was with me.)

KJV (1NT/1) <u>1 Corinthians 1:2</u> Unto the church of God which is at Corinth, to them that **are sanctified in Christ** Jesus, called to be saints, with all that in every place call upon the name of Jesus Christ our Lord, both their's and our's:)

KJV (3NT/5) <u>1 Corinthians 15:10</u> But **by the grace of God** I am what I am: and his grace which was bestowed upon me was not in vain; but I laboured more abundantly than they all: yet not I, but the grace of God which was with me.)

COM Clarke: <u>Heb 9:15-22</u> "The book of the law and **covenant**, to show that the covenant of grace is confirmed by the blood of Christ and made effectual to our good. [2.] The people, intimating that **the shedding of the blood of Christ** will be no advantage to us if it be not applied to us.")

KJV (1NT/1) <u>Hebrews 9:14</u> How much more shall **the blood of Christ**, who through the eternal Spirit offered himself **without spot** to God, purge your conscience from dead works to serve the living God?)

BOM <u>Moroni 10:34</u> And now I **bid** unto all, **farewell**. I soon go to rest in the **paradise of God**, until my spirit and body shall again reunite, and I am brought forth (1) triumphant (15th Century) through the air, to meet you before the pleasing bar of the great Jehovah, the *Eternal **Judge*** of both **quick and dead**. Amen.

KJV (1NT/4) <u>Luke 9:61</u> And another also said, Lord, I will follow thee; but let me first go **bid** them **farewell**, which are at home at my house.)

KJV (1NT/3) <u>Revelation 2:7</u> He that hath an ear, let him hear what the Spirit saith unto the churches; To him that overcometh will I give to eat of the tree of life, which is in the midst of the **paradise of God**.)

COM Gill: <u>1Co 15:57</u> "Over sin the sting of death, over the law the strength of sin, and over death and the grave; and which will be the ground and foundation of the above **triumphant** song in the resurrection morn," (Henry, Clarke, Wesley)

COM Clarke: <u>2Co 5:20</u> "Yet our almighty Lord, and our **eternal Judge**,")

KJV (1NT/1) <u>Acts 10:42</u> And he commanded us to preach unto the people, and to testify that it is he which was ordained of God to be the **Judge of quick and dead**.)

Chapter Five

The Use of the Bible

As you have been made aware Joseph Smith extensively utilized the commentaries I outlined to create the Book of Mormon. In addition Joseph Smith also utilized the Bible itself to create the Book of Mormon. As you may already be aware of from previous chapters Joseph Smith used a particular verse, paragraph, story or idea from the Bible and then went to the commentaries on that particular verse, paragraph, story or idea or visa-versa. In this chapter we will look more closely at Joseph Smith's use of the Bible to create the Book of Mormon.

It might be interesting to start out with some facts. As you know I took many years to go through each and every word of the Book of Mormon and as a result I can outline some facts that will give us some insight into how much Joseph Smith actually used the Bible to create the Book of Mormon.

For example Joseph Smith used 4970 phrases or words unique to the New Testament. In other words they were phrases not found in the Old Testament but only found in the New Testament. Now when I say words I do not mean just any type of word I mean unique or rare words. I want to clarify that the majority of these 4970 are phrases. Now I will not of course outline all 4970 but will give several of the more intriguing words and phrases. Out of the 4970 words and phrases only found in the New Testament Joseph Smith used 2532 unique words and phrases that are only found one time in the New Testament as in the example below. Now I think it is important to point out that parts of the Book of Mormon were supposed written at least 600-700 years before the New Testament and the Book of Mormon was written on another continent, supposedly written between 600BC to 400AD. And what document claiming to be unique, could ever contain this large number of unique phrases and words from another document without being considered plagiarism. Of course it is my contention that the Book of Mormon is indeed plagiarism, plagiarism by Joseph Smith of the Bible and the commentaries.

Now before we begin let me give you some additional statistics. Out of the 2532 unique words and phrases let us take a look at the books of the New Testament that they come from.

| Matthew | 450 times | | 1 Timothy | 18 times |

Luke	176 times	2 Timothy	30 times
John	254 times	Titus	7 times
Acts	303 times	Philemon	4 times
Romans	137 times	Hebrews	90 times
1 Corinthians	134 times	James	26 times
2 Corinthians	51 times	1 Peter	16 times
Galatians	44 times	2 Peter	27 times
Ephesians	69 times	1 John	21 times
Philippians	14 times	2 John	1 time
Colossians	16 Times	3 John	3 times
1 Thessalonians	17 times	Jude	2 times
2 Thessalonians	9 times	Revelation	279 times

Now as you can see he used certain books more often than others. Matthew 450 times, because it is the first book of the New Testament. Acts 303 times, because the Book of Mormon is, in a sense, the acts of the people of the Book of Mormon and hence fodder for writing the Book of Mormon. Revelations 279 times, because the Book of Mormon supposedly came about in the end times according to Joseph Smith. Thus he had to make the Book of Mormon and the events surrounding its coming forth match what Revelations says. John, 254 times, because it is routinely chosen as the most favorite book of the Bible and is the most "spiritual" as it relates to Christ of any of the Gospels.

Let me start by giving you an example of a unique phrase found only in The New Testament. For example 1 Nephi 2:18 and the verse Joseph Smith used from the New Testament Mark 3:5. I want to remind you of my coding. The coding will look similar to this (1NT/1) the first number is the number of times the word or phrase appears in the New Testament and the second number is the number of times the word appears in the Book of Mormon. So, (2NT/10) would indicate that the word or phrase appears two times in the New Testament and ten times in the Book of Mormon.

And now an example with an explanation: Note that my coding shows that this particular phrase only appears once in the New Testament hence 1NT and only once in the Book of Mormon hence the 1 after the /). To make it easier here I have removed the commentary references.

BOM 1 Nephi 2:18: But, behold, Laman and Lemuel would not hearken unto my words; and **being grieved because of the hardness of their hearts** I cried unto the Lord for them.

KJV Mark 3:5 (**1NT/1**) Mark 3:5 And when he had looked round about on them with anger, **being grieved for the hardness of their hearts,** he saith unto the man, Stretch forth thine hand.)

Obviously, and I think it can be stated without question; Joseph Smith took this phrase from Mark in the New Testament. The only place this phrase appears in the Bible. I could probably also safely conclude that this phrase does not exist anywhere originally outside of the Bible. It is important to remember that this part of Nephi was supposedly written 600-700 years before Mark even came into existence.

Now let us look at some others here by book of the New Testament used:

Matthew 450 times:

BOM 1 Nephi 10:18 For he is **the same yesterday, to-day, and forever**; and the way is **prepared for** all men **from the foundation of the world,** if it so be that they repent and come unto him.

> **KJV (1NT/14)** Matthew 25:34 Then shall the King say unto them on his right hand, Come, ye blessed of my Father, inherit the kingdom **prepared for you from the foundation of the world.**
>
> And if you haven't noticed a verse from Hebrews in the same 1 Nephi verse: **KJV (1NT/6)** Hebrews 13:8 Jesus Christ **the same yesterday,** and **to day, and for ever.**)

BOM 1 Nephi 12:9 And he said unto me: Thou rememberest **the twelve apostles of the Lamb**? Behold they are they who shall **judge the twelve tribes of Israel**; wherefore, the twelve ministers of thy seed shall be judged of them; for ye are of the house of Israel.

> **KJV (2NT/1)** Matthew 19:28 And Jesus said unto them, Verily I say unto you, That ye which have followed me, in the regeneration when the Son of man shall sit in the throne of his glory, ye also shall sit upon twelve thrones, **judging the twelve tribes of Israel.**)
>
> **Note**: You will notice also the quote from *The Book of Revelation*s also in the *New Testament* and again both written 600-700 years later than what the Book of Mormon claims this was written.
>
> **KJV (1NT/9)** Revelation 21:14 And the wall of the city had twelve foundations, and in them the names of **the twelve apostles of the Lamb.**)

BOM 1 Nephi 12:21 And I saw them gathered together in multitudes; and I saw **wars and rumors of wars** among them; and in **wars and rumors of wars** I saw many generations pass away.

> **KJV (2NT/6)** Matthew 24:6 And ye shall hear of **wars and rumours of wars**: see that ye be not troubled: for all these things must come to pass, but the end is not yet.)

BOM 1 Nephi 13:42 And the time cometh that he shall manifest himself unto all nations, both unto the Jews and also unto the Gentiles; and after he has manifested himself unto the Jews and also unto the Gentiles, then he shall manifest himself unto the Gentiles and also unto the Jews, and **the last shall be first, and the first shall be last**.

> **KJV (2NT/1)** Matthew 19:30 But many that are **first shall be last;**

and the last shall be first.)

BOM 1 Nephi 15:11 Do ye not remember the things which the Lord hath said? -- If ye will not harden your hearts, and **ask me in** faith, **believing** that **ye shall receive**, with diligence in keeping my commandments, surely these things shall be made known unto you.

    KJV (1NT/6) Matthew 21:22 And all things, whatsoever ye shall **ask in** prayer, **believing, ye shall receive**.)

BOM 1 Nephi 17:5 And we did come to the land which we called Bountiful, because of its much fruit and also **wild honey**; and all these things were prepared of the Lord that we might not perish. And we beheld the sea, which we called Irreantum, **which, being interpreted, is** many waters

    KJV (1NT/2) Matthew 1:23 Behold, a virgin shall be with child, and shall bring forth a son, and they shall call his name Emmanuel, **which being interpreted is**, God with us.)

    KJV By the way the phrase "wild honey" also comes from Matthew: **(2NT/1)** Matthew 3:4 And the same John had his raiment of camel's hair, and a leathern girdle about his loins; and his meat was locusts and **wild honey**.)

BOM 1 Nephi 18:13 Wherefore, they knew not whither they should (3) steer (12th Century) the ship, **insomuch that there arose a great storm**, yea, a **great** and terrible **tempest**, and we were driven back upon the waters for the space of three days; and they began to be (*11*) *frightened,* (*1666 AD*) exceedingly lest they should be drowned in the sea; nevertheless they did not loose me.

    KJV (1/2) Matthew 8:24 And, behold, there arose a **great tempest** in the sea, **insomuch that the ship** was covered with the waves: but he was asleep.)

    Note: A common trait of Joseph Smith was to use verses from different gospels about the same story and mix them together. In this story in 1 Nephi we are confronted with a story of a ship during a storm and in Matthew and Mark stories of a ship in a storm. Also note that the words in italics, meaning it is not found in the Bible, with numbers in front, the number of times the word was used, and the date the word came into use. Notice that the word "frightened" did not come into use until 55 years after the KJV of the Bible was written which came from the commentaries.

    KJV (1NT/2) Mark 4:37 And **there arose a great storm** of wind, and the waves beat into the **ship**, so that it was now full.)

BOM 1 Nephi 22:31 Wherefore, ye need not suppose that I and my father are the only ones that have testified, and also taught them. Wherefore, if ye shall be obedient to the commandments, and **endure to the end**, ye **shall be saved** at the last day. And thus it is. Amen.

KJV (1NT/8) Matthew 10:22 And ye shall be hated of all men for my name's sake: but he that **endure**th **to the end shall be saved**.)

BOM 2 Nephi 1:22 That ye may not be cursed with a *(5) sore cursing;* and also, that ye may not *(1) incur (15ᵗʰ Century) the displeasure of* a just God upon you, unto the destruction, yea, the eternal destruction of **both soul and body**.

KJV (1NT/4) (Note: Same context: Matthew 10:28 And fear not them which kill the body, but are not able to kill the soul: but rather fear him which is able to destroy **both soul and body** in hell.)

BOM 2 Nephi 4:24 And by day have I waxed bold in mighty prayer before him; yea, my voice have I sent up on high; and **angels came** down **and ministered unto** me.

KJV (1NT/2) Matthew 4:11 Then the devil leaveth him, and, behold, **angels came and ministered unto** him.)

BOM 2 Nephi 9:41 O then, my beloved brethren, come unto the Lord, the Holy One. Remember that his paths are righteous. Behold, the way for man is **narrow**, but it lieth in a **straight** course before him, and the keeper of the **gate** is the Holy One of Israel; and he employeth no servant there; and there is none other **way** save it be by the gate; for he cannot be deceived, for the Lord God is his name.

KJV (*Note: This verse is similar to* Matthew 7:14 Because strait is the gate, and **narrow** is the **way**, which leadeth unto life, and few there be that find it.)

BOM 2 Nephi 9:42 And whoso **knocketh, to him** will he **open**; and the wise, and the learned, and they that are rich, who are puffed up because of their learning, and their wisdom, and their riches -- yea, they are they whom he despiseth; and save they shall cast these things away, and consider themselves fools before God, and come down in the *(5) depths of humility,* he will not open unto them.

KJV (1NT/1) Matthew 7:8 For every one that asketh receiveth; and he that seeketh findeth; and **to him** that **knocketh** it shall be **open**ed.)

BOM 2 Nephi 9:43 But the things of **the wise and the prudent** shall be hid from them forever -- yea, that (30) happiness which is prepared for the saints.

KJV (Matthew 11:25 At that time Jesus answered and said, I thank thee, O Father, Lord of heaven and earth, because thou hast **hid** these **things from the wise and prudent**, and hast revealed them unto babes.)

BOM 2 Nephi 28:30 For behold, thus saith the **Lord** God: I will give **unto the children of men (22/131) line upon line, precept upon precept, here a little and there a little;** and blessed are those who hearken unto my precepts, and lend an ear unto my counsel, for they shall learn wisdom; for unto **him** that receiveth I will **give** more; and from them that shall say, We have enough,

from them **shall be taken away even that** which they have.

> **KJV (1NT/1)** <u>Matthew 13:12</u> For whosoever hath, to **him** shall be **give**n, and he shall have more abundance: but whosoever hath not, **from** him **shall be taken away even that** he **hath**.)
>
> **KJV** You will also notice the use of Isaiah in this verse: (1/1) <u>Isaiah 28:13</u> But the word of the **LORD** was **unto** them **precept upon precept, precept upon precept; line upon line, line upon line; here a little, and there a little**; that they might go, and fall backward, and be broken, and snared, and taken.)

BOM <u>2 Nephi 31:17</u> **There is nothing** which **is secret** save it **shall be revealed; there is** no work of darkness save it **shall be made manifest** in the light; **and there is nothing** which is sealed up**on the earth** save it **shall be loosed**.

> **KJV** A common tactic of Joseph Smith was to mix verses as in this case<u>: Matthew 10:26</u> Fear them not therefore: for **there is nothing** covered, that **shall** not **be revealed**; and hid, that shall not be known.)
>
> **KJV** (<u>Matthew 18:18</u> Verily I say unto you, Whatsoever ye shall bind on earth shall be bound in heaven: and whatsoever ye shall loose **on earth shall be loosed** in heaven.)
>
> **KJV** (<u>Luke 8:17</u> For **nothing is secret**, that **shall** not **be made manifest**; neither any thing hid, that shall not be known and come abroad.)

BOM <u>2 Nephi 31:15</u> And I heard a voice from the Father, saying: Yea, the **words** of my Beloved **are true and faithful. He that endureth to the end**, the same **shall be saved**.

> **KJV (1NT/1)** <u>Matthew 10:22</u> And ye shall be hated of all men for my name's sake: but **he that endureth to the end shall be saved**.)
>
> **KJV (1NT/1)** <u>Revelation 21:5</u> **And** he that sat upon the throne said, Behold, I make all things new. **And** he said unto me, Write: for these **words are true and faithful**.)

BOM <u>2 Nephi 22:9</u> I also have charity for the Gentiles. But behold, for none of these can I hope except they shall be reconciled unto Christ, and enter into the **narrow gate**, and walk in the **strait** path **which leads to life**, and continue in the path until the end of the day of (9) probation. (15th Century)

> **KJV (1NT/1)** <u>Matthew 7:14</u> Because **strait** is **the gate, and narrow** is the way, which **leadeth** unto **life**, and few there be that find it.)

BOM <u>Jacob 2:18</u> But before **ye seek** for riches, **seek ye** for **the kingdom of God**.

> **KJV (1NT/1)** <u>Matthew 6:33</u> But **seek ye** first **the kingdom of God**, and his righteousness; and all these things shall be added unto you.)

BOM <u>Jacob 5:35</u> And it came to pass that **the Lord of the vineyard said unto his** servant: The tree **profiteth me nothing**, and the roots thereof **profit**

me nothing so long as it shall **bring forth evil fruit.**

> **KJV (1NT/1)** Matthew 20:8 So when even was come, **the lord of the vineyard** saith **unto his** steward, Call the labourers, and give them their hire, beginning from the last unto the first.)
>
> **KJV (1NT/3)** Matthew 7:18 A good tree cannot **bring forth evil fruit**, neither can a corrupt tree **bring forth** good **fruit**.)
>
> **KJV (1NT/2)** 1 Corinthians 13:3 And though I bestow all my goods to feed the poor, and though I give my body to be burned, and have not charity, it **profiteth me nothing.**)

BOM Jacob 5:42 Behold, I knew that all the fruit of the vineyard, save it were these, had become corrupted. And now these which have once brought **forth good fruit** have also become corrupted; and now all the **tree**s of my vineyard are good for nothing save it be to be **hewn down and cast into the fire.**

> **KJV (2NT/13)** Matthew 7:19 Every **tree** that bringeth not **forth good fruit** is **hewn down, and cast into the fire.**)

BOM Enos 1:15 Wherefore, I knowing that the Lord God was able to preserve our records, I cried unto him continually, for he had said unto me: **Whatsoever thing ye shall ask in** faith, **believing** that **ye shall receive, in** the name of Christ, **ye shall receive** it.

> **KJV (1NT/1)** Matthew 21:22 And all **thing**s, **whatsoever ye shall ask in** prayer, **believing, ye shall receive.**)

BOM Mosiah 2:21 I say unto you that if ye should serve him who has created you from the beginning, and is preserving you from day to day, by lending you breath, that ye may live and move and do according to your own will, and even supporting you from one moment to another -- I say, if ye should serve him with all your whole souls yet **ye** would be **unprofitable servant**s.

> **KJV (1NT/2)** Matthew 25:30 And cast **ye** the **unprofitable servant** into outer darkness: there shall be weeping and gnashing of teeth.)

BOM Mosiah 3:18 For behold he judgeth, **and** his **judgment is just**; and the infant perisheth not that dieth in his infancy; but men **drink damnation to** their own souls **except** they humble themselves **and become as little children**, and believe that salvation **was, and is, and is to come**, in and through the atoning blood of Christ, **the Lord Omnipotent.**

> **KJV (1NT/1)** Matthew 18:3 And said, Verily I say unto you, **Except** ye be converted, **and become as little children**, ye shall not enter into the kingdom of heaven.)
>
> **KJV (1NT/1)** John 5:30 I can of mine own self do nothing: as I hear, I judge: **and** my **judgment is just**; because I seek not mine own will, but the will of the Father which hath sent me.)
>
> **KJV (1NT/3)** 1 Corinthians 11:29 For he that eateth and drinketh unworthily, eateth and **drink**eth **damnation to** himself, not discerning the Lord's body.)

KJV (1NT/1) Revelation 4:8 And the four beasts had each of them six wings about him; and they were full of eyes within: and they rest not day and night, saying, Holy, holy, holy, LORD God Almighty, which **was, and is, and is to come.**)

KJV (1NT/4) Revelation 19:6 And I heard as it were the voice of a great multitude, and as the voice of many waters, and as the voice of mighty thunderings, saying, Alleluia: for **the Lord** God **omnipotent** reigneth.)

BOM Mosiah 4:7 I say, that this is the man who receiveth salvation, through the atonement which was **prepared from the foundation of the world** for all mankind, which ever were since the fall of Adam, or who are, or who ever shall be, **even unto the end of the world.**

KJV (1/NT/14) Matthew 25:34 Then shall the King say unto them on his right hand, Come, ye blessed of my Father, inherit the kingdom **prepared** for you **from the foundation of the world.)**

KJV (1NT/1) Matthew 28:20 Teaching them to observe all things whatsoever I have commanded you: and, lo, I am with you always, **even unto the end of the world.** Amen.)

BOM Mosiah 5:11 And I would that ye should remember also, that this is the name that I said I should give unto you that never should be blotted out, except it be through transgression; therefore, **take heed that ye do not** transgress, that the name be not blotted out of your hearts.

KJV (1NT/1) Matthew 6:1 **Take heed that ye do not** your alms before men, to be seen of them: otherwise ye have no reward of your Father which is in heaven.)

BOM Mosiah 10:8 And it came to pass that they came up upon the north of the land of Shilom, with their numerous hosts, men armed with bows, and with arrows, and with swords, and with (11) cimeters (1548), and with stones, and with slings; and they had their heads shaved that they were naked; and they were girded with **a leathern girdle about** their **loins.**

KJV (1NT/1) Matthew 3:4 And the same John had his raiment of camel's hair, and **a leathern girdle about** his **loins**; and his meat was locusts and wild honey.)

BOM Mosiah 11:25 And except they **repent in sackcloth and ashes**, and cry mightily to the Lord their God, I will not hear their prayers, neither will I deliver them out of their afflictions; and thus saith the Lord, and thus hath he commanded me.

KJV (2NT/1) Matthew 11:21 Woe unto thee, Chorazin! woe unto thee, Bethsaida! for if the mighty works, which were done in you, had been done in Tyre and Sidon, they would have **repented** long ago **in sackcloth and ashes.**)

BOM Mosiah 17:1 **And** now **it came to pass that when** Abinadi **had finished**

these sayings, that the king commanded that the priests should take him and cause that he should be put to death.

> **KJV (1NT/1)** Matthew 19:1 **And it came to pass,** that **when** Jesus **had finished these sayings,** he departed from Galilee, and came into the coasts of Judaea beyond Jordan;)

BOM Mosiah 21:4 Yea, **all this was done that the** word of the Lord **might be fulfilled.**

> **KJV (1NT/1)** Matthew 26:56 But **all this was done, that the** scriptures of the prophets **might be fulfilled.** Then all the disciples forsook him, and fled.) (*Note: Joseph Smith obviously just changed "scriptures" to the more modern idea of "word of the Lord"*)

BOM Mosiah 26:27 **And then I will** confess **unto them** that **I never knew** them; and they shall **depart into everlasting fire prepared for the devil and his angels.**

> **KJV (1NT/1)** Matthew 7:23 **And then will I** profess **unto them, I never knew** you: **depart** from me, ye that work iniquity.)
>
> **KJV (1NT/1)** Matthew 25:41 Then shall he say also unto them on the left hand, **Depart** from me, ye cursed, **into everlasting fire, prepared for the devil and his angels:**)

BOM Alma 1:30 And thus, in their prosperous circumstances, they did not send away any who were **naked, or** that were **hungry, or** that were **athirst, or** that were sick, **or** that had not been nourished; and they did not set their hearts upon riches; therefore they were liberal to all, both old and young, both bond and free, both male and female, whether out of the church or in the church, having no respect to persons as to those who stood in need.

> **KJV** (1NT/1) Matthew 25:44 Then shall they also answer him, saying, Lord, when saw we thee an **hungred, or athirst, or** a stranger, **or naked, or sick, or** in prison, and did not minister unto thee?)

BOM Alma 5:52 **And again I say unto you**, the Spirit saith: Behold, **the ax is laid** at **the root of the tree**; therefore **every tree that bringeth not forth good fruit** shall be **hewn down and cast into the fire**, yea, a **fire** which cannot be consumed, even an **unquenchable fire**. Behold, and remember, the Holy One hath spoken it.

> **KJV (1NT/6)** Matthew 19:24 **And again I say unto you,** It is easier for a camel to go through the eye of a needle, than for a rich man to enter into the kingdom of God.)
>
> **KJV (2NT/1)** Matthew 3:10 And now also **the axe is laid** unto **the root of the trees:** therefore **every tree** which **bringeth not forth good fruit** is **hewn down, and cast into the fire.**)
>
> **KJV (2NT/13)** Matthew 7:19 **Every tree that bringeth not forth good fruit** is **hewn down, and cast into the fire.**)

KJV (2NT/5) <u>Luke 3:17</u> Whose fan is in his hand, and he will thoroughly purge his floor, and will gather the wheat into his garner; but the chaff he will burn with **fire unquenchable**.)

BOM <u>Alma 7:9</u> But behold, the Spirit hath said this much unto me, saying: Cry unto this people, **saying -- Repent ye,** and prepare the way of the Lord, and walk in **his paths,** which are **straight; for** behold, **the kingdom of heaven is at hand,** and the Son of God cometh upon the face of the earth.

KJV (3NT/24) <u>Matthew 3:2</u> And saying, **Repent ye**: for the kingdom of heaven is at hand.)

KJV (1NT/1) <u>Matthew 3:3</u> For this is he that was spoken of by the prophet Esaias, **saying,** The voice of one crying in the wilderness, **Prepare** ye **the way of the Lord,** make **his paths straight**.)

KJV (3NT/1) <u>Matthew 3:2</u> And **saying, Repent ye: for the kingdom of heaven is at hand**.)

BOM <u>Alma 7:19</u> For I perceive that ye are **in the paths of righteousness;** I perceive that ye are in the path which leads to the kingdom of God; yea, I perceive that ye are **making his paths straight.**

KJV (3NT/2) <u>Matthew 3:3</u> For this is he that was spoken of by the prophet Esaias, saying, The voice of one crying in the wilderness, Prepare ye the way of the Lord, **make his paths straight**.)

KJV (1/2) <u>Psalm 23:3</u> He restoreth my soul: he leadeth me **in the paths of righteousness** for his name's sake.)

BOM <u>Alma 7:25</u> And may the Lord bless you, and keep your garments (13) spotless (14th Century), that ye may at last be brought to **sit down with Abraham, Isaac, and Jacob,** and the **holy prophets** who **have been** ever **since the world began,** having your garments (13) spotless (14th Century) even as their garments are (13) spotless (14th Century), in the kingdom of heaven to go no more out.

KJV (1NT/2) <u>Matthew 8:11</u> And I say unto you, That many shall come from the east and west, and shall **sit down with Abraham, and Isaac, and Jacob,** in the kingdom of heaven.)

KJV (1NT/1) <u>Luke 1:70</u> As he spake by the mouth of his **holy prophets,** which **have been since the world began**:)

BOM <u>Alma 8:26</u> **And** now, Amulek, because thou hast fed me and taken me in, thou art blessed; for I **was an hungered,** for I **had fasted** many **days.**

KJV (1NT/4) <u>Matthew 4:2</u> **And** when he **had fasted** forty **days** and forty nights, he **was** afterward **an hungred**.)

BOM <u>Alma 9:15</u> Nevertheless **I say unto you,** that **it shall be more tolerable for** them in **the day of judgment than for you,** if ye remain in your sins, yea, and even **more tolerable for** them in this life than for you, except ye repent.

KJV (2NT/1) <u>Matthew 11:22</u> But **I say unto you, It shall be more tolerable for** Tyre and Sidon at **the day of judgment, than for you.**)

BOM <u>Alma 12:15</u> But this cannot be; we must come forth and stand before him in his glory, and in his power, and in his might, majesty, and dominion, and acknowledge to our everlasting shame that all his judgments are just; that he is just in all his works, and that he is merciful unto the children of men, and that he has all power to save every man that believeth on his name and **bring**eth **forth fruit meet for repentance.**

> **KJV (1NT/1)** <u>Matthew 3:8</u> **Bring forth** therefore **fruits meet for repentance**:)

BOM <u>Alma 14:17</u> And it came to pass that Alma and Amulek answered him nothing; and he smote them again, and **deliver**ed them **to the officer**s to **be cast into prison.**

> **KJV (1NT/1)** <u>Matthew 5:25</u> Agree with thine adversary quickly, whiles thou art in the way with him; lest at any time the adversary deliver thee to the judge, and the judge **deliver** thee **to the officer,** and thou **be cast into prison.**)

BOM <u>Alma 22:15</u> And it came to pass that after Aaron had expounded these things unto him, the king said: **What shall I do that I may have** this **eternal life** of which thou hast spoken? Yea, **what shall I do that I may** be **born of God,** having this wicked spirit rooted out of my breast, and receive his Spirit, **that I may be filled with joy,** that I may not be cast off at the last day? Behold, said he, I will give up all that I possess, yea, I will forsake my kingdom, that I may receive this great joy.

> **KJV (1NT/1)** <u>Matthew 19:16</u> And, behold, one came and said unto him, Good Master, **what** good thing **shall I do, that I may have eternal life**?)

> **KJV (5NT/9)** (Note: only in 1 John: <u>1 John 3:9</u> Whosoever is **born of God** doth not commit sin; for his seed remaineth in him: and he cannot sin, because he is **born of God.**)

> **KJV (1NT/1)** <u>2 Timothy 1:4</u> Greatly desiring to see thee, being mindful of thy tears, **that I may be filled with joy**;)

BOM <u>Alma 25:12</u> And he said unto the priests of Noah that their seed should cause many to be put to death, in the like manner as he was, and that they should be scattered abroad and slain, even as a sheep having no shepherd is driven and slain by wild beasts; and now behold, these words were verified, for they were driven by the Lamanites, and they were hunted, and they were smitten.

> **KJV (1NT/1)** <u>Matthew 9:36</u> But when he saw the multitudes, he was moved with compassion on them, because they fainted, and were scattered abroad, **as sheep having no shepherd.**)

BOM <u>Alma 26:7</u> But behold, they are in the hands of **the Lord of the harvest**, and they are his; and he **will raise** them **up at the last day.**

> **KJV (2NT/1)** <u>Matthew 9:38</u> Pray ye therefore **the Lord of the**

harvest, that he will send forth labourers into his **harvest.**)

KJV (5NT/49) <u>John 6:44</u> No man can come to me, except the Father which hath sent me draw him: and I **will raise** him **up at the last day.**)

BOM <u>Alma 31:10</u> Neither would they observe the (6) performances (15th Century) of the church, to continue in prayer and supplication to God daily, **that** they might **not enter into temptation.**

KJV (4NT/1) <u>Matthew 26:41</u> Watch and pray, **that** ye **enter not into temptation**: the spirit indeed is willing, but the flesh is weak.)

BOM <u>Alma 32:37</u> And after that they did separate themselves one from another, **taking no thought** for themselves **what** they should **eat, or what** they should **drink, or** what they should put on.

KJV (1NT/1) <u>Matthew 6:31</u> Therefore **take no thought,** saying, **What** shall we **eat?** or, **What** shall we **drink?** or, Wherewithal shall we be clothed?) (*Note: Note that this is even in the same order"*)

BOM <u>Alma 34:13</u> Therefore, it is expedient that there should be a great and last sacrifice; and then shall there be, or it is expedient there should be, a stop to the shedding of blood; then shall the law of Moses **be fulfilled**; yea, it shall **be all fulfilled**, every **jot** and **tittle,** and none shall have **pass**ed away.

KJV (1NT/1) <u>Matthew 5:18</u> For verily I say unto you, Till heaven and earth **pass,** one **jot** or one **tittle** shall in no wise **pass** from the law, till **all be fulfilled.**)

BOM <u>Alma 34:29</u> Therefore, if ye do not remember to be (1) charitable (14th Century), ye are as dross, which the (1) refiners (1582) do **cast out,** it being of no worth! and is **trodden under foot of men.**

KJV (1NT/3) <u>Matthew 5:13</u> Ye are the salt of the earth: but if the salt have lost his savour, wherewith shall it be salted? it is thenceforth good for nothing, but to be **cast out,** and to be **trodden under foot of men.**)

BOM <u>Alma 36:3</u> And now, O my son Alma, behold, thou art in thy youth, and therefore, I beseech of thee that thou wilt hear my words **and learn of me; for I** do know that whosoever shall put their trust in God shall be *(7) supported (14th Century)* in their trials, and their troubles, and their afflictions, and shall be lifted up at the last day.

KJV (1NT/1) <u>Matthew 11:29</u> Take my yoke upon you, **and learn of me; for I** am meek and lowly in heart: and ye shall find rest unto your souls.)

BOM <u>Alma 36:18</u> Now, as my mind caught hold upon this thought, I cried within my heart: O **Jesus, thou Son of God, have mercy on me,** who am **in the gall of bitterness, and** am (20) encircled (15th Century) about by the everlasting chains of death.

KJV (1NT/1) <u>Matthew 8:29</u> And, behold, they cried out, saying,

What have we to do with thee, **Jesus, thou Son of God**? art thou come hither to torment us before the time?)

KJV (6NT/1) Matthew 15:22 And, behold, a woman of Canaan came out of the same coasts, and **cried** unto him, saying, **Have mercy on me**, O Lord, thou son of David; my daughter is grievously vexed with a devil.)

KJV (1NT/5) Acts 8:23 For I perceive that thou art **in the gall of bitterness, and** in the bond of iniquity.)

BOM Alma 37:33 Preach unto them repentance, and faith on the Lord Jesus Christ; teach them to humble themselves and to be **meek and lowly in heart**; teach them to withstand every temptation of the devil, with their faith on the Lord Jesus Christ.

KJV (1NT/4) Matthew 11:29 Take my yoke upon you, and learn of me; for I am **meek and lowly in heart**: and ye shall find rest unto your souls.)

BOM Alma 37:34 Teach them to never be weary of good works, but to be **meek and lowly in heart**; for such **shall find rest to** their **souls**.

KJV (1NT/1) Matthew 11:29 Take my yoke upon you, and learn of me; for I am **meek and lowly in heart**: and ye **shall find rest** unto **your souls**.)

BOM Alma 40:13 And then shall it come to pass, that the spirits of the wicked, yea, who are evil -- for behold, they have no part nor portion of the Spirit of the Lord; for behold, they chose evil works rather than good; therefore the spirit of the devil did enter into them, and take possession of their house -- and these **shall be cast out into outer darkness; there shall be weeping, and wailing, and gnashing of teeth**, and this because of their own iniquity, being led captive by the will of the devil.

KJV (1NT/1) Matthew 8:12 But the children of the kingdom **shall be cast out into outer darkness: there shall be weeping and gnashing of teeth**.)

KJV (Matthew 13:42 And shall cast them into a furnace of fire: there shall be **wailing** and gnashing of teeth.)

BOM Alma 41:25 And **then shall the righteous shine forth in the kingdom of** God.

KJV (1NT/1) Matthew 13:43 **Then shall the righteous shine forth** as the sun **in the kingdom of** their Father. Who hath ears to hear, let him hear.)

BOM Alma 51:33 And it came to pass that when the night had come, Teancum and his servant stole forth and went out by night, and went into the camp of Amalickiah; and behold, sleep had (6) overpowered (1593) them because of their much (7) fatigue (1669), which was caused by the labors **and heat of the day**.

KJV (1NT/1) <u>Matthew 20:12</u> Saying, These last have wrought but one hour, and thou hast made them equal unto us, which have borne the burden **and heat of the day**) (Note: Same thought process here)

BOM <u>Alma 63:8</u> And it came to pass that they were never heard of more. And we suppose that they **were drowned in the depths of the sea**. And it came to pass that one other ship also did sail forth; and whither she did go we know not.

KJV (1NT/3) <u>Matthew 18:6</u> But whoso shall offend one of these little ones which believe in me, it were better for him that a millstone were hanged about his neck, and that he **were drowned in the depth of the sea.**)

BOM <u>Alma 3:30</u> And land their souls, yea, their immortal souls, at the right hand of God **in the kingdom of heaven, to sit down with Abraham, Isaac, and Jacob,** and with all our holy fathers, to go no more out.

KJV (1NT/2) <u>Matthew 8:11</u> And I say unto you, That many shall come from the east and west, and shall **sit down with Abraham, and Isaac, and Jacob, in the kingdom of heaven.**)

BOM <u>Alma 5:8</u> And now my sons, behold I have somewhat more to desire of you, which desire is, that ye may not do these things that ye may boast, but that ye may do these things to **lay up for yourselves** a **treasure in heaven**, yea, which is eternal, and which **fadeth not away**; yea, that ye may have that precious gift of eternal life, which we have reason to suppose hath been given to our fathers.

KJV (1NT/1) <u>Matthew 6:20</u> But **lay up for yourselves treasures in heaven**, where neither moth nor rust doth corrupt, and where thieves do not break through nor steal;)

KJV (2NT/1) <u>1 Peter 1:4</u> To an inheritance incorruptible, and undefiled, and that **fadeth not away**, reserved in heaven for you,)

BOM <u>Alma 5:32</u> And behold the voice came again, **saying: Repent ye, repent ye, for the kingdom of heaven is at hand**; and seek no more to destroy my servants. And it came to pass that the earth shook again, and the walls trembled.

KJV (1NT/1) <u>Matthew 3:2</u> And **saying, Repent ye: for the kingdom of heaven is at hand.**)

BOM <u>Alma 8:25</u> But behold, ye have rejected the truth, and rebelled against your holy God; and even at this time, instead of **laying up for yourselves treasures in heaven, where** nothing **doth corrupt, and where** nothing can come which is unclean, ye are heaping up for yourselves wrath against the day of judgment.

KJV (1NT/1) <u>Matthew 6:20</u> But **lay up for yourselves treasures in heaven, where** neither moth nor rust **doth corrupt, and where** thieves do not break through nor steal:)

BOM Helaman 10:7 Behold, I give unto you power, that **whatsoever ye shall** seal **on earth shall be** sealed **in heaven; and whatsoever ye shall loose on earth shall be loosed in heaven**; and thus shall ye have power among this people.

> **KJV (1NT/1)** Matthew 18:18 Verily I say unto you, **Whatsoever ye shall** bind **on earth shall be** bound **in heaven: and whatsoever ye shall loose on earth shall be loosed in heaven**)

BOM Alma 10:9 And **if ye shall say unto this mountain, Be thou cast** down and become smooth, **it shall be done.**

> **KJV (1NT/1)** Matthew 21:21 Jesus answered and said unto them, Verily I say unto you, If ye have faith, and doubt not, ye shall not only do this which is done to the fig tree, but also **if ye shall say unto this mountain, Be thou** removed, and be thou **cast** into the sea; **it shall be done**)

BOM Alma 13:29 *O* ye wicked **and perverse generation**; ye hardened and ye stiffnecked people, how long will ye suppose that the Lord will **suffer you?** Yea, **how long** will ye **suffer** yourselves to be led by foolish and **blind guides?** Yea, **how long** will ye choose **darkness rather than light?**

> **KJV (2NT/1)** Matthew 23:16 Woe unto you, ye **blind guides**, which say, Whosoever shall swear by the temple, it is nothing; but whosoever shall swear by the gold of the temple, he is a debtor!)
>
> **KJV (2NT/1)** Matthew 17:17 Then Jesus answered and said, **O** faithless **and perverse generation, how long** shall I be with you? **how long** shall I **suffer you?** bring him hither to me.)
>
> **KJV (1NT/1)** John 3:19 And this is the condemnation, that light is come into the world, and men loved **darkness rather than light,** because their deeds were evil.)

BOM Alma 14:25 And many **graves** shall be **opened, and** shall yield up **many** of their dead; and **many saints** shall **appear unto many.**

> **KJV (1NT/1)** Matthew 27:51-53 And, behold, the veil of the temple was **rent in twain** from the top to the bottom; and the earth did quake, and the rocks rent; And the **graves** were **opened; and many** bodies of the **saints** which slept arose, And came out of the **graves** after his resurrection, and went into the holy city, and **appear**ed **unto many.**)

BOM Alma 15:1 And now, my beloved brethren, behold, I declare unto you that except ye shall repent **your houses** shall be **left unto you desolate.**

> **KJV (2NT/1)** Matthew 23:38 Behold, **your house** is **left unto you desolate.**)

BOM Helaman 15:15 For behold, **had the mighty works been** (*29) shown* (12th Century) unto them which have been (*29) shown* (12th Century) unto you, yea, unto them who have (26) dwindled (1596 AD) in unbelief because of the traditions of their fathers, ye can see of yourselves that they never would again have (26) dwindled (1596 AD) in unbelief.

> **KJV (3NT/1)** *Note: Same idea here:* <u>Matthew 11:23</u> And thou, Capernaum, which art exalted unto heaven, shalt be brought down to hell: for if **the mighty works, which have been** done in thee, **had** been done in Sodom, it would have remained until this day.)

BOM <u>Alma 16:17</u> And now behold, saith the Lord, concerning the people of the Nephites: If they will not repent, and observe to do my will, I will utterly destroy them, saith the Lord, **because of their unbelief** notwithstanding the **many mighty works** which I have done among them; and as surely as the Lord liveth shall these things be, saith the Lord.

> **KJV (1NT/1)** <u>Matthew 13:58</u> And he did not **many mighty works** there **because of their unbelief.**)

BOM <u>3 Nephi 1:24</u> And there were no contentions, save it were a few that began to preach, *(2)* endeavoring (15th Century) to prove by the **scriptures** that it was no more expedient to observe the law of Moses. Now in this thing they did **err**, having **not** understood **the scriptures**.

> **KJV (1NT/1)** <u>Matthew 22:29</u> Jesus answered and said unto them, Ye do **err, not** knowing **the scriptures**, nor the power of God.).

BOM <u>3 Nephi 10:5</u> And again, **how oft would I have gathered** you **as a hen gathereth her chickens under her wings**, yea, **O** ye people of the house of Israel, who have fallen; yea, **O** ye people of the house of Israel, ye that dwell at **Jerusalem**, as ye that have fallen; yea, **how oft would I have gathered** you **as a hen gathereth her chickens, and ye would not**.

> **KJV (2NT/1)** (<u>Matthew 23:37</u> **O Jerusalem, Jerusalem**, thou that killest the prophets, and stonest them which are sent unto thee, **how oft**en would **I have gathered** thy children together, even **as a hen gathereth her chickens under her wings, and ye would not!**)

BOM <u>3 Nephi 10:14</u> And now, **whoso readeth, let him understand**; he that hath the scriptures, let him search them, and see and behold if all these deaths and destructions by fire, and by smoke, and by tempests, and by whirlwinds, and by the opening of the earth to receive them, and all these things are not unto the fulfilling of the prophecies of many of the holy prophets.

> **KJV (1NT/1)** <u>Matthew 24:15</u> When ye therefore shall see the abomination of desolation, spoken of by Daniel the prophet, stand in the holy place, (**whoso readeth, let him understand:**)

BOM <u>3 Nephi 11:7</u> Behold **my Beloved Son, in whom I am well pleased, in whom I** have glorified my name -- **hear** ye **him**.

> **KJV (1NT/1)** <u>Matthew 3:17</u> And lo a voice from heaven, saying, This is **my beloved Son, in whom I am well pleased.**)
>
> **KJV** (<u>Luke 9:35</u> And there came a voice out of the cloud, saying, This is **my beloved Son: hear him.**)

BOM 3 Nephi 11:25 **Having authority** given me of Jesus Christ, I **baptize you in the name of the Father, and of the Son, and of the Holy Ghost.** Amen.

> **KJV (1NT/4)** Matthew 7:29 For he taught them as one **having authority,** and not as the scribes.)
>
> **KJV (1NT/2)** Matthew 28:19 Go ye therefore, and teach all nations, **baptizing** them **in the name of the Father, and of the Son, and of the Holy Ghost:**)

BOM 3 Nephi 11:39 Verily, verily, I say unto you, that this is my doctrine, and whoso buildeth **upon this build**eth **upon** my **rock, and the gates of hell shall not prevail against** them.

> **KJV (1NT/1)** Matthew 16:18 And I say also unto thee, That thou art Peter, and **upon this rock** I will **build** my church; and **the gates of hell shall not prevail against** it.)

BOM 3 Nephi 11:40 And whoso shall declare **more** or less **than** this, and establish it for my doctrine, the same **cometh of evil,** and is not built upon my **rock**; but he buildeth upon a sandy foundation, and **the gates of hell** stand open to receive such when **the floods** come and the winds beat upon them.

> **KJV (1NT/1)** Matthew 5:37 But let your communication be, Yea, yea; Nay, nay: for whatsoever is **more than** these **cometh of evil.**)
>
> **KJV (1NT/4)** Matthew 16:18 And I say also unto thee, That thou art Peter, and upon this **rock** I will build my church; and **the gates of hell** shall not prevail against it.)
>
> **KJV (2NT/1)** Matthew 7:25 And the rain descended, and **the floods came, and the winds** blew, and **beat upon** that house; and it fell not: for it was founded **upon** a **rock.**)

BOM 3 Nephi 12:3-28

[**3**] Yea, **blessed are the poor in spirit** who come unto me, **for theirs is the kingdom of heaven.**

> **KJV (1NT/1)** Matthew 5:3 **Blessed are the poor in spirit: for theirs is the kingdom of heaven.**)

[**4**] And again, **blessed are** all **they that mourn, for they shall be comforted.**

> **KJV (1NT/1)** Matthew 5:4 **Blessed are they** that mourn: **for they shall be comforted.**)

[**5**] And **blessed are the meek, for they shall inherit the earth.**

> **KJV (1NT/1)** Matthew 5:5 **Blessed are the meek: for they shall inherit the earth.**)

[**6**] And **blessed are** all **they** who do **hunger and thirst after righteousness, for they shall be filled** with the **Holy Ghost.**

> **KJV (1NT/1)** Matthew 5:6 **Blessed are they** which **do hunger and thirst after righteousness: for they shall be filled.**)

[**7**] And **blessed are the merciful, for they shall obtain mercy.**

KJV (1NT/1) <u>Matthew 5:7</u> **Blessed are the merciful: for they shall obtain mercy.)**

[8] And **blessed are all the pure in heart, for they shall see God.**

KJV (1NT/1) <u>Matthew 5:8</u> **Blessed are the pure in heart: for they shall see God.)**

[9] And **blessed are all the peacemakers, for they shall be called the children of God.**

KJV (1NT/1) <u>Matthew 5:9</u> **Blessed are the peacemakers: for they shall be called the children of God.)**

[10] And **blessed are all they** who **are persecuted for** my name's **sake, for theirs is the kingdom of heaven.**

KJV (1NT/1) <u>Matthew 5:10</u> **Blessed are they** which **are persecuted for** righteousness' **sake: for theirs is the kingdom of heaven.)**

[11] And **blessed are ye when men shall revile you and persecute, and shall say all manner of evil against you falsely, for my sake;**

KJV (1NT/1) <u>Matthew 5:11</u> **Blessed are ye, when men shall revile you, and persecute** you, **and shall say all manner of evil against you falsely, for my sake.)**

[12] For ye shall have great joy **and be exceedingly glad, for great** shall be **your reward in heaven; for so persecuted they the prophets** who **were before you.**

KJV (1NT/1) <u>Matthew 5:12</u> **Rejoice, and be exceeding glad: for great** is **your reward in heaven: for so persecuted they the prophets** which **were before you.)**

[13] Verily, verily, I say unto you, I give unto you to be the **salt of the earth; but if the salt** shall lose its **savor wherewith shall** the earth **be salted?** The salt shall be **thenceforth good for nothing, but to be cast out and to be trodden under foot of men.**

KJV (1NT/3) <u>Matthew 5:13</u> **Ye are the salt of the earth: but if the salt** have lost his **savour, wherewith shall** it **be salted?** it is **thenceforth good for nothing, but to be cast out, and to be trodden under foot of men.)**

Note: Joseph Smith uses the term "wherewith shall the earth be salted?" instead of using the word "it" as it is in the KJV again his attempt at clarification.

[14] Verily, verily, I say unto you, I give unto you to be the light of this people. **A city that is set on a hill cannot be hid.**

KJV (1NT/1) <u>Matthew 5:14</u> **Ye are the light of the world. A city that is set on an hill cannot be hid.)**

[15] Behold, **do men light a candle and put it under a bushel?** Nay, **but on a candlestick, and it giveth light to all that are in the house;**

KJV (1NT/1) <u>Matthew 5:15</u> **Neither do men light a candle, and put**

it under a bushel, but on a candlestick; and it giveth light unto all that are in the house.)

[16] Therefore **let your light so shine before** this people, **that they may see your good works and glorify your Father** who **is in heaven.**

> KJV (1NT/1) <u>Matthew 5:16</u> **Let your light so shine before** men, **that they may see your good works, and glorify your Father** which **is in heaven.**)

[17] **Think not that I am come to destroy the law or the prophets. I am not come to destroy but to fulfil;**

> KJV (1NT/1) <u>Matthew 5:17</u> **Think not that I am come to destroy the law, or the prophets: I am not come to destroy, but to fulfil**)

[18] **For verily I say unto you,** one jot nor **tittle** hath not **pass**ed away **from the law,** but in me it hath **all been fulfilled.**

> KJV (1NT/1) <u>Matthew 5:18</u> **For verily I say unto you,** Till heaven and earth pass, **one jot** or one **tittle** shall in no wise **pass from the law,** till **all be fulfilled.**)

[19] And behold, I have given you the law and the commandments of my Father, that ye shall believe in me, and that ye shall repent of your sins, and come unto me with a broken heart and a contrite spirit. Behold, ye have the commandments before you, and the law is fulfilled.

[20] Therefore come unto me and be ye saved; **for** verily **I say unto you,** that except ye shall keep my commandments, which I have commanded you at this time, **ye shall in no case enter into the kingdom of heaven.**

> KJV (1NT/1) <u>Matthew 5:20</u> **For I say unto you,** That except your righteousness shall exceed the righteousness of the scribes and Pharisees, **ye shall in no case enter into the kingdom of heaven.**)

[21] **Ye have heard that it** hath **been said** by **them of old time,** and it is also written before you, that **thou shalt not kill, and whosoever shall kill shall be in danger of the judgment** of God;

> KJV (1NT/1) <u>Matthew 5:21</u> **Ye have heard that it** was **said of them of old time, Thou shalt not kill; and whosoever shall kill shall be in danger of the judgment:**)

[22] **But I say unto you, that whosoever is angry with his brother shall be in danger of** his **judgment. And whosoever shall say to his brother, Raca, shall be in danger of the council; and whosoever shall say, Thou fool, shall be in danger of hell fire.**

> KJV (1NT/1) <u>Matthew 5:22</u> **But I say unto you, That whosoever is angry with his brother** without a cause **shall be in danger of the judgment: and whosoever shall say to his brother, Raca, shall be in danger of the council: but whosoever shall say, Thou fool, shall be in danger of hell fire.**)

[23] **Therefore, if** ye shall come unto me, or shall desire to come unto me,

and rememberest that thy brother hast aught against thee –

> **KJV (1NT/1)** <u>Matthew 5:23</u> **Therefore if** thou bring thy gift to the altar, **and** there **rememberest that thy brother hath** ought **against thee.**)

[24] Go thy way unto **thy brother, and first be reconciled to thy brother, and then come** unto me with full purpose of heart, and I will receive you.

> **KJV (1NT/1)** <u>Matthew 5:24</u> Leave there thy gift before the altar, **and go thy way; first be reconciled to thy brother, and then come** and offer thy gift)

[25] Agree with thine adversary quickly while thou art in the way with him, lest at any time he shall get thee, **and thou** shalt **be cast into prison.**

> **KJV (1NT/1)** <u>Matthew 5:25</u> **Agree with thine adversary quickly, while**s **thou art in the way with him; lest at any time** the adversary deliver thee to the judge, and the judge deliver thee to the officer, **and thou be cast into prison.**)

[26] Verily, **verily, I say unto thee, thou shalt by no means come out thence until thou hast paid the uttermost** senine. And while ye are in prison can ye pay even one senine? Verily, verily, I say unto you, Nay.

> **KJV (1NT/1)** <u>Matthew 5:26</u> **Verily I say unto thee, Thou shalt by no means come out thence, till thou hast paid the uttermost** farthing.)

[27] Behold, it is written **by them of old time,** that **thou shalt not commit adultery;**

> **KJV (1NT/1)** <u>Matthew 5:27</u> Ye have heard that **it** was said **by them of old time, Thou shalt not commit adultery:**)

[28] But I say unto you, that whosoever looketh on a woman, to lust after her, hath committed adultery already in his heart.

> **KJV (1NT/1)** <u>Matthew 5:28</u> **But I say unto you, That whosoever looketh on a woman to lust after her hath committed adultery with her already in his heart.**)

BOM <u>3 Nephi 12:30-45</u>

[30] For it is better that ye should **deny** yourselves of these things, wherein ye will **take up** your **cross, than** that ye should **be cast into hell.**

> **KJV (1NT/1)** <u>Matthew 16:24</u> Then said Jesus unto his disciples, If any man will come after me, let him **deny** himself, and **take up** his **cross**, and follow me)
>
> **KJV (1NT/1)** <u>Matthew 18:9</u> And if thine eye offend thee, pluck it out, and cast it from thee: it is better for thee to enter into life with one eye, rather **than** having two eyes to **be cast into hell** fire.)

[31] It hath been written, that **whosoever shall put away his wife, let him give her a writing of divorcement.**

> **KJV (1NT/1)** <u>Matthew 5:31</u> **It hath been** said, **Whosoever shall put**

away his wife, let him give her a writing of divorcement:)
[32] Verily, verily, I say unto you, that whosoever shall put away his wife, saving for the cause of fornication, causeth her to commit adultery; and whoso shall marry her who is divorced committeth adultery.

KJV (1NT/1) <u>Matthew 5:32</u> But **I say unto you, That whosoever shall put away his wife, saving for the cause of fornication, causeth her to commit adultery: and whoso**ever **shall marry her that is divorced committeth adultery.**)

KJV (7NT/23) <u>John 8:34</u> Jesus answered them, **Verily, verily, I say unto you, Whosoever** committeth sin is the servant of sin.)

[33] And **again** it is written, **thou shalt not forswear thyself, but shalt perform unto the Lord thine oaths;**

KJV (1NT/1) <u>Matthew 5:33</u> **Again**, ye have heard that it hath been said by them of old time, **Thou shalt not forswear thyself, but shalt perform unto the Lord thine oaths:**)

[34] But verily, verily, I say unto you, swear not at all; neither by heaven, for it is God's throne;

KJV (1NT/1) <u>Matthew 5:34</u> **But I say unto you, Swear not at all; neither by heaven; for it is God's throne.**)

KJV (7NT/23) <u>John 8:34</u> Jesus answered them, **Verily, verily, I say unto you,** Whosoever committeth sin is the servant of sin.)

[35] Nor by the earth, for it is his footstool;

KJV (1NT/1) <u>Matthew 5:35</u> **Nor by the earth; for it is his footstool**: neither by Jerusalem; for it is the city of the great King.)

[36] Neither shalt thou swear by thy head, because thou canst not make one hair black or white;

KJV (1NT/1) <u>Matthew 5:36</u> **Neither shalt thou swear by thy head, because thou canst not make one hair white or black.**)

[37] But let your communication be Yea, yea; Nay, nay; for whatsoever cometh of more than these is evil.

KJV (1NT/1) <u>Matthew 5:37</u> **But let your communication be, Yea, yea; Nay, nay: for whatsoever is more than these cometh of evil.**)

[38] And behold, it is written, **an eye for an eye, and a tooth for a tooth;**

KJV (1NT/1) <u>Matthew 5:38</u> Ye have heard that it hath been said, **An eye for an eye, and a tooth for a tooth:**)

[39] But I say unto you, that ye shall **not resist evil, but whosoever shall smite thee on thy right cheek, turn to him the other also;**

KJV (1NT/1) <u>Matthew 5:39</u> **But I say unto you, That ye resist not evil: but whosoever shall smite thee on thy right cheek, turn to him the other also.**)

[40] And if any man will sue thee at the law and take away thy coat, let him have thy cloak also;

KJV (1NT/1) <u>Matthew 5:40</u> **And if any man will sue thee at the law, and take away thy coat, let him have thy cloak also.)**

[41] **And whosoever shall compel thee to go a mile, go with him twain.**

KJV (1NT/1) <u>Matthew 5:41</u> **And whosoever shall compel thee to go a mile, go with him twain.)**

[42] **Give to him that asketh thee, and from him that would borrow of thee turn not away.**

KJV (1NT/1) <u>Matthew 5:42</u> **Give to him that asketh thee, and from him that would borrow of thee turn not** thou **away)**

[43] **And behold it is written also, that thou shalt love thy neighbor and hate thine enemy;**

KJV (1NT/1) <u>Matthew 5:43</u>Ye have heard that it hath been said, **Thou shalt love thy neighbour, and hate thine enemy.)**

[44] **But I say unto you, love your enemies, bless them that curse you, do good to them that hate you, and pray for them who despitefully use you and persecute you;**

KJV (1NT/1) <u>Matthew 5:44</u> **But I say unto you, Love your enemies, bless them that curse you, do good to them that hate you, and pray for them which despitefully use you, and persecute you;)**

[45] **That ye may be the children of your Father** who **is in heaven; for he maketh his sun to rise on the evil and on the good.**

KJV (1NT/1) <u>Matthew 5:45</u> **That ye may be the children of your Father** which **is in heaven: for he maketh his sun to rise on the evil and on the good**, and sendeth rain on the just and on the unjust.)

BOM <u>3 Nephi 12:48</u> Therefore I would that ye should **be perfect even as** I, or **your Father** who **is in heaven is perfect**.

KJV (1NT/1) <u>Matthew 5:48</u> **Be** ye therefore **perfect, even** as **your Father** which **is in heaven is perfect.)**

BOM <u>3 Nephi 1-34</u>

[1] Verily, verily, I say that I would that ye should do alms unto the poor; but **take heed that ye do not your alms before men to be seen of them; otherwise ye have no reward of your Father** who **is in heaven.**

KJV (1NT/1) <u>Matthew 6:1</u> **Take heed that ye do not your alms before men, to be seen of them: otherwise ye have no reward of your Father** which **is in heaven.)**

[2] **Therefore, when** ye shall **do your alms do not sound a trumpet before you, as** will **hypocrites do in the synagogues and in the streets, that they may have glory of men. Verily I say unto you, they have their reward.**

KJV (1NT/1) <u>Matthew 6:2</u> **Therefore when** thou doest thine **alms, do not sound a trumpet before** thee, **as the hypocrites do in the synagogues and in the streets, that they may have glory of men.**

Verily I say unto you, They have their reward.)

[3] But when thou doest alms let not thy left hand know what thy right hand doeth;

    KJV (1NT/1) Matthew 6:3 But when thou doest alms, let not thy left hand know what thy right hand doeth:)

[4] That thine alms may be in secret; and thy Father who seeth in secret, himself shall reward thee openly.

    KJV (1NT/1) Matthew 6:4 That thine alms may be in secret: and thy Father which seeth in secret himself shall reward thee openly.)

[5] And when thou prayest thou shalt not do as the hypocrites, for they love to pray, standing in the synagogues and in the corners of the streets, that they may be seen of men. Verily I say unto you, they have their reward.

    KJV (1NT/1) Matthew 6:5 And when thou prayest, thou shalt not be as the hypocrites are: for they love to pray standing in the synagogues and in the corners of the streets, that they may be seen of men. Verily I say unto you, They have their reward.)

[6] But thou, when thou prayest, enter into thy closet, and when thou hast shut thy door, pray to thy Father who is in secret; and thy Father, who seeth in secret, shall reward thee openly.

    KJV (1NT/1) Matthew 6:6 But thou, when thou prayest, enter into thy closet, and when thou hast shut thy door, pray to thy Father which is in secret; and thy Father which seeth in secret shall reward thee openly.)

[7] But when ye pray, use not vain repetitions, as the heathen, for they think that they shall be heard for their much speaking.

    KJV (1NT/1) Matthew 6:7 But when ye pray, use not vain repetitions, as the heathen do: for they think that they shall be heard for their much speaking.)

[8] Be not ye therefore like unto them, for your Father knoweth what things ye have need of before ye ask him.

    KJV (1NT/1) Matthew 6:8 Be not ye therefore like unto them: for your Father knoweth what things ye have need of, before ye ask him.)

[9] After this manner therefore pray ye: Our Father who art in heaven, hallowed be thy name.

    KJV (1NT/1) (Matthew 6:9 After this manner therefore pray ye: Our Father which art in heaven, Hallowed be thy name.)

[10] Thy will be done on earth as it is in heaven.

    KJV (1NT/1) Matthew 6:10 Thy kingdom come, Thy will be done in earth, as it is in heaven.)

[11] And forgive us our debts, as we forgive our debtors.

> KJV (1NT/1) <u>Matthew 6:12</u> And forgive us our debts, as we forgive our debtors.)

[12] And lead us not into temptation, but deliver us from evil.

[13] For thine is the kingdom, and the power, and the glory, forever. Amen.

> KJV (1NT/1) <u>Matthew 6:13</u> And lead us not into temptation, but deliver us from evil: For thine is the kingdom, and the power, and the glory, for ever. Amen.)

> **Note:** The <u>doxology</u> as it is known (For thine is the kingdom, and the power, and the glory, for ever and ever. Amen.) was likely not present in the original version of what has become known as The Lord's Prayer, but was added to the Gospels as a result of its use in the liturgy of the early church. As a result of this knowledge, it is *not* included in many modern translations. Joseph Smith of course did not know this and thus added it here.

[14] For, if ye forgive men their trespasses your heavenly Father will also forgive you;

> KJV (1NT/1) <u>Matthew 6:14</u> For if ye forgive men their trespasses, your heavenly Father will also forgive you:)

[15] But if ye forgive not men their trespasses neither will your Father forgive your trespasses.

> KJV (1NT/1) <u>Matthew 6:15</u> But if ye forgive not men their trespasses, neither will your Father forgive your trespasses.)

[16] Moreover, when ye fast be not as the hypocrites, of a sad countenance, for they disfigure their faces that they may appear unto men to fast. Verily I say unto you, they have their reward.

> KJV (1NT/1) <u>Matthew 6:16</u> Moreover when ye fast, be not, as the hypocrites, of a sad countenance: for they disfigure their faces, that they may appear unto men to fast. Verily I say unto you, They have their reward.)

[17] But thou, when thou fastest, anoint thy **head, and wash thy face;**

> KJV (1NT/1) <u>Matthew 6:17</u> But thou, when thou fastest, anoint thine **head, and wash thy face;**)

[18] That thou appear not unto men to fast, but unto thy Father, who is in secret; and thy Father, who **seeth in secret, shall reward thee openly.**

> KJV (1NT/1) <u>Matthew 6:18</u> That thou appear not unto men to fast, but unto thy Father which is in secret: and thy Father, which seeth in secret, shall reward thee openly.)

[19] Lay not up for yourselves treasures upon earth, where moth and rust doth corrupt, and thieves break through and steal;

> KJV (1NT/1) <u>Matthew 6:19</u> Lay not up for yourselves treasures

upon earth, where moth and rust doth corrupt, and where thieves break through and steal:)

    COM Gill also leaves out the "where" in "where thieves" Gill: <u>Mat 6:19</u> "Where moth and rust doth corrupt, and thieves break through and steal")

[20] But lay up for yourselves treasures in heaven, where neither moth nor rust doth corrupt, and where thieves do not break through nor steal.

    KJV (1NT/1) <u>Matthew 6:20</u> **But lay up for yourselves treasures in heaven, where neither moth nor rust doth corrupt, and where thieves do not break through nor steal:)**

[21] For where your treasure is, there will your heart be also.

    KJV (2NT/1) <u>Matthew 6:21</u> **For where your treasure is, there will your heart be also.)**

[22] The light of the body is the eye; if, therefore, thine eye be single, thy whole body shall be full of light.

    KJV (1NT/1) <u>Matthew 6:22</u> **The light of the body is the eye: if therefore thine eye be single, thy whole body shall be full of light.)**

[23] But if thine eye be evil, thy whole body shall be full of darkness. If, therefore, the light that is in thee be darkness, how great is that darkness!

    KJV (1NT/1) <u>Matthew 6:23</u> **But if thine eye be evil, thy whole body shall be full of darkness. If therefore the light that is in thee be darkness, how great is that darkness!)**

[24] No man can serve two masters; for either he will hate the one and love the other, or else he will hold to the one and despise the other. Ye cannot serve God and Mammon.

    KJV (1NT/1) <u>Matthew 6:24</u> **No man can serve two masters: for either he will hate the one, and love the other; or else he will hold to the one, and despise the other. Ye cannot serve God and mammon.)**

[25] And now it came to pass that **when Jesus had spoken these words** he looked upon the twelve whom he had chosen, and said unto them: Remember the words which I have spoken. For behold, ye are they whom I have chosen to minister unto this people. **Therefore I say unto you, take no thought for your life, what ye shall eat, or what ye shall drink; nor yet for your body, what ye shall put on. Is not the life more than meat, and the body than raiment?**

    KJV (1NT/1) <u>Matthew 6:25</u> **Therefore I say unto you, Take no thought for your life, what ye shall eat, or what ye shall drink; nor yet for your body, what ye shall put on. Is not the life more than meat, and the body than raiment?)**

    KJV (1NT/10) <u>John 18:1</u> **When Jesus had spoken these words,** he went forth with his disciples over the brook Cedron, where was a garden, into the which he entered, and his disciples.)

[26] Behold the fowls of the air, for they sow not, neither do they reap nor gather into barns; yet your heavenly Father feedeth them. Are ye not much better than they?

> KJV (1NT/1) <u>Matthew 6:26</u> Behold the fowls of the air: **for they sow not, neither do they reap, nor gather into barns; yet your heavenly Father feedeth them. Are ye not much better than they?**)

[27] Which of you by taking thought can add one cubit unto his stature?

> KJV (1NT/1) <u>Matthew 6:27</u> **Which of you by taking thought can add one cubit unto his stature?**)

[28] And why take ye thought for raiment? Consider the lilies of the field how they grow; they toil not, neither do they spin;

> KJV (1NT/1) <u>Matthew 6:28</u> **And why take ye thought for raiment? Consider the lilies of the field, how they grow; they toil not, neither do they spin:**)

[29] And yet I say unto you, that even Solomon, in all his glory, was not arrayed like one of these.

> KJV (1NT/1) <u>Matthew 6:29</u> **And yet I say unto you, That even Solomon in all his glory was not arrayed like one of these.**)

[30] Wherefore, if God so clothe the grass of the field, which today is, and tomorrow is cast into the oven, even so will **he clothe you,** if ye are not **of little faith.**

> KJV (1NT/1) <u>Matthew 6:30</u> **Wherefore, if God so clothe the grass of the field, which** to day is, and to morrow is cast into the oven, shall **he** not much more **clothe you, O ye of little faith?**)

[31] Therefore take no thought, saying, What shall we eat? or, What shall we drink? or, Wherewithal shall we be clothed?

> KJV (1NT/1) <u>Matthew 6:31</u> **Therefore take no thought, saying, What shall we eat? or, What shall we drink? or, Wherewithal shall we be clothed?**)

[32] For your heavenly Father knoweth that ye have need of all these things.

> KJV (1NT/1) <u>Matthew 6:32</u> (For after all these things do the Gentiles seek:) **for your heavenly Father knoweth that ye have need of all these things.**)

[33] But seek ye first the kingdom of God and his righteousness, and all these things shall be added unto you.

> KJV (1NT/1) <u>Matthew 6:33</u> **But seek ye first the kingdom of God, and his righteousness; and all these things shall be added unto you.**)

[34] Take therefore no thought for the morrow, for the morrow shall take

thought for the things of itself. Sufficient is the day unto the evil thereof.

> KJV (1NT/1) <u>Matthew 6:34</u> **Take therefore no thought for the morrow: for the morrow shall take thought for the things of itself. Sufficient unto the day is the evil thereof.**)

BOM <u>3 Nephi 15:1-27</u>

[1] And now it came to pass that **when Jesus had spoken these words** he turned again to the multitude, and did open his mouth unto them again, saying: Verily, verily, I say unto you, **Judge not, that ye be not judged.**

> KJV (2NT/1) <u>Matthew 7:1</u> **Judge not, that ye be not judged.**)

> KJV (1NT/10) <u>John 18:1</u> **When Jesus had spoken these words,** he went forth with his disciples over the brook Cedron, where was a garden, into the which he entered, and his disciples.)

[2] **For with what judgment ye judge, ye shall be judged; and with what measure ye mete, it shall be measured to you again.**

> KJV (1NT/1) <u>Matthew 7:2</u> **For with what judgment ye judge, ye shall be judged: and with what measure ye mete, it shall be measured to you again.**)

[3] **And why beholdest thou the mote that is in thy brother's eye, but considerest not the beam that is in thine own eye?**

> KJV (1NT/1) <u>Matthew 7:3</u> **And why beholdest thou the mote that is in thy brother's eye, but considerest not the beam that is in thine own eye?**)

> **Note:** This verse is quoted two times in the NT one with the word "considerest" found in Matthew and the other with the word "perceivest" found in Luke Joseph Smith chose the verse with "considerest".

[4] **Or how wilt thou say to thy brother: Let me pull the mote out of thine eye -- and behold, a beam is in thine own eye?**

> KJV (1NT/1) <u>Matthew 7:4</u> **Or how wilt thou say to thy brother, Let me pull out the mote out of thine eye; and, behold, a beam is in thine own eye?**)

[5] **Thou hypocrite, first cast the beam out of thine own eye; and then shalt thou see clearly to cast the mote out of thy brother's eye.**

> KJV (1NT/1) <u>Matthew 7:5</u> **Thou hypocrite, first cast out the beam out of thine own eye; and then shalt thou see clearly to cast out the mote out of thy brother's eye.**)

[6] **Give not that which is holy unto the dogs, neither cast ye your pearls before swine, lest they trample them under their feet, and turn again and rend you.**

> KJV (1NT/1) <u>Matthew 7:6</u> **Give not that which is holy unto the dogs, neither cast ye your pearls before swine, lest they trample them under their feet, and turn again and rend you.**)

[7] Ask, and it shall be given unto you; seek, and ye shall find; knock, and it shall be opened unto you.

> KJV (1NT/1) <u>Matthew 7:7</u> Ask, and it shall be given you; seek, and ye shall find; knock, and it shall be opened unto you:)

[8] For every one that asketh, receiveth; and he that seeketh, findeth; and to him that knocketh, it shall be opened.

> KJV (2NT/1) <u>Matthew 7:8</u> For every one that asketh receiveth; and he that seeketh findeth; and to him that knocketh it shall be opened.)

[9] Or what man is there of you, who, if his son ask bread, will give him a stone?

> KJV (1NT/1) <u>Matthew 7:9</u> Or what man is there of you, whom if his son ask bread, will he give him a stone?)

[10] Or if he ask a fish, will he give him a serpent?

> KJV (1NT/1) <u>Matthew 7:10</u> Or if he ask a fish, will he give him a serpent?)

[11] If ye then, being evil, know how to give good gifts unto your children, how much more shall your Father who is in heaven give good things to them that ask him?

> KJV (1NT/1) <u>Matthew 7:11</u> If ye then, being evil, know how to give good gifts unto your children, how much more shall your Father which is in heaven give good things to them that ask him?)

[12] Therefore, all things whatsoever ye would that men should do to you, do ye even so to them, for this is the law and the prophets.

> KJV (1NT/1) <u>Matthew 7:12</u> Therefore all things whatsoever ye would that men should do to you, do ye even so to them: for this is the law and the prophets.)

[13] Enter ye in at the strait gate; for wide is the gate, and broad is the way, which leadeth to destruction, and many there be who go in thereat;

> KJV (1NT/1) <u>Matthew 7:13</u> Enter ye in at the strait gate: for wide is the gate, and broad is the way, that leadeth to destruction, and many there be which go in thereat:)

[14] Because strait is the gate, and narrow is the way, which leadeth unto life, and few there be that find it.

> KJV (1NT/1) <u>Matthew 7:14</u> Because strait is the gate, and narrow is the way, which leadeth unto life, and few there be that find it.)

[15] Beware of false prophets, who come to you in sheep's clothing, but inwardly they are ravening wolves.

> KJV (1NT/1) <u>Matthew 7:15</u> Beware of false prophets, which come to you in sheep's clothing, but inwardly they are ravening wolves.)

[16] Ye shall know them by their fruits. Do men gather grapes of thorns, or figs of thistles?

> **KJV (1NT/1)** <u>Matthew 7:16</u> Ye shall know them by their fruits. Do men gather grapes of thorns, or figs of thistles?)

[17] Even so every good tree bringeth forth good fruit; but a corrupt tree bringeth forth evil fruit.

> **KJV (1NT/1)** <u>Matthew 7:17</u> Even so every good tree bringeth forth good fruit; but a corrupt tree bringeth forth evil fruit.)

[18] A good tree cannot bring forth evil fruit, neither a corrupt tree bring forth good fruit.

> **KJV (1NT/1)** <u>Matthew 7:18</u> A good tree cannot bring forth evil fruit, neither can a corrupt tree bring forth good fruit.)

[19] Every tree that bringeth not forth good fruit is hewn down, and cast into the fire.

> **KJV (1NT/1)** <u>Matthew 7:19</u> Every tree that bringeth not forth good fruit is hewn down, and cast into the fire.)

[20] Wherefore, by their fruits ye shall know them.

> **KJV (1NT/1)** <u>Matthew 7:20</u> Wherefore by their fruits ye shall know them.)

[21] Not every one that saith unto me, Lord, Lord, shall enter into the kingdom of heaven; but he that doeth the will of my Father who is in heaven.

> **KJV (1NT/1)** <u>Matthew 7:21</u> Not every one that saith unto me, Lord, Lord, shall enter into the kingdom of heaven; but he that doeth the will of my Father which is in heaven.)

[22] Many will say to me in that day: Lord, Lord, have we not prophesied in thy name, and in thy name have cast out devils, and in thy name done many wonderful works?

> **KJV (1NT/1)** <u>Matthew 7:22</u> Many will say to me in that day, Lord, Lord, have we not prophesied in thy name? and in thy name have cast out devils? and in thy name done many wonderful works?)

[23] And then will I profess unto them: I never knew you; depart from me, ye that work iniquity.

> **KJV (1NT/1)** <u>Matthew 7:23</u> And then will I profess unto them, I never knew you: depart from me, ye that work iniquity.)

[24] Therefore, whoso heareth these sayings of mine and doeth them, I will liken him unto a wise man, who built his house upon a rock –

> **KJV (1NT/1)** <u>Matthew 7:24</u> Therefore whosoever heareth these sayings of mine, and doeth them, I will liken him unto a wise man, which built his house upon a rock:)

[25] And the rain descended, and the floods came, and the winds blew, and beat upon that house; and it fell not, for it was founded upon a rock.

> **KJV (1NT/1)** <u>Matthew 7:25</u> And the rain descended, and the

floods came, and the winds blew, and beat upon that house; and it fell not: for it was founded upon a rock.)

[26] And every one that heareth these sayings of mine and doeth them not shall be likened unto a foolish man, who built his house upon the sand –

> KJV (1NT/1) Matthew 7:26 And every one that heareth these sayings of mine, and doeth them not, shall be likened unto a foolish man, which built his house upon the sand:)

[27] And the rain descended, and the floods came, and the winds blew, and beat upon that house; and it fell, and great was the fall of it.

> KJV (1NT/1) Matthew 7:27 And the rain descended, and the floods came, and the winds blew, and beat upon that house; and it fell: and great was the fall of it.)

BOM 3 Nephi 15:1 And now it came to pass that when Jesus had ended these sayings he cast my eyes round about on the multitude, and said unto them: Behold, ye have heard the things which I taught before I ascended to my Father; therefore, whoso remembereth these sayings of mine and doeth them, him will I raise up at the last day.

> KJV (1NT/1) Matthew 7:28 And it came to pass, when Jesus had ended these sayings, the people were astonished at his doctrine:)
>
> KJV (1NT/1) John 20:17 Jesus saith unto her, Touch me not; for I am not yet ascended to my Father: but go to my brethren, and say unto them, I ascend unto my Father, and your Father; and to my God, and your God.)
>
> KJV (1NT/1) Matthew 7:24 Therefore whosoever heareth these sayings of mine, and doeth them, I will liken him unto a wise man, which built his house upon a rock:)
>
> KJV (1NT/1) John 6:44 No man can come to me, except the Father which hath sent me draw him: and I will raise him up at the last day.)

BOM 3 Nephi 15:10 Behold, I have given unto you the commandments; therefore keep my commandments. And this is the law and the prophets, for they truly testified of me.

> KJV (1NT/1) Matthew 7:12 Therefore all things whatsoever ye would that men should do to you, do ye even so to them: for this is the law and the prophets.)

BOM 3 Nephi 16:15 But if they will not turn unto me, and hearken unto my voice, I will suffer them, yea, I will suffer my people, O house of Israel, that they shall go through among them, and shall tread them down, and they shall be as salt that hath lost its savor, which is thenceforth good for nothing but to be cast out, and to be trodden under foot of my people, O house of Israel.

> KJV (1NT/3) Matthew 5:13 Ye are the salt of the earth: but if the salt have lost his savour, wherewith shall it be salted? it is

thenceforth **good for nothing, but to be cast out, and to be trodden under foot of** men.)

BOM 3 Nephi 17:1 Behold, now it came to pass that **when Jesus had spoken these words he** looked round about again on the multitude, and he said unto them: Behold, **my time is at hand**.

> **KJV (1NT/1)** Matthew 26:18 And he said, Go into the city to such a man, and say unto him, The Master saith, **My time is at hand**; I will keep the passover at thy house with my disciples.)
>
> **KJV (1NT/10)** John 18:1 **When Jesus had spoken these words**, he went forth with his disciples over the brook Cedron, where was a garden, into the which he entered, and his disciples.)

BOM 3 Nephi 18:13 But whoso among you shall do more or less than these are not **built upon** my **rock**, but are **built upon** a sandy foundation; and when the **rain descend**s, **and the floods** come, **and the winds** blow, **and beat upon** them, they shall **fall**, and **the gates of hell** are ready open to receive them.

> **KJV (1NT/1)** Matthew 7:27 And the **rain descend**ed, **and the floods** came, **and the winds** blew, **and beat upon** that house; and it fell: and great was the **fall** of it.)
>
> **KJV (1NT/4)** Matthew 16:18 And I say also unto thee, That thou art Peter, and **upon** this **rock** I will **build** my church; and **the gates of hell** shall not prevail against it.)
>
> **KJV (1NT/1)** Matthew 7:24 Therefore whosoever heareth these sayings of mine, and doeth them, I will liken him unto a wise man, which **built** his house **upon** a **rock**:)

BOM 3 Nephi 21:26 And then shall the work of the Father (17) commence (1340 AD) at that day, even when **this gospel shall be preached** among the remnant of this people. verily I say unto you, at that day shall the work of the Father (17) commence (1340 AD) among all the dispersed of my people, yea, even the tribes which have been lost, which the Father hath led away out of Jerusalem.

> **KJV (2NT/1)** Matthew 26:13 Verily I say unto you, Wheresoever **this gospel shall be preached** in the whole world, there **shall** also this, that this woman hath done, be told for a memorial of her.)

BOM 3 Nephi 27:2 And Jesus again showed himself unto them, for they were praying unto the Father in his name; and **Jesus came** and **stood in the midst of them, and** said **unto them: What will ye that I shall** give **unto you**?

> **KJV (1NT/1)** Luke 24:36 And as they thus spake, **Jesus** himself **stood in the midst of them, and** saith **unto them**, Peace be unto you.)
>
> **KJV (1NT/1)** Matthew 20:32 And Jesus stood still, and called them, and said, **What will ye that I shall** do **unto you**?)

BOM 3 Nephi 27:29 Therefore, **ask, and ye shall receive; knock, and it**

shall be opened unto you; for he that **asketh, receiveth; and** unto **him that knocketh, it shall be opened**.

> **KJV (1NT/1)** <u>John 16:24</u> Hitherto have ye asked nothing in my name: **ask, and ye shall receive**, that your joy may be full.)
>
> **KJV (1NT/1)** <u>Matthew 7:7</u> **Ask, and** it shall be given you; seek, and ye shall find; **knock, and it shall be opened unto you:**)
>
> **KJV (1NT/1)** <u>Matthew 7:8</u> **For** every one that **asketh receiveth**; **and** he that seeketh findeth; and to **him that knocketh it shall be opened**.)

BOM <u>3 Nephi 27:32</u> But behold, it sorroweth me because of the fourth generation from this generation, for they are led away captive by him even as was **the son of perdition**; for they will sell me for silver and for gold, and for that which **moth doth corrupt and** which **thieves** can **break through and steal**. And in that day will I visit them, even in turning their works upon their own heads.

> **KJV (1NT/1)** <u>Matthew 6:19</u> Lay not up for yourselves treasures upon earth, where **moth** and rust **doth corrupt, and** where **thieves break through and steal**:)
>
> **KJV (2NT/2)** <u>John 17:12</u> While I was with them in the world, I kept them in thy name: those that thou gavest me I have kept, and none of them is lost, but **the son of perdition**; that the scripture might be fulfilled.)

BOM <u>3 Nephi 27:33</u> And it came to pass that **when Jesus had ended these sayings** he said unto his disciples: **Enter ye in at the strait gate; for strait is the gate, and narrow is the way** that **leads to life, and few there be that find it**; but **wide is the gate, and broad the way which leads to death, and many there be** that travel therein, until **the night cometh**, wherein **no man can work**.

> **KJV (1NT/1)** <u>Matthew 7:28</u> And it came to pass, **when Jesus had ended these sayings**, the people were astonished at his doctrine:)
>
> **KJV (1NT/1)** <u>Matthew 7:13</u> **Enter ye in at the strait gate**: for **wide is the gate, and broad** is **the way**, that **lead**eth **to** destruction, **and many there be** which go in thereat:)
>
> **KJV (1NT/1)** <u>Matthew 7:14</u> Because **strait is the gate, and narrow is the way, which lead**eth **unto life, and few there be that find it**.)
>
> **KJV (1NT/1)** <u>John 9:4</u> I must work the works of him that sent me, while it is day: **the night cometh**, when **no man can work**.)

BOM <u>3 Nephi 28:35</u> And **it** would be **better for** them **if** they **had not been born**. For do ye suppose that ye can get rid of the justice of an offended God, who hath been trampled under feet of men, that thereby salvation might come?

> **KJV (1NT/1)** <u>Matthew 26:24</u> The Son of man goeth as it is written of him: but woe unto that man by whom the Son of man is betrayed! **it**

had **been** good **for** that man **if** he **had not been born.**)

BOM Mormon 8:30 And there **shall** also be heard **of wars, rumors of wars, and earthquakes in divers places.**

> **KJV (2NT/6)** Matthew 24:6 And ye **shall** hear **of wars and rumours of wars**: see that ye be not troubled: for all these things must come to pass, but the end is not yet.)

> **KJV (2NT/1)** Matthew 24:7 For nation shall rise against nation, and kingdom against kingdom: and there shall be famines, and pestilences, **and earthquakes**, **in divers places.**)

BOM Moroni 7:8 For behold, **if** a man **being evil give**th a **gift**, he doeth it **grudgingly**; wherefore it is counted unto him the same as if he had retained the gift; wherefore he is counted evil before God.

> **KJV (2NT/1)** Matthew 7:11 **If** ye then, **being evil**, know how to **give** good **gift**s unto your children, how much more shall your Father which is in heaven give good things to them that ask him?)

> **KJV (1NT/1)** 2 Corinthians 9:7 Every man according as he purposeth in his heart, so let him **give**; not **grudgingly**, or of necessity: for God loveth a cheerful giver.)

BOM Moroni 7:18 And now, my brethren, seeing that ye know the light by which ye may judge, which light is the light of Christ, see that ye do not judge wrongfully; **for with** that same **judgment** which **ye judge ye shall** also **be judged.**

> **KJV (1NT/1)** Matthew 7:2 **For with** what **judgment ye judge**, **ye shall be judged**: and with what measure ye mete, it shall be measured to you again.)

BOM Moroni 7:25 Wherefore, by the ministering of angels, and by **every word** which **proceeded** forth **out of the mouth of God,** men began to exercise faith in Christ; and thus by faith, they did lay hold upon every good thing; and thus it was until the coming of Christ.

> **KJV (1NT/1)** Matthew 4:4 But he answered and said, It is written, Man shall not live by bread alone, but by **every word** that **proceede**th **out of the mouth of God.**)

And now Mark whom Joseph Smith utilized 90 times where it was only found once in the New Testament.

BOM 1 Nephi 2:18 But, behold, Laman and Lemuel would not hearken unto my words; and **being grieved because of the hardness of their hearts** I cried unto the Lord for them.

> **KJV (1NT/1)** Mark 3:5 And when he had looked round about on them with anger, **being grieved for the hardness of their hearts,** he saith unto the man, Stretch forth thine hand.)

BOM 1 Nephi 11:6 And when I had spoken these words, the Spirit cried with a loud voice, saying: Hosanna to the Lord, the most high God; for he is God over all the earth, yea, even above all. And Blessed art thou, Nephi, because thou believest in the **Son of the most high God**; wherefore, thou shalt behold the things which thou hast desired.

> **KJV (1NT/1)** Mark 5:7 And cried with a loud voice, and said, What have I to do with thee, Jesus, thou **Son of the most high God**? I adjure thee by God, that thou torment me not.)

BOM 2 Nephi 1:1 And now it came to pass that after I, Nephi, had made an end of teaching my brethren, our father, Lehi, also spake many things unto them, and rehearsed unto **them, how great things the Lord** had **done for** them in bringing them out of the land of Jerusalem.

> **KJV (1NT/4)** Mark 5:19 Howbeit Jesus suffered him not, but saith unto him, Go home to thy friends, and tell **them how great things the Lord** hath **done for** thee, and hath had compassion on thee.)

BOM Alma 33:2 And Alma said unto them: Behold, ye have said that ye could not worship your God because ye are cast out of your synagogues. But behold, I say unto you, if ye suppose that ye cannot worship God, **ye do greatly err**, and ye ought to **search the scriptures**; if ye suppose that they have taught you this, ye do not understand them.

> **KJV (1NT/1)** Mark 12:27 He is not the God of the dead, but the God of the living: **ye** therefore **do greatly err**.)
>
> **KJV (1NT/2)** John 5:39 **Search the scriptures**; for in them ye think ye have eternal life: and they are they which testify of me.)

BOM Alma 38:4 For I know that thou wast in bonds; yea, and I also know that thou wast stoned **for the word's sake**; and thou didst bear all these things with patience because the Lord was with thee; and now thou knowest that the Lord did deliver thee.

> **KJV (1NT/1)** Mark 4:17 And have no root in themselves, and so endure but for a time: afterward, when affliction or persecution ariseth **for the word's sake**, immediately they are offended.)

BOM Alma 3:25 And so great was the prosperity of the church, and so many the blessings which were poured out upon the people, that even the high priests and the teachers **were** themselves **astonished beyond measure**.

> **KJV (1NT/1)** Mark 7:37 And **were beyond measure astonished**, saying, He hath done all things well: he maketh both the deaf to hear, and the dumb to speak.).

BOM Alma 8:12 And now behold, if God gave unto this man such power, then why should **ye dispute among yourselves**, and say that he hath given unto me no power whereby I may know concerning the judgments that shall come upon you except ye repent?

> **KJV (1NT/1)** Mark 9:33 And he came to Capernaum: and being in the house he asked them, What was it that **ye disputed among yourselves** by the way?)

BOM Alma 9:30 And he shall stand with fear, and **wist not what to say**. And behold, he shall deny unto you; and he shall make as if he were astonished; nevertheless, he shall declare unto you that he is innocent.

> **KJV (1NT/1)** Mark 9:6 For he **wist not what to say**; for they were sore afraid.)

BOM Helaman 14:20 But behold, as I said unto you concerning another sign, a sign of his death, behold, in that day that he shall suffer death **the sun shall be darkened and** refuse to **give** his **light** unto you; and also **the moon** and the stars; and there shall be no light upon the face of this land, even from the time that he shall suffer death, for the space of three days, to the time that he shall rise again from the dead.

> **KJV (1NT/1)** Mark 13:24 But in those days, after that tribulation, **the sun shall be darkened, and the moon** shall not **give** her **light**,)

BOM 3 Nephi 8:5 And it came to pass in the thirty and fourth year, in the first month, on the fourth day of the month, **there arose a great storm**, such an one as never had been known in all the land.

> **KJV (1NT/2)** Mark 4:37 And **there arose a great storm** of wind, and the waves beat into the ship, so that it was now full.)

BOM 3 Nephi 11:33 And whoso **believeth** in me, **and is baptized**, the same **shall be saved**; and they are they who **shall inherit the kingdom of God**.

> **KJV (1NT/1)** Mark 16:16 He that **believeth and is baptized shall be saved**; but he that believeth not shall be damned.)

> **KJV (1NT/2)** 1 Corinthians 6:10 Nor thieves, nor covetous, nor drunkards, nor revilers, nor extortioners, **shall inherit the kingdom of God**.)

BOM 3 Nephi 11:34 And whoso **believeth not** in me, and is not **baptized, shall be damned**.

> **KJV (1NT/1)** Mark 16:16 He that **believeth** and is **baptized shall** be saved; but he that **believeth not shall be damned**.)

BOM 3 Nephi 18:18 Behold, verily, verily, I say unto you, ye must **watch and pray** always **lest ye enter into temptation**; for **Satan desire**th **to have you, that he may sift you as wheat**.

> **KJV (1NT/1)** Mark 14:38 **Watch** ye **and pray, lest ye enter into temptation**. The spirit truly is ready, but the flesh is weak.)

> **KJV (1NT/1)** Luke 22:31 And the Lord said, Simon, Simon, behold, **Satan** hath **desired to have you, that he may sift you as wheat**:)

BOM Mormon 9:22 For behold, thus said **Jesus Christ, the Son of God**, unto his disciples who should tarry, yea, and also to all his disciples, in the hearing of the multitude: **Go ye into all the world, and preach the gospel to every creature**;

> **KJV (1NT/11)** Mark 1:1 The beginning of the gospel of **Jesus Christ, the Son of God**;)

KJV (1NT/1) Mark 16:15 And he said unto them, **Go ye into all the world, and preach the gospel to every creature.**)

BOM Mormon 9:23 And **he that believeth and is baptized shall be saved, but he that believeth not shall be damned;**

KJV (1NT/1) Mark 16:16 **He that believeth and is baptized shall be saved; but he that believeth not shall be damned.**)

BOM Mormon 9:24 **And these signs shall follow them that believe -- in my name shall they cast out devils; they shall speak with new tongues; they shall take up serpents; and if they drink any deadly thing it shall not hurt them; they shall lay hands on the sick and they shall recover;**

KJV (1NT/1) Mark 16:17 **And these signs shall follow them that believe; In my name shall they cast out devils; they shall speak with new tongues;)** **KJV (1NT/1)** Mark 16:18 **They shall take up serpents; and if they drink any deadly thing, it shall not hurt them; they shall lay hands on the sick, and they shall recover.**)

BOM Ether 5:18 Therefore, repent all ye ends of the earth, and come unto me, and believe in my gospel and be baptized in my name; for **he that believeth and is baptized shall be saved; but he that believeth not shall be damned**; and **signs shall follow them that believe in my name.**

KJV (1NT/1) Mark 16:16 **He that believeth and is baptized shall be saved; but he that believeth not shall be damned.**)

KJV (1NT/1) Mark 16:17 And these **signs shall follow them that believe; In my name** shall they cast out devils; they shall speak with new tongues;)

BOM Moroni 8:8 Listen to the words of Christ, your Redeemer, your Lord and your God. Behold, **I came** into the world **not to call the righteous but sinners to repentance**; the **whole need no physician, but they that are sick**; wherefore, little children are whole, for they are not capable of committing sin; wherefore the curse of Adam is taken from them in me, that it hath no power over them; and the law of circumcision is done away in me.

KJV (1NT/1) Mark 2:17 When Jesus heard it, he saith unto them, They that are **whole** have **no need of** the **physician, but they that are sick**: I **came not to call the righteous, but sinners to repentance.**)

BOM Moroni 9:16 And again, my son, there are many widows and their daughters who remain in Sherrizah; and that part of the provisions which the Lamanites did not carry away, behold, the army of Zenephi has carried away, and left them to wander whithersoever they can for food; and many old women do **faint by the way** and die.

KJV (1NT/1) Mark 8:3 And if I send them away fasting to their own houses, they will **faint by the way**: for divers of them came from far.)

And now Luke which he used 176 times.

BOM 1 Nephi 7:21 And it came to pass that I did **frankly forgive them** all that they had done, and I did exhort them that they would pray unto the Lord their God for forgiveness. And it came to pass that they did so. And after they had done praying unto the Lord we did again travel on our journey towards the tent of our father.

> **KJV (1NT/1)** Luke 7:42 And when they had nothing to pay, he **frankly forgave them** both. Tell me therefore, which of them will love him most?)

BOM 2 Nephi 2:30 I have spoken these few words unto you all, my sons, in the last days of my (9) probation; (15th Century) and I **have chosen the good part**, according to the words of the prophet. And I have none other (6) object (14th Century) save it be the everlasting welfare of your souls. Amen.

> **KJV (1NT/1)** Luke 10:42 But one thing is needful: and Mary **hath chosen that good part**, which shall not be taken away from her.)

BOM 2 Nephi 9:30 But **wo unto** the **rich**, who are rich as to the things of the world. For because they are **rich** they **despise the poor**, and they persecute the meek, and their hearts are upon their treasures; wherefore, their treasure is their God. And behold, their treasure shall perish with them also.

> **KJV (1NT/1)** Luke 6:24 But **woe unto** you that are **rich**! for ye have received your consolation.)
>
> **KJV (1NT/1)** James 2:6 But ye have **despised the poor**. Do not **rich** men oppress you, and draw you before the judgment seats?)

BOM 2 Nephi 9:34 Wo unto the liar, for he **shall be thrust down to hell**.

> **KJV (1NT/3)** Luke 10:15 And thou, Capernaum, which art exalted to heaven, **shalt be thrust down to hell**.)

BOM 2 Nephi 25:13 Behold, they will crucify him; and after he is **laid in a sepulcher** for the space of three days **he** shall **rise from the dead**, **with healing in his wings**; and all those who shall **believe on his name** shall be saved in the kingdom of God. Wherefore, my soul delighteth to prophesy concerning him, for I have seen his day, and **my** heart **doth magnify his holy name**.

> **KJV** (Luke 23:53 And he took it down, and wrapped it in linen, and **laid** it **in a sepulchre** that was hewn in stone, wherein never man before was laid.)
>
> **KJV (1NT/1)** Luke 24:46 And said unto them, Thus it is written, and thus it behooved Christ to suffer, and to **rise from the dead** the third day:)
>
> **KJV** (1/2) Malachi 4:2 But unto you that fear my name shall the Sun of righteousness arise **with healing in his wings**; and ye shall go forth, and grow up as calves of the stall.)
>
> **KJV (1NT/12)** John 1:12 But as many as received him, to them gave he power to become the sons of God, even to them that **believe on his**

name:)

KJV (1NT/1) <u>Luke 1:46</u> And Mary said, **My** soul **doth magnify** the Lord,)

KJV (<u>Luke 1:49</u> For he that is mighty hath done to me great things; and **holy is his name**)

BOM <u>2 Nephi 28:7</u> Yea, and there shall be many which shall say: **Eat, drink, and be merry, for tomorrow we die**; and it shall be well with us.

KJV (<u>Luke 12:19</u> And I will say to my soul, Soul, thou hast much goods laid up for many years; take thine ease, **eat, drink, and be merry.** <u>Isaiah 22:13</u> And behold joy and gladness, slaying oxen, and killing sheep, eating flesh, and drinking wine: **let us eat and drink; for to morrow we** shall **die.**)

Note: This is obviously supposed to be the OT verse of Isaiah 22:13 but Joseph Smith mistakenly utilizes the ending "and be merry" only found in Luke 12:19.

BOM <u>2 Nephi 28:8</u> And there shall also be many which shall say: **Eat, drink, and be merry**; nevertheless, fear God -- he will justify in committing a little sin ; yea, lie a little, take the advantage of one because of his words, **dig a pit for** thy neighbor; there is no harm in this; and do all these things, **for tomorrow we die**; and if it so be that we are guilty, God will **beat** us **with** a **few stripes**, and at last we shall be saved **in the kingdom of God**.

KJV (1NT/1) <u>Luke 12:19</u> And I will say to my soul, Soul, thou hast much goods laid up for many years; take thine ease, **eat, drink, and be merry.**)

KJV (2/2) <u>Isaiah 22:13</u> And behold joy and gladness, slaying oxen, and killing sheep, eating flesh, and drinking wine: let us eat and drink; **for to morrow we** shall **die.**)

KJV (1NT/1) <u>Luke 12:48</u> But he that knew not, and did commit things worthy of **stripes**, shall be **beat**en **with few stripes.** For unto whomsoever much is given, of him shall be much required: and to whom men have committed much, of him they will ask the more.)

KJV (<u>Luke 14:15</u> And when one of them that sat at meat with him heard these things, he said unto him, Blessed is he that shall eat bread **in the kingdom of God.**)

BOM <u>2 Nephi 30:1</u> And now behold, my beloved brethren, I would speak unto you; for I, Nephi, would not suffer that ye should suppose that ye are more righteous than the Gentiles shall be. For behold, **except ye** shall keep the commandments of God **ye shall all likewise perish**; and because of the words which have been spoken ye need not suppose that the Gentiles are utterly destroyed.

KJV (1NT/1) <u>Luke 13:3</u> I tell you, Nay: but, **except ye** repent, **ye shall all likewise perish.**)

BOM 2 Nephi 30:17 **There is nothing** which **is secret** save it **shall be revealed**; there is no work of darkness save it shall **be made manifest** in the light; and there is nothing which is sealed upon the earth save it **shall be loosed**.

> **KJV** (Luke 8:17 For **nothing** is **secret**, that **shall** not **be made manifest**; neither any thing hid, that shall not be known and come abroad.)
>
> **KJV** (Matthew 10:26 Fear them not therefore: for **there is nothing** covered, that **shall** not **be revealed**; and hid, that shall not be known.)
>
> **KJV** (Matthew 18:18 Verily I say unto you, Whatsoever ye shall bind on earth shall be bound in heaven: and whatsoever ye shall loose on earth **shall be loosed** in heaven.)

BOM 2 Nephi 31:8 Wherefore, after he was baptized with water **the Holy Ghost descended upon him** in the form of **a dove**.

> **KJV (1NT/1)** Luke 3:22 And **the Holy Ghost descended** in a bodily shape like **a dove upon him**, and a voice came from heaven, which said, Thou art my beloved Son; in thee I am well pleased.

BOM Enos 1:5 **And there came a voice** unto me, **saying**: Enos, **thy sins are forgiven thee, and thou shalt be blessed**.

> **KJV (2NT/1)** Luke 9:35 **And there came a voice** out of the cloud, **saying**, This is my beloved Son: hear him.)
>
> **KJV (1NT/1)** Luke 5:20 And when he saw their faith, he said unto him, Man, **thy sins are forgiven thee**.)
>
> **KJV (1NT/1)** Luke 14:14 **And thou shalt be blessed**; for they cannot recompense thee: for thou shalt be recompensed at the resurrection of the just.)

BOM Mosiah 3:10 And he shall **rise the third day from the dead**; and behold, he standeth to judge the world; and behold, all these things are done that a righteous judgment might come upon the children of men.

> **KJV (1NT/1)** Luke 24:46 And said unto them, Thus it is written, and thus it behooved Christ to suffer, and to **rise from the dead the third day**:)

BOM Mosiah 9:2 Therefore, I contended with my brethren in the wilderness for I would that our ruler should make a (3) treaty (14th Century) with them; but he being **an austere** and a bloodthirsty **man** commanded that I should be slain; but I was rescued by the shedding of much blood; for father fought against father, and brother against brother, until the greater number of our army was destroyed in the wilderness; and we returned, those of us that were spared, to the land of Zarahemla, to (3) relate (1530) that tale to their wives and their children.

> **KJV (2NT/1)** Only in Luke Luke 19:21 For I feared thee, because thou art **an austere man**: thou takest up that thou layedst not down,

and reapest that thou didst not sow.)

BOM Mosiah 11:14 And it came to pass that he placed his heart upon his riches, and he spent his time in **riotous living** with his wives and his concubines; and so did also his priests spend their time with harlots.

> **KJV (1NT/1)** Luke 15:13 And not many days after the younger son gathered all together, and took his journey into a far country, and there wasted his substance with **riotous living**.)

BOM Mosiah 17:7 And he said unto him: Abinadi, we have found **an accusation against** thee, and thou art worthy of death.

> **KJV (1NT/1)** Luke 6:7 And the scribes and Pharisees watched him, whether he would heal on the sabbath day; that they might find **an accusation against** him.)

BOM Mosiah 20:13 **And** they took **him and bound up his wounds, and brought him** before Limhi, and said: Behold, here is the king of the Lamanites; he having received a wound has fallen among their dead, and they have left him; and behold, we have brought him before you; and now let us slay him

> **KJV (1NT/1)** Luke 10:34 **And** went to **him, and bound up his wounds,** pouring in oil and wine, and set him on his own beast, **and brought him** to an inn, and took care of him.)

BOM Alma 10:17 Now they knew not that Amulek could know of their designs. But it came to pass as they began to question him, he **perceived their thoughts,** and he **said unto them:** O ye wicked and **perverse generation,** ye lawyers and hypocrites, for ye are laying the foundation of the devil; for ye are laying traps and snares to catch the holy ones of God.

> **KJV (1NT/1)** Luke 5:22 But when Jesus **perceived their thoughts,** he answering **said unto them,** What reason ye in your hearts?)

> **KJV (2NT/1)** Matthew 17:17 Then Jesus answered and said, **O** faithless and **perverse generation,** how long shall I be with you? how long shall I suffer you? bring him hither to me.)

BOM Alma 11:44 Now, this (19) restoration (14th Century) shall come to all, both old and young, both bond and free, both male and female, both the wicked and the righteous; and even there shall not so much as a **hair of** their **head**s be lost; but every thing shall be restored to its perfect frame, as it is now, or in the body, and shall be brought and be (1) arraigned (14th Century) before the Son, and God the Father, and the Holy Spirit, which is one Eternal God, to be judged according to their works, whether they be good or whether they be evil.

> **KJV** (Luke 21:18 But there shall not an **hair of** your **head** perish.)

BOM Alma 13:22 Yea, and the voice of the Lord, by the mouth of angels, doth declare it unto all nations; yea, doth declare it, that they may have glad **tidings of great joy**; yea, and he doth sound these glad tidings among all his people, yea, even to them that are **scattered abroad upon the face of the earth**; wherefore they have come unto us.

> **KJV (1NT/1)** <u>Luke 2:10</u> And the angel said unto them, Fear not: for, behold, I bring you good **tidings of great joy**, which shall be to all people.)
>
> **KJV** (1/8) <u>Genesis 11:4</u> And they said, Go to, let us build us a city and a tower, whose top may reach unto heaven; and let us make us a name, lest we be **scattered abroad upon the face of the** whole **earth.**)

BOM <u>Alma 16:17</u> That they might not be hardened against the word, that they might not be unbelieving, and go on to destruction, but that they might **receive the word with joy**, and as a branch be grafted into **the true vine**, that they might enter into the rest of the Lord their God.

> **KJV (1NT/1)** <u>Luke 8:13</u> They on the rock are they, which, when they hear, **receive the word with joy**; and these have no root, which for a while believe, and in time of temptation fall away.)
>
> **KJV (1NT/2)** <u>John 15:1</u> I am **the true vine**, and my Father is the husbandman.)

BOM <u>Alma 16:14</u> And **angel**s did appear unto men, wise men, and did declare **unto them** glad **tidings of great joy**; thus in this year the scriptures began to be fulfilled.

> **KJV (1NT/1)** <u>Luke 2:10</u> And the **angel** said **unto them**, Fear not: for, behold, I bring you good **tidings of great joy**, which shall be to all people.)

BOM <u>3 Nephi 11:37</u> And again I say unto you, ye must repent, and become **as a little child**, and be baptized in my name, or ye can **in nowise** receive these things.

> **KJV (1NT/1)** <u>Luke 18:17</u> Verily I say unto you, Whosoever shall not receive the kingdom of God **as a little child** shall **in no wise** enter therein)

BOM <u>3 Nephi 17:7</u> Have ye any that are sick among you? **Bring them hither.** Have ye any that are lame, or **blind**, or **halt**, or **maimed**, or leprous, or that are withered, or that are deaf, or that are afflicted in any manner? Bring them hither and I will heal them, for I have compassion upon you; my bowels are filled with mercy.

> **KJV (1NT/1)** <u>Luke 14:21</u> So that servant came, and shewed his lord these things. Then the master of the house being angry said to his servant, Go out quickly into the streets and lanes of the city, and bring in hither the poor, and the **maimed**, and **the halt**, and the **blind**.)
>
> **KJV (1NT/3)** <u>Matthew 14:18</u> He said, **Bring them hither** to me.)

BOM <u>3 Nephi 17:10</u> And they did all, both they who had been healed and they who were whole, bow down at his feet, and did worship him; and as many as could come for the multitude did **kiss his feet**, insomuch that they did bathe **his feet with** their **tears**.

> **KJV (1NT/1)** <u>Luke 7:38</u> And stood at **his feet** behind him weeping, and began to wash **his feet with tears**, and did wipe them with the hairs of her head, and **kiss**ed **his feet**, and anointed them with the ointment.)

BOM <u>3 Nephi 18:7</u> And **this** shall ye **do in remembrance of** my body, which I have (*29) shown* (12th Century) unto you. And it shall be a testimony unto the Father that ye do always remember me. And if ye do always remember me ye shall have my Spirit to be with you.

> **KJV (1NT/1)** <u>Luke 22:19</u> And he took bread, and gave thanks, and brake it, and gave unto them, saying, This is my body which is given for you: **this do in remembrance of** me.)

BOM <u>3 Nephi 18:11</u> And this shall ye always do to those who repent and are baptized in my name; and ye shall **do it in remembrance of my blood, which** I have **shed for you**, that ye may witness unto the Father that ye do always remember me. And if ye do always remember me ye shall have my Spirit to be with you.

> **KJV (1NT/1)** <u>Luke 22:19</u> And he took bread, and gave thanks, and brake it, and gave unto them, saying, This is my body which is given for you: this **do in remembrance of** me.)

> **KJV (1NT/1)** <u>Luke 22:20</u> Likewise also the cup after supper, saying, This cup is the new testament in **my blood, which** is **shed for you**.)

BOM <u>3 Nephi 19:38</u> And it came to pass that when Jesus had touched them all, **there came a cloud and overshadowed** the multitude that they could not see Jesus.

> **KJV (1NT/1)** <u>Luke 9:34</u> While he thus spake, **there came a cloud, and overshadowed** them: and they feared as they entered into the **cloud**.)

BOM <u>3 Nephi 23:6</u> And now it came to pass (452/1353) that when Jesus had said these words he said unto them again, after he had **expounded all the scriptures unto them** which they had received, he said unto them: Behold, other scriptures I would that ye should write, that ye have not.

> **KJV (1NT/2)** <u>Luke 24:27</u> And beginning at Moses and all the prophets, he **expounded unto them** in **all the scriptures** the things concerning himself.)

BOM <u>3 Nephi 27:2</u> And Jesus again showed himself unto them, for they were praying unto the Father in his name; **and Jesus came** and **stood in the midst of them, and** said **unto them**: **What will ye that I shall** give **unto you**?

> **KJV (1NT/1)** <u>Luke 24:36</u> And as they thus spake, **Jesus** himself **stood in the midst of them, and** saith **unto them**, Peace be unto you.)

KJV (1NT/1) <u>Matthew 20:32</u> And **Jesus** stood still, and called them, **and said, What will ye that I** shall do **unto you?**)

BOM <u>Mormon 5:8</u> And now behold, I, Mormon, do not desire to harrow up the souls of men in casting before them such an *(47) awful (13th Century)* scene of blood and *(5) carnage (1656)* as **was laid before** mine **eyes**; but I, knowing that these things must surely be made known, and that all things which are hid must be revealed **upon the house-tops –**

> **KJV (1NT/1)** <u>Luke 12:3</u> Therefore whatsoever ye have spoken in darkness shall be heard in the light; and that which ye have spoken in the ear in closets shall be proclaimed upon the **housetops**.)
>
> **KJV** (1/1) <u>Ezra 3:12</u> But many of the priests and Levites and chief of the fathers, who were ancient men, that had seen the first house, when the foundation of this house **was laid before** their **eyes**, wept with a loud voice; and many shouted aloud for joy:)

BOM <u>Ether 4:16</u> And then shall my revelations which I have caused to be written by my servant John be unfolded (4) in the eyes of all the people. Remember, **when ye see these things, ye** shall **know** that **the time is at hand** that they shall be made manifest in very deed.

> **KJV (1NT/1)** <u>Luke 21:31</u> So likewise ye, **when ye see these things** come to pass, **know ye** that **the** kingdom of God is nigh **at hand**.)
>
> **KJV (2NT/7)** <u>Revelation 1:3</u> Blessed is he that readeth, and they that hear the words of this prophecy, and keep those things which are written therein: for **the time is at hand**.)

BOM <u>Moroni 7:10</u> Wherefore, **a man being evil** cannot do **that which is good**; neither will he **give** a **good gift**.

> **KJV (1NT/1)** <u>Luke 6:45</u> **A** good **man** out of the **good** treasure of his heart bringeth forth **that which is good**; and an evil man out of the evil treasure of his heart bringeth forth that which is evil: for of the abundance of the heart his mouth speaketh)
>
> **KJV (2NT/1)** <u>Matthew 7:11</u> If ye then, **being evil**, know how to **give good gift**s unto your children, how much more shall your Father which is in heaven give good things to them that ask him?)

And now The Gospel of John 254 times.

The Intro to the Book of Mormon

An account of Lehi and his wife Sariah and his four sons, being called, **(beginning at the eldest)** Laman, Lemuel, Sam, and Nephi. The Lord warns Lehi to depart out of the land of Jerusalem, because he prophesieth unto the people concerning their iniquity and they seek to destroy his life. He taketh **three days' journey into the wilderness** with his family. Nephi taketh his brethren and returneth to the land of Jerusalem after the record of the Jews. The account of their sufferings. They take the daughters of Ishmael to wife. They take their families and depart into the wilderness. Their sufferings and afflictions in the wilderness. The course of their travels. They come to the large waters. Nephi's brethren rebel against him. He (2) confoundeth them, and buildeth a ship. They **call the name of the place** Bountiful. They cross the large waters into the promised land, and so forth. This is according to the account of Nephi; or in other words, I, Nephi, wrote this record.

> **KJV (1NT/1)** John 8:9 And they which heard it, being convicted by their own conscience, went out one by one, **beginning at the eldest**, even unto the last: and Jesus was left alone, and the woman standing in the midst.)
>
> **KJV (2/1)** Exodus 8:27 We will go **three days' journey into the wilderness**, and sacrifice to the LORD our God, as he shall command us.)
>
> **KJV (8/4)** Genesis 32:30 And Jacob **called the name of the place** Peniel: for I have seen God face to face, and my life is preserved.)

BOM 1 Nephi 1:3 And I know that the **record** which I make **is true**; and I make it **with mine own hand**; and I make it according to my knowledge.

> **KJV (1NT/3)** John 8:14 Jesus answered and said unto them, Though I bear **record** of myself, yet my **record is true**:)
>
> **KJV (5NT/9)** in context 1 Corinthians 16:21 The salutation of me Paul **with mine own hand**.)

BOM 1 Nephi 4:13 Behold the Lord slayeth the wicked to bring forth his righteous purposes. It is better **that one man should perish** than that a **nation** should (26) dwindle (1596 AD) and **perish** in unbelief

> **KJV** (John 11:50 Nor consider that it is expedient for us, **that one man should die** for the people, and that the whole **nation perish** not.")

BOM 1 Nephi 10:8 Yea, even he should go forth and **cry in the wilderness: Prepare ye the way of the Lord, and make his paths straight**; for there **standeth one among you whom ye know not; and he is mightier than I, whose shoe's latchet I am not worthy to unloose**. And much spake my father concerning this thing.

> **KJV (1NT/1)** John 1:25-27 And they asked him, and said unto him, Why baptizest thou then, if thou be not that Christ, nor Elias, neither that prophet? John answered them, saying, I baptize with water: but **there standeth one among you, whom ye know not; He it is, who coming after me is preferred before me, whose shoe's latchet I am not worthy to unloose**.)
>
> **KJV (3NT/2)** John 1:23 He said, I am the voice of one **crying in the wilderness, Make straight** the way of the Lord, as said the prophet Esaias.)
>
> **KJV (1NT/1)** Luke 3:4 As it is written in the book of the words of Esaias the prophet, saying, The voice of one **crying in the**

wilderness, Prepare ye the way of the Lord, make his paths straight.)

BOM 1 Nephi 10:9 And my father said he should **baptize in Bethabara, beyond Jordan**; and he also said he should **baptize with water**; even that he should **baptize** the Messiah with water.

KJV (John 1:28 These things were done in **Bethabara beyond Jordan**, where John was **baptizing**.)

KJV (2NT/1) John 1:26 John answered them, saying, I **baptize with water**: but there standeth one among you, whom ye know not;)

BOM 1 Nephi 10:10 And after he had baptized the Messiah with water, he should behold and **bear record** that he had baptized **the Lamb of God, who should take away the sins of the world**.

KJV (**4NT/30**) John 8:14 Jesus answered and said unto them, Though I **bear record** of myself, yet my record is true: for I know whence I came, and whither I go; but ye cannot tell whence I come, and whither I go.)

KJV (**1NT/3**) John 1:29 The next day John seeth Jesus coming unto him, and saith, Behold the **Lamb of God, which taketh away the sin of the world**.)

BOM 1 Nephi 11:30 And it came to pass that the angel spake unto me again, saying: Look! And I looked, and I beheld the **heavens open** again, **and** I saw **angels descending upon the** children of men; and they did minister unto them.

KJV (**1NT/1**) John 1:51 And he saith unto him, Verily, verily, I say unto you, Hereafter ye shall see **heaven open, and** the **angels** of God ascending and **descending upon the** Son of man.)

BOM 1 Nephi 1:41 And they must come according to the words which shall be established by the mouth of the Lamb; and the words of the Lamb shall be made known in the records of thy seed, as well as in the records of **the twelve apostles of the Lamb**; wherefore they both shall be established in one; for **there** is **one** God **and one Shepherd** over all the earth.

KJV (**1NT/5**) John 10:16 And other sheep I have, which are not of this fold: them also I must bring, and they shall hear my voice; and **there** shall be **one** fold, **and one shepherd**.)

KJV (**1NT/9**) Revelation 21:14 And the wall of the city had twelve foundations, and in them the names of **the twelve apostles of the Lamb**.)

BOM 1 Nephi 17:28 And ye also know that they were fed with **manna in the wilderness**.

KJV (**1NT/1**) John 6:49 Your fathers did eat **manna in the wilderness**, and are dead.)

BOM 1 Nephi 17:48 And now it came to pass that when I had spoken these words, they were angry with me, and were desirous to throw me into the depths of the sea; and as they came forth to lay their hands upon me I spake unto them, saying: In the name of the Almighty God, I command you that ye **touch me not, for I am** filled with the power of God, even unto the consuming of my flesh; and whoso shall lay his hands upon me shall wither even as a dried reed; and he shall be as naught before the power of God, for God shall smite him.

> **KJV (1NT/2)** John 20:17 Jesus saith unto her, **Touch me not; for I am** not yet ascended to my Father: but go to my brethren, and say unto them, I ascend unto my Father, and your Father; and to my God, and your God.)

BOM 1 Nephi 22:25 And he gathereth his children from **the four quarters of the earth**; and he numbereth **his sheep**, and **they know** him; **and there shall be one fold and one shepherd**; and he shall feed his sheep, and in him they **shall find pasture**.

> **KJV (1NT/1)** John 10:4 And when he putteth forth **his** own **sheep**, he goeth before them, and the **sheep** follow him: for **they know** his voice.)

> **KJV (1NT/5)** John 10:16 And other sheep I have, which are not of this fold: them also I must bring, and they shall hear my voice; **and there shall be one fold, and one shepherd**.)

> **KJV (1NT/6)** Revelation 20:8 And shall go out to deceive the nations which are in **the four quarters of the earth**, Gog, and Magog, to gather them together to battle: the number of whom is as the sand of the sea.)

> **KJV (1NT/1)** John 10:9 I am the door: by me if any man enter in, he shall be saved, and **shall** go in and out, and **find pasture**.)

BOM 2 Nephi 2:6 Wherefore, redemption cometh in and through the Holy Messiah; for he is **full of grace and truth**.

> **KJV (1NT/1)** John 1:14 And the Word was made flesh, and dwelt among us, (and we beheld his glory, the glory as of the only begotten of the Father,) **full of grace and truth**.)

BOM 2 Nephi 2:8 Wherefore, how great the (2) importance (1508) to make these things known unto the inhabitants of the earth, that they may know that there is no flesh that can dwell in the presence of God, save it be through the (5) merits, (14th Century) and mercy, and grace of the Holy Messiah, who **lay**eth **down his life** according to the flesh, and **take**th **it again** by the power of the Spirit, that he may bring to pass the resurrection of the dead, being **the first that should rise**.

> **KJV (1NT/1)** John 15:13 Greater love hath no man than this, that a man **lay down his life** for his friends.)

> **KJV (1NT/1)** John 10:17 Therefore doth my Father love me, because

I lay down my life, that I might **take it again**.)

KJV (1NT/1) Acts 26:23 That Christ should suffer, and that he should be **the first that should rise** from the dead, and should shew light unto the people, and to the Gentiles.)

BOM 2 Nephi 2:18 And because he had **fallen from heaven**, and had become miserable forever, he sought also the misery of all mankind. Wherefore, he said unto Eve, yea, even **that old serpent**, who is **the devil**, who is **the father of all lies**, wherefore he said: partake of the forbidden fruit, and **ye shall not die**, but **ye shall be as** God, **knowing good and evil**.

KJV (1NT/2) John 8 44 Ye are of your father the devil, and the lusts of your father ye will do. He was a murderer from the beginning, and abode not in the truth, because there is no truth in him. When he speaketh a lie, he speaketh of his own: **for he is a liar, and the father of it**.)

KJV (1/3) Isaiah 14:12 How art thou **fallen from heaven**, O Lucifer, son of the morning! how art thou cut down to the ground, which didst weaken the nations!)

KJV (2NT/2) Revelation 12:9 And the great dragon was cast out, **that old serpent**, called **the Devil**, and Satan, which deceiveth the whole world: he was cast out into the earth, and his angels were cast out with him.)

KJV (1/1) Genesis 3:3-4 And the **serpent** said unto the woman, **Ye shall not** surely **die**: For God doth know that in the day ye eat thereof, then your eyes shall be opened, and **ye shall be as** gods, **knowing good and evil**.)

BOM 2 Nephi 2:25 Adam fell that men might be; and men are, **that they might have** joy.

KJV (John 10:10 The thief cometh not, but for to steal, and to kill, and to destroy: I am come **that they might have** life, and that they might have it more abundantly.)

BOM 2 Nephi 2:29 And not choose eternal death according to **the will of the flesh** and the evil which is therein, which giveth the spirit of the devil power to (1) captivate, (1555 AD) to bring you down to hell, that he may reign over you in his own kingdom.

KJV (1NT/1) John 1:13 Which were born, not of blood, nor of **the will of the flesh**, nor of the will of man, but of God.)

BOM 2 Nephi 25:2 For I, Nephi, have not taught them many things concerning the manner of the Jews; for their works were works of darkness, and their doings were doings of abominations.

KJV (1NT/5) John 19:40 Then took they the body of Jesus, and wound it in linen clothes with the spices, as **the manner of the Jews** is to bury.)

BOM 2 Nephi 15:12 But, behold, they **shall have wars, and rumors of wars**; and when the day cometh that **the Only Begotten of the Father**, yea, even the **Father of heaven and of earth,** shall manifest himself unto them in the flesh, behold, they will reject him, because of their iniquities, and the hardness of their hearts, and the stiffness of their necks.

> **KJV (1NT/4)** John 1:14 And the Word was made flesh, and dwelt among us, (and we beheld his glory, the glory as of **the only begotten of the Father**,) full of grace and truth.)
>
> **KJV (2NT/6)** Matthew 24:6 And ye **shall** hear of **wars and rumours of wars**: see that ye be not troubled: for all these things must come to pass, but the end is not yet.)
>
> **KJV (2NT/5)** Matthew 11:25 At that time Jesus answered and said, I thank thee, O **Father**, Lord **of heaven and earth**, because thou hast hid these things from the wise and prudent, and hast revealed them unto babes.)

BOM 2 Nephi 25:18 Wherefore, he shall bring forth his **words** unto them, which **words shall judge** them at **the last day**, for they shall be given them for the purpose of (10) convincing (1530 AD) them of the true Messiah who was rejected by them; and unto the *(10) convincing* (1530 AD of them that they need not look forward any more for a Messiah to come, for there should not any come, save it should be a false Messiah which should deceive the people; for there is save one Messiah spoken of by the prophets, and that Messiah is he who should be rejected of the Jews.

> **KJV (1NT/1)** John 12:48 He that rejecteth me, and receiveth not my **words, hath** one that judgeth him: the word that I have spoken, the same **shall judge** him in **the last day**.)

BOM 2 Nephi 26:29 And now behold, I say unto you that the right way is to believe in Christ, and deny him not; and Christ is the Holy One of Israel: wherefore ye must bow down before him, and worship him with all your might, mind, and strength, and your whole soul; and if ye do this ye shall **in nowise** be **cast out**.

> **KJV (1NT/1)** John 6:37 All that the Father giveth me shall come to me; and him that cometh to me I will **in no wise cast out**.)

BOM 2 Nephi 26:10 And when these things have passed away a speedy destruction, cometh unto my people; for, notwithstanding the pains of my soul, I have seen it; wherefore, I know that it shall come to pass; and they sell themselves for naught; for, for the reward of their pride and their foolishness they shall reap destruction; for because they yield unto the devil and choose works of **darkness rather than light**, therefore they must go down to hell.

> **KJV** (John 3:19 And this is the condemnation, that **light** is come into the world, and men loved **darkness rather than light**, because their deeds were evil.)

BOM 2 Nephi 26:24 He doeth not anything save it be for the benefit of the world; **for** he **love**th **the world**, even **that he lay**eth **down his** own **life** that he may **draw all men unto** him. Wherefore, he commandeth none that they shall not partake of his salvation.

> **KJV (1NT/1)** John 3:16 For God so **loved the world, that he** gave his only begotten Son, that whosoever believeth in him should not perish, but have everlasting life.)
>
> **KJV (1NT/1)** John 15:13 Greater love hath no man than this, that a man lay **down his life** for **his** friends.)
>
> **KJV (1NT/3)** John 12:32 And I, if I be lifted up from the earth, will **draw all men unto** me.)

BOM 2 Nephi 26:26 Behold, hath he commanded any that they should depart out of the synagogues, or out of the houses of worship? Behold, I say unto you, Nay.

> **KJV (1NT/1)** John 16:2 **They** shall put you **out of the synagogues**: yea, the time cometh, that whosoever killeth you will think that he doeth God service.)

BOM 2 Nephi 29:8 Wherefore murmur ye, because that ye shall receive more of my word? Know ye not that **the testimony of two** nations **is** a witness unto you that I am God, that I remember one nation like unto another? Wherefore, I speak the same words unto one nation like unto another. And when the two nations shall run together **the testimony of the two** nations shall run together also.

> **KJV (1NT/2) John 8:17** It is also written in your law, that **the testimony of two** men **is** true.)

BOM 2 Nephi 33:2 But behold, there are many that harden their hearts against the Holy Spirit, that it **hath no place in** them; wherefore, they cast many things away which are written and esteem them as things of naught.

> **KJV (1NT/7)** John 8:37 I know that ye are Abraham's seed; but ye seek to kill me, because my word **hath no place in** you.)

BOM 2 Nephi 33:3 But **I**, Nephi, **have written what I have written**, and I esteem it as of great worth and especially unto my people. For I pray continually for them by day, and mine eyes water my pillow by night, because of them; and I cry unto my God in faith, and I know that he will hear my cry.

> **KJV (1NT/1)** John 19:22 Pilate answered, **What I have written I have written**.)

BOM 2 Nephi 33:12 And **I pray the Father** in the name of Christ that many of us, if not all, may be saved in his kingdom at that great and last day.

> **KJV (1NT/1)** John 14:16 And **I** will **pray the Father**, and he shall give you another Comforter, that he may abide with you for ever;)

BOM Jacob 4:12 And now, beloved, **marvel not that I** tell you these things; for why not speak of the atonement of Christ, and attain to a **perfect**

knowledge of him, as to attain to the knowledge of a resurrection and **the world to come**?

> **KJV (1NT/1)** John 3:7 **Marvel not that I** said unto thee, Ye must be born again.)

> **KJV (1NT/14)** Acts 24:22 And when Felix heard these things, having more **perfect knowledge** of that way, he deferred them, and said, When Lysias the chief captain shall come down, I will know the uttermost of your matter.)

> **KJV (5NT/1)** Matthew 12:32 And whosoever speaketh a word against the Son of man, it shall be forgiven him: but whosoever speaketh against the Holy Ghost, it shall not be forgiven him, neither in this world, neither in **the world to come**.)

BOM Enos 1:27 And I soon go to **the place of my rest**, which is with my Redeemer; for I know that in him I shall rest. And I rejoice in the day when my **mortal** shall **put on immortality**, and shall stand before him; then shall I see his face with pleasure, and he will say unto me: Come unto me, ye blessed, there is **a place prepared for you** in the mansions of my Father. Amen.

> **KJV (1NT/1)** John 14:2 In my Father's house are many **mansions**: if it were not so, I would have told you. I go to **prepare a place for you**.)

> **KJV (2/1)** Isaiah 66:1 Thus saith the LORD, The heaven is my throne, and the earth is my footstool: where is the house that ye build unto me? and where is **the place of my rest**?)

> **KJV (2NT/3)** 1 Corinthians 15:53 For this corruptible must put on incorruption, and **this mortal** must **put on immortality**.)

BOM Mosiah 1:8 **And many** more things did king Benjamin teach his sons, **which are not written in this book.**

> **KJV (1NT/2)** John 20:30 **And many** other signs truly did Jesus in the presence of his disciples, **which are not written in this book**:)

BOM Mosiah 9:21 Yea, they are as a wild flock which **fleeth** from **the shepherd, and scattereth**, and are driven, and are devoured by the beasts of the forest.

> **KJV (1NT/1)** John 10:12 But he that is an hireling, and not **the shepherd**, whose own the sheep are not, seeth the wolf coming, and leaveth the sheep, and **fleeth**: and the wolf catcheth them, **and scattereth** the sheep.)

BOM Mosiah 10:8 And it came to pass that they came up upon the north of the land of Shilom, with their numerous hosts, men armed with bows, and with arrows, and with swords, and with(11) cimeters (1548), and with stones, and with slings; and they had their heads shaved that they were naked; and they were girded with **a leathern girdle about** their **loins**.

> **KJV (1NT/1)** Matthew 3:4 And the same John had his raiment of

camel's hair, and **a leathern girdle about** his **loins**; and his meat was locusts and wild honey.)

BOM Mosiah 12:25 And now Abinadi said unto them: Are you priests, and pretend to teach this people, and to understand the spirit of prophesying, and yet desire to know of me what **these things** mean?

> **KJV** (*Note how similar:* (1NT/1) John 3:10 Jesus answered and said unto him, Art thou a master of Israel, and knowest not **these things**?)

BOM Mosiah 13:3 Touch me not, for God shall smite you if ye lay your hands upon me, for I have not delivered the message which the Lord sent me to deliver; neither have I told you that which ye requested that I should tell; therefore, God will not suffer that I shall be destroyed at this time.

> **KJV** (**1NT/2**) John 20:17 Jesus saith unto her, **Touch me not**; **for** I am not yet ascended to my Father: but go to my brethren, and say unto them, I ascend unto my Father, and your Father; and to my God, and your God.)

BOM Mosiah 13:12 And now, ye **remember that I said unto you: Thou shall not make unto thee any graven image, or any likeness** of things which are **in heaven above, or** which are **in the earth beneath, or** which are **in the water under the earth**.

> **KJV** (**1NT/2**) John 15:20 **Remember** the word **that I said unto you**, The servant is not greater than his lord. If they have persecuted me, they will also persecute you; if they have kept my saying, they will keep yours also.)
>
> **KJV** (1/1) Deuteronomy 5:8 **Thou shalt not make thee any graven image, or any likeness of** any **thing** that is **in heaven above, or** that is **in the earth beneath, or** that is **in the water**s beneath **the earth**:) (Exodus 20:4 **Thou shalt not make unto thee any graven image, or any likeness of** any **thing** that is in **heaven above, or** that is **in the earth beneath, or** that is **in the water under the earth**.)
>
> Note: It is interesting that in Mosiah 12:36 where Joseph Smith uses this verse he did not add "or which are in the water under the earth" Also here he uses "shall" instead of "shalt".

BOM Mosiah 12:36 Thou shalt not make unto thee any graven image, or any likeness of any thing in heaven above, or things which are in the earth beneath.)

BOM Mosiah 26:21 And he that will **hear my voice shall** be **my sheep**; and him shall ye receive into the church and him will I also receive.

> **KJV** (**1NT/1**) John 10:16 And other **sheep** I have, which are not of this fold: them also I must bring, and they **shall hear my voice**; and there shall be one fold, and one shepherd.)

BOM Mosiah 27:25 And the Lord said unto me: **Marvel not that** all mankind, yea, men and women, **all nations, kindreds, tongues, and people must be**

born again; yea, born of God, changed from their carnal and fallen state, to a state of righteousness, being redeemed of God, becoming his sons and daughters;

> **KJV (1NT/1)** John 3:7 **Marvel not that** I said unto thee, Ye must be born again.)

> **KJV (1NT/8)** Revelation 7:9 After this I beheld, and, lo, a great multitude, which no man could number, of **all nations, and kindreds, and people, and tongues**, stood before the throne, and before the Lamb, clothed with white robes, and palms in their hands;)

> **KJV (1NT/1)** John 3:7 Marvel not that I said unto thee, Ye **must be born again**.)

> **Note**: It is interesting that Joseph Smith utilizes the only instance of "born of the Spirit" when also in the next verse of John is the phrase "Marvel not that" and below continuing this verse with "must be born again".

BOM Alma 4:27 For every man **receiveth wages** of him whom he **listeth** to obey, and this according to the words of **the spirit of prophecy**; therefore let it be **according to the truth**. And thus endeth the fifth year of the reign of the judges.

> **KJV (1NT/1)** John 4:36 And he that reapeth **receiveth wages**, and gathereth fruit unto life eternal: that both he that soweth and he that reapeth may rejoice together.)

> **KJV (2NT/5)** John 3:8 The wind bloweth where it **listeth**, and thou hearest the sound thereof, but canst not tell whence it cometh, and whither it goeth: so is every one that is born of the Spirit.)

> **KJV (1NT/18)** Revelation 19:10 And I fell at his feet to worship him. And he said unto me, See thou do it not: I am thy fellowservant, and of thy brethren that have the testimony of Jesus: worship God: for the testimony of Jesus is **the spirit of prophecy**.

> **KJV (1NT/7)** Galatians 2:14 But when I saw that they walked not uprightly **according to the truth** of the gospel, I said unto Peter before them all, If thou, being a Jew, livest after the manner of Gentiles, and not as do the Jews, why compellest thou the Gentiles to live as do the Jews?)

BOM Alma 5:48 I say unto you, that I know of myself that whatsoever I shall say unto you, concerning that which is to come, is true; And I say unto you, that I know that Jesus Christ shall come, yea, the Son, **the Only Begotten of the Father, full of grace**, and mercy, **and truth**. And behold, it is he that cometh to **take away the sins of the world**, yea, the sins of every man who steadfastly believeth on his name.

> **KJV (1NT/4)** John 1:14 And the Word was made flesh, and dwelt among us, (and we beheld his glory, the glory as of **the only begotten**

of the Father,) **full of grace and truth**.)

KJV (**1NT/7**) <u>John 1:29</u> The next day John seeth Jesus coming unto him, and saith, Behold the **Lamb of God, which taketh away the sin of the world.**)

BOM <u>Alma 9:26</u> And not many days hence **the Son of God shall come in his glory; and** his glory shall be the glory of **the Only Begotten of the Father, full of grace**, equity, **and truth**, full of patience, mercy, and long-suffering, quick to hear the cries of his people and to answer their prayers.

KJV (**1NT/1**) <u>Matthew 25:31</u> When the **Son of** man **shall come in his glory, and** all the holy angels with him, then shall he sit upon the throne of **his glory**:)

KJV (**1NT/4**) <u>John 1:14</u> And the Word was made flesh, and dwelt among us, (and we beheld his glory, the glory as of **the only begotten of the Father,**) **full of grace and truth**.)

BOM <u>Alma 11:2</u> Now if a man owed another, and he would not pay that which he did owe, he was complained of to the judge; and the judge executed authority, and sent forth officers that the man should be brought before him; and he judged the man according to the law and the evidences which were brought against him, and thus the man was compelled to pay that which he owed, or be stripped, or be cast out from among the people as **a thief and a robber**.

KJV (**1NT/1**) <u>John 10:1</u> Verily, verily, I say unto you, He that entereth not by the door into the sheepfold, but climbeth up some other way, the same is **a thief and a robber**.)

BOM <u>Alma 13:31</u> And Alma spake many more words unto the people, **which are not written in this book.**

KJV (**1NT/3**) <u>John 20:30</u> And many other signs truly did Jesus in the presence of his disciples, **which are not written in this book**:)

BOM <u>Alma 19:5</u> Therefore, if this is the case, I would that ye should go in and see my husband, for he has been laid upon his bed for the space of two days and two nights; and some say that he is not dead, but others say that he is dead and that **he stinketh**, and that he ought to be placed in the sepulchre; but as for myself, to me he doth not stink.

KJV (**1NT/1**) <u>John 11:39</u> Jesus said, Take ye away the stone. Martha, the sister of him that was dead, saith unto him, Lord, by this time **he stinketh**: for he hath been dead four days.)

BOM <u>Alma 20:23</u> Now the king, fearing he should lose his life, said: If thou wilt spare me I will grant unto thee **whatsoever thou wilt ask, even to half of the kingdom.**

KJV (**1NT/1**) <u>John 11:22</u> But I know, that even now, **whatsoever thou wilt ask** of God, God will give it thee.)

KJV (**3/1**) <u>Esther 5:3</u> Then said the king unto her, What wilt thou, queen Esther? and what is thy request? it shall be **even** given thee **to the half of the kingdom**.)

BOM Alma 43:10 For they knew that if they should fall into the hands of the Lamanites, that whosoever should **worship God in spirit and in truth**, the true and the living God, the Lamanites would destroy.

> **KJV (2NT/2)** John 4:24 **God** is a Spirit: and they that **worship** him must **worship** him **in spirit and in truth**.)

BOM Alma 6:34 And thus we see that the Nephites did begin to (26) dwindle (1596 AD) in unbelief, and grow in wickedness and abominations, while the Lamanites began to grow exceedingly in the knowledge of their God; yea, they did begin to keep his statutes and commandments, and to **walk in truth** and uprightness before him.

> **KJV (1NT/1)** 3 John 1:4 I have no greater joy than to hear that my children **walk in truth**.)

BOM Alma 8:17 Yea, and behold, **Abraham saw** of his coming, **and was** filled with **glad**ness and did rejoice.

> **KJV (1NT/1)** John 8:56 Your father **Abraham** rejoiced to see my day: and he **saw** it, **and was glad**.)

BOM Alma 10:1 And it came to pass that there arose **a division among the people**, insomuch that they divided hither and thither and went their ways, leaving Nephi alone, as he was standing in the midst of them.

> **KJV (1NT/3)** John 7:43 So there was **a division among the people** because of him.)
>
> **KJV (2/5)** 2 Kings 2:8 And Elijah took his mantle, and wrapped it together, and smote the waters, and **they** were **divided hither and thither**, so that they two went over on dry ground.)

BOM Alma 11:16 But behold, the power of God was with him, and they could not take him to **cast him into prison**, for he was taken by the Spirit and **conveyed away** out of the midst of them.

> **KJV (1NT/1)** John 5:13 And he that was healed wist not who it was: for Jesus had **conveyed** himself **away**, a multitude being in that place)
>
> **KJV (1NT/3)** Matthew 18:30 And he would not: but went **and cast him into prison**, till he should pay the debt.)

BOM Alma 12:26 Yea, who shall be (9) consigned (1528*) to a state of endless misery,* fulfilling the words which say: **They that have done good** shall have everlasting **life; and they that have done evil** shall have everlasting **damnation**. And thus it is. Amen.

> **KJV (1NT/1)** John 5:29 And shall come forth; **they that have done good**, unto the resurrection of **life**; and **they that have done evil**, unto the resurrection of **damnation**.)

BOM Alma 13:29 **O ye** wicked and **perverse generation**; ye hardened and ye stiffnecked people, **how long** will ye suppose that the Lord will **suffer you**? Yea, **how long** will ye **suffer** yourselves to be led by foolish and **blind guides**? Yea, **how long** will ye choose **darkness rather than light**?

> **KJV (1NT/1)** John 3:19 And this is the condemnation, that light is come into the world, and men loved **darkness rather than light**, because their deeds were evil.)

> **KJV (2NT/1)** Matthew 23:16 Woe unto you, ye **blind guides**, which say, Whosoever shall swear by the temple, it is nothing; but whosoever shall swear by the gold of the temple, he is a debtor!)

> **KJV (2NT/1)** Matthew 17:17 Then Jesus answered and said, **O faithless and perverse generation, how long** shall I be with you? **how long** shall I **suffer you**? bring him hither to me.)

BOM Alma 14:8 And it shall come to pass **that whosoever** shall **believe** on **the Son of God**, the same shall **have everlasting life**.

> **KJV (2NT/3)** John 3:16 For God so loved the world, that he gave his only begotten Son, **that whosoever believe**th in him should not perish, but **have everlasting life**.)

BOM Helaman 14:28 And the angel said unto me that many **shall see greater things than these, to the intent that** they **might** believe that these signs and these wonders should come to pass upon all the face of this land, **to the intent that** there should be no cause for unbelief among the children of men --

> **KJV (1NT/1)** John 1:50 Jesus answered and said unto him, Because I said unto thee, I saw thee under the fig tree, believest thou? thou **shalt see greater things than these**.)

> **KJV (6/7)** 2 Samuel 17:14 And Absalom and all the men of Israel said, The counsel of Hushai the Archite is better than the counsel of Ahithophel. For the LORD had appointed to defeat the good counsel of Ahithophel, **to the intent that** the LORD **might** bring evil upon Absalom.)

BOM Helaman 16:1 And now, it came to pass that there were many who heard the words of Samuel, the Lamanite, which he spake upon the walls of the city. And as many as believed on his word went forth and **sought for** Nephi; and when they had come forth **and found him** they **confessed** unto him their sins **and denied not**, desiring that they might be baptized unto the Lord.

> **KJV (1NT/1)** John 1:20 And he **confessed, and denied not**; but confessed, I am not the Christ.)

> **KJV (1NT/1)** Acts 12:19 And when Herod had **sought for** him, **and found him** not, he examined the keepers, and commanded that they should be put to death. And he went down from Judaea to Caesarea, and there abode.)

BOM 3 Nephi 9:15 Behold, I am **Jesus Christ the Son of God**. I **created the**

heavens **and the earth,** and all things that in them are. I was with the Father from the beginning. **I am in the Father, and the Father in me**; and in me hath the Father glorified his name.

> **KJV (1NT/1)** John 14:10 Believest thou not that **I am in the Father, and the Father in me**? the words that I speak unto you I speak not of myself: but the Father that dwelleth in me, he doeth the works.)

> **KJV (1NT/11)** Mark 1:1 The beginning of the gospel of **Jesus Christ, the Son of God**;)

> **KJV (1/2)** Genesis 1:1 In the beginning God created the heaven and the earth.)

BOM 3 Nephi 9:17 And **as many as** have **received** me, **to them** have I given **to become the sons of God**; and **even** so will I to as many as shall **believe on** my **name**, for behold, by me redemption cometh, and in me is the law of Moses fulfilled.

> **KJV (1NT/1)** John 1:12 But **as many as received** him, to them gave he power **to become the sons of God**, **even** to them that **believe on** his **name**:)

BOM 3 Nephi 9:18 **I am the light** and **the life of the world. I am Alpha and Omega, the beginning and the end**.

> **KJV (1NT/1)** John 8:12 Then spake Jesus again unto them, saying, **I am the light of the world**: he that followeth me shall not walk in darkness, but shall have **the light of life**)

> **KJV (1NT/1)** Revelation 22:13 **I am Alpha and Omega, the beginning and the end**, he first and the last.)

BOM 3 Nephi 9:22 Therefore, **whoso** repenteth and cometh unto me **as a little child**, him will I receive, for **of such is the kingdom of God**. Behold, for such I have laid **down my life**, and have **take**n **it** up **again**; therefore repent, and come unto me ye ends of the earth, and be saved.

> **KJV (1NT/1)** John 10:17 Therefore doth my Father love me, because **I lay down my life**, that I might **take it again**)

> **KJV (2NT/1)** Mark 10:15 Verily I say unto you, **Whoso**ever shall not receive the kingdom of God **as a little child**, he shall not enter therein.)

> **KJV (2NT/1)** Mark 10:14 But when Jesus saw it, he was much displeased, and said unto them, Suffer the little children to come unto me, and forbid them not: **for of such is the kingdom of God**.)

BOM 3 Nephi 10:10 And the earth did cleave together again, that it stood; and the mourning, and the **weep**ing, and the wailing of the people who were *spared alive* did cease; and their mourning was **turned into joy**, and their **lament**ations into the praise and thanksgiving unto the Lord Jesus Christ, their Redeemer.

> **KJV (1NT/1)** John 16:20 Verily, verily, I say unto you, That ye shall

weep and **lament**, but the world shall rejoice: and ye shall be sorrowful, but your sorrow shall be **turned into joy**.)

BOM 3 Nephi 11:11 And behold, **I am the light and the life of the world**; and I have drunk out of that bitter cup which the Father hath given me, and have glorified the Father in taking upon me the sins of the world, in the which I have suffered **the will of the Father** in all things from the beginning.

> **KJV (1NT/2)** John 8:12 Then spake Jesus again unto them, saying, **I am the light of the world**: he that followeth me shall not walk in darkness, but shall have the **light of life**.)

> **KJV (1NT/5)** John 5:30 I can of mine own self do nothing: as I hear, I judge: and my judgment is just; because I seek not mine own will, but **the will of the Father** which hath sent me.)

BOM 3 Nephi 11:12 And it came to pass that **when Jesus had spoken these words** the whole multitude fell to the earth; for they remembered that it had been prophesied among them that Christ should show himself unto them after his (4) ascension (14th Century) into heaven.

> **KJV (1NT/10)** John 18:1 **When Jesus had spoken these words**, he went forth with his disciples over the brook Cedron, where was a garden, into the which he entered, and his disciples.)

BOM 3 Nephi 11:14 Arise and come forth unto me, that ye may **thrust** your **hand**s **into my side**, and also that ye may feel the **prints of the nails** in my hands and in my feet, that ye may know that I am the God of Israel, and the God of the whole earth, and have been slain for the sins of the world.

> **KJV (1NT/1)** John 20:27 Then saith he to Thomas, Reach hither thy finger, and behold my **hand**s; and reach hither thy **hand**, and **thrust** it **into my side**: and be not faithless, but believing.)

> **KJV (1NT/1)** John 20:25 The other disciples therefore said unto him, We have seen the LORD. But he said unto them, Except I shall see in his **hands** the **print of the nails**, and put my finger into the **print of the nails**, and **thrust** my **hand into his side**, I will not believe.)

BOM 3 Nephi 11:27 And after this manner did shall ye baptize in my name; for behold, verily I say unto you, that the Father, and the Son, and the **Holy Ghost** are one; and **I am in the Father, and the Father in me**, and the **Father and I are one**.

> **KJV (2NT/1)** John 14:10 Believest thou not that **I am in the Father, and the Father in me**? the words that I speak unto you I speak not of myself: but the Father that dwelleth in me, he doeth the works.)

> **KJV (1NT/1)** John 10:30 **I and my Father are one**)

BOM 3 Nephi 15:1 **And now it came to pass** that **when Jesus had ended these sayings** he cast my eyes round about on the multitude, and said unto them: Behold, ye have heard the things which I taught before **I ascended to my Father**; therefore, **whoso** remembereth **these sayings of mine and doeth**

them, him will I raise up at the last day.

> KJV (1NT/1) John 20:17 Jesus saith unto her, Touch me not; for **I am not yet ascended to my Father**: but go to my brethren, and say unto them, I ascend unto my Father, and your Father; and to my God, and your God.)

> KJV (1NT/1) Matthew 7:28 **And it came to pass, when Jesus had ended these sayings**, the people were astonished at his doctrine:)

> KJV (1NT/1) Matthew 7:24 Therefore **whoso**ever heareth **these sayings of mine, and doeth them**, I will liken him unto a wise man, which built his house upon a rock:)

> KJV (1NT/1) John 6:44 No man can come to me, except the Father which hath sent me draw him: and **I will raise him up at the last day**.)

BOM 3 Nephi 15:3 And he said unto them: **Marvel not that I said unto** you that **old things** had **passed away**, and that **all things** had **become new**.

> KJV (1NT/1) John 3:7 **Marvel not that I said unto** thee, Ye must be born again.)

> KJV (1NT/1) 2 Corinthians 5:17 Therefore if any man be in Christ, he is a **new** creature: **old things** are **passed away**; behold, **all things** are **become new**.)

BOM 3 Nephi 15:12 **Ye are my disciples**; and **ye are** a **light unto this people**, who are a remnant of the house of Joseph.

> KJV (1NT/1) John 13:35 By this shall all men know that **ye are my disciples**, if ye have love one to another.)

> KJV (1NT/1) Matthew 5:14 **Ye are** the **light** of the world. A city that is set on an hill cannot be hid.)

BOM 3 Nephi 15:17 That **other sheep I have which are not of this fold; them also I must bring, and they shall hear my voice; and there shall be one fold, and one shepherd.**

> KJV (1NT/5) John 10:16 And **other sheep I have, which are not of this fold: them also I must bring, and they shall hear my voice; and there shall be one fold, and one shepherd.**)

BOM 3 Nephi 17:3 Therefore, go ye unto your homes, and ponder upon the things which I have said, and **ask of the Father, in my name**, that ye may understand, and prepare your minds for the morrow, and I come unto you again.

> KJV (1NT/1) John 15:16 Ye have not chosen me, but I have chosen you, and ordained you, that ye should go and bring forth fruit, and that your fruit should remain: that whatsoever ye shall **ask of the Father in my name**, he may give it you.)

BOM 3 Nephi 17:4 But now **I go unto the Father**, and also to show myself unto the lost tribes of Israel, for they are not lost unto the Father, for he knoweth whither he hath taken them.

> **KJV (1NT/3)** <u>John 14:28</u> Ye have heard how I said unto you, I go away, and come again unto you. If ye loved me, ye would rejoice, because I said, **I go unto the Father**: for my Father is greater than I.)

BOM <u>3 Nephi 17:14</u> And it came to pass that when they had knelt upon the ground, **Jesus groaned** within himself, and said: Father, I am **troubled** because of the wickedness of the people of the house of Israel.

> **KJV (1NT/1)** <u>John 11:33</u> When **Jesus** therefore saw her weeping, and the Jews also weeping which came with her, he **groaned** in the spirit, and was **troubled**.)

BOM <u>3 Nephi 17:21</u> And **when he had said these words**, he **wept**, and the multitude bare record of it, and he took their little children, one by one, and blessed them, and prayed unto the Father for them.

> **KJV (1NT/6)** <u>John 7:9</u> **When he had said these words** unto them, he abode still in Galilee.)

> **KJV (1NT/1)** <u>John 11:35</u> **Jesus wept.**)

BOM <u>3 Nephi 18:12</u> And **I give unto you a commandment that ye** shall do these things. And if ye shall always do these things blessed are ye, for ye are built upon my rock.

> **KJV (1NT/1)** <u>John 13:34</u> **A** new **commandment** I **give unto you, That ye** love one another; as I have loved you, that ye also love one another.)

BOM <u>3 Nephi 18:16</u> And as I have prayed among you even so shall ye pray in my church among my people who do repent and are baptized in my name. Behold **I am the light**; I have set an example for you.

> **KJV (2NT/1)** <u>John 8:12</u> Then spake Jesus again unto them, saying, **I am the light** of the world: he that followeth me shall not walk in darkness, but shall have the light of life.)

BOM <u>3 Nephi 18:20</u> And **whatsoever ye shall ask the Father in my name**, which is right, **believing** that **ye shall receive**, behold it shall be given unto you.

> **KJV (1NT/1)** <u>John 16:23</u> And in that day ye shall ask me nothing. Verily, verily, I say unto you, **Whatsoever ye shall ask the Father in my name**, he will give it you.)

> **KJV (1NT/6)** <u>Matthew 21:22</u> And all things, **whatsoever ye shall ask** in prayer, **believing, ye shall receive**.)

BOM <u>3 Nephi 19:4</u> And it came to pass that on the morrow, when the multitude was gathered together, behold, Nephi and his brother **whom he had raised from the dead**, whose name was Timothy, and also his son, whose name was Jonas, and also Mathoni, and Mathonihah, his brother, and Kumen, and Kumenonhi, and Jeremiah, and Shemnon, and Jonas, and Zedekiah, and Isaiah -- now these were the names of the disciples whom Jesus had chosen --

and it came to pass that they went forth and stood in the midst of the multitude.

> **KJV (1NT/1)** John 12:9 Much people of the Jews therefore knew that he was there: and they came not for Jesus' sake only, but that they might see Lazarus also, **whom he had raised from the dead.**)

BOM 3 Nephi 19:20 **Father, I thank thee that thou hast** given the **Holy Ghost (89NT/95)** unto these whom I have chosen; and it is because of their belief in me that I have chosen them **out of the world**.

> **KJV (1NT/2)** John 11:41 Then they took away the stone from the place where the dead was laid. And Jesus lifted up his eyes, and said, Father, **I thank thee that thou hast** heard me.)
>
> **KJV (1NT/1)** John 17:6 I have manifested thy name unto the men which thou gavest me **out of the world**: thine they were, and thou gavest them me; and they have kept thy word.)

BOM 3 Nephi 19:23 And now Father, I pray unto thee for them, and also for all those who shall believe on their words, that they may believe in me, **that I may be in** them **as thou, Father, art in me, that** we **may be one**.

> **KJV (1NT/1)** John 17:21 **That** they all **may be one**; **as thou, Father, art in me,** and I in thee, **that** they also **may be one** in us: that the world may believe that thou hast sent me.)

BOM 3 Nephi 19:29 Father, **I pray not for the world, but for** those whom **thou hast given me** out of the world, because of their faith, that they may be purified in me, that I may be in them **as thou, Father, art in me**, that we **may be one**, that **I** may be **glorified in them**.

> **KJV (1NT/1)** John 17:9 I pray for them: **I pray not for the world, but for** them which **thou hast given me;** for they are thine.)
>
> **KJV (1NT/1)** John 17:21 That they all may be one; **as thou, Father, art in me,** and I in thee, that they also **may be one** in us: that the world may believe that thou hast sent me.)
>
> **KJV (1NT/1)** John 17:10 And all mine are thine, and thine are mine; and **I am glorified in them**.)

BOM 3 Nephi 8:20 And he said unto them: **He that eateth this bread eateth** of my body to his soul; and he that **drinketh** of this wine **drinketh** of **my blood** to his soul; and his soul **shall never hunger** nor **thirst**, but shall be filled.

> **KJV (1NT/1)** John 6:58 This is that bread which came down from heaven: not as your fathers did eat manna, and are dead: **he that eateth of this bread** shall live for ever.)
>
> **KJV (1NT/1)** John 6:56 **He that eateth** my flesh, and **drinketh my blood**, dwelleth in me, and I in him.)
>
> **KJV (1NT/1)** John 6:35 And Jesus said unto them, I am the **bread** of life: he that cometh to me shall **never hunger**; and he that believeth

on me shall never **thirst**.)

BOM 3 Nephi 26:5 If **they** be **good, to the resurrection of** everlasting **life**; and if **they** be **evil, to the resurrection of damnation**; being on a (1) parallel (1549), the one on the one hand and the other on the other hand, according to the mercy, and the justice, and the holiness **which is in Christ**, who was before the world began.

> **KJV** (**1NT/1**) John 5:29 And shall come forth; **they** that have done **good**, un**to the resurrection of life**; and **they** that have done **evil**, un**to the resurrection of damnation**.)
>
> **KJV** (**7NT/8**) Romans 8:39 Nor height, nor depth, nor any other creature, shall be able to separate us from the love of God, **which is in Christ** Jesus our Lord.)

BOM 3 Nephi 27:14 And my Father sent me that I might be **lifted up** upon the cross; and after that I had been **lifted up** upon the cross, that I might **draw all men unto me**, that as I have been lifted up by men even so should men be lifted up by the Father, to stand before me, to be judged of their works, whether they be good or whether they be evil --

> (**1NT/1**) John 12:32 And I, if I **be lifted up** from the earth, will **draw all men unto me**.)

BOM 3 Nephi 27:28 And now **I go unto the Father**. And **verily I say unto you, whatsoever** things ye **shall ask the Father in my name** shall be **given** unto you.

> **KJV** (**1NT/3**) John 14:28 Ye have heard how I said unto you, I go away, and come again unto you. If ye loved me, ye would rejoice, because I said, **I go unto the Father**: for my Father is greater than I.)
>
> **KJV** (**1NT/1**) John 16:23 And in that day ye shall ask me nothing. **Verily, verily, I say unto you, Whatsoever ye shall ask the Father in my name**, he will **give** it you.)

BOM 3 Nephi 27:30 And now, behold, my joy is great, even unto fulness, because of you, and also this generation; yea, and even the Father rejoiceth, and also **all the holy angels**, because of you and this generation; for **none of them** are **lost**.

> **KJV** (**1NT/1**) Matthew 25:31 When the Son of man shall come in his glory, and **all the holy angels** with him, then shall he sit upon the throne of his glory:)
>
> **KJV** (**1NT/2**) John 17:12 While I was with them in the world, I kept them in thy name: those that thou gavest me I have kept, and **none of them** is **lost**, but the son of perdition; that the scripture might be fulfilled.)

BOM 3 Nephi 28:33 And **it came to pass** that when **Jesus had ended these sayings** he said unto his disciples: **Enter ye in at the strait gate; for strait is the gate, and narrow is the way** that **leads to life, and few there be that**

find it; but **wide is the gate, and broad the way** which **leads** to death, **and many there be** that **travel** therein, until **the night cometh**, wherein **no man can work**.

> **KJV (1NT/1)** John 9:4 I must work the works of him that sent me, while it is day: **the night cometh**, when **no man can work**.)

> **KJV (1NT/1)** Matthew 7:28 And it came to pass, **when Jesus had ended these sayings**, the people were astonished at his doctrine:)

> **KJV (1NT/1)** Matthew 7:13 **Enter ye in at the strait gate**: for **wide is the gate, and broad** is **the way**, that **lead**eth to destruction, **and many there be** which go in thereat:)

> **KJV (1NT/1)** Matthew 7:14 Because **strait is the gate, and narrow is the way**, which **lead**eth un**to life, and few there be that find it**.)

BOM 3 Nephi 28:7 Therefore, more blessed are ye, for ye **shall never taste of death**; but ye shall live to behold all the doings of the Father unto the children of men (22/131), even until all things shall be fulfilled according to **the will of the Father**, when I shall come in my glory with **the powers of heaven**.

> **KJV (1NT/1)** John 8:52 Then said the Jews unto him, Now we know that thou hast a devil. Abraham is dead, and the prophets; and thou sayest, If a man keep my saying, he **shall never taste of death**.)

> **KJV (1NT/5)** John 5:30 I can of mine own self do nothing: as I hear, I judge: and my judgment is just; because I seek not mine own will, but **the will of the Father** which hath sent me.)

> **KJV (1NT/1)** Luke 21:26 Men's hearts failing them for fear, and for looking after those things which are coming on the earth: for **the powers of heaven** shall be shaken.)

BOM Ether 8:15 And it came to pass that thus they did agree with Akish. And Akish did administer unto them the oaths which were given by them of old who also sought power, which had been handed down even from Cain, who **was a murderer from the beginning**.

> **KJV (1NT/1)** John 8:44 Ye are of your father the devil, and the lusts of your father ye will do. He **was a murderer from the beginning**, and abode not in the truth, because there is no truth in him. When he speaketh a lie, he speaketh of his own: for he is a liar, and the father of it.)

BOM Ether 8:25 For it cometh to pass that whoso buildeth it up seeketh to overthrow the freedom of all lands, nations, and countries; and it bringeth to pass the destruction of all people, for it is built up by **the devil**, who is the **father of all lies**; even that same **liar** who beguiled our first parents, yea, even that same **liar** who hath caused man to commit **murder from the beginning**; who hath hardened the hearts of men that they have murdered the prophets, and stoned them, and cast them out from the beginning.

> **KJV (1NT/2)** John 8 44 Ye are of your father **the devil**, and the lusts

of your father ye will do. He was a **murderer from the beginning**, and abode not in the truth, because there is no truth in him. When he speaketh a lie, he speaketh of his own: **for he is a liar, and the father of it.**)

BOM Moroni 7:26 And after that he came men also were saved by faith in his name; and by faith, they **become the sons of God**. And as sure as Christ liveth he spake these words unto our fathers, saying: **Whatsoever** thing **ye shall ask the Father in my name**, which is good, in faith **believing** that **ye shall receive**, behold, it shall be done unto you.

> **KJV (1NT/3)** John 1:12 But as many as received him, to them gave he power to **become the sons of God**, even to them that believe on his name:)

> **KJV (1NT/1)** John 16:23 And in that day ye shall ask me nothing. Verily, verily, I say unto you, **Whatsoever ye shall ask the Father in my name**, he will give it you.)

> **KJV (1NT/6)** Matthew 21:22 And all things, whatsoever ye shall ask in prayer, **believing, ye shall receive**.)

BOM Moroni 8:48 Wherefore, **my beloved brethren**, pray unto the Father with all the (4) energy (1655) of heart, that ye may be filled with this **love**, which he **hath bestowed upon** all who are true followers of his Son, Jesus Christ; that ye may become **the sons of God; that when he shall appear we shall be like him, for we shall see him as he is**; that we may have this **hope**; that we may be **purified even as he is pure**. Amen.

> **KJV (1NT/1)** 1 John 3:1 Behold, what manner of **love** the Father **hath bestowed upon** us, that we should be called **the sons of God**: therefore the world knoweth us not, because it knew him not.)

> **KJV (1NT/1)** 1 John 3:2 Beloved, now are we the sons of God, and it doth not yet appear what we shall be: but we know **that, when he shall appear, we shall be like him**; **for we shall see him as he is**.)

> **KJV (1NT/1)** 1 John 3:3 And every man that hath this **hope** in him purifieth himself, **even as he is pure**.)

> **KJV (4NT/60)** James 1:19 Wherefore, **my beloved brethren**, let every man be swift to hear, slow to speak, slow to wrath:)

BOM Moroni 10:26 And may the grace of God the Father, whose throne is high in the heavens, and our Lord Jesus Christ, who **sitteth on the right hand of** his power, until all things shall become subject unto him, be, and **abide with you forever**. Amen.

> **KJV (1NT/1)** John 14:16 And I will pray the Father, and he shall give you another Comforter, that he may **abide with you for ever**;)

> **KJV** (1NT/1) Colossians 3:1 If ye then be risen with Christ, seek those things which are above, where Christ **sitteth on the right hand of** God.)

Now that we have finished with the Gospels let us now look at the other books of the New Testament. Again I will remind you that I will not be giving every use by Joseph Smith of these books but some of the more interesting and noteworthy uses.

Let us begin with The Book of Acts which you will remember was used in the Book of Mormon where it was only found in one place in the New Testament. Used 303 times in the Book of Mormon.

BOM 1 Nephi 5:8 And she spake, saying: **Now I know of a surety that the Lord hath** commanded my husband to flee into the wilderness, yea, and **I** also **know of a surety that the Lord hath** protected my sons, and **delivered them out of the hand**s of Laban, and given them power whereby they could accomplish **the thing which the Lord hath commanded** them. And after this manner of language did she speak.

> **KJV (1NT/2)** Acts 12:11 And when Peter was come to himself, he said, **Now I know of a surety, that the LORD hath** sent his angel, and **hath delivered me out of the hand of** Herod, and from all the expectation of the people of the Jews.

> **KJV** (3/2) Exodus 16:16 This is **the thing which the LORD hath commanded**, Gather of it every man according to his eating, an omer for every man, according to the number of your persons; take ye every man for them which are in his tents.)

BOM 1 Nephi 11:1 For it came to pass after I had desired to know the things that my father had seen, and believing that the Lord was **able to make** them **known unto me**, as I sat (4) pondering (14th Century) in mine heart I was **caught away in the Spirit of the Lord**, yea, into an exceedingly high mountain, which I never had before seen, and upon which I never had before set my foot.

> **KJV (1NT/1)** Acts 8:39 And when they were come up out of the water, **the Spirit of the Lord caught away** Philip, that the eunuch saw him no more: and he went on his way rejoicing.)

> **KJV** (2/1) Daniel 2:26 The king answered and said to Daniel, whose name was Belteshazzar, Art thou **able to make known unto me** the dream which I have seen, and the interpretation thereof?)

BOM 1 Nephi 11:2 And **the Spirit said unto** me: **Behold**, what **desirest thou**?

> **KJV (2NT/5)** Acts 8:29 Then **the Spirit said unto** Philip, Go near, and join thyself to this chariot.)

> **KJV** (2/8) Psalm 51:6 **Behold, thou desirest** truth in the inward parts: and in the hidden part thou shalt make me to know wisdom.)

BOM 1 Nephi 13:27 And all this have they done that they might **pervert the right ways of the Lord**, that they might blind the eyes and harden **the hearts of the children of men.**

KJV (1NT/2) <u>Acts 13:10</u> And said, O full of all subtilty and all mischief, thou child of the devil, thou enemy of all righteousness, wilt thou not cease to **pervert the right ways of the Lord**?)

KJV (2/14) <u>Proverbs 15:11</u> Hell and destruction are before the LORD: how much more then **the hearts of the children of men**?)

BOM <u>1 Nephi 15:18</u> Wherefore, our father hath not spoken of our seed alone, but also of all the house of Israel, (4) pointing (14th Century) to the covenant which should be fulfilled in the latter days; **which covenant the Lord made to our father Abraham, saying: In thy seed shall all the kindreds of the earth be blessed.**

KJV (1NT/1) <u>Acts 3:25</u> Ye are the children of the prophets, and **of the covenant which God made with our fathers, saying unto Abraham**, And **in thy seed shall all the kindreds of the earth be blessed.**)

BOM <u>1 Nephi 22:9</u> And it shall also be of worth unto the Gentiles; and not only unto the Gentiles but unto all the house of Israel, unto the making known **of the covenant**s of the Father of heaven **unto Abraham, saying: In thy seed shall all the kindreds of the earth be blessed.**

KJV (1NT/1) <u>Acts 3:25</u> Ye are the children of the prophets, and **of the covenant** which God made with our fathers, **saying unto Abraham**, And **in thy seed shall all the kindreds of the earth be blessed.**)

Note: Here he quotes the paraphrased version that is found in Acts written hundreds of years later.

BOM <u>1 Nephi 22:18</u> Behold, my brethren, I say unto you, that these **things must shortly come**; yea, even **blood, and fire, and vapor of smoke** must come; and **it must needs be** upon the face of this earth; and it cometh unto men according to the flesh if it so be that they will harden their hearts against the Holy One of Israel.

KJV (1NT/1) <u>Acts 2:19</u> And I will shew wonders in heaven above, and signs in the earth beneath; **blood, and fire, and vapour of smoke**:

Note: Acts 2:19 is a paraphrase of <u>Joel 2:30</u> And I will shew wonders in the heavens and in the earth, **blood, and fire, and pillars of smoke**. You will note that the BOM uses "vapor" like Acts and not "pillars" as Joel.

KJV (<u>Revelation 1:1</u> The Revelation of Jesus Christ, which God gave unto him, to shew unto his servants **things which must shortly come** to pass; and he sent and signified it by his angel unto his servant John:)

BOM <u>1 Nephi 22:20</u> And the Lord will surely prepare a way for his people, unto the fulfilling of the words of **Moses**, which he spake, saying: **A prophet**

shall the Lord your God raise up unto you, like unto me; him shall ye hear
in all things whatsoever he shall say unto you. And it shall come to pass
that all those who will not hear that prophet shall be cut off from among the
people.

> Note: Big problem here as you can see the original found in
> Deuteronomy is paraphrased in Acts but the one in Acts is quoted
> here. –
>
> KJV Acts 3:22 For Moses truly said unto the fathers, A prophet
> shall the Lord your God raise up unto you of your brethren, like
> unto me; him shall ye hear in all things whatsoever he shall say
> unto you. Deuteronomy 18:15 The LORD thy God will raise up unto
> thee a Prophet from the midst of thee, of thy brethren, like unto me;
> unto him ye shall hearken;)
>
> KJV (1NT/1) Acts 3:23 And it shall come to pass, that every soul,
> which will not hear that prophet, shall be destroyed from among
> the people)
>
> KJV Deuteronomy 18:19 And it shall come to pass, that whosoever
> will not hearken unto my words which he shall speak in my name, I
> will require it of him.)

BOM 2 Nephi 9:23 And he commandeth all men that they must repent, and
be baptized in his name, having perfect faith in the Holy One of Israel, or
they cannot be saved in the kingdom of God.

> KJV (1NT/2) Acts 17:30 And the times of this ignorance God
> winked at; but now commandeth all men every where to repent:)
>
> KJV (1NT/1) Acts 19:5 When they heard this, they were baptized in
> the name of the Lord Jesus.)
>
> KJV (2NT/9) Acts 15:1 And certain men which came down from
> Judaea taught the brethren, and said, Except ye be circumcised after
> the manner of Moses, ye cannot be saved.)

BOM 2 Nephi 9:33 Wo unto the uncircumcised of heart, for a knowledge of
their iniquities shall smite them at the last day.

> Note: "uncircumcised heart" is also found in OT, this verse in the NT
> coincides with the flow of these verses in 2 Nephi.
>
> KJV Acts 7:51 Ye stiffnecked and uncircumcised in heart and ears,
> ye do always resist the Holy Ghost: as your fathers did, so do ye.)

BOM 2 Nephi 9:40 O, my beloved brethren, give ear to my words.
Remember the greatness of the Holy One of Israel. Do not say that I have
spoken hard things against you; for if ye do, ye will revile against the truth; for
I have spoken the words of your Maker. I know that the words of truth and
soberness. are hard against all uncleanness; but the righteous fear them not,
for they love the truth and are not shaken.

> KJV (1NT/1) Acts 26:25 But he said, I am not mad, most noble

Festus; but speak forth **the words of truth and soberness**.)

KJV (**4NT/60**) James 1:19 Wherefore, **my beloved brethren**, let every man be swift to hear, slow to speak, slow to wrath:)

KJV (1/3) Psalm 5:1 **Give ear to my words**, O LORD, consider my meditation.)

BOM 2 Nephi 9:44 O, **my beloved brethren**, remember my words. Behold, I take off my garments, and I shake them before you; I pray **the God of my salvation** that he view me with his all-searching eye; wherefore, ye shall know at the last day, when all men shall be judged of their works, that the God of Israel did witness that I **shook** your iniquities from my soul, and that I stand with brightness before him, and am rid of **your blood**.

KJV (*Note: Please note how similar these two acts are.* Acts 18:6 And when they opposed themselves, and blasphemed, he **shook** his raiment, and said unto them, **Your blood** be upon your own heads; I am clean; from henceforth I will go unto the Gentiles.)

KJV (Psalm 18:46 The LORD liveth; and blessed be **my** rock; and let **the God of my salvation** be exalted.)

KJV (**4NT/60**) James 1:19 Wherefore, **my beloved brethren**, let every man be swift to hear, slow to speak, slow to wrath:)

BOM 2 Nephi 25:20 **And now**, my **brethren**, , I have spoken plainly that ye cannot err . And as the Lord God liveth that brought Israel up out of the land of Egypt, and gave unto Moses power that he should heal the nations after they had been bitten by the (6) poisonous (1580) serpents if they would cast their eyes unto the serpent which he did raise up before them, and also gave him power that he should **smite the rock and** the **water** should come forth; yea, behold I say unto you, that as these things are true, and as the Lord God liveth, **there is none other name given under heaven** save it be this Jesus Christ, of which I have spoken, **whereby** man can **be saved**.

KJV (**3NT/19**) Acts 3:17 **And now, brethren**, I wot that through ignorance ye did it, as did also your)

KJV (**1NT/1**) Acts 4:12 Neither is there salvation in any other: for **there is none other name under heaven given** among men, **whereby** we must **be saved**.)

KJV (1/1) Exodus 17:6 Behold, I will stand before thee there upon the rock in Horeb; and thou shalt **smite the rock, and** there shall come **water** out of it, that the people may drink. And Moses did so in the sight of the elders of Israel.)

BOM Jacob 6:5 Wherefore, my beloved brethren, I beseech of you in **words of soberness**; that ye would repent, and come with full purpose of heart, and cleave unto God as he cleaveth unto you. And while his arm of mercy is extended towards you in the light of the day, harden not your hearts.

KJV (**1NT/8**) Acts 26:25 But he said, I am not mad, most noble

Festus; but speak forth the **words of** truth and **soberness**.)

BOM <u>Jarom 1:12</u> And it came to pass that by so doing they kept them from being destroyed upon the face of the land; for they did **prick their heart**s with the word, continually stirring them up unto repentance.

> **KJV (1NT/1)** <u>Acts 2:37</u> Now when they heard this, they were **prick**ed in **their heart**, and said unto Peter and to the rest of the apostles, Men and brethren, what shall we do?)

BOM <u>Mosiah 4:14</u> And ye will not suffer your children that they go hungry, or naked; neither will ye suffer that they transgress the laws of God, and fight and quarrel one with another, and serve the devil, who is the master of sin, or who is the evil spirit which hath been spoken of by our fathers, he being an **enemy** to **all righteousness**.

> **KJV (1NT/1)** <u>Acts 13:10</u> And said, O full of all subtilty and all mischief, thou child of the devil, thou **enemy** of **all righteousness**, wilt thou not cease to pervert the right ways of the Lord?)

BOM <u>Mosiah 13:8</u> Yea, and my words **fill** you **with wonder and amazement**, and with anger.

> **KJV (1NT/2)** <u>Acts 3:10</u> And they knew that it was he which sat for alms at the Beautiful gate of the temple: and they were **fill**ed **with wonder and amazement** at that which had happened unto him.)

BOM <u>Mosiah 11:18</u> And after Alma had said these words, both Alma and Helam were buried in the water; and they arose and came forth **out of the water rejoicing**, being **filled with the Spirit**.

> **KJV (1NT/1)** <u>Acts 8:39</u> And when they were come up **out of the water**, the Spirit of the Lord caught away Philip, that the eunuch saw him no more: and he went on his way **rejoicing**.)

> **KJV (1NT/4)** (<u>Ephesians 5:18</u> And be not drunk with wine, wherein is excess; but be **filled with the Spirit**;)

BOM <u>Mosiah 18:18</u> And it came to pass that Alma, having authority from God, ordained priests; even one priest to every fifty of their number did he ordain to preach unto them, and to teach them concerning **the things pertaining to the kingdom of God**.

> **KJV (1NT/1)** <u>Acts 1:3</u> To whom also he shewed himself alive after his passion by many infallible proofs, being seen of them forty days, and speaking of **the things pertaining to the kingdom of God**)

BOM <u>Mosiah 19:3</u> And the lesser part began to **breathe out threatenings against the** king, and there began to be *a great contention* among them.

> **KJV (1NT/5)** <u>Acts 9:1</u> And Saul, yet **breathing out threatenings** and slaughter **against the** disciples of the Lord, went unto the high priest,)

BOM <u>Mosiah 20:17</u> Now when Gideon had heard these things, he being **the king's captain**, he went forth and said unto the king: I pray thee forbear, and do not search this people, and **lay not this** thing **to their charge**.

> **KJV (1NT/1)** <u>Acts 7:60</u> And he kneeled down, and cried with a loud voice, Lord, **lay not this** sin **to their charge**. And when he had said this, he fell asleep.)
>
> **KJV** (1/1) <u>Daniel 2:15</u> He answered and said to Arioch **the king's captain**, Why is the decree so hasty from the king? Then Arioch made the thing known to Daniel.)

BOM <u>Mosiah 23:13</u> And now as ye have been delivered by the power of God out of these bonds; yea, even out of the hands of king Noah and his people, and also from **the bonds of iniquity**, even so I desire that ye should **stand fast in** this **liberty wherewith** ye have been **made free**, and that ye trust no man to be a king over you.

> **KJV (1NT/4)** <u>Acts 8:23</u> For I perceive that thou art in the gall of bitterness, and in **the bond of iniquity**.)
>
> **KJV (1NT/3)** <u>Galatians 5:1</u> **Stand fast** therefore **in** the **liberty wherewith** Christ hath **made** us **free**, and be not entangled again with the yoke of bondage.)

BOM <u>Mosiah 25:7</u> And now, when Mosiah had **made an end of reading** the records, his people who tarried in the land were struck **with wonder and amazement**.

> **KJV (1NT/2)** <u>Acts 3:10</u> And they knew that it was he which sat for alms at the Beautiful gate of the temple: and they were filled **with wonder and amazement** at that which had happened unto him.)
>
> **KJV** (1/1) <u>Jeremiah 51:63</u> And it shall be, when thou hast **made an end of reading** this book, that thou shalt bind a stone to it, and cast it into the midst of Euphrates:)

BOM <u>Mosiah 27:13</u> Nevertheless he cried again, saying: Alma, a**rise and stand** forth, for **why persecutest thou the church of God**? For the Lord hath said: This is my church, and will establish it; and nothing shall overthrow it, save it is the transgression of my people.

> **KJV (1NT/1)** <u>Acts 26:16</u> But **rise, and stand** upon thy feet: for I have appeared unto thee for this purpose, to make thee a minister and a witness both of these things which thou hast seen, and of those things in the which I will appear unto thee;)
>
> **Note**: Throughout this section is the same idea of that of Paul who persecuted the church, hence Joseph Smith using this verse.
>
> **KJV (3NT/1)** <u>Acts 9:4</u> And he fell to the earth, and heard a voice saying unto him, Saul, Saul, **why persecutest thou** me?)

BOM <u>Mosiah 27:29</u> My soul hath been redeemed from **the gall of bitterness** and **bonds of iniquity**. I was in the darkest abyss; but now I behold the marvelous light of God. My soul was (7) racked (15th Century) with eternal torment; but I am snatched, and my soul is pained no more.

KJV (1NT/5) <u>Acts 8:23</u> For I perceive that thou art in **the gall of bitterness**, and in the **bond of iniquity**.)

BOM <u>Alma 3:4</u> And the Amlicites were (9) distinguished (1561) from the Nephites, for they had marked themselves with red in their foreheads after the manner of the Lamanites; nevertheless they had not **shorn** their **head**s like unto the Lamanites.

KJV (1NT/3) <u>Acts 18:18</u> And Paul after this tarried there yet a good while, and then took his leave of the brethren, and sailed thence into Syria, and with him Priscilla and Aquila; having **shorn** his **head** in Cenchrea: for he had a vow.)

BOM <u>Alma 5:39</u> And now if ye are not the sheep of the good shepherd, of what fold are ye? Behold, I say unto you, that the devil is your shepherd, and ye are of his fold; and now, who can deny this? Behold, I say unto you, whosoever denieth this is a liar and a **child of the devil**.

KJV (1NT/3) <u>Acts 13:10</u> And said, O full of all subtilty and all mischief, thou **child of the devil**, thou enemy of all righteousness, wilt thou not cease to pervert the right ways of the Lord?)

BOM <u>Alma 5:54</u> Yea, will ye (9) persist (1538) in supposing that ye are better one than another; yea, will ye (9) persist (1538) in the persecution of your brethren, who humble themselves and do walk after the holy order of God, wherewith they have been brought into this church having been **sanctified by the Holy** Spirit, and they do bring forth **works** which are **meet for repentance** —

KJV (1NT/2) <u>Acts 26:20</u> But shewed first unto them of Damascus, and at Jerusalem, and throughout all the coasts of Judaea, and then to the Gentiles, that they should repent and turn to God, and do **works meet for repentance**.)

KJV (1NT/3) <u>Romans 15:16</u> That I should be the minister of Jesus Christ to the Gentiles, ministering the gospel of God, that the offering up of the Gentiles might be acceptable, being **sanctified by the Holy** Ghost.)

BOM <u>Alma 7:10</u> And behold, he shall be born of Mary, at Jerusalem which is the land of our forefathers, she being a virgin, a precious and chosen vessel, who shall be overshadowed and conceive by the power of the **Holy Ghost (89NT/95)**, and bring forth a son, yea, even the Son of God.

KJV (1NT/2) <u>Acts 9:15</u> But the Lord said unto him, Go thy way: for he is a **chosen vessel** unto me, to bear my name before the Gentiles, and kings, and the children of Israel:)

BOM <u>Alma 8:27</u> And Alma **tarried many days** with Amulek before he began **to preach unto the people**.

KJV (1NT/1) <u>Acts 9:43</u> And it came to pass, that he **tarried many days** in Joppa with one Simon a tanner.)

KJV (1NT/10) <u>Acts 10:42</u> And he commanded us to **preach unto the people**, and to testify that it is he which was ordained of God to be the Judge of quick and dead.)

BOM <u>Alma 10:12</u> And now, when Amulek had spoken these words the people began to be astonished, seeing there was more than one witness who testified of **the things whereof** they were **accused**, and also of the things which were to come, according to the spirit of prophecy which was in them.

KJV (1NT/1) <u>Acts 26:2</u> I think myself happy, king Agrippa, because I shall answer for myself this day before thee touching all **the things whereof** I am **accused** of the Jews;)

BOM <u>Alma 12:2</u> Now the words that Alma spake unto Zeezrom were heard by the people round about; for the multitude was great, and he **spake on this wise**:

KJV (1NT/1) <u>Acts 7:6</u> And God **spake on this wise**, That his seed should sojourn in a strange land; and that they should bring them into bondage, and entreat them evil four hundred years.)

BOM <u>Alma 12:3</u> Now Zeezrom, seeing that thou hast been taken in thy lying and craftiness, for **thou hast not lied unto men** only **but** thou hast lied **unto God**; for behold, he knows all thy thoughts, and thou seest that thy thoughts are made known unto us by his Spirit;

KJV (1NT/1) <u>Acts 5:4</u> Whiles it remained, was it not thine own? and after it was sold, was it not in thine own power? why hast thou conceived this thing in thine heart? **thou hast not lied unto men, but unto God.**)

BOM <u>Alma 30:57</u> Now the knowledge of what had happened unto Korihor was **immediately published throughout all the** land; yea, the proclamation was sent forth by the chief judge to all the people in the land, declaring unto those who had believed in the words of Korihor that they must speedily repent ,lest the same judgments would come unto them.

KJV (1NT/1) <u>Acts 13:49</u> And the word of the Lord was **published throughout all the** region.)

BOM <u>Alma 34:23</u> Yea, cry unto him against **the devil**, who is an **enemy to all righteousness**.

KJV (1NT/1) <u>Acts 13:10</u> And said, O full of all subtilty and all mischief, thou child of **the devil**, thou **enemy of all righteousness**, wilt thou not cease to pervert the right ways of the Lord?)

BOM <u>Alma 41:11</u> And now, my son, all men that are in a state of nature, or I would say, in a carnal state, are **in the gall of bitterness and in the bonds of iniquity**; they are **without God in the world**, and they have gone contrary to the nature of God; therefore, they are in a state contrary to the nature of (30) happiness (15th Century).

KJV (1NT/3) <u>Acts 8:23</u> For I perceive that thou art **in the gall of**

bitterness, and in the bond of iniquity.)

KJV (1NT/1) Ephesians 2:12 That at that time ye were **without Christ**, being aliens from the commonwealth of Israel, and strangers from the covenants of promise, having no hope, **and without God in the world**:)

BOM Alma 48:13 Yea, and he was a man who was firm in the faith of Christ, and he **had sworn with an oath** to defend his people, his rights, and his country, and his religion, even to the loss of his blood.

KJV (1NT/2) Acts 2:30 Therefore being a prophet, and knowing that God **had sworn with an oath** to him, that of the fruit of his loins, according to the flesh, he would raise up Christ to sit on his throne;)

BOM Alma 54:21 Yea, they were men **of truth and soberness**, for they had been taught to keep the commandments of God and to **walk uprightly** before him.

KJV (1NT/1) Acts 26:25 But he said, I am not mad, most noble Festus; but speak forth the words **of truth and soberness**.)

KJV (2/5) Psalm 84:11 For the LORD God is a sun and shield: the LORD will give grace and glory: no good thing will he withhold from them that **walk uprightly**.)

BOM Alma 56:50 The army of Antipus being weary, because of their long march in so short a space of time, were about to fall into the hands of the Lamanites; and had I not returned with my two thousand they would have **obtained their purpose**.

KJV (1NT/1) Acts 27:13 And when the south wind blew softly, supposing that they had **obtained their purpose**, loosing thence, they sailed close by Crete.)

BOM Helaman 5:45 And behold, the Holy Spirit of God did come down from heaven, and did enter into their hearts, and they were filled as if with fire, and they could **speak forth** marvelous **words**.

KJV (1NT/2) Acts 26:25 But he said, I am not mad, most noble Festus; but **speak forth** the **words** of truth and soberness.)

BOM Alma 9:21 But Nephi said unto them: O ye fools, ye **uncircumcised** of **heart**, ye blind, **and ye stiffnecked** people, do ye know how long the Lord your God will suffer you that ye shall go on in this your way of sin?

KJV (1NT/1) Acts 7:51 **Ye stiffnecked and uncircumcised** in **heart** and ears, ye do always resist the Holy Ghost: as your fathers did, so do ye.)

BOM Helaman 16:23 And notwithstanding the **signs and** the **wonders** which were **wrought among the people** of the Lord, and the many miracles which they did, Satan did get great hold upon the hearts of the people upon all the face of the land.

KJV (1NT/1) Acts 5:12 And by the hands of the apostles were many

signs and wonders wrought among the people; (and they were all with one accord in Solomon's porch.)

BOM 3 Nephi 11:5 And again the third time they did hear the voice, and did open their ears to hear it; and their eyes were towards the sound thereof; and they did **look steadfastly towards heaven**, from whence the sound came

> **KJV (1NT/1)** Acts 1:10 And while they **look**ed **stedfastly toward heaven** as he went up, behold, two men stood by them in white apparel;)

BOM 3 Nephi 11:32 And this is my doctrine, and it is the doctrine which the Father hath given unto me; and I bear record of the Father, and the Father beareth record of me, and the **Holy Ghost** beareth record of the Father and me; and I bear record that the Father **commandeth all men, everywhere, to repent** and believe in me.

> **KJV (1NT/2)** Acts 17:30 And the times of this ignorance God winked at; but now **commandeth all men every where to repent**:)

BOM 3 Nephi 19:21 Father, **I pray thee that thou** wilt give the Holy Ghost unto all them that shall believe in their words.

> **KJV (1NT/1)** Acts 24:4 Notwithstanding, that I be not further tedious unto thee, **I pray thee that thou** wouldest hear us of thy clemency a few words.)

BOM 3 Nephi 20:23 Behold, I am he of whom **Moses** spake, saying: **A prophet shall the Lord your God raise up unto you of your brethren, like unto me; him shall ye hear in all things whatsoever he shall say unto you**. And it shall come to pass that every soul who will not hear that prophet shall be cut off from among the people.

> **KJV (1NT/1)** Acts 3:22 For **Moses** truly said unto the fathers, **A prophet shall the Lord your God raise up unto you of your brethren, like unto me; him shall ye hear in all things whatsoever he shall say unto you.**)

> **Note**: Of course here is the original in Deuteronomy that the writer of Acts just paraphrases Joseph Smith mistakenly uses the verse of Acts. Deuteronomy 18:15The LORD thy God will **raise up unto** thee a **Prophet** from the midst of thee, of thy brethren, **like unto me**; **unto** him ye shall hearken;)

BOM 3 Nephi 20:25 And behold, **ye are the children of the prophets; and** ye are of the house of Israel; **and** ye are **of the covenant which** the Father **made with** your **fathers, saying unto Abraham: And in thy seed shall all the kindreds of the earth be blessed.**

> **KJV (1NT/1)** Acts 3:25 **Ye are the children of the prophets, and of the covenant which** God **made with** our **fathers, saying unto Abraham, And in thy seed shall all the kindreds of the earth be blessed.**)

BOM 3 Nephi 20:27 And after that ye were blessed then (3) fulfilleth the Father the covenant which he made with **Abraham**, saying: **In thy seed shall all the kindreds of the earth be blessed** -- unto the pouring out of the **Holy Ghost** through me upon the Gentiles, which blessing upon the Gentiles shall make them mighty above all, unto the scattering of my people, O house of Israel.

> **KJV** Note: Joseph Smith is using Acts which writer uses his own words to say what is found in Genesis 12:3 And I will bless them that bless thee, and curse him that curseth thee: and in thee shall all families **of the earth be blessed**.)
>
> **KJV (1NT/1)** Acts 3:25 Ye are the children of the prophets, and of the covenant which God made with our fathers, saying unto **Abraham**, And **in thy seed shall all the kindreds of the earth be blessed**.)

BOM 3 Nephi 21:9 For in that day, **for my sake shall** the Father **work a work**, which shall be a great and **a marvelous work among** them; and there shall be among them those who **will not believe** it, **although a man shall declare it unto** them.

> **Note**: Note the similarities between these two verses one in the NT the other in the OT and note that Joseph Smith uses words out of each:
>
> **KJV (1NT/1)** Acts 13:41 Behold, ye despisers, and wonder, and perish: for I **work a work** in your days, a work which ye shall in no wise **believe, though a man declare it unto** you. Habakkuk 1:5 Behold ye among the heathen, and regard, and wonder marvelously: for I will **work a work** in your days which ye **will not believe**, though it be told you.)
>
> **KJV (2NT/1)** Matthew 10:39 He that findeth his life shall lose it: and he that loseth his life **for my sake shall** find it.)
>
> **KJV (1/7)** Isaiah 29:14 Therefore, behold, I will proceed to do **a marvellous work among** this people, even **a marvellous work** and a wonder: for the wisdom of their wise men shall perish, and the understanding of their prudent men shall be hid.)

BOM 3 Nephi 27:19 And they taught, and did minister one to another; and they **had all things common** among them, every man dealing justly, one with another.

> **KJV (2NT/2)** Acts 2:44 And all that believed were together, and **had all things common**;)

BOM Mormon 8:29 Yea, it shall come in a day when there shall be heard of **fires**, and tempests, **and vapors of smoke** in foreign lands;

> **KJV (1NT/1)** Acts 2:19 And I will shew wonders in heaven above, and signs in the earth beneath; blood, and **fire, and vapour of**

smoke:)

BOM Mormon 8:31 Yea, it shall come in a day when there shall be great pollutions upon the face of the earth; there shall be murders, and robbing, and lying, and deceivings, and whoredoms, and all manner of abominations; when there shall be many who will say, Do this, or do that, and it (12) mattereth not, for the Lord will uphold such at the last day But wo unto such for they are **in the gall of bitterness and in the bonds of iniquity**.

> **KJV (1NT/3)** Acts 8:23 For I perceive that thou art **in the gall of bitterness, and in the bond of iniquity**.)

BOM Mormon 9:18 And who shall say that Jesus Christ did not many mighty miracles? And there **were many** mighty miracles **wrought by the hands of the apostles**.

> **KJV (1NT/1)** Acts 5:12 And **by the hands of the apostles were many** signs and wonders **wrought** among the people; (and they were all with one accord in Solomon's porch.)

BOM Mormon 9:21 Behold, I say unto you that whoso believeth in Christ, **doubting nothing**, whatsoever he shall ask the Father in the name of Christ it shall be granted him; and this promise is unto all, even unto the ends of the earth.

> **KJV (1NT/2)** Acts 10:20 Arise therefore, and get thee down, and go with them, **doubting nothing**: for I have sent them.)

BOM Mormon 9:26 And now, behold, who can stand against the works of the Lord? Who can deny his sayings? Who will rise up against the almighty power of the Lord? Who will despise the works of the Lord? Who will despise the children of Christ? Behold, all **ye** who are **despisers** of the works of the Lord, for ye shall **wonder and perish**.

> **KJV (2NT/1)** Acts 13:41 Behold, **ye despisers**, and **wonder, and perish**: for I work a work in your days, a work which ye shall in no wise believe, though a man declare it unto you.)

BOM Ether 9:30 And it came to pass that there began to **be** a **great dearth** upon the land, and the inhabitants began to be destroyed exceedingly fast because of the dearth, for there was no rain upon the face of the earth.

> **KJV (1NT/1)** Acts 11:28 And there stood up one of them named Agabus, and signified by the Spirit that there should **be great dearth** throughout all the world: which came to pass in the days of Claudius Caesar.)

BOM Moroni 3:1 The manner which the disciples, who were **called the elders of the church**, ordained priests and teachers –

> **KJV (1NT/1)** Acts 20:17 And from Miletus he sent to Ephesus, and **called the elders of the church**.)

BOM Moroni 7:32 And by so doing, the Lord God prepareth the way **that the residue of men** may have faith in Christ, that the Holy Ghost may have place in their hearts, according to the power thereof; and after this manner did bringeth to pass the Father, the covenants which he hath made unto the children of men.

> **KJV (1NT/1)** <u>Acts 15:17</u> **That the residue of men** might seek after the Lord, and all the Gentiles, upon whom my name is called, saith the Lord, who doeth all these things.)

BOM <u>Moroni 8:12</u> But little children are alive in Christ, even from the foundation of the world; if not so, God is a partial God, and also a changeable God, and a **respecter to persons**; for how many little children have died without baptism!

> **KJV (1NT/1)** <u>Acts 10:34</u> Then Peter opened his mouth, and said, Of a truth I perceive that God is no **respecter of persons**:)

BOM <u>Moroni 8:14</u> Behold I say unto you, that he that (7) supposeth that little children need baptism is **in the gall of bitterness and in the bonds of iniquity**, for he hath neither **faith, hope,** nor **charity**; wherefore, should he be cut off while in the thought, he must go down to hell.

> **KJV (1NT/3)** <u>Acts 8:23</u> For I perceive that thou art **in the gall of bitterness, and in the bond of iniquity**.)
>
> **KJV (1NT/1)** <u>1 Corinthians 13:13</u> And now abideth **faith**, **hope**, **charity**, these three; but the greatest of these is charity.)

BOM <u>Moroni 9:6</u> And now, my beloved son, notwithstanding their hardness, let us labor diligently; for if we should cease to labor, we should be brought under condemnation; for we have a labor to perform whilst in this tabernacle of clay, that we may conquer the **enemy of all righteousness**, and rest our souls in the kingdom of God.

> **KJV (1NT/1)** <u>Acts 13:10</u> And said, O full of all subtilty and all mischief, thou child of the devil, thou **enemy of all righteousness**, wilt thou not cease to pervert the right ways of the Lord?)

BOM <u>Moroni 10:34</u> And now I bid unto all, farewell. I soon go to rest in the **paradise of God**, until my spirit and body shall again reunite, and I am brought forth (1) triumphant (15th Century) through the air, to meet you before the pleasing bar of the great Jehovah, the Eternal Judge of both **quick and dead**. Amen.

> **KJV (1NT/1)** <u>Acts 10:42</u> And he commanded us to preach unto the people, and to testify that it is he which was ordained of God to be the Judge of **quick and dead**.)
>
> **KJV (1NT/3)** <u>Revelation 2:7</u> He that hath an ear, let him hear what the Spirit saith unto the churches; To him that overcometh will I give to eat of the tree of life, which is in the midst of the **paradise of God**.)

And now Romans 137 times

BOM <u>1 Nephi 2:11</u> Now this he spake because of the stiffneckedness (4) of

Laman and Lemuel; for behold they did murmur in many things against their father, because he was a visionary (1648 AD) man, and had led them out of the land of Jerusalem, to leave the land of their inheritance, and their **gold**, and their **silver**, and their **precious things**, to perish in the wilderness. And this they said he had done because of the **foolish imaginations** of his **heart**.

> **KJV** (Romans 1:21 Because that, when they knew God, they glorified him not as God, neither were thankful; but became vain in their **imaginations**, and their **foolish heart** was darkened.)
>
> **KJV** (8/22) 2 Chronicles 21:3 And their father gave them great gifts of **silver**, and of **gold, and** of **precious things**, with fenced cities in Judah:)

BOM 1 Nephi 10:12 Yea, even my father spake much concerning the Gentiles, and also concerning the house of Israel, that they should be compared like unto an olive-tree, whose **branches** should **be broken off** and should be **scattered upon all the face of the earth**.

> **KJV** Note: See Romans 11:16-20 Romans 11:17 And if some of the **branches be broken off**, and thou, being a wild olive tree, wert grafted in among them, and with them partakest of the root and fatness of the **olive tree**;)
>
> **KJV** (1/6) Genesis 11:8 So the LORD **scattered** them abroad from thence **upon the face of all the earth**: and they left off to build the city.)

BOM 1 Nephi 10:14 And after the house of Israel should be scattered they should be gathered together again; or, in fine, after the Gentiles had received the fulness of the Gospel, **the natural branches of the olive-tree**, or the remnants of the house of Israel, should be **grafted in**, or **come to the knowledge of the** true Messiah, their Lord and their Redeemer.

> **KJV** (1NT/1) Romans 11:24 For if thou wert cut out **of the olive tree** which is wild by nature, and wert grafted contrary to nature into a good **olive tree**: how much more shall these, which be **the natural branches**, be **grafted in**to their own **olive tree**?)
>
> **KJV** (1NT/10) 2 Timothy 3:7 Ever learning, and never able to **come to the knowledge of the** truth.)

BOM 1 Nephi 11:22 And I answered him, saying: Yea, it is the love of God, which **shed**deth itself **abroad in the hearts of the children of men**; wherefore, it is the most desirable above all things.

> **KJV** (*Note: The similar verse here:* (1NT/1) Romans 5:5 And hope maketh not ashamed; because **the love of God** is **shed abroad in** our **hearts** by the Holy Ghost which is given unto us.)
>
> **KJV** (Proverbs 15:11 Hell and destruction are before the LORD: how much more then **the hearts of the children of men**?)

BOM 1 Nephi 15:7 And they said: Behold, we cannot understand the words which our father hath spoken concerning **the natural branches** of the **olive-**

tree, and also concerning the Gentiles.

> **KJV (1NT/1)** <u>Romans 11:24</u> For if thou wert cut out of the olive tree which is wild by nature, and wert grafted contrary to nature into a good olive tree: how much more shall these, which be the **natural branches**, be grafted into their own **olive tree**?)

BOM <u>1 Nephi 15:13</u> And now, the thing which our father meaneth concerning the **grafting** in of **the natural branches** through **the fulness of the Gentiles**, is, that in the latter days, when our seed shall have (26) dwindled (1596 AD) **in unbelief**, yea, for the space of many years, and many generations after the Messiah shall be manifested in body unto the children of men, then shall the fulness of the Gospel, of the Messiah come unto the Gentiles, and from the Gentiles unto the remnant of our seed --

> **KJV (1NT/1)** <u>Romans 11:24</u> For if thou wert cut out of the olive tree which is wild by nature, and wert **grafted** contrary to nature into a good **olive tree**: how much more shall these, which be **the natural branches**, be grafted into their own **olive tree**?)
>
> **KJV (1NT/2)** <u>Romans 11:25</u> For I would not, brethren, that ye should be ignorant of this mystery, lest ye should be wise in your own conceits; that blindness in part is happened to Israel, until **the fulness of the Gentiles** be come in.)
>
> **KJV (3NT/26)** <u>Romans 11:23</u> And they also, if they abide not still **in unbelief**, shall be grafted in: for God is able to graft them in again.)

BOM <u>1 Nephi 15:16</u> Behold, I say unto you, Yea; they shall be remembered again among the house of Israel; they shall **be grafted in**, being a **natural branch** of the **olive-tree**, into the **true olive-tree**.

> **KJV (1NT/1)** <u>Romans 11:24</u> For if thou wert cut out of the olive tree which is wild by nature, and wert grafted contrary to nature into a **good olive tree**: how much more shall these, which be the **natural branches**, be **grafted** into their own **olive tree**?)
>
> **KJV (2NT/3)** <u>Romans 11:19</u> Thou wilt say then, The branches were broken off, that I might **be grafted in**.)

BOM <u>2 Nephi 2:5</u> And men are instructed sufficiently that they know good from evil. And the law is given unto men. And **by the law no flesh is justified**; or, **by the law** men are cut off. Yea, by the temporal law they were cut off; and also, by the spiritual law they perish from that which is good, and become miserable forever.

> **KJV (1NT/1)** <u>Romans 3:20</u> Therefore **by** the deeds of **the law** there shall **no flesh be justified** in his sight: for **by the law** is the knowledge of sin.)

BOM <u>2 Nephi 4:17</u> Nevertheless, notwithstanding the great goodness of the Lord, in showing me his great and marvelous works, my heart exclaimeth: ("exclaim" 1570 AD) **O wretched man that I am!** Yea, my heart sorroweth because of my flesh; my soul grieveth because of mine iniquities.

> **KJV (1NT/1)** Romans 7:24 **O wretched man that I am!** who shall deliver me from the body of this death?)

BOM 2 Nephi 9:6 For as **death** hath **passed upon all men**, to fulfil the merciful plan of the great Creator, there must needs be a power of resurrection, and the resurrection must needs come unto man by reason of the fall; and the fall came **by reason of transgression**; and because man became fallen they were cut off from the presence of the Lord.

> **KJV (1NT/1)** Romans 5:12 Wherefore, as by one man sin entered into the world, and death by sin; and so **death passed upon all men**, for that all have sinned:)
>
> **KJV (1/1)** Daniel 8:12 And an host was given him against the daily sacrifice **by reason of transgression**, and it cast down the truth to the ground; and it practised, and prospered.)

BOM 2 Nephi 9:22 And he suffereth this that the resurrection might pass **upon all men, that all** might stand before him at **the great and judgment day.**

> **KJV (1NT/1)** Romans 5:12 Wherefore, as by one man sin entered into the world, and death by sin; and so death **passed upon all men**, for **that all** have sinned:)
>
> **KJV Note:** This did not make sense at first for example it seemed like a grammatical error until I read the following verse, he there fore is concluding the "great day" and "judgment day" with this sentence.
>
> Jude 1:6 And the angels which kept not their first estate, but left their own habitation, he hath reserved in everlasting chains under darkness unto **the judgment** of the **great day.**)

BOM 2 Nephi 9:25 Wherefore, he has given a law; and where there is no law given there is no punishment; and where there is no punishment **there is no condemnation**; and where there is no condemnation the mercies of the Holy One of Israel have (15) claim (14th Century) upon them, because of the atonement; for they are delivered by the power of him.

> **KJV (1NT/1)** Romans 8:1 **There is** therefore now **no condemnation** to them which are in Christ Jesus, who walk **not** after the flesh, but after the Spirit.)

BOM 2 Nephi 9:39 O, **my beloved brethren**, remember the (2) awfulness (13th Century) in transgressing against that Holy God, and also the (2) awfulness (13th Century) of yielding to the enticings of that cunning one. Remember, **to be carnally-minded is death**, and **to be spiritually-minded is life** eternal.

> **KJV (1NT/1)** Romans 8:6 For **to be carnally minded is death; but to be spiritually minded is life and peace.**)
>
> **KJV (4NT/60)** James 1:19 Wherefore, **my beloved brethren**, let

every man be swift to hear, slow to speak, slow to wrath:)

BOM 2 Nephi 9:47 But behold, my brethren, is it expedient that I should awake you to an (47) awful (13th Century) (1) reality (1550 AD) of these things? Would I harrow (Note: used in this context 14th Century) up your souls if **your minds** were **pure**? Would I be plain unto you according to the plainness of the truth if ye were **freed from sin**?

> **KJV (1NT/1)** Romans 6:7 For he that is dead is **freed from sin**.)
>
> **KJV (1NT/1)** 2 Peter 3:1 This second epistle, beloved, I now write unto you; in both which I stir up **your pure minds** by way of remembrance:)

BOM 2 Nephi 25:25 For, for this end was the law given; **wherefore the law** hath **become dead** unto us, and we are **made alive in Christ** because of our faith; yet we keep the law because of the commandments.

> **KJV (1NT/1)** Romans 7:4 **Wherefore**, my brethren, ye also are **become dead** to **the law** by the body of Christ; that ye should be married to another, even to him who is raised from the dead, that we should bring forth fruit unto God.)
>
> **KJV (1NT/1)** 1 Corinthians 15:22 For as in Adam all die, even so **in Christ** shall all be **made alive**.
>
> **KJV** Romans 6:11 Likewise reckon ye also yourselves to be dead indeed unto sin, but **alive** unto God through Jesus **Christ** our Lord.)

BOM 2 Nephi 28:11 Yea, **they** have **all gone out of the way; they** have **become** corrupted.

> **KJV (1NT/1)** Romans 3:12 **They** are **all gone out of the way, they** are together **become** unprofitable; there is none that doeth good, no, not one.)

BOM Jacob 1:19 And we did **magnify** our **office** unto the Lord, taking upon us the (2) responsibility (1786), answering the sins of the people upon our own heads if we did not teach them the word of God with all diligence; wherefore, by laboring with our might their blood might not come upon our garments; otherwise their blood would come upon our garments, and we would not be found (13) spotless (14th Century) at the last day.

> **KJV (1NT/1)** Romans 11:13 For I speak to you Gentiles, inasmuch as I am the apostle of the Gentiles, I **magnify** mine **office**:)

BOM Jacob 2:2 Now, **my beloved brethren**, I, Jacob, according to the (2) responsibility (1786), which I am under to God, to **magnify mine office** with soberness, and that I might rid my garments of your sins, I come up into the temple this day that I might declare unto you the word of God.

> **KJV (1NT/1)** Romans 11:13 For I speak to you Gentiles, inasmuch as I am the apostle of the Gentiles, I **magnify** mine **office**:)
>
> **KJV (4NT/60)** James 1:19 Wherefore, **my beloved brethren**, let every man be swift to hear, slow to speak, slow to wrath:)

BOM <u>Jacob 4:8</u> Behold, great and marvelous are the works of the Lord. **How unsearchable are the depth**s of the mysteries of him; and it is impossible that man should **find out** all **his ways**. And no man knoweth of his ways save it be revealed unto him; wherefore, brethren, despise not the revelations of God.

> **KJV** (**1NT/1**) <u>Romans 11:33</u> O the **depth** of the riches both of the wisdom and knowledge of God! **how unsearchable are** his judgments, and **his ways** past **finding out**!)

BOM <u>Jacob 6:4</u> And how merciful is our God unto us, for he remembereth the house of Israel, both roots and branches; and he **stretch**es **forth** his **hands** unto them **all the day long**; and they are a stiffnecked and a **gainsaying people**; but as many as will not harden their hearts shall be saved in the kingdom of God.

> **KJV** (**1NT/1**) <u>Romans 10:21</u> But to Israel he saith, **All day long** I have **stretch**ed **forth** my **hands** unto a disobedient and **gainsaying people**.)

BOM <u>Omni 1:22</u> It also spake a few words concerning his fathers. And his first parents came out from the tower, at the time the Lord confounded the language of the people; and the **severity of** the Lord **fell up**on **them** according to his judgments, which are just; and their bones lay scattered in the land northward.

> **KJV** (**1NT/1**) <u>Romans 11:22</u> Behold therefore the goodness and **severity of** God: **on them** which **fell**, **severity**; but toward thee, goodness, if thou continue in his goodness: otherwise thou also shalt be cut off.)

BOM <u>Mosiah 4:13</u> And ye will not have a mind to injure one another, but to **live peaceably**, and to **render to every man according to** that which is **his** due.

> **KJV** (**1NT/1**) <u>Romans 12:18</u> If it be possible, as much as lieth in you, **live peaceably** with all men.)

> **KJV** (**1NT/1**) <u>Romans 2:6</u> Who will **render to every man according to his** deed.)

BOM <u>Mosiah 4:18</u> **But** I say unto you, **O man**, whosoever doeth this the same hath great cause to repent; and except he repenteth of that which he hath done he perisheth forever, and hath no interest in the kingdom of God.

> **KJV** (**1NT/1**) <u>Romans 9:20</u> Nay **but**, **O man**, who art thou that repliest against God? Shall the thing formed say to him that formed it, Why hast thou made me thus?)

BOM <u>Mosiah 4:20</u> And behold, even at this time, ye have been calling on his name, and begging for a remission of your sins. And has he suffered that ye have begged in vain? Nay; he has poured out his Spirit upon you, and has caused that your hearts should **be filled with joy**, and has caused **that** your **mouth**s should **be stopped** that ye could not find utterance, so was exceedingly great was your joy.

> **KJV (1NT/1)** <u>Romans 3:19</u> Now we know that what things soever the law saith, it saith to them who are under the law: **that** every **mouth** may **be stopped**, and all the world may become guilty before God.)

> **KJV (1NT/9)** <u>2 Timothy 1:4</u> Greatly desiring to see thee, being mindful of thy tears, that I may **be filled with joy**;)

BOM <u>Mosiah 18:17</u> And they were called **the church of God**, or **the church of Christ**, from that time forward. And it came to pass that whosoever was baptized by the power and authority of God was added to his church.

> **KJV (1NT/4)** <u>Romans 16:16</u> Salute one another with an holy kiss. **The churches of Christ** salute you.)

> **KJV (8NT/31)** <u>Acts 20:28</u> Take heed therefore unto yourselves, and to all the flock, over the which the Holy Ghost hath made you overseers, to feed **the church of God**, which he hath purchased with his own blood.)

BOM <u>Mosiah 27:31</u> Yea, **every knee shall bow, and every tongue confess** before him. Yea, even at the last day, when all men shall stand to be judged of him, then shall they confess that he is God; then shall they confess, who live **without God in the world,** that the judgment of an **everlasting punishment** is just upon them; and they shall quake, and tremble, and (6) shrink (13th Century) beneath the (3) glance (15th Century) of his all-searching eye.

> **KJV (1NT/1)** <u>Romans 14:11</u> For it is written, As I live, saith the Lord, **every knee shall bow** to me, **and every tongue shall confess** to God.)

> **KJV (1NT/1)** <u>Ephesians 2:12</u> That at that time ye were without Christ, being aliens from the commonwealth of Israel, and strangers from the covenants of promise, having no hope, **and without God in the world**:)

> **KJV (1NT/2)** <u>Matthew 25:46</u> And these shall go away into **everlasting punishment**: but the righteous into life eternal.)

BOM <u>Alma 1:30</u> And thus, in their prosperous circumstances, they did not send away any who were **naked,** or that were **hungry,** or that were **athirst,** or that were **sick,** or that had not been nourished; and they did not *set their hearts upon riches*; therefore they were liberal to all, both old and young, both bond and free, both male and female, whether out of the church or in the church, having **no respect** to **persons** as to those who stood in need.

> **KJV (3NT/1)** <u>Romans 2:11</u> For there is **no respect** of **persons** with God.)

> **KJV (1NT/1)** <u>Matthew 25:44</u> Then shall they also answer him, saying, Lord, when saw we thee an **hungred**, or **athirst**, or a stranger, or **naked**, or **sick**, or in prison, and did not minister unto thee?)

BOM <u>Alma 5:54</u> Yea, will ye (9) persist (1538) in supposing that ye are better one than another; yea, will ye (9) persist (1538) in the persecution of your brethren, who humble themselves and do walk after the holy order of God, wherewith they have been brought into this church (76/259), having been **sanctified by the Holy** Spirit, and they do bring forth **works** which are **meet for repentance** –

> **KJV (1NT/3)** <u>Romans 15:16</u> That I should be the minister of Jesus Christ to the Gentiles, ministering the gospel of God, that the offering up of the Gentiles might be acceptable, being **sanctified by the Holy** Ghost.)

> **KJV (1NT/2)** <u>Acts 26:20</u> But shewed first unto them of Damascus, and at Jerusalem, and throughout all the coasts of Judaea, and then to the Gentiles, that they should repent and turn to God, and do **works meet for repentance.**)

BOM <u>Alma 13:12</u> Now they, after **being sanctified by the Holy Ghost**, having their garments made white, being pure and (13) spotless (14th Century) before God, could not look upon sin save it were with (2) abhorrence (1660); and there were many, exceedingly great many, who were made pure and entered into the rest of the Lord their God.

> **KJV (1NT/1)** <u>Romans 15:16</u> That I should be the minister of Jesus Christ to the Gentiles, ministering the gospel of God, that the offering up of the Gentiles might be acceptable, **being sanctified by the Holy Ghost.**)

BOM <u>Alma 36:4</u> And I would not that ye think that I know of myself -- not of the temporal but of the spiritual, not of the **carnal mind** but of God.

> **KJV (1NT/2)** <u>Romans 8:7</u> Because the **carnal mind** is enmity against God: for it is not subject to the law of God, neither indeed can be.)

BOM <u>Alma 42:26</u> And thus God bringeth about his great and eternal purposes; which were **prepared from the foundation of the world**. And thus cometh about the salvation and the redemption of men, and also their **destruction and misery**.

> **KJV (1NT/1)** <u>Romans 3:16</u> **Destruction and misery** are in their ways:)

> **KJV (1/NT/14)** <u>Matthew 25:34</u> Then shall the King say unto them on his right hand, Come, ye blessed of my Father, inherit the kingdom **prepared** for you **from the foundation of the world.**)

BOM <u>Alma 47:36</u> Now these (20) dissenters (1639), having the same instruction and the same information of the Nephites, yea, having been instructed in the same knowledge of the Lord, nevertheless, it is strange to (3) relate (1530), not long after their dissensions they became more **hardened and impenitent**, and more wild, wicked and (6) ferocious (1646) than the

Lamanites -- drinking in with the traditions of the Lamanites; giving way to (1) indolence (1710),and all manner of lasciviousness; yea, entirely forgetting the Lord their God.

> **KJV (1NT/1)** <u>Romans 2:5</u> But after thy **hard**ness **and impenitent** heart treasurest up unto thyself wrath against the day of wrath and revelation of the righteous judgment of God;)

BOM <u>Helaman 6:2</u> For behold, there were many of the Nephites who had become **hard**ened **and impenitent** and (2) grossly (14th Century) wicked, insomuch (20/181) that they did reject the word of God and all the preaching and prophesying which did come among them.

> **KJV (1NT/1)** <u>Romans 2:5</u> But after thy **hard**ness **and impenitent** heart treasurest up unto thyself wrath against the day of wrath and revelation of the righteous judgment of God;)

BOM <u>Alma 6:17</u> For behold, the Lord had blessed them so long with **the riches of the world** that they had not been stirred up to anger, to wars, nor to bloodshed; therefore they began to set their hearts upon their riches; yea, they began to seek to get gain that they might be lifted up one above another; therefore they began to commit secret murders, and to rob and to (12) plunder (1632), that they might get gain.

> **KJV (1NT/1)** <u>Romans 11:12</u> Now if the fall of them be **the riches of the world**, and the diminishing of them the riches of the Gentiles; how much more their fulness?")

BOM <u>3 Nephi 7:24</u> **Now I would have you** to remember also, that there were none who were brought unto repentance who were not **baptized with water**.

> **KJV (1NT/1)** <u>Romans 1:13</u> **Now I would** not **have you** ignorant, brethren, that oftentimes I purposed to come unto you, (but was let hitherto,) that I might have some fruit among you also, even as among other Gentiles.)
>
> **KJV (2NT/4)** <u>Acts 1:5</u> For John truly **baptized with water**; but ye shall be baptized with the Holy Ghost not many days hence)

BOM <u>3 Nephi 8:4</u> And there began to be great **doubt**ings and **disputations** among the people, notwithstanding so many signs had been given.

> **KJV (1NT/1)** <u>Romans 14:1</u> Him that is weak in the faith receive ye, but not to **doubt**ful **disputations**.)

BOM <u>3 Nephi 16:4</u> And I command you that ye shall write these sayings after I am gone, that if it so be that my people at Jerusalem, they who have seen me and been with me in my ministry, do not **ask the Father in my name**, that they may receive a knowledge of you by the **Holy Ghost**, and also of the other tribes whom they know not of, that these sayings which ye shall write shall be kept and shall be manifested unto the Gentiles, that through **the fulness of the Gentiles**, the remnant of their seed, who shall be scattered forth upon the face of the earth **because of their unbelief**, may be brought in, or may be brought to a knowledge of me, their Redeemer.

> **KJV (1NT/2)** Romans 11:25 For I would not, brethren, that ye should be ignorant of this mystery, lest ye should be wise in your own conceits; that blindness in part is happened to Israel, until **the fulness of the Gentiles** be come in.)

> **KJV (1NT/1)** John 16:23 And in that day ye shall **ask** me nothing. Verily, verily, I say unto you, Whatsoever ye shall **ask the Father in my name**, he will give it you.)

> **KJV (2NT/5)** Matthew 13:58 And he did not many mighty works there **because of their unbelief**.)

BOM 3 Nephi 28:31 Therefore, great and marvelous works shall be wrought by them, before the great and coming day when all people must surely **stand before the judgment-seat of Christ**;

> **KJV (1NT/4)** Romans 14:10 But why dost thou judge thy brother? or why dost thou set at nought thy brother? for we shall all **stand before the judgment seat of Christ**.)

BOM Mormon 3:15 **Vengeance is mine**, and **I will repay**; and because this people repented not after I had delivered them, behold, they shall be cut off from the face of the earth.

> **KJV (1NT/2)** Romans 12:19 Dearly beloved, avenge not yourselves, but rather give place unto wrath: for it is written, **Vengeance is mine; I will repay**, saith the Lord.)

BOM Moroni 7:7 For behold, **it** is not **counted unto him for righteousness**.

> **KJV (1NT/1)** Romans 4:3 For what saith the scripture? Abraham believed God, and **it** was **counted unto him for righteousness**.)

BOM Moroni 10:25 And wo be unto the children of men if this be the case; for there shall be **none that doeth good among you, no not one**. For if there be one among you **that doeth good**, he shall work by the power and gifts of God.

> **KJV (3/1)** Romans 3:12 They are all gone out of the way, they are together become unprofitable; **there** is **none that doeth good**, no, not one.)

BOM Moroni 10:26 And wo unto them who shall do these things away and die, for they die in their sins, and they cannot be saved in the kingdom of God; and I speak it according to the words of **Christ**; and **I lie not**.

> **KJV (1NT/1)** Romans 9:1 I say the truth in **Christ, I lie not**, my conscience also bearing me witness in the Holy Ghost,)

BOM Moroni 10:28 I declare these things unto the fulfilling of the prophecies. And behold, they shall proceed forth out of the mouth **of the everlasting God**; and his word shall hiss forth from generation to generation.

> **KJV (1NT/2)** Romans 16:26 But now is made manifest, and by the scriptures of the prophets, according to the commandment **of the**

everlasting God, made known to all nations for the obedience of faith:)

And now 1 Corinthians 134 times

BOM 1 Nephi 3:7 And it came to pass that I, Nephi, said unto my father: I will go and do the things which the Lord hath commanded, for I know that the Lord giveth no commandments unto the children of men, save he shall prepare a way for them that they may accomplish the thing which he commandeth them.

> **KJV Note:** This verse sounds a lot like the following verse *in* 1 Corinthians 10:13 There hath no temptation taken you but such as is common to man: but God is faithful, who will not suffer you to be tempted above that ye are able; but will with the temptation also make a way to escape, that ye may be able to bear it.)

BOM 1 Nephi 22:17 Wherefore, he will preserve the righteous by his power, even if it so be that the fulness of his wrath must come, and the righteous be preserved, even unto the destruction of their enemies by fire. Wherefore, the righteous need not fear; for thus **saith the prophet**, they **shall be saved**, even if it so be **as by fire.**

> **KJV (1NT/1)** 1 Corinthians 3:15 If any man's work shall be burned, he shall suffer loss: but he himself **shall be saved**; yet so **as by fire.**)
>
> **KJV (1NT/7)** Acts 7:48 Howbeit the most High dwelleth not in temples made with hands; as **saith the prophet,**)

BOM 2 Nephi 2:27 Wherefore, men are free according to the flesh; and **all things are** given them which are **expedient** unto man. And they are free to choose liberty and eternal life, through the great **Mediator** of all **men**, or to choose captivity and death, according to the captivity and power of the devil; for he seeketh that all men might be miserable like unto himself.

> **KJV (1NT/1)** 1 Corinthians 10:23 **All things are** lawful for me, but **all things** are not **expedient**: all things are lawful for me, but all things edify not.)
>
> **KJV** (1 Timothy 2:5 For there is one God, and one **mediator** between God and **men**, the man Christ Jesus;)

BOM 2 Nephi 9:7 Wherefore, it must needs be an infinite atonement -- save it should be an infinite atonement **this corruption** could not **put on incorruption**. Wherefore, the first judgment which came upon man must needs have remained to an endless *(2) duration. (14ᵗʰ Century)* And if so, this flesh must have laid down to rot and to (2) crumble (1570AD) to its mother earth, to rise no more.

> **KJV (1NT/1)** 1 Corinthians 15:53 For this corruptible must **put on incorruption**, and this mortal must put on immortality.)

BOM 2 Nephi 9:28 O that cunning plan of the evil one! O the (1) vainness (14ᵗʰ Century), and the (1) frailties, (14ᵗʰ Century) and the foolishness of men!

When they are learned they think they are **wise**, and they hearken not unto the counsel of God, for they set it aside, supposing they know of themselves, wherefore, their **wisdom is foolishness** and it profiteth them not. And they shall perish.

> **KJV (1NT/1)** 1 Corinthians 3:19 For the **wisdom** of this world **is foolishness** with God. For it is written, He taketh the **wise** in their own craftiness.)

BOM 2 Nephi 9:43 But the things **of the wise** and **the prudent** shall be **hid from** them forever -- yea, that (30) happiness (15th Century) which is prepared for the saints.

> **KJV (Note: Again a mixture of two verses: (1NT/1)** 1 Corinthians 1:19 For it is written, I will destroy the wisdom **of the wise**, and will bring to nothing the understanding of **the prudent**.
>
> **KJV** Matthew 11:25 At that time Jesus answered and said, I thank thee, O Father, Lord of heaven and earth, because thou hast **hid** these **things from the wise** and **prudent**, and hast revealed them unto babes.)

BOM 2 Nephi 6:30 Behold, the Lord hath forbidden this thing; wherefore, the Lord God hath given a commandment that all men should have **charity**, which **charity** is love, and except they should have **charity** they were **nothing**. Wherefore, if they should **have charity** they would not suffer the laborer in Zion to perish.

> **KJV (1NT/1)** 1 Corinthians 13:2 And though I have the gift of prophecy, and understand all mysteries, and all knowledge; and though I have all faith, so that I could remove mountains, and **have** not **charity**, I am **nothing**.)

BOM 2 Nephi 31:13 Wherefore, my beloved brethren, I know that if ye shall follow the Son, **with** full **purpose of heart**, acting no hypocrisy and no (1) deception (15th Century) before God, but with (6) *real (14th Century)* intent, repenting of your sins, witnessing unto the Father that ye are willing to take upon you the name of Christ, by baptism -- yea, by following your Lord and your Savior **down into the water**, according to his word; behold, then shall ye receive the **Holy Ghost** yea, then cometh the baptism of fire and of the **Holy Ghost**; and then can ye **speak with the tongue of angels**, and shout praises unto the Holy One of Israel.

> **KJV (1NT/3)** 1 Corinthians 13:1 Though I **speak with the tongues** of men and **of angels**, and have not charity, I am become as sounding brass, or a tinkling cymbal.
>
> **KJV (1NT/2)** Acts 8:38 And he commanded the chariot to stand still: and they went **down** both **into the water**, both Philip and the eunuch; and he baptized him.)
>
> **KJV** Acts 11:23 Who, when he came, and had seen the grace **of** God,

was glad, and exhorted them all, that **with purpose of heart** they would cleave unto the Lord.)

BOM Jacob 2:19 And after ye have obtained a **hope in Christ** ye shall obtain riches, if ye seek them; and ye will seek them for the intent to do good -- to clothe the naked, and to feed the hungry, and to liberate the captive, and administer relief to the sick and the afflicted.

> **KJV (1NT/1)** 1 Corinthians 15:19 If in this life only we have **hope in Christ**, we are of all men most miserable.)

BOM Jacob 5:32 But behold, this time it hath brought forth much fruit, and there is none of it which is good. And behold, there are all kinds of bad fruit; and **it profiteth me nothing**, notwithstanding all our labor; and now it grieveth me that I should lose this tree.

> **KJV (1NT/2)** 1 Corinthians 13:3 And though I bestow all my goods to feed the poor, and though I give my body to be burned, and have not charity, **it profiteth me nothing**.)

BOM Enos 1:27 And I soon go to the place of my rest, which is with my Redeemer; for I know that in him I shall rest. And I rejoice in the day when my **mortal** shall put **on immortality**, and shall stand before him; then shall I see his face with pleasure, and he will say unto me: Come unto me, ye blessed, there is **a place prepared for you** in the **mansions** of my Father. Amen.

> **KJV (2NT/3)** 1 Corinthians 15:53 For this corruptible must put on incorruption, and **this mortal** must **put on immortality**.)

> **KJV (1NT/1)** John 14:2 In my Father's house are many **mansions**: if it were not so, I would have told you. I go to **prepare a place for you**.)

BOM Omni 1:25 And it came to pass that I began to be old; and, having no seed, and knowing king Benjamin to be a just man before the Lord, wherefore, I shall deliver up these plates unto him, exhorting all men to come unto God, the Holy One of Israel, and believe in prophesying, and in revelations, and in the ministering of angels, and in the gift of **speaking with tongues**, and in the gift of interpreting languages, and in all things which are good; for there is nothing which is good save it comes from the Lord; and that which is evil cometh from the devil.

> **KJV (1NT/3)** 1 Corinthians 14:6 Now, brethren, if I come unto you **speaking with tongues**, what shall I profit you, except I shall speak to you either by revelation, or by knowledge, or by prophesying, or by doctrine?)

BOM Mosiah 2:33 For behold, there is a wo pronounced upon him who listeth to obey that spirit; for if he listeth to obey him, and remaineth and dieth in his sins, the same **drinketh damnation to** his own soul; for he receiveth for his wages an **everlasting punishment**, having transgressed the law of God contrary to his own knowledge.

KJV (1NT/3) 1 Corinthians 11:29 For he that eateth and **drinketh** unworthily, eateth and **drinketh damnation** to himself, not discerning the Lord's body.)

KJV (1NT/2) Matthew 25:46 And these shall go away into **everlasting punishment**: but the righteous into life eternal.)

BOM Mosiah 3:16 And even if it were possible that little children could sin they could not be saved; but I say unto you they are blessed; for behold, **as in Adam**, or by nature, they fall, **even so** the blood of Christ (3) atoneth for their sins.

KJV (1NT/1) 1 Corinthians 15:22 For **as in Adam** all die, **even so** in Christ shall all be made alive.)

BOM Mosiah 4:27 And see that **all** these **things** are **done** in wisdom and order; for it is not requisite that a man should run faster than he has strength. And again, it is expedient that he should be diligent, that thereby he might win the prize; therefore, **all things** must **be done in order**.

KJV (1NT/1) 1 Corinthians 14:40 Let **all things be done** decently and **in order**.)

BOM Mosiah 5:15 Therefore, **I would that ye** should be steadfast, and (5) immovable (14th Century), **always abounding in good works**, that Christ, **the Lord God Omnipotent**, may seal you his, that you may be brought to heaven, that ye may have **everlasting salvation** and eternal life, through the wisdom, and power, and justice, and mercy of him who created all things, in heaven and in earth, who is God above all. Amen.

KJV (1NT) 1 Corinthians 15:58 Therefore, my beloved brethren, **be** ye **stedfast**, unmoveable, **always abounding in** the **work** of the Lord, forasmuch as ye know that your labour is not in vain in the Lord.)

KJV (16NT/11) Matthew 5:16 Let your light so shine before men, that they may see your **good works**, and glorify your Father which is in heaven.)

KJV (1/2) Isaiah 45:17 But Israel shall be saved in the LORD with an **everlasting salvation**: ye shall not be ashamed nor confounded world without end.)

KJV (1NT/2) Revelation 19:6 And I heard as it were the voice of a great multitude, and as the voice of many waters, and as the voice of mighty thunderings, saying, Alleluia: for the Lord God omnipotent reigneth.)

KJV (2NT/56) 1 Corinthians 14:5 **I would that ye** all spake with tongues but rather that ye prophesied: for greater is he that prophesieth than he that speaketh with tongues, except he interpret, that the church may receive edifying.)

BOM Mosiah 8:17 But A seer can know of things which are past, and also of things which are to come, and by them shall all things be revealed, or, rather, shall secret things be made manifest, and **hidden things** shall come **to light**, and things which are not known shall be made known by them, and also things shall be made known by them which otherwise could not be known.

    KJV (1NT/1) 1 Corinthians 4:5 Therefore judge nothing before the time, until the Lord come, who both will bring **to light** the **hidden things** of darkness, and will make manifest the counsels of the hearts: and then shall every man have praise of God.)

BOM Mosiah 16:7 And if Christ had not **risen from the dead**, or have broken the bands of death. that the **grave** should have no **victory**, and that **death** should have no **sting**, there could have been no resurrection.

    KJV (1NT/1) 1 Corinthians 15:55 O **death,** where is thy **sting**? O **grave**, where is thy **victory**?)

    KJV (10NT/4) Matthew 27:64 Command therefore that the sepulchre be made sure until the third day, lest his disciples come by night, and steal him away, and say unto the people, He is **risen from the dead**: so the last error shall be worse than the first.)

BOM Mosiah 16:8 But there is a resurrection, therefore the **grave** hath no **victory**, and the **sting** of **death is swallowed up in** Christ.

    KJV (1NT/1) 1 Corinthians 15:54 So when this corruptible shall have put on incorruption, and this mortal shall have put on immortality, then shall be brought to pass the saying that is written, **Death is swallowed up in victory.**)

BOM Mosiah 16:10 Even **this mortal shall put on immortality, and this corruption shall put on incorruption**, and shall be brought to stand before the bar of God, to be **judged** of him **according to their works whether** they **be good or whether** they **be evil** –

    KJV (1NT/1) 1 Corinthians 15:54 So when **this corruptible shall** have **put on incorruption, and this mortal shall** have **put on immortality**, then shall be brought to pass the saying that is written, Death is swallowed up in victory.)

    KJV (3NT/13) Revelation 20:13 And the sea gave up the dead which were in it; and death and hell delivered up the dead which were in them: and they were **judged** every man **according to their works**.)

    KJV (2/5) Ecclesiastes 12:14 For God shall bring every work into judgment, with every secret thing, **whether** it **be good, or whether** it **be evil**.)

BOM Mosiah 26:25 And it shall come to pass that when **the** second **trump shall sound** then shall they that never knew me come forth and shall stand before me.

    KJV (1NT/1) 1 Corinthians 15:52 In a moment, in the twinkling of an eye, at **the** last **trump**: for the trumpet **shall sound**, and the dead shall be raised incorruptible, and we shall be changed.)

BOM Alma 1:25 Now this was a great trial to those that did **stand fast in the faith**; nevertheless, they were **steadfast**, and (5) immovable (14th Century) in keeping the commandments of God, and they bore with patience the persecution which was heaped upon them.

> **KJV (1NT/3)** 1 Corinthians 16:13 Watch ye, **stand fast in the faith**, quit you like men, be strong.)

> **KJV (1NT/4)** 1 Corinthians 15:58 Therefore, my beloved brethren, be ye **stedfast**, **unmoveable**, always abounding in the work of the Lord, forasmuch as ye know that your labour is not in vain in the Lord.)

BOM Alma 5:15 Do ye exercise faith in the redemption of him who created you? Do you look forward with an eye of faith, and view this mortal body raised in immortality, and this **corruption raised in incorruption**, to **stand before God**, to be judged **according to** the **deeds** which have been done in the mortal body?

> **KJV (1NT/1)** 1 Corinthians 15:42 So also is the resurrection of the dead. It is sown in **corruption**; it is **raised in incorruption**:)

> **KJV (1NT/8)** Revelation 20:12 And I saw the dead, small and great, **stand before God**; and the books were opened: and another book was opened, which is the book of life: and the dead were judged out of those things which were written in the books, according to their works.)

> **KJV (1NT/1)** Romans 2:6 Who will render to every man **according** to his **deeds**:)

BOM Alma 5:47 And moreover, I say unto you that it has thus been revealed unto me, that the words which have been spoken by our fathers are true, even so according to **the spirit of prophecy** which is in me, which is also by **the manifestation of the Spirit** of God.

> **KJV (1NT/3)** 1 Corinthians 12:7 But **the manifestation of the Spirit** is given to every man to profit withal.)

> **KJV (1/18)** Revelation 19:10 And I fell at his feet to worship him. And he said unto me, See thou do it not: I am thy fellowservant, and of thy brethren that have the testimony of Jesus: worship God: for the testimony of Jesus is **the spirit of prophecy**.)

BOM Alma 7:23 And now I would that ye should be humble, and be submissive and gentle; easy to be entreated; full of patience and long-suffering; being **temperate in all things**; being diligent in keeping the commandments of God at all times; asking for whatsoever things ye stand in need, both spiritual and temporal; always returning thanks unto God for whatsoever things ye do receive.

> **KJV (1NT/2)** 1 Corinthians 9:25 And every man that striveth for the

mastery is **temperate in all things**. Now they do it to obtain a corruptible crown; but we an incorruptible.)

BOM <u>Alma 7:24</u> And see that ye have **faith, hope, and charity**, and then ye will always abound in good works.

> **KJV (1NT/1)** <u>1 Corinthians 13:13</u> And now abideth **faith, hope, charity**, these three; but the greatest of these is **charity**)

BOM <u>Alma 13:28</u> But that ye would humble yourselves before the Lord, and call on his holy name, and **watch and pray** continually, that ye may not be tempted above that which ye can bear, and thus be led by the Holy Spirit, becoming humble, meek, submissive, patient, full of love and all long-suffering;

> **KJV (1NT/1)** <u>1 Corinthians 10:13</u> There hath no temptation taken you but such as is common to man: but God is faithful, who will not suffer you to be **tempted above that ye** are able; but will with the temptation also make a way to escape, that ye may be able to **bear** it.)
>
> **KJV (1NT/1)** <u>Luke 21:36</u> **Watch** ye therefore, **and pray** always, **that ye may** be accounted worthy to escape all these things that shall come to pass, and to stand before the Son of man.)
>
> **KJV (2NT/1)** <u>Matthew 26:41</u> **Watch and pray**, that ye enter not into temptation: the spirit indeed is willing, but the flesh is weak.)

BOM <u>Alma 22:14</u> And since man had fallen he could not (2) merit (14th Century) anything of himself; but the sufferings and death of Christ atone for their sins, through faith and repentance, and so forth; and that he breaketh the bands of death, that the grave shall have no **victory**, and that the **sting** of **death** should be **swallowed up** in the hopes of glory; and Aaron did expound all these things unto the king.

> **KJV (1NT/1)** <u>1 Corinthians 15:55</u> "Where, O **death**, is your **victory**? Where, O **death**, is your **sting**?")
>
> **KJV (1NT/1)** <u>1 Corinthians 15:54</u> When the perishable has been clothed with the imperishable, and the mortal with immortality, then the saying that is written will come true: "**Death** has been **swallowed up** in **victory**.")

BOM <u>Alma 27:28</u> And they did look upon shedding the blood of their brethren with the greatest (2) abhorrence (1660; and they never could be prevailed upon to take up arms their brethren; and they never did look upon death with any degree of terror, for their hope and (3) views (1523 AD) of Christ and the resurrection; therefore, **death** was **swallowed up** to them by the **victory** of Christ over it.

> **KJV (1NT/2)** <u>1 Corinthians 15:54</u> So when this corruptible shall have put on incorruption, and this mortal shall have put on immortality, then shall be brought to pass the saying that is written, **Death** is **swallowed up** in **victory**.)

BOM Alma 31:1 Now it came to pass that after the end of Korihor, Alma having received tidings that the Zoramites were **pervert**ing **the ways of the Lord**, and that Zoram, who was their leader, was leading the hearts of the people to bow down to **dumb idols**, his heart again began to sicken because of the iniquity of the people.

> **KJV (1NT/1)** 1 Corinthians 12:2 Ye know that ye were Gentiles, carried away unto these **dumb idols**, even as ye were **led**.)

> **KJV (1NT/1)** Acts 13:10 And said, O full of all subtilty and all mischief, thou child of the devil, thou enemy of all righteousness, wilt thou not cease to **pervert the** right **ways of the Lord**?)

BOM Alma 32:23 And now, he imparteth his word by angels unto men, yea, not only men but women also. Now this is not all; little children do have words given unto them many times which **confound the wise** and the learned.

> **KJV (1NT/3)** 1 Corinthians 1:27 But God hath chosen the foolish things of the world to **confound the wise**; and God hath chosen the weak things of the world to **confound** the things which are mighty.)

BOM Alma 40:2 Behold, I say unto you, that there is no resurrection -- or, I would say, in other words, that **this mortal** does not **put on immortality**, this corruption does not **put on incorruption** – until after the coming of Christ.

> **KJV (2NT/3)** 1 Corinthians 15:53 For this corruptible must **put on incorruption**, and **this mortal** must **put on immortality**.)

BOM Alma 45:17 And now, **when** Alma **had said these words** he blessed the **church**, yea, all those who should **stand fast in the faith** from that time henceforth.

> **KJV (1NT/3)** 1 Corinthians 16:13 Watch ye, **stand fast in the faith**, quit you like men, be strong.)

> **KJV (1NT/1)** Acts 28:29 **And when** he **had said these words**, the Jews departed, and had great reasoning among themselves.)

BOM 3 Nephi 17:16 And after this manner did do they bear record: The **eye hath** never **seen, neither** hath the **ear heard**, before, so great and marvelous things as we saw and heard Jesus speak unto the Father;

> **KJV (1NT/1)** 1 Corinthians 2:9 But as it is written, **Eye hath** not **seen**, nor **ear heard**, neither have entered into the heart of man, the things which God hath prepared for them that love him.)

> **KJV (1/1)** Isaiah 64:4 For since the beginning of the world men have not **heard**, nor perceived by the **ear**, **neither hath** the **eye seen**, O God, beside thee, what he **hath** prepared for him that waiteth for him.)

BOM 3 Nephi 18:29 **For** whoso **eateth and drinketh** my flesh and blood unworthily **eateth and drinketh damnation to** his soul; therefore if ye know that a man is unworthy to eat and drink of my flesh and blood ye shall forbid him.

KJV (1NT/1) 1 Corinthians 11:29 For he that **eateth and drinketh unworthily, eateth and drinketh damnation to** himself, not discerning the Lord's body.)

BOM 3 Nephi 20:36 And **then shall be brought to pass that** which **is written**: Awake, awake again, and **put on thy strength, O Zion; put on thy beautiful garments, O Jerusalem, the holy city, for henceforth there shall no more come into thee the uncircumcised and the unclean.**

KJV (1NT/1) 1 Corinthians 15:54 So when this corruptible shall have put on incorruption, and this mortal **shall** have put on immortality, **then shall be brought to pass** the saying **that is written**, Death is swallowed up in victory.)

KJV (1/1) Isaiah 52:1 **Awake, awake; put on thy strength, O Zion; put on thy beautiful garments, O Jerusalem, the holy city: for henceforth there shall no more come into thee the uncircumcised and the unclean.**)

BOM 3 Nephi 28:8 And ye shall never endure **the pains of death**; but when I shall come in my glory ye **shall be changed in the twinkling of an eye** from mortality to immortality; and then shall ye be blessed in the kingdom of my Father.

KJV (1NT/1) 1 Corinthians 15:52 In a moment, **in the twinkling of an eye**, at the last trump: for the trumpet shall sound, and the dead shall be raised incorruptible, and we **shall be changed**.)

KJV (1NT/3) Acts 2:24 Whom God hath raised up, having loosed **the pains of death**: because it was not possible that he should be holden of it.)

BOM Mormon 6:23 **Know ye not that ye are** in the hands **of God**? Know ye not that he hath all power, and at his great command the earth **shall be rolled together as a scroll**?

KJV (1NT/1) 1 Corinthians 3:16 **Know ye not that ye are** the temple **of God**, and that the Spirit of God dwelleth in you?)

KJV (1/2) Isaiah 34:4 And all the host of heaven shall be dissolved, and the heavens **shall be rolled together as a scroll**: and all their host shall fall down, as the leaf falleth off from the vine, and as a falling fig from the fig tree.)

BOM Mormon 9:7 And again I speak unto you who deny the revelations of God, and say that they are done away, that there are no revelations, nor prophecies, nor gifts, nor healing, nor **speaking with tongues**, and the **interpretation of tongues**;

KJV (1NT/3) 1 Corinthians 14:6 Now, brethren, if I come unto you **speaking with tongues**, what shall I profit you, except I shall speak to you either by revelation, or by knowledge, or by prophesying, or by doctrine?)

KJV (1NT/2) 1 Corinthians 12:10 To another the working of miracles; to another prophecy; to another discerning of spirits; to another divers kinds of tongues; to another the **interpretation** of tongues:)

BOM Mormon 9:13 And because of the redemption of man, which came by Jesus Christ, they are brought back into the presence of the Lord; yea, this is wherein all men are redeemed, because the death of Christ bringeth to pass the resurrection, which bringeth to pass a redemption from an endless sleep, from which sleep all men shall be (8) awakened (12ᵗʰ Century) by the power of God when **the trump shall sound**; and they shall come forth, **both small and great,** and all shall stand before his bar, being redeemed and loosed from this eternal band of death, which death is a temporal death.

KJV (1NT/1) 1 Corinthians 15:52 In a moment, in the twinkling of an eye, at the last **trump**: for the trumpet **shall sound**, and the dead shall be raised incorruptible, and we shall be changed.)

KJV (*Note: Same idea:* (2NT/1) Revelation 13:16 And he causeth all, **both small and great**, rich and poor, free and bond, to receive a mark in their right hand, or in their foreheads:)

BOM Ether 12:11 Wherefore, by faith was the law of Moses given. But in the gift of his Son hath God prepared **a more excellent way**; and it is by faith that it hath been fulfilled.

KJV (1NT/1) 1 Corinthians 12:31 But covet earnestly the best gifts: and yet shew I unto you **a more excellent way**.)

BOM Ether 12:28 Behold, I will show unto the Gentiles their weakness and I will show unto them that **faith, hope** and **charity** bringeth unto me -- the fountain of all righteousness.

KJV (1NT/1) 1 Corinthians 13:13 And now abideth **faith, hope, charity**, these three; but the greatest of these is **charity**.)

BOM Ether 12:37 And it came to pass that the Lord said unto me: If they **have not charity** it (12) mattereth not unto thee, **thou hast been faithful**; wherefore, thy garments shall be made clean. And because thou hast seen thy **weakness** thou shalt be **made strong**, even unto the sitting down in the place which **I** have **prepared** in the **mansions** of **my Fath**er.

KJV (1NT/1) 1 Corinthians 13:2 And though I have the gift of prophecy, and understand all mysteries, and all knowledge; and though I have all faith, so that I could remove mountains, and **have not charity**, I am nothing.)

KJV (3NT/4) Matthew 25:23 His lord said unto him, Well done, good and **faithful** servant; **thou hast been faithful** over a few things,)

KJV (1NT/4) Hebrews 11:34 Quenched the violence of fire, escaped the edge of the sword, out of **weakness** were **made strong**, waxed valiant in fight, turned to flight the armies of the aliens.)

KJV (1NT/1) <u>John 14:2</u> In **my Father**'s house are many **mansions**: if it were not so, I would have told you. **I** go to **prepare** a **place** for you.)

BOM <u>Moroni 7:1</u> And now I, Moroni, write a few of the words of my father Mormon, which he spake concerning **faith, hope, and charity**; for after this manner did he speak unto the people, as **he taught them in** the **synagogue** which they had built for the place of worship.

> **KJV (1NT/1)** <u>1 Corinthians 13:13</u> And now abideth **faith, hope, charity**, these three; but the greatest of these is **charity**.)

> **KJV (1NT/1)** <u>Matthew 13:54</u> And when he was come into his own country, **he taught them in** their **synagogue**, insomuch that they were astonished, and said, Whence hath this man this wisdom, and these mighty works?)

BOM <u>Moroni 7:6</u> For behold, God hath said a man **being evil** cannot do that which is **good**; for if he offereth a gift, or prayeth unto God, except he shall do it with *real* (*14th Century)* intent **it profiteth** him **nothing**.

> **KJV (1NT/2)** <u>1 Corinthians 13:3</u> And though I bestow all my goods to feed the poor, and though I give my body to be burned, and have not charity, **it profiteth** me **nothing**.)

> **KJV (1NT/1)** <u>Matthew 12:34</u> O generation of vipers, how can ye, **being evil**, speak **good** things? for out of the abundance of the heart the mouth speaketh.)

BOM <u>Moroni 7:16</u> For behold, the Spirit of Christ **is given to every man**, that he may know good from evil; wherefore, I show unto you the way to judge; for every thing which inviteth to do good, and to persuade to believe in Christ, is sent forth by the power and gift of Christ; wherefore ye may know with a **perfect knowledge** it is of God.

> **KJV (1NT/1)** <u>1 Corinthians 12:7</u> But the manifestation of **the Spirit is given to every man** to profit withal.)

> **KJV (1NT/14)** <u>Acts 24:22</u> And when Felix heard these things, having more **perfect knowledge** of that way, he deferred them, and said, When Lysias the chief captain shall come down, I will know the uttermost of your matter.)

BOM <u>Moroni 7:44</u> If so, his faith and hope is vain, for none is **acceptable before God**, save the **meek and lowly in heart**; and if a man be **meek and lowly in heart**, and confesses by the power of the **Holy Ghost** that Jesus is the Christ, he must needs have **charity**; for if he **have not charity** he is **nothing**; wherefore he **must needs have charity**.

> **KJV (1NT/2)** <u>1 Corinthians 13:2</u> And though I have the gift of prophecy, and understand all mysteries, and all knowledge; and though I have all faith, so that I could remove mountains, and **have**

not charity, I am **nothing**.)

KJV (1NT/1) 1 Timothy 5:4 But if any widow have children or nephews, let them learn first to shew piety at home, and to requite their parents: for that is good and **acceptable before God**.)

KJV (1NT/4) Matthew 11:29 Take my yoke upon you, and learn of me; for I am **meek and lowly in heart**: and ye shall find rest unto your souls.)

BOM Moroni 7:45 And **charity suffereth long, and is kind, and envieth not**, and **is not puffed up, seeketh not her own, is not easily provoked, thinketh no evil**, and **rejoiceth not in iniquity but rejoiceth in the truth, beareth all things, believeth all things, hopeth all things, endureth all things.**

KJV (1NT/1) 1 Corinthians 13:4-8 **Charity suffereth long, and is kind;** charity **envieth not**; charity vaunteth not itself, **is not puffed up**, Doth not behave itself unseemly, **seeketh not her own, is not easily provoked, thinketh no evil; Rejoiceth not in iniquity, but rejoiceth in the truth; Beareth all things, believeth all things, hopeth all things, endureth all things.**)

BOM Moroni 7:46 Wherefore, **my beloved brethren**, if ye **have not charity**, ye are **nothing**, for **charity never faileth**. Wherefore, cleave unto charity, which is the greatest of all, for all things must fail --

KJV (1NT/2) 1 Corinthians 13:2 And though I have the gift of prophecy, and understand all mysteries, and all knowledge; and though I have all faith, so that I could remove mountains, and **have not charity**, I am **nothing**.)

KJV (1NT/1) 1 Corinthians 13:8 **Charity never faileth**: but whether there be prophecies, they shall fail; whether there be tongues, they shall cease; whether there be knowledge, it shall vanish away.)

KJV (4NT/60) James 1:19 Wherefore, **my beloved brethren**, let every man be swift to hear, slow to speak, slow to wrath:)

BOM Moroni 10:8 And again, I exhort you, my brethren, that ye deny not the gifts of God, for they are many; and they come from the same God. And there are different ways that these gifts are administered; **but it is the same God** who **worketh all in all**; and they are given by the **manifestations of the Spirit** of God unto men, to profit them.

KJV (1NT/1) 1 Corinthians 12:6 And there are diversities of operations, **but it is the same God** which **worketh all in all**.)

KJV (1NT/1) 1 Corinthians 12:7 But **the manifestation of the Spirit** is given to every man **to profit** withal.)

BOM Moroni 10:9-10 **For** behold, **to one is given by the Spirit** of God, that he may teach **the word of wisdom**;

BOM Moroni 10:10 And **to another**, that he may teach **the word of**

knowledge by the same Spirit;

> **KJV (1NT/1)** 1 Corinthians 12:8 **For** to **one is given by the Spirit the word of wisdom; to another the word of knowledge by the same Spirit;)**

BOM Moroni 10:11 And **to another**, exceedingly great **faith**; and **to another, the gifts of healing by the same Spirit;**

> **KJV (1NT/1)** 1 Corinthians 12:9 **To another faith by the same Spirit**; to another **the gifts of healing by the same Spirit;)**

BOM Moroni 10:12 And again, **to another**, that he may **work** mighty **miracles;**

BOM Moroni 10:13 And again, **to another**, that he may **prophesy** concerning all things;

BOM Moroni 10:14 And again, **to another**, the beholding of angels and ministering **spirits;**

BOM Moroni 10:15 And again, **to another**, all **kinds of tongues;**

BOM Moroni 10:16 And again, **to another, the interpretation** of languages and of **divers kinds of tongues.**

> **KJV (1NT/1)** 1 Corinthians 12:10 **To another** the **work**ing of **miracles; to another prophecy; to another** discerning of **spirits; to another divers kinds of tongues; to another the interpretation of tongues.)**

BOM Moroni 10:17 And all these gifts come by the **Spirit** of Christ; and they come un**to every man severally**, according **as he will.**

> **KJV (1NT/1)** 1 Corinthians 12:11 But **all these** worketh that one and the selfsame **Spirit**, dividing **to every man severally as he will.)**

2 Corinthians 51 times

BOM 1 Nephi 15:31 And they said unto me: Doth this thing mean the torment of the body in the days of (9) probation, (15th Century) or doth it mean the final state of the soul after the death of the **temporal** body, or doth it speak of **the things which are temporal**?

> **KJV (1NT/1)** 2 Corinthians 4:18 While we look not at the things which are seen, but at the things which are not seen: for **the things which are** seen are **temporal**; but the things which are not seen are eternal.)

BOM 2 Nephi 1:23 Awake, my sons; put on the **armor of righteousness.** Shake off the chains of with which ye are bound, and come forth **out of obscurity**, and arise from the dust.

> **KJV (1NT/1)** 2 Corinthians 6:7 By the word of truth, by the power of God, by the **armour of righteousness** on the right hand and on the left,)

> **KJV (1/3)** Isaiah 29:18 And in that day shall the deaf hear the words of the book, and the eyes of the blind shall see **out of obscurity**, and

out of darkness.)

BOM 2 Nephi 9:9 And our spirits must have become like unto him, and we become devils, angels to a devil, to be shut out from the presence of our God, and to remain with the **father of lies**, in misery, like unto himself; yea, to that being who beguiled our first parents, who **transformeth** himself nigh unto **an angel of light**, and stirreth up the children of men unto secret (21) combinations (14th Century) of murder and all manner of secret works of darkness.

> **KJV** (**1NT/1**) 2 Corinthians 11:14 And no marvel; for Satan himself is **transformed into an angel of light**.)
>
> **KJV** (John 8:44 Ye are of your **father** the **devil**, and the lusts of your **father** ye will do. He was a murderer from the beginning, and abode not in the truth, because there is no truth in him. When he speaketh a lie, he speaketh of his own: for he is a **liar**, and the **father** of it.)

BOM 2 Nephi 9:15 And it shall come to pass that when all men shall have passed from this first death unto life, insomuch as they have become immortal, they must **appear before the judgment-seat** of the Holy One of Israel; and then cometh the judgment, and then must they be judged according to the holy judgment of God.

> **KJV** (**1NT/1**) 2 Corinthians 5:10 For we must all **appear before the judgment seat** of Christ; that every one may receive the things done in his body, according to that he hath done, whether it be good or bad.)

BOM Jacob 2:7 And also it grieveth me that I must use so much **boldness of speech** concerning you, before your wives and your children, many of whose feelings are exceedingly tender and chaste and delicate before God, which thing is pleasing unto God;

> **KJV** (**1NT/1**) 2 Corinthians 7:4 Great is my **boldness of speech** toward you, great is my glorying of you: I am filled with comfort, I am exceeding joyful in all our tribulation.)

BOM Jacob 3:12 And now I, Jacob, spake many more things unto the people of Nephi, warning them against **fornication and lasciviousness**, and every kind of sin, telling them the (47) awful (13th Century) (4) consequences (14th Century) of them.

> **KJV** (**2NT/1**) 2 Corinthians 12:21 And lest, when I come again, my God will humble me among you, and that I shall bewail many which have sinned already, and have not repented of the uncleanness and fornication and lasciviousness which they have committed.)

BOM Mosiah 18:10 Now I say unto you, if this be the desire of your hearts, what have you against being **baptized in the name of** the Lord, as a witness before him that ye have entered into a covenant with him, that ye will serve him and keep his commandments, that he may pour out his Spirit **more**

abundantly upon **you**?

> **KJV (1NT/1)** 2 Corinthians 2:4 For out of much affliction and anguish of heart I wrote unto you with many tears; not that ye should be grieved, but that ye might know the love which I have **more abundantly** unto **you**.)

> **KJV (4NT/6)** Acts 19:5 When they heard this, they were **baptized in the name of** the Lord Jesus.)

BOM Mosiah 18:27 And again Alma commanded that the people of the church should impart of their substance, every one according to that which he had; if he **have more abundantly** he should impart more abundantly; and of him that had but little, but little should be required; and to him that had not should be given.

> **KJV (1NT/2)** 2 Corinthians 2:4 For out of much affliction and anguish of heart I wrote unto you with many tears; not that ye should be grieved, but that ye might know the love which I **have more abundantly** unto you.)

> **KJV** (*Note: Similar idea here:* Luke 19:26 For I say unto you, That unto every one which hath shall be given; and from him that hath not, even that he hath shall be taken away from him.)

BOM Mosiah 27:26 And thus they become **new creature**s; and unless they do this, they can in nowise **inherit the kingdom of God**.

> **KJV (2NT/1)** 2 Corinthians 5:17 Therefore if any man be in Christ, he is a **new creature**: old things are passed away; behold, all things are become new.)

> **KJV (4NT/13)** 1 Corinthians 6:9 Know ye not that the unrighteous shall not **inherit the kingdom of God**? Be not deceived: neither fornicators, nor idolaters, nor adulterers, nor effeminate, nor abusers of themselves with mankind,)

BOM Alma 5:57 **And now I say unto you**, all you that are desirous to follow the voice of **the good shepherd**, **come** ye **out from** the wicked, and **be ye separate**, and **touch not** their **unclean thing**s; and behold, their **names** shall be **blotted out**, that the names of the wicked shall not be numbered among the names of the righteous, that the word of God may be fulfilled, which saith: The names of the wicked shall not be mingled with the names of my people;

> **KJV (1NT/1)** 2 Corinthians 6:17 Wherefore **come out from** among them, **and be ye separate**, saith the Lord, and **touch not** the **unclean thing**; and I will receive you.)

> **KJV (1NT/18)** Acts 5:38 **And now I say unto you**, Refrain from these men, and let them alone: for if this counsel or this work be of men, it will come to nought:)

> **KJV (2NT/8)** John 10:11 I am **the good shepherd**: the **good shepherd** giveth his life for the sheep.)

KJV (6/8) <u>Psalm 109:13</u> Let his posterity be cut off; and in the generation following let their **name** be **blotted out.**)

BOM <u>Alma 18:23</u> And the king answered him, and said: Yea, I will believe all thy words. And thus he was **caught with guile.**

KJV (**1NT/1**) <u>2 Corinthians 12:16</u> But be it so, I did not burden you: nevertheless, being crafty, I **caught** you **with guile.**)

BOM <u>Alma 29:9</u> I know that which the Lord hath commanded me, and **I glory** in it. **I** do **not glory** of **myself, but I glory in** that which the Lord hath commanded me; yea, and this is my glory, that perhaps I may be an instrument in the hands of God to bring some soul to repentance; and this is my joy.

KJV (**1NT/1**) <u>2 Corinthians 12:5</u> Of such an one will **I glory:** yet **of myself I** will **not glory, but in** mine infirmities.)

BOM <u>Helaman 11:19</u> And behold, Lehi, his brother, **was not a whit behind** him as to **things pertaining to** righteousness.

KJV (**1NT/1**) <u>2 Corinthians 11:5</u> For I suppose I **was not a whit behind** the very chiefest apostles.)

KJV (**4NT/9**) <u>Acts 1:3</u> To whom also he shewed himself alive after his passion by many infallible proofs, being seen of them forty days, and speaking of the **things pertaining to** the kingdom of God)

BOM <u>3 Nephi 13:37</u> **Old things are** done **away,** and **all things** have **become new.**

KJV (**1NT/1**) <u>2 Corinthians 5:17</u> Therefore if any man be in Christ, he is a new creature: **old things are** passed **away**; behold, **all things** are **become new.**)

BOM <u>3 Nephi 15:2</u> And it came to pass that when Jesus had said these words he perceived that there were some among them who marveled, and wondered what he would concerning the law of Moses; for they understood not the saying that **old things** had **passed away,** and that **all things** had **become new.**

KJV (**1NT/1**) <u>2 Corinthians 5:17</u> Therefore if any man be in Christ, he is a **new** creature: **old things** are **passed away**; behold, **all things** are **become new.**)

BOM <u>3 Nephi 28:15</u> And **whether** they were **in the body or out of the body,** they could not **tell**; for it did seem unto them like a (2) transfiguration of them, that they were changed from this body of flesh into an immortal state, that they could behold the things of God.

KJV (**2NT/1**) <u>2 Corinthians 12:2</u> I knew a man in Christ above fourteen years ago, (**whether in the body,** I cannot tell; **or** whether **out of the body,** I cannot **tell**: God knoweth;) such an one caught up to the third heaven.)

BOM <u>Mormon 8:35</u> Behold, **I** speak unto **you as if** ye **were present,** and yet ye are not. But behold, Jesus Christ hath (*29) shown* (12th Century) you unto me, and I know your doing.

KJV (1NT/1) 2 Corinthians 13:2 **I** told you before, and foretell **you**, as if I **were present**, the second time; and being absent now I write to them which heretofore have sinned, and to all other, that, if I come again, I will not spare:)

BOM Ether 12:26 And when I had said this, Lord spake unto me, saying: **Fools mock**, but they shall mourn; and **my grace is sufficient for** the meek, that they shall take no advantage of your weakness;

KJV (1NT/2) 2 Corinthians 12:9 And he said unto me, **My grace is sufficient for** thee: for my strength is made perfect in weakness. Most gladly therefore will I rather glory in my infirmities, that the power of Christ may rest upon me.)

KJV (1/1) Proverbs 14:9 **Fools** make a **mock** at sin: but among the righteous there is favour.)

BOM Ether 13:9 And there shall be **a new heaven and a new earth**; and they shall be like unto the **old** save the **old** have **passed away**, and **all things** have **become new**.

KJV (1NT/1) 2 Corinthians 5:17 Therefore if any man be in Christ, he is a **new** creature: **old things** are **passed away**; behold, **all things** are **become new**.)

KJV (1NT/1) Revelation 21:1 And I saw **a new heaven and a new earth**: for the first heaven and the first earth were passed away; and there was no more sea.)

BOM Moroni 7:8 For behold, **if** a man **being evil give**th a **gift**, he doeth it **grudgingly**; wherefore it is counted unto him the same as if he had retained the gift; wherefore he is counted evil before God.

KJV (1NT/1) 2 Corinthians 9:7 Every man according as he purposeth in his heart, so let him **give**; not **grudgingly**, or of necessity: for God loveth a cheerful giver.)

KJV (2NT/1) Matthew 7:11 **If** ye then, **being evil**, know how to **give** good **gift**s unto your children, how much more shall your Father which is in heaven give good things to them that ask him?

And now Galatians 44 times

BOM 2 Nephi 10:16 Wherefore, he that fighteth against Zion, both **Jew** and **Gentile**, both **bond** and **free**, both **male** and **female**, shall perish; for they are they who are the whore of all the earth; for they who are not for me are against me, saith our God.

KJV (1NT/1) Galatians 3:28 There is neither **Jew** nor Greek, there is neither **bond** nor **free**, there is neither **male** nor **female**: for ye are all one in Christ Jesus.)

Note: If this is God speaking why would he say "saith our God"?

BOM Mosiah 4:15 But ye will teach them to walk in the ways of **truth and soberness**; ye will teach them to **love one another**, and to **serve one another**.

> **KJV (1NT/1)** <u>Galatians 5:13</u> For, brethren, ye have been called unto liberty; only use not liberty for an occasion to the flesh, but by **love serve one another.**)

> **KJV (1NT/1)** <u>Acts 26:25</u> But he said, I am not mad, most noble Festus; but speak forth **the** words **of truth and soberness.**)

BOM <u>Mosiah 13:7</u> Ye see that ye have not power to slay me, therefore I finish my message. Yea, and I perceive that it cuts you to your hearts **because I tell you the truth** concerning your iniquities.

> **KJV (1NT/2)** <u>Galatians 4:16</u> Am I therefore become your enemy, **because I tell you the truth?**)

BOM <u>Mosiah 18:8</u> And it came to pass that he said unto them: Behold, here are the waters of Mormon (for thus were they called) and now, as ye are desirous to come into the fold of God, and to be called his people, and are willing to **bear one another's burdens**, that they may be light;

> **KJV (1NT/1)** <u>Galatians 6:2</u> **Bear** ye **one another's burdens**, and so fulfil the law of Christ.)

BOM <u>Mosiah 23:13</u> And now as ye have been delivered by the power of God out of these bonds; yea, even out of the hands of king Noah and his people, and also from **the bonds of iniquity,** even so **I desire that ye** should **stand fast in** this **liberty wherewith** ye have been **made free**, and that ye trust no man to be a king over you.

> **KJV (1NT/3)** <u>Galatians 5:1</u> **Stand fast** therefore **in** the **liberty wherewith** Christ hath **made** us **free**, and be not entangled again with the yoke of bondage.)

> **KJV (1NT/10)** <u>Ephesians 3:13</u> Wherefore **I desire that ye** faint not at my tribulations for you, which is your glory.)

> **KJV (1NT/4)** <u>Acts 8:23</u> For I perceive that thou art in the gall of bitterness, and in **the bond of iniquity.**)

BOM <u>Alma 44:2</u> Behold, we have not come out to battle against you that we might shed your blood for power; neither do we desire to bring any one to **the yoke of bondage.** But this is the very cause for which ye have come against us; yea, and ye are angry with us because of our religion.

> **KJV (1NT/5)** <u>Galatians 5:1</u> **Stand fast** therefore in the liberty wherewith Christ hath made us free, and be not entangled again with **the yoke of bondage.**)

BOM <u>Alma 59:40</u> But behold, they have received many wounds; nevertheless they **stand fast in** that **liberty wherewith** God **has made** them **free**; and they are (13) strict (15th Century) to remember the Lord their God from day to day; yea, they do observe to **keep his statutes, and his judgments, and his commandments** continually; and their faith is strong in the prophecies concerning that which is to come.

> **KJV (1NT/3)** <u>Galatians 5:1</u> **Stand fast** therefore **in the liberty**

wherewith Christ **hath made** us **free**, and be not entangled again with **the yoke of bondage**.)

KJV (2/1) Deuteronomy 26:17 Thou hast avouched the LORD this day to be thy God, and to walk in his ways, and to **keep his statutes, and his commandments, and his judgments**, and to hearken unto his voice:)

BOM Alma 61:9 And now, in your epistle you have (1) censured (1587) me, but it (12) mattereth not; I am not angry, but do rejoice in the greatness of your heart. I, Pahoran, do not seek for power, save only to retain my judgment-seat that I may preserve the rights and the liberty of my people. My soul **stand**eth **fast in** that **liberty in** the which God **hath made us free**.

KJV (1NT/1) Galatians 5:1 **stand fast** therefore **in the liberty** wherewith Christ **hath made us free**, and be not entangled again with the yoke of bondage.)

BOM Alma 61:21 See that ye strengthen Lehi and Teancum in the Lord; tell them to fear not, for God will deliver them, yea, and also all those who **stand fast in** that **liberty wherewith** God **hath made** them **free**. And now I close mine epistle to my beloved brother, Moroni.

KJV (1NT/3) Galatians 5:1 **Stand fast** therefore **in the liberty wherewith** Christ **hath made** us **free**, and be not entangled again with **the yoke of bondage**.)

BOM Ether 4:8 And he that will contend against the word of the Lord, **let him be accursed**; and he that shall deny these things, let him be accursed; for unto them will I show no greater things, saith Jesus Christ; for **I am he** who **speak**eth.

KJV (2NT/1) Galatians 1:8 But though we, or an angel from heaven, preach any other gospel unto you than that which we have preached unto you, **let him be accursed**.)

KJV (1/1) Isaiah 52:6 Therefore my people shall know my name: therefore they shall know in that day that **I am he** that doth **speak**: behold, it is I.)

And now Ephesians 69 times

BOM 1 Nephi 15:24 And I said unto them that it was the word of God, and whose would hearken unto the word of God, and would hold fast unto it, they would never perish; neither could the temptations and the **fiery darts of the** adversary (22) overpower (1593 AD) them unto blindness, to lead them away to destruction.

KJV (1NT/1) Ephesians 6:16 Above all, taking the shield of faith, wherewith ye shall be able to quench all the **fiery darts of the** wicked.)

BOM 2 Nephi 1:14 **Awake! and arise from the dust**, and hear the words of a trembling parent, whose (5) limbs (12th Century) ye must soon lay down in the cold and silent grave, from whence no traveler can return; a few more days and **I go the way of all the earth**.

> **KJV (1NT/1)** <u>Ephesians 5:14</u> Wherefore he saith, **Awake** thou that sleepest, and **arise from the** dead, and Christ shall give thee light.)
>
> **KJV** (1/1) <u>1 Kings 2:2</u> **I go the way of all the earth**: be thou strong therefore, and shew thyself a man;)

BOM <u>2 Nephi 10:22</u> For behold, the Lord God has led away from time to time from the house of Israel, **according to his will** and **pleasure**. And now behold, the Lord remembereth all them who have been broken off, wherefore he remembereth us also.

> **KJV (1NT/5)** <u>Ephesians 1:9</u> Having made known unto us the mystery of his **will, according to his** good **pleasure** which he hath purposed in himself:)

BOM <u>2 Nephi 32:21</u> And now, behold, my beloved brethren, this is the way; and **there is none other** way nor **name given under heaven whereby** man can be saved in the kingdom of God. And now, behold, this is **the doctrine of Christ**, and the only and true doctrine of the Father, **and of the Son, and of the Holy Ghost**, which is one God, **without end. Amen.**

> **KJV (1NT/1)** <u>Ephesians 3:21</u> Unto him be glory in the church by Christ Jesus throughout all ages, world **without end. Amen**.)
>
> **KJV (1NT/1)** <u>Acts 4:12</u> Neither is there salvation in any other: for **there is none other name under heaven given** among men, **whereby** we must **be saved**.)
>
> **KJV (2NT/7)** <u>2 John 1:9</u> Whosoever transgresseth, and abideth not in **the doctrine of Christ**, hath not God. He that abideth in **the doctrine of Christ**, he hath both the Father and the Son.)
>
> **KJV (1NT/2)** <u>Matthew 28:19</u> Go ye therefore, and teach all nations, baptizing them in the name of the Father, **and of the Son, and of the Holy Ghost**:)

BOM <u>Enos 1:1</u> Behold, it came to pass that I, Enos, knowing my father that he was a just man -- for he taught me in his language, and also **in the nurture and admonition of the Lord** -- and blessed be the name of my God for it –

> **KJV (1NT/1)** <u>Ephesians 6:4</u> And, ye fathers, provoke not your children to wrath: but bring them up **in the nurture and admonition of the Lord**.)
>
> **Note**: Isn't it interesting that this verse in Ephesians was given to tell "fathers" to bring up children "in the admonition of the Lord" when this is exactly what this verse in Enos is saying, the he was "taught" in the same thing.

BOM <u>Mosiah 26:37</u> And it came to pass that Alma did (1) regulate (15th Century) all the affairs of the church; and they began again to have peace and to prosper exceedingly in the affairs of the church, **walk**ing **circumspectly**

before God, receiving many, and baptizing many.

> **KJV (1NT/1)** <u>Ephesians 5:15</u> See then that ye **walk circumspectly**, not as fools, but as wise,)

BOM <u>Helaman 3:29</u> Yea, we see that whosoever will may lay hold upon the word of God, which **is quick and powerful**, which shall **divide asunder** all the cunning and the snares and **the wiles of the devil**, and lead the man of Christ in a strait and narrow course across that everlasting gulf of misery which is prepared to engulf the wicked –

> **KJV (1NT/1)** <u>Ephesians 6:11</u> Put on the whole armour of God, that ye may be able to stand against **the wiles of the devil**.)

> **KJV (1NT/1)** <u>Hebrews 4:12</u> For **the word of God is quick, and powerful**, and sharper than any twoedged sword, piercing even to the **divid**ing **asunder** of soul and spirit, and of the joints and marrow, and is a discerner of the thoughts and intents of the heart.)

BOM <u>Helaman 15:5</u> And I would that ye should behold that the more part of them are in the path of their duty, and they do **walk circumspectly** before God, and they do observe to keep his commandments and his statutes and his judgments according to the law of Moses.

> **KJV (1NT/1)** <u>Ephesians 5:15</u> See then that ye **walk circumspectly**, not as fools, but as wise,)

And now Philippians 14 times

BOM <u>Alma 10:4</u> And behold, I am also a man **of no** small **reputation** among all those who know me; yea, and behold, I have many kindreds and friends, and I have also acquired much riches by the hand of my industry.

> **KJV (1NT/1)** <u>Philippians 2:7</u> But made himself **of no reputation**, and took upon him the form of a servant, and was made in the likeness of men:)

BOM <u>Alma 34:37</u> And now, my beloved brethren, I desire that ye should remember these things, and that ye should **work out your salvation with fear** before God, and that ye should no more deny the coming of Christ;

> **KJV (1NT/10)** <u>Ephesians 3:13</u> Wherefore **I desire that ye** faint not at my tribulations for you, which is your glory.)

> **KJV (1NT/1)** <u>Philippians 2:12</u> Wherefore, my beloved, as ye have always obeyed, not as in my presence only, but now much more in my absence, **work out your** own **salvation with fear** and trembling.)

BOM <u>3 Nephi 27:31</u> Behold, **I would** that **ye should understand**; for I mean them who are now alive of this generation; and none of them are lost; and in them I have fulness of joy.

> **KJV (1NT/1)** <u>Philippians 1:12</u> But **I would ye should understand**, brethren, that the things which happened unto me have fallen out rather unto the furtherance of the gospel;)

BOM <u>Mormon 9:27</u> O then despise not, and wonder not, but hearken unto the words of the Lord, and **ask the Father in** the **name** of Jesus for what things soever ye shall stand in need. Doubt not, but be believing, and begin as in times of old, and come unto the Lord with all your heart, and **work out your own salvation with fear and trembling** before him.

> **KJV (1NT/1)** <u>Philippians 2:12</u> Wherefore, my beloved, as ye have always obeyed, not as in my presence only, but now much more in my absence, **work out your own salvation with fear and trembling**.)
>
> **KJV (1NT/1)** <u>John 16:23</u> And in that day ye shall ask me nothing. Verily, verily, I say unto you, Whatsoever ye shall **ask the Father in** my **name**, he will give it you.)

BOM <u>Moroni 7:41</u> And what is it that ye shall hope for? Behold I say unto you that ye shall have hope through the atonement of Christ **and the power of his resurrection**, to be raised unto life eternal, and this because of your faith in him **according to the promise**.

> **KJV (1NT/1)** <u>Philippians 3:10</u> That I may know him, **and the power of his resurrection**, and the fellowship of his sufferings, being made conformable unto his death;)
>
> **KJV (2NT/1)** <u>Galatians 3:29</u> And if ye be Christ's, then are ye Abraham's seed, and heirs **according to the promise**.)

And now Colossians 16 Times

BOM <u>Mosiah 4:30</u> But this much I can tell you, that if ye do not watch yourselves, and your thoughts, and your words, and your deeds, and observe the commandments of God, and **continue in the faith** of what **ye have heard** concerning the coming of our Lord, even unto the end of your lives, ye must perish. And now, **O man**, remember, and perish not.

> **KJV (1NT/1)** <u>Colossians 1:23</u> If ye **continue in the faith** grounded and settled, and be not moved away from the hope of the gospel, which **ye have heard**, and which was preached to every creature which is under heaven; whereof I Paul am made a minister;)
>
> **KJV (9/3)** <u>Micah 6:8</u> He hath shewed thee, **O man**, what is good; and what doth the LORD require of thee, but to do justly, and to love mercy, and to walk humbly with thy God?)

BOM <u>Mosiah 18:21</u> And he commanded them that there should be no contention one with another, but that they should look forward with one eye, having one faith and one baptism, having their **hearts knit together in** unity and **in love** one towards another.

> **KJV (1NT/1)** <u>Colossians 2:2</u> That their **hearts** might be comforted, being **knit together in love**, and unto all riches of the full assurance of understanding, to the acknowledgement of the mystery of God, and of the Father, and of Christ;)

BOM <u>3 Nephi 19:26</u> And Jesus said unto them: Pray on; nevertheless they did not cease to pray.

> **KJV (1NT/2)** <u>Colossians 1:9</u> For this cause we also, since the day we heard it, do **not cease to pray** for you, and to desire that ye might be filled with the knowledge of his will in all wisdom and spiritual understanding;)

BOM <u>Mosiah 10:26</u> And may the grace of God the Father, whose **throne** is high **in the heavens**, and our Lord Jesus Christ, who **sitteth on the right hand of** his power, until all things shall become subject unto him, be, and **abide with you forever**. Amen.

> **KJV** (1NT/1) <u>Colossians 3:1</u> If ye then be risen with Christ, seek those things which are above, where Christ **sitteth on the right hand of** God.)
>
> **KJV** (16/8) (<u>Psalm 103:19</u> The LORD hath prepared his **throne in the heavens**; and his kingdom ruleth over all.)
>
> **KJV (1NT/1)** <u>John 14:16</u> And I will pray the Father, and he shall give you another Comforter, that he may **abide with you for ever**;)

And now 1 Thessalonians 17 times

BOM <u>Mosiah 26:39</u> And they did admonish their brethren; and they were also admonished, every one **by the word of God**, according to his sins, or to the sins which he had committed, being commanded of God to **pray without ceasing**, and to give thanks in all things.

> **KJV (5NT/3)** <u>Romans 10:17</u> So then faith cometh by hearing, and hearing **by the word of God**.)
>
> **KJV (1NT/1)** <u>1 Thessalonians 5:17</u> **Pray without ceasing**.)

BOM <u>Alma 29:1</u> O that I were an angel, and could have the wish of mine heart, that I might go forth and speak **with the trump of God, with** a **voice** to shake the earth, and cry repentance unto every people!

> **KJV (1NT/1)** <u>1 Thessalonians 4:16</u> For the Lord himself shall descend from heaven with a shout, **with** the **voice** of the archangel, and **with the trump of God**: and the dead in Christ shall rise first:)

And now 2 Thessalonians 9 times

BOM <u>Alma 12:6</u> And behold I say unto you all that this was a snare of the adversary, which he has laid to catch this people, that he might bring you into subjection unto him, that he might encircle you about with his chains, that he might chain you down to **everlasting destruction**, according to the power of his captivity.

> **KJV (1NT/9)** <u>2 Thessalonians 1:9</u> Who shall be punished with **everlasting destruction** from the presence of the Lord, and from the glory of his power;)

And now 1 Timothy 18 times

BOM <u>2 Nephi 9:21</u> And he **cometh into the world** that he may **save all men** if they will **hearken unto his voice**; for behold, he suffereth the pains of all men, yea, the pains of **every living creature**, both men, women, and children, who belong to the family of Adam.

> **KJV (1NT/1)** 1 Timothy 2:4 Who will have **all men** to be **saved**, and to come unto the knowledge of the truth.)
>
> **KJV (2NT/1)** John 1:9 That was the true Light, which lighteth every man that **cometh into the world**.)
>
> **KJV** (1/3) Deuteronomy 26:17 Thou hast avouched the LORD this day to be thy God, and to walk in his ways, and to keep his statutes, and his commandments, and his judgments, and to **hearken unto his voice**:)
>
> **KJV** (7/1) Genesis 1:21 And God created great whales, and **every living creature** that moveth, which the waters brought forth abundantly, after their kind, and **every** winged fowl after his kind: and God saw that it was good.)

BOM 2 Nephi 28:12 Because of pride, and because of **false teachers**, and false doctrine, their churches have become corrupted, and their churches are **lifted up**; because of **pride** they **are puffed up.**

> **KJV** (1 Timothy 3:6 Not a novice, lest being **lifted up** with **pride** he fall into the condemnation of the devil.)
>
> **KJV (1NT/1)** 2 Peter 2:1 But there were **false** prophets also among the people, even as there shall be **false teachers** among you, who privily shall bring in damnable heresies, even denying the Lord that bought them, and bring upon themselves swift destruction.)
>
> **KJV (6NT/9)** 1 Corinthians 4:18 Now some **are puffed up**, as though I would not come to you.)

BOM Jacob 1:16 Yea, and they also began to search much gold and silver, and began to be **lifted up** somewhat in **pride**.

> **KJV (1NT/1)** 1 Timothy 3:6 Not a novice, lest being **lifted up** with **pride** he fall into the condemnation of the devil.)

BOM Mosiah 2:27 Therefore, as I said unto you that I had served you, walking with a clear conscience before God, even so I at this time have caused that ye should assemble yourselves together, that I might be **found blameless**, and that your blood should not come upon me, when I shall stand to be judged of God of the things whereof he hath commanded me concerning you.

> **KJV (1NT/2)** 1 Timothy 3:10 And let these also first be proved; then let them use the office of a deacon, being **found blameless**.)

BOM Mosiah 12:30 **Know ye not that I speak the truth**? Yea, ye know that **I speak the truth**; and you ought to tremble before God.

> **KJV (1NT/2)** 1 Timothy 2:7 Whereunto I am ordained a preacher, and an apostle, (**I speak the truth** in Christ, and lie not;) a teacher of the Gentiles in faith and verity.)
>
> **KJV** (17/11) 2 Samuel 3:38 And the king said unto his servants,

Know ye not that there is a prince and a great man fallen this day in Israel?)

And now 2 Timothy 30 times

BOM 1 Nephi 2:19 And it came to pass that the Lord spake unto me, saying: Blessed art thou, Nephi, because of thy faith, for thou hast **sought me diligently**, with lowliness of heart.

> **KJV (1NT/1)** 2 Timothy 1:17 But, when he was in Rome, he **sought me** out very **diligently**, and found me.)

BOM 2 Nephi 25:28 And now behold, my people, ye are a stiffnecked people; wherefore, I have spoken plainly unto you, that ye cannot (1) misunderstand. (13th Century) And the words which I have spoken shall stand as **a testimony against** you; for they are sufficient to teach any man the right way; for the right way is to believe in Christ and **deny him** not; for by denying him ye **also deny** the prophets and the law.

> **KJV (1NT/1)** 2 Timothy 2:12 If we suffer, we shall also reign with him: if we **deny him**, he **also** will **deny** us:)

> **KJV (4NT/5)** Luke 9:5 And whosoever will not receive you, when ye go out of that city, shake off the very dust from your feet for **a testimony against** them.)

BOM Jarom 1:11 Wherefore, the prophets, and the priests, and the teachers, did labor diligently, **exhort**ing **with all long-suffering** the people to diligence; teaching the law of Moses, and the intent for which it was given; persuading them to look forward unto the Messiah, and believe in him to come as though he already was. And after this manner did they teach them.

> **KJV (1NT/1)** 2 Timothy 4:2 Preach the word; be instant in season, out of season; reprove, rebuke, **exhort with all long suffering** and doctrine.)

BOM Mosiah 3:4 For the Lord hath heard thy prayers, and hath judged of thy righteousness, and hath sent me to declare unto thee that thou mayest rejoice; and that thou mayest declare unto thy people, **that** they **may** also **be filled with joy**.

> **KJV (1NT/1)** 2 Timothy 1:4 Greatly desiring to see thee, being mindful of thy tears, **that I may** be **filled with joy**;)

And now Titus 7 times

BOM Alma 5:16 I say unto you, can you imagine to yourselves that ye hear the voice of the Lord, saying unto you, in that day: Come unto me ye blessed, for behold, your works have been the **works of righteousness** upon the face of the earth?

> **KJV (1NT/3)** Titus 3:5 Not by **works of righteousness** which we have done, but according to his mercy he saved us, by the washing of regeneration, and renewing of the Holy Ghost;)

BOM Alma 24:7 **Now, these are the words** which he said unto the people concerning the matter: **I thank my God**, my beloved people, that **our great God** has in goodness sent these our brethren, the Nephites, unto us to preach unto us, and to convince us **of the traditions of our wicked fathers**.

> **KJV (1NT/2)** Titus 2:13 while we wait for the blessed hope—the glorious appearing of **our great God** and Savior, Jesus Christ,)
>
> **KJV (1/8)** Jeremiah 29:1 **Now these are the words** of the letter that Jeremiah the prophet sent from Jerusalem unto the residue of the elders which were carried away captives, and to the priests, and to the prophets, and to all the people whom Nebuchadnezzar had carried away captive from Jerusalem to Babylon;)
>
> **KJV (5NT/3)** Romans 1:8 [*Paul's Longing to Visit Rome*] First, **I thank my God** through Jesus Christ for all of you, because your faith is being reported all over the world.)
>
> **KJV (1NT/20)** Galatians 1:14 And profited in the Jews' religion above many my equals in mine own nation, being more exceedingly zealous **of the traditions of** my **fathers**.)

And now Philemon 4 times

BOM 1 Nephi 10:1 And now I, Nephi, proceed to give an account upon these plates of my (10) proceedings (14ᵗʰ Century), and my reign and ministry; wherefore, to proceed with **mine account**, I must speak somewhat of the things of my father, and also of my brethren.

> **KJV (1NT/3)** Philemon 1:18 If he hath wronged thee, or oweth thee ought, put that on **mine account**;)

BOM Helaman 3:35 Nevertheless they did fast and pray oft, and did wax stronger and stronger in their humility, and firmer and firmer in the faith of Christ, unto the filling their souls with **joy and consolation**, yea, even to the purifying and the sanctification of their hearts, which sanctification cometh because of their yielding their hearts unto God.

> **KJV (1NT/1)** Philemon 1:7 For we have great **joy and consolation** in thy love, because the bowels of the saints are refreshed by thee, brother.)

And now Hebrews 90 times

BOM 1 Nephi 5:5 But behold, I have obtained a **land of promise**, in the which things I do rejoice; yea, and I know that the Lord will deliver my sons out of the hands of Laban, and bring them down again unto us in the wilderness.

> **KJV (1NT/22)** Hebrews 11:9 By faith he sojourned in the **land of promise**, as in a strange country, dwelling in tabernacles with Isaac and Jacob, the heirs with him of the same **promise**:)

BOM 1 Nephi 10:17 And it came to pass after I, Nephi, having heard all the words of my father, concerning the things which he saw in a vision, and also the things which he spake by the power of the **Holy Ghost**, which power he received by faith on the Son of God -- and the Son of God was the Messiah who should come -- I, Nephi, was desirous also that I might see, and hear, and know of these things, by the power of the **Holy Ghost** which is the gift of God unto all those who **diligently seek him**, as well in **times of old** as in the time that he should manifest himself unto the children of men.

> **KJV** (Hebrews 11:6 But without faith it is impossible to please him: for he that cometh to God must believe that he is, and that he is a rewarder of them that **diligently seek him**.)

> **KJV** (1/5) Psalm 44:1 We have heard with our ears, O God, our fathers have told us, what work thou didst in their days, in the **times of old**.)

BOM 1 Nephi 10:18 For he is **the same yesterday, to-day, and forever**; and the way is **prepared for** all men **from the foundation of the world**, if it so be that they repent and come unto him.

> **KJV** (**1NT/6**) Hebrews 13:8 Jesus Christ **the same yesterday**, and **to day, and for ever**.)

> **KJV** (**1NT/14**) Matthew 25:34 Then shall the King say unto them on his right hand, Come, ye blessed of my Father, inherit the kingdom **prepared for you from the foundation of the world**.)

BOM 2 Nephi 1:25 And **I exceedingly fear and** tremble because of you, lest he shall suffer again; for behold, ye have accused him that he sought **power and authority over** you; but I know that he hath not sought for power nor authority over you, but he hath sought the glory of God, and your own eternal welfare.

> **KJV** (**1NT/1**) Hebrews 12:21 And so terrible was the sight, that Moses said, **I exceedingly fear and** quake:)

> **KJV** (**2NT/5**) Luke 9:1 Then he called his twelve disciples together, and gave them **power and authority over** all devils, and to cure diseases.)

BOM 2 Nephi 2:4 And thou hast beheld in thy youth his glory; wherefore, thou art blessed even as they unto whom he shall minister in the flesh; for the Spirit is **the same, yesterday, today, and forever**.

> **KJV** (**1NT/6**) Hebrews 13:8 Jesus Christ **the same yesterday**, and **to day, and for ever**.)

BOM 2 Nephi 3:13 And **out of weakness** he shall be **made strong,** in that day when my work shall (17) commence (1340 AD) among all my people, unto the (5) restoring (14th Century) thee, O house of Israel, saith the Lord.

> **KJV** (**1NT/4**) Hebrews 11:34 Quenched the violence of fire, escaped the edge of the sword, **out of weakness** were **made strong**, waxed valiant in fight, turned to flight the armies of the aliens.)

BOM 2 Nephi 3:21 Because of their faith their words shall proceed forth out of my mouth unto their brethren who are **the fruit of thy loins**; and the

weakness of their words will I make **strong** in their faith, unto the remembering of my covenant which I made unto thy fathers.

> KJV (**1NT/4**) <u>Hebrews 11:34</u> Quenched the violence of fire, escaped the edge of the sword, out of **weakness** were made **strong**, waxed valiant in fight, turned to flight the armies of the aliens.)
>
> KJV (**1NT/13**) <u>Acts 2:30</u> Therefore being a prophet, and knowing that God had sworn with an oath to him, that of **the fruit of** his **loins**, according to the flesh, he would raise up Christ to sit on his throne;)

BOM <u>2 Nephi 4:18</u> I am (3) en**compassed** (14th Century) **about**, because of the temptations **and the sins which do so easily beset** me.

> KJV (1/1) <u>Hebrews 12:1</u> Wherefore seeing we also are **compassed about** with so great a cloud of witnesses, let us lay aside every weight, **and the sin which doth so easily beset us**, and let us run with patience the race that is set before us,)

BOM <u>2 Nephi 9:18</u> But, behold, the righteous, the saints of the Holy One of Israel, they who have believed in the Holy One of Israel, they who have **endured the cross**es of the world, and **despised the shame** of it, they **shall inherit the kingdom of God**, which was **prepared for** them **from the foundation of the world**, and their **joy shall be full** forever.

> KJV (**1NT/1**) <u>Hebrews 12:2</u> Looking unto Jesus the author and finisher of our faith; who for the joy that was set before him **endured the cross, despising the shame**, and is set down at the right hand of the throne of God.)
>
> KJV (**1NT/2**) <u>1 Corinthians 6:10</u> Nor thieves, nor covetous, nor drunkards, nor revilers, nor extortioners, **shall inherit the kingdom of God**.)
>
> KJV (**1/NT/14**) <u>Matthew 25:34</u> Then shall the King say unto them on his right hand, Come, ye blessed of my Father, inherit the kingdom **prepared for** you **from the foundation of the world**.)
>
> KJV (**1NT/2**) <u>John 16:24</u> Hitherto have ye asked nothing in my name: ask, and ye **shall** receive, that your **joy** may **be full**.)

BOM <u>2 Nephi 25:8</u> Wherefore, they are of worth unto the children of men, and he that (7) supposeth that they are not, unto them will I **speak particularly**, and (1) confine (1400 AD) the words unto mine own people; for I know that they shall be of great worth unto them in the last days; for in that day shall they understand them; wherefore, for their good have I written them.

> KJV (**1NT/1**) <u>Hebrews 9:5</u> And over it the cherubims of glory shadowing the mercyseat; of which we cannot now **speak particularly**.)

BOM <u>2 Nephi 33:4</u> And I know that the Lord God will consecrate my prayers for the gain of my people. And the words which I have written in **weakness** will be **made strong** unto them; for it persuadeth them to do good; it maketh known unto them of their fathers; and it speaketh of Jesus, and persuadeth them to believe in him, and to **endure to the end**, which is **life eternal**.

> **KJV (1NT/4)** <u>Hebrews 11:34</u> Quenched the violence of fire, escaped the edge of the sword, out of **weakness** were **made strong**, waxed valiant in fight, turned to flight the armies of the aliens.)
>
> **KJV (1NT/8)** <u>Matthew 10:22</u> And ye shall be hated of all men for my name's sake: but he that **endure**th **to the end** shall be saved.)
>
> **KJV (***Note: The similarity between the meaning of these two verses:*** <u>John 5:39</u> Search the scriptures; for in them ye think ye have **eternal life**: and they are they which testify of me.)

BOM <u>Jacob 1:7</u> Wherefore we labored diligently among our people, that we might persuade them to come unto Christ, and partake of **the goodness of God**, that they might **enter into his rest, lest by any means** he should swear in his wrath they should not enter in, as **in the provocation in the days of temptation** while the children of Israel were **in the wilderness**.

> **KJV (1NT/3)** <u>Hebrews 3:18</u> And to whom sware he that they should not **enter into his rest**, but to them that believed not?)
>
> **KJV (1NT/1)** <u>Hebrews 3:8</u> Harden not your hearts, **as in the provocation, in the day of temptation in the wilderness:**)
>
> **KJV (2/5)** <u>Psalm 52:1</u> Why boastest thou thyself in mischief, O mighty man? **the goodness of God** endureth continually.)
>
> **KJV (3NT/7)** <u>1 Corinthians 8:9</u> But take heed **lest by any means** this liberty of yours become a stumblingblock to them that are weak.)

BOM <u>Jacob 6:6</u> Yea, **today, if ye will hear his voice, harden not your hearts; for why will ye die**?

> **KJV (2NT/1)** <u>Hebrews 3:15</u> While it is said, **To day if ye will hear his voice, harden not your hearts**, as in the provocation.)
>
> **KJV (2/1)** <u>Ezekiel 18:31</u> Cast away from you all your transgressions, whereby ye have transgressed; and make you a new heart and a new spirit: **for why will ye die**, O house of Israel?)

BOM <u>Jacob 6:7</u> For behold, after ye have been nourished by **the good word of God all the day long**, will ye **bring forth evil fruit**, that ye must be **hewn down and cast into the fire**?

> **KJV (1NT/2)** <u>Hebrews 6:5</u> And have tasted **the good word of God**, and the powers of the world to come,)
>
> **KJV (13/12)** <u>Psalm 35:28</u> And my tongue shall speak of thy righteousness and of thy praise **all the day long**.)
>
> **KJV (1NT/3)** <u>Matthew 7:18</u> A good tree cannot **bring forth evil fruit**, neither can a corrupt tree bring forth good fruit.)
>
> **KJV (2NT/13)** <u>Matthew 7:19</u> Every **tree** that **bring**eth not **forth** good fruit is **hewn down, and cast into the fire**.)

BOM <u>Mosiah 4:9</u> Believe in God; **believe that he is, and that he** created all things, both in heaven and in earth; believe that he has all wisdom, and all power, both in heaven and in earth; believe that man doth not comprehend all the things which the Lord can comprehend.

> KJV (1NT/1) Hebrews 11:6 But without faith it is impossible to please him: for he that cometh to God must **believe that he is, and that he** is a rewarder of them that diligently seek him.)

BOM Mosiah 5:13 For how knoweth a man the master whom he has not served, and who is a stranger unto him, and is far from **the thoughts and intents of** his **heart**?

> KJV (1NT/3) Hebrews 4:12 For the word of God is quick, and powerful, and sharper than any twoedged sword, piercing even to the dividing asunder of soul and spirit, and of the joints and marrow, and is a discerner of **the thoughts and intents of** the **heart**.)

BOM Mosiah 7:10 And now, I desire to know the cause whereby ye were so bold as to come near the walls of the city, when I, myself, was with my (30) guards (15th Century) **without the gate**?

> KJV (1NT/2) Hebrews 13:12 Wherefore Jesus also, that he might sanctify the people with his own blood, suffered **without the gate**.)

BOM Mosiah 13:28 And moreover, I say unto you, that salvation doth not come by the law alone; and were it not for the atonement, which God himself shall make for the **sins and iniquities** of his people, that they must (6) unavoidably (1577) perish, notwithstanding the law of Moses.

> KJV (1NT/9) Hebrews 10:17 And their **sins and iniquities** will I remember no more.)

BOM Mosiah 15:8 And thus God breaketh the bands of death, having gained the victory over death; giving the Son power to **make intercession for** the children of men --

> KJV (1NT/2) Hebrews 7:25 Wherefore he is able also to save them to the uttermost that come unto God by him, seeing he ever liveth to **make intercession for** them.)

BOM Mosiah 17:14 Therefore, if ye teach the law of Moses, also teach that it is **a shadow of** those **things** which are **to come** –

> KJV (1NT/1) Hebrews 10:1 For the law having a **shadow of** good **things to come**, and not the very image of the things, can never with those sacrifices which they offered year by year continually make the comers thereunto perfect.)

BOM Mosiah 27:15 And now behold, can ye dispute **the power of God**? For behold, doth not my **voice shake the earth**? And can ye not also behold me before you? And I am sent from God.

> KJV (1NT/1) Hebrews 12:26 Whose **voice** then shook **the earth**: but now he hath promised, saying, Yet once more I **shake** not the **earth** only, but also heaven.)

KJV (11NT/48) <u>Matthew 22:29</u> Jesus answered and said unto them, Ye do err, not knowing the scriptures, nor **the power of God**.)

BOM <u>Alma 7:15</u> Yea, I say unto you come and fear not, and **lay aside every sin, which easily doth beset you**, which doth bind you **down to destruction**, yea, come and go forth, and show unto your God that ye are willing to repent of your sins and enter into a covenant with him to keep his commandments, and witness it unto him this day by going into the waters of baptism.

> **KJV (1NT/1)** <u>Hebrews 12:1</u> Wherefore seeing we also are compassed about with so great a cloud of witnesses, let us **lay aside every** weight, and the **sin which doth** so **easily beset** us, and let us run with patience the race that is set before us,)

> **KJV (1/3)** <u>Psalm 73:18</u> Surely thou didst set them in slippery places: thou castedst them **down into destruction**.)

BOM <u>Alma 12:27</u> But behold, it was not so; but **it** was **appointed unto men** that they must **die**; and **after** death, they must come to **judgment**, even that same judgment of which we have spoken, which is the end.

> **KJV (1NT/1)** <u>Hebrews 9:27</u> And as **it** is **appointed unto men** once to **die**, but **after** this the **judgment**;)

BOM <u>Alma 12:35</u> And whosoever will **harden** his **heart** and will do iniquity, behold, **I swear in my wrath** that he **shall not enter into my rest**.

> **KJV (1NT/1)** <u>Hebrews 3:11</u> So **I sware in my wrath**, They **shall not enter into my rest**.)

BOM <u>Alma 12:36</u> **And now**, my **brethren**, behold I say unto you, that if ye will **harden your hearts** ye shall not enter into the rest of the Lord; therefore your iniquity provoketh him that he sendeth down his wrath upon you as in the first **provocation**, yea, according to his word in the last **provocation** as well as the first, to the **everlasting destruction** of your souls; therefore, according to his word, unto the last death, as well as the first.

> **KJV (1NT/1)** <u>Hebrews 3:8</u> **Harden** not **your hearts**, as in the **provocation**, in the day of temptation in the wilderness:)

> **KJV (3NT/19)** <u>Acts 3:17</u> **And now, brethren**, I wot that through ignorance ye did it, as did also your)

> **KJV (1NT/9)** <u>2 Thessalonians 1:9</u> Who shall be punished with **everlasting destruction** from the presence of the Lord, and from the glory of his power;)

BOM <u>Alma 13:7</u> This high priesthood being after the order of his Son, which order was **from the foundation of the world**; or in other words, being without **beginning of days or end of** years, being prepared from eternity to all eternity, **according to** his **foreknowledge** of all things —

> **KJV (1NT/2)** <u>Hebrews 7:3</u> Without father, without mother, without descent, having neither **beginning of days**, nor **end of** life; but made like unto the Son of God; abideth a priest continually.)

KJV (6NT/22) <u>Matthew 13:35</u> That it might be fulfilled which was spoken by the prophet, saying, I will open my mouth in parables; I will utter things which have been kept secret **from the foundation of the world**.)

KJV (1NT/1) <u>1 Peter 1:2</u> Elect **according to** the **foreknowledge** of God the Father, through sanctification of the Spirit, unto obedience and sprinkling of the blood of Jesus Christ: Grace unto you, and peace, be multiplied.)

BOM <u>Alma 13:9</u> Thus they become **high priests forever, after the order of** the Son, **the Only Begotten of the Father**, who is without **beginning of days or end of** years, who is **full of grace**, equity, **and truth**. And thus it is. Amen.

KJV (2NT/1) <u>Hebrews 5:10</u> Called of God an **high priest after the order of** Melchisedec.)

KJV (1NT/2) <u>Hebrews 7:3</u> Without father, without mother, without descent, having neither **beginning of days**, n**or end of** life; but made like unto the Son of God; abideth a priest continually.)

KJV (1NT/4) <u>John 1:14</u> And the Word was made flesh, and dwelt among us, (and we beheld his glory, the glory as of **the only begotten of the Father**,) **full of grace and truth**.)

BOM <u>Alma 13:15</u> And it was this same Melchizedek to whom Abraham paid tithes; yea, even our father Abraham paid tithes of one-**tenth part of all** he possessed.

KJV (<u>Genesis 14:20</u> And blessed be the most high God, which hath delivered thine enemies into thy hand. And he gave him tithes of all.)

KJV (1NT/1) <u>Hebrews 7:2</u> To whom also Abraham gave a **tenth part of all**; first being by interpretation King of righteousness, and after that also King of Salem, which is, King of peace;)

BOM <u>Alma 13:18</u> But **Melchizedek** having exercised mighty faith, and received the office of the high priesthood according to the holy order of God, did preach repentance unto his people. And behold, they did repent; and **Melchizedek** did establish peace in the land in his days; therefore he was **called the prince of peace**, for he was the **king of Salem**; and he did reign under his father.

KJV (1NT/1) <u>Hebrews 7:1</u> For this Melchisedec, **king of Salem**, priest of the most high God, who met Abraham returning from the slaughter of the kings, and blessed him;)

KJV (1NT/1) <u>Hebrews 7:2</u> To whom also Abraham gave a tenth part of all; first being by interpretation King of righteousness, and after that also **King of Salem**, which is, **King of peace**;)

KJV (1/1) <u>Genesis 14:18</u> And **Melchizedek king of Salem** brought forth bread and wine: and he was the priest of the most high God.)

KJV (1/1) <u>Isaiah 9:6</u> For unto us a child is born, unto us a son is given: and the government shall be upon his shoulder: and his name shall be **called** Wonderful, Counsellor, The mighty God, The everlasting Father, **The Prince of Peace**.)

BOM <u>Alma 18:32</u> And Ammon said: Yea, and he looketh down upon all the children of men; and he knows all **the thoughts and intents of the heart**; for by his hand were they all created from the beginning.

> **KJV (1NT/3)** <u>Hebrews 4:12</u> For the word of God is quick, and powerful, and sharper than any twoedged sword, piercing even to the dividing asunder of soul and spirit, and of the joints and marrow, and is a discerner of **the thoughts and intents of the heart**.)

BOM <u>Alma 24:30</u> And thus we can plainly discern, that after a people have been **once enlightened** by the Spirit of God, and have had great knowledge, of **things pertaining to** righteousness, and then have fallen away into sin and transgression, they become more hardened, and thus their state becomes worse than though they had never known these things.

> **KJV (1NT/2)** <u>Hebrews 6:4</u> For it is impossible for those who were **once enlightened**, and have tasted of the heavenly gift, and were made partakers of the Holy Ghost,)

> **KJV (4NT/9)** <u>Acts 1:3</u> To whom also he shewed himself alive after his passion by many infallible proofs, being seen of them forty days, and speaking of the **things pertaining to** the kingdom of God)

BOM <u>Alma 32:21</u> And now as I said concerning faith -- faith is not to have a **perfect knowledge** of things; therefore if ye have **faith** ye **hope for things** which are **not seen**, which are true.

> **KJV (1NT/1)** <u>Hebrews 11:1</u> Now faith is the substance of **things hoped for**, the evidence of **things not seen**.)

> **KJV (1NT/14)** <u>Acts 24:22</u> And when Felix heard these things, having more **perfect knowledge** of that way, he deferred them, and said, When Lysias the chief captain shall come down, I will know the uttermost of your matter.)

BOM <u>Alma 40:14</u> Now this is the state of the souls of the wicked, yea, in darkness, and a state of (47) awful (13th Century, **fearful looking for** the **fiery indignation** of the wrath of God upon them; thus they remain in this state, as well as the righteous **in paradise**, until the time of their resurrection.

> **KJV (1NT/1)** <u>Hebrews 10:27</u> But a certain **fearful looking for** of judgment and **fiery indignation**, which shall devour the adversaries.)

> **KJV (3NT/5)** <u>Luke 23:43</u> And Jesus said unto him, Verily I say unto thee, Today shalt thou be with me in **paradise**.)

BOM <u>Helaman 3:29</u> Yea, we see that whosoever will may lay hold upon the word of God, which **is quick and powerful**, which shall **divide asunder** all the cunning and the snares and **the wiles of the devil**, and lead the man of Christ in a strait and narrow course across that everlasting gulf of misery which is prepared to engulf the wicked –

> **KJV (1NT/1)** <u>Hebrews 4:12</u> For **the word of God is quick, and powerful**, and sharper than any twoedged sword, piercing even to the **divid**ing **asunder** of soul and spirit, and of the joints and marrow, and is a discerner of the thoughts and intents of the heart.)
>
> **KJV (1NT/1)** <u>Ephesians 6:11</u> Put on the whole armour of God, that ye may be able to stand against **the wiles of the devil**.)

BOM <u>Helaman 12:8</u> For behold, the dust of the earth moveth **hither and thither, to the dividing asunder**, at the command of our great and everlasting God.

> **KJV (1NT/1)** <u>Hebrews 4:12</u> For the word of God is quick, and powerful, and sharper than any twoedged sword, piercing even **to the dividing asunder** of soul and spirit, and of the joints and marrow, and is a discerner of the thoughts and intents of the heart.)
>
> **KJV (2/5)** <u>2 Kings 2:8</u> And Elijah took his mantle, and wrapped it together, and smote the waters, and they were divided **hither and thither**, so that they two went over on dry ground.)

BOM <u>Alma 15:3</u> Yea, wo unto this people who are called the people of Nephi except they shall repent, when they shall see all these signs and wonders which shall be showed unto them; for behold, they have been a chosen people of the Lord; yea, the people of Nephi hath he **loved**, and also hath **he chasten**ed them; yea, in the days of their iniquities hath he **chasten**ed them because **he loveth** them.

> **KJV (1NT/1)** <u>Hebrews 12:6</u> For whom the Lord **loveth he chasten**eth, and scourgeth every son whom he receiveth)

BOM <u>3 Nephi 18:28</u> And now behold, this is the commandment which I give unto you, that ye shall not suffer any one knowingly to **partake of** my **flesh and blood** unworthily, when ye shall minister it;

> **KJV (1NT/1)** <u>Hebrews 2:14</u> Forasmuch then as the children are **partaker**s **of flesh and blood**, he also himself likewise took part of the same; that through death he might destroy him that had the power of death, that is, the devil;)

BOM <u>4 Nephi 1:3</u> And they **had all things common** among them; therefore there were not **rich and poor, bond and free**, but they were all made free, and **partakers of the heavenly gift**.

> **KJV (1NT/2)** <u>Hebrews 6:4</u> For it is impossible for those who were once enlightened, and have tasted **of the heavenly gift**, and were made **partakers** of the Holy Ghost,)
>
> **KJV (1NT/1)** <u>Revelation 13:16</u> And he causeth all, both small and great, **rich and poor, free and bond**, to receive a mark in their right hand, or in their foreheads:)
>
> **KJV (2NT/2)** <u>Acts 2:44</u> And all that believed were together, and **had**

all things common;)

BOM Ether 12:4 Wherefore, whoso believeth in God might with surety hope for a better world, yea, even a place **at the right hand of God**, which hope cometh of faith, maketh **an anchor** to **the souls** of men, which would make them sure and steadfast, **always abounding in** good works, being led to glorify God.

> **KJV (1NT/1)** Hebrews 6:19 **Which hope** we have as **an anchor** of **the soul**, both sure and stedfast, and which entereth into that within the veil;)

> **KJV (1NT/4)** Romans 8:34 Who is he that condemneth? It is Christ that died, yea rather, that is risen again, who is even **at the right hand of God**, who also maketh intercession for us.)

> **KJV (1NT/1)** 1 Corinthians 15:58 Therefore, my beloved brethren, be ye stedfast, unmoveable, **always abounding in** the work of the Lord, forasmuch as ye know that your labour is not in vain in the Lord.)

BOM Ether 12:6 And now, I, Moroni, would speak somewhat concerning these things; I would show unto the world that **faith is things** which are **hoped for** and **not seen**; wherefore, dispute not because ye see not, for ye receive no witness until after **the trial of your faith**.

> **KJV (1NT/1)** Hebrews 11:1 Now **faith is** the substance of **things hoped for**, the evidence of things **not seen**.)

> **KJV (1NT/1)** 1 Peter 1:7 That **the trial of your faith**, being much more precious than of gold that perisheth, though it be tried with fire, might be found unto praise and honour and glory at the appearing of Jesus Christ:)

BOM Ether 12:8 But because of the faith of men he has (29) shown (12th Century) himself unto the world, and glorified the name of the Father, and prepared a way that thereby others might be **partakers of the heavenly gift**, that they might **hope for** those **things** which they have **not seen**.

> **KJV (1NT/2)** Hebrews 6:4 For it is impossible for those who were once enlightened, and have tasted **of the heavenly gift**, and were made **partakers of** the Holy Ghost,)

> **KJV (1NT/1)** Hebrews 11:1 Now faith is the substance of **things hoped for**, the evidence of **things not seen**.)

BOM Moroni 6:4 And after they had been received unto baptism, and were wrought upon and cleansed by the power of the **Holy Ghost**, they were numbered among the people of **the church of Christ**; and their names were taken, that they might be remembered and nourished by **the good word of God**, to keep them in the right way, to keep them continually watchful unto prayer, (5) relying (1574) alone upon the (5) merits (15th Century) of Christ, who was **the author and the finisher of** their **faith**.

KJV (1NT/1) Hebrews 12:2 Looking unto Jesus **the author and finisher of** our **faith**; who for the joy that was set before him endured the cross, despising the shame, and is set down at the right hand of the throne of God.)

KJV (1NT/2) Hebrews 6:5 And have tasted **the good word of God**, and the powers of the world to come,)

KJV (1NT/24) Romans 15:13 Now the God of hope fill you with all joy and peace in believing, that ye may abound in hope, through **the power of the Holy Ghost.**)

KJV (1NT/4) Romans 16:16 Salute one another with an holy kiss. **The churches of Christ** salute you.)

BOM Moroni 7:27 Wherefore, my beloved brethren, have miracles ceased because Christ hath ascended into heaven, and hath **sat down on the right hand of God,** to (15) claim (14th Century) of the Father his rights of mercy which he hath upon the children of men?

KJV (1NT/1) Hebrews 10:12 But this man, after he had offered one sacrifice for sins for ever, **sat down on the right hand of God**;)

BOM Moroni 10:33 And again, if ye **by the grace of God** are perfect in Christ, and deny not his power, then **are** ye **sanctified in Christ by the grace of God**, through the shedding of **the blood of Christ**, which is in the covenant of the Father unto the remission of your sins, that ye become holy, **without spot**.

KJV (1NT/1) Hebrews 9:14 How much more shall **the blood of Christ**, who through the eternal Spirit offered himself **without spot** to God, purge your conscience from dead works to serve the living God?)

KJV (3NT/5) 1 Corinthians 15:10 But **by the grace of God** I am what I am: and his grace which was bestowed upon me was not in vain; but I laboured more abundantly than they all: yet not I, but the grace of God which was with me.)

KJV (1NT/1) 1 Corinthians 1:2 Unto the church of God which is at Corinth, to them that **are sanctified in Christ** Jesus, called to be saints, with all that in every place call upon the name of Jesus Christ our Lord, both their's and our's:)

KJV (3NT/5) 1 Corinthians 15:10 But **by the grace of God** I am what I am: and his grace which was bestowed upon me was not in vain; but I laboured more abundantly than they all: yet not I, but the grace of God which was with me.)

And now James 26 times

BOM 2 Nephi 4:35 Yea, **I know that God will give liberally to him that asketh.** Yea, my God will give me, if I **ask** not **amiss**; therefore I will lift up my voice unto thee; yea, I will cry unto thee, my God, the rock of my righteousness. Behold, my voice shall forever ascend up unto thee, my rock and mine everlasting God. Amen.

> KJV (1NT/1) James 1:5 If any of you lack wisdom, **let him ask of God, that giveth to all men liberally**, and upbraideth not; and it shall be given him.)

> KJV (1NT/1) James 4:3 Ye ask, and receive not, because ye **ask amiss**, that ye may consume it upon your lusts.)

BOM 2 Nephi 9:30 But **wo unto** the **rich**, who are rich as to **the things of the world**. For because they are **rich** they **despise the poor**, and they persecute the meek, and their hearts are upon their treasures; wherefore, their treasure is their God. And behold, their treasure shall perish with them also.

> KJV (1NT/1) James 2:6 But ye have **despised the poor**. Do not **rich** men oppress you, and draw you before the judgment seats?)

> KJV (1NT/1) Luke 6:24 But **woe unto** you that are **rich**! for ye have received your consolation.)

> KJV (1NT/3) 1 Corinthians 7:34 There is difference also between a wife and a virgin. The unmarried woman careth for the things of the Lord, that she may be holy both in body and in spirit: but she that is married careth for **the things of the world**, how she may please her husband.)

BOM Jacob 4:5 Behold, they believed in Christ and worshiped the Father in his name, and also we **worship the Father** in his name. And for this intent we keep the law of Moses, it (4) pointing (14th Century) our souls to him; and for this cause it is sanctified unto us for righteousness, even as it was accounted unto Abraham in the wilderness to be obedient unto the commands of God in offering up his son Isaac, which is a **similitude of God** and **his Only Begotten Son**.

> KJV (1NT/1) James 3:9 Therewith bless we God, even the Father; and therewith curse we men, which are made after the **similitude of God**.)

> KJV (5NT/5) John 3:16 For God so loved the world, that he gave **his only begotten Son**, that whosoever believeth in him should not perish, but have everlasting life.)

> KJV (1NT/2) John 4:21 Jesus saith unto her, Woman, believe me, the hour cometh, when ye shall neither in this mountain, nor yet at Jerusalem, **worship the Father**.)

BOM Mosiah 6:14 And again, doth a man take an ass which belongeth to his neighbor, and keep him? I say unto you, Nay; he will not even suffer that he shall feed among his flocks, but will drive him away, and cast him out. I say unto you, that **even so shall it be** among you if ye know not the **name by which ye are called**.

> KJV (1NT/2) James 2:7 Do not they blaspheme that worthy **name by**

the which ye are called?)
KJV (**1NT/1**) Matthew 12:45 Then goeth he, and taketh with himself seven other spirits more wicked than himself, and they enter in and dwell there: and the last state of that man is worse than the first. **Even so shall it be** also unto this wicked generation.)

BOM Mosiah 8:11 And again, they have brought swords, the (4) hilts (uncertain origin) thereof have perished, and the blades thereof were **cankered** with **rust**; and there is no one in the land that is able to interpret the language or the engravings that are on the plates. Therefore I said unto thee: Canst thou translate?

KJV (**1NT/1**) James 5:3 Your gold and silver is **cankered**; and the **rust** of them shall be a witness against you, and shall eat your flesh as it were fire. Ye have heaped treasure together for the last days.)

BOM Alma 7:20 I perceive that it has been made known unto you, by the testimony of his word, that he cannot walk in **crooked paths**; neither doth he vary from that which he hath said; neither hath he a **shadow of turning** from the right to the left, or from that which is right to that which is wrong; therefore, his course is one eternal round.

KJV **Note**: Note the same meaning in "doth not vary" and this verse in James "with whom is no variableness": (**1NT/1**) James 1:17 Every good gift and every perfect gift is from above, and cometh down from the Father of lights, with whom is no variableness, neither **shadow of turning**.)

KJV (1/1) Isaiah 59:8 The way of peace they know not; and there is no judgment in their goings: they have made them **crooked paths**: whosoever goeth therein shall not know peace.)

BOM Alma 16:18 Now those priests who did go forth among the people did preach against all (9) lyings, and deceivings, and envyings, and strifes, and malice, and revilings, and stealing, robbing, (11) plundering (1632), murdering, committing adultery, and all manner of lasciviousness, crying that **these things ought not so to be** –

KJV (**1NT/1**) James 3:10 Out of the same mouth proceedeth blessing and cursing. My brethren, **these things ought not so to be**.)

BOM Alma 6:8 And it came to pass (452/1353) that the Lamanites did also go whithersoever they would, whether it were among the Lamanites or among the Nephites; and thus they did have free (1) intercourse (15th Century) **one with another**, to **buy and** to **sell, and** to **get gain,** according to their desire.

KJV (**1NT/1**) James 4:13 Go to now, ye that say, To day or to morrow we will go into such a city, and continue there a year, and **buy and sell, and get gain**:)

BOM Helaman 13:2 And in the days of your poverty ye shall **cry unto the Lord**; and in vain shall ye cry, for your desolation is already come upon you, and your destruction is made sure; and then shall ye **weep and howl** in that day, saith the Lord of Hosts. And then shall ye lament, and say:

> KJV (**1NT/2**) <u>James 5:1</u> Go to now, ye rich men, **weep and howl** for your miseries that shall come upon you.)
>
> KJV (**7/20**) <u>Psalm 107:19</u> Then they **cry unto the LORD** in their trouble, and the saveth hem out of their distresses.)

BOM <u>Mormon 9:9</u> For do we not read that God is **the same yesterday, today, and forever**, and in him there **is no variableness neither shadow of** changing?

> KJV **Note:** Joseph Smith says "do we not read" James for example was written on another continent they could not have read. (**1NT/1**) <u>James 1:17</u> Every good gift and every perfect gift is from above, and cometh down from the Father of lights, with whom **is no variableness, neither shadow of** turning.)
>
> KJV (**1NT/6**) <u>Hebrews 13:8</u> Jesus Christ **the same yesterday**, and **to day, and for ever**.)

BOM <u>Mormon 9:28</u> Be wise in the days of your probation; (15th Century) strip yourselves of **all uncleanness**; **ask** not, **that ye may consume it on your lusts**, but ask with a (9) firmness (14th Century) (4) unshaken, that ye will yield to no temptation, but that ye will serve the true and living God

> KJV (**1NT/1**) <u>James 4:3</u> Ye **ask**, and receive not, because ye **ask** amiss, **that ye may consume it** upon **your lusts**.)
>
> KJV (**3NT/2**) <u>Ephesians 5:3</u> But fornication, and **all uncleanness**, or covetousness, let it not be once named among you, as becometh saints;)

BOM <u>Moroni 10:8</u> And I would exhort you, my beloved brethren, that ye remember that **every good gift cometh** of Christ.

> KJV (**1NT/1**) <u>James 1:17</u> **Every good gift** and every perfect gift is from above, and **cometh** down from the Father of lights, with whom is no variableness, neither shadow of turning.)

And now 1 Peter 16 times

BOM <u>1 Nephi 19:24</u> Wherefore I spake unto them, saying: Hear ye the words of the prophet, ye who are a **remnant of the house of Israel**, a **branch** who have been **broken off**; hear ye the words of the prophet, which were written unto all the house of Israel, and liken them unto yourselves, that ye may have hope as well as your brethren from whom ye have been **broken off; for after this manner** has the prophet written.

> KJV (**1NT/4**) <u>1 Peter 3:5</u> **For after this manner** in the old time the holy women also, who trusted in God, adorned themselves, being in subjection unto their own husbands;)
>
> KJV (**1/9**) <u>Isaiah 46:3</u> Hearken unto me, O house of Jacob, and all the **remnant of the house of Israel**, which are borne by me from the

belly, which are carried from the womb:)

  KJV (1NT/1) <u>Romans 11:19</u> Thou wilt say then, The **branch**es were **broken off**, that I might be grafted in.)

BOM <u>1 Nephi 22:22</u> And the righteous need not fear, for they are those who **shall not be confounded.** But it is the kingdom of the devil, which shall be built up **among the children of men**, which kingdom is established among them which **are in the flesh** –

  KJV (1NT/1) <u>1 Peter 2:6</u> Wherefore also it is contained in the scripture, Behold, I lay in Sion a chief corner stone, elect, precious: and he that believeth on him **shall not be confounded.**)

  KJV (2/30) <u>Psalm 21:10</u> Their fruit shalt thou destroy from the earth, and their seed from **among the children of men.**)

  KJV (1NT/3) <u>Romans 8:8</u> So then they that **are in the flesh** cannot please God.)

BOM <u>Alma 13:3</u> And this is the manner after which they were ordained -- being called and **prepared from the foundation of the world according to the foreknowledge of God**, on account of their exceeding faith and good works; in the first place being left to choose good or evil; therefore they having chosen good, and exercising exceedingly great faith, are **called with a holy calling**, yea, with that **holy calling** which was prepared with, and according to, a (4) preparatory (15th Century) redemption for such.

  KJV (1NT/1) <u>1 Peter 1:2</u> Elect **according to the foreknowledge of God** the Father, through sanctification of the Spirit, unto obedience and sprinkling of the blood of Jesus Christ: Grace unto you, and peace, be multiplied.)

  KJV (1/NT/14) <u>Matthew 25:34</u> Then shall the King say unto them on his right hand, Come, ye blessed of my Father, inherit the kingdom **prepared** for you **from the foundation of the world.)**

  KJV (1NT/6) <u>2 Timothy 1:9</u> Who hath saved us, and **called** us with an **holy calling**, not according to our works, but according to his own purpose and grace, which was given us in Christ Jesus before the world began,)

BOM <u>Alma 16:14</u> And as many as would hear their words, unto them they did impart the word of God, **without** any **respect of persons**, continually.

  KJV (1NT/1) <u>1 Peter 1:17</u> And if ye call on the Father, who **without respect of persons** judgeth according to every man's work, pass the time of your sojourning here in fear:)

BOM <u>Alma 18:41</u> And he began to cry unto the Lord, saying: O Lord, have mercy; **according to** thy **abundant mercy** which thou hast had upon the people of Nephi, have upon me, and my people.

  KJV (1NT/1) <u>1 Peter 1:3</u> Blessed be the God and Father of our Lord Jesus Christ, which **according to** his **abundant mercy** hath begotten us again unto a lively hope by the resurrection of Jesus Christ from the dead,)

BOM 3 Nephi 6:13 Some were **lifted up** in **pride**, and others were (*1*) *exceedingly humble;* some did return **railing for railing**, while others would receive **railing** and persecution and all manner of afflictions, and would not turn and revile again, but were humble and penitent before God.

> **KJV (1NT/1)** 1 Peter 3:9 Not rendering evil for evil, or **railing for railing**: but contrariwise blessing; knowing that ye are thereunto called, that ye should inherit a blessing.)

> **KJV (1NT/4)** 1 Timothy 3:6 Not a novice, lest being **lifted up** with **pride** he fall into the condemnation of the devil.)

BOM 3 Nephi 7:21 And it came to pass that the thirty and first year did pass away, and there **were but few** who were converted unto the Lord; but as many as were converted **did** truly **signify** unto the people that they had been visited by the power and Spirit of God, which was in Jesus Christ, in whom they believed.

> **KJV (1NT/1)** 1 Peter 1:11 Searching what, or what manner of time the Spirit of Christ which was in them **did signify**, when it testified beforehand the sufferings of Christ, and the glory that should follow.)

> **KJV (1/4)** 1 Chronicles 16:19 When ye **were but few**, even a few, and strangers in it.)

BOM 3 Nephi 21:27 Yea, the work shall (17) commence (1340 AD) among all the dispersed of my people, with the Father to prepare the way whereby they may come unto me, that they may **call on the Father** in my name.

> **KJV (1NT/2)** 1 Peter 1:17 And if ye **call on the Father**, who without respect of persons judgeth according to every man's work, pass the time of your sojourning here in fear:)

BOM Ether 12:6 And now, I, Moroni, would speak somewhat concerning these things; I would show unto the world that **faith is things** which are **hoped for** and **not seen**; wherefore, dispute not because ye see not, for ye receive no witness until after **the trial of your faith**.

> **KJV (1NT/1)** 1 Peter 1:7 That **the trial of your faith**, being much more precious than of gold that perisheth, though it be tried with fire, might be found unto praise and honour and glory at the appearing of Jesus Christ:)

> **KJV (1NT/1)** Hebrews 11:1 Now **faith is** the substance of **things hoped for**, the evidence of things **not seen**.)

And now 2 Peter 27 times

BOM 1 Nephi 2:24 And if it so be that they **rebel against me**, they shall be a scourge unto thy seed, to **stir** them **up in** the ways of **remembrance**.

> **KJV (1NT/7)** 2 Peter 1:13 Yea, I think it meet, as long as I am in this tabernacle, to **stir** you **up** by putting you **in remembrance**;)

KJV (1/3) <u>Hosea 7:14</u> And they have not cried unto me with their heart, when they howled upon their beds: they assemble themselves for corn and wine, and they **rebel against** me.)

BOM <u>1 Nephi 8:23</u> And it came to pass that there arose a **mist of darkness** yea, even an exceedingly great **mist of darkness**; insomuch that they who had (14) commenced (14th Century) in the path did lose their way, that they wandered off and were lost.

> **KJV** (**1NT/4**) <u>2 Peter 2:17</u> These are wells without water, clouds that are carried with a tempest; to whom the **mist of darkness** is reserved for ever)

BOM <u>1 Nephi 13:37</u> And blessed are they who shall seek to bring forth my Zion at that day, for they shall have the gift and the power of the **Holy Ghost**; and if they **endure unto the end** they shall be lifted up at the last day, and **shall be saved** in **the everlasting kingdom of** the Lamb; and whoso shall **publish peace, yea, tidings** of **great joy, how beautiful upon the mountains** shall they be.

> **KJV** (**1NT/1**) <u>2 Peter 1:11</u> For so an entrance shall be ministered unto you abundantly into **the everlasting kingdom of** our Lord and Saviour Jesus Christ.)
>
> **KJV** (**2NT/1**) <u>Matthew 24:13</u> But he that shall **endure unto the end**, the same **shall be saved**.)
>
> **KJV** (<u>Isaiah 52:7</u> **How beautiful upon the mountains** are the feet of him that bringeth good tidings, that **publisheth peace**; that **bringeth good tidings of** good, that publisheth salvation; that saith unto Zion, Thy God reigneth!)
>
> **KJV** (<u>Luke 2:10</u> And the angel said unto them, Fear not: for, behold, I bring you good **tidings of great joy**, which shall be to all people.)

BOM <u>1 Nephi 15:3</u> For he truly spake many great **things** unto them, **which** were **hard to be understood**, save a man should (8) inquire (1290) of the Lord; and they being hard in their hearts, therefore they did not look unto the Lord as they ought.

> **KJV** (**1NT/1**) <u>2 Peter 3:16</u> As also in all his epistles, speaking in them of these **things**; in **which** are some things **hard to be understood**, which they that are unlearned and unstable wrest, as they do also the other scriptures, unto their own destruction.)

BOM <u>1 Nephi 22:23</u> For the time speedily shall come that all churches which are built up to get gain, and all those who are built up to get power over the flesh, and those who are built up to become (3) popular (1548) in the eyes of the world, and those who seek **the lusts of the flesh** and **the things of the world**, and to do all manner of iniquity; yea, in fine, all those who belong to the kingdom of the devil are they who need fear, and tremble, and quake; they are those who must be brought low in the dust; they are those who must be

consumed as stubble; and this is according to the words of the prophet.

> **KJV (1NT/1)** <u>2 Peter 2:18</u> For when they speak great swelling words of vanity, they allure through **the lusts of the flesh**, through much wantonness, those that were clean escaped from them who live in error.)
>
> **KJV (1NT/3)** <u>1 Corinthians 7:34</u> There is difference also between a wife and a virgin. The unmarried woman careth for the things of the Lord, that she may be holy both in body and in spirit: but she that is married careth for **the things of the world**, how she may please her husband.)
>
> **KJV (1/1)** <u>Exodus 15:7</u> And in the greatness of thine excellency thou hast overthrown them that rose up against thee: thou sentest forth thy wrath, which **consumed** them **as stubble**.)

BOM <u>2 Nephi 9:47</u> But behold, my brethren, is it expedient that I should awake you to an (47) awful (13th Century) (1) reality (1550 AD) of these things? Would I harrow (Note: used in this context 14th Century) up your souls if **your minds** were **pure**? Would I be plain unto you according to the plainness of the truth if ye were **freed from sin**?

> **KJV (1NT/1)** <u>2 Peter 3:1</u> This second epistle, beloved, I now write unto you; in both which I stir up **your pure minds** by way of remembrance:)
>
> **KJV (1NT/1)** <u>Romans 6:7</u> For he that is dead is **freed from sin**.)

BOM <u>2 Nephi 28:12</u> Because of pride, and because of **false teachers**, and false doctrine, their churches have become corrupted, and their churches are lifted up; because of pride they are puffed up.

> **KJV (1NT/1)** <u>2 Peter 2:1</u> But there were **false** prophets also among the people, even as there shall be **false teachers** among you, who privily shall bring in damnable heresies, even denying the Lord that bought them, and bring upon themselves swift destruction.)

BOM <u>Alma 30:31</u> And he did rise up in **great swelling words** before Alma, and did revile against the priests and teachers, accusing them of leading away the people after the silly **traditions of** their **fathers**, for the sake of (1) glutting (14th Century) on the labors of the people.

> **KJV (2NT/1)** <u>2 Peter 2:18</u> For when they speak **great swelling words** of vanity, they allure through the lusts of the flesh, through much wantonness, those that were clean escaped from them who live in error.)
>
> **KJV (1NT/20)** <u>Galatians 1:14</u> And profited in the Jews' religion above many my equals in mine own nation, being more exceedingly zealous of the **traditions of** my **fathers**.)

BOM <u>3 Nephi 7:8</u> And thus six years had not passed away since the more part of the people had turned from their righteousness, like **the dog to his vomit**, or like **the sow** to her **wallowing in the mire.**

> **KJV (1NT/1)** 2 Peter 2:22 But it is happened unto them according to the true proverb, **The dog** is **turned to his** own **vomit** again; and **the sow** that was washed **to her wallowing in the mire.**)

BOM 3 Nephi 26:3 And he did **expound all things, even from the beginning** until the time that he should **come in his glory** -- yea, even all things which should come **upon the face of the earth**, even until **the elements** should **melt with fervent heat,** and **the earth** should **be** (1) wrapt **together as a scroll,** and **the heavens** and the **earth** should **pass away;**

> **KJV (1NT/1)** 2 Peter 3:10 But the day of the Lord will come as a thief in the night; in the which **the heavens** shall pass away with a great noise, and **the elements** shall **melt with fervent heat, the earth** also and the works that are therein shall be burned up.)
>
> **KJV** (1/5) Isaiah 48:5 I have **even from the beginning** declared it to thee; before it came to pass I shewed it thee: lest thou shouldest say, Mine idol hath done them, and my graven image, and my molten image, hath commanded them.)
>
> **KJV (1NT/1)** Matthew 25:31 When the Son of man shall **come in his glory**, and all the holy angels with him, then shall he sit upon the throne of **his glory**:)
>
> **KJV** (12/26) Numbers 12:3 Now the man Moses was very meek, above all the men which were **upon the face of the earth**.)
>
> **KJV** (1/1) Isaiah 34:4 And all the host of heaven shall be dissolved, and the heavens shall **be** rolled **together as a scroll**: and all their host shall fall down, as the leaf falleth off from the vine, and as a falling fig from the fig tree.)

BOM 3 Nephi 27:27 And know ye that ye shall be judges of this people, according to the judgment which I shall give unto you, which shall be just. Therefore, **what manner of** men **ought ye to be**? Verily I say unto you, even as I am.

> **KJV (1NT/1)** 2 Peter 3:11 Seeing then that all these things shall be dissolved, **what manner of** persons **ought ye to be** in all holy conversation and godliness,)

BOM Mormon 9:2 Behold, will ye believe in the day of your visitation – behold, when the Lord shall come, yea, even that great day when the earth **shall be rolled together as a scroll, and the elements shall melt with fervent heat,** yea, in that great day when ye shall be brought to stand before the Lamb of God -- then will ye say that there is no God?

> **KJV (2NT/1)** 2 Peter 3:10 But the day of the Lord will come as a thief in the night; in the which the heavens shall pass away with a great noise, **and the elements shall melt with fervent heat,** the earth also and the works that are therein shall be burned up.)

KJV (1/2) Isaiah 34:4 And all the host of heaven shall be dissolved, and the heavens **shall be rolled together as a scroll**: and all their host shall fall down, as the leaf falleth off from the vine, and as a falling fig from the fig tree.)

KJV (**2NT/1**) Isaiah 10:3 And what will ye do in the **day of visitation**, and in the desolation which shall come from far? to whom will ye flee for help? and where will ye leave your glory?)

And now 1 John 21 times

BOM 2 Nephi 9:20 O how great the holiness of our God! For he **knoweth all things,**

KJV (**1NT/6**) 1 John 3:20 For if our heart condemn us, God is greater than our heart, and **knoweth all things.**)

BOM Alma 7:14 **Now I say unto you** that ye must repent, and be born again; for the Spirit saith if ye are not **born again** ye cannot **inherit the kingdom** of heaven; therefore come and be baptized unto repentance, that ye may be washed from your sins, that ye may have faith on **the Lamb of God,** who **taketh away the sins of the world, the Lamb of God** who is **mighty to save** and **to cleanse from all unrighteousness.**

KJV (**1NT/1**) 1 John 1:9 If we confess our sins, he is faithful and just to forgive us our sins, and **to cleanse** us **from all unrighteousness**.)

KJV (**1NT/18**) Acts 5:38 And **now I say unto you**, Refrain from these men, and let them alone: for if this counsel or this work be of men, it will come to nought:)

KJV (**2NT/2**) John 3:7 Marvel not that I said unto thee, Ye must **be born again.**)

KJV (**4NT/13**) 1 Corinthians 6:9 Know ye not that the unrighteous shall not **inherit the kingdom of** God? Be not deceived: neither fornicators, nor idolaters, nor adulterers, nor effeminate, nor abusers of themselves with mankind,)

KJV (**1NT/1**) John 1:29 The next day John seeth Jesus coming unto him, and saith, Behold **the Lamb of God**, which **taketh away the sin of the world**.)

KJV (1/3) Isaiah 63:1 Who is this that cometh from Edom, with dyed garments from Bozrah? this that is glorious in his apparel, travelling in the greatness of his strength? I that speak in righteousness, **mighty to save**.)

BOM Alma 26:2 And now, I ask, **what** great blessings has he **bestowed upon us**? Can ye tell?

KJV (**1NT/1**) 1 John 3:1 Behold, **what** manner of love the Father hath **bestowed upon us**, that we should be called the sons of God: therefore the world knoweth us not, because it knew him not.)

BOM Helaman 6:3 Nevertheless, the people of the church did have great joy because of the conversion of the Lamanites, yea, because of the church of God, which had been established among them. And they did **fellowship one with another** and did rejoice one **with another**, and did have great joy.

> **KJV (1NT/1)** 1 John 1:7 But if we walk in the light, as he is in the light, we have **fellowship one with another**, and the blood of Jesus Christ his Son cleanseth us from all sin.)

BOM Moroni 7:48 Wherefore, my beloved brethren, pray unto the Father with all the (4) energy (1655) of heart, that ye may be filled with this **love**, which he **hath bestowed upon** all who are true followers of his Son, Jesus Christ; that ye may become **the sons of God; that when he shall appear we shall be like him, for we shall see him as he is**; that we may have this **hope**; that we may be **purifi**ed **even as he is pure**. Amen.

> **KJV (1NT/1)** 1 John 3:1 Behold, what manner of **love** the Father **hath bestowed upon** us, that we should be called **the sons of God**: therefore the world knoweth us not, because it knew him not.)

> **KJV (1NT/1)** 1 John 3:2 Beloved, now are we the sons of God, and it doth not yet appear what we shall be: but we know **that, when he shall appear, we shall be like him; for we shall see him as he is**.)

> **KJV (1NT/1)** 1 John 3:3 And every man that hath this **hope** in him **purifi**eth himself, **even as he is pure**.)

BOM Moroni 8:16 Wo be unto them that shall **pervert the ways of the Lord** after this manner did, for they shall perish except they repent. hold, I **speak with boldness**, having authority from God; and I fear not what man can do; for **perfect love casteth out** all **fear**.

> **KJV (1NT/1)** 1 John 4:18 There is no fear in love; but **perfect love casteth out fear**: because fear hath torment. He that feareth is not made perfect in love.)

> **KJV (1NT/1)** Acts 13:10 And said, O full of all subtilty and all mischief, thou child of the devil, thou enemy of all righteousness, wilt thou not cease to **pervert the** right **ways of the Lord**?)

> **KJV (1NT/1)** Acts 4:29 And now, Lord, behold their threatenings: and grant unto thy servants, that **with** all **boldness** they may **speak** thy word,)

BOM Moroni 10:6 And whatsoever thing is good is **just and true**; wherefore, nothing that is good **denieth the** Christ, but **acknowledgeth** that he is.

> **KJV (1NT/1)** 1 John 2:23 Whosoever **denieth the** Son, the same hath not the Father: he that **acknowledgeth** the Son hath the Father also.)

> **KJV (1NT/6)** Revelation 15:3 And they sing the song of Moses the servant of God, and the song of the Lamb, saying, Great and marvellous are thy works, Lord God Almighty; **just and true** are thy ways, thou King of saints.)

And now 2 John 1 time
BOM <u>Mosiah 26:29</u> **Therefore I say unto you**, Go; and **whosoever transgresseth** against me, him shall ye judge according to the sins which he has committed; and if he confess his sins before thee and me, and repenteth in the sincerity of his heart, him shall ye forgive, and I will forgive him also.

> **KJV (1NT/1)** <u>2 John 1:9</u> **Whosoever transgresseth**, and abideth not in the doctrine of Christ, hath not God. He that abideth in the doctrine of Christ, he hath both the Father and the Son.)

> **KJV (3NT/6)** <u>Matthew 6:25</u> **Therefore I say unto you**, Take no thought for your life, what ye shall eat, or what ye shall drink; nor yet for your body, what ye shall put on. Is not the life more than meat, and the body than raiment?)

And Now 3 John 3 times
BOM <u>Helaman 6:34</u> And thus we see that the Nephites did begin to (26) dwindle (1596 AD) in unbelief, and grow in wickedness and abominations, while the Lamanites began to grow exceedingly in the knowledge of their God; yea, they did begin to keep his statutes and commandments, and to **walk in truth** and uprightness before him.

> **KJV (1NT/1)** <u>3 John 1:4</u> I have no greater joy than to hear that my children **walk in truth**.)

BOM <u>Moroni 9:24</u> And if it so be that they perish, we know that many of our brethren have deserted over unto the Lamanites, and many more will also desert over unto them; wherefore, write **somewhat a few things**, if thou art spared and I shall perish and not see thee; **but I trust that I** may **see thee** soon; for I have sacred records that I would deliver up unto thee.

> **KJV (1NT/1)** <u>3 John 1:14</u> **But I trust** I shall shortly **see thee**, and we shall speak face to face. Peace be to thee. Our friends salute thee. Greet the friends by name.)

> **KJV (4NT/2)** <u>Matthew 25:21</u> His lord said unto him, Well done, thou good and faithful servant: thou hast been faithful over **a few things**, I will make thee ruler over many things: enter thou into the joy of thy lord.)

Jude 2 times
BOM <u>2 Nephi 28:19</u> For the kingdom of the devil must shake, and they which belong to it must needs be stirred up unto repentance, or the devil will (4) grasp (16th Century) them with his **everlasting chains**, and they be stirred up to anger, and perish;

> **KJV (1NT/2)** <u>Jude 1:6</u> And the angels which kept not their first estate, but left their own habitation, he hath reserved in **everlasting chains** under darkness unto the judgment of the great day.)

Revelation 279 times
BOM <u>1 Nephi 1:14</u> And it came to pass that when my father had read and seen

many **great and marvelous** things, he did (6) exclaim (1570 AD) many things unto the Lord; such as: **Great and marvelous are thy works, O Lord God Almighty!** Thy throne is high in the heavens, and thy power, and goodness, and mercy are over **all the inhabitants of the earth**, and, because thou art merciful, thou wilt not suffer those who come unto thee that they shall perish!

> **KJV (1NT/1)** <u>Revelation 15:3</u> And they sing the song of Moses the servant of **God**, and the song of the Lamb, saying, **Great and marvellous are thy works, Lord God Almighty**; just and true are thy ways, thou King of saints.
>
> **KJV (1NT/25)** <u>Revelation 15:3</u> And they sing the song of Moses the servant of God, and the song of the Lamb, saying, **Great and marvellous** are thy works, Lord God Almighty; just and true are thy ways, thou King of saints.)
>
> **KJV (4/3)** <u>Psalm 33:14</u> From the place of his habitation he looketh upon **all the inhabitants of the earth**.)

BOM <u>1 Nephi 5:18</u> That these plates of brass should go forth unto **all nations, kindreds, tongues, and people** who were of his seed.

> **KJV (1NT/8)** <u>Revelation 7:9</u> After this I beheld, and, lo, a great multitude, which no man could number, of **all nations, and kindreds, and people, and tongues**, stood before the throne, and before the Lamb, clothed with white robes, and palms in their hands;)

BOM <u>1 Nephi 7:13</u> And if it so be we shall obtain the land of promise; and ye shall know at some future (14th Century) period (1530 AD) that **the word of** the Lord **shall be fulfilled** concerning the destruction of Jerusalem, for **all things** which the Lord hath spoken concerning the destruction of Jerusalem, **must be fulfilled**.

> **KJV (1NT/1)** <u>Revelation 17:17</u> For God hath put in their hearts to fulfil his will, and to agree, and give their kingdom unto the beast, until **the word**s of God **shall be fulfilled**.)
>
> **KJV (1NT/2)** <u>Luke 24:44</u> And he said unto them, These are the words which I spake unto you, while I was yet with you, that **all things must be fulfilled**, which were written in the law of Moses, and in the prophets, and in the psalms, concerning me.)

BOM <u>1 Nephi 11:34</u> And after he was slain I saw the multitudes of the earth, that they were **gathered together to fight** against the **apostles of the Lamb**; for thus were **the twelve** called by the angel of the Lord.

> **KJV (1NT/9)** <u>Revelation 21:14</u> And the wall of the city had twelve foundations, and in them the names of **the twelve apostles of the Lamb**.)
>
> **Note**: "Called by the angel of the Lord" to explain how he could possibly know this hundreds of years before they existed.
>
> **KJV (1/2)** <u>1 Samuel 13:5</u> And the Philistines **gathered** themselves

together to fight with Israel, thirty thousand chariots, and six thousand horsemen, and people as the sand which is on the sea shore in multitude: and they came up, and pitched in Michmash, eastward from Bethaven.)

BOM 1 Nephi 11:35 And the multitude of the earth was gathered together; and I beheld that they were in a large and *spacious* (*14ᵗʰ Century*) building, like unto the building which my father saw. And the angel of the Lord spake unto me again, saying: Behold the world and the wisdom thereof; yea, behold the house of Israel hath **gathered together to fight** against **the twelve apostles of the Lamb.**

> **KJV (1NT/9)** Revelation 21:14 And the wall of the city had twelve foundations, and in them the names of **the twelve apostles of the Lamb.**)
>
> **KJV** (1/2) 1 Samuel 13:5 And the Philistines **gathered** themselves **together to fight** with Israel, thirty thousand chariots, and six thousand horsemen, and people as the sand which is on the sea shore in multitude: and they came up, and pitched in Michmash, eastward from Bethaven.)

BOM 1 Nephi 11:36 And it came to pass that I saw and bear record, that the great and spacious (14ᵗʰ Century) building was the pride of the world; and it fell, and the fall thereof was exceedingly great And the angel of the Lord spake unto me again, saying: Thus shall be the destruction of **all nations, kindreds, tongues, and people** that shall fight against **the twelve apostles of the Lamb**.

> **KJV (1NT/8)** Revelation 7:9 After this I beheld, and, lo, a great multitude, which no man could number, of **all nations, and kindreds, and people, and tongues**, stood before the throne, and before the Lamb, clothed with white robes, and palms in their hands;)
>
> **KJV (1NT/9)** Revelation 21:14 And the wall of the city had twelve foundations, and in them the names of **the twelve apostles of the Lamb.**)

BOM 1 Nephi 12:1 And it came to pass that the angel said unto me: Look, and behold thy seed, and also the seed of thy brethren. And I looked and beheld the land of promise; and I beheld **multitudes of people**, yea, even as it were **in number** as many **as the sand of the sea**.

> **KJV (1NT/2)** Revelation 20:8 And shall go out to deceive the nations which are in the four quarters of the earth, Gog, and Magog, to **gather** them **together to battle**: the **number** of whom is **as the sand of the sea.**)
>
> **KJV (1NT/3)** Matthew 4:25 And there followed him great **multitudes of people** from Galilee, and from Decapolis, and from Jerusalem, and from Judaea, and from beyond Jordan.)

BOM 1 Nephi 12:11 And the angel said unto me: Look! And I looked, and beheld three generations pass away in righteousness; and their garments were white even like unto **the Lamb of God**. And the angel said unto me: These are **made white in the blood of the Lamb**, because of their faith in him.

> **KJV (1NT/2)** Revelation 7:14 And I said unto him, Sir, thou knowest. And he said to me, These are they which came out of great tribulation, and have washed their robes, and **made** them **white in the blood of the Lamb**.)
>
> **KJV (2NT/35)** John 1:29 The next day John seeth Jesus coming unto him, and saith, Behold **the Lamb of God**, which taketh away the sin of the world.)

BOM 1 Nephi 13:34 And it came to pass that the angel of the Lord spake unto me, saying: Behold, saith **the Lamb of God**, after I have visited **the remnant of the house of Israel** -- and this remnant of whom I speak is the seed of thy father -- wherefore, after I have visited them in judgment, and smitten them by the hand of the Gentiles, and after the Gentiles do stumble exceedingly , because of the most plain and precious parts of the gospel of the Lamb which have been kept back by that abominable church (76/259), which is **the mother of harlots**, saith the Lamb –I will be merciful unto the Gentiles in that day, insomuch that I will bring forth unto them, in mine own power, much of my gospel, which shall be plain and precious, saith the Lamb.

> **KJV (1NT/3)** Revelation 17:5 And upon her forehead was a name written, MYSTERY, BABYLON THE GREAT, THE **MOTHER OF HARLOTS** AND ABOMINATIONS OF THE EARTH.)
>
> **KJV (2NT/35)** John 1:29 The next day John seeth Jesus coming unto him, and saith, Behold **the Lamb of God**, which taketh away the sin of the world.)
>
> **KJV (1/9)** Isaiah 46:3 Hearken unto me, O house of Jacob, and all the **remnant of the house of Israel**, which are borne by me from the belly, which are carried from the womb:)

BOM 1 Nephi 14:9 And it came to pass that he said unto me: Look, and behold that great and abominable church, which is the **mother of abominations**, whose founder is the devil.

> **KJV (1NT/4)** Revelation 17:5 And upon her forehead was a name written, MYSTERY, BABYLON THE GREAT, THE **MOTHER OF** HARLOTS AND **ABOMINATIONS** OF THE EARTH.)

BOM 1 Nephi 14:10 And he said unto me: Behold there are save two churches only; the one is the church of **the Lamb of God**, and the other is the church of the devil; wherefore, whoso belongeth not to the church of the Lamb of God belongeth to that great church, which is the **mother of abominations**; and she is **the whore** of all the earth.

> **KJV** (Revelation 17:15 And he saith unto me, The waters which thou

sawest, where **the whore** sitteth, are peoples, and multitudes, and nations, and tongues.)

KJV **(1NT/4)** Revelation 17:5 And upon her forehead was a name written, MYSTERY, BABYLON THE GREAT, THE **MOTHER OF** HARLOTS AND **ABOMINATIONS** OF THE EARTH.)

KJV **(2NT/35)** John 1:29 The next day John seeth Jesus coming unto him, and saith, Behold **the Lamb of God**, which taketh away the sin of the world.)

BOM 1 Nephi 14:11 And it came to pass that I looked and beheld **the whore** of all the earth, and **she sat upon many waters**; and she had **dominion over all the earth**, among **all nations, kindreds, tongues, and people**.

KJV **(1NT/2)** Revelation 17:1 And there came one of the seven angels which had the seven vials, and talked with me, saying unto me, Come hither; I will shew unto thee the judgment of the great **whore that sitteth upon many waters**:)

And...KJV (1NT/8) Revelation 7:9 After this I beheld, and, lo, a great multitude, which no man could number, of **all nations, and kindreds, and people, and tongues**, stood before the throne, and before the Lamb, clothed with white robes, and palms in their hands;)

KJV **(1/1)** Genesis 1:26 And God said, Let us make man in our image, after our likeness: and let them have **dominion** over the fish of the sea, and over the fowl of the air, and over the cattle, and **over all the earth**, and over every creeping thing that creepeth upon the earth.)

BOM 1 Nephi 14:12 And it came to pass that I beheld the church of **the Lamb of God**, and its numbers were few, because of the wickedness and abominations of **the whore** who **sat upon many waters**; ; nevertheless, I beheld that the **church** of the Lamb, who were the saints of God, were also upon all the face of the earth; and their dominions **upon the face of the earth** were small, because of the wickedness **of the great whore** whom I saw.

KJV **(1NT/2)** Revelation 17:1 And there came one of the seven angels which had the seven vials, and talked with me, saying unto me, Come hither; I will shew unto thee the judgment of the great **whore that sitteth upon many waters**:)

KJV **(2NT/35)** John 1:29 The next day John seeth Jesus coming unto him, and saith, Behold **the Lamb of God**, which taketh away the sin of the world.)

KJV **(12/26)** Numbers 12:3 Now the man Moses was very meek, above all the men which were **upon the face of the earth**.)

BOM 1 Nephi 14:15 And it came to pass that I beheld that **the wrath of God** was **poured out** upon that great and abominable church, insomuch that there were **wars and rumors of wars** among all the nations and kindreds of the earth.

> **KJV (1NT/1)** <u>Revelation 14:10</u> The same shall drink of the wine of **the wrath of God**, which is **poured out** without mixture into the cup of his indignation; and he shall be tormented with fire and brimstone in the presence of the holy angels, and in the presence of the Lamb:)
>
> **KJV (2NT/6)** <u>Matthew 24:6</u> And ye shall hear of **wars and rumours of wars**: see that ye be not troubled: for all these things must come to pass, but the end is not yet.)

BOM <u>1 Nephi 15:30</u> And I said unto them that our father also saw that the justice of God did also divide the wicked from the righteous; and the brightness thereof was like unto the brightness of a flaming fire, which **ascendeth up** unto God **forever and ever**, and hath no end.

> **KJV (1NT/6)** <u>Revelation 14:11</u> And the smoke of their torment **ascendeth up for ever and ever**: and they have no rest day nor night, who worship the beast and his image, and whosoever receiveth the mark of his name.)

BOM <u>1 Nephi 15:33</u> Wherefore, if they should die in their wickedness they must be cast off also, as to the things which are spiritual, which are pertaining to righteousness; wherefore, they must be brought to **stand before God**, to be judged of their works; and if their works have been filthiness they **must needs be filthy**; and if they be **filthy it must needs be that** they cannot dwell in the kingdom of God; if so, the kingdom of God must be filthy also.

> **KJV (1NT/8)** <u>Revelation 20:12</u> And I saw the dead, small and great, **stand before God**; and the books were opened: and another book was opened, which is the book of life: and the dead were judged out of those things which were written in the books, according to their works.)
>
> **KJV (1NT/1)** <u>Revelation 22:11</u> He that is unjust, let him be unjust still: and he which is **filthy**, let him be **filthy** still: and he that is righteous, let him be righteous still: and he that is holy, let him be holy still.)
>
> **KJV (1NT/14)** <u>Matthew 18:7</u> Woe unto the world because of offences! for **it must needs be that** offences come; but woe to that man by whom the offence cometh!)

BOM <u>1 Nephi 19:16</u> Yea, then will he remember **the isles of the sea**; yea, and all the people who are of the house of Israel, will I gather in, saith the Lord, according to the words of the prophet Zenos, **from the four quarters of the Earth**.

> **KJV (1NT/6)** <u>Revelation 20:8</u> And shall go out to deceive the nations which are in **the four quarters of the earth**, Gog, and Magog, to gather them together to battle: the number of whom is as the sand of the sea.)

KJV (2/8) <u>Isaiah 24:15</u> Wherefore glorify ye the LORD in the fires, even the name of the LORD God of Israel in **the isles of the sea**.)

BOM <u>1 Nephi 22:18</u> Behold, my brethren, I say unto you, that these **things must shortly come**; yea, even **blood, and fire, and vapor of smoke** must come; and it must needs be upon the face of this earth; and it cometh unto men **according to the flesh** if it so be that they will harden their hearts against the Holy One of Israel.

KJV (<u>Revelation 1:1</u> The Revelation of Jesus Christ, which God gave unto him, to shew unto his servants **things which must shortly come** to pass; and he sent and signified it by his angel unto his servant John:)

KJV (**1NT/1**) <u>Acts 2:19</u> And I will shew wonders in heaven above, and signs in the earth beneath; **blood, and fire, and vapour of smoke**:

KJV Note: Acts 2:19 is a paraphrase of <u>Joel 2:30</u> And I will shew wonders in the heavens and in the earth, **blood, and fire, and pillars of smoke**.

Note: You will note that the BOM uses "vapor" like Acts and not "pillars" as Joel.

KJV (**1NT/7**) <u>Matthew 18:7</u> Woe unto the world because of offences! for **it must needs be** that offences come; but woe to that man by whom the offence cometh!)

BOM <u>1 Nephi 22:26</u> And because of the righteousness of his people, **Satan** has no power; wherefore, he cannot **be loosed** for the space of many years; for he **hath no power** over the hearts of the people, for they dwell in righteousness, and the Holy One of Israel reigneth.

KJV (**1NT/1**) <u>Revelation 20:7</u> And when the thousand years are expired, **Satan** shall **be loosed** out of his prison,)

KJV (**1NT/2**) <u>Revelation 20:6</u> Blessed and holy is he that hath part in the first resurrection: on such the second death **hath no power**, but they shall be priests of God and of Christ, and shall reign with him a thousand years.)

BOM <u>2 Nephi 2:9</u> Wherefore, he is **the first-fruits unto God**, inasmuch as he shall **make intercession for** all the children of men; and they that believe in him shall be saved.

KJV (**1NT/1**) <u>Revelation 14:4</u> These are they which were not defiled with women; for they are virgins. These are they which follow the Lamb whithersoever he goeth. These were redeemed from among men, being **the firstfruits unto God** and to the Lamb.)

KJV (**2NT/1**) *Note: Same idea:* <u>Romans 8:34</u> Who is he that condemneth? It is Christ that died, yea rather, that is risen again, who is even at the right hand of God, who also **maketh intercession for**

us.)

BOM 2 Nephi 2:18 And because he had **fallen from heaven**, and had become miserable forever, he sought also the misery of all mankind. Wherefore, he said unto Eve, yea, even **that old serpent**, who is **the devil**, who is the **father of all lies**, wherefore he said: partake of the forbidden fruit, and **ye shall not die**, but **ye shall be as** God, **knowing good and evil.**

> **KJV (2NT/2)** Revelation 12:9 And the great dragon was cast out, **that old serpent**, called **the Devil**, and Satan, which deceiveth the whole world: he was cast out into the earth, and his angels were cast out with him.)

> **KJV (1/3)** Isaiah 14:12 How art thou **fallen from heaven**, O Lucifer, son of the morning! how art thou cut down to the ground, which didst weaken the nations!)

> **KJV (1NT/2)** John 8 44 Ye are of your father the devil, and the lusts of your father ye will do. He was a murderer from the beginning, and abode not in the truth, because there is no truth in him. When he speaketh a lie, he speaketh of his own: **for he is a liar, and the father of it.**)

> **KJV (1/1)** Genesis 3:3-4 And the **serpent** said unto the woman, **Ye shall not** surely **die**: For God doth know that in the day ye eat thereof, then your eyes shall be opened, and **ye shall be as** gods, **knowing good and evil.**)

BOM 2 Nephi 6:4 And now, behold, I would speak unto you concerning **things which are, and which are** to come; wherefore, I will read you the words of Isaiah. And they are the words which my brother has desired that I should speak unto you. And I speak unto you for your sakes, that ye may learn and glorify the name of your God.

> **KJV (1NT/1)** Revelation 1:19 Write the **things which** thou hast seen, and the **things which are**, and the **things which** shall be hereafter;)

BOM 2 Nephi 9:11 And because of the way of deliverance of our God, the Holy One of Israel, this death, of which I have spoken, which is the temporal, shall **deliver up** its **dead**; which death is the grave.

> **KJV (1NT/3)** Revelation 20:13 And the sea gave **up the dead** which were in it; and death and hell **delivered up the dead** which were in them: and they were judged every man according to their works.)

BOM 2 Nephi 9:12 And this death **of which I have spoken**, which is the spiritual death, shall **deliver up** its **dead**; which spiritual death, is hell; wherefore, **death and hell** must **deliver up** their **dead**, and hell must deliver up its captive spirits, and the grave must deliver up its captive bodies, and the bodies and the spirits of men will be restored one to the other; and it is by the power of the resurrection of the Holy One of Israel.

KJV (1NT/3) <u>Revelation 20:13</u> And the sea gave **up** the **dead** which were in it; and death and hell **delivered up the dead** which were in them: and they were judged every man according to their works.)

KJV (1NT/3) <u>Revelation 20:13</u> And the sea gave **up** the **dead** which were in it; and death and hell **delivered up the dead** which were in them: and they were judged every man according to their works.)

KJV (1/13) <u>Exodus 32:34</u> Therefore now go, lead the people unto the place **of which I have spoken** unto thee: behold, mine Angel shall go before thee: nevertheless in the day when I visit I will visit their sin upon them.)

BOM <u>2 Nephi 9:16</u> And assuredly, **as the Lord liveth**, for the Lord God hath spoken it, and it is his eternal **word**, which cannot pass away, that they who are **righteous** shall **be righteous still**, and they who are **filthy** shall **be filthy still**; wherefore, they who are filthy are **the devil and his angels**; and they shall go away **into everlasting fire; prepared for** them; and their **torment** is as **a lake of fire** and **brimstone**, whose flame **ascendeth up forever and ever** and has no end.

KJV (1NT/1) <u>Revelation 22:11</u> He that is unjust, let him be unjust still: **and** he which is **filthy**, let him **be filthy still: and** he that is **righteous**, let him **be righteous still**: and he that is holy, let him be holy **still**.)

KJV (<u>Revelation 20:10</u> And the devil that deceived them was cast into the **lake of fire and brimstone**, where the beast and the false prophet are, and shall be tormented day and night **for ever and ever**. <u>Revelation 14:11</u> And the smoke of their **torment ascendeth up for ever and ever**: and they have no rest day nor night, who worship the beast and his image, and whosoever receiveth the mark of his name.)

KJV (27/17) <u>1 Samuel 29:6</u> Then Achish called David, and said unto him, **Surely, as the LORD liveth**, thou hast been upright, and thy going out and thy coming in with me in the host is good in my sight: for I have not found evil in thee since the day of thy coming unto me unto this day: nevertheless the lords favour thee not.)

KJV (1NT/1) <u>Matthew 24:35</u> Heaven and earth shall **pass away**, but my **words** shall **not pass away**.)

KJV (1NT/2) <u>Matthew 25:41</u> Then shall he say also unto them on the left hand, Depart from me, ye cursed, into everlasting fire, prepared for **the devil and his angels**:)

BOM <u>2 Nephi 9:46</u> Prepare your souls for that glorious day when justice shall be administered unto the righteous, even **the day of judgment**, that ye may not (6) shrink (13th Century) with (47) awful (13th Century) fear; that ye may not remember your (47) awful (13th Century) guilt in perfectness, and be constrained to (6) exclaim (1570 AD) **Holy, holy are thy judgments, O Lord**

God Almighty -- but I know my guilt; I **transgressed thy law** and my transgressions are mine; and the devil hath obtained me, that I am a prey to his (47) awful (13th Century) misery.

> **KJV** (Revelation 4:8 And the four beasts had each of them six wings about him; and they were full of eyes within: and they rest not day and night, saying, Holy, **holy, holy, LORD God Almighty**, which was, and is, and is to come.

> **KJV** (Revelation 16:7 And I heard another out of the altar say, Even so, **Lord God Almighty**, true and righteous **are thy judgments**.)

> **KJV** (Revelation 11:17 Saying, We give thee thanks, **O LORD God Almighty**, which art, and wast, and art to come; because thou hast taken to thee thy great power, and hast reigned.)

> **KJV** (**8NT/4**) Matthew 11:22 But I say unto you, It shall be more tolerable for Tyre and Sidon at **the day of judgment**, than for you.)

> **KJV** (1/1) Daniel 9:11 Yea, all Israel have **transgressed thy law**, even by departing, that they might not obey thy voice; therefore the curse is poured upon us, and the oath that is written in the law of Moses the servant of God, because we have sinned against him.,)

BOM 2 Nephi 28:23 Yea, they are (1) grasped (16th Century) with **death, and hell; and death, and hell, and the devil**, and all that have been seized therewith must **stand before** the **throne** of God, and be **judged according to their works**, from whence they must go into the **place prepared** for them, even a **lake of fire and brimstone,** which is endless torment.

> **KJV Note:** This entire verse is a reiteration of the following verses in Revelation chapter 20: Revelation 20:10 **And the devil** that deceived them was cast into the **lake of fire and brimstone**, where the beast and the false prophet are, and shall be **torment**ed day and night for ever and ever. Revelation 20:11 And I saw a great white **throne**, and him that sat on it, from whose face the earth and the heaven fled away; and there was found no place for them. Revelation 20:12 And I saw the dead, small and great, **stand before God**; and the books were opened: and another book was opened, which is the book of life: and the dead were **judged** out of those things which were written in the books, **according to their works**. Revelation 20:13 And the sea gave up the dead which were in it; **and death and hell** delivered up the dead which were in them: and they were **judged** every man **according to their works**. Revelation 20:14 And **death and hell** were cast into the **lake of fire**. This is the second death. Revelation 20:15 And whosoever was not found written in the book of life was cast into the **lake of fire**.)

> **KJV** (**1NT/1**) Revelation 12:6 And the woman fled into the wilderness, where she hath a **place prepared** of God, that they should

feed her there a thousand two hundred and threescore days.)
BOM 2 Nephi 29:11 For I command all men, both in the east and in the west, and in the north, and in the south, and in the islands of the sea, that they shall write the words which I speak unto them; for **out of the books which** shall be **written** I will **judge the world, every man according to their works**, according to that which is written.

> **KJV (1NT/1)** Revelation 20:12 And I saw the dead, small and great, stand before God; and the **books** were opened: and another **book** was opened, which is the book of life: and the dead were **judge**d **out of** those things **which** were **written** in the **books, according to their works**.)

> **KJV (1NT/1)** Revelation 20:13 And the sea gave up the dead which were in it; and death and hell delivered up the dead which were in them: and they were judged **every man according to their works**.)

> **KJV** (Psalm 98:9 Before the LORD; for he cometh to **judge the** earth: with righteousness shall he **judge the world**, and the people with equity.)

BOM 2 Nephi 31:15 And I heard a voice from the Father, saying: Yea, the **words** of my Beloved **are true and faithful. He that endureth to the end**, the same **shall be saved**.

> **KJV (1NT/1)** Revelation 21:5 **And** he that sat upon the throne said, Behold, I make all things new. **And** he said unto me, Write: for these **words are true and faithful**.)

> **KJV (1NT/1)** Matthew 10:22 And ye shall be hated of all men for my name's sake: but **he that endureth to the end shall be saved**.)

BOM Jacob 3:11 O my brethren, **hearken unto my words**; (3) arouse (1593) the (3) faculties (14th Century) of your souls; shake yourselves that ye may awake from the slumber of death; and loose yourselves from **the pains of hell** that ye may not become angels to the devil, to be **cast into** that **lake of fire and brimstone** which **is the second death**.

> **KJV (1NT/1)** Revelation 20:14 And death and hell were cast into the **lake of fire**. This **is the second death**.)

> **KJV (2NT/1)** Revelation 20:10 And the devil that deceived them was **cast into the lake of fire and brimstone**, where the beast and the false prophet are, and shall be tormented day and night for ever and ever.)

> **KJV** (1/14) Deuteronomy 18:19 And it shall come to pass, that whosoever will not **hearken unto my words** which he shall speak in my name, I will require it of him.)

> **KJV** (1/4) Psalm 116:3 The sorrows of death compassed me, and **the pains of hell** gat hold upon me: I found trouble and sorrow.)

BOM Jacob 6:10 And according to the power of justice, for justice cannot be denied, ye must go away **into** that **lake of fire and brimstone**, whose flames are **unquenchable**, and whose smoke **ascendeth up forever and ever**, which **lake of fire and brimstone** is endless **torment**.

> **KJV (1NT/1)** Revelation 20:10 And the devil that deceived them was cast **into** the **lake of fire and brimstone**, where the beast and the false prophet are, and shall be tormented day and night for ever and ever.)

> **KJV (1NT/6)** Revelation 14:11 And the smoke of their **torment ascendeth up for ever and ever**: and they have no rest day nor night, who worship the beast and his image, and whosoever receiveth the mark of his name.)

> **KJV (2NT/5)** Luke 3:17 Whose fan is in his hand, and he will thoroughly purge his floor, and will gather the wheat into his garner; but the chaff he will burn with fire **unquenchable**.)

BOM Mosiah 3:6 For behold, **the time cometh**, and is not far distant, that with power, **the Lord Omnipotent** who **reigneth**, who **was, and is** from all eternity to all eternity, shall come down from heaven **among the children of men**, and shall dwell in a tabernacle of clay, and shall go forth amongst men, working mighty miracles, such as **heal**ing **the sick, rais**ing **the dead**, causing **the lame to walk, the blind to** receive their sight, and **the deaf to hear**, and curing **all manner of disease**s.

> **KJV (1NT/4)** Revelation 19:6 And I heard as it were the voice of a great multitude, and as the voice of many waters, and as the voice of mighty thunderings, saying, Alleluia: for **the Lord** God **omnipotent reigneth**.)

> **KJV (1NT/1)** Revelation 4:8 And the four beasts had each of them six wings about him; and they were full of eyes within: and they rest not day and night, saying, Holy, holy, holy, LORD God Almighty, which **was, and is**, and is to come.)

> **KJV (2/30)** Psalm 21:10 Their fruit shalt thou destroy from the earth, and their seed from **among the children of men**.)

> **KJV (1NT/2)** Matthew 10:8 **Heal the sick**, cleanse the lepers, **raise the dead**, cast out devils: freely ye have received, freely give.)

> **KJV (1NT/2)** Matthew 15:31 Insomuch that the multitude wondered, when they saw the dumb to speak, the maimed to be whole, **the lame to walk, and the blind to** see: and they glorified the God of Israel.)

> **KJV (1NT/2)** Mark 7:37 And were beyond measure astonished, saying, He hath done all things well: he maketh both **the deaf to hear**, and the dumb to speak.)

> **KJV (2NT/4)** Matthew 10:1 And when he had called unto him his twelve disciples, he gave them power against unclean spirits, to cast them out, and to heal all manner of sickness and **all manner of**

disease.)

KJV (2NT/15) <u>John 16:2</u> They shall put you out of the synagogues: yea, **the time cometh**, that whosoever killeth you will think that he doeth God service.)

BOM <u>Mosiah 3:18</u> For behold he judgeth, **and** his **judgment is just**; and the infant perisheth not that dieth in his infancy; but men **drink damnation to** their own souls except they humble themselves **and become as little children**, and believe that salvation **was, and is, and is to come**, in and through the atoning blood of Christ, **the Lord Omnipotent**.

> **KJV (1NT/1)** <u>Revelation 4:8</u> And the four beasts had each of them six wings about him; and they were full of eyes within: and they rest not day and night, saying, Holy, holy, holy, LORD God Almighty, which **was, and is, and is to come**.)
>
> **KJV (1NT/4)** <u>Revelation 19:6</u> And I heard as it were the voice of a great multitude, and as the voice of many waters, and as the voice of mighty thunderings, saying, Alleluia: for **the Lord** God **omnipotent** reigneth.)
>
> **KJV (1NT/1)** <u>John 5:30</u> I can of mine own self do nothing: as I hear, I judge: **and** my **judgment is just**; because I seek not mine own will, but the will of the Father which hath sent me.)
>
> **KJV (1NT/3)** <u>1 Corinthians 11:29</u> For he that eateth and drinketh unworthily, eateth and **drink**eth **damnation to** himself, not discerning the Lord's body.)
>
> **KJV (1NT/1)** <u>Matthew 18:3</u> And said, Verily I say unto you, **Except** ye be converted, **and become as little children**, ye shall not enter into the kingdom of heaven.)

BOM <u>Mosiah 15:24</u> And these are those who have **part in the first resurrection**; and these are they that have died before Christ came, in their ignorance, not having salvation declared unto them. And thus the Lord bringeth about the (19) restoration (14th Century) of these; and they have a **part in the first resurrection**, or have eternal life, being redeemed by the Lord.

> **KJV (1NT/3)** <u>Revelation 20:6</u> Blessed and holy is he that hath **part in the first resurrection**: on such the second death hath no power, but they shall be priests of God and of Christ, and shall reign with him a thousand years.)

BOM <u>Mosiah 16:9</u> He is the light and the life of the world; yea, a light that is endless, that can never be darkened; yea, and also a life which is endless, that **there** can **be no more death**.

> **KJV (1NT/1)** <u>Revelation 21:4</u> And God shall wipe away all tears from their eyes; and **there** shall **be no more death**, neither sorrow, nor crying, neither shall there be any more pain: for the former things

are passed away.)

BOM <u>Alma 5:34</u> Yea, he saith: Come unto me and ye shall partake of the fruit of **the tree of life**; yea, ye shall eat and drink of the **bread** and **the waters of life freely**;

> **KJV (2NT/2)** <u>Revelation 22:17</u> And the Spirit and the bride say, Come. And let him that heareth say, Come. And let him that is athirst come. And whosoever will, let him take **the water of life freely**.)
>
> **KJV (2NT/1)** <u>John 6:48</u> I am that **bread of life**.)
>
> **KJV** (6/15) <u>Genesis 2:9</u> And out of the ground made the LORD God to grow every tree that is pleasant to the sight, and good for food; **the tree of life** also in the midst of the garden, and the tree of knowledge of good and evil.)

BOM <u>Alma 7:21</u> And he doth not dwell in unholy temples; neither can filthiness or anything which is unclean be received into the kingdom of God; **therefore I say unto you the time shall come**, yea, and it shall be **at the last day**, that **he** who **is filthy** shall remain in his **filth**iness.

> **KJV** (*Note: Same idea:* <u>Revelation 22:11</u> He that is unjust, let him be unjust still: and **he** which **is filthy**, let him be **filthy** still: and he that is righteous, let him be righteous still: and he that is holy, let him be holy still.)
>
> **KJV (3NT/6)** <u>Matthew 6:25</u> **Therefore I say unto you**, Take no thought for your life, what ye shall eat, or what ye shall drink; nor yet for your body, what ye shall put on. Is not the life more than meat, and the body than raiment?)
>
> **KJV (1NT/7)** <u>John 16:4</u> But these things have I told you, that when **the time shall come**, ye may remember that I told you of them. And these things I said not unto you at the beginning, because I was with you.)
>
> **KJV (5NT/49)** <u>John 6:44</u> No man can come to me, except the Father which hath sent me draw him: and I will raise him up **at the last day**.)

BOM <u>Alma 9:20</u> Yea, after having been such a **highly favored** people of the Lord; yea, after having been favored above **every** other **nation, kindred, tongue,** or **people**; after having had all things made known unto them, according to their desires, and their faith, and prayers, of that **which** has been, and **which is**, and **which is to come**;

> **KJV (1NT/1)** <u>Revelation 14:6</u> And I saw another angel fly in the midst of heaven, having the everlasting gospel to preach unto them that dwell on the earth, and to **every nation**, and **kindred**, and **tongue**, and **people**,)
>
> **KJV (1NT/1)** <u>Revelation 4:8</u> And the four beasts had each of them six wings about him; and they were full of eyes within: and they rest

not day and night, saying, Holy, holy, holy, LORD God Almighty, **which** was, and **is**, and **is to come**.)
KJV (1NT/7) <u>Luke 1:28</u> And the angel came in unto her, and said, Hail, thou that art **highly favoured**, the Lord is with thee: blessed art thou among women.)

BOM <u>Alma 11:22</u> And Amulek said unto him: Yea, if it be according to the Spirit of the Lord, which is in me; for I shall say nothing which is contrary to the Spirit of the Lord. And Zeezrom said unto him: Behold, here are six onties of silver, **and all these will I give thee if thou wilt** deny the existence *of a Supreme Being.*
KJV (1NT/1) <u>**Matthew 4:9**</u> And saith unto him, **All these things will I give thee, if thou wilt** fall down and worship me.)

BOM <u>Alma 11:39</u> And Amulek said unto him: Yea, he is the very Eternal **Father of heaven and of earth**, and all things which in them are; he is **the beginning and the end, the first and the last;**
KJV (1NT/1) <u>Revelation 22:13</u> I am Alpha and Omega, the **beginning and the end, the first and the last**.)
KJV (2NT/5) <u>Matthew 11:25</u> At that time Jesus answered and said, I thank thee, O **Father**, Lord **of heaven and earth**, because thou hast hid these things from the wise and prudent, and hast revealed them unto babes.)

BOM <u>Alma 12:8</u> And Zeezrom began to inquire of them diligently, that he might know more concerning the kingdom of God. And he said unto **BOM** Alma: What does this mean which Amulek hath spoken concerning **the resurrection of the dead**, that all shall **rise from the dead**, both the just and the unjust, and are brought to **stand before God**, to be **judged according to their works**?
KJV (3NT/13) <u>Revelation 20:13</u> And the sea gave up the dead which were in it; and death and hell delivered up the dead which were in them: and they were **judged** every man **according to their works**.)
KJV (1NT/8) <u>Revelation 20:12</u> And I saw the dead, small and great, **stand before God**; and the books were opened: and another book was opened, which is the book of life: and the dead were judged out of those things which were written in the books, according to their works.)
KJV (6NT/17) <u>Matthew 22:31</u> But as touching **the resurrection of the dead,** have ye not read that which was spoken unto you by God, saying,)
KJV (3NT/7) <u>Luke 24:46</u> And said unto them, Thus it is written, and thus it behooved Christ to suffer, and to **rise from the dead** the third day:)

BOM <u>Alma 12:14</u> For our words will condemn us, yea, all our works will condemn us; we shall not be found (13) spotless (14th Century); and our thoughts will also condemn us; and in this (47) awful (13th Century) state we shall not dare to look up to our God; and we **would fain** be glad if we could command **the rocks and** the **mountains** to **fall** up**on us** to **hide us from** his presence.

> **KJV (1NT/1)** <u>Revelation 6:16</u> And said to **the mountains and rocks, Fall on us,** and **hide us from** the face of him that sitteth on the throne, and from the wrath of the Lamb:)
>
> **KJV (2/1)** <u>Job 27:22</u> For God shall cast upon him, and not spare: he **would fain** flee out of his hand.)

BOM <u>Alma 12:24</u> And we see that death comes upon mankind, yea, the death which has been spoken of by Amulek, which is the temporal death; nevertheless there was a **space** granted unto man in which he might **repent**; therefore this life became a (4) probationary (15th Century) state; a time to prepare to meet God; a time to prepare for that endless state which has been spoken of by us, which is after **the resurrection of the dead.**

> **KJV (1NT/1)** <u>Revelation 2:21</u> And I gave her **space** to **repent** of her fornication; and she repented not.)
>
> **KJV (6NT/17)** <u>Matthew 22:31</u> But as touching **the resurrection of the dead,** have ye not read that which was spoken unto you by God, saying,)

BOM <u>Alma 13:11</u> Therefore they were called after this holy order, and were sanctified, and their garments were **washed white** through **the blood of the Lamb.**

> **KJV (1NT/1)** <u>Revelation 7:14</u> And I said unto him, Sir, thou knowest. And he said to me, These are they which came out of great tribulation, and have **washed** their robes, and **made** them **white** in **the blood of the Lamb.**)

BOM <u>Alma 16:19</u> **Holding forth things which must shortly come**; yea, **holding forth** the coming of the Son of God, his sufferings and death, and also **the resurrection of the dead.**

> **KJV (1NT/2)** <u>Revelation 1:1</u> The Revelation of Jesus Christ, which God gave unto him, to shew unto his servants **things which must shortly come** to pass; and he sent and signified it by his angel unto his servant John:)
>
> **KJV (6NT/17)** <u>Matthew 22:31</u> But as touching **the resurrection of the dead,** have ye not read that which was spoken unto you by God, saying,)
>
> **KJV (1NT/2)** <u>Philippians 2:16</u> **Holding forth the** word of life; that I may rejoice in the day of Christ, that I have not run in vain, neither laboured in vain.)

BOM <u>Alma 17:21</u> And now after the church had been established throughout all the land -- having **got the victory over** the devil, and the word of God being preached in its purity in all the land, and the Lord pouring out his blessings upon the people -- thus ended the fourteenth year of the reign of the judges over the people of Nephi.

> **KJV** (1NT/1) <u>Revelation 15:2</u> And I saw as it were a sea of glass mingled with fire: and them that had **gotten the victory over the** beast, and over his image, and over his mark, and over the number of his name, stand on the sea of glass, having the harps of God.)

BOM <u>Alma 26:5</u> Behold, the field was ripe, and blessed are ye, for ye did **thrust in** the **sickle**, and did **reap** with your might, yea, **all the day long** did ye labor; and behold the number of your sheaves! And they shall be gathered into the garners, that they are not wasted.

> **KJV** (**1NT/1**) <u>Revelation 14:15</u> And another angel came out of the temple, crying with a loud voice to him that sat on the cloud, **Thrust in** thy **sickle**, and **reap**: for the time is come for thee to **reap**; for the harvest of the earth is ripe.)

> **KJV** (13/12) <u>Psalm 35:28</u> And my tongue shall speak of thy righteousness and of thy praise **all the day long**.)

BOM <u>Alma 31:26</u> **And** he lifted up his **voice** to heaven, and **cried, saying: O, how long, O Lord**, wilt **thou** suffer that thy servants shall **dwell** here below in the flesh, to behold such gross wickedness **among the children of men**?

> **KJV** (**1NT/1**) <u>Revelation 6:10</u> **And** they **cried** with a loud **voice, saying, How long, O Lord**, holy and true, dost **thou** not judge and avenge our blood on them that **dwell** on the earth?)

> **KJV** (2/30) Psalm 21:10 Their fruit shalt thou destroy from the earth, and their seed from **among the children of men**.)

BOM <u>Alma 33:42</u> And because of your diligence and your faith and your patience with the word in nourishing it, that it may take root in you, behold, **by and by** ye shall pluck the fruit thereof, which is **most precious**, which is sweet above all that is sweet, and which is white above all that is white, yea, and pure above all that is pure; and ye shall feast upon this fruit even until ye are filled, that ye **hunger** not, **neither shall** ye **thirst**.

> **KJV** (**1NT/1**) <u>Revelation 7:16</u> They shall **hunger** no more, **neither thirst** any more; **neither shall** the sun light on them, nor any heat.)

> **KJV** (**2NT/10**) <u>Revelation 18:12</u> The merchandise of gold, and silver, and precious stones, and of pearls, and fine linen, and purple, and silk, and scarlet, and all thyine wood, and all manner vessels of ivory, and all manner vessels of **most precious** wood, and of brass, and iron, and marble,)

> **KJV** (**1NT/5**) <u>Matthew 13:21</u> Yet hath he not root in himself, but dureth for a while: for when tribulation or persecution ariseth because of the word, **by and by** he is offended.)

BOM <u>Alma 37:31</u> Yea, and cursed be the land forever and ever unto those workers of darkness and secret (21) combinations (14th Century), even unto destruction, **except they repent** before they **are fully ripe.**

> **KJV (1NT/14)** <u>Revelation 2:22</u> Behold, I will cast her into a bed, and them that commit adultery with her into great tribulation, **except they repent** of their deeds.)

> **KJV (1NT/5)** <u>Revelation 14:18</u> And another angel came out from the altar, which had power over fire; and cried with a loud cry to him that had the sharp sickle, saying, Thrust in thy sharp sickle, and gather the clusters of the vine of the earth; for her grapes **are fully ripe.**)

BOM <u>Helaman 10:6</u> Behold, thou art Nephi, and I am God. Behold, I declare it unto thee **in the presence of** mine **angels,** that ye shall **have power** over this people, and shall **smite the earth with** famine, and with pestilence, and destruction, according to the wickedness of this people.

> **KJV (1NT/1)** <u>Revelation 11:6</u> These **have power** to shut heaven, that it rain not in the days of their prophecy: and have power over waters to turn them to blood, and to **smite the earth with** all plagues, as often as they will.)

> **KJV (2NT/1)** <u>Revelation 14:10</u> The same shall drink of the wine of the wrath of God, which is poured out without mixture into the cup of his indignation; and he shall be tormented with fire and brimstone **in the presence of** the holy **angels,** and in the **presence** of the Lamb:)

BOM <u>3 Nephi 9:2</u> **Wo, wo, wo unto this people**; wo unto **the inhabitants of the** whole earth except they shall repent; for the devil laugheth, and his angels rejoice, because of the slain of the fair sons and daughters of my people; and it is because of their iniquity and abominations that they are fallen!

> **KJV (1NT/1)** <u>Revelation 8:13</u> And I beheld, and heard an angel flying through the midst of heaven, saying with a loud voice, **Woe, woe, woe, to the inhabiters of the earth** by reason of the other voices of the trumpet of the three angels, which are yet to sound!)

> **KJV (9/43)** <u>Jeremiah 21:8</u> And **unto this people** thou shalt say, Thus saith the LORD; Behold, I set before you the way of life, and the way of death.)

BOM <u>3 Nephi 9:18</u> **I am the light** and **the life of the world. I am Alpha and Omega, the beginning and the end.**

> **KJV (1NT/1)** <u>Revelation 22:13</u> **I am Alpha and Omega, the beginning and the end**, the first and the last.)

> **KJV (1NT/1)** <u>John 8:12</u> Then spake Jesus again unto them, saying, **I am the light of the world**: he that followeth me shall not walk in darkness, but shall have **the light of life**)

BOM <u>3 Nephi 10:12</u> And it was the more righteous part of the people who were saved, and it was they who received the prophets and stoned them not;

and it was they who had not **shed the blood of** the **saints**, who were spared –

> KJV **(1NT/1)** <u>Revelation 16:6</u> For they have **shed the blood of saints** and prophets, and thou hast given them blood to drink; for they are worthy.)

BOM <u>3 Nephi 11:8</u> And it came to pass, as they understood they cast their eyes up again towards heaven; and behold, they saw a Man **descending out of heaven;** and he was **clothed** in a **white robe**; and he came down and **stood in the midst of them**; and the eyes of the whole multitude were turned upon him, and they durst not open their mouths, even one to another, and **wist not what** it meant, for they thought it was an angel that had appeared unto them.

> KJV **(1NT/4)** <u>Revelation 21:10</u> And he carried me away in the spirit to a great and high mountain, and shewed me that great city, the holy Jerusalem, **descending out of heaven** from God,)
>
> KJV **(3NT/3)** <u>Revelation 7:9</u> After this I beheld, and, lo, a great multitude, which no man could number, of all nations, and kindreds, and people, and tongues, stood before the throne, and before the Lamb, **clothed** with **white robe**s, and palms in their hands;)
>
> KJV **(1NT/2)** <u>Luke 24:36</u> And as they thus spake, Jesus himself **stood in the midst of them**, and saith unto them, Peace be unto you.)
>
> KJV **(1NT/1)** <u>Mark 9:6</u> For he **wist not what** to say; for they were sore afraid.)

BOM <u>4 Nephi 1:3</u> And they **had all things common** among them; therefore there were not **rich and poor, bond and free**, but they were all made free, and **partakers of the heavenly gift**.

> KJV **(1NT/1)** <u>Revelation 13:16</u> And he causeth all, both small and great, **rich and poor, free and bond**, to receive a mark in their right hand, or in their foreheads:)
>
> KJV **(2NT/2)** <u>Acts 2:44</u> And all that believed were together, and **had all things common**;)
>
> KJV **(1NT/2)** <u>Hebrews 6:4</u> For it is impossible for those who were once enlightened, and have tasted **of the heavenly gift**, and were made **partakers** of the Holy Ghost,)

BOM <u>Mormon 9:14</u> And then cometh the judgment of the Holy One upon them; and then cometh the time that **he that is filthy** shall **be filthy still**; **and he that is righteous** shall **be righteous still**; he that is happy shall be happy still; and he that is unhappy shall be unhappy still.

> KJV **(1NT/1)** <u>Revelation 22:11</u> He that is unjust, let him be unjust **still**: and **he** which **is filthy**, let him **be filthy still**: **and he that is righteous**, let him **be righteous still**: and he that is holy, let him be holy **still**.)

BOM <u>Ether 3:1</u> And it came to pass that the brother of Jared, (now the number of the vessels which had been prepared was eight) went forth unto the mount, which they called the mount Shelem, because of its exceeding height, and did molten out of a rock sixteen small stones; and they were white and clear, even **as transparent glass**; and he did carry them in his hands upon the top of the mount, and cried again unto the Lord, saying:

> **KJV (1NT/1)** Revelation 21:21 And the twelve gates were twelve pearls: every several gate was of one pearl: and the street of the city was pure gold, **as** it were **transparent glass**.)

BOM Ether 13:3 And that it was the place of the **New Jerusalem**, which should **come down out of heaven**, and the **holy sanctuary of the Lord**.

> **KJV (2NT/8)** Revelation 21:2 And I John saw the holy city, **new Jerusalem, com**ing **down** from God **out of heaven**, prepared as a bride adorned for her husband.)
>
> **KJV** (5/1) Numbers 19:20 But the man that shall be unclean, and shall not purify himself, that soul shall be cut off from among the congregation, because he hath defiled the **sanctuary of the LORD**: the water of separation hath not been sprinkled upon him; he is unclean.)

BOM Ether 13:9 And there shall be **a new heaven and a new earth**; and they shall be like **unto** the **old** save the **old** have **passed away**, and **all things** have **become new**.

> **KJV (1NT/1)** Revelation 21:1 And I saw **a new heaven and a new earth**: for the first heaven and the first earth were **passed away**; and there was no more sea.)
>
> **KJV (1NT/1)** 2 Corinthians 5:17 Therefore if any man be in Christ, he is a **new** creature: **old things** are **passed away**; behold, **all things** are **become new**.)

Now that we have finished the numerous uses of phrases used in the Book of Mormon and only found only one time in the New Testament. I just want to outline some of the large numbers of phrases found only one time from the Old Testament. Now space will not allow me to show them all here so I will give you the book of the Old Testament and the number of time Joseph Smith used a phrase from that book to compile the Book of Mormon. It is important to remember that the books that appear after Jeremiah should not be found in the Book of Mormon since the supposed writers of the Book of Mormon left for the "promised land" after that time. Some scholars believe that even parts of Jeremiah should not be included as it is believed they also were written after the time the characters in the Book of Mormon left Jerusalem for the "promised land". He used a total of 132 phrases, not including more common words. These 132 single use phrases from the Old Testament after Jeremiah should not, as those from the New Testament, even be in the Book of Mormon as they appear in time after the characters of the Book of Mormon left Jerusalem. Now if you include these with those of the

New Testament (2532) you have 2,664, a staggering number even though we are not even including phrases that may appear more than once in the Bible. This means that he utilized 2,644 phrases and key words from books of the Bible that he should not have used, for to the characters of the Book of Mormon, a continent away, they did not even exist. This again, as everything we have outlined, is staggering evidence that the Book of Mormon is a fake.

You will note that he uses phrase from Malachi the last book of the Old Testament 42 times. He does this as a result of trying to use "end time" meanings in his interpretations of the "end times" as it relates to him and the Book of Mormon.

You will also notice that he utilizes Isaiah 608 times, well over any other book. This is a result, as you may have noticed in chapter two, of using Isaiah and its prophesies as the basis for the Book of Mormon and its coming forth. Remember the "isles of the sea". I have charted the books of the Old Testament for you and the number of times key words and phrases were used in the Book of Mormon.

Book	Times	Book	Times
Genesis	75 times	Proverbs	26 times
Exodus	65 times	Ecclesiastes	13 times
Leviticus	4 times	Song of Solomon	1 time
Numbers	20 times	Isaiah	608 times
Deuteronomy	46 times	Jeremiah	82 times
Joshua	4 times	Lamentations	16 times
Judges	5 times	Ezekiel	26 times
Ruth	1 time	Daniel	22 times
1 Samuel	27 times	Hosea	12 times
2 Samuel	18 times	Joel	8 times
1 Kings	54 times	Amos	3 times
2 Kings	17 times	Obadiah	0 times
1 Chronicles	9 times	Jonah	2 times
2 Chronicles	11 times	Micah	16 times
Ezra	2 times	Nahum	0 times
Nehemiah	10 times	Habakkuk	2 times
Esther	4 times	Zephaniah	2 times
Job	21 times	Haggai	1 time
Psalm	118 times	Zechariah	8 times
	Malachi	42 times	

To end this chapter Joseph Smith used key words and phrases from the Bible, that are found only once in the Bible, 4023 times. I am not counting all those key words and phrases from the Bible that are found more than once in the BOM which total in the tens of thousands.

Chapter Six

The Use of the Bible in Detail

Now that we have looked at how Joseph Smith used the New and Old Testaments in short or used verses of The Old and New Testaments to enhance the Book of Mormon and have also looked at how Joseph Smith used the commentaries to create parts of the Book of Mormon, let us now look at how he utilized the Bible and the commentaries to create entire stories. I would like to point out as I have throughout this book that I don't see how you could have read this far and still believe that the Book of Mormon is divine in any way and that it was not written by Joseph Smith.

Also, let us start with a simple example of how Joseph Smith took verses or ideas from the Bible to create his own stories or ideas in the Book of Mormon. Let us look at 1 Nephi 3:7 And it came to pass that I, Nephi, said unto my father: I will go and do the things which the Lord hath commanded, *for I know that the Lord giveth no commandments unto the children of men save he shall prepare a way for them that they may accomplish the thing which he commandeth them.*

As you will note I have used italics on the area we will look be looking into. Many of you who are familiar with the Bible already know what verse this sounds like. 1 Corinthians 10:13

1 Corinthians 10:13 There hath no temptation taken you but such as is common to man: but God is faithful, who will not suffer you to be tempted above that ye are able; but will with the temptation also make a way to escape, that ye may be able to bear it.

As you can see Joseph Smith took the idea behind this verse in 1 Corinthians and utilized it to make his own verse in the Book of Mormon. This is a small example but Joseph Smith also did this type of manipulation on a much grander scale and again it would be impossible to recount them all in this book but I will hit several of them here and suggest you pick up my CD or go to the website to obtain more detail.

The Use of the Book of Revelation

As you we have already noted Joseph Smith used several books of the Bible more often than others. One of those books was The Book of Revelation. Please note that Revelations was written over 700 years after 1 Nephi and therefore the Book of Mormon should not contain exact quotes from Revelation but it does. The use of the commentaries creates no doubts that the quotes were copied from Revelation. Here we will take a look in more detail at how Joseph Smith used this book to create long sections of the Book of

Mormon. We will begin by looking at **BOM** 1 Nephi chapter 14.

BOM 1 Nephi 14:9 And it came to pass that he said unto me: Look, and behold that great and abominable church, which is the **mother of abominations**, whose founder is the devil.

> **KJV (1NT/4)** Revelation 17:5 And upon her forehead was a name written, MYSTERY, BABYLON THE GREAT, THE **MOTHER OF** HARLOTS AND **ABOMINATIONS** OF THE EARTH.)
>
> **Note**: Many people of Joseph Smith's day and just prior believed that the Catholic church was the "abominable church" as can be counted in the commentaries, as here in Gill: (I have added italics for emphasis:
>
> **KJV** Rev 17:4 "and this being a golden cup may design the external lustre and splendour of the worship of the *church of Rome*, by which many have been drawn into a compliance with it, which is attended with many *abominable*,"

BOM 1 Nephi 14:10 And he said unto me: Behold there are save two churches only; the one is the church of **the Lamb of God**, and the other is the church of the devil; wherefore, whoso belongeth not to the church of **the Lamb of God** belongeth to that great church, which is the **mother of abominations**; and she is **the whore** of all the earth.

> **KJV (1NT/4)** Revelation 17:5 And upon her forehead was a name written, MYSTERY, BABYLON THE GREAT, THE **MOTHER OF** HARLOTS AND **ABOMINATIONS** OF THE EARTH.)
>
> **KJV** (Revelation 17:15 And he saith unto me, The waters which thou sawest, where **the whore** sitteth, are peoples, and multitudes, and nations, and tongues.)
>
> **KJV (2NT/35)** John 1:29 The next day John seeth Jesus coming unto him, and saith, Behold **the Lamb of God**, which taketh away the sin of the world.)

BOM 1 Nephi 14:11 And it came to pass that I looked and beheld **the whore** *of all the earth*, and **she sat upon many waters**; and she had **dominion over all the earth**, among **all nations, kindreds, tongues, and people.**

> **KJV (1NT/2)** Revelation 17:1 And there came one of the seven angels which had the seven vials, and talked with me, saying unto me, Come hither; I will shew unto thee the judgment of the great **whore that sitteth upon many waters**:)
>
> **KJV (1NT/8)** Revelation 7:9 After this I beheld, and, lo, a great multitude, which no man could number, of **all nations, and kindreds, and people, and tongues**, stood before the throne, and before the Lamb, clothed with white robes, and palms in their hands;)
>
> **KJV** (1/1) Genesis 1:26 And God said, Let us make man in our image, after our likeness: and let them have **dominion** over the fish of

the sea, and over the fowl of the air, and over the cattle, and **over all the earth**, and over every creeping thing that creepeth upon the earth.)

COM Gill: Rev 17:1 "her *sitting* here may be in allusion to the posture of harlots plying of men; or may denote her ease, rest, and grandeur, sitting as a queen; and is chiefly expressive of her power and *dominion over* the kings and *nations of the earth*,"

Note: Notice that Gill state the same thing that Joseph Smith does in 1 Nephi 14:71, that the whore had "dominion over" the whole earth.

BOM 1 Nephi 14:12 And it came to pass that I beheld the church of **the Lamb of God**, and its numbers were few, because of the *wickedness and abominations* of **the whore** who **sat upon many waters**; nevertheless, I beheld that the church of **the Lamb**, who were *the saints of God,* were also upon all the face of the earth; and their dominions upon the face of the earth were small, because of the *wickedness* **of the great whore** whom I saw.

KJV (1NT/2) Revelation 17:1 And there came one of the seven angels which had the seven vials, and talked with me, saying unto me, Come hither; I will shew unto thee the judgment of the great **whore that sitteth upon many waters**:)

KJV (2NT/1) Revelation 17:1 And there came one of the seven angels which had the seven vials, and talked with me, saying unto me, Come hither; I will shew unto thee the judgment **of the great whore** that sitteth upon many waters:)

COM Gill: Rev 18:6 "not in the cup of her *abominations*, her errors, idolatries, *and wickedness*; but in the cup of afflictions and trouble,"

Note: Notice how Gill's commentary on Revelations specifically on "the whore" says the same thing about her, "abominations and wickedness".

COM Wesley: Rev 18:6 "Others; in particular, *the saints of God.*" (Henry, Clarke)

BOM 1 Nephi 14:13 And it came to pass that I beheld that the great **mother of abominations** did *gather together* multitudes upon the face of all the earth, among all *the nations of the Gentiles, to fight against* the **Lamb of God**.

KJV (1NT/4) Revelation 17:5 And upon her forehead was a name written, MYSTERY, BABYLON THE GREAT, THE **MOTHER OF** HARLOTS AND **ABOMINATIONS** OF THE EARTH.)

COM Also notice how this fits with the next few verses. Gill: Rev 16:14 "that is, they will persuade them to *gather together, to fight against the saints*, the Gentile Christians in the several parts of the world, and the Jewish Christians, now settled in their own land; and this will be the battle of the Lord, who is God Almighty, and it will be fighting against him; and therefore the attempt must be vain and fruitless, and issue in the ruin of those who are gathered to it, who will be deceived and drawn into it by these diabolical spirits: and this is called "the battle of that great day of God"; not of the day of judgment, for it will be before that time; but of *that day* of vengeance upon all the remains of his and his church's enemies, both Pagan, Papal, and Mahometan, who will for this purpose be gathered together; "which", as the Ethiopic version renders it, "God has appointed".)

COM Henry: <u>Eze 39:1-7</u> "in the isles, that is, *the nations of the Gentiles*." (Clarke)

Note: We already discussed in the first chapter why Joseph Smith uses the phrase "nations of the gentiles".

BOM <u>1 Nephi 14:14</u> And it came to pass that I, Nephi, beheld the power of **the Lamb of God**, that it descended upon the saints of the church of **the Lamb**, and upon the covenant people of the Lord, who were **scattered upon all the face of the earth**; and they were armed with righteousness and with **the power of God** in **great glory**.

> **KJV (11NT/48)** <u>Matthew 22:29</u> Jesus answered and said unto them, Ye do err, not knowing the scriptures, nor **the power of God**.)
>
> **KJV (2NT/6)** <u>Matthew 24:30</u> And then shall appear the sign of the Son of man in heaven: and then shall all the tribes of the earth mourn, and they shall see the Son of man coming in the clouds of heaven with **power and great glory**.)
>
> **KJV (1/6)** <u>Genesis 11:8</u> So the LORD **scattered** them abroad from thence **upon the face of all the earth**: and they left off to build the city.)

BOM <u>1 Nephi 14:15</u> And it came to pass that I beheld that **the wrath of God** was **poured out** upon that great and abominable church, insomuch that there were **wars and rumors of wars** among all the **nations and kindreds of the earth**.

> **KJV (1NT/1)** <u>Revelation 14:10</u> The same shall drink of the wine of **the wrath of God**, which is **poured out** without mixture into the cup of his indignation; and he shall be tormented with fire and brimstone in the presence of the holy angels, and in the presence of the Lamb:)
>
> **KJV (2NT/6)** <u>Matthew 24:6</u> And ye shall hear of **wars and rumours of wars**: see that ye be not troubled: for all these things must come to pass, but the end is not yet.)

BOM <u>1 Nephi 14:16</u> And as there began to be **wars and rumors of wars** among all the nations which belonged to the **mother of abominations**, the angel spake unto me, saying: Behold, **the wrath of God** is upon the **mother of harlots**; and behold, **thou seest** all these things –

> **KJV (10/14)** <u>Rev 14:19</u> - The great winepress of **the wrath of**

God...)

KJV (15/10) <u>Rev 1:11</u> - Saying, I am Alpha and Omega, the first and the last and, what **thou seest**, write in a book;)

BOM <u>1 Nephi 14:17</u> And when **the day cometh that** the **wrath of God is poured out** upon the **mother of harlots**, which is the great and **abominable** church of all the earth, whose founder is the devil, then, at that day, *(5) the work of the Father* shall (17) commence (1340 AD), in preparing the way for the fulfilling of his covenants, which he hath made to his people who are of the house of Israel.

> **KJV (1NT/1)** <u>Revelation 14:10</u> The same shall drink of the wine of the **wrath of God, which is poured out** without mixture into the cup of his indignation; and he shall be tormented with fire and brimstone in the **presence** of the holy angels, and in the **presence** of the Lamb:)
>
> **KJV** (1/9) <u>Malachi 4:1</u> For, behold, **the day cometh, that** shall burn as an oven; and all the proud, yea, and all that do wickedly, shall be stubble: and **the day that cometh** shall burn them up, saith the LORD of hosts, that it shall leave them neither root nor branch.)
>
> **KJV (1NT/3)** <u>Revelation 17:5</u> And upon her forehead was a name written, MYSTERY, BABYLON THE GREAT, THE **MOTHER OF HARLOTS** AND ABOMINATIONS OF THE EARTH.)
>
> **COM** Henry: <u>Col 1:12-29</u> "It is spoken of as *the work of the Father*,")

BOM <u>1 Nephi 14:18</u> And it came to pass that the angel spake unto me, saying: Look!

BOM <u>1 Nephi 14:19</u> **And I looked and** beheld a man, and he was dressed in a **white robe.**

> **KJV** (9/14) <u>Revelation 6:8</u> **And I looked, and** behold a pale horse: and his name that sat on him was Death, and Hell followed with him. And power was given unto them over the fourth part of the earth, to kill with sword, and with hunger, and with death, and with the beasts of the earth.)
>
> **KJV (3NT/3)** <u>Revelation 7:9</u> After this I beheld, and, lo, a great multitude, which no man could number, of all nations, and kindreds, and people, and tongues, stood before the throne, and before the Lamb, clothed with **white robe**s, and palms in their hands;)

BOM <u>1 Nephi 14:20</u> **And the angel said unto me**: Behold one of **the twelve apostles of the Lamb.**

> **KJV** <u>Revelation 17:7</u> **And the angel said unto me**, Wherefore didst thou marvel? I will tell thee the mystery of the woman, and of the beast that carrieth her, which hath the seven heads and ten horns.
>
> **KJV (1NT/9)** <u>Revelation 21:14</u> And the wall of the city had twelve foundations, and in them the names of **the twelve apostles of the**

Lamb.)

BOM 1 Nephi 14:21 Behold, he shall see and write the remainder of these things; yea, and also many things which have been.

BOM 1 Nephi 14:22 And he shall also write concerning **the end of the world**.

> **KJV Note:** Even though this phrase exists twice in the OT it does not have the same meaning as it has in the NT verses: **(5NT/2)** Matthew 13:49 So shall it be at **the end of the world**: the angels shall come forth, and sever the wicked from among the just,)
>
> **Note**: This is obviously a reference to John and The Book of Revelation. Which of course Joseph Smith has been quoting from.

BOM 1 Nephi 14:23 Wherefore, the things which he shall write are **just and true**; and behold they are written in the book **which thou** beheld proceeding out of the mouth of the Jew; and at the time they proceeded out of the mouth of the Jew, or, at the time the book proceeded out of the mouth of the Jew, the things which were written were *plain and pure,* and **most precious** and easy to the understanding of all men.

> **Note the Jew is John the Revelator: KJV (1NT/6)** Revelation 15:3 And they sing the song of Moses the servant of God, and the song of the Lamb, saying, Great and marvellous are thy works, Lord God Almighty; **just and true** are thy ways, thou King of saints.)
>
> **KJV** Revelation 17:12 And the ten horns **which thou** sawest are ten

kings, which have received no kingdom as yet; but receive power as kings one hour with the beast.

> **COM** Henry: 1Co 3:18-20 "*plain and pure* Christianity will be likely to be despised by those who can suit their doctrines to the corrupt taste of their hearers,")
>
> **KJV (2NT/10)** Revelation 18:12 The merchandise of gold, and silver, and precious stones, and of pearls, and fine linen, and purple, and silk, and scarlet, and all thyine wood, and all manner vessels of ivory, and all manner vessels of **most precious** wood, and of brass, and iron, and marble,)

Joseph Smith used Revelation extensively through 1 Nephi chapters 10,11,12,13, and 14. 2 Nephi chapter 9, Mosiah chapter 3, and of course used here and there throughout the Book of Mormon. Space constraints make it impossible to keep going.

The made up Prophets and New Testament Theology

From 1 Nephi chapter 19 through 1 Nephi chapter 22 the Book of Mormon claims to quote from four prophets including Moses. But the other three are made up. One is called Zenos, as you have already been made aware was made up from the commentaries, and Zenock, which is obviously made up from the commentaries and which has the name Zeno as we have already covered. Here he just adds "ck" to the end. The other prophet is Neum, which is found in Clarke and as you will see in the names chapter is a Hebrew word Joseph Smith commonly used Hebrew to make up names and words. (Clarke: "who use their tongues, נאם וינאמו vaiyinamu **neum**, and solemnly pronounce,")

Now when Joseph Smith claims that the writer of this section is quoting from these prophets it is interesting to note that they are living more than 600 years before the New Testament was written. So here I will outline many of the New Testament phrases and theologies that could only come from the New Testament and should therefore not be found in this section of the Book of Mormon and not at all from "prophets of old" as he calls Zenos, Zenock, Neum and Moses.

"to be crucified", (1) **"vapor of"**, (1) **"saith the prophet"**, (1) **"the rocks rend"**, (1) **"power and glory"**, (1) **"from the four quarters of the Earth"**, (1) **"every nation, kindred, tongue and people"**, (1) **"branch broken off"**, (1) **"for after this manner"**, "according to the flesh", "things pertaining to", **"the more part"**, (1) **"shall be hated of all men"**, (1) **"things of which are temporal"**, "the time cometh", (1) **"unto Abraham, saying: In thy seed shall all the kindreds of the earth be blessed."**, (1) **"all the kindreds of the earth be blessed"**, (1) **"pervert the right ways of the Lord"**, (1) **"and great shall be the fall of it."**, (1) **"the wrath of God shall be poured out"**, (1) **"shall be saved,** even if it so be, **as by fire"**, (1) **"blood, and fire, and vapor of smoke"**, (1) **"it must needs be"**, (1) **"A prophet shall the Lord your God raise up unto you, like unto me; him shall ye hear in all things whatsoever he shall say unto you."**, (1) **"And it shall come to pass that** all those who **will not hear that prophet shall be"**, (1) **"shall not be confounded."**, "the devil", (1) **"get gain"**, (1) **"the lusts of the flesh"**, (1) **"the things of the world"**, (1) **"dominion, and might, and power, and great glory"**, (1) **"the four quarters of the earth"**, (1) **"his sheep,** and **they know"**, (1) **"and there shall be one fold and one shepherd"**, (1) **"shall find pasture"**, (1) **Satan...be loosed"**, (1) **"for the space of"**, (1) **"hath no power"**, (1) **"I would that ye"**, (1) **"endure to the end,** ye **shall be saved"**, **"at the last day"**, **"thus it is"**.)

All these phrases come from the New Testament and can in no way be attributed to prophets over 600 years ago, especially with such a large number of key phrases from the New Testament. An example of a short section made up from a section of the New Testament.

Joseph Smith many times took sections of the Bible to create small sections of the Book of Mormon. Of course he attempted as much as possible not to be too blatant with this as he would have been found out more readily. This is an example of one such instance found in Enos 1:5-8 and outlines the use of Luke to create these verses.

BOM Enos 1:5 And **there came a voice** unto me, **saying: Enos, thy sins are**

forgiven thee, and thou shalt be blessed.

> **KJV (2NT/1)** <u>Luke 9:35</u> And **there came a voice** out of the cloud, **saying,** This is my beloved Son: hear him.)
>
> **KJV (1NT/1)** <u>Luke 5:20</u> And when he saw their faith, he said unto him, Man, **thy sins are forgiven thee**.)
>
> **KJV (1NT/1)** <u>Luke 14:14</u> **And thou shalt be blessed**; for they cannot recompense thee: for thou shalt be recompensed at the resurrection of the just.)

BOM <u>Enos 1:6</u> And I, Enos, knew that God could not lie; wherefore, my guilt was swept away.

BOM <u>Enos 1:7</u> And I said: Lord, how is it done?

BOM <u>Enos 1:8</u> And he said unto me: *because of thy faith* in Christ, whom thou hast never before heard nor seen. And many years pass away before he shall manifest himself in the flesh; wherefore, go to, **thy faith hath made thee whole**.

> **KJV (5NT/1)** <u>Luke 8:48</u> And he said unto her, Daughter, be of good comfort: **thy faith hath made thee whole**; go in peace.)
>
> **Note:** As you can see he used Luke for this small section but again I give this as an example as he did this throughout the Book of Mormon and space restraints make it impossible to show here.

And now a more blatant use of the New Testament.

In 3 Nephi chapters 12 through chapter 15 the Book of Mormon Jesus after his resurrection in the Holy Land comes and visit those in the Americas. What is interesting is that Jesus supposedly, in most cases word for word, says what is written in Matthew chapter 5 verse three all the way through Matthew chapter 7:27. Now because of space constraints I can't detail them all here but for the most part it is an actual quote from Matthew 5:3 through Matthew 7:27. I will outline some interesting points during of this section here.

To start let us look at the beginning of 3 Nephi 12 were Jesus is giving what is know in the Bible as the Sermon on the Mount.

BOM <u>3 Nephi 12:3</u> Yea, **blessed are the poor in spirit** who come unto me, **for theirs is the kingdom of heaven**.

> **KJV (1NT/1)** <u>Matthew 5:3</u> **Blessed are the poor in spirit: for theirs is the kingdom of heaven.**)

BOM <u>3 Nephi 12:4</u> And again, **blessed are** all **they that mourn, for they shall be comforted**.

> **KJV (1NT/1)** <u>Matthew 5:4</u> **Blessed are they that mourn: for they shall be comforted.**)

BOM <u>3 Nephi 12:5</u> And **blessed are the meek, for they shall inherit the earth**.

> **KJV (1NT/1)** <u>Matthew 5:5</u> **Blessed are the meek: for they shall inherit the earth.**)

BOM 3 Nephi 12:6 And **blessed are** all **they** who do **hunger and thirst after righteousness, for they shall be filled** with the Holy Ghost.

KJV (1NT/1) Matthew 5:6 **Blessed are they** which **do hunger and thirst after righteousness: for they shall be filled.**)

Notice that he makes minor changes as he sees fit. Such as verse six where in the original the ending is "they shall be filled" and Joseph Smith adds "with the Holy Ghost". Now what is very interesting is that this is known as the "Sermon on the Mount" and this sermon can be found in Luke chapter six. So why would Jesus visit another land and only say what he said in a Gospel that had yet to be written and in fact was written sometime after his death, and almost exactly as it is found in the Gospel of Matthew and not in the way it is found in the Gospel of Luke. Precisely because he didn't, Joseph Smith was writing a fake book and copied it from only the Gospel of Matthew and not for example Luke as that account has differences as we will see.

Here is Luke's version: Luke 6:20 And he lifted up his eyes on his disciples, and said, **Blessed** be ye poor: for yours is the kingdom of God.

And here is Joseph Smith's version:

BOM 3 Nephi 12:3 Yea, **blessed are the poor in spirit** who come unto me, **for theirs is the kingdom of heaven.**

And now Matthew's version. KJV (1NT/1) Matthew 5:3 **Blessed are the poor in spirit: for theirs is the kingdom of heaven.**)

Can it be any more obvious that Joseph Smith copied this from Matthew. Well to "add fuel to the fire" as they say, let us look at another.

Another change:

BOM 3 Nephi 12:10 And **blessed are** all **they** who **are persecuted for** my name's **sake, for theirs is the kingdom of heaven.**

KJV (1NT/1) Matthew 5:10 **Blessed are they** which **are persecuted for** righteousness' sake: **for theirs is the kingdom of heaven.**)

Another change:

BOM 3 Nephi 12:12 For ye shall have great joy **and be exceedingly glad, for great** shall be **your reward in heaven; for so persecuted they the prophets** who **were before you.**

KJV (1NT/1) Matthew 5:12 Rejoice, **and be exceeding glad: for great** is **your reward in heaven: for so persecuted they the prophets** which **were before you.**)

Of interest.

BOM 3 Nephi 12:13 **Verily, verily, I say unto you,** I give unto you to be **the salt of the earth; but if the salt** shall lose its **savor wherewith shall** the earth **be salted?** The salt shall be **thenceforth good for nothing, but to be cast out and to be trodden under foot of men.**

Note: Joseph Smith uses the term "wherewith shall the earth be salted?" instead of using the word "it" as it is in the King James

Version of the Bible again his attempt at clarification as he did on many occasions.

KJV (1NT/23) John 5:24 **Verily, verily, I say unto you, He that** heareth my word, and believeth on him that sent me, hath everlasting life, and shall not come into condemnation; but is passed from death unto life.)

KJV (1NT/3) Matthew 5:13 Ye **are the salt of the earth: but if the salt** have lost his **savour, wherewith shall** it **be salted?** it is **thenceforth good for nothing, but to be cast out, and to be trodden under foot of men.**)

Additional change.

BOM 3 Nephi 12:14 **Verily, verily, I say unto you,** I give unto you to be the light of this people. **A city that is set on a hill cannot be hid.**

KJV (1NT/1) Matthew 5:14 Ye are the light of the world. **A city that is set on an hill cannot be hid.**)

BOM 3 Nephi 12:18 **For verily I say unto you, one jot** nor **tittle** hath not passed away **from the law,** but in me it hath **all been fulfilled.**

KJV (1NT/1) Matthew 5:18 **For verily I say unto you,** Till heaven and earth pass, **one jot** or one **tittle** shall in no wise **pass from the law,** till **all be fulfilled.**)

Now Joseph Smith skips Matthew 5:19 and goes straight to verse twenty. Which says this:

"Whosoever therefore shall break one of these least commandments, and shall teach men so, he shall be called the least in the kingdom of heaven: but whosoever shall do and teach them, the same shall be called great in the kingdom of heaven."

He replaces this with 3 Nephi 12 :20 and 21 which both talk about the law and what is interesting is that he includes the verse in Matthew where he picks back up with Matthew 5:20.

BOM 3 Nephi 12:19 And behold, I have given you the law and the commandments of my Father, that ye shall **believe in me,** and that ye shall repent of your sins, and come unto me with **a broken heart and a contrite spirit.** Behold, ye have the commandments before you, and the law is fulfilled.

KJV (2NT/8) Matthew 18:6 But whoso shall offend one of these little ones which **believe in me,** it were better for him that a millstone were hanged about his neck, and that he were drowned in the depth of the sea.)

KJV (1/6) Psalm 34:18 The LORD is nigh unto them that are of **a broken heart; and** saveth such as be of **a contrite spirit.**)

BOM 3 Nephi 12:20 Therefore come unto me and be ye saved; **for verily I say unto you,** that except ye shall **keep my commandments,** (which I have commanded you at this time, **ye shall in no case enter into the kingdom of**

heaven.

> **KJV (1NT/1)** <u>Matthew 5:20</u> **For I say unto you**, That except your righteousness shall exceed the righteousness of the scribes and Pharisees, **ye shall in no case enter into the kingdom of heaven**.)
>
> **Note**: I have bolded "keep my commandments" and "for verily I say unto you" as they are both quotes of Jesus.

In this next verse Joseph Smith has to add a few words because we already know that he said in the beginning of the Book of Mormon that they took the books of the Torah with them.

BOM 3 Nephi 12:21 **Ye have heard that it** hath been **said** by **them of old time**, and it is also written before you, that **thou shalt not kill, and whosoever shall kill shall be in danger of the judgment** of God;

> **KJV (1NT/1)** <u>Matthew 5:21</u> **Ye have heard that it** was **said** of **them of old time, Thou shalt not kill; and whosoever shall kill shall be in danger of the judgment**:)

And now more changes:

BOM 3 Nephi 12:23 **Therefore, if** ye shall come unto me, or shall desire to come unto me, **and rememberest that thy brother hast aught against thee-**

> **KJV (1NT/1)** <u>Matthew 5:23</u> **Therefore if** thou bring thy gift to the altar, **and** there **rememberest that thy brother hath** ought **against thee.**)

BOM 3 Nephi 12:24 **Go thy way** unto **thy brother, and first be reconciled to thy brother, and then come** unto me with full purpose of heart, and I will receive you.

> **KJV (1NT/1)** <u>Matthew 5:24</u> Leave there thy gift before the altar, **and go thy way; first be reconciled to thy brother, and then come** and offer thy gift)
>
> **Note:** Notice that Joseph Smith left out the entire concept of "the gift".

BOM 3 Nephi 12:25 **Agree with thine adversary quickly while thou art in the way with him, lest at any time** he shall get thee, **and thou** shalt **be cast into prison**.

> **KJV (1NT/1)** <u>Matthew 5:25</u> **Agree with thine adversary quickly, while**s thou art in the way with him; **lest at any time** the adversary deliver thee to the judge, and the judge deliver **thee** to the officer, **and thou be cast into prison**.)

BOM 3 Nephi 12:26 **Verily, verily, I say unto thee, thou shalt by no means come out thence** until **thou hast paid the uttermost** senine. And while ye are in prison can ye pay even one senine? **Verily, verily, I say unto you,** Nay.

> **KJV (1NT/1)** <u>Matthew 5:26</u> **Verily I say unto thee, Thou shalt by no means come out thence, till thou hast paid the uttermost** farthing

Note: Obviously Joseph Smith changes the Bible money word "farthing" which was the smallest Roman coin in use and replaces it with a "senine" from the Book of Mormon. The problem is that the context of the saying is to say that, in our more modern terms, the last penny or the least in the monetary system. The problem with the "senine" is that it is not the least in value in the Book of Mormon monetary system. The farthing was 1/64 the value of a denarius which was the value of a days wage at the time. Now according to Alma 11:3 the "senine" was the value of a days wage which is equal to a Denarius.

Note: Out of the 23 times Joseph Smith uses verily, verily, I say unto" this is the only time he uses the same phrase as here in John:

KJV (1NT/1) John 3:5 Jesus answered, **Verily, verily, I say unto thee**, Except a man be born of water and of the Spirit, he cannot enter into the kingdom of God.)

Examples of using stories in the Bible to create his own stories.

Joseph Smith utilized Bible stories on several occasions to create his own stories. In other words he would follow the basic outline of the story but in his case he would actually use words and phrases from those Bible stories which gives us the evidence that he used them to begin with. We will begin by using the story of Jesus begin turned over to face his enemies.

BOM Mosiah 17:6 And after three days, having counseled with his priests, he caused that he should again be brought before him.

Note: Here we have the same thing happening to Jesus with the priests as is happening to Abinadi in this Book of Mormon story. Jesus was taken before the priests and questioned as is Abinadi.

BOM Mosiah 17:7 And he said unto him: Abinadi, we have found **an accusation against** thee, and thou art **worthy of death**.

KJV (1NT/1) Luke 6:7 And the scribes and Pharisees watched him, whether he would heal on the sabbath day; that they might find **an accusation against** him.)

KJV (Luke 23:15 No, nor yet Herod: for I sent you to him; and, lo, nothing **worthy of death** is done unto him.)

Note: Now Jesus also was taken before the King in his case Pilate and in Abinadi's case King Noah. Here in Luke 23:15 we have Pilate saying he did "nothing worthy of death" hence Joseph Smith using "worthy of death" in his story of Abinadi.

BOM Mosiah 7:8 For thou hast said that God himself should come down among the children of men; and now, for this cause thou shalt be put to death unless thou wilt recall all the words which thou hast **spoken evil** concerning me and my people.

KJV (John 18:23 Jesus answered him, If I have **spoken evil**, bear witness of the evil: but if well, why smitest thou me?)

Note: Here the same story of Jesus' time leading up to his crucifixion. Here he is before the High Priest just before he is sent to Pilate when the guard strikes him.

BOM Mosiah 17:9 Now Abinadi said unto him: I say unto you, I will not recall the words which I have spoken unto you concerning this people, for they are true; and **that ye may know** of their surety I have suffered myself that I have fallen into your hands.

KJV (John 19:4 Pilate therefore went forth again, and saith unto them, Behold, I bring him forth to you, **that ye may know** that I find no fault in him.)

Note: Obviously this verse of John is also during the time Jesus was before Pilate. Jesus also let himself "fall into" their hands.

BOM Mosiah 17:10 Yea, and I will suffer even until death, and I will not recall my words, and they shall stand as **a testimony against** you. And if ye slay me ye will shed innocent blood, and this shall also stand as **a testimony against** you at the last day.

KJV (4NT/1) Mark 6:11 And whosoever shall not receive you, nor hear you, when ye depart thence, shake off the dust under your feet for **a testimony against** them. Verily I say unto you, It shall be more tolerable for Sodom and Gomorrha in the day of judgment, than for that city.

KJV (7/2) Proverbs 6:17 A proud look, a lying tongue, and hands that **shed innocent blood**,)

Note: Obviously the same meaning with this verse in Mark where Jesus basically says the same thing and obviously Jesus was "innocent blood" that was "shed".

BOM Mosiah 17:11 And now king Noah was about to **release him**, for he feared his word; for he feared that the judgments of God would come upon him.

KJV (2NT/1) Luke 23:16 I will therefore chastise him, and **release him**.)

Note: This verse in Luke is also where Jesus was going to be released by King Pilate even though the priests wanted him killed as with King Noah above. And as you will see below the King bowed to the cries of the group against him.

BOM Mosiah 17:12 But the priests lifted up their voices against him, and **began to accuse him, saying**: He has reviled the king. Therefore the king was stirred up in anger against him, and he **delivered him up** that he might be slain.

KJV Luke 23:2 And they **began to accuse him, saying**, We found this fellow perverting the nation, and forbidding to give tribute to

Caesar, saying that he himself is Christ a King.)

KJV (2NT/2) John 18:30 They answered and said unto him, If he were not a malefactor, we would not have **delivered him up** unto thee.)

Note: Again this is similar to Jesus story even though Pilate wanted to let Jesus go the priests rose up in anger against the idea. It is interesting that the verse in John outlined above is also a part of the story of Jesus before Pilate and the priest turning him over to the King.

BOM Mosiah 17:13 And it came to pass that they **took** him **and bound him, and scourged** his skin with (1) faggots (14th Century), yea, even unto death.

KJV (1NT/1) John 18:12 Then the band and the captain and officers of the Jews **took** Jesus, **and bound him**,)

KJV John 19:1 Then Pilate therefore took Jesus, **and scourged** him)

Note: Notice how this verse includes a verse from John 18 as above and of course this is the same story of Jesus' end. Also notice that the words are that Abinadi is "scourged" also done to Jesus as outlined in the verse of John 19:1.

Now if we skip to Mosiah 17:19, by the way in-between these verses Joseph Smith gives us a similar dissertation by Abinadi to that of Jesus, we can see that Abinadi end's his death in a similar way to how the Gospels account Jesus ended his.

BOM Mosiah 17:19 Thus God executeth vengeance upon those that destroy his people. O God, receive my soul.

KJV Luke 23:46 And when Jesus had cried with a loud voice, he said, Father, into thy hands I commend my spirit: and having said thus, he gave up the ghost.)

Note: Notice the similarity of "O God, receive my soul" and "Father, into thy hands I commend my spirit".

Now we will look at a small use of the story of Paul's conversion by Jesus from Mosiah chapter 27 when Alma experiences a similar event. But in our case Joseph Smith makes the mistake of copying some of the words and phrases from the similar Paul event.

BOM Mosiah 27:10 And now it came to pass that while he was going about to destroy the church of God, for he did go about secretly with the sons of Mosiah seeking to destroy the church, and to lead astray the people of the Lord, contrary to the commandments of God, or even the king --

BOM Mosiah 27:11 And as I said unto you, as they were going about rebelling against God , behold, the angel of the Lord appeared unto them; and he descended as it were in a cloud; and he spake as it were with a voice of thunder, which caused the earth to shake upon which they stood;

Note: Now Paul and his companions where on their way attempting to "destroy the church" just as Alma and the Sons of Mosiah. And also were met with someone from heaven. In one case Jesus and the other an "angel of the Lord"

BOM Mosiah 27:12 And so great was their astonishment, that they **fell to the earth**, and understood not the words which he spake unto them.

> **Note:** As you can see below Paul also "fell to the earth" but in this case there is a difference in what happened next. Those who were with Paul heard a voice but did not see anyone but in the Sons of Mosiah case they saw someone but could not understand the words that he spoke.
>
> **KJV** Acts 9:4 And he **fell to the earth**, and heard a voice saying unto him, Saul, Saul, why persecutest thou me?
>
> **KJV** Acts 9:7 And the men which journeyed with him stood speechless, hearing a voice, but seeing no man.

BOM Mosiah 27:13 Nevertheless he cried again, saying: Alma, a**rise and stand** forth, for **why persecutest thou the church of God**? For the Lord hath said: This is **my church**, and I will establish **it**; and nothing **shall** overthrow **it**, save it is the transgression of my people.

> **KJV (1NT/1)** Acts 26:16 But **rise, and stand** upon thy feet: for I have appeared unto thee for this purpose, to make thee a minister and a witness both of these things which thou hast seen, and of those things in the which I will appear unto thee;)
>
> **KJV (3NT/1)** Acts 9:4 And he fell to the earth, and heard a voice saying unto him, Saul, Saul, **why persecutest thou** me?)
>
> **Note**: Notice that Paul also persecuting the church.
>
> **KJV (8NT/31)** Acts 20:28 Take heed therefore unto yourselves, and to all the flock, over the which the Holy Ghost hath made you overseers, to feed **the church of God**, which he hath purchased with his own blood.)
>
> **Note:** Also notice that the meaning of the last sentence is quite similar to that of a statement of Jesus in Matthew. Joseph Smith, as we have learned, just varies the wording. This is too similar to be just coincidence. For acts "why persecutest thou me" or the church and Joseph Smith uses the same phrase but just clarifies it "why persecutest thou the church of God".
>
> **KJV** Matthew 16:18 And I say also unto thee, That thou art Peter, and upon this rock I will build **my church**; and the gates of hell **shall** not prevail against **it**.

BOM Mosiah 27:14 And again, the angel said: Behold, the Lord hath heard the prayers of his people, and also the prayers of his servant, Alma, who is thy father; for he has prayed with much faith concerning thee **that thou mightest be** brought to **the knowledge of the truth**; therefore, **for this purpose** have I come to convince thee of the power and authority of God, that the prayers of his servants might be answered according to their faith.

> **KJV** (2/6) Psalm 51:4 Against thee, thee only, have I sinned, and done this evil in thy sight: **that thou mightest be** justified when **thou** speakest, and be clear when **thou** judgest.)
>
> **KJV** (3NT/15) 1 Timothy 2:4 Who will have all men to be saved, and to come unto **the knowledge of the truth**.)
>
> **KJV** (2NT/1) Acts 26:16 But rise, and stand upon thy feet: for I have appeared unto thee **for this purpose**, to make thee a minister and a witness both of these things which thou hast seen, and of those things in the which I will appear unto thee;)
>
> **Note**: This verse is also from the same story of Paul's conversion but Paul, much later in the Bible, retells the story to Felix of what happened to him when Christ first appeared to him. So of course this could only mean that it was cross referenced and Joseph Smith new both instances of this story.

BOM Mosiah 27:16 Now I say unto thee: Go, and remember the captivity of thy fathers in the land of Helam, and in the land of Nephi; and remember **how great things he** has **done for** them; for they were in bondage, and he has delivered them. And now I say unto thee, Alma, **go thy way**, and seek to destroy the church no more, that their prayers may be answered, and this even if thou wilt of thyself be cast off.

> **KJV** (1/1) 1 Samuel 12:24 Only fear the LORD, and serve him in truth with all your heart: for consider **how great things he** hath **done for** you.)
>
> **KJV** Acts 9:15 But the Lord said unto him, **Go thy way**: for he is a chosen vessel unto me, to bear my name before the Gentiles, and kings, and the children of Israel:

BOM Mosiah 17:19 And now the astonishment of Alma was so great that he became dumb, that he could not open his mouth; yea, and he became weak, even that he could not move his hands; therefore he was taken by those that were with him, and carried helpless, even until he was laid before his father.

> **Note**: Notice below that Paul lost his sight but Alma became dumb as stated above Joseph Smith just made slight variations on the story. By the way Paul was also "astonished".
>
> **KJV** Acts 9:9 And he was three days without sight, and neither did eat nor drink.

Now we have another story this time in Alma that is similar to the story of Lazarus being raised from the dead by Jesus. In the story in Alma a king known as Lamoni, dies and is raised from the dead just as Lazarus. Let's look at the similarities and Joseph Smith's use of words and phrases from the New Testament. We start with Alma 18:42.

BOM <u>Alma 19:42</u> And now, when he had said this, he fell unto the earth, as if he were dead.

BOM <u>Alma 19:43</u> And it came to pass that his servants took him and carried him in unto his wife, and laid him upon a bed; and he lay as if he were dead for the space of two days and two nights; and his wife, and his sons, and his daughters mourned over him, after the manner of the Lamanites, greatly lamenting his loss.

BOM <u>Alma 19:5</u> Therefore, if this is the case, I would that ye should go in and see my husband, for he has been laid upon his bed for the space of two days and two nights; and some say that he is not dead, but others say that he is dead and that **he stinketh,** and that he ought to be placed in the sepulchre; but as for myself, to me he doth not stink.

> **Note**: Notice here that both accounts have people worrying that the dead, for days, "stinketh", but in both it is "he stinketh".
>
> **KJV (1NT/1)** <u>John 11:39</u> Jesus said, Take ye away the stone. Martha, the sister of him that was dead, saith unto him, Lord, by this time **he stinketh**: for he hath been dead four days.)

BOM <u>Alma 19:7</u> Therefore, what the queen desired of him was his only desire. Therefore, he went in to see the king according as the queen had desired him; and he saw the king, and he knew that he was not dead.

BOM <u>Alma 19:8</u> And he said unto the queen: He **is not dead, but** he **sleepeth** in God, and on the morrow he **shall rise again**; therefore bury him not.

> **Note:** The verses below from the New Testament are from the story of Lazarus.
>
> **KJV (3NT/1)** <u>Matthew 9:24</u> He said unto them, Give place: for the maid **is not dead, but sleepeth**. And they laughed him to scorn)
>
> **KJV (1NT/1)** <u>John 11:23</u> Jesus saith unto her, Thy brother **shall rise again.**)
>
> **Note**: I want to stress here, as I have every so often throughout the book, after reading the similarity between this verse and what Joseph Smith wrote how can there be any doubt as to the authenticity of the Book of Mormon "He is not dead but sleepeth" from a raising of the dead story by Jesus and "shall rise again" from the story of Lazarus, being raised from the dead are beyond coincidence.

BOM <u>Alma 19:9</u> And Ammon said unto her: **Believest thou this?** And she said unto him: I have had no witness save thy word, and the word of our servants; nevertheless I believe that it shall be according as thou hast said.

> **Note**: Jesus asked this of Lazarus' sister. Ammon asks the same thing of the Queen.
>
> **KJV (1NT/2)** <u>John 11:26</u> And whosoever liveth and believeth in me shall never die. **Believest thou this?**)

BOM <u>Alma 19:10</u> And Ammon said unto her: **Blessed art thou** because of thy exceeding faith; I say unto thee, woman, there has not been such **great faith** among all the people of the Nephites.

> **Note**: And now as filler Joseph Smith uses ideas and words of Jesus. Notice how similar the words relating to not finding such "great faith".
>
> **KJV** (Matthew 16:17 And Jesus answered and said unto him, **Blessed art thou**, Simon Barjona: for flesh and blood hath not revealed it unto thee, but my Father which is in heaven.
>
> **KJV (2NT/6)** Matthew 8:10 When Jesus heard it, he marvelled, and said to them that followed, Verily I say unto you, I have not found so **great faith**, no, not in Israel.)

Now as usual I could keep going but I do not have enough room to outline all uses of the Bible stories to create the Book of Mormon stories. In fact he took many story ideas from the Old Testament. But again space will not allow me to go into them in detail; perhaps in the next book.

I wanted to add this here as it is interesting.

> **Note**: This as it explains is God talking to Nephi. The problem is that God uses phrases from Matthew in which Jesus is talking to his apostles.

BOM Alma 10:6 Behold, thou art Nephi, and I am God. Behold, I declare it unto **thee in the presence of** mine **angels**, that ye shall **have power** over this people, and shall **smite the earth with** famine, and with pestilence, and destruction, according to the wickedness of this people.

> **KJV (2NT/1)** Revelation 14:10 The same shall drink of the wine of the wrath of God, which is poured out without mixture into the cup of his indignation; and he shall be tormented with fire and brimstone **in the presence of** the holy **angels**, and in the **presence** of the Lamb:)
>
> **KJV (1NT/1)** Revelation 11:6 These **have power** to shut heaven, that it rain not in the days of their prophecy: and have power over waters to turn them to blood, and to **smite the earth with** all plagues, as often as they will.)

BOM Alma 10:7 Behold, I give unto you power, that **whatsoever ye shall** seal **on earth shall be** sealed **in heaven; and whatsoever ye shall loose on earth shall be loosed in heaven**; and thus shall ye have power among this people.

> **KJV (1NT/1)** Matthew 18:18 Verily I say unto you, **Whatsoever ye shall** bind **on earth shall be** bound **in heaven: and whatsoever ye shall loose on earth shall be loosed in heaven**)

BOM Alma 10:8 And thus, **if ye shall say unto this** temple it shall be **rent in twain, it shall be done**.

> **KJV (1NT/1)** Matthew 21:21 Jesus answered and said unto them, Verily I say unto you, If ye have faith, and doubt not, ye shall not

only do this which is done to the fig tree, but also **if ye shall say unto this** mountain, Be thou removed, and be thou cast into the sea; **it shall be done**)

KJV (2NT/6) Matthew 27:51 And, behold, the veil of the temple was **rent in twain** from the top to the bottom; and the earth did quake, and the rocks rent;)

BOM Alma 10:9 And **if ye shall say unto this mountain, Be thou cast** down and become smooth, **it shall be done**.

KJV (1NT/1) Matthew 21:21 Jesus answered and said unto them, Verily I say unto you, If ye have faith, and doubt not, ye shall not only do this which is done to the fig tree, but also **if ye shall say unto this mountain, Be thou** removed, and be thou **cast** into the sea; **it shall be done**)

Chapter Seven

How it was done in Detail

Now from Jacob 5 thru Jacob 6:7 Joseph Smith tells the story of a "lord of the vineyard". This of course is similar to the New Testament story from Jesus of a "lord of the vineyard" and Paul's story of the Olive Tree in Romans. Joseph Smith combined the two to create this story with his own variations. Joseph Smith obviously used the New Testament for much of the creation of this story but he also used the commentaries as you will soon see. As an early example Joseph Smith uses the phrase "master of the vineyard" which is used by the commentaries as an additional explanation for the "lord of the vineyard". So either Joseph Smith made up "master of the vineyard" or he got it from the commentaries as you will see, the later is the truth.

Instead of quoting uses of the Bible every time they appear such as the phrase "Lord of the Vineyard" I will show you where that is and then just bold it thereafter.

BOM Jacob 5:1 Behold, my brethren, **do ye not remember** to have read the words of the prophet Zenos, which he spake unto the house of Israel, saying:

> **KJV (1NT/7)** Mark 8:18 Having eyes, see ye not? and having ears, hear ye not? and **do ye not remember**?)

BOM Jacob 5:2 Hearken, **O ye house of Israel**, and hear the words of me, a prophet of the Lord.

> **KJV** (4/4) Ezekiel 20:44 And ye shall know that I am the LORD when I have wrought with you for my name's sake, not according to your wicked ways, nor according to your corrupt doings, **O ye house of Israel**, saith the Lord GOD.)

BOM Jacob 5:3 For behold, thus saith the Lord, I will liken thee, O house of Israel, like unto a **tame olive-tree**, which a man took and nourished in his **vineyard**; and it grew, and *waxed old, and began to decay.*

> **KJV (2NT/5)** James 3:8 But the tongue can no man **tame**; it is an unruly evil, full of deadly poison.)
>
> **KJV** (4/3) Genesis 18:12 Therefore Sarah laughed within herself, saying, After I am **waxed old** shall I have pleasure, my lord being old also?)
>
> **COM** Henry: Psa 89:38-52 "and yet **waxed old and began to decay** already.")

Here in Jacob 5:1-3 Joseph Smith is telling us it is the "Prophet Zenos" who is speaking for the Lord. It is important to note, for those of you who don't know the Bible, that Zenos is not a prophet of the Bible in fact he is someone Joseph Smith made up. It is interesting then that, since we know that the entire Book of Mormon was made up by Joseph Smith and that this story of "the master of the vineyard" is also made up by using the commentaries and the Bible, that the word "Zeno" appears in each of the commentaries. (See also the chapter on name usage in the Book of Mormon)

> **COM** Gill: <u>Mat 9:11</u> "And indeed this was not only the sense of the Jews, but also of other people, according to those words of ***Zeno*** the poet,"

You will note in the next example that Joseph Smith took the idea of the olive tree in Romans and added the story of the parable of "The Lord of the Vineyard" found in Matthew, Mark and Luke. It is interesting that Joseph Smith changes "the Lord of the vineyard" to "the master of the vineyard" found only in the commentary of Gill: It is also interesting that you can cross reference Gill's commentary on the olive-tree of Romans with that of the lord of the vineyard found in Matthew. Again this is beyond coincidence.

> **COM** Gill: <u>Mat 20:8</u> "Sooner than this, one that was hired for a day, could not demand it; nor was ***the master of the vineyard***, who hired him, obliged to pay him till the sun was set (t), which was the time of his going ***forth*** from his labour")

BOM <u>Jacob 5:4</u> And **it came to pass** (452/1353) that (*2) the master of the vineyard* went forth, and he saw that his **olive-tree** began to decay; and he said: I will prune it, and **dig about it**, and nourish it, that **perhaps** it may **shoot forth** young and tender **branches**, and it perish not.

> **COM** Gill: <u>Mat 20:8</u> "Sooner than this, one that was hired for a day, could not demand it; nor was **the master of the vineyard,** who hired him, obliged to pay him till the sun was set (t), which was the time of his going forth from his labour")
>
> **COM** Gill: <u>Mat 24:32</u> "**and putteth forth leaves**; from the ***tender branches***, which swell, and open, and put forth buds, leaves, and fruit:")
>
> **KJV** From "the lord of the vineyard" parable: (**1NT/2**) <u>Luke 13:8</u> And he answering said unto him, Lord, let it alone this year also, till I shall **dig about it**, and dung it:)
>
> **KJV** (**3NT/43**) <u>Acts 8:22</u> Repent therefore of this thy wickedness, and pray God, if **perhaps** the thought of thine heart may be forgiven thee.)
>
> **KJV** (1/1) <u>Ezekiel 36:8</u> But ye, O mountains of Israel, ye shall **shoot forth** your **branches**, and yield your fruit to my people of Israel; for they are at hand to come.)

KJV Also from "the lord of the vineyard" parable: (Luke 21:30 When they now **shoot forth**, ye see and know of your own selves that summer is now nigh at hand.)

BOM Jacob 5:5 And **it came to pass** (452/1353) that he pruned it, and digged about it, and nourished it (*16) according to his word.*

    COM Clarke: Luk 1:38 "Done unto her **according to his word**." (Henry).

BOM Jacob 5:6 And **it came to pass** (452/1353) that **after many days** it began to put forth somewhat a little, young and tender branches; but behold, the (2) main (12th Century) top thereof began to perish.

    KJV (5/5) Ezekiel 38:8 **After many days** thou shalt be visited: in the latter years thou shalt come into the land that is brought back from the sword, and is gathered out of many people, against the mountains of Israel, which have been always waste: but it is brought forth out of the nations, and they shall dwell safely all of them.)

    Note: You can tell when Joseph Smith makes up most of the wording because it usually doesn't make much sense: "somewhat a little" or "the main top thereof")

BOM Jacob 5:7 And **it came to pass** (452/1353) that (*2) the master of the vineyard* saw it, and he said unto his servant: **It grieveth me** that I should lose this tree; wherefore, go and pluck the **branches** from **a wild olive-tree**, and **bring them hither** unto me; and we will pluck off those (2) main (12th Century) branches which are beginning to *wither away*, and we will **cast them into the fire** that **they may be burned**.

    COM Gill: Mat 20:8 "Sooner than this, one that was hired for a day, could not demand it; nor was **the master of the vineyard**, who hired him, obliged to pay him till the sun was set (t), which was the time of his going forth from his labour")

    KJV (1/12) Ruth 1:13 Would ye tarry for them till they were grown? would ye stay for them from having husbands? nay, my daughters; for **it grieveth me** much for your sakes that the hand of the LORD is gone out against me.)

    KJV (**1NT/5**) Romans 11:17 And if some of the **branches** be broken off, and thou, being a **wild olive tree**, wert grafted in among them, and with them partakest of the root and fatness of the olive tree;)

    KJV (**1NT/2**) Matthew 14:18 He said, **Bring them hither to me**.)

    KJV (**1NT/1**) John 15:6 If a man abide not in me, he is cast forth as a branch, and is **wither**ed; and men gather them, and **cast them into the fire**, and **they are burned**.)

    COM Gill: Joh 15:6 "And is withered. Some versions, as the Arabic, Syriac, and Persic, read this as an epithet of the word "branch", thus; "the branch that is withered"; expressing the condition the branch is in before it is cast forth out of the vineyard, and the reason of its being cast forth: but others read it as a new and distinct predicate of the branch, showing the case it is in, immediately upon its being cast forth: it may be cut off, and cast out with its leaves upon it, though without fruit; but as soon as ever it is ejected, it **withers away**.")

BOM Jacob 5:8 And behold, saith **the Lord of the vineyard**, I take away many of these young and tender branches, and I will graft them whithersoever I will; and it (12) mattereth not that (*37) if it so be* that the root of this tree will perish, I may preserve the fruit thereof unto myself; wherefore, I will take these young and tender branches, and I will graft them whithersoever I will.

> **KJV (4NT/33)** Luke 20:13 Then said **the lord of the vineyard**, What shall I do? I will send my beloved son: it may be they will reverence him when they see him.)

Now from here on we will look at the rest of this chapter of Jacob 5. As we have noted Joseph mixed in the use of Romans and the "natural branch" with that of the parable of "the lord of the vineyard". Here will see that Joseph Smith's story in Jacob is similar to that of the parable of "the lord of the vineyard" while mixing in his theory on Romans.

BOM Jacob 5:9 Take thou the **branches** of the **wild olive-tree**, and **graft** them **in**, *in the stead* thereof; and these which I have plucked off I will cast into the fire and burn them, *that they may not (5) cumber (14th Century) the ground* of my vineyard.

> **Note** in this verse the use of a unique word "cumber". This word is not found in the KJV of the Bible. You will notice that this word is part of a phrase found in Gill. Now this commentary of Gill is about another parable related to a vineyard which Joseph Smith would have easily cross referenced.
>
> **COM** Gill: Luk 13:7 "or "*that it may not cumber*"; or "render *the ground* useless", as read the Arabic version, and one of Beza's copies; for unfruitful trees suck up the juices of the earth, and draw away nourishment from other trees that are near them, and so make the earth barren, and not only hurt other trees, but stand in the way and place of fruitful ones; and therefore it is best to cut them down.")
>
> **Note**: It is interesting that Luke 13:7 uses the KJV word "cumbereth" "cut it down, why cumbereth it the ground?", while Joseph Smith uses exactly what is in Gill instead.
>
> **Note:** You will also note that in the above verse Joseph Smith states that "the **branches** of the **wild olive-tree**," would **be grafted in** "in the stead" which is exactly what the commentary of Gill also says.
>
> **COM** Gill: Rom 11:17 "grafted amongst them; meaning either the broken branches, *in* whose *stead* they were grafted; the Syriac version favours this sense, reading it בדוכתיהון, "in their place"; as also in

Rom_11:19; and so the Ethiopic version: or rather the believing Jews, of whom the first Gospel church and churches consisted; for the Jews first trusted in Christ, received the firstfruits of the Spirit, and were first incorporated into a Gospel church state; and then *the Gentiles* which believed were received among them. The first coalition of Jews and Gentiles, or the ingrafting of *the Gentiles in among the* Jews that believed, was at Antioch, when dropping their distinctive names of Jews and Gentiles, they took the common name of Christians, Act_11:19. So that this is not to be understood of an ingrafting into Christ unless by a visible profession, but of being received into a Gospel church state; which is signified by the "olive tree" in the next clause: ")

KJV (1NT/5) Romans 11:17 And if some of the **branches** be broken off, and thou, being a **wild olive tree**, wert **graft**ed **in** among them, and with them partakest of the root and fatness of the **olive tree**;)

BOM Jacob 5:10 And **it came to pass** (452/1353) that the servant of **the Lord of the vineyard** did according to the word of **the Lord of the vineyard**, and **grafted in** the **branches** of **the wild olive-tree**.

KJV (4NT/33) Luke 20:13 Then said **the lord of the vineyard**, What shall I do? I will send my beloved son: it may be they will reverence him when they see him.)

KJV (1NT/5) Romans 11:17 And if some of the **branches** be broken off, and thou, being a **wild olive tree**, wert **graft**ed **in** among them, and with them partakest of the root and fatness of the olive tree;)

BOM Jacob 5:11 And **the Lord of the vineyard** caused that it should be digged about, and pruned, and nourished, saying unto his servant: **It grieveth me** that I should lose this tree; wherefore, that **perhaps** I might preserve the roots thereof that they perish not, that I might preserve them unto myself, I have done this thing.

KJV (1/12) Ruth 1:13 Would ye tarry for them till they were grown? would ye stay for them from having husbands? nay, my daughters; for **it grieveth me** much for your sakes that the hand of the LORD is gone out against me.)

KJV (3NT/43) Acts 8:22 Repent therefore of this thy wickedness, and pray God, if **perhaps** the thought of thine heart may be forgiven thee.)

BOM Jacob 5:12 Wherefore, **go thy way**; watch the tree, and nourish it, according to my words.

KJV (*Note: Part of the vineyard parable:* Matthew 20:14 Take that thine is, and **go thy way**: I will give unto this last, even as unto thee.)

BOM Jacob 5:13 And these will I place in the nethermost part of my vineyard, whithersoever I will, it (12) mattereth not unto thee; and I do it that I may preserve unto myself **the natural branches** of the tree; and also, that I may lay up fruit thereof against the season, unto myself; for **it grieveth me** that I should lose this tree and the fruit thereof.

> **KJV (2NT/16)** <u>Romans 11:24</u> For if thou wert cut out of the olive tree which is wild by nature, and wert grafted contrary to nature into a good olive tree: how much more shall these, which be **the natural branches**, be grafted into their own olive tree?)
>
> **KJV** (1/12) <u>Ruth 1:13</u> Would ye tarry for them till they were grown? would ye stay for them from having husbands? nay, my daughters; for **it grieveth me** much for your sakes that the hand of the LORD is gone out against me.)

BOM <u>Jacob 5:14</u> And **it came to pass** (452/1353) that **the Lord of the vineyard** went his way, and hid **the natural branches** of the tame olive-tree in the nethermost parts of the vineyard, *some in one and some in another*, **according to his will** and **pleasure**.

> **KJV (4NT/33)** <u>Luke 20:13</u> Then said **the lord of the vineyard**, What shall I do? I will send my beloved son: it may be they will reverence him when they see him.)
>
> **KJV (2NT/16)** <u>Romans 11:24</u> For if thou wert cut out of the olive tree which is wild by nature, and wert grafted contrary to nature into a good olive tree: how much more shall these, which be **the natural branches**, be grafted into their own olive tree?)
>
> **COM** Henry: <u>Jer 29:8-14</u> "Though they are dispersed, **some in one** country **and some in another**, he will gather them from all the places whither they are driven," (Gill, Clarke, Wesley)
>
> **KJV (1NT/5)** <u>Ephesians 1:9</u> Having made known unto us the mystery of his **will**, **according to his** good **pleasure** which he hath purposed in himself:)

BOM <u>Jacob 5:15</u> And it came to pass (452/1353) that a long time passed away, and **the Lord of the vineyard** said unto his servant: Come, let us go down **into the vineyard**, that we may *labor* **in the vineyard**.

> **KJV (4NT/33)** <u>Luke 20:13</u> Then said **the lord of the vineyard**, What shall I do? I will send my beloved son: it may be they will reverence him when they see him.)
>
> **KJV (2NT/4)** <u>Matthew 20:4</u> And said unto them; Go ye also **into the vineyard**, and whatsoever is right I will give you. And they went their way.")
>
> **COM** Gill: <u>Mat 20:4</u> "**into the vineyard**, the church, to **labour** there;")

BOM <u>Jacob 5:16</u> And it came to pass (452/1353) that **the Lord of the vineyard**, and also the servant, went down **into the vineyard** to labor. And **it came to pass** (452/1353) that the servant said unto his master: Behold, look here; behold the tree.

Same as above see Jacob 5:15

BOM Jacob 5:17 And **it came to pass** (452/1353) that **the Lord of the vineyard** looked and beheld the **tree in the which** the wild olive branches had been grafted; and it had sprung forth and begun to bear **fruit**. And he beheld **that it was good**; and the fruit thereof was like unto the natural fruit.

> **KJV** (14/28) Genesis 1:29 And God said, Behold, I have given you every herb bearing seed, which is upon the face of all the earth, and every tree, **in the which** is the **fruit** of a **tree** yielding seed; to you it shall be for meat.)
>
> **KJV** (6/3) Genesis 1:4 And God saw the light, that **it was good**: and God divided the light from the darkness.)

BOM Jacob 5:18 And he said unto the servant: Behold, the branches of the wild tree have taken hold of the **moisture** of the root thereof, that the root thereof hath brought forth **much strength**; and because of the **much strength** of the root thereof the wild branches have brought forth tame fruit. Now, if we had not grafted in these branches, the tree thereof would have perished. And now, behold, I shall lay up **much fruit**, which the tree thereof hath brought forth; and the fruit thereof I shall lay up against the season, unto mine own self.

> **KJV** (Luke 8:6 And some fell upon a rock; and as soon as it was sprung up, it withered away, because it lacked **moisture**.)
>
> **KJV** (1/6) Psalm 33:16 There is no king saved by the multitude of an host: a mighty man is not delivered by **much strength**.)
>
> **KJV** (3NT/12) John 12:24 Verily, verily, I say unto you, Except a corn of wheat fall into the ground and die, it abideth alone: but if it die, it bringeth forth **much fruit**.)

BOM Jacob 5:19 And **it came to pass** (452/1353) that **the Lord of the vineyard** said unto the servant: Come, let us go to the nethermost part of the vineyard, and behold if the natural branches of the tree have not brought **forth much fruit** also, that I may lay up of the fruit thereof against the season, unto mine own self.

> **KJV** (3NT/12) John 12:24 Verily, verily, I say unto you, Except a corn of wheat fall into the ground and die, it abideth alone: but if it die, it bringeth **forth much fruit**.)

BOM Jacob 5:20 And **it came to pass** (452/1353) that they went forth whither the master had hid the natural branches of the tree, and he said unto the servant: Behold these; and he beheld the first that it had brought **forth much fruit**; and he beheld also **that it was good**. And he said unto the servant: Take of the fruit thereof, and lay it up against the season, that I may preserve it unto mine own self; for behold, said he, this long time have I nourished it, and it hath brought **forth much fruit**.

KJV (3NT/12) <u>John 12:24</u> Verily, verily, I say unto you, Except a corn of wheat fall into the ground and die, it abideth alone: but if it die, it bringeth **forth much fruit**.)

KJV (6/3) <u>Genesis 1:4</u> And God saw the light, that **it was good**: and God divided the light from the darkness.)

BOM <u>Jacob 5:21</u> And **it came to pass** (452/1353) that the servant said unto his master: How comest thou hither to plant this tree, or this branch of the tree? For behold, it was the poorest spot in all the land of thy vineyard.

BOM <u>Jacob 5:22</u> And **the Lord of the vineyard** said unto him: Counsel me not; I knew that it was a poor *(5) spot of ground;* wherefore, I said unto thee, I have nourished it this long time, and thou beholdest that it hath brought **forth much fruit**.

> **COM** Gill: <u>Mat 20:1</u> "Perhaps it may not be worth while to observe, how large a **spot of ground**, set with vines, was, by them, called a vineyard: it is frequently said by them")

> **KJV (3NT/12)** <u>John 12:24</u> Verily, verily, I say unto you, Except a corn of wheat fall into the ground and die, it abideth alone: but if it die, it bringeth **forth much fruit**.)

BOM <u>Jacob 5:23</u> And **it came to pass** (452/1353) that **the Lord of the vineyard** said unto his servant: Look hither; behold I have planted another branch of the tree also; and thou knowest that this *(5) spot of ground;* was poorer than the first. But, behold the tree. I have nourished it this long time, and it hath brought **forth much fruit**; therefore, gather it, and lay it up against the season, that I may preserve it unto mine own self.

> Same as above see Jacob 5:22

BOM <u>Jacob 5:24</u> And **it came to pass** (452/1353) that **the Lord of the vineyard** said again unto his servant: Look hither, and behold another branch also, which I have planted; behold that I have nourished it also, and it hath brought forth fruit.

BOM <u>Jacob 5:25</u> And he said unto the servant: Look hither and behold the last. Behold, this have I planted in a good *(5) spot of ground;* and I have nourished it this long time, and only a part of the tree hath brought forth tame fruit, and the other part of the tree hath brought forth wild fruit; behold, I have nourished this tree like unto the others.

> **COM** Gill: <u>Mat 20:1</u> "Perhaps it may not be worth while to observe, how large a **spot of ground**, set with vines, was, by them, called a vineyard: it is frequently said by them")

BOM <u>Jacob 5:26</u> And **it came to pass** (452/1353) that **the Lord of the vineyard** said unto the servant: Pluck off the branches that have not **brought forth good fruit**, and **cast them into the fire**.

> **KJV** (<u>Matthew 13:8</u> But other fell into **good** ground, and **brought forth fruit**, some an hundredfold, some sixtyfold, some thirtyfold.)

KJV (<u>John 15:6</u> If a man abide not in me, he is cast forth as a branch, and is withered; and men gather them, and **cast them into the fire**, and they are burned.)

BOM <u>Jacob 5:27</u> But behold, the servant said unto him: Let us prune it, and **dig about it**, and nourish it a little longer, that perhaps it may bring forth good fruit unto thee, that thou canst lay it up against the season.

KJV (1NT/2) <u>Luke 13:8</u> And he answering said unto him, Lord, let it alone this year also, till I shall **dig about it**, and dung it:)

BOM <u>Jacob 5:28</u> And **it came to pass** (452/1353) that **the Lord of the vineyard** and the servant of **the Lord of the vineyard** did nourish all the fruit of the vineyard.

KJV (1NT/1) <u>Mark 12:2</u> And at the season he sent to the husbandmen a servant, that he might receive from the husbandmen of **the fruit of the vineyard**.

BOM <u>Jacob 5:29</u> And **it came to pass (452/1353)** that a long time had passed away, and **the Lord of the vineyard** said unto his servant: Come, let us go down **into the vineyard**, that we may *labor* again in the vineyard. For behold, **the time draweth near**, and the end soon cometh; wherefore, I must lay up fruit against the season, unto mine own self.

KJV (2NT/4) <u>Matthew 20:4</u> And said unto them; Go ye also **into the vineyard**, and whatsoever is right I will give you. And they went their way.")

KJV (1NT/1) <u>Luke 21:8</u> And he said, Take heed that ye be not deceived: for many shall come in my name, saying, I am Christ; and **the time draweth near**: go ye not therefore after them.)

COM Gill: <u>Mat 20:4</u> "**into the vineyard**, the church, to **labour** there;")

BOM <u>Jacob 5:30</u> And it came to pass that **the Lord of the vineyard** and the **servant** went down **into the vineyard**; and they came to the tree whose **natural branches** had been **broken off**, and the **wild branches** had been **grafted in;** and behold all sorts of **fruit** did *(5) cumber* (*14ᵗʰ Century)* the tree.

BOM <u>Jacob 5:31</u> And it came to pass that **the Lord of the vineyard** did taste of the **fruit**, every sort according to its number. And **the Lord of the vineyard** said: Behold, this long time have we nourished this **tree**, and I have laid up unto myself against the season **much fruit**.

BOM <u>Jacob 5:32</u> But behold, this time it hath brought **forth much fruit**, and there is none of it which is good. And behold, there are all kinds of *bad fruit*; and **it profiteth me nothing**, notwithstanding all our **labor**; and now it grieveth me that I should lose this **tree**.

KJV (1NT/2) <u>1 Corinthians 13:3</u> And though I bestow all my goods to feed the poor, and though I give my body to be burned, and have not charity, **it profiteth me nothing**.)

COM Gill: <u>Luk 6:43</u> "for as that cannot be called a good tree, which *brings forth bad fruit*; so such men cannot be accounted good men,")

BOM <u>Jacob 5:33</u> And **the Lord of the vineyard** said unto the **servant**: What shall we do unto the tree, that I may preserve again **good fruit** thereof unto mine own self?

BOM <u>Jacob 5:34</u> And the servant said unto his master: Behold, because thou didst **graft in** the **branches** of the **wild olive-tree** they have nourished the **root**s, that they are alive and they have not perished; wherefore thou beholdest that they are yet **good**.

> **KJV (1NT/5)** <u>Romans 11:17</u> And if some of the **branches** be broken off, and thou, being a **wild olive tree**, wert **grafted in** among them, and with them partakest of the **root** and fatness of the olive tree;)

BOM <u>Jacob 5:35</u> And it came to pass that **the Lord of the vineyard** said **unto his servant**: The **tree profiteth me nothing**, and the roots thereof **profit me nothing** so long as it shall **bring forth evil fruit**.

> **KJV (1NT/1)** <u>Matthew 20:8</u> So when even was come, **the lord of the vineyard** saith **unto his** steward, Call the labourers, and give them their hire, beginning from the last unto the first.)
>
> **KJV (1NT/2)** <u>1 Corinthians 13:3</u> And though I bestow all my goods to feed the poor, and though I give my body to be burned, and have not charity, it **profiteth me nothing**.)
>
> **KJV (1NT/3)** <u>Matthew 7:18</u> A good tree cannot **bring forth evil fruit**, neither can a corrupt tree bring forth good fruit.)

BOM <u>Jacob 5:36</u> Nevertheless, I know that the **root**s are good, and for mine own purpose I have preserved them; and because of their much strength they have hitherto **brought forth**, from the **wild branches**, **good fruit**.

BOM <u>Jacob 5:37</u> But behold, the **wild branches** have grown and have (4) *overrun* the **root**s thereof; and because that the **wild branches** have overcome the **root**s thereof it hath **brought forth** much **evil fruit**; and because that it hath **brought forth** so much **evil fruit** thou beholdest that it (11) beginneth to perish; and it will soon become ripened, that it may be **cast into the fire**, except we should do something for it to preserve it.

> **COM** Gill: <u>Mat 13:7</u> " such was not this piece of ground, it was *overrun* with them, not on the surface of the earth, but within it: for it follows," (Clarke, Henry)

BOM <u>Jacob 5:38</u> And it came to pass that **the Lord of the vineyard** said unto his servant: Let us go down into the nethermost parts of **the vineyard**, and behold if **the natural branches** have also **brought forth evil fruit**.

BOM <u>Jacob 5:39</u> And it came to pass that they went down into the nethermost parts of the vineyard. And it came to pass that they beheld that the **fruit of the natural branches** had become corrupt also; yea, the first and the second and also the last; and they had all become corrupt.

BOM Jacob 5:40 And the wild **fruit** of the last had overcome that part of the **tree** which **brought forth good fruit**, even that the **branch** had **withered away** and died.
BOM Jacob 5:41 And it came to pass that **the Lord of the vineyard** wept, and said unto the **servant**: What could I have done more for my **vineyard**?
BOM Jacob 5:42 Behold, I knew that all **the fruit of the vineyard**, save it were these, had become corrupted. And now these which have once **brought forth good fruit** have also become corrupted; and now all the **tree**s of my **vineyard** are **good for nothing** save it be to be **hewn down and cast into the fire**.

> **KJV (1NT/1)** Matthew 7:19 Every **tree** that bringeth not **forth good fruit** is **hewn down, and cast into the fire**.)

BOM Jacob 5:43 And behold this last, whose branch hath withered away, I did plant in a good *(5) spot of ground;* yea, even that which was choice unto me *(18) above all other* parts of the land of my vineyard.

> **COM** Gill: Mat 20:1 "Perhaps it may not be worth while to observe, how large a **spot of ground**, set with vines, was, by them, called a vineyard: it is frequently said by them")
> **COM** Clarke: Mat 10:25 **"above all other** things, fruit." (Henry, Wesley)

BOM Jacob 5:44 And thou (2) beheldest (***Note: Not found in Wesley, Clarke, Henry,** Gill **or KJV)** that I also cut down that which cumbered this *(5) spot of ground* , that I might plant this tree in the *stead* thereof.

> **COM** Gill: Mat 20:1 "Perhaps it may not be worth while to observe, how large a **spot of ground**, set with vines, was, by them, called a vineyard: it is frequently said by them")
> **COM** Gill: Luk 13:7 "or "that it may not **cumber**"; or "render **the ground** useless", as read the Arabic version, and one of Beza's copies; for unfruitful trees suck up the juices of the earth, and draw away nourishment from other trees that are near them, and so make the earth barren, and not only hurt other trees, but stand in the way and place of fruitful ones; and therefore it is best to cut them down.")
> **COM** Gill: Rom 11:17**graft**ed amongst them; meaning either the broken branches, in whose **stead** they were grafted; the Syriac version favours this sense, reading it בדוכתיהון, "in their place"; as also in Rom 11:19;)

BOM Jacob 5:45 And thou (2) beheldest that a part thereof **brought forth good fruit**, and a part thereof **brought forth** wild **fruit**; and because I plucked not the branches thereof and **cast them into the fire**, behold, they have overcome the good branch that it hath **withered away**.
BOM Jacob 5:46 And now, behold, notwithstanding all the care which we have taken of my **vineyard**, the **tree**s thereof have become corrupted, that they

bring forth no **good fruit**; and these I had hoped to preserve, to have laid up **fruit** thereof against the season, unto mine own self. But, behold, they have become like unto the **wild olive-tree**, and *they are of no worth* ! but to be **hewn down and cast into the fire**; and it grieveth me that I should lose them.

> **KJV** (1/6) <u>Isaiah 14:10</u> All they shall speak and say unto thee, Art thou also become weak as we? art thou **become like unto** us?)
>
> **KJV (1NT/5)** <u>Romans 11:17</u> And if some of the branches be broken off, and thou, being a **wild olive tree**, wert grafted in among them, and with them partakest of the root and fatness of the olive tree;)
>
> **KJV (2NT/13)** <u>Matthew 7:19</u> Every tree that bringeth not forth good fruit is **hewn down, and cast into the fire**.)
>
> **KJV** (1/12) <u>Ruth 1:13</u> Would ye tarry for them till they were grown? would ye stay for them from having husbands? nay, my daughters; for **it grieveth me** much for your sakes that the hand of the LORD is gone out against me.)
>
> **COM** Clarke: <u>Rom 12:16</u> "However, it argues one important fact, that such persons are conscious that **they are of no worth** and of no consequence in Themselves,")

BOM <u>Jacob 5:47</u> But what could I have done more in my vineyard? Have I (1) slackened (13th Century) mine hand, that I have not nourished it, Nay, I have nourished it, and I have digged about it, and I have pruned it, and I have (2) dunged it; and I have stretched forth mine hand almost **all the day long**, and the end **draweth nigh**. And **it grieveth me** that I should **hew down** all **the tree**s of my vineyard, **and cast them into the fire** that **they** should be **burned**. Who is it that has corrupted my vineyard?

> **COM** Gill: <u>Mat 11:3</u> "though some have thought, that John's faith was somewhat **slackened**;" (Wesley, Clarke)
>
> **KJV** (2/2) <u>Daniel 4:14</u> He cried aloud, and said thus, **Hew down the tree**, and cut off his branches, shake off his leaves, and scatter his fruit: let the beasts get away from under it, and the fowls from his branches:)
>
> **KJV (1NT/1)** <u>John 15:6</u> If a man abide not in me, he is cast forth as a branch, and is withered; and men gather them, **and cast them into the fire**, and **they** are **burned**.)
>
> **COM** Gill: <u>Isa 61:11</u> "being enclosed, and better taken care of, and well watered, and **dunged**, and cultivated; seeds sown in such a rich soil spring up freely, strongly, and constantly:")
>
> **KJV** (13/12) <u>Psalm 35:28</u> And my tongue shall speak of thy righteousness and of thy praise **all the day long**.)
>
> **KJV** (*Note: Only found once in OT:* (4/4) <u>Psalm 88:3</u> For my soul is full of troubles: and my life **draweth nigh** unto the grave.)
>
> **KJV** (1/12) <u>Ruth 1:13</u> Would ye tarry for them till they were grown?

would ye stay for them from having husbands? nay, my daughters; for **it grieveth me** much for your sakes that the hand of the LORD is gone out against me.)

BOM Jacob 5:48 And it came to pass that the **servant** said unto his **master**: Is it not the *loftiness* of thy **vineyard** -- have not the **branches** thereof overcome the **root**s which are good? And because the **branches** have overcome the **root**s thereof, behold they grew faster than the strength of the **root**s, taking strength unto themselves. Behold, I say, is not this the cause that the **tree**s of thy **vineyard** have become corrupted?

> **COM** Note the same ideas here and using the same word "loftiness": Gill: Mat 7:19 - Every tree that bringeth not forth good fruit,.... Every preacher and teacher that does not bring the Gospel of Christ with him, and plainly and faithfully preach it to the people, sooner or later, is *hewn down*: however he may have appeared as a tall lofty cedar, and have carried it with a high hand against Christ and his Gospel, spoke "great swelling words of vanity", and behaved with much "*loftiness*" and "haughtiness"; yet the time comes on, when all this is bowed and made low, "and the Lord alone is exalted": such preachers are either cut off from the churches of Christ, or *hewn down* by death, and *cast into the fire*; into the fire of hell; into the lake of fire and brimstone, "where the beast and false prophet shall be".")

BOM Jacob 5:49 And **it came to pass (452/1353)** that **the Lord of the vineyard** said unto the servant: Let us go to and **hew down the trees** of the vineyard and cast them into the fire, that they shall not *(5) cumber (14th Century) the ground* of my vineyard, for I have done all. What could I have done more for my vineyard?

> **KJV** (2/2) Daniel 4:14 He cried aloud, and said thus, **Hew down the tree**, and cut off his branches, shake off his leaves, and scatter his fruit: let the beasts get away from under it, and the fowls from his branches:)

> **COM** Gill: Luk 13:7 "or "that it may **not cumber**"; or "render **the ground** useless", as read the Arabic version, and one of Beza's copies; for unfruitful trees suck up the juices of the earth, and draw away nourishment from other trees that are near them, and so make the earth barren, and not only hurt other trees, but stand in the way and place of fruitful ones; and therefore it is best to cut them down.")

BOM Jacob 5:50 But, behold, the servant said unto **the Lord of the vineyard**: Spare it *a little longer*.

BOM Jacob 5:51 And the Lord said: Yea, I will spare it *a little longer*, for it grieveth me that I should lose the **tree**s of my **vineyard**.

> **COM** Gill: Mat 18:35 "and the debtor or tenant, utterly insolvent, prayed for *a little longer* time, hoping God would enable him to pay

thee all;

BOM Jacob 5:52 Wherefore, let us take of the **branches** of these which I have planted in the nethermost parts of my **vineyard**, and let us **graft** them into the **tree** from whence they came; and let us pluck from the **tree** those **branches** whose **fruit** is most bitter, and *graft* in **the natural branches** of the **tree** *in* the *stead* thereof.

> **COM** Gill: Rom 11:17 *graft*ed amongst them; meaning either the broken **branches**, in whose *stead* they were *graft*ed; the Syriac version favours this sense, reading it בדוכתיהון, "in their place"; as also in Rom 11:19;)

BOM Jacob 5:53 And this will I do that the **tree** may not perish, that, perhaps, I may preserve unto myself the **root**s thereof for mine own purpose.

BOM Jacob 5:54 And, behold, the **root**s of **the natural branches** of the **tree** which I planted whithersoever I would are yet alive; wherefore, that I may preserve them also for mine own purpose, I will take of the **branches** of this **tree**, and I will **graft** them in unto them.

Yea, I will **graft** in unto them the **branches** of their mother tree, that I may preserve the **root**s also unto mine own self, that when they shall be sufficiently strong perhaps they may **bring forth good fruit** unto me, and I may yet have glory in the **fruit** of my **vineyard**.

BOM Jacob 5:55 And it came to pass that they took from the natural **tree** which had become **wild**, and **grafted in** unto the natural **tree**s, which also had become **wild**.

BOM Jacob 5:56 And they also took of the natural **tree**s which had become **wild**, and **grafted into** their mother **tree**.

BOM Jacob 5:57 And **the Lord of the vineyard** said unto the **servant**: Pluck not the **wild branches** from the trees, save it be those which are most bitter; and in them ye shall **graft** according to that which I have said.

BOM Jacob 5:58 And we will nourish again the **tree**s of the **vineyard**, and we will trim up the **branches** thereof; and we will pluck from the **tree**s those **branches** which are ripened, that must perish, and **cast them into the fire**.

BOM Jacob 5:59 And this I do that, perhaps, the **root**s thereof may take strength because of their goodness; and because of the change of the **branches**, that the **good** may overcome the evil.

BOM Jacob 5:60 And because that I have preserved **the natural branches** and the **root**s thereof, and that I have **grafted in the natural branches** again into their mother **tree**, and have preserved the **root**s of their mother **tree**, that, perhaps, the **tree**s of my **vineyard** may **bring forth** again **good fruit**; and that I may have joy again in the **fruit** of my **vineyard**, and, perhaps, that I may rejoice exceedingly that I have preserved the **root**s and the **branches** of the first fruit --

> **KJV** (1/9) Job 3:22 Which **rejoice exceedingly**, and are glad, when

they can find the grave?)

BOM Jacob 5:61 Wherefore, go to, and call servants, that we may labor diligently with our might in the vineyard, that we may prepare the way, that I may bring forth again the natural fruit, which natural fruit is good and the **most precious** (*1*) *above all other fruit.*

> **KJV (2NT/10)** Revelation 18:12 The merchandise of gold, and silver, and precious stones, and of pearls, and fine linen, and purple, and silk, and scarlet, and all thyine wood, and all manner vessels of ivory, and all manner vessels of **most precious** wood, and of brass, and iron, and marble,)
>
> **COM** Clarke: Mat 10:25 " **above all other** things, **fruit**." (Henry, Wesley)

BOM Jacob 5:62 Wherefore, let us go to and labor with our might this last time, for behold the end **draweth nigh**, and this is for the last time that I shall prune my vineyard.

> **KJV** (*Note: Only found once in OT:* (4/4) Psalm 88:3 For my soul is full of troubles: and my life **draweth nigh** unto the grave.)

BOM Jacob 5:63 **Graft** in the **branches**; begin at **the last** that they may be **first**, and that **the first** may **be last**, and *dig about* the trees, both old and young, **the first and the last**; **and the last and the first**, that all may be nourished once again for the last time.

> **KJV** (4NT/1) Matthew 20:16 So **the last shall be first**, and **the first last**: for many be called, but few chosen.)

BOM Jacob 5:64 Wherefore, *dig about* them, and prune them, and *dung* them once more, for the last time, for the end **draweth nigh**. And if it be so that these last *grafts* shall grow, and **bring forth** the **natural fruit**, then shall ye prepare the way for them, that they may grow.

> **KJV** (*Note: Only found once in OT:* (4/4) Psalm 88:3 For my soul is full of troubles: and my life **draweth nigh** unto the grave.)

BOM Jacob 5:65 And as they begin to grow ye shall clear away **the branches** which *bring forth bitter fruit*, according to the strength of the **good** and the size thereof; and ye shall not clear away the bad thereof all at once, lest the **root**s thereof should be too strong for the **graft**, and the **graft** thereof shall perish, and I lose the **tree**s of my **vineyard**.

> **COM** Gill: Heb 12:15 "and is apt to spring up, and ***bring forth bitter fruit***, and gives trouble both to a man's self and others;")

BOM Jacob 5:65 For **it grieveth me** that I should lose the trees of my vineyard; wherefore ye shall clear away the bad according as the good shall grow, that the root and the top may be equal in strength, until the good shall overcome the bad, and the bad be **hewn down and cast into the fire**, *that* they (*5*) *cumber* (*14th Century) not the ground* of my vineyard; and thus will I sweep away the bad out of my vineyard.

KJV (1/12) <u>Ruth 1:13</u> Would ye tarry for them till they were grown? would ye stay for them from having husbands? nay, my daughters; for **it grieveth me** much for your sakes that the hand of the LORD is gone out against me.)

KJV (**2NT/13**) <u>Matthew 7:19</u> Every tree that bringeth not forth good fruit is **hewn down, and cast into the fire.**)

COM Gill: <u>Luk 13:7</u> "or "**that** it may **not cumber**"; or "render **the ground** useless", as read the Arabic version, and one of Beza's copies; for unfruitful trees suck up the juices of the earth, and draw away nourishment from other trees that are near them, and so make the earth barren, and not only hurt other trees, but stand in the way and place of fruitful ones; and therefore it is best to cut them down.")

BOM <u>Jacob 5:67</u> And **the branches** of the **natural tree** will I **graft** in again into the **natural tree**;

BOM <u>Jacob 5:68</u> And the **branches** of the **natural tree** will I **graft** into **the natural branches** of the **tree**; and thus will I bring them together again, that they shall **bring forth** the **natural fruit**, and they shall be one.

BOM <u>Jacob 5:69</u> And the bad shall be cast away, yea, even out of all the land of my **vineyard**; for behold, only this once will I prune my **vineyard**.

BOM <u>Jacob 5:70</u> And it came to pass that **the Lord of the vineyard** sent his **servant**; and the **servant** went and did as the Lord had commanded him, and brought other servants; and they were few.

BOM <u>Jacob 5:71</u> And **the Lord of the vineyard** said unto them: Go to, and **labor in the vineyard**, with your might. For behold, this is the last time that I shall nourish my **vineyard**; for the end is **nigh at hand**, and the season speedily cometh; and if ye labor with your might with me ye shall have joy in the fruit which I shall lay up unto myself against the time which will soon come.

KJV (5/?) <u>Luke 21:31</u> So likewise ye, when ye see these things come to pass, know ye that the kingdom of God is **nigh at hand**.

BOM <u>Jacob 5:72</u> And it came to pass that the servants did go and **labor** with their mights; and **the Lord of the vineyard** labored also with them; and they did obey the commandments of **the Lord of the vineyard** in all things.

BOM <u>Jacob 5:73</u> And there began to be the **natural fruit** again in **the vineyard**; and **the natural branches** began to *grow and thrive exceedingly*; and the **wild branches** began to be plucked off and to be **cast away**; and they did keep the **root** and the top thereof equal, according to the strength thereof.

BOM <u>Jacob 5:74</u> And thus they labored, **with all diligence**, according to the commandments of **the Lord of the vineyard**, even until the bad had been cast away out of the vineyard, and the Lord had preserved unto himself that the trees had become again the natural fruit; and they became like unto one body; and the fruits were equal; and **the Lord of the vineyard** had preserved unto himself the natural fruit, which was **most precious** unto him from the beginning.

> KJV (1/10) Proverbs 4:23 Keep thy heart **with all diligence**; for out of it are the issues of life.)
>
> KJV (2NT/10) Revelation 18:12 The merchandise of gold, and silver, and precious stones, and of pearls, and fine linen, and purple, and silk, and scarlet, and all thyine wood, and all manner vessels of ivory, and all manner vessels of **most precious** wood, and of brass, and iron, and marble,)

BOM Jacob 5:75 And **it came to pass (452/1353)** that when **the Lord of the vineyard** saw that his fruit was good, and that his vineyard was no more corrupt, he called up his servants, and said unto them: Behold, for this last time have we nourished my vineyard; and thou beholdest that I have done according to my will; and I have preserved the natural fruit, that it is good, even like as it was in the beginning. And **Blessed art thou**; for because ye have been diligent in laboring with me in my vineyard, and have kept my commandments, and have brought unto me again the natural fruit, that my vineyard is no more corrupted, and the bad is cast away, behold ye shall have joy with me because of the fruit of my vineyard.

> KJV (5/14) Psalm 119:12 **Blessed art thou**, O LORD: teach me thy statutes.)

BOM Jacob 5:76 For behold, **for a long time** will I lay up of the fruit of my vineyard unto mine own self against the season, which speedily cometh; and for the last time have I nourished my vineyard, and pruned it, and dug about it, and (2) dunged it; wherefore I will lay up unto mine own self of the fruit, **for a long time**, according to that which I have spoken.

> KJV (1NT/3) Luke 20:9 Then began he to speak to the people this parable; A certain man planted a vineyard, and let it forth to husbandmen, and went into a far country **for a long time**.)
>
> COM Gill: Isa 61:11 "being enclosed, and better taken care of, and well watered, and **dunged**, and cultivated; seeds sown in such a rich soil spring up freely, strongly, and constantly:")

BOM Jacob 5:77 And when **the time cometh** that evil fruit shall again come into my vineyard, then will I cause the good and the bad to be gathered; and the good will I preserve unto myself, and the bad will I cast away into its own place. And then cometh the season and the end; and my vineyard will I cause to be burned with fire.

> KJV (2NT/15) John 16:2 They shall put you out of the synagogues: yea, **the time cometh**, that whosoever killeth you will think that he doeth God service.)

Jacob 6

BOM Jacob 6:1 And now, behold, my brethren, as I said unto you that I would prophesy, behold, this is my prophecy -- that the things which this prophet Zenos spake, concerning the house of Israel, **in the which** he likened them unto a **tame** olive-tree, must **surely come to pass**.

> **KJV** (1/5) 1 Kings 13:32 For the saying which he cried by the word of the LORD against the altar in Bethel, and against all the houses of the high places which are in the cities of Samaria, shall **surely come to pass**.)

> **KJV** (14/28) Genesis 1:29 And God said, Behold, I have given you every herb bearing seed, which is upon the face of all the earth, and every tree, **in the which** is the fruit of a tree yielding seed; to you it shall be for meat.)

> **KJV** (**2NT/5**) James 3:8 But the tongue can no man **tame**; it is an unruly evil, full of deadly poison.)

BOM Jacob 6:2 And the **day that** he **shall set his hand again the second time to recover** his people, is the day, yea, even the last time, that the servants of the Lord shall go forth in his power, to nourish and prune his vineyard; and after that the end soon cometh.

> **KJV** (1/1) Isaiah 11:11 And it shall come to pass in that **day, that the** Lord **shall set his hand again the second time to recover** the remnant of his people, which shall be left, from Assyria, and from Egypt, and from Pathros, and from Cush, and from Elam, and from Shinar, and from Hamath, and from the islands of the sea.)

BOM Jacob 6:3 And how blessed are they who have labored diligently in his vineyard; and how cursed are they who shall be cast out into their own place! And the **world shall be burned** with **fire**.

> **KJV** (Note: Matthew 13:40 As therefore the tares are gathered and **burned** in the **fire**; so **shall** it be in the end of this **world**.)

BOM Jacob 6:4 And how merciful is our God unto us, for he remembereth the house of Israel, both roots and branches; and he **stretch**es **forth** his **hands** unto them **all the day long**; and *they are a stiffnecked* and a **gainsaying people**; but as many as will not **harden their hearts** shall be saved in the kingdom of God.

> **KJV** (**1NT/1**) Romans 10:21 But to Israel he saith, **All day long** I have **stretched forth** my **hands** unto a disobedient and **gainsaying people**.)

> **Note:** Notice in Gill's commentary that he quotes a phrase similar in structure to that of Joseph Smith above.

> **COM** Gill: Rom 10:21 "The Lord's "stretching out his hands all the day long" to them,". Instead of "all the day long" first as it is in Romans he structures it after the stretching of the hands phrase as does Gill's commentary. Also notice in the same commentary Gill describes them as "stiffnecked" as does Joseph Smith above. "but

they were **a stiffnecked** and rebellious people, uncircumcised in heart and ears;")

KJV (1/24) Joshua 11:20 For it was of the LORD to **harden their hearts**, that they should come against Israel in battle, that he might destroy them utterly, and that they might have no favour, but that he might destroy them, as the LORD commanded Moses.)

BOM Jacob 6:5 Wherefore, **my beloved brethren**, I beseech of you in **words of soberness**; that ye would repent, and come *(6) with full purpose of heart* , and *cleave* unto God as he cleaveth unto you. And while his arm of mercy is extended towards you in *the light of the day*, **harden not your hearts**.

KJV (**4NT/60**) James 1:19 Wherefore, **my beloved brethren**, let every man be swift to hear, slow to speak, slow to wrath:)

KJV (**1NT/8**) Acts 26:25 But he said, I am not mad, most noble Festus; but speak forth the **words of** truth and **soberness**.)

COM Gill: Psa 104:22 "So wicked men do not care for **the light of the day**, nor do false teachers choose to come to the light of the word;" (Clarke, Wesley)

Note: Note that this phrase is also in the commentary of Gill regarding the comments of Jesus on a "branch" that "cannot bear fruit" the whole idea behind these verses.

COM Gill: Joh 15:4 "The former of these is an exhortation to continue in the exercise of faith and love upon Christ, holding to him the head, **cleaving** to him **with full purpose of heart**, and so deriving life, grace, strength, and nourishment from him; the latter is a promise encouraging to the former; for as Christ is formed in the hearts of his people, he continues there as the living principle of all grace.,")

BOM Jacob 6:6 Yea, **today, if ye will hear his voice, harden not your hearts; for why will ye die**?

KJV (**2NT/1**) Hebrews 3:15 While it is said, **To day if ye will hear his voice, harden not your hearts**, as in the provocation.)

KJV (2/1) Ezekiel 18:31 Cast away from you all your transgressions, whereby ye have transgressed; and make you a new heart and a new spirit: **for why will ye die**, O house of Israel?)

BOM Jacob 6:7 For behold, after ye have been nourished by **the good word of God all the day long**, will ye **bring forth evil fruit**, that ye must be **hewn down and cast into the fire**?

KJV (**1NT/2**) Hebrews 6:5 And have tasted **the good word of God**, and the powers of the world to come,)

KJV (13/12) Psalm 35:28 And my tongue shall speak of thy righteousness and of thy praise **all the day long**.)

KJV (**1NT/3**) Matthew 7:18 A good tree cannot **bring forth evil fruit**, neither can a corrupt tree bring forth good fruit.)

KJV (2NT/13) Matthew 7:19 Every tree that bringeth not forth good fruit is **hewn down, and cast into the fire**.)

Now a very long quote from the commentary of Henry on Romans 11:1-32. I know this is quite long but I want you to see the similarities here with what Henry has written and what Joseph Smith has written in the Book of Mormon. Here are just some of those similarities.

The Gentiles are grafted in from a wild olive into an original olive.

Both accounts want to maintain the main root.

Both accounts have branches broken off which are know as the Jews.

Both accounts state that the grafted in branch can partake of what comes from the root.

Both accounts say that there are those that are first or the first-fruits.

Both have the idea that the branches can be holy because the root is holy.

As you read Jacob 5 and the commentary below you will see the many similarities. I will bold and italicize the words and phrases which are found in both the commentary and in the Book of Mormon*'s* Jacob 5.

First, The privilege which the Gentiles had by being taken into the church. They were *grafted in* (Rom_11:17), as a *branch* of a *wild olive* into a *good olive*, which is contrary to the way and custom of the husbandman, who *grafts* the *good olive* into *the bad;* but those that God *grafts* into the church he finds *wild* and barren, and *good* for nothing. Men *graft* to mend the *tree*; but God *grafts* to mend the *branch*. 1. The church of God is an *olive-tree*, flourishing and fruitful as an olive (Psa_52:8; Hos_14:6), the *fruit* useful for the honour both of God and man, Jdg_9:9. 2. Those that are out of the church are as *wild olive-tree*s, not only useless, but what they do produce is sour and unsavoury: *Wild by nature,* Rom_11:24. This was the state of the poor Gentiles, that wanted church privileges, and in respect of real sanctification; and it is the *natural* state of every one of us, to be *wild* by nature. 3. Conversion is the grafting in of *wild branches* into the *good olive*. We must be cut off from the old stock, and be brought into union with a new *root*. 4. Those that are *grafted into the good olive-tree* partake of the *root* and fatness of the olive. It is applicable to a saving union with Christ; all that are by a lively faith *grafted into* Christ partake of him as the *branches* of the *root* - receive from his fulness. But it is here spoken of a visible church-membership, from which the Jews were as *branches broken off*; and so the Gentiles were *grafted in*, *autois - among those* that continued, or in the room of those that were *broken off*. The Gentiles, being *grafted into* the church, partake of the same privileges that the Jews did, *the root and fatness.* The *olive-tree* is the visible church (called so Jer_11:16); the *root* of this *tree* was Abraham, not the *root* of communication, so Christ only is the *root*, but the *root* of administration, he being the first with whom the covenant was so solemnly made. Now the believing Gentiles partake of this *root*: *he also is a son of Abraham* (<u>Luk_19:9</u>), the *blessing of Abraham comes upon the Gentiles* (<u>Gal_3:14</u>), the same fatness of the *olive-tree*, the same for substance, special protection, lively oracles, means of salvation, a standing ministry, instituted ordinances; and, among the rest, the visible church-membership of their infant seed, which was part of the fatness of the *olive-tree* that the Jews had, and cannot be imagined to be denied to the Gentiles.

Secondly, A caution not to abuse these privileges. 1. "Be not proud (<u>Rom_11:18</u>): *Boast not against the **branches***. Do not therefore trample upon the Jews as a reprobate people, nor insult over those that are *broken off*, much less over those that do continue." Grace is given, not to make us proud, but to make us thankful. The law of faith excludes all boasting either of ourselves or against others. "Do not say (<u>Rom_11:19</u>): *They were **broken off** that I might be **grafted in**;* that is, do not think that thou didst merit more at the hand of God than they, or didst stand higher in his favour." "But remember, *thou bearest not the **root**, but the **root** thee.* Though thou art *grafted* in, thou art still but a *branch* borne by the *root*; nay, and an en*grafted branch*, brought into the *good olive* contrary to nature (<u>Rom_11:24</u>), not free-born, but by an act of grace enfranchised and *natural*ized. Abraham, the *root* of the Jewish church, is not beholden to thee; but thou art greatly obliged to him, as the trustee of the covenant and the father of many nations. Therefore, *if thou boast,* know (this word must be supplied to clear the sense) *thou bearest not the **root** but the **root** thee.*" 2. "Be not secure (<u>Rom_11:20</u>): *Be not high-minded, but fear.* Be not too confident of your own strength and standing." A holy fear is an excellent preservative against high-mindedness: happy is the man that thus feareth always. We need not fear but God will be true to his word; all the danger is lest we be false to ours. *Let us therefore fear,* <u>Heb_4:1</u>. The church of Rome now boasts of a patent of perpetual preservation; but the apostle here, in his epistle to that church when she was in her infancy and integrity, enters an express caveat against that boast, and all claims of that kind. - *Fear* what? "Why fear lest thou commit a forfeiture as they have done, lest thou lose the privileges thou now enjoyest, as they have lost theirs." The evils that befall others should be warnings to us. *Go* (saith God to Jerusalem <u>Jer_7:12</u>), and *see what I did to* Shiloh; so now, let all the churches of God go and see what he did to Jerusalem, and what is become of the day of their visitation, that we may hear and fear, and take heed of Jerusalem's sin. The patent which churches have of their privileges is not for a certain term, nor entailed upon them and their heirs; but it runs as long as they carry themselves well, and no longer. Consider, (1.) "How they were *broken off*. It was not undeservedly, by an act of absolute sovereignty and prerogative, but *because of unbelief*." It seems, then, it is possible for churches that have long stood by faith to fall into such a state of infidelity as may be their ruin. Their unbelief did not only provoke God to cut them off, but they did by this cut themselves off; it was not only the meritorious, but the formal cause of their separation. "Now, thou art liable to the same infirmity and corruption that they fell by." Further observe, They were **natural branches** (Rom_11:21), not only interested in Abraham's covenant, but descending from Abraham's loins, and so born upon the premises, and thence had a kind of tenant-right: yet, when they sunk into unbelief, God did not spare them. Prescription, long usage, the faithfulness of their ancestors, would not secure them. It was in vain to plead, though they insisted much upon it, that they were Abraham's seed, Mat_3:9; Joh_8:33. It is true they were the husbandmen to whom **the vineyard** was first let out; but, when they forfeited it, it was justly taken from them, Mat_21:41, Mat_21:43. This is called here *severity*, Rom_11:22. God laid righteousness to the line and judgment to the plummet, and dealt with them according to their sins. Severity is a word that sounds harshly; and I do not remember that it is any where else in scripture ascribed to God; and it is here applied to the unchurching of the Jews. God is most severe towards those that have been in profession nearest to him, if they rebel against him, Amo_3:2. Patience and privileges abused turn to the greatest wrath. Of all judgments, spiritual judgments are the sorest; for of these he is here speaking, Rom_11:8. (2.) "How thou standest, thou that art en**grafted** in." He speaks to the Gentile churches in general, though perhaps tacitly reflecting on some particular person, who might have expressed some such pride and triumph in the Jews' rejection. "Consider then," [1.] "By what means thou standest: *By faith,* which is a depending grace, and fetches in strength from heaven. Thou dost not stand in any strength of thy own, of which thou mightest be confident: thou art no more than the free grace of God makes thee, and his grace is his own, which he gives or withholds at pleasure. That which ruined them was unbelief, and by faith thou standest; therefore thou hast no faster hold than they had, thou standest on no firmer foundation than they did." [2.] "On what terms (Rom_11:22): *Towards thee goodness, if thou continue in his goodness,* that is, continue in a dependence upon and compliance with the free grace of God, the want of which it was that ruined the Jews - if thou be careful to keep up thine interest in the divine favour, by being continually careful to please God and fearful of offending him." The sum of our duty, the condition of our happiness, is to keep ourselves in the love of God. *Fear the Lord and his goodness.* Hos_3:5.

III. Another thing that qualified this doctrine of the Jews' rejection is that, though for the present they are **cast** off, yet the rejection is not final; but, when the fulness of time is come, they will be taken in again. They are not **cast** off for ever, but mercy is remembered in the midst of wrath. Let us observe,

1. How this conversion of the Jews is here described. (1.) It is said to be their fulness (Rom_11:12), that is, the addition of them to the church, the filling up again of that place which became vacant by their rejection. This

would be the enriching of the world (that is, the church in the world) with a great deal of light and strength and beauty. (2.) It is called the receiving of them. The conversion of a soul is the receiving of that soul, so the conversion of a nation. They shall be received into favour, into the church, into the love of Christ, whose arms are stretched out for the receiving of all those that will come to him. And this will be as *life from the dead* - so strange and surprising, and yet withal so welcome and acceptable. The conversion of the Jews will bring great joy to the church. See <u>Luk 15:32</u>, *He was dead, and is alive;* and therefore *it was meet we should make merry and be glad.* (3.) It is called the **graft**ing *of them in again* (<u>Rom 11:23</u>), into the church, from which they had been **broken off**. That which is **grafted in** receives sap and virtue from the **root**; so does a soul that is truly **grafted into** the church receive life, and strength, and grace from Christ the quickening **root**. They shall be **grafted into** *their own* **olive-tree** (<u>Rom 11:24</u>); that is, into the church of which they had formerly been the most eminent and conspicuous members, to retrieve those privileges of visible church-membership which they had so long enjoyed, but have now sinned away and forfeited by their unbelief. (4.) It is called the *saving of all Israel,* <u>Rom 11:26</u>. True conversion may well be called salvation; it is salvation begun. See <u>Act 2:47</u>. The adding of them to the church is the saving of them: *tous sōzōmenous*, in the present tense, *are saved*. When conversion-work goes on, salvation-work goes on.

2. What it is grounded upon, and what reason we have to look for it.

(1.) Because of the holiness of the ***first-fruits*** and the ***root***, <u>Rom 11:16</u>. Some by the ***first-fruits*** understand those of the Jews that were already converted to the faith of Christ and received into the church, who were as the ***first-fruits*** dedicated to God, as earnests of a more plentiful and sanctified harvest. A good beginning promises a good ending. Why may we not suppose that others may be savingly wrought upon as well as those who are already brought in? Others by the ***first-fruits*** understand the same with the ***root***, namely, the patriarchs, Abraham, Isaac, and Jacob, from whom the Jews descended, and with whom, as the prime trustees, the covenant was deposited: and so they were the ***root*** of the Jews, not only as a people, but as a church. Now, if they were holy, which is not meant so much of inherent as of federal holiness - if they were in the church and in the covenant - then we have reason to conclude that God hath a kindness for the *lump* - the body of that people; and for the **branches** - the particular members of it. The Jews are in a sense a holy nation (<u>Exo 19:6</u>), being descended from holy parents. Now it cannot be imagined that such a holy nation should be totally and finally **cast** off. This proves that the seed of believers, as such, are within the pale of the visible church, and within the verge of the covenant, till they do, by their unbelief, throw themselves out; for, *if the* **root** *be holy, so are the* **branches**. Though real qualifications are not propagated, yet relative privileges are. Though a wise man does not beget a wise man, yet a free man begets a free man. Though grace does not run in the blood, yet external privileges do (till they are forfeited), even to a thousand generations. Look how they will answer it another day that cut off the entail, by turning the seed of the faithful out of the church, and so not allowing the blessing of Abraham to come upon the Gentiles. The Jewish **branches** are reckoned holy, because the **root** was so. This is expressed more plainly (Rom_11:28): *They are beloved for the fathers' sakes.* In this love to the fathers the first foundation of their church-state was laid (Deu_4:37): *Because he loved they fathers, therefore he chose their seed after them.* And the same love would revive their privileges, for still the ancient loving-kindness is remembered; they are *beloved for the fathers' sakes.* It is God's usual method of grace. Kindness to the children for the father's sake is therefore called the *kindness of God,* 2Sa_9:3, 2Sa_9:7. Though, as concerning the gospel (namely, in the present dispensation of it), they are enemies to it *for your sakes,* that is, for the sake of the Gentiles, against whom they have such an antipathy; yet, when God's time shall come, this will wear off, and God's love to their fathers will be remembered. See a promise that points at this, Lev_26:42. The iniquity of the fathers is visited but to the third and fourth generation; but there is mercy kept for thousands. Many fare the better for the sake of their godly ancestors. It is upon this account that the church is called their own *olive-tree.* Long it had been their own peculiar, which is some encouragement to us to hope that there may be room for them in it again, for old acquaintance-sake. That which hath been may be again. Though particular persons and generations wear off in unbelief, yet there having been a national church-membership, though for the present suspended, we may expect that it will be revived.

(2.) Because of the power of God (Rom_11:23): *God is able to **graft** them in again.* The conversion of souls is a work of almighty power; and when they seem most hardened, and blinded, and obstinate, our comfort is that God is able to work a change, able to **graft** those in that have been long **cast out and withered.** When the house is kept by the strong man armed, with all his force, yet God is stronger than he, and is able to dispossess him. The condition of their restoration is faith: *If they abide not still in unbelief.* So that nothing is to be done but to remove that unbelief that is the great obstacle; and God is able to take that away, though nothing less than an almighty power will do it, the same power that raised up Christ from the dead, Eph_1:19, Eph_1:20. Otherwise, can these dry bones live?

(3.) Because of the grace of God manifested to the Gentiles. Those that have themselves experienced the grace of God, preventing, distinguishing grace, may thence take encouragement to hope well concerning others. This is his argument (Rom_11:24): "If thou wast **grafted into** a **good olive,** that was **wild** by nature, much more shall these that were the **natural branches**, and may therefore be presumed somewhat nearer to the divine acceptance." This is a suggestion very proper to check the insolence of those Gentile Christians that looked with disdain and triumph upon the condition of the rejected Jews, and trampled upon them; as if he had said, "Their condition, bad as it is, is not so bad as yours was before your conversion; and therefore why may it not be made as *good* as yours is?" This is his argument (Rom_11:30, Rom_11:31): *As you in times past have not,* etc. It is *good* for those that have found mercy with God to be often thinking what they were in time past, and how they obtained that mercy. This would help to soften our censures of those that still continue in unbelief, and quicken our prayers for them. He argues further from the occasion of the Gentiles' call, that is, the unbelief of the Jews; thence it took rise: "*You have obtained mercy through their unbelief;* much more shall they obtain mercy through your mercy. If the putting out of their candle was the lighting of yours, by that power of God which brings *good* out of *evil*, much more shall the continued light of your candle, when God's time shall come, be a means of lighting theirs again." "*That through your mercy they might obtain mercy,* that is, that they may be beholden to you, as you have been to them." He takes it for granted that the believing Gentiles would do their utmost endeavour to work upon the Jews - that, when God had persuaded Japhet, Japhet would be labouring to persuade Shem. True grace hates monopolies. Those that have found mercy themselves should endeavour that through their mercy others also may obtain mercy."

Chapter Eight

The Mistake of King James English

More evidence of Joseph Smith writing the Book of Mormon can be found in a common mistake made by authors who write books that attempt to maintain the language of a specific time period. For example imagine trying to write a book where the setting and characters of your book take place in 17th Century England. You would need to do a significant amount of research in order to make sure you used the common phrases and words of that day. In addition you would also have to go to great lengths to ensure that you did not add words and phrases from today when you wrote your book and of course you would do this in order to maintain an aire of reality. Ask any author who has attempted to do this and they can tell you how difficult this truly is.

So one of the major problems of the Book of Mormon is that it was written in King James English. Why write the Book of Mormon in King James English when it would have made sense to translate it into the language of Joseph Smith's day that is 1800's American English? The reason is obvious, he wanted his book to sound "religious" and as you will note in this book he utilized the King James Bible, for much of the Book of Mormon and just for this reason. Note that The King James English Version of the Bible was originally published in 1611.

If he hadn't used King James English he would not have been able to utilize the Bible. Therefore not only did he use King James English so that it would sound religious, he in a sense had to use King James English or he would not have been able to use the Bible or create the Book of Mormon. This use of King James English was a common occurrence during Joseph Smith's time as many upstart religions and those claiming the ability to prophecy would write their works in the Bible's King James English so that their works would sound religious. Even groups in our modern day attempt the same aire of religious authenticity by utilizing King James English. This would be the equivalent of finding an ancient Greek manuscript today and translating it into King James English instead of modern English it wouldn't make much sense to do this but this is preciously what Joseph Smith did as well as other religious startups of the day and even our day.

Now not only should the use of King James English throw up a major road block as to the authenticity of the Book of Mormon, the mistakes Joseph Smith made in his attempt to utilize King James English speak should seal the fate of the Book of Mormon as a fake and clearly indicate that Joseph Smith wrote it, as if we haven't proven this fact already. We will look at several of those mistakes here in this chapter.

First let us look at the use of certain words and how they relate to time. If Joseph Smith translated in King James English then it should be safe to say that all of it should be in King James English. In fact this should indicate that we should not be able to find words written after 1611, the year the King James English Bible was published, otherwise why write or translate the Book of Mormon into King James English to begin with. In other words the use of one negates the use of the other. In fact there are so many words not found in the King James Bible that are used in the Book of Mormon that it would be impossible to outline them all here. It is also interesting that almost every one of these words, we will look at a few later, although excluded because of time, can be found in the commentaries as a result of the time they were written and the fact that Joseph Smith utilized the commentaries to write the Book of Mormon. I will therefore outline a few for you with the number of times used the Book of Mormon in parentheses, one place it appears in the Book of Mormon, the word itself, and its etymology or date of use.

(18) 1 Nephi 1:8 "surrounded" (circa 1616)
(5) 1 Nephi 1:8 "attitude" (1668)
(3) 1 Nephi 2:11 "visionary" (1648)
(11) 1 Nephi 4:28 "frightened" (1666)
(5) 1 Nephi 11:16 "condescension" (1647)
(4) 1 Nephi 15:35 "preparatory" (1762)
(1) 1 Nephi 16:19 "fatigued" (1693)
(4) 1 Nephi 16:24 "energy" (1655)
(7) 1 Nephi 16:35 "fatigue" (1669)
(4) 1 Nephi 17:8 "construct" (1663 AD)
(1) 2 Nephi 11:4 "typifying" (1634)
(4) 2 Nephi 28:14 "instances" (1657 AD)
(1) 2 Nephi 28:21 "lull" (1650 AD)
(1) Jacob 1:15 "indulge" (1623)
(2) Jacob 1:19 "responsibility" (1786)
(1) Jacob 2:9 "consoling" (1693)
(2) Jacob 3:1 "console" (1664)
(1) Jacob 7:26 "lonesome" (1647)
(6) Enos 1:20 "ferocious" (1646)

(1) Jarom 1:8 "machinery" (1687)
(2) Omni 1:29 "considerable" (1619)
(12) Mosiah 2:13 "plunder" (1632)
(3) Mosiah 4:5 "nothingness" (1631)
(1) Mosiah 10:19 "stimulate" (1619)
(3) Mosiah 11:8 "ornamented" (1720)
(3) Mosiah 11:11 "breastwork" (1642)
(1) Mosiah 15:5 "disowned" (1649)
(1) Mosiah 18:34 "apprised" (1694)
(1) Mosiah 20:11 "exerted" (1681)
(2) Mosiah 21:25 "previous" (1625)
(1) Mosiah 29:36 "enumerated" (1616)
(1) Mosiah 29:38 "anxious" (1616)
(5) Alma 12:1 "consciousness" (1632)
(2) Alma 13:12 "abhorrence" (1660)
(1) Alma 17:15 "indolent" (1663)
(1) Alma 22:3 "generosity" (1616)
(5) Alma 25:6 "disbelieve" (1644)
(3) Alma 28:2 "tremendous" (1632)
(1) Alma 30:16 "frenzied" (1796)
(1) Alma 30:16 "derangement" (1776)
(1) Alma 30:28 "whims" (1697)
(1) Alma 31:5 "tendency" (1628)
(20) Alma 31:8 "dissenters" (1639)
(1) Alma 36:14 "inexpressible" (1625)
(2) Alma 43:27 "secreted" (1707)
(6) Alma 45:21 "regulation" (1665)
(1) Alma 46:7 "precarious" (1646)
(1) Alma 47:36 "indolence" (1710)
(1) Alma 48:21 "reluctantly" (1667)
(3) Alma 49:2 "stationed" (1748)
(2) Alma 50:3 "pickets" (1702)
(2) Alma 52:21 "decoy" (1641)
(2) Alma 55:24 "liberated" (1623)
(1) Alma 58:9 "embarrassments" (1729)
(5) 3 Nephi 2:11 "carnage" (1656)
(1) 3 Nephi 3:16 "exert" (1681)
(1) 3 Nephi 4:19 "scantiness" (1660)

As you can see Joseph Smith utilized many words from after the time the King James Version of the Bible was written. There can only be one conclusion from this. That Joseph Smith faked the Book of Mormon. Again if the Book of Mormon was to be translated into King James English then it should contain the same King James English style of words throughout the entire translation especially, unlike the King James Version, that the Book of Mormon was translated by one person. Remember it is in the translation not in the original wording that makes the difference. Again, The King James Version was translated by many different people hence you will find differences but because the Book of Mormon was translated by one person there should not be discrepancies in King James English. I will give you just some of the many examples here. It is important to remember that when you are faking a book as large a book as the Book of Mormon it would be nearly impossible to remember to use the same style throughout the entire work, especially when it was written over several years.

To start you with an example the word "cometh" is King James style and appears in the Book of Mormon 127 times and appears in the King James Bible 268 times. The word "comes" which is the modern way of saying "cometh" appears in the Book of Mormon six times and does not appear in the King James Bible even once. The reason it doesn't appear even once in the King James Bible is because it was written when people only used the word "cometh". The word "comes" was not utilized during this time period. So, essentially Joseph Smith made six mistakes. These six mistakes add to the proof, outlined in this book, that Joseph Smith wrote the Book of Mormon. Now let us look at just a few more of these mistakes. I will outline them with the number of times they appear in the Book of Mormon first and immediately after this the word and then how many times the word appears in the King James Bible then the alternate modern word and how many times Joseph Smith made the mistake of using that word.

(127) "cometh" (268) - "comes" (6)
(11) "giveth" (119) - "gives" (2)
(10) "leadeth" (14) - "leads" (5)
(10) "divideth" (1) - "divides" (2)
(1) "containeth" (1) - "contains" (2)
(131) "goeth" (4) – "goes" (3)
(19) "belongeth" (5) – "belongs" (2)
(6) "cutteth" (1) – "cuts" (1)
(6) "thinketh" (4) – "thinks" (1)
(100) "knoweth" (45) – "knows" (5)
(2) "grieveth" (15) – "grieves" (1)
(5) "suffereth" (12) – "suffers" (1)
(9) "bindeth" (2) – "binds" (1)
(14) "leadeth" (10) – "leads" (5)
(36) "remaineth" (5) – "remains" (1)

(57) "dwelleth" (7) – "dwells" (1)

(31) "causeth" (5) – "causes" (1)

Note: Although the word "causes" appears in the King James Version it is used as a noun.

(31) "exerciseth" (2) – "exercises" (1)

(0) "mattereth" (12) ("matters" not as a noun) (2)

Note: Even though "mattereth" does not appear in the King James Bible Joseph Smith got it from another source, as you will see, but failed to utilize the correct form twice.

(848) "hast" (149) "has" (449)

Now Joseph Smith therefore made 492 mistakes by not using the proper King James English form.

Now you might want to ask yourself, "Why did Joseph Smith make these mistakes?" When we take a look at the mistakes outlined above two reasons become obvious. Reason one is that he made up the section in which the word appears himself instead of copying it from the Bible or commentaries. His thought process, the process needed to make up the section, thus distracted him and he therefore forgot to use the King James style. This is a common mistake of authors attempting to write in a specific time frame.

Reason two is simple; he copied the word directly from the commentaries. Let us look at a couple of these reasons in detail.

First we will look at (5) "suffereth" (12) – "suffers" (1). Now why did Joseph Smith correctly use the word "suffereth" twelve times but used "suffers" mistakenly once? He copied it from a commentary. When we look at the verse in the Book of Mormon where we find that he used the word "suffers", we can see its related use in the commentary. I have italicized the similar uses.

BOM 1 Nephi 19:12 "And all these things must surely come, saith the prophet Zenos. And the rocks of the earth must rend; and because of the groanings of the earth, many of the kings of the isles of the sea shall be wrought upon by the Spirit of God, to exclaim The God of nature **suffers**."

> **COM** Gill: <u>Acts 17:34</u> ""It is reported of him, that being at Heliopolis in Egypt, along with Apollophanes, a philosopher, at the time of Christ's sufferings, he should say concerning the unusual eclipse that then was, that "a God unknown, and clothed with flesh, suffered", on whose account the whole world was darkened; or, as, others affirm, he said, "either *the God of nature suffers*, or the frame of the world will be dissolved"":"

As you can see the entire story line matches both the Book of Mormon verse and the commentary in Gill. Therefore the only explanation for Joseph Smith making this mistake is that he copied this phrase from the commentaries. In addition note that Joseph Smith states, "many of the kings of the isles of the sea shall be wrought upon by the Spirit of God, to exclaim…" to exclaim "the God of nature suffers". He knew that this was a unique quote and needed, as he had done many times before in the Book of Mormon, to explain how, if anyone found it, it could possibly be in the Book of Mormon so he must state that they were able to do this by "the Spirit of God. What he should have written was "the God of nature suffereth" but of course he copied it from the commentaries so he wrote the copied phrase "the God of nature suffers".

Now let us look at the word "come". Joseph Smith should have used the word "cometh" instead of "comes" as "comes" is the modern form of the King James English word "cometh".

BOM 2 Nephi 9:2 "That he has spoken unto the Jews, by the mouth of his holy prophets, even from the beginning down, from generation to generation, *until the time comes*."

Now a quote from Gill: Note that even Gill gives the King James English way of saying this as well as the modern way.

> **COM** Gill: Mat 23:39 "till ye shall say, blessed is he that cometh in the name of the Lord; that is, **until the time comes**, that the fulness of the Gentiles shall be brought in, and all Israel shall be saved, the Jews shall be converted, and seek the Lord their God,")…"

Notice that he utilized the word "come" because it was used by Gill. Let us look at another:

BOM Alma 12:24 "And we see that *death comes upon* mankind, yea, the death which has been spoken of by Amulek,…"

And now the quote from Gill:

> **COM** Gill: Jam 1:13-18 "There is a death upon the soul, and *death comes upon* the body. And, besides death spiritual and temporal, the wages of sin is eternal death too."

Now we can see examples of where he utilized the proper King James English form of the word by copying from the King James Bible. Note: The phrase "the time cometh" only appears in the New Testament.

BOM 1 Nephi 13:42 "And **the time cometh** that he shall manifest himself unto all nations, both unto the Jews and also unto the Gentiles;…"

> **KJV** John 16:2 "They shall put you out of the synagogues: yea, **the time cometh**, that whosoever killeth you will think that he doeth God service."

Notice here that he is using a phrase from John and therefore he utilizes the correct word "cometh". Instead of the mistake he used above where he uses "comes".

And another example:

BOM 2 Nephi 9:21 "And he **cometh into the world**…"

KJV John 1:9 "That was the true Light, which lighteth every man that **cometh into the world**."

Now let us look at another word, "dwells" instead of the proper King James English word "dwelleth".

BOM Alma 18:30 "And Ammon said unto him: The *heavens* is a place *where God dwells* and all his holy angels."

Now the quote in the commentary of Gill:

COM Gill: Heb 11:10 "or else the ultimate glory of the saints in *heaven, where God dwells*, and keeps his palace; and which will be the dwelling place of the saints" This phrase and idea also appears in Henry's commentary.

I hope it is obvious why he made this mistake. He was copying the same words from the commentary and so made the mistake of using the more modern commentary word "dwells" instead of the word he should have used the King James English word "dwelleth" which the King James Bible uses 57 times and Joseph Smith himself used seven times in the Book of Mormon.

And now lets look at another keeping in mind that he used the more modern word because it comes from the commentaries; "cuts" instead of the proper King James English word "cutteth".

BOM Mosiah 13:7 "Ye see that ye have not power to slay me, therefore I finish my message. Yea, and I perceive that it *cuts* you *to* your *heart*s because I tell you the truth concerning your iniquities."

COM Gill: Eph 6:17 "the word of God is compared to a "sword", for its two edges, the law and Gospel; the one convicts of sin, and *cuts to the heart* for it, and the other cuts down all the goodliness of man;"

As you can see the reason he made the mistake of using the word "cuts" one time but correctly used the word "cutteth" six times in the Book of Mormon is because he copied it from the commentaries.

Now that we have looked at a few of the modern words Joseph Smith utilized from the commentaries let us look at variations in style for words in close proximity to each other. These again are mistakes, mistakes he again makes in regard to King James English utilizing one style and then another in verses in close proximity to each other and even the same sentence. This again is a problem of attempting to makeup parts of the Book of Mormon and utilizing the King James Bible and the commentaries. These mistakes were not done in the King James Bible. Let us look at some of those examples. Joseph Smith also made these mistakes for the same reasons I outlined above. Again there are so many examples of this that I will only outline a few here.

"intrigue amongst" vs. "intrigue among"

BOM Alma 53:8 "on account of some intrigue amongst the Nephites"

BOM Alma 53:9 "and intrigue among themselves"

BOM Alma 53:9 "iniquity amongst themselves"

As you can see Joseph Smith should have used "amongst" in each case especially when they are so close together. Let us look at a few others.

"divideth the lands" vs. "divides the land"

The King James Version of the Bible does not use the word "divides".

BOM Ether 2:13 "And now I proceed with my record; for behold, it came to pass that the Lord did bring Jared and his brethren forth even to that great sea which *divideth the lands*. And as they came to the sea they pitched their tents; and they called the name of the place Moriancumer; and they dwelt in tents, and dwelt in tents upon the seashore for the space of four years."

BOM Ether 10:20 "And they built a great city by the narrow neck of land, by the place where the sea *divides the land*."

"containeth" vs. "contains"

The King James Version of the Bible does not use the word "contains".

BOM 1 Nephi 13:23 "And he said: Behold it proceedeth out of the mouth of a Jew. And I, Nephi, beheld it; and he said unto me: The book that thou beholdest is a record of the Jews, which *contains* the covenants of the Lord, which he hath made unto the house of Israel; and it also *containeth* many of the prophecies of the holy prophets; and it is a record like unto the engravings which are upon the plates of brass, save there are not so many; nevertheless, they contain the covenants of the Lord, which he hath made unto the house of Israel; wherefore, they are of great worth unto the Gentiles."

"goeth" vs. "goes"

The King James Version of the Bible does not use the word "goes".

BOM Alma 12:15 "And thus, according to his word the earth *goeth* back, and it appeareth unto man that the sun standeth still; yea, and behold, this is so; for surely it is the earth that moveth and not the sun."

BOM Mosiah 16:5 "But remember that he that persists in his own carnal nature, and *goes* on in the ways of sin and rebellion against God, remaineth in his fallen state and the devil hath all power over him. Therefore, he is as though there was no redemption made, being an enemy to God; and also is the devil an enemy to God."

"repenteth" vs. "repents"

The King James Version of the Bible does not use the word "repents".

BOM Mosiah 26:29 "Therefore I say unto you, Go; and whosoever transgresseth against me, him shall ye judge according to the sins which he has committed; and if he confess his sins before thee and me, and *repenteth* in the sincerity of his heart, him shall ye forgive, and I will forgive him also."

BOM Mosiah 26:21 "And ye shall also forgive one another your trespasses; for verily I say unto you, he that forgiveth not his neighbor's trespasses when he says that he *repents*, the same hath brought himself under condemnation."

"the time cometh" vs. "the time comes"

The King James Version of the Bible does not use the word "comes".

BOM <u>Mosiah 29:27</u> "And if *the time comes* that the voice of the people doth choose iniquity, then is the time that the judgments of God will come upon you; yea, then is the time he will visit you with great destruction even as he has hitherto visited this land."

BOM <u>Mosiah 3:5</u> "For behold, *the time cometh*, and is not far distant, that with power, the Lord Omnipotent who reigneth, who was, and is from all eternity to all eternity, shall come down from heaven among the children of men, and shall dwell in a tabernacle of clay, and shall go forth amongst men, working mighty miracles, such as healing the sick, raising the dead, causing the lame to walk, the blind to receive their sight, and the deaf to hear, and curing all manner of diseases."

"thinketh" vs. "thinks"

The King James Version of the Bible does not use the word "thinks".

BOM <u>1 Nephi 17:17</u> "And when my brethren saw that I was about to build a ship, they began to murmur against me, saying: Our brother is a fool, for he *thinketh* that he can build a ship; yea, and he also *thinketh* that he can cross these great waters."

BOM <u>2 Nephi 5:3</u> "Yea, they did murmur against me, saying: Our younger brother *thinks* to rule over us; and we have had much trial because of him; wherefore, now let us slay him, that we may not be afflicted more because of his words. For behold, we will not have him to be our ruler; for it belongs unto us, who are the elder brethren, to rule over this people."

"curseth the land" vs. "curse the land"

BOM <u>1 Nephi 17:38</u> "And he leadeth away the righteous into precious lands, and the wicked he destroyeth, and *curseth the land* unto them for their sakes."

BOM <u>1 Nephi 17:35</u> "Behold, the Lord esteemeth all flesh in one; he that is righteous is favored of God. But behold, this people had rejected every word of God, and they were ripe in iniquity; and the fulness of the wrath of God was upon them; and the Lord did *curse the land* against them, and bless it unto our fathers; yea, he did *curse* it against them unto their destruction, and he did bless it unto our fathers unto their obtaining power over it."

"which giveth" vs. "which gives"

The King James Version of the Bible does not use the word "gives".

BOM <u>2 Nephi 2:28</u> "And they shall contend one with another; and their priests shall contend one with another, and they shall teach with their learning, and deny the Holy Ghost, *which giveth* utterance."

BOM <u>1 Nephi 19:4</u> "Wherefore, I, Nephi, did make a record upon the other plates, which **gives** an account, or *which gives* a greater account of the wars and contentions and destructions of my people. And this have I done, and commanded my people what they should do after I was gone; and that these plates should be handed down from one generation to another, or from one prophet to another, until further commandments of the Lord."

"that causeth" vs. "that causes"

Note: The Bible uses "causes" as a noun only.

BOM Alma 18:16 "And it came to pass that Ammon, being filled with the Spirit of God, therefore he perceived the thoughts of the king. And he said unto him: Is it because thou hast heard that I defended thy servants and thy flocks, and slew seven of their brethren with the sling and with the sword, and smote off the arms of others, in order to defend thy flocks and thy servants; behold, is it this *that causeth* thy marvelings?"

BOM Alma 30:35 "Then why sayest thou that we preach unto this people to get gain, when thou, of thyself, knowest that we receive no gain? And now, believest thou that we deceive this people, *that causes* such joy in their hearts?"

"yieldeth" vs. "yields"

The King James Version of the Bible does not use the word "yields".

BOM Mosiah 15:5 "And thus the flesh becoming subject to the Spirit, or the Son to the Father, being one God, suffereth temptation, and *yieldeth* not to the temptation, but suffereth himself to be mocked, and scourged, and cast out, and disowned by his people."

BOM Mosiah 3:19 "For the natural man is an enemy to God, and has been from the fall of Adam, and will be, forever and ever, unless he *yields* to the enticings of the Holy Spirit, and putteth off the natural man and becometh a saint through the atonement of Christ the Lord, and becometh as a child, submissive, meek, humble, patient, full of love, willing to submit to all things which the Lord seeth fit to inflict upon him, even as a child doth submit to his father."

"enacteth laws" vs. "enacts laws"

The King James Version of the Bible does not use the word "enacts".

BOM Mosiah 29:23 "And he *enacteth laws*, and sendeth them forth among his people, yea, laws after the manner of his own wickedness; and whosoever doth not obey his laws he causeth to be destroyed; and whosoever doth rebel against him he will send his armies against them to war, and if he can he will destroy them; and thus an unrighteous king doth pervert the ways of all righteousness."

BOM Alma 4:16 "And he selected a wise man who was among the elders of the church, and gave him power according to the voice of the people, that he might have power to *enact laws* according to the laws which had been given, and to put them in force according to the wickedness and the crimes of the people."

"and thus endeth the" vs. "and thus ended the"

BOM Alma 4:10 "*And thus ended the eighth* year of the reign of the judges; and the wickedness of the church was a great stumbling-block to those who did not belong to the church; and thus the church began to fail in its progress."

BOM Alma 3:27 "For every man receiveth wages of him whom he listeth to obey, and this according to the words of the spirit of prophecy; therefore let it be according to the truth. *And thus endeth the* fifth year of the reign of the judges."

It is important to note here that Joseph Smith used the phrase "thus endeth the" four times and each time in Alma. He used the phrase "thus ended the" 39 times and 22 of those times were in Alma. Of course this change should not have happened especially in the same book, the Book of Alma. Joseph Smith used the phrase so often that he mistakenly used "thus ended" four times.

"comprehendeth all" vs. "comprehend all"

BOM Alma 26:35 "Now have we not reason to rejoice? Yea, I say unto you, there never were men that had so great reason to rejoice as we, since the world began; yea, and my joy is carried away, even unto boasting in my God; for he has all power, all wisdom, and all understanding; he *comprehendeth all* things, and he is a merciful Being, even unto salvation, to those who will repent and believe on his name."

BOM Mosiah 4:9 "Believe in God; believe that he is, and that he created all things, both in heaven and in earth; believe that he has all wisdom, and all power, both in heaven and in earth; believe that man doth not *comprehend all* the things which the Lord can *comprehend*."

"it appeareth" vs. "it appears"

The King James Version of the Bible does not use the word "appears".

BOM Alma 12:15 "And thus, according to his word the earth goeth back, and *it appeareth* unto man that the sun standeth still; yea, and behold, this is so; for surely it is the earth that moveth and not the sun."

BOM 1 Nephi 1:3 "Wherefore, the things of which I have read are things pertaining to things both temporal and spiritual; for *it appears* that the house of Israel, sooner or later, will be scattered upon all the face of the earth, and also among all nations."

Now as I said in the first chapter I want to show you the only words not found in the commentaries or The King James Version of the Bible that Joseph Smith utilized.

I will start by using the more modern words or words that do not appear or attempt to be King James English. I will not include names and places. There should of course be some words in such a large made-up book as the Book of Mormon that would not be in either the commentaries or The King James Version of the Bible, as in the case of Joseph Smith using words common to his day. Note that there are only 20 of these words that do not appear in either out of the entire Book of Mormon. But as you will see there are some circumstances that make this number even smaller.

(2) luster (1522)

From the Christian sermons and books of the day.

(1) preparator (1762)

This word comes from 1 Nephi 15:35 which was changed from the 1920 version of the Book of Mormon in the 1981 version to the word "foundation". This makes sense with the commentaries and is the reason I could not find this word in the commentaries.

BOM 1 Nephi 15:35 And there is a place prepared, yea, even that awful hell of which I have spoken, and the devil is the **preparator** of it; wherefore the final state of the souls of men is to dwell in the kingdom of God, or to be cast out because of that justice of which I have spoken.

COM Henry: Joh 20:26-31 "because he was to be not only the founder of it, but **the foundation of it** for its constant support," (Gill, Clarke)

(1) pointers (1574)

As in a compass. Used by many seafaring seamen of Joseph Smith's day.

(2) simpleness (13th Century)

Used in hymns of Joseph Smith's day

(1) vainness (14th Century)

Again from the Christian sermons and books of the day.

(1) sobbings (13th Century)

Used in many of the sermons of famous ministers of Joseph Smith's day.

(1) pester (1533)

As used by Joseph Smith in the Book of Mormon related to bugs a common saying during his day. Don't let the bugs "pester" you.

(1) hinderment

Could not find this word in any of the dictionaries, including the 1828 Webster's Dictionary.

(9) lyings

Found in the Nicene Fathers

(2) marvelings

Could not find this word in any of the dictionaries, including the 1828 Webster's Dictionary.

(1) frenzied (1796)

Obviously a word that came into existence just before the writing of the Book of Mormon.

(1) overbearance

Could not find this word in any of the dictionaries, including the 1828 Webster's Dictionary.

(2) consignation (1528)

Word used in many Christian books of Joseph Smith's day, as an example: Holy Dying, by Jeremy Taylor (1613-1667)

(2) pickets (1702)

As in a picket fence used in Joseph Smith's day.

(1) quarrelings

Again from the Christian sermons and books of the day.

(2) murderings

Again from the Christian sermons and books of the day.

(2) unwearyingness

Could not find this word in any of the dictionaries, including the 1828 Webster's Dictionary.

(1) magics (14th Century)

Could not find this word in any of the dictionaries, including the 1828 Webster's Dictionary.

(1) molder (14th Century)

A common word of the day.

Now we will look at the numerous King James Style words that Joseph Smith used, of which there are 39. Now these words do not appear in the dictionaries, or in the commentaries or in the King James Version of the Bible. Now there are several choices for their existence: he made them up even though they may be found elsewhere; he heard them used a lot in the sermons of his day; again many sermons utilized King James English style words, or he got them from a specific source. It is nearly impossible to prove any of these therefore I list them with a source that I found them in below.

Confoundeth

Found in the Nicene Fathers

Mattereth

Found in the Nicene Fathers

Tortureth

Found in Frances Bacon

Yoketh

Found in Shakespeare

Numbereth

Found in the Nicene Fathers

Mixeth

Found in the Nicene Fathers

Behooveth

Found in the Nicene Fathers

Transformeth

Found in the Nicene Fathers

Employeth

Found in John Calvin

Manifesteth
Found in the Nicene Fathers

Inviteth
Found in the Nicene Fathers

Cheateth
Found in many poems

Whispereth
Found in Sermons from the 1600's

Covenanteth
Hard to find

Burdeneth
Found in the Nicene Fathers

Counseleth
Could not find

Beginneth
Found in the Nicene Fathers

Beheldest
Found in books from the 12th and 13th centuries

Wondereth
Found in the Nicene Fathers

Pretendeth
Sermons of the day

Granteth
Found in the Nicene Fathers

Trampleth
Found in the Nicene Fathers

Enacteth
Found in the Nicene Fathers

Mingleth
Found in the Nicene Fathers

Granteth
Found in the Nicene Fathers

Allotteth
Sermons of the day

Decreeth
Found in the Nicene Fathers

Imparteth
Found in the Nicene Fathers

Swelleth
Found in the Nicene Fathers

Sprouteth

Sermons of the day
Scorcheth
Found in the Nicene Fathers
Murdereth
Found in John Calvin
Overpowereth
Hard to find
Claimeth
Found in the Nicene Fathers
Fulfilleth
Found in the Nicene Fathers
Spurneth
Found in the Nicene Fathers
Sweepeth
Found in the Nicene Fathers
Inviteth
Found in the Nicene Fathers
Advocateth
Found in Sermons from the 1640's.

Chapter Nine

Why Joseph Smith Used Words That Were Developed After the King James Version of the Bible

Previously we looked at many words that were developed after the King James Version of the Bible was complied in 1611. If you will remember in the chapter "The Mistake of Using King James English" I wrote the following; "First let us look at the use of certain words and how they relate to time. If Joseph Smith translated in King James English then it should be safe to say that all of it should be in King James English. In fact this should indicate that we should not be able to find words written after 1611 otherwise why write or translate the Book of Mormon into King James English to begin with. In other words the use of one negates the other."

Now in this chapter we will go into more detail on the reasons why Joseph Smith utilized words that should not appear in the Book of Mormon. In-other-words, words that appear in history after 1611 AD.

Just so you know I painstakingly tried to find these words and more especially the phrases you will see below in hundreds of books, articles, poems and songs. The result, more evidence that indeed Joseph Smith used these commentaries to create the Book of Mormon. I rarely found the key phrases and when I did they did not come from the same sources. In other words the results were arbitrary but not so with the commentaries I have outlined and as you have seen.

Note that I have given the number of times the word appears in the Book of Mormon in parentheses. In addition I have given a source of the word found in the commentaries. I will exclude the details that I have normally used in the analysis of the Book of Mormon, such as King James Bible verses or other commentary uses.

Surrounded (circa 1616)
BOM 1 Nephi 1:8: **surrounded** (circa 1616) **with**

COM Clarke: Act 26:22 "Preaching before kings, rulers, priests, and peasants; fearing no evil, though ever **surrounded with** evils;")

BOM Mosiah 7:7 and they were *(5)* *(18)* **surrounded** *(circa 1616)* ***by the*** king's guard, and were taken, and were bound, and were committed to prison.

> **COM** Clarke: Act 21:40 "Where he was out of the reach of the mob, and was **surrounded by the** Roman soldiers."(Henry)

BOM Mosiah 21:5 And now the afflictions of the Nephites were great, and there was no way that they could deliver themselves out of their hands, for the Lamanites had *(18)* **surrounded** *(circa 1616)* ***them on every side.***

> **COM** Henry: 2Ki 25:1-7 "Formerly Jerusalem had been compassed with the favour of God as with a shield, but now their defense had departed from them and their enemies **surrounded them on every side.**")

BOM Alma 22:32 and the land of Zarahemla were nearly *(18)* **surrounded** *(circa 1616)* ***by water,***

> **COM** Clarke: Job 28:28 "Though this has been already explained, let the reader farther consider that, as fishes are **surrounded by water,** and live and move in it, which is a much denser medium than our atmosphere;")

BOM Alma 47:14 And it came to pass that Lehonti came down with his men and *(18)* **surrounded** *(circa 1616)* the men of Amalickiah, so that before they awoke at the dawn of day *(6)* ***they were*** *(18)* **surrounded** *(circa 1616),* by the armies of Lehonti.

> **COM** Henry: Jos 19:1-9 "The cities of Simeon were scattered in Judah, with which tribe **they were surrounded,** except on that side towards the sea. (Clarke)

(5) 1 Nephi 1:8 "attitude" (1668)

BOM 1 Nephi 1:8 in the *(5)* ***attitude*** *(1668)* *of* singing and praising their God.

> **COM** Clarke: 1Pe 1:12 "There is evidently an allusion here to **the attitude of** the cherubim who stood at the ends of the ark of the covenant,")

(3) 1 Nephi 2:11 "visionary" (1648)

BOM 1 Nephi 2:11 because he was *(3)* ***a visionary*** *(1648 AD)* man,

> **COM** Gill: Jer 13:7 "this digging was in **a visionary** way;" (Clarke, Wesley)

(11) 1 Nephi 4:28 "frightened" (1666)

BOM 1 Nephi 18:13 Wherefore, they knew not whither they should the ship, insomuch that there arose a great storm, yea, a great and terrible tempest, and we were driven back upon the waters for the space of three days; and they began to be *(1)* *(11)* ***frightened,*** *(1666 AD)* exceedingly lest they should be drowned in the sea; nevertheless they did not loose me.

> **COM** This is from the same story as that of Jesus on the boat during the fierce storm a similar story to that here. Henry: Mar 6:45-56

"They were **frightened** at the sight of him, supposing him to have been an apparition;" (Gill, Clarke)

BOM Mosiah 23:27 But Alma went forth and stood among them, and exhorted them that they *should not be (11) frightened, (1666 AD)* but that they should remember the Lord their God and he would deliver them.

> **COM** Henry: Isa 10:24-34 "Note, We **should not be frightened** at those enemies that can do no more than frighten us.")

(5) 1 Nephi 11:16 "condescension" (1647)

BOM 1 Nephi 11:16 And he said unto me: Knowest thou the *(2) (5) condescension (1647 AD) of God?*

> **COM** Clarke: Eph 3:8 "and the amazing **condescension of God**," (Wesley, Henry)

BOM 2 Nephi 4:26 O then, if I have seen so great things, if the Lord *in his (5) condescension (1647 AD)* unto the children of men hath visited men in so much mercy, why should my heart weep and my soul linger in the valley of sorrow, and my flesh **waste away**, and my strength slacken, because of mine afflictions?

> **COM** Henry: Luk 9:57-62 "He glories in his **condescension** towards us, not only to the meanness of our nature, but to the meanest condition in that nature, to testify his love to us,")

BOM Jacob 4:7 Nevertheless, the Lord God showeth us our weakness that we may know that it is by his grace, and *his great (2) condescensions (1647 AD)* unto the children of men, that we have power to do these things.

> **COM** Gill: Luk 15:20 "and of **his great condescension** and grace to fall on that neck which had been like an iron sinew,")

1 Nephi 15:35 "preparatory" (1762)

BOM Alma 12:26 "tree of life they would have been forever miserable, having *no (4) preparatory* (15th Century) state;"

> **COM** Gill: Tit 3:4 "when these persons were in the full career of sin, and so had done **no preparatory** works, or had any previous qualifications and dispositions for the grace of God:" (Clarke, Henry)

1 Nephi 16:19 "fatigued" (1693)

BOM 1 Nephi 16:19 And it came to pass that we did return without food to our families, and being *(1) much (1) fatigued, (1693)* because of their journeying, they did suffer much for the want of food.

> **COM** Henry: Jdg 8:4-17 "They were faint, and yet pursuing, **much fatigued** with what they had done" (Gill, Clarke,)

(4) "energy" (1655)

BOM 1 Nephi 16:24 And it came to pass that he did inquire of the Lord, for they had humbled themselves because of my words; for I did say many things unto them in *(2) the (4) energy (1655) of my* soul.

> **COM** Clarke: Joh 14:20 "for I will live in you by **the energy of my**

Spirit,")

BOM <u>Alma 5:43</u> And now, my brethren, I would that ye should hear me, for I speak in *(2) the (4) energy (1655) of my Spirit*; for behold, I have spoken unto you plainly that ye cannot err, or have spoken according to the commandments of God.

> **COM** Clarke: <u>Joh 14:20</u> "for I will live in you by **the energy of my Spirit**,")

BOM <u>Mormon 2:23</u> And it came to pass that I did speak unto my people, and did urge them *with great (4) energy (1655)*, that they would stand boldly before the Lamanites and fight for their wives, and their children, and their houses, and their homes.

> **COM** Gill: <u>Act 2:2</u> "and works with great energy upon the minds of men;")

(7) "fatigue" (1669)

BOM <u>1 Nephi 16:35</u> And it came to pass that the daughters of Ishmael did mourn exceedingly, because of the loss of their father, and because of their afflictions in the wilderness; and they did murmur against my father, because he had brought them out of the land of Jerusalem, saying: Our father is dead; yea, and we have wandered much in the wilderness, and we have suffered much affliction, *hunger, thirst, and (7) fatigue (1669);* and after all these sufferings we must perish in the wildernes with hunger.

BOM <u>Mosiah 3:7</u> And lo, he shall suffer temptations, and pain of body, *hunger, thirst, and (7) fatigue (1669)*, even more than man can suffer, except it be unto death; for behold, blood cometh from every pore so great shall be his anguish for the wickedness and the abominations of his people.

BOM <u>Alma 17:5</u> Now these are the circumstances which attended them in their journeyings, for they had many afflictions; they did suffer much, both in body and in mind, such as *hunger, thirst and (7) fatigue (1669),* and also much labor in the spirit.

BOM <u>Mosiah 7:16</u> And now, king Limhi commanded his guards that they should no more bind Ammon nor his brethren, but caused that they should go to the hill which was north of Shilom, and bring their brethren into the city, that thereby they might eat, and drink, and rest themselves from the labors of their journey; for they had suffered many things; they had suffered *hunger, thirst, and (7) fatigue (1669).*

> **COM** Gill: <u>2Co 4:16</u> "we are oftentimes in a very distressed condition through **hunger**, **thirst**, nakedness, and want of the common necessaries of life; our bodies are almost worn out with **fatigue**, labour, and sorrow;")

BOM <u>Alma 51:33</u> And it came to pass that when the night had come, Teancum and his servant stole forth and went out by night, and went into the camp of Amalickiah; and behold, sleep had overpowered them because of their *much* (*7) fatigue* (*1669*), which was caused by the labors and heat of the day.

COM Gill: Dan 3:3 "and with **much fatigue** and trouble")

BOM Alma 60:3 And now behold, I say unto you that myself, and also my men, and also Alma and his men, have suffered exceedingly great sufferings; yea, even hunger, thirst, and (7) **fatigue** (1669), and all manner of afflictions of every kind.

(4) "construct" (1663 AD)

BOM 1 Nephi 17:8 And it came to pass that the Lord spake unto me, saying: Thou shalt (*4) construct* (*1663 AD*) a ship, after the manner which I shall show thee, that I may carry thy people across these waters.

> COM Clarke: Exo 2:3 "Of the papyrus itself they **construct** sailing vessels.")

(1) "typifying" (1634)

BOM 2 Nephi 11:4 Behold, my soul delighteth in proving unto my people the truth of the coming of Christ; for, for this end hath the law of Moses been given; and all things which have been given of God from the beginning of the world, unto man, are the (*1) typifying* (*1634*) of him.

> COM Henry: Isa 65:8-10 "the land of promise, **typifying** the covenant of grace," (Clarke, Wesley)

(4) "instances" (1657 AD)

BOM 2 Nephi 28:14 they are led, that in (*4) many instances* (*1657 AD*) they do err because they are taught by the precepts of men.

BOM Alma 31:11 Yea, in fine, they did pervert the ways of the Lord in very (4) *many instances* (*1657 AD*); therefore, for this cause, Alma and his brethren went into the land to preach the word unto them.

BOM Alma 34:6 And ye also beheld that my brother has proved unto you, in (*4) many instances* (*1657 AD*), that the word is in Christ unto salvation.

BOM Alma 37:6 Now ye may suppose that this is foolishness in me; but behold I say unto you, that by small and simple things are great things brought to pass; and small means in (*4) many instances* (*1657 AD*) doth confound the wise.

> COM Henry: Isa 26:12-19 "That God had in **many instances** been very gracious to them and had done great things for them." (Clarke, Wesley)

(1) "lull" (1650 AD)

BOM 2 Nephi 28:21 And others will he pacify, *and* (*1) lull* (*1650 AD*) them away into carnal security, that they will say: All is well in Zion; yea, Zion prospereth, all is well -- and thus the devil cheateth their souls, and leadeth them away carefully down to hell.

> COM Clarke: Zep 3:4 "**and lull** the people into spiritual slumber." (Henry)

(2) "indulge" (1623)

BOM Jacob 1:15 And now it came to pass that the people of Nephi, under the reign of the second king, began to grow hard in their hearts, *and (2) indulge (1623) themselves* somewhat in wicked practices, such as like unto David of old desiring many wives and concubines, and also Solomon, his son.

BOM Alma 1:32 For those who did not belong to their church did *(2) indulge (1623) themselves in* sorceries, and in idolatry or idleness, and in babblings, and in envyings and strife; wearing costly apparel; being lifted up in the pride of their own eyes; persecuting, lying, thieving, robbing, committing whoredoms, and murdering, and all manner of wickedness; nevertheless, the law was put in force upon all those who did transgress it, inasmuch as it was possible.

> **COM** Gill: Job 21:7 "and **indulge themselves in** all the gratifications of sensual pleasures and delights;" (Clarke, Henry)

Jacob 1:19 "responsibility" (1786)

BOM Jacob 1:19 And we did magnify our office unto the Lord, taking upon us the *(2) responsibility (1786),* answering the sins of the people upon our own heads if we did not teach them the word of God with all diligence; wherefore, by laboring with our might their blood might not come upon our garments; otherwise their blood would come upon our garments, and we would not be found spotless at the last day.

> **COM** Clarke: Act 20:28 "it is an office of most awful **responsibility**;")

Jacob 2:9 "consoling" (1693)

BOM Jacob 2:9 Wherefore, it burdeneth my soul that I should be constrained, because of the strict commandment which I have received from God, to admonish you according to your crimes, to enlarge the wounds of those who are already wounded, instead of *(1) consoling (1693)* and healing their wounds; and those who have not been wounded, instead of feasting upon the pleasing word of God have daggers placed to pierce their souls and wound their delicate minds.

> **COM** Clarke: Eze 33:10 "In such circumstances how **consoling** is that word: "Come unto me, all ye who are heavy laden, and I will give you rest!")

Jacob 3:1 "console" (1664)

BOM Jacob 3:1 But behold, I, Jacob, would speak unto you that are pure in heart. Look unto God with firmness of mind, and pray unto him with exceeding faith, and he will *(2) console (1664)* you in your afflictions, and he will plead your cause, and send down justice upon those who seek your destruction.

BOM Alma 56:11 Nevertheless, we may *(2) console (1664)* ourselves in this point, that they have died in the cause of their country and of their God, yea, and they are happy.

COM Clarke: <u>Job 16:2</u> "ye see me in affliction; ye should endeavor to **console** me.")

Jacob 7:26 "lonesome" (1647)

BOM <u>Jacob 7:26</u> And it came to pass that I, Jacob, began to be old; and the record of this people being kept on the other plates of Nephi, wherefore, I conclude this record, declaring that I have written according to the best of my knowledge, by saying that the time passed away with us, and also our lives passed away like as it were unto us a dream, we being *a (1) lonesome (1647)* and a solemn people, wanderers, cast out from Jerusalem, born in tribulation, in a wilderness, and hated of our brethren, which caused wars and contentions; wherefore, we did mourn out our days.

> **COM** Gill: <u>Mal 1:3</u> "a **lonesome** desolate wilderness; no otherwise diversified than by plains covered with sand," (Clarke)

Enos 1:20 "ferocious" (1646)

BOM <u>Enos 1:20</u> And I bear record that the people of Nephi did seek diligently to restore the Lamanites unto the true faith in God. But our labors were vain; their hatred was fixed, and they were led by their evil nature that they became *wild, and (6) ferocious (1646),* and a bloodthirsty people, full of idolatry and filthiness; feeding upon beasts of prey; dwelling in tents, and wandering about in the wilderness with a short skin girdle about their loins and their heads shaven; and their skill was in the bow, and in the cimeter, and the ax. And many of them did eat nothing save it was raw meat; and they were continually seeking to destroy us.

> **COM** Clarke: <u>Deu 7:22</u> "And as **wild and ferocious** animals might be expected to multiply where either there are no inhabitants,")

BOM <u>Mosiah 17:17</u> Yea, and ye shall be smitten on every hand, and shall be driven and scattered to and fro , even as a wild flock is driven by *wild and (6) ferocious* (1646) *beasts*.

> **COM** Clarke: <u>Jdg 15:4</u> "In other countries, where **ferocious beasts** were less numerous,")

BOM <u>Alma 17:14</u> And assuredly it was great, for they had undertaken to preach the word of God to a wild and a hardened and *a (6) ferocious (1646),* people; a people who delighted in murdering the Nephites, and robbing and plundering them; and their hearts were set upon riches, or upon gold and silver, and precious stones; yet they sought to obtain these things by murdering and plundering, that they might not labor for them with their own hands.

> **COM** Clarke: <u>Gen 14:16</u> "All who read the account must be in pain for the fate of wives and daughters fallen into the hands of **a ferocious**, licentious, and victorious soldiery.")

Jarom 1:8 "machinery" (1687)

BOM <u>Jarom 1:8</u> And we multiplied exceedingly, and spread upon the face of the land, and became exceedingly rich in gold, and in silver, and in precious things, and in fine workmanship of wood, in buildings, and in *(1)* **machinery** *(1687)*, and also in iron and copper, and brass and steel, making all manner of tools of every kind to till the ground, and weapons of war -- yea, the sharp pointed arrow, and the quiver, and the dart, and the javelin, and all preparations for war.

> **COM** Clarke: <u>Exo 26:1</u> "what could be done by hand, without the use of complex **machinery**,")

Omni 1:29 "considerable" (1619)

BOM <u>Omni 1:29</u> And it came to pass that they also took others to a *(2)* ***considerable*** *(1619)* **number**, and took their journey again into the wilderness.

> **COM** Gill: <u>Act 9:2</u> "and for this purpose he must take with him a **considerable number** of men;" (Henry, Clarke, Wesley)

BOM <u>Alma 56:37</u> Yea, even ***to a (2) considerable*** *(1619)* ***distance***, insomuch (20/181) that when they saw the army of Antipus pursuing them, with their might, they did not turn to the right nor to the left, but pursued their march in a straight course after us; and, as we suppose, it was their intent to slay us before Antipus should overtake them, and this that they might not be surrounded by our people.

> **COM** Clarke: <u>Exo 33:7</u> "This is now removed **to a considerable distance** from the camp," (Gill, Henry)

(12) Mosiah 2:13 "plunder" (1632)

BOM <u>Mosiah 2:13</u> Neither have I suffered that ye should be confined in dungeons, nor that ye should make slaves one of another, nor that ye should murder, or *(12)* ***plunder*** *(1632)*, or steal, or commit adultery; nor even have I suffered that ye should commit any manner of wickedness, and have taught you that ye should keep the commandments of the Lord, in all things which he hath commanded you –

> **COM** Gill: <u>2Ki 13:21</u> "one of the bands of the Moabites, which came to rob and **plunder**, and which was about the place where they intended to bury the man;" (Clarke)

BOM <u>Mosiah 10:17</u> And thus they have taught their children that they should hate them, and that they should murder them, and that they should ***rob and*** *(12)* ***plunder*** *(1632)* them, and do all they could to destroy them; therefore they have an eternal hatred towards the children of Nephi.

> **COM** Gill: <u>2Ki 13:21</u> "one of the bands of the Moabites, which came to **rob and plunder**, and which was about the place where they intended to bury the man;" (Clarke)

Mosiah 4:5 "nothingness" (1631)

BOM <u>Mosiah 4:5</u> For behold, if the knowledge of the goodness of God at this time has awakened you to ***a sense of*** your *(3)* ***nothingness*** *(1631)*, and your worthless and *fallen state* --

> **COM** Gill: <u>2Sa 7:20</u> "to express his **sense of** his own **nothingness**

and unworthiness," (Clarke)

BOM Mosiah 4:11 And again I say unto you as I have said before, that as ye have come to the knowledge of the glory of God, or if ye have known of his goodness and have tasted of his love, and have received a remission of your sins, which causeth such exceedingly great joy in your souls, even so I would that ye should remember, and always retain in remembrance, the greatness of God; , and your own *(3) nothingness (1631)*, and his goodness and long-suffering towards you, unworthy creatures, and humble yourselves even in the depths of humility, calling on the name of the Lord daily, and standing steadfastly in the faith of that which is to come, which was spoken by the mouth of the angel.

> **COM** Gill: 2Sa 7:20 "to express his sense of his own **nothingness** and unworthiness," (Clarke)

BOM Alma 12:7 O how great is the *(3) nothingness (1631)* of the children of men; yea, even they are less than the dust of the earth.

> **COM** Gill: 2Sa 7:20 "to express his sense of his own **nothingness** and unworthiness," (Clarke)

Mosiah 10:19 "stimulate" (1619)

BOM Mosiah 10:19 And now I, Zeniff, after having told all these things unto my people concerning the Lamanites, I did *(1) stimulate (1619)* them to go to battle with their might, putting their trust in the Lord; therefore, we did contend with them, face to face.

> **COM** Gill: Jer 3:12 "and to **stimulate** Judah to repentance, and to turn unto the Lord:" (Clarke)

(3) Mosiah 11:8 "ornamented" (1720)

BOM Mosiah 11:8 And it came to pass that king Noah built many elegant and spacious buildings; and he *(3) ornamented (1720)* them *with* fine work of wood, and of all manner of *precious* things, of *gold, and of silver*, and of iron, and of brass, and of ziff, and of copper;

> **COM** Gill: Exo 15:22 "**ornamented** with **gold and silver**, and **precious** stones; or as others," (Clarke)

BOM Mosiah 11:9 And he also built him a spacious palace, and a throne in the midst thereof, all of which was of fine wood and was *(3) ornamented (1720) with gold and silver and with precious* things.

BOM Alma 31:28 Behold, O my God, their costly apparel, and their ringlets, and their bracelets, and their ornaments of gold, and all their precious things which they are *(3) ornamented (1720) with*; and behold, their hearts are set upon them, and yet they cry unto thee and say -- We thank thee, O God, for we are a chosen people unto thee, while others shall perish.

> **COM** Gill: Exo 15:22 "ornamented with gold and silver, and precious stones; or as others," (Clarke)

(3) Mosiah 11:11 "breastwork" (1642)

BOM <u>Mosiah 11:11</u> And the seats which were set apart for the high priests, which were above all the other seats, he did ornament with pure gold; and he caused a *(3) breastwork (1642)* to be built before them, that they might rest their bodies and their arms upon while they should speak lying and vain words to his people.

> **COM** Wesley: <u>Deu 22:8</u> "A battlement - A fence or breastwork, because the roofs of their houses were made flat, that men might walk on them.")

BOM <u>Alma 53:4</u> And he caused that they should build a *(3) breastwork (1642)* of timbers upon the inner bank of the ditch; and they cast up dirt out of the ditch against the *(3) breastwork (1642)* of timbers; and thus they did cause the Lamanites to labor until they had encircled the city of Bountiful round about with a strong wall of timbers and earth, to an exceeding height.

> **COM** Wesley: <u>Deu 22:8</u> "A battlement - A fence or **breastwork**, because the roofs of their houses were made flat, that men might walk on them.")

(1) Mosiah 15:5 "disowned" (1649)

BOM <u>Mosiah 15:5</u> And thus the flesh becoming subject to the Spirit, or the Son to the Father, being one God, suffereth temptation, and yieldeth not to the temptation, but suffereth himself to be mocked, and scourged, and cast out, and *(1) disowned (1649) by* his people.

> **COM** Henry: <u>Jos 7:1-5</u> "and he was not as yet separated from them, nor **disowned by** them." Clarke, Gill, Wesley)

(1) Mosiah 18:34 "apprised" (1694)

BOM <u>Mosiah 18:34</u> And it came to pass that Alma and the people of the Lord were *(1) apprised (1694) of the* coming of the king's army; therefore they took their tents and their families and departed into the wilderness.

> **COM** Gill: <u>Act 27:31</u> "were not **apprised of the** danger," (Clarke, Henry)

(1) Mosiah 20:11 "exerted" (1681)

BOM <u>Mosiah 20:11</u> And it came to pass that the people of Limhi began to drive the Lamanites before them; yet they were not half so numerous as the Lamanites. But they fought for their lives, and for their wives, and for their children; therefore *they (1) exerted (1681) themselves* and like dragons did they fight.

> **COM** Gill: <u>1Ki 1:49</u> "had **they exerted themselves** according to their character, betaken themselves to arms, and put themselves at the head of their troops in favour of Adonijah" (Clarke)

(2) Mosiah 21:25 "previous" (1625)

BOM <u>Mosiah 21:25</u> Now king Limhi had sent, *(2) previous (1625) to the coming of* Ammon, a small number of men to search for the land of Zarahemla; but they could not find it, and they were lost in the wilderness.

Timothy W. Henline

COM Gill: Rev 21:27 "cannot design any state of the church **previous to the coming of** Christ and the first resurrection:")

(1) Mosiah 29:36 "enumerated" (1616)

BOM Mosiah 29:36 Yea, all his iniquities and abominations, and all the wars, and contentions, and bloodshed, and the stealing, and the plundering, and the committing of whoredoms, and all manner of iniquities which cannot be *(1) enumerated (1616)* -- telling them that these things ought not to be, that they were expressly *repugnant to the commandments of God.*

COM Henry, Gill, Clarke, Wesley)

(1) Mosiah 29:38 "anxious" (1616)

BOM Mosiah 29:38 Therefore they relinquished their desires for a king, and became *(1) exceedingly (1) anxious (1616)* that every man should have an equal chance throughout all the land; yea, and every man expressed a willingness to answer for his own sins.

COM Clarke: 2Co 7:5 "So **exceedingly anxious** was he to know the success of his first epistle to them.")

(5) Alma 12:1 "consciousness" (1632)

BOM Alma 12:1 Now Alma, seeing that the words of Amulek had silenced Zeezrom, for he beheld that Amulek had caught him in his lying and deceiving to destroy him, and seeing that he began to tremble under *(4) a (5) consciousness (1632) of his guilt*, he opened his mouth and began to speak unto him, and to establish the words of Amulek, and to explain things beyond, or to unfold the scriptures beyond that which Amulek had done.

COM Gill: Job 16:6 "and if he was silent, that was interpreted a **consciousness of his guilt**;")

BOM Alma 14:6 And it came to pass that Zeezrom was astonished at the words which had been spoken; and he also knew concerning the blindness of the minds, which he had caused among the people by his lying words; and his soul began to be harrowed up under *a (5) consciousness (1632) of his* own *guilt*; yea, he began to be encircled about by the pains of hell.

COM Gill: Job 16:6 "and if he was silent, that was interpreted a **consciousness of his guilt**;")

BOM Mormon 9:3 Then will ye longer deny the Christ, or can ye behold the Lamb of God? Do ye suppose that ye shall dwell with him under *a (5) consciousness (1632) of your guilt*? Do ye suppose that ye could be happy to dwell with that holy Being, when your souls are racked with a *(5) consciousness (1632) of guilt* that ye have ever abused his laws?

COM Gill: Job 16:6 "and if he was silent, that was interpreted a **consciousness of his guilt**;")

(2) Alma 13:12 "abhorrence" (1660)

BOM Alma 13:12 Now they, after being sanctified by the Holy Ghost, having their garments made white, being pure and spotless before God, could not look upon sin save it were *with* (*2*) *abhorrence* (*1660*); and there were many, exceedingly great many , who were made pure and entered into the rest of the Lord their God.

> COM Clarke: Isa 3:8 "And he cannot look upon iniquity but **with abhorrence**;" Henry, Wesley, Gill)

BOM Alma 27:28 And they did look upon shedding the blood of their brethren *with the greatest* (*2*) *abhorrence* (*1660*); and they never could be prevailed upon to take up arms against their brethren; and they never did look upon death with any degree of terror, for their hope and views of Christ and the resurrection; therefore, death was swallowed up to them by the victory of Christ over it.

> COM Henry: Rom 6:1-23 "are to be rejected **with the greatest abhorrence**;)

(1) Alma 17:15 "indolent" (1663)

BOM Alma 17:15 Thus they were a very (*1*) *indolent* (*1663*) *people*, many of whom did worship idols, and the curse of God had fallen upon them because of the traditions of their fathers; notwithstanding the promises of the Lord were extended unto them on the conditions of repentance.

> COM Gill: Jer 49:31 "they were not an **indolent people**, that lived an idle and inactive life;")

(1) Alma 22:3 "generosity" (1616)

BOM Alma 22:3 And now, O king, if thou wilt spare our lives, we will be thy servants. And the king said unto them: Arise, for I will grant unto you your lives, and I will not suffer that ye shall be my servants; but I will insist that ye shall administer unto me; for I have been somewhat troubled in mind because of the (*1*) *generosity* (*1616*) *and* the *greatness of* the words of thy brother Ammon; and I desire to know the cause why he has not come up out of Middoni with thee.

> COM Gill: 1Sa 14:43 "represents him speaking with a **generosity and greatness** of soul,")

(5) Alma 25:6 "disbelieve" (1644)

BOM Alma 25:6 For many of them, after having suffered much loss and so many afflictions (0/8), began to be stirred up in remembrance of the words which Aaron and his brethren had preached to them in their land; therefore they began to (*5*) *disbelieve* (*1644*) *the* traditions of their fathers, and to believe in the Lord, and that he gave great power unto the Nephites; and thus there were many of them converted in the wilderness.

> COM Gill: Amo 9:10 "even all such who are notorious sinners, abandoned to their lusts, obstinate and incorrigible; live in sin, and continue therein; repent not of sin, **disbelieve the** prophets of the Lord, and defy his threatenings, and put away the evil day far from them:") Clarke, Henry, Wesley)

BOM <u>Alma 33:14</u> Now behold, my brethren, I would ask if ye have read the scriptures? If ye have, how can ye *(5) disbelieve (1644)* on the Son of God? **(43NT/49)**

  COM Gill: <u>Joh 16:9</u> "to persons enjoying a Gospel revelation; that such who **disbelieve** the Messiah, shall die in their sins;" Clarke, Henry, Wesley)

 (3) Alma 28:2 "tremendous" (1632)

BOM <u>Alma 28:2</u> And thus there was a *(3) tremendous (1632)* battle; yea, even such an one as never had been known among all the people in the land from the time Lehi left Jerusalem; yea, and tens of thousands of the Lamanites were slain and scattered abroad.

BOM <u>Alma 28:3</u> Yea, and also there was a *(3) tremendous (1632)* slaughter among the people of Nephi; nevertheless, the Lamanites were driven and scattered, and the people of Nephi returned again to their land.

  COM Gill, Clarke, Henry, Wesley)

BOM <u>Mormon 8:2</u> And now it came to pass that after the ***great and*** *(3) tremendous (1632)* battle at Cumorah, behold, the Nephites who had escaped into the country southward were hunted by the Lamanites, until they were all destroyed.

  COM Gill: <u>Psa 96:9</u> "the name of the Lord shall be **great and tremendous** among the Gentiles;")

  <u>**Alma 30:16 "frenzied" (1796)**</u>

  <u>**Alma 30:16 "derangement" (1776)**</u>

BOM <u>Alma 30:16</u> Ye look forward and say that ye see a remission of your sins.

 But behold, it is the effect of a (1) **frenzied** (1796) mind; and this *(1) derangement (1776) of* your ***mind*s** comes because of the traditions of your fathers, which lead you away into a belief of things which are not so.

  COM Clarke: <u>Act 12:25</u> "This argues such blindness of understanding, hardness of heart, and **derangement of mind**,")

 (1) Alma 30:28 "whims" (1697)

BOM <u>Alma 30:28</u> Yea, they durst not make use of that which is their own lest they should offend their priests, who do yoke them according to their desires, and have brought them to believe, by their traditions and their dreams and their *(1) whims (1697)* and their visions and their pretended mysteries, that they should, if they did not do according to their words, offend some unknown being, who they say is God -- a being who never has been seen or known, who never was nor ever will be.

  COM Gill: <u>Luk 24:11</u> "Luk 24:11 - And their words seemed to them as idle tales,.... As fabulous things, as mere **whims**, and the fancies of their brains:") Clarke, Henry)

 (1) Alma 31:5 "tendency" (1628)

BOM <u>Alma 31:5</u> And now, as the preaching of the word had a **great** *(1)* **tendency** *(1628)* to lead the people to do that which was just -- yea, it had had more powerful effect upon the minds of the people than the sword, or anything else, which had happened unto them -- therefore Alma thought it was expedient that they should try the virtue of the word of God.

> **COM** Henry: <u>Mar 6:7-13</u> "The great design of the gospel preachers, and the **great tendency** of gospel preaching, should be, to bring people to repentance," (Clarke)

(20) Alma 31:36 "dissenters" (1639)

BOM <u>Alma 31:36</u> Now these *(20)* **dissenters** *(1639),* having the same instruction and the same information of the Nephites, yea, having been instructed in the same knowledge of the Lord, nevertheless, it is strange to relate, not long after their dissensions they became more hardened and impenitent, and more wild, wicked and ferocious than the Lamanites -- drinking in with the traditions of the Lamanites; giving way to indolence, and all manner of lasciviousness; yea, entirely forgetting the Lord their God.

There are 20 uses of the word "dissenters" in the Book of Mormon. The word is found in Clarke, Gill.

(1) Alma 36:14 "inexpressible" (1625)

BOM <u>Alma 36:14</u> Yea, and I had murdered many of his children, or rather led them away unto destruction; yea, and in fine so great had been my iniquities, that the very thought of coming into the presence of my God did rack my soul with *(1)* **inexpressible** *(1625)* horror.

> **COM** Gill: <u>Rom 3:16</u> "the destruction of the body and soul in hell, which will be attended with endless and **inexpressible** misery." Henry, Clarke, Wesley)

(2) Alma 43:27 "secreted" (1707)

BOM <u>Alma 42:27</u> And it came to pass that Moroni caused that his army should be *(2)* **secreted** *(1707)* in the valley which was near the bank of the river, Sidon, which was on the west of the river Sidon in the wilderness.

> **COM** Clarke: <u>Eze 39:12</u> "Many of the Syrian soldiers had **secreted** themselves in different places during the pursuit after the battle, where they died of their wounds, of hunger, and of fatigue; so that they were not all found and buried till seven months after the defeat of the Syrian army.")

BOM <u>Alma 58:17</u> Now Gid and his men were on the right and the others on the left; and when they had thus *(2)* **secreted** *(1707)* **themselves**, behold, I remained, with the remainder of my army, in that same place where we had first pitched our tents against the time that the Lamanites should come out to battle.

> **COM** Clarke: <u>Eze 39:12</u> "Many of the Syrian soldiers had **secreted themselves** in different places during the pursuit after the battle,

where they died of their wounds, of hunger, and of fatigue; so that they were not all found and buried till seven months after the defeat of the Syrian army.")

(2) Alma 45:21 "regulation" (1665)

BOM <u>Alma 45:21</u> For behold, because of their wars with the Lamanites and the many little dissensions and disturbances which had been among the people, it became expedient that the word of God (45/89) should be declared among them, yea, and that a *(2) regulation (1665)* should be made throughout the church.

> **COM** Henry: <u>Heb 7:11-28</u> "a new priesthood must be under a new **regulation," (*Clarke,* Gill*)*

BOM <u>Alma 62:44</u> And Pahoran did return to his judgment-seat and Alma did take upon him again to preach unto the people the word of God; for because of so many wars and contentions it had become expedient that a *(2) regulation (1665)* should be made again in the church.

> **COM** Henry: <u>Heb 7:11-28</u> "a new priesthood must be under a new **regulation,"** (Clarke, Gill)

(1) Alma 46:7 "precarious" (1646)

BOM <u>Alma 47:7</u> And there were many in the church who believed in the flattering words of Amalickiah, therefore they dissented even from the church; and thus were the affairs of the people of Nephi *(1) exceedingly (1) **precarious** (1646) and dangerous,* notwithstanding their great victory which they had had over the Lamanites, and their great rejoicings which they had had because of their deliverance by the hand of the Lord.

> **COM** Henry: <u>1Ti 2:2</u> "Rebellions and insurrections seldom terminate even in political good; and even where the government is radically bad, revolutions themselves are most **precarious and** hazardous.")

Alma 48:21 "reluctantly" (1667)

BOM <u>Alma 48:21</u> But, as I have said, in the latter end of the nineteenth year, yea, notwithstanding their peace amongst themselves, they were compelled *(1) reluctantly (1667)* to contend with their brethren, the Lamanites.

> **COM** Clarke: <u>Exo 17:3</u> "This shows that they had left Egypt **reluctantly;**")

(3) Alma 49:2 "stationed" (1748)

BOM <u>Alma 49:2</u> And behold, the city had been rebuilt, and Moroni had *(3) stationed (1748)* an **army** by the borders of the city, and they had cast up dirt around about to shield them from the arrows and the stones of the Lamanites; for behold, they fought with stones and with arrows.

BOM Alma 56:34 And now, in the city Antiparah were *(3) **stationed** (1748)* the strongest *army* of the Lamanites; yea, the most numerous.

BOM <u>Alma 4:7</u> And there they did fortify against the Lamanites, from the west sea, even unto the east; it being a day's journey for a Nephite, on the line which they had fortified and *(3)* **stationed** *(1748)* their armies to defend their north country.

> **COM** Gill: <u>Jdg 20:21</u> "and in and about which they had **stationed** their whole **army** of 26,000 men:" (Clarke)

(2) Alma 50:3 "pickets" (1702)

(2) Alma 52:21 "decoy" (1641)

BOM <u>Alma 52:21</u> And it came to pass that Moroni, having no hopes of meeting them upon fair grounds, therefore, he resolved upon a plan that he might *(2)* **decoy** *(1641)* the Lamanites out of their strongholds.

> **COM** These next few verses match perfectly this story including using the word "decoy": Clarke: <u>Jos 8:10</u> "There is no doubt that Joshua had left the rest of the army so disposed and ready, part of it having probably advanced towards Ai, that he might easily receive reinforcements in case of any disaster to the thirty thousand which had advanced against the city; and this consideration will serve to remove a part of the difficulty which arises from <u>Jos 8:1</u>, <u>Jos 8:3</u>, <u>Jos 8:10</u>, collated with other parts of this chapter. Had he brought all his troops in sight, the people of Ai would not have attempted to risk a battle, and would consequently have kept within their walls, from which it was the object of Joshua to **decoy** them. See the preceding observations, particularly <u>Jos 8:10-12</u> (note).")

BOM <u>Alma 58:1</u> And behold, now it came to pass that our next object was to obtain *the city* of Manti; but behold, there was no way that we could lead them out of the city by our small bands. For behold, they remembered that which we had hitherto done; therefore we could not *(2)* **decoy** *(1641)* **them** away from their strongholds.

> **COM** Gill: <u>Jer 41:6</u> "Hearing there was such a number of men upon the road to Jerusalem, in such a habit, and upon such a design, he thought it advisable to go out and meet them, and stop them, and **decoy them** into **the city**, and there destroy them; lest, if they should have got any hint of what had been done by him, they should spread it, and raise the country upon him, before he had executed his whole design:")

(2) Alma 55:24 "liberated" (1623)

BOM <u>Alma 55:24</u> Now behold, this was the desire of Moroni. He took them prisoners of war, and took possession of the city, and caused that all the prisoners should *be (2)* **liberated** *(1623)*, who were Nephites; and they did join the army of Moroni, and were a great strength to his army.

> **COM** Clarke: <u>Phi 1:25</u> "Convinced that it is necessary that I should live longer, for the spreading and defense of the Gospel, I am persuaded that I shall now **be liberated**.")

BOM <u>Alma 9:18</u> And it came to pass that the five were *(2)* **liberated** *(1623)* on the day of the burial. Nevertheless, they did rebuke the judges in the words which they had spoken against Nephi, and did contend with them one by one, insomuch that they did confound them .

> **COM** Clarke: <u>Phi 1:25</u> "Convinced that it is necessary that I should live longer, for the spreading and defense of the Gospel, I am persuaded that I shall now be liberated.")

(1) Alma 58:9 "embarrassments" (1729)

BOM <u>Alma 58:9</u> And now the cause of these our (*1*) ***embarrassments*** (*1729*), or the cause why they did not send more strength unto us, we knew not; therefore we were grieved and also filled with fear, lest by any means the judgments of God should come upon our land, to our overthrow and utter destruction .

> **COM** Clarke: <u>1Sa 17:58</u> "the attempts of clearing it from its **embarrassments** would have been attended with very great difficulties;" (Henry, Gill)

(5) 3 Nephi 2:11 "carnage" (1656)

BOM <u>3 Nephi 2:11</u> And it came to pass in the thirteenth year there began to be wars and contentions throughout all the land; for the Gadianton robbers had become so numerous, and did slay so many of the people, and did lay waste so many cities, and did spread so much death *and* (*5*) ***carnage*** (*1656*) throughout the land, that it became expedient that all the people, both the Nephites and the Lamanites, should take up arms against them.

> **COM** Gill: <u>Isa 26:21</u> "unless this should rather denote the great effusion of blood and **carnage** that will be made, so that the earth will not be able to drink it in, and the slain will lie unburied on it;" (Clarke)

BOM <u>Mormon 2:8</u> But behold, the land was filled with robbers and with Lamanites; and notwithstanding the great destruction which hung over my people, they did not repent of their evil doings; therefore there was (*3*) ***blood and*** (*5*) ***carnage*** (*1656*) spread throughout all the face of the land, both on the part of the Nephites and also on the part of the Lamanites; and it was one complete revolution throughout all the face of the land.

> **COM** Gill: <u>Isa 26:21</u> "unless this should rather denote the great effusion of **blood and carnage** that will be made")

BOM <u>Mormon 4:11</u> And it is impossible for the tongue to describe, or for man to write a perfect description of the horrible scene of the (*3*) ***blood and*** (*5*) ***carnage*** (*1656*) which was among the people, both of the Nephites and of the Lamanites; and every heart was hardened, so that they delighted in the shedding of blood continually.

> **COM** Gill: <u>Isa 26:21</u> "unless this should rather denote the great effusion of **blood and carnage** that will be made")

BOM <u>Mormon 5:8</u> And now behold, I, Mormon, do not desire to harrow up the souls (5) of men in casting before them such an awful scene of (3) **blood and** (5) **carnage** (*1656*) as was laid before mine eyes; but I, knowing that these things must surely be made known, and that all things which are hid must be revealed upon the house-tops –

BOM Ether 14:21 And so *great and lasting* had been the war, and so long had been the scene of (3) *bloodshed and* (5) *carnage* (*1656*), that the whole face of the land was covered with the bodies of the dead.

> **COM** Gill: Isa 26:21 "unless this should rather denote the great effusion of **blood and carnage** that will be made")

(1) 3 Nephi 3:16 "exert" (1681)

BOM 3 Nephi 3:16 And so great and marvelous were the words and prophecies of Lachoneus that they did cause fear to come upon all the people; and they did (*1*) *exert* (*1681*) *themselves* in their might to do according to the words of Lachoneus.

> **COM** Gill: Rev 11:11 "they shall now rise in high spirits, and bravely **exert themselves** in the cause of Christ;" (Clarke, Henry)

(1) 3 Nephi 4:19 "scantiness" (1660)

BOM 3 Nephi 4:19 And because of *the* (*1*) *scantiness* (*1660*) *of provisions* among the robbers -- for behold, they had nothing save it were meat for their subsistence, which meat they did obtain in the wilderness;

> **COM** Gill: Mar 8:21 "or that I concerned myself about **the scantiness of** your **provisions**,")

Now that we have looked at the words that appear in history after 1611AD and are not found in the King James Version of the Bible, I want to touch briefly on those words that also do not appear in the Book of Mormon but do appear in history before 1611AD. There are so many that I could not possibly outline them all here. I will therefore give you a few examples so that you can see that even though the words do not appear in The King James Version of the Bible you can see that he got these words from the commentaries.

(7) obliged (14ᵗʰ Century)

BOM 1 Nephi 3:26 And it came to pass that we did flee before the servants of Laban, and we were (*7*) *obliged* (*14ᵗʰ Century*) *to leave* behind our (9) *property* (*14ᵗʰ Century*) and it fell into the hands of Laban.

> **COM** Clarke: Exo 2:25 "and his being **obliged to leave** Egypt was undoubtedly a powerful means to wean his heart from a land in which he had at his command all the advantages and luxuries of life."(Gill, Henry)

(5) cavity (1541 AD)

BOM 1 Nephi 3:27 And it came to pass that we fled into the wilderness, and the servants of Laban did not overtake us, and we hid ourselves (5) *in the* (5) *cavity* (*1541 AD) of* a rock.

COM Wesley: Psa 109:18 "Water **in the cavity of** the belly,")
    (1) future (14ᵗʰ Century) period (1530 AD)
BOM 1 Nephi 7:13 And if it so be that we are faithful to him, we shall obtain the land of promise; and ye shall know at some *(1) future (14ᵗʰ Century) period (1530 AD)* that the word of the Lord shall be fulfilled concerning the destruction of Jerusalem, for all things which the Lord hath spoken concerning the destruction of Jerusalem, must be fulfilled.

    COM Clarke: Rom 9:33 "to which, at a certain **future period**, they shall again be restored.")

    (2) methought (before 12ᵗʰ Century) and (1) dreary (before 12ᵗʰ Century)
BOM 1 Nephi 8:4 But behold, Laman and Lemuel, I fear exceedingly because of you; for behold, *(2) methought (before 12ᵗʰ Century)* I saw in my dream, a dark and *(1) dreary (before 12ᵗʰ Century) wilderness.*

    COM Henry: Jdg 7:9-15 "He dreamed that he saw a barley-cake come rolling down the hill into the camp of the Midianites, and "**methought**," says he (for so we speak in telling our dreams),")
    COM Clarke: Eze 19:13 "and which, compared with their own land, was to them a **dreary wilderness**.")

    (6) unavoidably (1577)
BOM 1 Nephi 15:4 And now I, Nephi, was grieved because of the hardness of their hearts, and also, because of the things which I had seen, and knew they *(5) must (6) unavoidably (1577)* come to pass because of the great wickedness of the children of men.

    COM Henry: Jer 50:21-32 "Babylon's pride **must unavoidably** be her ruin;" (Clarke, Gill, Wesley)

    (19) restoration (15ᵗʰ Century)
BOM 1 Nephi 15:19 And it came to pass that I, Nephi, spake much unto them concerning these things; yea, I spake unto them concerning *(2) the (19) restoration of the Jews* in the latter days.

    COM Gill: Rom 9:25 "on the one hand salvation should come to the Gentiles, through the fall of the Jews, and they should obtain mercy through their unbelief; and on the other hand that **the restoration of the Jews** should be as life from the dead to the Gentiles;" (Henry, Clarke)

    (2) fertile (15ᵗʰ Century)
BOM 1 Nephi 16:14 And it came to pass that we did take our bows and our arrows, and go forth into the wilderness to slay food for our families; and after we had slain food for our families we did return again to our families in the wilderness, to the place of Shazer. And we did go forth again in the wilderness, following the same direction, keeping in *(1) the most (2) fertile (15ᵗʰ Century) parts of* the wilderness, which were in the borders near the Red

Sea.

> **COM** Clarke: <u>Isa 65:10</u> "Two of **the most fertile parts of** Judea;")

(29) shown (12ᵗʰ Century)

BOM <u>1 Nephi 17:9</u> And I said: Lord, whither shall I go that I may find ore to molten, that I may make tools to *(4) construct (1663 AD)* the ship after the manner which *(1) thou hast (29) shown (12ᵗʰ Century) unto me?*

> **COM** Joseph Smith uses the Henry paraphrase of the verse of Acts 23:22 which uses "thou hast showed": Henry: <u>Act 23:12-35</u> "See that thou tell no man that **thou hast shown** these things **unto me**,")

(1) big (14ᵗʰ Century)

BOM <u>1 Nephi 17:20</u> And thou art like unto our father, led away by the foolish imaginations of his heart; yea, he hath led us out of the land of Jerusalem, and we have wandered in the wilderness for these many years; and our women have toiled, being *(1) big (14ᵗʰ Century) with child;* and they have borne children in the wilderness and suffered all things, save it were death; and it would have been better that they had died before they came out of Jerusalem than to have suffered these afflictions.

> **COM** Gill: <u>Rom 8:22</u> "it was like a woman **big with child**, ready to bring forth many sons to God;" (Henry, Clarke)

(1) sick-beds. (14ᵗʰ Century)

BOM <u>1 Nephi 18:17</u> Now my father, Lehi, had said many things unto them, and also unto the sons of Ishmael; but, behold, they did breathe out much threatenings against anyone that should speak for me; and my parents being stricken in years, and having suffered much grief because of their children, they were brought down, yea, even *(1) upon their (1) sick-beds. (14ᵗʰ Century)*

> **COM** Henry: <u>Psa 149:1-5</u> "**Upon their sick-beds**, their death-beds, let them sing the praises of their God.")

(1) incur (15ᵗʰ Century)

BOM <u>2 Nephi 1:22</u> That ye may not be cursed with a sore cursing; and also, that ye may not *(1) incur (15ᵗʰ Century) the displeasure of* a just *God* upon you, unto the destruction, yea, the eternal destruction of both soul and body.

> **COM** Clarke: <u>Jer 33:9</u> "and tremble lest they should **incur the displeasure of** your **God** by doing you any kind of evil." (Henry, Gill)

(9) probation, (15ᵗʰ Century)

BOM <u>2 Nephi 2:21</u> And the days of the children of men were prolonged, according to the will of God, that they might repent while in the flesh; wherefore, their state became a *state of (9) probation, (15ᵗʰ Century)* and their time was lengthened, according to the commandments which the Lord God gave unto the children of men. For he gave commandment that all men must repent; for he showed unto all men that they were lost, because of the transgression of their parents.

COM Henry: <u>1Co 3:22</u> "as the grand **state of** your **probation**" (Clarke)

(1) innocence, (14ᵗʰ Century)

BOM <u>2 Nephi 2:23</u> And they would have had no children; wherefore they would have remained *(1)* **in a state of** *(1)* **innocence**, *(14ᵗʰ Century)* having no joy, for they knew no misery; doing no good, for they knew no sin.

> **COM** Gill: <u>Gen 2:17</u> "and may have regard to more deaths than one; not only a corporeal one, which in some sense immediately took place, man became at once a mortal creature, who otherwise continuing **in a state of innocence**, and by eating of the tree of life, he was allowed to do, would have lived an immortal life;" (Henry, Wesley, Clarke)

(3) encompassed (14ᵗʰ Century)

BOM <u>2 Nephi 4:18</u> I am *(3)* *(3)* **encompassed** *(14ᵗʰ Century)* **about**, because of the temptations and the sins which do so easily beset me.

> **COM** Gill: <u>Heb 4:15</u> "there was no sin in his nature; though he was **encompassed about** with infirmities, yet not with sinful infirmities, only sinless ones ;")

(2) duration. (14ᵗʰ Century)

BOM <u>2 Nephi 9:7</u> Wherefore, it must needs be an infinite atonement -- save it should be an infinite atonement this corruption could not put on incorruption. Wherefore, the first judgment which came upon man must needs have remained to an *(1)* **endless** *(2)* **duration**. *(14ᵗʰ Century)* And if so, this flesh must have laid down to rot and to (2) crumble (1570AD) to its mother earth, to rise no more.

> **COM** Clarke: <u>Rev 1:4</u> "the **endless duration** that shall be when time is no more." (Henry)

(4) unshaken (Middle English) and (5) merits (15ᵗʰ Century)

BOM <u>2 Nephi 31:19</u> And now, my beloved brethren, after ye have gotten into this strait and narrow path, I would ask if all is done? Behold, I say unto you, Nay; for ye have not come thus far save it were by the word of Christ with (4) **unshaken** *(Middle English)* **faith in him** (5) *relying* *(1574)* wholly *(2)* **upon the** (5) **merits** *(15ᵗʰ Century)* of him who is mighty to save.

> **COM** John Gill: <u>Phi 1:20</u> "professing his constant and **unshaken faith in him**, and sealing the Gospel by his blood, with the greatest cheerfulness.")
>
> **COM** Henry: <u>Heb 9:1-7</u> "grounded **upon the merits** and satisfaction of his sacrifice,")

(9) probation. (15ᵗʰ Century)

BOM <u>2 Nephi 33:9</u> I also have charity for the Gentiles. But behold, for none of these can I hope except they shall be reconciled unto Christ, and enter into the narrow gate, and walk in the strait path which leads to life, and *continue in* *the path* until *the end* of ***the day of*** *(9)* ***probation.*** (15th Century)

> COM Clarke: <u>Mat 8:12</u> "and now **the day of probation** is ended,) (Clark: Gen 19:38 "To begin in the good way is well; to continue in the path is better; and to persevere unto the end, best of all.")

(2) protector (14th Century)

BOM <u>Jacob 1:10</u> The people having loved Nephi exceedingly, he having been a ***great*** *(2)* ***protector*** *(14th Century)*, for them, having wielded the sword of Laban in their defence, and having labored in all his days for their welfare –

> COM Henry: <u>Dan 10:10-21</u> "Here is Michael our prince, the **great protector** of the church,")

(1) adieu. (14th Century)

BOM <u>Jacob 7:27</u> And I, Jacob, saw that I must soon go down to my grave; wherefore, I said unto my son Enos: Take these plates. And I told him the things which my brother Nephi had commanded me, and he promised obedience unto the commands. And I make an end of my writing upon these plates, which writing has been small; and *to the (1) reader (12th Century)* I bid farewell, hoping that many of my brethren may read my words. Brethren, (1) **adieu.** (14th Century)

> COM It is highly unlikely that a Jewish man living around 500 BC would know such a word. It cannot be just an interpretation of a word that a Jewish man would have used as there are many other words utilized in the KJV that mean "farewell" including "farewell" even though it is only found in the NT, but why break with precedent here. It is also interesting to note that Henry, Clarke, and Gill all use the word. Gill: Job 2:9 "take thy farewell of him (l); bid adieu to him and all religion, and so die; "Note: Henry: <u>Act 15:29</u> "God be with you! corrupted now into good by to ye! And of the same meaning with **adieu!** a Dieu, to God; that is, I commend you to God. All these terms savour not only of good will, or benevolence, but also of piety.")

(2) doom (12th Century)

BOM <u>Mosiah 2:39</u> And now I say unto you, that mercy hath no *(15) claim (14th Century)* on that man; therefore his ***final*** *(2)* ***doom*** *(12th Century)* is to endure a never-ending torment.

> COM Henry: <u>Rom 14:1-23</u> "expecting our **final doom** from him, which will be eternally conclusive.")

(1) pore (14th Century)

BOM <u>Mosiah 3:7</u> And lo, he shall suffer temptations, and pain of body, hunger, thirst, and *(7) fatigue (1669)*, even more than man can suffer, except it be unto death; for behold, blood cometh from ***every*** *(1)* ***pore*** *(14th Century)*, so great shall be his anguish for the wickedness and the abominations of his people.

> COM As the Mosiah verse above they both talk of Christ's suffering.

Gill: Luk 22:39-46 "**Every pore** was as it were a bleeding wound, and his blood stained all his raiment.")

(7) supported (14th Century) and (1) laziness (1549)

BOM Mosiah 11:6 Yea, and thus they were *(7) supported (14th Century) in their (1) laziness (1549),* and in their idolatry, and in their whoredoms, by the taxes which king Noah had put upon his people; thus did the people *(5) labor exceedingly* to support iniquity.

> **COM** Henry: Jer 5:25-31 "The priests bear rule by their means; they **supported** themselves in their grandeur and wealth, **their laziness** and luxury, their impositions and oppressions, by the help of the false prophets and their interest in the people.")

(2) types (15th Century)

BOM Mosiah 13:31 But behold, I say unto you, that all these things were *(2) types (15th Century) of things* to come.

> **COM** Gill: Mat 13:35 "the very historical facts recorded of the people of Israel, were **types of things** future under the Gospel dispensation:")

(1) endlessly (12th century)

BOM Mosiah 16:4 Thus all mankind were lost; and behold, they would have been *(1) endlessly (12th century) lost* were it not that God redeemed his people from their lost and fallen state.

> **COM** Clarke: 1Co 15:54 "God is represented as swallowing him up; or that eternity gulps him down; so that he is **endlessly lost** and absorbed in its illimitable waste.")

(4) subjecting

BOM Mosiah 21:13 And they did humble themselves even to the dust, *(4) subjecting themselves to the yoke of* bondage, submitting themselves to be smitten, and to be driven to and fro , and burdened, according to the desires of their enemies.

> **COM** Gill: Col 2:23 "or rather in **subjecting themselves to the yoke of** the law,)

(6) disturbance (13th Century)

BOM Mosiah 21:22 And it came to pass that there was *no more (6) disturbance (13th Century)* between the Lamanites and the people of Limhi, even until the time that Ammon and his brethren came into the land.

> **COM** Henry: Jdg 8:22-28 "The Midianites that had been so vexatious gave them **no more disturbance**. Gideon,")

(1) interposition (14th Century)

BOM Mosiah 29:19 And were it not for the *(1) interposition (14th Century)* of their all-wise Creator, and this because of their sincere repentance, *they (5) must (6) unavoidably (1577)* remain in bondage until now.

> **COM** Gill: Exo 34:28 "all which must be ascribed to the miraculous

interposition of God in the support of him;" Clarke, Henry, Wesley)

(1) disadvantages (14th Century)

BOM Mosiah 29:35 And he also unfolded (4) unto them all the *(1) disadvantages (14th Century)* ***they labored under***, by having an unrighteous king to rule over them;

> COM Henry: Act 11:19-26 "considering the outward **disadvantages they laboured under**:")

(1) repugnant (15th Century)

BOM Mosiah 29:36 Yea, all his iniquities and abominations, and all the wars, and contentions, and bloodshed, and the stealing, and the *(11) plundering (1632)*, and the committing of whoredoms, and all manner of iniquities which cannot be *(1) enumerated (1616)* -- telling them that these things ought not to be, that they were expressly *(1)* ***repugnant** (15th Century) to the commandments of God*.

> COM Gill: Rom 15:2 "nor in anything **repugnant** to the commands of God,")

(1) ignominious (15th Century)

BOM Alma 1:15 And it came to pass that they took him; and his name was Nehor; and they carried him upon the top of the hill Manti, and there he was caused, or rather did acknowledge, between the heavens and the earth, that what he had taught to the people was contrary to the word of God; and there he suffered ***an** (1)* ***ignominious** (15th Century)* ***death***.

> COM Henry: Luk 24:36-49 "Redeemer that it dares face those daring enemies of his that had put him to **an ignominious death**," (Henry, Clarke)

(1) tribunal (1526)

BOM Alma 5:18 Or otherwise, can ye imagine yourselves brought ***before the** (1)* ***tribunal** (1526)* ***of God*** with your souls *filled with guilt and (3) remorse (14th Century)*, having a remembrance of all your guilt, yea, a perfect remembrance of all your wickedness, yea, a remembrance that ye have *(3) set at (3) defiance (15th Century)* the commandments of God?

> COM Clarke: Mat 26:39 "The whole world are here represented as standing guilty and condemned **before the tribunal of God**;" (Gill, Henry)

(1) arraigned (14th Century)

BOM Alma 11:44 Now, this *(19) restoration (14th Century)* shall come to all, both old and young, both bond and free, both male and female, both the wicked and the righteous; and even there shall not so much as a hair of their heads be lost; but every thing shall be restored to its perfect frame, as it is now, or in the body, and shall be brought and be *(1)* ***arraigned** (14th Century)* ***before the*** bar of Christ the Son, and God the Father, and the Holy Spirit, which is one Eternal God, to be judged according to their works, whether they be good or whether they be evil.

  COM Henry: <u>Luk 22:54-62</u> "at the time when he was **arraigned before the** high priest," (Clarke, Gill)

 (2) subtlety, (14ᵗʰ Century)

BOM <u>Alma 12:4</u> And thou seest that we know that thy plan was a very subtle plan, as to *(1) the (2) subtlety, (14ᵗʰ Century) of the devil* , for to lie and to deceive this people that thou mightest set them against us, to revile us and to cast us out –

  COM Clarke: <u>Eph 5:33</u> "**the subtlety of the devil** in deceiving Eve." (word subtlety Henry, Wesley)

 (2) martyrdom (12ᵗʰ Century)

BOM <u>Alma 14:9</u> And it came to pass that they took Alma and Amulek, and carried them forth to the place of *(2) martyrdom (12ᵗʰ Century)*, that they might witness the destruction of those who were consumed by fire.

  COM "martyrdom", as of course most of the words here, is a modern concept. Henry, Clarke, Wesley, Gill)

 (1) baseness (14ᵗʰ Century)

BOM <u>Alma 17:9</u> And it came to pass that they journeyed many days in the wilderness, and they fasted much and prayed much that the Lord would grant unto them a portion of his Spirit to go with them, and abide with them, that they might be an instrument in the hands of God to bring, if it were possible, their brethren, the Lamanites, to the knowledge of the truth, to the knowledge of *the (1) baseness (14ᵗʰ Century) of* the traditions of their fathers, which were not correct.

  COM Henry: <u>Isa 16:6-14</u> "forgetting **the baseness of** their origin" (Gill, Clarke, Wesley)

 (4) correspondence (15ᵗʰ Century)

BOM <u>Alma 24:18</u> And they began to be a very industrious people; yea, and they were friendly with the Nephites; therefore, they *did open a (4) correspondence (15ᵗʰ Century) with* them, and the curse of God did no more follow them.

  COM Henry: <u>Luk 3:21-38</u> "to **open a correspondence** with the heavenly Canaan.")

 (1) grossest (14ᵗʰ Century)

BOM <u>Alma 26:24</u> For they said unto us: Do ye suppose that ye can bring the Lamanites to the knowledge of the truth? Do ye suppose that ye can convince the Lamanites of the incorrectness of the traditions of their fathers, as stiffnecked a people as they are; whose hearts delight in the shedding of blood; whose days have been spent in *the (1) grossest (14ᵗʰ Century) iniquity*; whose ways have been the ways of a transgressor from the beginning? Now my brethren, ye remember that this was their language.

  COM Gill: <u>Mic 2:1</u> "they do not pray to him, and therefore are bold and daring to perpetrate **the grossest iniquity**,")

(1) privation (14th Century)

BOM Alma 26:28 And now behold, we have come, and been forth amongst them; and we have been patient in our sufferings, and we have suffered *every (1) privation (14th Century)*; yea, we have traveled from house to house, *(5) relying (1574)* upon the mercies of the world -- not upon the mercies of the world alone but upon the mercies of God.

> **COM** Clarke: 1Ki 21:4 "**Every privation** and cross makes an unholy soul unhappy;")

(2) abhorrence (1660) and (3) views (1523 AD)

BOM Alma 27:28 And they did look upon shedding the blood of their brethren *with the greatest (2) abhorrence (1660)*; and they never could be prevailed upon to take up arms against their brethren; and they never did look upon death with any degree of terror, for their hope and *(3) views (1523 AD) of Christ* and the resurrection; therefore, death was swallowed up to them by the victory of Christ over it.

> **COM** Henry: Rom 6:1-23 "are to be rejected **with the greatest abhorrence;**)
>
> **COM** Gill: Isa 56:7 "by giving them **views** of Christ, his love and loveliness, fulness, grace, and righteousness: by favouring them with the consolations of his Spirit, and his gracious influences; and by showing them their interest in the blessings of grace and glory:")

(1) infidelity (15th Century) and (1) infirm (15th Century)

BOM Alma 31:30 O Lord God, how long wilt thou suffer that such *wickedness and (1) infidelity (15th Century)* shall be among this people? O Lord, wilt thou give me strength, that I may bear with mine infirmities. For I am *(1) infirm (15th Century)*, and such wickedness among this people doth pain my soul.

> **COM** Clarke: Joh 5:31-47 "To this testimony he annexes a reproof of their **infidelity** and wickedness in four instances; particularly,")
>
> **COM** Clarke: 2Co 11:30 "The verb ασθενεω signifies to be weak, **infirm**, sick, poor, despicable through poverty, etc. And in a few places it is applied to weakness in the faith, to young converts, who are poor in religious knowledge, not yet fully instructed in the nature of the Gospel;" (Henry, Gill, Wesley)

(2) unpardonable (15th Century)

BOM Alma 39:6 For behold, if ye deny the **Holy Ghost** when it once has had place in you, and ye know that ye deny it, behold, this is a *sin* which is *(2) unpardonable (15th Century)*; yea, and whosoever murdereth against the light and knowledge of God, it is not easy for him to obtain forgiveness; yea, I say unto you, my son, that it is not easy for him to obtain a forgiveness.

> **COM** Note that "**unpardonable** sin" is a modern phrase: Gill: Mar

<u>3:30</u> "and so were guilty of the sin against the Holy Ghost; the unpardonable sin, for which there is no remission:" (Clarke, Henry)

(1) wrested (12th Century)

BOM <u>Alma 41:1</u> And now, my son, I have somewhat to say concerning the *(19) restoration (14th Century)* of which has been spoken; for behold, some have *(1)* ***wrested*** *(12th Century)* ***the scriptures*** , and have gone far astray because of this thing. And I perceive that thy mind has been *(3) worried (13th Century)* also concerning this thing. But behold, I will explain it unto thee.

> **COM** Gill: <u>1Ti 1:7</u> "**wrested the Scriptures** to their own destruction, and that of others; they were ignorant of the things they talked of,")

(2) unalterable (1611)

BOM <u>Alma 41:8</u> Now, the *decrees of God* are *(2)* **unalterable** *(1611)*; therefore, the way is prepared that whosoever will may walk therein and be saved.

> **COM** Gill: <u>2Pe 2:4</u> "by the everlasting, **unalterable**, and inscrutable purposes and **decrees of God**,")

(3) remorse (14th Century) and (6) affixed, (1533 AD)

BOM <u>Alma 42:18</u> Now, there was a punishment *(6)* ***affixed****, (1533 AD)*, and a just law given, which brought *(3)* ***remorse*** *(14th Century) of conscience* unto man.

> **COM** Clarke: <u>Luk 16:23</u> "and find themselves in torments, under dreadful gnawings, and **remorse of conscience**; and having a terrible sensation of divine wrath" (Gill, Henry, Wesley)

> **COM** Clarke: <u>Joh 3:33</u> "and such instrument is considered as fully confirmed by having the testator's seal **affixed** to it," (Henry, Gill, Wesley)

(3) murderous (1535)

BOM <u>Alma 43:6</u> And now, as the Amalekites were of a more wicked and *(3)* ***murderous*** *(1535) disposition* than the Lamanites were, in and of themselves, therefore, Zerahemnah appointed chief captains over the Lamanites, and they were all Amalekites and Zoramites.

> **COM** Clarke: <u>Eze 19:14</u> "A vindictive and **murderous disposition** has taken hold:")

(7) obliged (14th Century)

BOM <u>Alma 43:14</u> Now those descendants were as numerous, *(13) nearly (1561)*, as were the Nephites; and thus the Nephites were *(7)* ***obliged*** *(14th Century) to contend with* their brethren, even unto bloodshed.

> **COM** Clarke: <u>2Ti 1:18</u> "triumphing over sufferings and death; perfectly unshaken, unstumbled, with the evils with which he is **obliged to contend**,")

(1) monarchy (14th Century)

BOM <u>Alma 43:45</u> Nevertheless, the Nephites were inspired by a better cause, for they were not fighting for (*1*) **monarchy** (*14th Century)* nor power but they were fighting for their homes and their liberties, their wives and their children, and their all, yea, for their rites of worship and their church.

COM A modern idea: Clarke, Henry, Wesley, Gill)

(1) serviceable (14th Century)

BOM Alma 48:19 Now behold, Alma and his brethren were no **less** (*1*) ***serviceable*** (*14th Century)* unto the people than was Moroni; for they did preach the word of God, and they did baptize unto repentance all men whosoever would hearken unto their words.

> COM Henry: Eze 27:1-25 "in making one country to abound in one commodity and another in another, and all more or **less serviceable** either to the necessity or to the comfort or ornament of human life." (Clarke, Gill)

(1) appellation (15th Century)

BOM Alma 51:21 And thus Moroni put an end to those king-men, that there were not any *know*n **by the** (*1*) ***appellation*** (*15th Century)* of king-men; and thus he put an end to the stubbornness and the pride of those people who professed the blood of nobility; but they were brought down to humble themselves like unto their brethren, and to fight valiantly for their freedom from bondage.

> COM Clarke: Act 8:3 "and are known in ecclesiastical history **by the appellation** of Zealots or Sicarii.")

(1) embassies (1534)

BOM Alma 52:20 And it came to pass they sent (*1*) ***embassies*** (*1534)* to the army of the Lamanites, which protected the city of Mulek, to their leader, whose name was Jacob, desiring him that he would come out with his armies to meet them upon the plains between the two cities. But behold, Jacob, who was a Zoramite, would not come out with his army to meet them upon the plains.

> COM Gill: Isa 39:1 "he sent letters and a present to Hezekiah; by his ambassadors, which was always usual in **embassies** and visits" (Henry)

(1) undaunted (1587)

BOM Alma 57:20 And as the remainder of our army were about to give way before the Lamanites, behold, those two thousand and sixty were ***firm and*** (*1*) ***undaunted*** (*1587).*

> COM Gill: Gen 49:24 "and so his posterity were unmoved and unshaken, and stood **firm and undaunted**, notwithstanding the powerful enemies they had to deal with, until they were wholly subdued")

(1) exactness (1533)

BOM Alma 57:21 Yea, and they did obey and observe to *perform* every word of command *with* *(1) exactness (1533)*; yea, and even according to their faith it was done unto them; and I did remember the words which they said unto me that their mothers had taught them.

> **COM** Henry: <u>1Ch 23:1-23</u> "that the service might be performed both with expedition and **with exactness**." (Clarke, Gill, Wesley)

(3) embassy (1534)

BOM <u>Alma 58:4</u> And it came to pass that I thus did send *an (3) embassy (1534)* to the governor of our land, to acquaint him concerning the affairs of our people. And it came to pass that we did wait to receive provisions and strength from the land of Zarahemla.

> **COM** Gill: <u>2Sa 10:1</u> "David sent an **embassy** to their king," Henry, Clarke, Wesley)

(1) sallying (1560) and (7) stratagem (15ᵗʰ Century) and (1) retreats (14ᵗʰ Century)

BOM <u>Alma 58:6</u> And the Lamanites were *(1) sallying (1560)* forth against us from time to time, resolving *by (7) stratagem (15ᵗʰ Century)* to destroy us; nevertheless we could not come to battle with them, because of *their (1) retreats (14ᵗʰ Century)* and their strongholds.

> **COM** Gill: <u>Jer 14:18</u> "who by **sallying** out of the city upon them," (Henry, Wesley, Clarke)
>
> **COM** Henry: <u>Jos 8:3-22</u> "We have here an account of the taking of Ai **by stratagem**. The stratagem here used, we are sure, was lawful and good;" (Clarke, Gill, Wesley)
>
> **COM** Clarke: <u>1Sa 4:2</u> "There is no doubt that both the Philistines and Israelites had what might be called the art of war, according to which they marshalled their troops in the field, constructed their camps, and conducted their **retreats**, sieges, etc.; but we know not the principles on which they acted." (Henry)

(4) pretended (15ᵗʰ Century)

BOM <u>Alma 9:27</u> Has Nephi, *the (4) pretended (15ᵗʰ Century) prophet*, who doth prophesy so much evil concerning this people, agreed with **thee**, in the which ye have murdered Seezoram, who is your brother?

> **COM** Henry: <u>Neh 6:10-14</u> "**The pretended prophet** was Shemaiah," (Clarke)

(1) havoc, (15ᵗʰ Century)

BOM <u>Alma 11:27</u> Now behold, these robbers did make *great (1) havoc, (15ᵗʰ Century)* yea, even great destruction among the people of Nephi, and also among the people of the Lamanites.

> **COM** Gill: <u>Rev 6:8</u> "under him thirty tyrants sprung up together in the empire, who made **great havoc** before they were cut off;" (Henry)

(1) furthermost (15ᵗʰ Century)

BOM <u>3 Nephi 4:23</u> And it came to pass that Zemnarihah did give command unto his people that they should withdraw themselves from the siege, and march into the *(1) furthermost (15ᵗʰ Century) parts of* the land northward.

> **COM** Gill: <u>Isa 13:5</u> "from the ends of the earth; the **furthermost parts of** it,")

(2) infest (1602)

BOM <u>Mormon 1:18</u> And these Gadianton robbers, who were among the Lamanites, did *(2) (2) infest (1602) the land;,* insomuch that the inhabitants thereof began to hide up their treasures in the earth; and they became slippery, because the Lord had cursed the land, that they could not hold them, nor retain them again.

> **COM** Clarke: <u>Exo 8:3</u> "The expression, bring forth abundantly, not only shows the vast numbers of those animals, which should now **infest the land**,")

(2) repulsed (15ᵗʰ Century)

BOM <u>Mormon 4:8</u> And it came to pass that they *were (2) repulsed (15ᵗʰ Century)* and driven back by the Nephites. And when the Nephites saw that they had driven the Lamanites they did again boast of their own strength; and they went forth in their own might, and took possession again of the city Desolation.

> **COM** Note: Gill: <u>Act 28:12</u> "it was again assaulted by the Athenians, who were **repulsed**, and entirely conquered," (Henry, Clarke)

(2) chastity (13ᵗʰ Century)

BOM <u>Moroni 9:9</u> And notwithstanding this great abomination of the Lamanites, it doth not exceed that of our people in Moriantum. For behold, many of the daughters of the Lamanites have they taken prisoners; and after depriving them of that which was most dear and precious above all things, which is *(2) chastity (13ᵗʰ Century) and virtue –*

> **COM** Gill: <u>Num 5:12</u> "the sin of adultery, which is a going aside out of the way of virtue and **chastity**,")

(1) triumphant (15ᵗʰ Century)

BOM <u>Moroni 10:34</u> And now I bid unto all, farewell. I soon go to rest in the paradise of God, until my spirit and body shall again reunite, and I am brought forth *(1) triumphant (15ᵗʰ Century)* through the air, to meet you before the pleasing bar of the great Jehovah, the Eternal Judge of both quick and dead. Amen.

> **COM** Gill: <u>1Co 15:57</u> "Over sin the sting of death, over the law the strength of sin, and over death and the grave; and which will be the ground and foundation of the above **triumphant** song in the resurrection morn," (Henry, Clarke, Wesley)

Chapter Ten

Joseph Smith's Use of Names

Joseph Smith had an interesting prospect ahead of him when writing the Book of Mormon. As you have seen there is not much that we could consider unique in the Book of Mormon. Joseph Smith utilized the King James Bible and the commentaries for much of his work. But, as we have seen, when he did attempt to make up sections utilizing King James English he made many mistakes. Now let us look at how he came up with names for use in the Book of Mormon not only as places but also as people. the Book of Mormon contains 337 proper names. So let us first look at those that could have come from the King James Bible in the direct sense the actual word.

King James Bible Names

Leah (coin)   Alma 11:17
KJV Genesis 29:16 And Laban had two daughters: the name of the elder was **Leah**, and the name of the younger was Rachel.

Ammah   Alma 20:2
KJV 2 Samuel 2:24 Joab also and Abishai pursued after Abner: and the sun went down when they were come to the hill of **Ammah**, that lieth before Giah by the way of the wilderness of Gibeon.

Nimrah   Ether 9:8
KJV Numbers 32:3 Ataroth, and Dibon, and Jazer, and **Nimrah**, and Heshbon, and Elealeh, and Shebam, and Nebo, and Beon,

Ramah   Ether 15:11
KJV Joshua 18:25 Gibeon, and **Ramah**, and Beeroth,

Nephi   I Nephi 1:1
KJV 1 Chronicles 5:19 And they made war with the Hagarites, with Jetur, and **Nephi**sh, and Nodab.

KJV Nehemiah 7:52 The children of Besai, the children of Meunim, the children of **Nephi**shesim,
  Variation:
  Zenephi   Moroni 9:16

Lehi   I Nephi 1:4
KJV Judges 15:9 Then the Philistines went up, and pitched in Judah, and spread themselves in **Lehi**.
  Note: Used 4 times in the OT in Judges as the name of a place. Used 130 times in the BOM. The name means Jawbone in Hebrew and is an unlikely choice for a name of a Jew.

Lemuel   I Nephi 2:5
KJV Proverbs 31:1 The words of king **Lemuel**, the prophecy that his mother taught him.

Sam   I Nephi 2:5
KJV Genesis 36:36 And Hadad died, and **Sam**lah of Masrekah reigned in his stead.
KJV Judges 13:24 And the woman bare a son, and called his name **Sam**son: and the child grew, and the LORD blessed him.
KJV 1 Samuel 2:18 But **Sam**uel ministered before the LORD, being a child, girded with a linen ephod.

Laban   I Nephi 3:3
KJV Genesis 24:29 And Rebekah had a brother, and his name was **Laban**: and **Laban** ran out unto the man, unto the well.

Ishmael   I Nephi 7:2
KJV Genesis 16:11 And the angel of the LORD said unto her, Behold, thou art with child and shalt bear a son, and shalt call his name **Ishmael**; because the LORD hath heard thy affliction.

Bountiful   **I Nephi 17:5**
KJV (2/37) Proverbs 22:9 He that hath a **bountiful** eye shall be blessed; for he giveth of his bread to the poor.)

Jacob   I Nephi 18:7
KJV Genesis 25:31 And **Jacob** said, Sell me this day thy birthright.)

Joseph   I Nephi 18:7
KJV Genesis 30:24 And she called his name **Joseph**; and said, The LORD

shall add to me another son.

Alma   Mosiah 17:2
KJV 1 Chronicles 2:11 And Nahshon begat Salma, and Salma begat Boaz,

Gideon   Mosiah 19:4
KJV Judges 6:11 And there came an angel of the LORD, and sat under an oak which was in Ophrah, that pertained unto Joash the Abiezrite: and his son **Gideon** threshed wheat by the winepress, to hide it from the Midianites.

Ammon   Mosiah 27:34
KJV Genesis 19:38 And the younger, she also bare a son, and called his name Benammi: the same is the father of the children of **Ammon** unto this day.

Aaron   Mosiah 27:34
KJV Exodus 4:29 And Moses and **Aaron** went and gathered together all the elders of the children of Israel:

Sidon (site)   Alma 2:15
A city in the Bible
KJV Matthew 15:21 Then Jesus went thence, and departed into the coasts of Tyre and **Sidon**.

Chemish   Omni 1:8
KJV 2 Chronicles 35:20 Necho king of Egypt came up to fight against Car**chemish** by Euphrates;

Zarahemla   Omni 1:12
KJV Genesis 38:30...and his name was called **Zarah**;...
Note: Obviously using "Zara" and the variation of **Sheml**on (site)   Mosiah 10:7

Benjamin   Omni 1:23
KJV Genesis 35:18 And it came to pass, as her soul was in departing, (for she died) that she called his name Benoni: but his father called him **Benjamin**.

Helorum   Mosiah 1:2
KJV Numbers 1:9 Of Zebulun; Eliab the son of **Helon**.
KJV Leviticus 24:11 ...and his mother's name *was* **Shelo**mith, the daughter of Dibri, of the tribe of Dan;...
COM Gill: **Isa 47:13** "Tigurine version; "contemplatores co**elorum**","

Alma　　Mosiah 1:2
KJV 2Samuel 10:16 …and they came to **Helam**;…

Laman　　I Nephi 2:5
KJV Esther 3:1　After these things did King Ahasuerus promote H**aman** the son of Hammedatha the Agagite;

Helem　　Mosiah 7:6
KJV 1 Chronicles 7:35 And the sons of his brother **Helem**; Zophah, and Imna, and Shelesh, and Amal.

Hem　　Mosiah 7:6
KJV Genesis 36:22 And the children of Lotan were Hori and **Hem**am; and Lotan's sister was Timna

Noah　　Mosiah 7:9
KJV Genesis 5:29 And he called his name **Noah**, saying, This same shall comfort us concerning our work and toil of our hands, because of the ground which the LORD hath cursed.

Zeniff　　Mosiah 7:9
KJV Joshua 15:37 **Zen**an, and Hadashah, and Migdalgad…
　　　　Variation:
　　　　Ziff (metal)　Mosiah 11:3

Mormon　　Words of Mormon
KJV Deuteronomy 3:8 from the river of Arnon unto Mount He**rmon**;

Himni　　Mosiah 27:34
KJV Joshua 19:43 And Elon and T**himn**athah…

Abinadi　　Mosiah 11:20
KJV 1 Samuel 7:1 And the men of Kirjathjearim came, and fetched up the ark of the LORD, and brought it into the house of **Abinadab** in the hill, and sanctified Eleazar his son to keep the ark of the LORD.
　　　And
KJV Song of Solomon 6:12 Or ever I was aware, my soul made me like the chariots of **Amminadi**b.
　　　Variations:
　　　Abinadom　　Omni 1:10
　　　Aminadi　　Alma 10:2

Amnihu (site) Alma 2:15
Aminadab Alma 5:39

Zeram Alma 2:22
KJV Joshua 7:1 ...for Achan, the son of Carmi, the son of Zabdi, the son of **Zerah**, of the tribe of Judah, took of the accursed thing;...

Shum (coin) Alma 11:5
KJV 1 Chronicles 2:53 And the families of Kirjathjearim; the Ithrites, and the Puhites, and the **Shum**athites, and the Mishraites; of them came the Zareathites, and the Eshtaulites,

Lamoni Alma 17:21
Note: A possible variation on "Lamanites" in addition we have the oft used "omni" move around for the ending.

Sebus (site) Alma 17:26

KJV Joshua 9:1 ...the Hittite, and the Amorite, the Canaanite, the Perizzite, the Hivite, and the **Jebus**ite, heard thereof;...

Abish Alma 19:16
KJV 1 Samuel 26:6 Then answered David and said to Ahimelech the Hittite, and to **Abish**ai the son of Zeruiah, brother to Joab, saying, Who will go down with me to Saul to the camp? And **Abish**ai said, I will go down with thee.

Gazelem Alma 37:23
KJV 2Samuel 5:25 ...and smote the Philistines from Geba until thou come to **Gaze**r;
KJV Joshua 15:24 Ziph, and **T**e**lem**, and Bealoth, ...

Liahona Alma 37:38
Note: "Liah" is used often in Bible names.
KJV 2 Kings 8:26 ... and his mother's name was Atha**liah** the daughter of Omri king of Israel;...
KJV 1 Chronicles 8:17-18 ...Hezeki, Heber, Ishmerai, Jez**liah**, and Jobab, were the sons of Elpaal...
KJV 2 Kings 10:15 ... he lighted on Je**hona**dab the son of Rechab coming to meet him;...

Lehonti Alma 47:10
Note: A variation on "Lehi"; I Nephi 1:4 which we have already looked at and

"Onti" (coin); Alma 11:6

Antipas (site) Alma 47:7
KJV Revelation 2:13 I know thy works, and where thou dwellest, even where Satan's seat is: and thou holdest fast my name, and hast not denied my faith, even in those days wherein **Antipas** was my faithful martyr, who was slain among you, where Satan dwelleth.
> Variation:
> **Antipus**   Alma 56:9

Judea (site) Alma 56:9
KJV Ezra 5:8 Be it known unto the king, that we went into the province of **Judea**, to the house of the great God, which is builded with great stones, and timber is laid in the walls, and this work goeth fast on, and prospereth in their hands.

Samuel   Alma 13:2
KJV 1 Samuel 1:20 Wherefore it came to pass, when the time was come about after Hannah had conceived, that she bare a son, and called his name **Samuel**, saying, Because I have asked him of the LORD.

Gilgal (site) III Nephi 9:6
KJV Deuteronomy 11:30 Are they not on the other side Jordan, by the way where the sun goeth down, in the land of the Canaanites, which dwell in the champaign over against **Gilgal**, beside the plains of Moreh?

Josh   III Nephi 9:10
KJV Exodus 17:9 And Moses said unto **Josh**ua, Choose us out men, and go out, fight with Amalek: to morrow I will stand on the top of the hill with the rod of God in mine hand.

Gad   III Nephi 9:10
KJV Genesis 30:11 And Leah said, A troop cometh: and she called his name **Gad**.

Timothy   III Nephi 19:4
Note: Timothy is a Greek name and should not be found obviously in the Book of Mormon.
KJV 2 Corinthians 1:1 Paul, an apostle of Jesus Christ by the will of God, and **Timothy** our brother, unto the church of God which is at Corinth, with all the saints which are in all Achaia:

Jonas   III Nephi 19:4
KJV Matthew 12:39 But he answered and said unto them, An evil and adulterous generation seeketh after a sign; and there shall no sign be given to it, but the sign of the prophet **Jonas**:

Shim (site)   Mormon 1:3
KJV Genesis 46:13 And the sons of Issachar; Tola, and Phuvah, and Job, and **Shim**ron.

Joshua (site)   Mormon 2:6
KJV Exodus 17:9 And Moses said unto **Joshua**, Choose us out men, and go out, fight with Amalek: to morrow I will stand on the top of the hill with the rod of God in mine hand.

Shem (site)   Mormon 2:20
KJV Genesis 5:32 And Noah was five hundred years old: and Noah begat **Shem**, Ham, and Japheth.

Boaz (site)   Mormon 4:20
KJV Ruth 2:1 And Naomi had a kinsman of her husband's, a mighty man of wealth, of the family of Elimelech; and his name was **Boaz**.

Ether   Ether 1:2
KJV Joshua 15:42 Libnah, and **Ether**, and Ashan,

Seth   Ether 1:10
KJV Genesis 4:25 And Adam knew his wife again; and she bare a son, and called his name **Seth**: For God, said she, hath appointed me another seed instead of Abel, whom Cain slew.

Heth   Ether 1:16
KJV Genesis 10:15 And Canaan begat Sidon his first born, and **Heth**,

Lib   Ether 1:17
KJV Exodus 6:17 The sons of Gershon; **Lib**ni, and Shimi, according to their families.

Kish   Ether 1:18
KJV 1 Samuel 9:1 Now there was a man of Benjamin, whose name was **Kish**, the son of Abiel, the son of Zeror, the son of Bechorath, the son of Aphiah, a Benjamite, a mighty man of power.

Levi   Ether 1:20
KJV Genesis 29:34 And she conceived again, and bare a son; and said, Now this time will my husband be joined unto me, because I have born him three sons: therefore was his name called **Levi**.

Omer   Ether 1:29
KJV Exodus 16:16 This is the thing which the LORD hath commanded, Gather of it every man according to his eating, an **omer** for every man, according to the number of your persons; take ye every man for them which are in his tents.

Kib   Ether 1:31
KJV Numbers 11:34 And he called the name of that place **Kib**rothhattaavah: because there they buried the people that lusted.

Jared   Ether 1:32
KJV Genesis 5:15 And Mahalaleel lived sixty and five years, and begat **Jared**:

Esrom   Ether 8:4
KJV Matthew 1:3 And Judas begat Phares and Zara of Thamar; and Phares begat **Esrom**; and **Esrom** begat Aram;

Gilead   Ether 14:8
KJV Genesis 31:21 So he fled with all that he had; and he rose up, and passed over the river, and set his face toward the mount **Gilead**.

Shiz   Ether 14:17
KJV 1 Chronicles 11:42 Adina the son of **Shiz**a the Reubenite, a captain of the Reubenites, and thirty with him,

Amaleki   Omni 1:12
KJV Genesis 14:7 And they returned, and came to Enmishpat, which is Kadesh, and smote all the country of the **Amaleki**tes, and also the Amorites, that dwelt in Hazezontamar.
    Variation
    Amlici   Alma 2:1   A variation on pronunciation

Luram   Moroni 9:2
KJV 2Chronicles 2:3 And Solomon sent to H**uram** the king of Tyre, saying, As thou didst deal with David my father, and didst send him cedars to build him a house to dwell therein, *even so deal with me.*

Emer   Ether 1:28
KJV 1Ki 16:24 And he bought the hill of Samaria of **Sh**em**er**, for two talents of silver,....

Shurr (site)   Ether 14:28
KJV Gen 10:11 Out of that land went forth **A**sh**ur**,....

Pagag   Ether 6:25
KJV 1Samuel 15:8 And he took **Agag** the king of the Amalekites alive,....

Agosh (site)   Ether 14:15
KJV Genesis 45:10 And thou shall dwell in the land of **Gosh**en,....

Jashon (site)   Mormon 2:16
KJV 1Chronicles 12:6 Elkanah, and Jesiah, and Azareel, and Joezer, and **Jasho**beam, the Korhites.
      Variation:
      Jershon (site) Alma 27:22

Ezias   Alma 8:20
KJV Matthew 1:8 ...And Joram begat **Ozias**;...

Pahoran   Alma 50:40
KJV Exo 8:32 - Pharaoh hardened his heart at this time also
Note: A common trait of Joseph Smith was to take from one word and make a variant. In most words he would just add or remove a letter but in several he moved them around such as in this instance. Notice that all you need to do to create this word is take the word "pharaoh" switch the "ah" to "ha" leave the move the "rao" around to make "ora" and add an "n" which "h" in type is similar to "n".

Hagoth   Alma 63:5
      Variation:
      Jacobugath   III Nephi 9:9   (site)
      Note: Again take the common name "Jacob" change the "o" in "Ogath" to "u" and you have "Jacobugath". It is interesting that in the Hatch cemetery in Attica, NY there is a John Jacob Gath who died 14 Feb 1881 and was 53 yrs 6 mos 3 days.

Ogath   Ether 15:10
Note: More moving around of letters. Take "Hagoth" remove the first "h" and

then just reverse "ago" to "oga".

Now as you may have noticed Joseph Smith on occasion would take some words and change the spelling but essentially keep the same pronunciation. Let us look at a few of those with Bible references.

Now we have listed 49 here of the 337 names which leaves us with 288 names to go. So now let us look at the variations of these names which we can then eliminate.

We will do this by looking at how Joseph Smith came up with the variations. Joseph Smith had an intriguing way of making up names, take for example ending words with "ah" or "hah". Now you might ask why he did this. Well the answer is simple and actually what you would want to attempt to do if you were making up names from another source, utilize that source. This is exactly what Joseph Smith did with the Bible. Many of the names that appear in the Bible end with "ah" or "hah" or in some cases "iah" as well as other common endings for names. So when we take off his additions of "ah" or "hah" we are left with the source for the names. Some are easy to eliminate such as "Nephihah" take off the "hah" and we have "Nephi". Now to find his source for the word Nephi and thus Nephihah we look at the Bible and the commentaries particularly: "**Nephi:** (1 Chronicles 5:19 And they made war with the Hagarites, with Jetur, and **Nephi**sh, and Nodab. Nehemiah 7:52 The children of Besai, the children of Meunim, the children of **Nephi**shesim,)

It is also interesting to note that the Bible has 19 names that end in "hah" and not one of them has the shorter version of the name without the "hah". For example we would have the name Nephihah but there would not be such a name as Nephi. It is also interesting to note that there is not one single place name in the Bible that ends with "hah" but Joseph Smith names a place "Limhah".

Names that end in "hah"

Nephihah   Alma 4:17
    As noted above.

Ammonihah   Alma 8:6
    A variation on: Ammon   Mosiah 27:34
    KJV Deuteronomy 2:20 (That also was accounted a land of giants: giants dwelt therein in old time; and the **Ammoni**tes call them Zamzummims;

Zemnarihah   III Nephi 4:17
    KJV Joshua 18:22 And Betharabah, and **Zemarai**m, and Bethel,

Limhah (site) Mormon 6:14
"lim" is too common to look up but an obviously easy word to create.

Orihah Ether 1:32
Also a variation on "Onihah"
KJV Job 9:9 Which maketh Arcturus, **Ori**on, and Pleiades, and the chambers of the south.

Mahah Ether 6:14
KJV Genesis 5:12 And Cainan lived seventy years and begat **Maha**laleel:

Onihah (site) III Nephi 9:7
Take parts of Mor**oni**, or Math**oni** or Lam**oni** or Midd**oni**

The following have additions of "hah" but are not from the Bible but from commentaries

Ahah Ether 1:9
COM Gill: **Jer 1:6** "The word אהה, "Ah", or "**Ahah**", is used in distress and grief, as Kimchi observes")

Mathonihah III Nephi 19:4
A variation on Mathoni III Nephi 19:4
COM Gill: **Jos 13:27** "which in the same Talmud is **Amatho** or Amathus, which Jerom says (r) is a village beyond Jordan, twenty one miles from Pella to the south, though he places it in the tribe of Reuben") (Gill: **Jos 18:26** "it was about eight miles from Gibeah; it was near Ra**mathon**,")

Cumenihah Mormon 6:14
A variation on: **Cumeni** (site) Alma 56:14
COM Henry: **1Co 16:10-12** "He was but a young man, and alone, as E**cumeni**us observes.") (Gill: **2Co 12:4** "and so Oe**cumeni**us, "he was caught up unto the third heaven, and so again from thence into paradise";

And we end with the last word with the "hah" addition.

Moronihah Alma 62:43
A variation on **Moroni**
Note: An addition to Moroni which appears in the BOM. When you read

the first verse Moronihah appears in you can see why: "And Moroni yielded up the command of his armies into the hands of his son, whose name was Moronihah;"

With this we eliminate 13 more. We are now down to 275 names left.

Names that end in "ah" or "nah"

Giddonah   Alma 10:2
    Variations:
    Gidgiddoni   III Nephi 3:18 Created by using the ending of Moroni
    Gidgiddonah   Mormon 6:13   (site)   Created by using the name Johnah
    Giddianhi   III Nephi 3:9   Created by using Nephi
    Amgid   Ether 10:32   Created by using for example "Ammah" and of course "Gid" words.

    KJV Joshua 12:21 The king of Taanach, one; the king of Me**giddo**, one;

Limnah (coin)   Alma 11:5
    Variations: **Lim**hi   Mosiah 7:9, **Lim**her   Alma 2:22

Rabbanah   Alma 18:13
    COM Clarke: **Mat 23:7** "There are three words used among the Jews as titles of dignity, which they apply to their doctors - Rabh, Rabbi, and **Rabban**;"

Ammah   Alma 20:2
    KJV 2 Samuel 2:24 Joab also and Abishai pursued after Abner: and the sun went down when they were come to the hill of **Ammah**, that lieth before Giah by the way of the wilderness of Gibeon.

Onidah (site)   Alma 32:4
    Note: There are hundreds of "onid" in all commentaries. Clarke: **Lam 5:12** "In this way they treated Histiaeus of Miletum, and Le**onida**s of Lacedaemon")

Zerahemnah   Alma 43:5
    KJV Genesis 36:13 And these are the sons of Reuel; Nahath, and **Zerah**, Shammah, and Mizzah: these were the sons of Bashemath Esau's wife.

Riplah (site) Alma 43:31
   KJV Genesis 10:3 And the sons of Gomer; Ashkenaz, and **Rip**hath, and Togarmah.

Antiparah   Alma 56:14
   KJV Acts 23:31 Then the soldiers, as it was commanded them, took Paul, and brought him by night to **Antipa**tris.

Gadiomnah   III Nephi 9:8
   KJV Deuteronomy 3:12 And this land, which we possessed at that time, from Aroer, which is by the river Arnon, and half mount Gilead, and the cities thereof, gave I unto the Reubenites and to the **Gadi**tes.

Cumorah (site) Mormon 6:2
   COM Clarke: **Psa 9:20** "shithah Yehovah **morah** lahe") (Gill: **Jdg 7:3** "the hill of Moreh")
   Note: Notice how similar the sounds are "the hill of Moreh" from the commentary of Gill and "the hill Cumorah" from the Book of Mormon. This, as you will see, was a common practice of Joseph Smith. He would take words from one source and change the spelling but keep the same pronunciation.
   Note: Another posiblility is that it is a change on Gomorrah of Sodom and Gomorrah fame.
   KJV Gen 10:19 - And the border of the Canaanites was from Sidonas thou goest unto Sodom and **Gomorrah**, and Admah and Zeboim;

Gidgiddonah   Mormon 6:13
   Variations: **Giddonah**   Alma 10:2
   KJV Numbers 1:11 Of Benjamin; Abidan the son of **Gide**oni.
   KJV Zechariah 12:11 In that day shall there be a great mourning in Jerusalem, as the mourning of Hadadrimmon in the valley of Me**giddon**.
   COM Clarke: Deu 10:22 "thence to Hor-ha**gidg**ad")
   COM Clarke: Jdg 3:22 "The original, פרשדונה parshe**donah**, occurs only here,")

Lamah (site) Mormon 6:14
   Note: Too many to look up and easy to create. "lamah" is also a Hebrew word.

Amnigaddah   Ether 1:14
   KJV 2 Samuel 3:2 And unto David were sons born in Hebron: and his
   LJV firstborn was **Amn**on, of Ahinoam the Jezreelitess;

KJV Joshua 15:27 And Hazar**gaddah**, and Heshmon, and Bethpalet,
COM Clarke: Zep 3:10 "which flows into the Lake Sirbonis; Trajanus **Amni**s, which flows into the Red Sea")
COM Clarke: Isa 66:9 "the breaking forth of the liquor *amnii*.")

Gilgah   Ether 6:14
KJV Deuteronomy 11:30 Are they not on the other side Jordan, by the way where the sun goeth down, in the land of the Canaanites, which dwell in the champaign over against **Gilga**l, beside the plains of Moreh?

Sherrizah   Moroni 9:7
KJV 1 Chronicles 7:24 (And his daughter was **Sher**ah, who built Bethhoron the nether, and the upper, and Uzzensherah.)

With this we eliminate 21 more. We are now down to 254 names left.

Words that end in "iah".

The "iah" ending is the most common Bible name ending.

Sariah   I Nephi 2:5
KJV Genesis 17:15 And God said unto Abraham, As for **Sar**ai thy wife, thou shalt not call her name **Sar**ai, but **Sar**ah shall her name be.

Mosiah   Omni 1:12
KJV Exodus 2:10 And the child grew, and she brought him unto Pharaoh's daughter, and he became her son. And she called his name **Mos**es: and she said, Because I drew him out of the water.

Amalickiah   Alma 46:3
KJV Genesis 14:7 And they returned, and came to Enmishpat, which is Kadesh, and smote all the country of the **Amale**kites, and also the Amorites, that dwelt in Hazezontamar.

With this we eliminate 3 more. We are now down to 251 names left.

Words with "ton"

Another common practice of Joseph Smith was to end words with "ton". There is not a single Bible name that ends with "ton" but it was common in Joseph Smith's day to name places with "ton" for example Washington or Charleston

Morianton   Alma 50:25
> **COM** Clarke: Ezr 1:2 "Indians, Saci, Cilicians, Paphlagonians, **Morian**drians, and many others.")
> **KJV** Genesis 22:2 And he said, Take now thy son, thine only son Isaac, whom thou lovest, and get thee into the land of **Moria**h; and offer him there for a burnt offering upon one of the mountains which I will tell thee of.

Gadianton   Alma 2:4
> **KJV** Deuteronomy 3:12 And this land, which we possessed at that time, from Aroer, which is by the river Arnon, and half mount Gilead, and the cities thereof, gave I unto the Reubenites and to the **Gadi**tes.

Corianton   Alma 31:7
> **KJV** Numbers 11:7 And the manna *was* as **corian**der seed
> **Note:** There are only two names in the Bible that start with "cor" and they are both in the New Testament.
> Variations:
>> **Coriantor**   Ether 1:6
>>> Obviously a variation on "Corianton"
>> **Coriantumr**   Omni 1:21
>>> Obviously a variation on "Corianton". No Bible names have a "umr" ending. He came up with it by taking "umer" below as an example and removed the vowel "e".
>> **Moriancumer**   Ether 2:13
>>> (site) A variation on "Coriantumr"
>> **Moriantum**   Moroni 9:9
>>> A variation on "Moriancumer"
>>> **COM** Clarke: "Medes, Persians, Hyrcanians, Armenians, Syrians, Assyrians, Arabians, Cappadocians, Phrygians, Lydians Phoenicians, Babylonians, Bactrians, Indians, Saci, Cilicians, Paphlagonians, **Morian**drians,")
>> **Corihor**   Ether 7:3
>>> Another variation
>> **Cohor**   Ether 7:15
>>> And another variation of the previous "Corihor"

With this we eliminate 3 more. We are now down to 248 names left.

Words that end in "ron"

Ammaron   IV Nephi 1:47
    KJV 2 Samuel 2:24 Joab also and Abishai pursued after Abner: and the
    sun went down when they were come to the hill of **Amma**h, that lieth
    before Giah by the way of the wilderness of Gibeon.
        Variations:
        Amaron   Omni 1:3
        Amoron   Moroni 9:7
            Also see "Moron" below

Siron (site)   Alma 39:3
    Obviously simple to create.

Moron   Ether 1:7
    A variation on Moroni

Emron   Moroni 9:2
    Obviously simple to create.
    KJV Joshua 15:45 **Ekron**, with her towns and her villages:

Words ending in "non".

Minon (site)   Alma 2:24
    KJV Genesis 36:41 Duke Aholibamah, duke Elah, duke **Pinon**,
    COM Gill: 2Sa 13:20 "he calls him **Aminon**, for so it is in the Hebrew
    text")

Shemnon   III Nephi 19:4
    KJV Genesis 5:32 And Noah was five hundred years old: and Noah begat
    Shem, Ham, and Japheth.
    COM Gill: Mat 1:13-15 ""Zorobabel, Hananiah, Jesaiah, Rephaiah,
    Arnon, Obadiah, Shecaniah, **Shemn**igh, Neariah, Elioenai, Anani; this is
    the king Messiah, who is to be revealed.")

Words ending in "lon"

Shemlon (site) Mosiah 10:7
    Also as variation of "Shemnon" above.
    KJV Genesis 5:32 And Noah was five hundred years old: and Noah begat
    Shem, Ham, and Japheth.

Amulon   Mosiah 23:31
    A variation on "Amulek" which we will look at later.

Shiblon (coin) Alma 11:15
> **KJV** Numbers 32:38 And Nebo, and Baalmeon, (their names being changed,) and **Shib**mah: and gave other names unto the cities which they builded.
> Variation:
> **Shiblum** (coin) Alma 11:16
> **Shiblom** (site) Mormon 6:14

Heshlon (site) Ether 13:28
> **KJV** Numbers 21:25 And Israel took all these cities: and Israel dwelt in all the cities of the Amorites, in **Hesh**bon, and in all the villages thereof.

Words ending in "lom".

Shilom (site) Mosiah 7:5
> This is actually a variation "Shiblon" above.
> **Note**: According to Hitchcock's Bible Name Dictionary "Shilom" is a Biblical word. It means "tarrying; peace-maker"
> **KJV** Genesis 46:24 And the sons of Naphtali; Jahzeel, and Guni, and Jezer, and **Shill**em.
> **KJV** Genesis 49:10 The sceptre shall not depart from Judah, nor a lawgiver from between his feet, until **Shil**oh come; and unto him shall the gathering of the people be.

Shimnilom Alma 23:12 (Site)
> Obviously a variation on the above
> **KJV** Genesis 46:13 And the sons of Issachar; Tola, and Phuvah, and Job, and **Shim**ron.

Ablom Ether 9:3
> Obviously very easy to create.

Curelom Ether 9:19 (animal)
> Very east to create. Take the word "cure" and then add "lom"

Words ending in "nor".

The Bible has only one name that ends in "nor" Acts 6:5 And the saying pleased the whole multitude: and they chose Stephen, a man full of faith and of the Holy Ghost, and Philip, and Prochorus, and **Nicanor**, and Timon, and Parmenas, and Nicolas a proselyte of Antioch:

Amnor   Alma 2:22
Obviously easy to create.
KJV 2 Samuel 3:2 And unto David were sons born in Hebron: and his firstborn was **Amno**n, of Ahinoam the Jezreelitess;

Kimnor   Ether 8:10
Obviously easy to create.
Variation
Kim   Ether 1:21

Comnor   Ether 14:28
Obviously easy to create.
Variation
Com   Ether 1:12
You will notice that "Com" comes before "Comnor" so he took "Com" and added the "nor".

Words ending in "rom"

Jarom   Jarom 1:1
Obviously easy to create
KJV Genesis 5:15 And Mahalaleel lived sixty and five years, and begat **Jar**ed:

Zeezrom   Alma 10:31
KJV Judges 7:25 And they took two princes of the Midianites, Oreb and **Zee**b; and they slew Oreb upon the rock Oreb, and **Zee**b they slew at the winepress of **Zee**b, and pursued Midian, and brought the heads of Oreb and **Zee**b to Gideon on the other side Jordan.
Variation:
Ezrom (coin)   Alma 11:6   Even though we have the "Esrom" from the Bible below I think this is more obvious than any that it was created by using "Zeezrom"
KJV Matthew 1:3 And Judas begat Phares and Zara of Thamar; and Phares begat **Esrom**; and **Esrom** begat Aram;

Corom   Ether 1:19
Obviously very easy to create and "cor" names in the Bible are only in the New Testament and there are only two.

Words ending in "om".

Nahom (Site)   I Nephi 16:34
  KJV Genesis 11:22 And Serug lived thirty years, and begat **Nahor**:
  KJV Nahum 1:1
  The burden of Nineveh. The book of the vision of **Nahum** the Elkoshite.

Sidom (site)   Alma 15:1
  KJV Genesis 10:15 And Canaan begat **Sido**n his first born, and Heth,

Hearthom   Ether 1:16
  Obviously take the word "hearth" and add "om". As you may have
  noticed Joseph Smith did this with many common words.
  KJV Genesis 18:6 And Abraham hastened into the tent unto Sarah, and
  said, Make ready quickly three measures of fine meal, knead it, and make
  cakes upon the **hearth**.

Jacom   Ether 6:14
  Genesis 25:31 And **Jaco**b said, Sell me this day thy birthright.

Words with "oni"

  Another common ending for Joseph Smith to use was "oni". We have
already looked at the following; Lamoni   Alma 17:21; which was a variation
on Lamanites, Ammonihah Alma 8:6 ; which was a variation on: Ammon;
Mosiah 27:34 and adding the common "hah" ending, Onihah (site) III Nephi
9:7; again just adding the "hah" ending, Onidah (site)   Alma 32:4: which is an
variation on Onihah (site) III Nephi 9:7, Mathonihah III Nephi 19:4: which
was a variation on Mathoni III Nephi 19:4 and adding the "hah" ending,
Moronihah Alma 62:43 which was a variation on Moroni, Gidgiddoni III
Nephi 3:18: which was a variation on Gidgiddonah Mormon 6:13: and other
"gid" words. There are only three names in the Bible that end in "oni"

Middoni   Alma 20:2
  KJV Joshua 15:61 In the wilderness, Betharabah; **Midd**in, and Secacah;
  KJV Joshua 10:3   Wherefore **Adoni**zedek king of Jerusalem sent to
  Hoham king of Hebron
Moroni   Words of Mormon
  The word Moroni I believe came from the following in Gill: "Deu 34:6:
  "if Moses is the same with the Osiris of the Egyptians, as some think (f),
  it may be observed, that his grave is said to be unknown to the Egyptians,
  as Diodorus Siculus (g) and Strabo (h) both affirm; and the grave of
  Moses is unknown, even unto this our day: for though no longer ago than

in the year 1655, in the month of October, it was pretended to be found by some **Maronite** shepherds on Mount Nebo,"

Now if you take the word "Maronite" as I have bolded above and change the "a" to "o" and remove the "te" at the end you have "Moroni". This was a common tactic of Joseph Smith as he made up words.

Mathoni   III Nephi 19:4
Obviously easy to create, take "math" and add "oni". I like to think here that Joseph Smith was having a hard time coming up with name so he was looking at a math book and said "Yes, I will take "math" and add "oni"."

Words utilizing "cum"

Cumeni (site)   Alma 56:14
COM Clarke: Joh 20:28 "and the fifth E**cumeni**c council," (Gill, Henry, Wesley)
    Variation
                Pacumeni   Alma 1:3
                Obviously a variation on "Cumeni" above.

Mocum (site)   III Nephi 9:7
Obviously easy to create.

Words that begin with "rip"

Ripliancum   Ether 15:8 (site)
Using the "cum" ending but a variation on the other "rip" words.

Riplah (site)   Alma 43:31
Using the "rip" and ending with the "lah" which we already covered

Riplakish   Ether 1:23
This is a variation on "Riplah" above and an addition of "kish" which we will look at next.

Words with "kish"

Akish   Ether 8:10
KJV 1 Samuel 9:3 And the asses of **Kish** Saul's father were lost. And **Kish** said to Saul his son, Take now one of the servants with thee, and

arise, go seek the asses.
Obviously easy to create.

Kishkumen Alma 1:9
A variation on "kish" but also using "kumen" which we will look at next.

Words using "kumen"
We already looked at "Kishkumen" now we will look at the other words with "kumen"

Kumen III Nephi 19:4
"Kumen" was a German word and a family name.

Kumenonhi III Nephi 19:4
This word ends with "hi" such as in Nephi which words we will look at next.

Words ending in "hi"

Limhi Mosiah 7:9
We already looked at "Nephi" above.
Variation:
Limher Alma 2:22
Obviously simple to create by adding the word "her".

Words with "she".

Now let us look at words using the word "she". Variations we already looked at: Shem (site); Mormon 2:20, Sherrizah; Moroni 9:7,Shemnon; III Nephi 19:4, Shemlon (site); Mosiah 10:7

Shelem (site) Ether 3:1
KJV 1 Chronicles 26:14 And the lot eastward fell to **Shelem**iah. Then for Zechariah his son, a wise counsellor, they cast lots; and his lot came out northward.

Sherem Jacob 7:1
A variation on the Shemer again as Joseph Smith has done many times take "rem" in "Shemer" and reverse to "mer" and you have "Sherem".
KJV 1Kings 16:24 And he bought the hill of Samaria of **She**mer, for two talents of silver,....
Variations:

Sheum (food)   Mosiah 9:9
Shez   Ether 1:24
KJV Nehamia 11:24
And Pethahiah the son of Me**shez**abeel, of the children of Zerah, the son of Judah,....

Words with "anti".

Now let us look at "anti" which of course is easily recognizable in the Bible such as the "Anti-Christ" We already looked at "Antipas" and "Antipus". Only New Testament words use "anti"

Ani-Anti   Alma 21:11
Obviously this is simple to create.

Antionah   Alma 12:20
Take "Anti" and "Jonah" and you have "Antionah"
KJV Acts 6:5 And the saying pleased the whole multitude: and they chose Stephen, a man full of faith and of the Holy Ghost, and Philip, and Prochorus, and Nicanor, and Timon, and Parmenas, and Nicolas a proselyte of **Antio**ch:

Antionum   Alma 31:3   (site)
A variation on "Antionah". Take "anti" and add "onum" found in many Greek words found in the commentaries such as in Gill: **Gen 14:3** ""in valle occa**tionum**"" There are no Bible words that end in "onum" precisely because it is used in Greek words. As you will see there are several that utilize Greek.
   Variation:
   Antion (coin)   Alma 11:19
   Antum (site)   Mormon 1:3

Manti (site)   Alma 1:15
   COM Gill: **Lev 6:13** "the Grecians have many traces of this continual fire on the altar among them: at **Manti**nia, as Pausanias")

Words with "eantu"

It is interesting that several words contain "eantu".

Irreantum   I Nephi 17:5   (site)

COM Gill: <u>Psa 67:3</u> ""confit**eantur**""
Variation:
Seantum   <u>Alma 9:26</u>
Obviously a variation on Irreantum, in this case it follows the several
"se" words he used such as Seezoram Alma 9:23, Senum (coin) Alma
11:3 , Senine (coin) Alma 11:3, and Seon (coin) Alma 11:5

Archeantus   <u>Moroni 9:2</u>
COM Gill: <u>Pro 13:11</u> ""Usque ad manum", Mont**antus**."

Words with "zoram"

Zoram   <u>I Nephi 4:35</u>
Note: Easy to take "Zorah" and change the "h" to "m".
KJV <u>Joshua 19:41</u> And the coast of their inheritance was **Zorah**, and
Eshtaol, and Irshemesh,
Variations:
Cezoram   <u>Alma 5:1</u>
Seezoram   <u>Alma 9:23</u>   Can you "see" how easy it would be to
create this word.

Words with "Mulek".

Mulek   <u>Mosiah 25:2</u>
A very simple word to create take "mule" and then add a "k".
Variations:
Melek (site)   <u>Alma 8:3</u>
Amulek   <u>Alma 8:21</u>

Muloki   <u>Alma 20:2</u>
With similar endings to "Amaleki" <u>Omni 1:12</u>

Unique Words

Now let us look at some words that are rather unique. Words that don't
have a direct correlation to the Bible or the commentaries.

Paanchi   <u>Alma 1:3</u>
KJV <u>Genesis 41:45</u> Pharaoh gave Joseph the name Zaphenath-
paaneah and gave him a wife, Asenath daughter of Potiphera, priest
at On. And Joseph went throughout the land of Egypt.
COM Gill: <u>Gen 29:9</u> "the same is related of the seven children of the

king of Thebes, of Antiphus the son of Priam, and of **Anchi**ses, Aeneas's father (g).")
KJV 2 Samuel 23:35 Hezrai the Carmelite, **Paa**rai the Arbite,

Pachus   Alma 62:6
KJV John 18:10 Then Simon Peter having a sword drew it, and smote the high priest's servant, and cut off his right ear. The servant's name was Mal**chus**.
COM Gill: Act 28:13 "About the isle of Sicily, from Syracuse to **Pach**inus, the promontory of the island:")
COM There are many words in Gill that end in "achus"
COM Gill: Gen 10:7 "out of Arabia thither, where he finds a city called Samydace, and a river, Samyd**achus**,")

Lachoneus   III Nephi 1:1
KJV Joshua 10:3 ...and unto Japhia king of **Lach**ish;...
COM Clarke: Jos 2:1 "Nymphodorus, quoted by the ancient scholiast on the Oedipus Col**oneus** of Sophocles,"
Note: Most "oneus" ending words are Greek in origin.

Tubaloth   Alma 1:16
KJV Genesis 10:2 The sons of Japheth; Gomer, and Magog, and Madai, and Javan, and **Tubal**, and Meshech, and Tiras.
KJV Joshua 15:24 Ziph,....and Telem and Be**aloth**;

Korihor   Alma 30:12
KJV Gen 36:5 And Aholibamah bare Jeush, and Jaalam, and **Kor**ah,....
KJV Joshua 13:3 From S**ihor**, which *is* before Egypt,....

Rameumptom   Alma 31:21   (site)
KJV Genesis 47:11 ...in the best of the land, in the land of **Rame**ses, as Pharaoh commanded;...
Note: This word is very unique as no word in the Bible has a similar ending but if you will note this ending is similar to the word symptom. So if you take "Rameses" above add a "u" and the ending of the word symptom.

Isabel   Alma 39:3
Obviously Isabel was a common name of Joseph Smith's America.

Deseret   Ether 2:3   (insect)
Obviously easy to create, take "desert" and add an "e".

Shared   Ether 13:23

Obviously a modern word.

Angola (site) Mormon 2:4

Angola is the name of a city in New York not far from where Joseph Smith grew up. Since my relatives are from New York, and I used to live in upstate New York, I would pass Angola on my way to visit them.

Direct from the commentaries

Zenos   I Nephi 19:10

  COM Gill: Gen 10:4 "places in the island of Cyprus, a city there being called Citium, from whence was **Zeno** the Citian:" (Clarke, Henry, Wesley)

    Variation:

  Zenock   I Nephi 19:10

Neum   I Nephi 19:10

  COM Clarke: "who use their tongues, וינאמו נאם vaiyinamu **neum**, and solemnly pronounce,"

    Variation:

  Jeneum (site) Mormon 6:14

Neas (food)   Mosiah 9:9

  KJV Although this word does appear in a name in the New Testament, Act 9:34 "And Peter said unto him, Ae**neas**," I believe it is not from here but from the commentaries.

  BOM Mosiah 9:9 And we began to till the ground, yea, even with all manner of seeds, with seeds of **corn**, and of **wheat**, and of **barley**, and with neas, and with sheum, and with seeds of all manner of fruits; and we did begin to multiply and prosper in the land.

  COM Notice that this part of Gill uses the same vegetables in the same order: and if you just take away the b in beans and move the n you get neas. In addition Joseph Smith ends with "all manner of fruits" and this ends with a similar idea "and various fruits": Gill: Gen 1:29 "and both these take in all kind of vegetables, all herbs, plants, roots, even **corn**, **wheat**, **barley**, pease, beans, &c. and the various **fruits** of all sorts of trees,")

Omni   Jarom 1:15

  COM Gill: Jer 29:4 ""universae migrationi", Schmidt; "**omni**

transmigrationi", Pagninus, Montanus." (Clarke, Henry)
   Variation:
   Omner   Mosiah 27:34
   Take "Omni" remove the "l" and add the common ending "er".

And we have a variation on the "omner" with Teomner Alma 58:16

Gimgimno   III Nephi 9:8   (site)
   Note: Again the common mixing tactic of Joseph Smith. Take the ending
   of this word it is really "omni" just mixed into "imno"
   KJV 2Ch 28:18 …and **Gim**zo also, and the villages thereof;…

Gadiomnah   III Nephi 9:8   (site)
   Note: And now another one in the same verse: Notice the "omni" use and
   then attaching the common "ah" ending of Bible words and BOM words.
   Also notice the common beginning "Gad" such as from the Bible **KJV**
   Genesis 30:11 "And Leah said, A troop cometh: and she called his name
   Gad." And Joseph Smith's common use of the word as follows:
   Gadiomnah: III Nephi 9:8 and Gadianton; Alma 2:4. Which then brings
   us to the next word he creates in the same verse.

Gadiandi   III Nephi 9:8   (site)
   Note: Take the "Gadi" out of "Gadiomnah" and add "andi" which can be
   found in many common words or a similar ending from the commentaries
   such as Henry: 2Sa 12:15-25 *"Favores sunt ampliandi")*

Nehor   Alma 1:15
   COM Gill: Mat 1:1 "The tradition of R. **Nehor**ai says,"

Senum (coin)   Alma 11:3
   COM Gill: Job 3:19 "Mista **senum** ac juvenum densantur funera"."
   (Clarke)
      Variation:
      Senine (coin)   Alma 11:3
      Note: As we already mentioned Joseph Smith used "se" in front of
      several words in this case he just took the number "nine" and added
      the "se".
      Seon (coin)   Alma 11:5
      COM Gill: Deu 4:48 "In the Septuagint version it is called **Seon**,"
      (Clarke)

Ethem   Ether 1:8

COM Clarke: <u>Lam 4:1</u> "**kethem**, that which was stamped to make it current," (Gill)
KJV Could be a variation on: <u>Exodus 13:20</u> And they took their journey from Succoth, and encamped in **Etham**, in the edge of the wilderness.

Zerin (site)   <u>Ether 12:30</u>
Zerin is a city in Israel in old times was known as Jezreel
COM Clarke: <u>Dan 2:27</u> "but גזרין **gazerin** is the name of another class of those curious artists,"
KJV <u>Genesis 36:13</u> And these are the sons of Reuel; Nahath, and **Zerah**, Shammah, and Mizzah: these were the sons of Bashemath Esau's wife.

Shule   <u>Ether 1:30</u>
COM Gill: <u>Deu 30:4</u> "Great Britain, reckoned formerly the uttermost part of the earth, as **Thule**,"
KJV Could be a variation on: <u>1 Chronicles 7:36</u> The sons of Zophah; Suah, and Harnepher, and **Shual**, and Beri, and Imrah,

Chapter Ten

The Translation

If you will remember in the first chapter I explained that I would explain how Joseph Smith translated the Book of Mormon when you have had a better understanding of just how he complied the Book of Mormon. As you have seen he complied the Book of Mormon by utilizing the commentaries and the Bible. . If you will remember Joseph Smith claimed to have his first visit in 1820 and the Book of Mormon was published in 1830. You will also remember that Joseph Smith had, as we discussed, at the least five and a half years to accomplish this, again more than enough time to compile the Book of Mormon with the aide of the commentaries and the Bible. Now that he had finished the Book of Mormon he had to fake a translation of the plates. This he did quite easily as we will see.

In December of 1827 Joseph Smith translated a few of the characters from the plates he did this with the aide of his wife Emma and her brother Reuben Hale who acted as scribes for Joseph. Now in this beginning translation Joseph Smith separated himself from the scribes by a blanket thus making it very easy for him to take his work, complied from the commentaries and the Bible and just say word for word what he wrote. The reason we are given that he did this was so that no one could see the gold plates.

Now from April 12 to June 14, 1828, Martin Harris acted as a scribe for Joseph Smith during the translation process. On July 15 Martin Harris lost 116 pages of the translation. This caused Joseph Smith to be "chastened by the Lord" and the plates were taken back. Joseph Smith was completely devastated by this loss. During this time Joseph Smith would translate by putting the "interpreters" into a hat and then dictating to the scribes what to write. Again why a hat? It could easily hold his work compiled from the commentaries and the Bible without anyone seeing it. Now it is important that we look a little closer at the 116 lost pages that were "lost forever". Why was Joseph Smith so devastated by this? Why couldn't they just retranslate these 116 pages? Wouldn't God be able to do this with no problem? The reason I believe they couldn't just retranslate was that these were 116 pages from Joseph Smith's work from the commentaries and the Bible. I believe that Joseph Smith would destroy this work as he would translate to lessen the chance of anyone finding out what he was doing. This would explain why it was impossible to retranslate the 116 pages. Remember there were no copiers or copying technology that we take for granted. Writing 116 pages by hand, let alone the entire *Book of* Mormon, would have taken countless hours to complete. Joseph Smith only had his one hand written copy and this is why he was so devastated at the loss of the 116 pages and this is why they were "lost forever".

When it came to names, we have already seen how Joseph Smith came up with the names of the Book of Mormon, Joseph Smith would say the name and the scribe would try to spell it phonetically and then Joseph Smith would verify the spelling. This of course he could do because he had his made up names in front of him from his work. This was similar to the entire process in that Joseph Smith would read 20 or so words and then the scribe would read back the words for verification. Again this was easy for Joseph Smith to verify as he had his work in front of him. Joseph Smith's wife Emma also stated that after a meal or a night's rest Joseph would begin again without being told where to begin. In other words Joseph Smith could begin right were he left off the next time they started translating. Not difficult to do when you have the work in front of you.

So quite simply it was very easy for Joseph Smith to use his work made up from the commentaries and the Bible in the "translation" process of the Book of Mormon. And it also explains his use of a "curtain" a "hat" and in addition his extreme sense of loss at the loss "forever" of the 116 pages.

Chapter Eleven

The Miscellaneous Chapter

The following are notes I took while producing and researching this book. I and many others have found the notes to be so interesting that I have included them here.

-The BOM first published in 1830.

-Adam Clarke's Commentary finished NT in 1810 and OT in 1825.

-Matthew Henry's *Exposition of the Old and New Testaments* (1708-1710)

-John Gill's *An Exposition of the* New Testament (3 vols., 1746-1748), with his *Exposition of the* Old Testament (6 vols., 1748-1763)

-The word "desirous" found only six times in the KJV five of those in the NT but used 63 times in the BOM.

-The phrase "beheld myself" seems to make no sense. How can one behold oneself? 1Nephi 8:7 And it came to pass (452/1353) that as I followed him I beheld myself that I was in a dark and dreary waste.

-"for the space of" used once in the KJV but 69 times in the Book of Mormon. Including "for the space of nine moons" and "for the space of twenty and two years" Mosiah 10:3 "for the space of two days and two nights" Mosiah 27:23 "for the space of an hour" Alma 18:14 "for the space of a long time" 3 Nephi 6:17 "for the space of forty and two years" Ether 10:8

-The following section I found to be very interesting. As there where many words that were used a staggering amount of times in the Book of Mormon as compared to the King James Bible. This would tend to lead one to believe that the book was again faked. It is a common fault of writers to use certain words too many times throughout their work. For example I have a tendency to use the phrase "of course" too much. The problem with the Book of Mormon is that it is claimed to be written by many people yet this phrase tendency occurs throughout the Book of Mormon, which indicates a single writer, which has already, I believe, been proven. I will bold some of the more prominent examples below.

As an example "for behold" was only used 28 times in the Bible but Joseph Smith used it 260 times from beginning to end of the Book of Mormon.

The same applies with "but behold", only 8 times in the Bible but 251 times in the Book of Mormon again, from beginning to end which signifies a single writer for the entire book.

Look up and count the words in the BOM and KJV:

Wherefore (KJV 344 : BOM 419)
For behold (KJV 28: BOM 260)
Come to pass (KJV 159 : BOM 90)
But behold (KJV 8 : BOM 241)
Yea (KJV 1065 : BOM 1663)
Nevertheless (KJV 97 : 178)
Wo (KJV 101 : BOM 2)
wo be unto (KJV 2 : BOM 7)
know ye not (KJV 17 : BOM 11)
need not suppose (KJV 0 : BOM 6)
suppose (KJV 18 only once in OT: BOM 104)
beloved brethren (KJV 4 Only in NT : BOM 65)
I would speak (KJV 1 : BOM 10)
save it be (KJV 0 : BOM 47)
at that day (KJV 12 : BOM 23)
make an end (KJV 8 : BOM 16)
my soul delighteth (KJV 1 : BOM 11)
children of men (KJV 23 : BOM 131)
would that ye (KJV 2 only in NT : BOM 57)
baptize (KJV 59 only in NT : BOM 113)
the lamb of God (KJV 2 only in NT : BOM 35)
notwithstanding (KJV 36: BOM 67)
Holy Ghost (KJV 89 only in NT : BOM 95)
doctrine of Christ (KJV 2 only in NT : BOM 7)
maketh (KJV 117 : BOM 8)
speaketh (KJV 66 : BOM 12)
Jesus (KJV 943 : BOM 188)
Land of Promise (KJV 1 only in NT : BOM 22)
If it so be (KJV 0 : BOM 37)
Face of this land (KJV 0 : BOM 12)
Save it were (KJV 0 : BOM 76)
Insomuch (KJV 20 : BOM 181)
marvelous work (KVV 1 : BOM 9)
records (KJV 2 : BOM 78)

Joseph Smith loved to use Wo, he utilized it 88 times, wo, wo, the double wo is used six times in fact one time he used it three times in a row, as does only Revelations in the King James Version of the Bible.

3 Nephi 9:2 **Wo, wo,** wo unto this people; wo unto the inhabitants of the whole earth except they shall repent; for the devil laugheth, and his angels rejoice, because of the slain of the fair sons and daughters of my people; and it is because of their iniquity and abominations that they are fallen!

2 Nephi 28:15 O the wise, and the learned, and the rich, that are puffed up in the pride of their hearts, and all those who preach false doctrines, and all those who commit whoredoms, and pervert the right way of the Lord, wo, wo, wo be unto them, saith the Lord God Almighty, for they shall be thrust down to hell!

Ezekiel 16:23 And it came to pass after all thy wickedness, (**woe, woe** unto thee! saith the LORD GOD;)

Revelation 8:13 And I beheld, and heard an angel flying through the midst of heaven, saying with a loud voice, **Woe, woe, woe,** to the inhabiters of the earth by reason of the other voices of the trumpet of the three angels, which are yet to sound!

Joseph Smith liked the word "exceedingly" exceedingly much, sorry, even though it appears in the KJV only 40 times he utilized it 267 times with many phrases not found in the KJV nor in the commentaries. Again he used these phrases throughout the entire Book of Mormon which points to one user as the author of the Book of Mormon. I have put a "?" in front of the ones that are obviously made up, in other words they don't seem to make sense.

tremble exceedingly (3)
exceedingly young (1)
exceedingly glad (4) Clarke (1) Henry (7) Bible (1) OT
exceedingly sorrowful (14) – Henry (14)
exceedingly great (57) – Clarke (3) Henry (28)
exceedingly fine (4) -- Clarke (1)
exceedingly frightened (1)
rejoice exceedingly
exceedingly wroth
fear exceedingly (5)
exceedingly great joy (11)
? exceedingly great mist of darkness
exceedingly feared (1) – Clarke, Gill, **Wesley (1) each**
exceedingly high Mountain (2) – Henry (1)
exceedingly fair (7) – Henry (5) Clarke (1)
exceedingly great many (3)
? stumble **exceedingly**
? blessed of the Lord **exceedingly**

murmur exceedingly (1)
exceedingly difficult (1) – Clarke (6)
mourn exceedingly (3)
? chasten them **exceedingly**
exceedingly rejoiced (4) – Clarke (1) Gill *(1) Bible (1) OT*
frightened exceedingly (1)
exceedingly sore (15)
? swollen exceedingly (1)
grow exceedingly (4) – Gill **(2)**
-exceedingly fear and tremble
prosper exceedingly (8)
exceedingly many (4) – Henry (1)
loved Nephi **exceedingly**
exceedingly tender (1) – Clarke (1) Henry (2)
? grow and thrive exceedingly (1)
astonished exceedingly (6)
? exceedingly great plainness of speech (1)
exceedingly merciful (1)
exceedingly strict (1) – Clarke (1)
? exceedingly more numerous (3)
multiplied exceedingly – (2) Clarke (2) Gill *(2) Henry (3) – Bible (1) OT*
exceedingly rich (9) – Henry (2)
rejoiced exceedingly (1) – Clarke (2) Gill **(3)**
labor exceedingly (5)
exceedingly rejoice (1) – Henry (1) Gill **(1) Clarke (1)**
exceedingly fear (1) – Clarke (5) Gill *(2) Henry (6) Wesley (1) Bible (NT)*
exceedingly numerous (4) – Clarke (1) Henry (1)
more exceedingly (1) – Gill *(2) Henry (20) Bible (2) NT*
exceedingly great faith (2)
weep exceedingly (1)
exceedingly angry (7)
exceedingly sharp (2)
worn exceedingly (1)
labored exceedingly (1) – Gill **(1)**
exceedingly afraid (4) – Gill *(2) Henry (1) Bible (2) OT*
fight exceedingly (1)
exceedingly great strength and courage (1)
exceedingly fast (3)
exceedingly great riches (4)
exceedingly great care (1)
? exceedingly precarious and dangerous (1)

exceedingly astonished (3)
exceedingly great prosperity (3)
exceedingly fearful (1)
? exceedingly valiant for courage (1)
exceedingly strong (6) – Clarke (7)
exceedingly desirous (1) – Gill (1)
exceedingly great slaughter (2)
exceedingly great sufferings (1)
exceedingly great neglect (3)
exceedingly great courage (1)
affrighted exceedingly (1)
exceedingly great length (2)
exceedingly curious (2)
exceedingly large (1) – Henry (1)
? exceedingly great speed (1)
exceedingly bloody (1)
exceedingly expert (3)
? exceedingly great distance (1)
exceedingly scarce (1) – Clarke (3)
? exceedingly great pride (1)
shook exceedingly (2)
shine exceedingly (1)
? exceedingly great power (2)
flourish exceedingly (1)
exceedingly wicked (3) – Clarke (4) Gill (2) Henry (1)
? exceedingly great peace (1)
? exceedingly great band of robbers (1)
exceedingly great praise (1)
exceedingly humble (1)
exceedingly great quaking (1)
exceedingly dry (1)
exceedingly great number (1)
multiply exceedingly (2) – Gill (1) Henry (1) Wesley (1)
exceedingly great anger (1)
? exceedingly tight (1)
exceedingly old (3)
exceedingly great wickedness (1)
exceedingly great age (1)
exceedingly beautiful (1) – Clarke (1)
exceedingly industrious (1)
exceedingly great war (1)
rend the air exceedingly (1)

exceedingly fierce (1) – Clarke (1)
grieveth me exceedingly (1)
exceedingly anxious (1) – Clarke (1)
slay them exceedingly (1)

He also loved the phrase "as it were". Again as this phrase appears throughout the entire Book of Mormon from beginning to end, 76 times, this would indicate that one person wrote the entire Book of Mormon. As I have stated earlier I have a habit of using the phrase "of course" in fact I had to go back through this entire work and remove the numerous times I used it. **Note**: This phrase is quite unique and found in works such as The Scarlet Letter, and Geofffrey Chaucer, The Canterbury Tales, The Reeves Prologue noted here: "**Save it were** only old Oswald the reeve, Because he was a carpenter by craft."

Joseph Smith also like the phrase "one with another". This phrase is used 9 times in the KJV of the Bible and 29 times in the Book of Mormon.

Disputing one with another (1)
Consult one with another (1)
Contend one with another (3)
Peace one with another (1)
Quarrel one with another (1)
Anger one with another (3)
Contention one with another (1)
Friendly one with another (1)
Trade one with another (1)
Impart the word of God one with another (1)
Wonderful contentions one with another (1)
Contend mightily one with another (1)
Fellowship one with another (1)
Rejoice one with another (1)
Free intercourse one with another (1)
Covenant one with another (2)
War one with another (2)
Marveling and wondering one with another (1)
Conversing one with another (1)
Dealing justly one with another (2)
Sell and traffic one with another (1)
Speak one with another (1)

Joseph Smith also liked utilizing titles. Titles:

The Holy One of Israel (KJV 30 : BOM 40)
Holy Ghost (KJV 89 only in NT : BOM 95)
Jesus (KJV 943 : BOM 188)
Jesus Christ (KJV 187 : BOM 69)
Jesus the Christ (KJV 1 : BOM 0)
Spirit of the Lord (KJV 31 : BOM 40)
Messiah (KJV 2 : BOM 32) (Messiah only in OT and only in Daniel)
Spirit of God (KJV 26 : BOM 20)
Adam and Eve (KJV 0 : BOM 2) (In the commentaries)
the holy prophets (KJV 2NT : BOM 19) (Only in NT)
the Lord God (KJV 465 : BOM 112)
Gentiles (KJV 141 : BOM 121)
the Lamb of God (KJV 2NT : BOM 35)
Redeemer (KJV 18 : BOM 41)
children of men (KJV 23 : BOM 131)
twelve apostles (KJV 3NT : BOM 9)
Savior (KJV 37 : BOM 12)
The Devil (KJV 44NT : BOM 94) (Only in NT)
Almighty God (KJV 3 : BOM 4)
God of Israel (KJV 201 : BOM 11) If BOM characters are direct from
Jerusalem this should have been a big number instead of only 11.
God of our fathers (KVJ 7 : BOM 1)
Holy One of Israel (KJV 31 : BOM 40)
Satan   (KJV 48 : BOM 26)
just God (KJV 1 : BOM 6)
Holy Messiah (KJV 0 : BOM 2)
Mighty God (KJV 9 : BOM 3)
Mighty One of Jacob (KJV 2 : BOM 2)
Eternal God (KJV 1 : BOM 7)
angel of light (KJV 1 : BOM 1)
captive spirits (KJV 0 : BOM 1)
devil of all devils (KJV 0 : BOM 1)
Lord of Hosts (KJV 235 : BOM 52) If BOM characters are direct from
Jerusalem this should have been a big number.
Jesus is the very Christ (KJV 0 : BOM 1)
God of miracles (KJV 0 : BOM 7)
house of Israel (KJV 146 : BOM 122)
hand of the Lord (KJV 38 : BOM 26)
kingdom of God (KJV 68NT : BOM 38) Only in NT
false teachers (KJV 1NT : BOM 1) Only in NT
Lord God of Hosts (KJV 28 : BOM 5) If BOM characters are direct from

Jerusalem this should have been a big number.
Bible (KJV 0 : BOM 11)
ancient covenant people (KJV 0 : BOM 2)
Creator (KJV 10 : BOM 5)
all-powerful Creator of heaven and earth (KJV 0 : BOM 1)
Maker (KJV 19 : BOM 6)
great Creator (KJV 0 : BOM 3) (Gill 2, Henry 17, Clarke 5)
Lord of the vineyard (KJV 4NT : BOM 33) This fits with the chapters showing him making up a story on a "Lord of the vineyard"
unprofitable servants (KJV 1NT : BOM 2)
heavenly Father KJV 6NT : BOM 4)
the evil spirit (KJV 6 : BOM 5)
unholy temples (KJV 0 : BOM 4)
Lord Omnipotent (KJV 0 : BOM 4)
the Lord Jesus Christ (KJV 26NT : BOM 11)
the Son of God (KJV 44 : BOM 49) Only one outside NT and that is in Daniel.
the master of sin (KJV 0 : BOM 1)
God above all (KJV 1 : BOM 1)
seer (KJV 26 : BOM 10)
teachers (KJV 13 : BOM 30)
cunning people (KJV 0 : BOM 1)
the enemy of God (KJV 1NT : BOM 1)
all-wise Creator (KJV 0 : BOM 1)
high priest (KJV 72 : BOM 19) If BOM characters are direct from Jerusalem this should have been a big number.
the people of God (KJV 5 : BOM 9)
captains (KJV 102 : BOM 27)
higher captains (KJV 0 : BOM 1)
chief captains (KJV 2NT : BOM 22)
elders (KJV 175 : BOM 9) If BOM characters are direct from Jerusalem this should have been a big number.
murderers (KJV 9 : BOM 11)
child of the devil (KJV 1NT : BOM 3)
the Holy One (KJV 49 : BOM 40)
the good shepherd (KJV 2NT : BOM 8)
the spirit of prophecy (KJV 1NT : BOM 18)
stiffnecked people (KJV 6 : BOM 14)
the holy ones of God (KJV 0 : BOM 1)
lawyers (KJV 5NT : BOM 17)
the adversary (KJV 2NT : BOM 1)
Only Begotten Son (KJV 5NT : BOM 5)

Only Begotten of the Father (KJV 1NT : BOM 4)
king of Salem (KJV 3 : BOM 1)
holy scriptures (KJV 2NT : BOM 5)
the word of God (KJV 45 : BOM 89)
fellow-servants (KJV 4NT : BOM 1)
Lord of the harvest (KJV 2NT : BOM 1)
his holy name (KJV 5 : BOM 6)
Most High God (KJV 11 : BOM 6)
the creature (KJV 3 : BOM 4)
a lying spirit (KJV 4 : BOM 1)
Refiners (KJV 1 : BOM 1)
the days of Adam (KJV 1 : BOM 2)
merciful God (KJV 1 : BOM 2)
Christians (KJV 1 : BOM 4)
men of God (KJV 1 : BOM 1)
child of hell (KJV 1 : BOM 2)
everlasting Maker (KJV 1 : BOM 1)
rock of our Redeemer (KJV 0 : BOM 1)
Well Beloved (KJV 2 : BOM 1)
the holy ones (KJV 1 : BOM 2)

Titles from the Commentaries

Now below are titles that do not appear in the King James Version of the Bible but have their source in the commentaries. You will notice how many there are but I have not taken the time to find all of them. Many are very unique and this alone should be evidence enough that Joseph Smith used the commentaries to create the Book of Mormon.

Eternal Father (KJV 0 : BOM 13) (Gill 0, Henry 3, Clarke 0)
the great Creator (KJV 0 : BOM 2) (Gill 1, Henry 13, Clarke 3)
mother earth (KJV 0 : BOM 3) (Gill 2, Henry 0, Clarke 4)
God of nature (KJV 0 : BOM 1) (Gill 52, Henry 4, Clarke 79)
true and living God (KJV 0 : BOM 9) (Gill 32, Henry 31, Clarke 1)
The Great Mediator (KJV 0 : BOM 2) (Gill 1, Henry 11, Clarke 7)
the father of lies (KJV 0 : BOM 1) (Gill 16, Henry 13, Clarke 5)
first parents (KJV 0 : BOM 13) (Gill 48, Henry 62, Clarke 16)
the evil one (KJV 0 : BOM 7) (Gill 23, Henry 8, Clarke 6)
cunning one (KJV 0 : BOM 1) (Gill 1, Henry 0, Clarke 0)
true Messiah (KJV 0 : BOM 3) (Gill 182, Henry 24, Clarke 18)
Christ is the Holy One of Israel (KJV 0 : BOM 1) (Gill 0, Henry 1, Clarke 0)

humble followers of Christ (KJV 0 : BOM 1) (Gill 2, Henry 0, Clarke 0)
the kingdom of the devil (KJV 0 : BOM 5) (Gill 0, Henry 4, Clarke 0)
the lost tribes (KJV 0 : BOM 3) (Gill 0, Henry 0, Clarke 1)
the Creator of all things (KJV 0 : BOM 2) (Gill 18, Henry 4, Clarke 7)
the master of the vineyard (KJV 0 : BOM 2) (Gill 2, Henry 0, Clarke 0)
the bar of God (KJV 0 : BOM 5) (Gill 5, Henry 1, Clarke 2)
the Father of all things (KJV 0 : BOM 1) (Gill 0, Henry 0, Clarke 1)
wise people (KJV 0 : BOM 1) (Gill 1, Henry 2, Clarke 1)
the rising generation (KJV 0 : BOM 3) (Gill 1, Henry 20, Clarke 2)
vilest of sinners (KJV 0 : BOM 1) (Gill 10, Henry 2, Clarke 1)
chief judge (KJV 0 : BOM 44) (Gill 4, Henry 2, Clarke 0)
tribunal of God (KJV 0 : BOM 1) (Gill 4, Henry 1, Clarke 5)
the order of God (KJV 0 : BOM 2) (Gill 11, Henry 1, Clarke 38)
a holy man (KJV 0 : BOM 4) (Gill 7, Henry 2, Clarke 13)
Supreme Being (KJV 0 : BOM 1) (Gill 13, Henry 0, Clarke 66)
the plan of redemption (KJV 0 : BOM 13) (Gill 1, Henry 0, Clarke 1)
indolent people (KJV 0 : BOM 1) (Gill 1, Henry 0, Clarke 0)
the curse of God (KJV 0 : BOM 2) (Gill 23, Henry 33, Clarke 9)
Great Spirit (KJV 0 : BOM 8) (Gill 0, Henry 0, Clarke 1)
the light of the glory of God (KJV 0 : BOM 1) (Gill 1, Henry 0, Clarke 5)
our great God (KJV 0 : BOM 2) (Gill 0, Henry 1, Clarke 0)
fold of God (KJV 0 : BOM 4) (Gill 0, Henry 0, Clarke 1)
the sword of his justice (KJV 0 : BOM 2) (Gill 1, Henry 5, Clarke 0)
the penitent (KJV 0 : BOM 2) (Gill 5, Henry 25, Clarke 25)
merciful Being (KJV 0 : BOM 1) (Gill 0, Henry 0, Clarke 2)
Supreme Creator (KJV 0 : BOM 1) (Gill 0, Henry 1, Clarke 0)
holy commandments (KJV 0 : BOM 1) (Gill 2, Henry 0, Clarke 0)
holy writ (KJV 0 : BOM 1) (Gill 0, Henry 2, Clarke 2)
the restoration (KJV 0 : BOM 10) (Gill 36, Henry 24, Clarke 55)
decrees of God (KJV 0 : BOM 3) (Gill 49, Henry 4, Clarke 3)
the nature of God (KJV 0 : BOM 1) (Gill 13, Henry 9, Clarke 16)
plan of salvation (KJV 0 : BOM 3) (Gill 2, Henry 0, Clarke 7)
fallen man (KJV 0 : BOM 1) (Gill 12, Henry 35, Clarke 16)
spiritual death (KJV 0 : BOM 8) (Gill 18, Henry 7, Clarke 2)
probationary state (KJV 0 : BOM 3) (Gill 0, Henry 0, Clarke 2)
true believers in Christ (KJV 0 : BOM 3) (Gill 43, Henry 0, Clarke 2)
powers of hell (KJV 0 : BOM 1) (Gill 2, Henry 14, Clarke 0)
Spirit of freedom (KJV 0 : BOM 2) (Gill 2, Henry 0, Clarke 0)
holy fathers (KJV 0 : BOM 2) (Gill 2, Henry 0, Clarke 1)
Eternal Head (KJV 0 : BOM 1) (Gill 0, Henry 0, Clarke 1)
the great commander (KJV 0 : BOM 1) (Gill 0, Henry 2, Clarke 0)

Why are things like "make an abridgement" and "wherefore" in the introduction, and are exactly the same in the BOM itself?

Note: Joseph Smith utilizes the phrase "according to the spirit of prophecy" 18 times and "spirit of revelation" 9 times this of course is his attempt to try to give us an explanation as to why the source, whether it be Lehi, Nephi or other BOM characters, who tell us about Jesus, and many other coming events such as the coming of the United States of America, could possibly know such things.